THE
Complete Cook

by Pat Jester

Published by HPBooks®
P.O. Box 5367, Tucson, AZ 85703   602/888-2150
ISBN 0-89586-235-2
Library of Congress Catalog Card Number 84-81383
© 1984 HPBooks, Inc. Printed in the U.S.A.

Cover Photo: Pork Rib Crown Roast, page 64.

Sweet-Glazed Acorn Squash and Piquant-Glazed Beets, page 356.

Special thanks to the following organizations for use of photographs and line art:
National Live Stock and Meat Board
American Dairy Association
National Turkey Federation

Contents

ANOTHER BEST-SELLING VOLUME FROM HPBooks®

Publisher: Rick Bailey; Editorial Director: Retha M. Davis
Editors: Judith Wesley Allen, Veronica Durie
Art Director: Don Burton; Book Design: Leslie Sinclair
Typography: Cindy Coatsworth, Michelle Claridge
Research Assistants: Karla Tillotson, Carol Miller, Diann Peyton
Food Stylists: Mable Hoffman, Pat Jester, Karla Tillotson,
Carol Miller, Diann Peyton
Photography: Bob Hawks; George de Gennaro Studios

Shown on the following pages: Strawberry Cheesecake, page 440.

Pat Jester

Pat Jester is the author of three HPBooks bestsellers: *Microwave Cookbook—The Complete Guide, Brunch Cookery* and *Easy Suppers.*

Pat has an extensive background in food and nutrition. For many years she was a food editor for Better Homes and Gardens. Pat has also worked as a dietitian in several health-care institutions. Employing a staff of home economists, Pat now runs her own company, Creative Foods, Ltd., in West Des Moines, Iowa. With test kitchens and a photography studio at her disposal, Pat works on recipe testing and development and does food styling for photographic projects.

The Complete Cook is the result of two years of dedicated and inspired work by Pat and her staff.

Come into My Kitchen

Welcome! Pull up a chair and examine *The Complete Cook*—a down-to-earth cookbook that combines the best of old-fashioned cooking with exciting new improvements.

Between these covers you will find a large collection of classic, familiar recipes—some simple, some fancy. This is the cookbook you will refer to again and again, whether you want to make a pie like Grandma used to make, or you need help with a cooking technique. It is a basic cookbook you can rely on to provide tried-and-true recipes and tips.

● **An Exciting Improvement**—But the best is yet to come. *The Complete Cook* introduces a new recipe design tailored for today's cook—*you*. This new design allows you to adapt a recipe, if you wish, and make it *your own*. It helps you become the accomplished, creative cook you want to be.

The unique recipe concept is flexible enough to take beginners by the hand through every cooking step, or to inspire experienced cooks to individualize recipes. Here is how it works.

● **Look for Basic**—The key to the new recipe design lies in the word *Basic*. You may have noticed that many recipe titles in this book begin with the word Basic. These recipe titles, such as Basic Ground-Meat Sandwiches, below, are *variable recipes*. They provide a framework for you to use in preparing the dish. Your finished dish depends on how you choose to complete the recipe's building blocks—the *variable ingredients*.

● **Variable Ingredients**—The recipe for Basic Ground-Meat Sandwiches has six variable ingredients: ground meat, chopped vegetables, cooking sauce, dried leaf herb or spice, shredded cheese and

Basic Ground-Meat Sandwiches

SERVINGS	8	4
INGREDIENTS		
ground meat	1 lb.	8 oz.
chopped vegetables	1 cup	1/2 cup
cooking sauce	1 cup	1/2 cup
Worcestershire sauce	2 teaspoons	1 teaspoon
dried leaf herb or ground spice	1 teaspoon	1/2 teaspoon
dry mustard	1 teaspoon	1/2 teaspoon
taco shells or hamburger buns, split	8	4
shredded cheese	1/2 cup (2 oz.)	1/4 cup (1 oz.)
toppings, see suggestions below	to garnish	to garnish
SKILLET	11-inch skillet	8-inch skillet
TIME AT MEDIUM HIGH	9 to 10 minutes	6 to 7 minutes
TIME AT MEDIUM LOW	10 minutes	10 minutes

Crumble ground meat into a skillet, see size in chart above. Add chopped vegetables. Cook over Medium-High heat for time in chart above or until meat is browned and vegetables are tender, stirring often. Drain off fat. Stir in cooking sauce, Worcestershire sauce, herb or spice and dry mustard; mix well. Bring to a boil. Reduce heat to Medium Low. Simmer, uncovered, 10 minutes or until flavors blend and meat mixture is thick, stirring occasionally. Spoon into taco shells or hamburger buns. Sprinkle with cheese. Garnish with toppings according to suggestions below.

Suggested Combinations

Tacos: Use ground beef or fresh bulk pork sausage. Use chopped onion and canned chopped green chilies for vegetables. Use taco sauce for cooking sauce. Use chili powder for spice. Serve in taco shells. Use Cheddar cheese. Garnish with shredded lettuce, chopped tomatoes and guacamole dip.

Sloppy Joes: Use ground beef. Use chopped onion and chopped celery for vegetables. Use barbecue sauce for cooking sauce. Use oregano for herb. Serve in hamburger buns. Use mozzarella cheese. Garnish with chopped tomatoes and sliced black or green olives.

toppings. What you choose for each ingredient can vary, depending on your food preferences and what foods you have on hand.

● **Suggested Combinations**—To help new cooks fill in the blanks, *Suggested Combinations* appear at the end of each Basic recipe. Each combination offers ideas for variable ingredients with complementary flavors. These combinations are our favorite ways to prepare the recipe.

Notice that these are only suggestions. A novice cook can use a suggested combination in its entirety for a foolproof recipe. A more experienced cook can use the suggestions as a tool to inspire creativity.

● **Ingredient Suggestions**—Look at the examples in the ground-meat sandwich recipe. The Suggested Combinations list *Tacos* and *Sloppy Joes* as two possibilities. The first ingredient is *ground meat*. Tacos have ground beef or sausage; Sloppy Joes have ground beef. If you want to experiment, the term "ground meat" might encourage you to dream up your own delicious creation using, for example, ground veal or ham.

Suggestions for *chopped vegetables*, the second ingredient, are onion and green chilies for Tacos, or onion and celery for Sloppy Joes. How much to use of each one is a matter of personal taste. I have listed the suggestions in the decreasing order in which we used them. In this case, we used more onion than green chilies in the tacos. If you are experimenting, think of vegetables that sound good for your own combination. How about fresh mushroom slices and grated carrot to go with veal, or chopped green pepper and zucchini for ham?

Cooking sauce, the third ingredient, becomes taco sauce for Tacos or barbecue sauce for Sloppy Joes. As a complement to your new creation, you might try mushroom sauce with veal, or seafood-cocktail sauce for ham.

The seasoning, *dried leaf herb or ground spice*, translates into chili powder for Tacos and oregano for Sloppy Joes. Dill weed would go well with veal and thyme with ham. There are many choices, but you get the idea.

Suggestions for *shredded cheese*, another ingredient, are Cheddar for Tacos and mozzarella for Sloppy Joes. If you do not have mozzarella in the refrigerator, but you have a little Monterey Jack cheese—use it! That is the idea behind these recipes. How about a more sophisticated bleu cheese for your veal sandwich, and Muenster for the ham?

Our final building block—*toppings*—are built-in garnishes that are so important in taste and eye appeal. Tacos are topped with lettuce, chopped tomatoes and guacamole dip, while Sloppy Joes have chopped tomatoes and sliced olives. For the upscale veal sandwich, you might garnish with fresh watercress and enoki mushrooms. Onion rings and chopped pickle could be the final touch for more robust ham.

What's the end result? Diverse sandwiches made from similar ingredients. This is cooking at its best—made possible with flexibility and creativity.

● **Select-A-Size™ Recipes**—Another significant improvement this cookbook offers you is a choice of how many servings to make. The ingredients are divided for you, and you have at least two recipe-size choices. The amount for each ingredient is listed under the serving-size column.

Likewise, the cookware size and approximate timings for each step in the recipe are shown in the serving-size column. The timing benefit is twofold. It is a guide for cooking foods to optimum doneness. It also helps you get all the food done and on the table at the same time—no small feat!

● **Classic Recipes**—Not all recipes in the book are "Basic" recipes. Many stand on their own as time-honored classics. These recipes do not have variable ingredients. The clue to the new-format recipes is the title word, *Basic*.

There you have it—a cookbook that combines the old with the new. Prepare recipes in the quantity that is right for your needs. You have maximum flexibility in ingredients and creativity.

I have always believed this kind of approach is what makes a good cook. After adding many of these recipes to your collection, I think you will agree.

Tacos and Sloppy Joes, pages 7 and 152.

Just Between Us Cooks

A quick look through these pictorial tips may save the tears from the stew. It was probably plenty salty anyway. Which brings me to my first point. While these recipes are by no means low in sodium, most have reduced salt, sugar and fat content. I think this makes good nutritional sense. You may have to adjust your taste buds at first. If you stick with it, you will miss the unnecessary salt, sugar and fat less and less—and you will probably be better off for it.

I have tried to estimate servings in a somewhat generous manner. However, four recipe servings will not feed four hungry teen-age boys. That is where our exclusive Select-A-Size™ recipes can help. If your starving family of four eats the equivalent of six normal servings, follow the appropriate column to prepare six servings.

Confusion always arises over where the comma is placed in ingredient lists. It is an important point.

Consider whipping cream. If the ingredient is listed as *1/2 cup whipping cream, whipped,* this indicates you measure the cream *before* you whip it. If the ingredient states *1/2 cup whipped cream,* you measure the cream *after* it is whipped.

To maximize energy savings, I have specified when to preheat or not preheat the oven. Generally, most baked goods, such as cakes, pies and breads, are best baked in a preheated oven. Most roasts, poultry and casseroles, however, don't seem to mind a chilly start. If the recipe tells you to preheat the oven, please do so—it is essential to success. If the recipe tells you not to preheat the oven, you may preheat if you wish—but you will waste energy. Also, cooking time will be about 5 to 10 minutes less for dishes cooked less than 1 hour. Preheating seemed to have little or no effect on timings for long-cooking items, such as roasts or turkey.

Cook's Glossary

Oven—Arrange utensils in the oven to allow for maximum air circulation. Stagger utensils on oven racks so one is not directly above another. Generally, place utensils on center oven rack, near center of rack. Overbrowning may occur if food is placed toward back of oven or if utensils are too close to sides of oven. Most recipes do not require a preheated oven. See the discussion above about when to preheat oven.

Range—The burner should fit the bottom of the pan you are using. Do not place a small pan on a large burner or vice versa. Our timings were determined using electric ranges. Because gas ranges provide immediate heat, timings on these ranges may be slightly less. Our burner settings are High, Medium High, Medium, Medium Low or Low. Your range may use a numbering or other system. To find the equivalent setting, consider your hottest setting equal to High, and determine the other settings from that point.

Boiling vs. simmering—When boiling, a mixture should have bubbles rising continually to the top and breaking on the surface, as above. When simmering, a mixture should have smaller bubbles forming more slowly and collapsing below the surface. If a mixture must simmer a long time, it may be necessary to adjust the heat down to prevent the mixture from boiling. Most recipes recommend Medium-Low heat to simmer food. You may have to adjust the heat slightly up or down to simmer food on your range.

Utensils—Use water to determine the volume of casseroles. Fill casserole with a measured amount of water. Pie plates vary dramatically in size. Recipes were tested using pie plates with the following volumes: 10-inch pie plate = 5-1/2 cups, 9-inch pie plate = 4 cups, and 7-inch pie plate = 2-1/2 cups. Measure the dimensions of a utensil inside the rim at the top. A *baking pan* indicates a *metal* utensil was used for testing. A *baking dish* means *ovenware glass* was used. You can substitute ovenware pottery for glassware. Times between metal and glass utensils are not interchangeable; glass bakes faster.

Preparing utensils—Grease utensils only when specified in the recipe. Use a pastry brush or piece of paper towel to apply a light coating of shortening, butter or margarine over inside of utensil. Do not use vegetable oil. For cakes, add about 1 tablespoon flour to greased pan. Tilt, turn and tap pan so flour coats entire inside surface. Brush a light coating of vegetable oil on inside of gelatin molds. This makes molded items easier to remove without breaking their shapes.

Covering—Cover a dish only when stated in the recipe. A saucepan or casserole is usually covered with a matching lid. Timings assume a tight-fitting lid is used, not a "borrowed" lid that allows heat to escape. Baking dishes may be covered with a piece of foil crimped over the edge to hold in as much heat as possible. If the recipe does not say to cover dish, assume it cooks uncovered. Oven-roasting bags are another way to cook foods covered in the oven.

Cook's Glossary

Electric mixer—Recipes were tested using a counter-top electric mixer. Beating times are given at high, medium or low speeds. To use a mixer with numbers or other speed designations, simply identify the highest speed, the lowest speed and the speed closest to the middle. Timings for a small hand-held mixer will be longer, while timings for a heavy-duty, institutional-type mixer will be less. Use the large 3-quart or small 1-1/2-quart mixer bowls specified in recipes for accurate beating times and best results.

Measuring—Use glass measuring cups for liquid ingredients. Bend down and read the measurement at eye level. Spoon dry ingredients into graduated measuring cups. Granular foods, such as sugar and flour, should be leveled off with the straight edge of a knife. Dry or liquid ingredients may be measured with measuring spoons. Measure liquid ingredients level full. Use the straight edge of a knife to level off dry ingredients, such as baking powder. Do not pack foods down in measuring cups. Brown sugar is the only exception.

Cutting up—*Chop* foods in small irregular pieces with a knife. *Slice* foods to a uniform thickness with a knife. *Mince* some flavoring ingredients, such as garlic, by chopping in tiny pieces. *Cube* foods in reasonably even blocks with a knife. *Snip* ingredients, such as fresh herbs, dried fruit or dried meat, with scissors before measuring. Egg slicers are handy gadgets for cutting eggs or soft vegetables, such as mushrooms, in even slices.

Cutting in—Use two flatware knives or a pastry blender to cut in shortening, butter, margarine or lard into dry ingredients. The recipe will state how small the fat particles should be in the end. In pie crust, for example, shortening is cut into flour mixture until most of the mixture resembles peas. This means shortening particles can be of varying sizes, with the largest being the size of a large pea. This same technique is used for biscuits, some quick breads and some crumb toppings.

Stirring—Use a circular motion to stir a mixture with a spoon or other utensil. To *mix well,* combine until ingredients are evenly distributed in each other. To *blend,* stir ingredients until mixture is homogeneous or the same throughout. To *beat,* stir vigorously in a motion that incorporates air. To *whisk,* use a wire whisk to stir. Whisking is especially useful for stirring ingredients that might lump, such as flour, or that are difficult to blend together, such as milk and canned cream soup.

Folding—Use a folding action to combine ingredients to retain volume or texture. Often recipes call for *folding* ingredients into beaten egg whites to retain volume. Gently spoon other ingredients over beaten egg whites. Using a rubber spatula, make a vertical cut down through egg whites, then move spatula along bottom of bowl, up side of bowl and over top of egg whites. Give bowl a quarter turn and repeat circular motion.

Shredding—Hold the shredder at an angle and push food across the oval-shaped cutting holes with a downward motion. *Grating* is done the same way, using a cutting device with very small, round, cutting holes. Use a hand shredder or food processor to shred cheese, citrus peel and carrots. A shredder makes long, thin, narrow pieces. A grater makes very fine pieces. Citrus peel and hard cheese, such as Parmesan, are often grated. Shredding cheese with a food processor provides a fluffier product.

Sieving—Use a sieve or strainer to separate solids and liquid. Many recipes include spinach that has been pressed in a sieve to remove liquid so spinach will not make finished dish watery. Large sieves make quick work of draining cooked pasta or vegetables. Egg yolks may be forced through a sieve with a spoon to make a garnish. Or, vegetables or fruits may be pressed through a sieve to puree them. Sieves can also be used for sifting cake flour or powdered sugar. Do not sift flour, except cake flour, before measuring.

Cook's Glossary

Steam—Place food on a rack or in a perforated basket in a saucepan or skillet. Pour water to a depth of about 1 inch. Water must be below basket. Bring mixture to a boil over High heat. Cover tightly. Reduce heat to Medium and cook until tender. Water should boil hard enough to make steam escape from under lid. Do not lift lid to check for doneness too soon or too much steam will escape and affect cooking time. Steam chicken, fish, seafood or vegetables.

Poach—Place food in seasoned liquid. Bring to a boil over High heat. Cover tightly. Reduce heat to Medium Low. Simmer so small bubbles form and break below surface of liquid. Poach eggs, fish, seafood, fruit or chicken. Poaching liquid may be strained through cheesecloth and used as broth in soups and sauces, or as a sauce for the fruit. Discard poaching liquid from eggs.

Boil—Place food in a large amount of liquid or enough liquid to cover food. Bring to a boil over High heat. Large bubbles should break on surface of mixture at this point. Cover tightly. Reduce heat to Medium or Medium Low and cook until tender. This method is often used for vegetables and seafood. Pasta is boiled, uncovered, in a large amount of water over Medium-High heat until tender.

Cook in liquid—Place food in a large amount of liquid. This differs from braising, in which a small amount of cooking liquid is used. Bring to a boil over High heat. Reduce heat. Simmer until tender. This method is most often used for soups. If meat, chicken or fish is used, the resulting cooked liquid is called *broth*. This is a good way to precook or parboil pork or beef ribs. This method is also used for salty items, such as corned beef, and for foods that need rehydrating, such as dried beans.

Braise—Place food in a small amount of seasoned liquid. Bring to a boil over High heat. Cover tightly. Reduce heat and cook slowly over Medium-Low heat on the range or in a 350F (175C) oven. Braising is a slow-cooking method to develop flavors and make food fork-tender. Try braising pot roasts, stew, Swiss steak, chops, shanks, chicken or fish. Oven-cooking bags are a good way to braise foods in the oven.

Oven-braise—Place food in a very small amount of seasoned liquid in an ovenproof skillet or Dutch oven. Cover and bake in a 350F (175C) oven. Roasting bags provide an easy way to oven-braise; the bag forms the cover and eliminates messy cleanup. Place food in a floured bag set in a baking dish. Add a small amount of liquid and seasonings. Cut 6 (1/2-inch) slits in top of bag. Tie bag securely with an ovenproof twist tie or string. Oven-braise stew, pot roasts, ribs and fish.

Stir-fry—Cook thinly sliced food very quickly in a small amount of hot oil over Medium-High heat, stirring and tossing food constantly. Foods are often cooked in small batches and then all are combined. Woks are traditionally used for stir-frying, but a heavy skillet is a good alternative. Foods are cut to expose as much surface area as possible for faster cooking. Meat, chicken, shrimp and vegetables are all delicious stir-fried.

Deep-fry—Cook food, usually with a crumb coating, in deep hot oil at 350F (175C) to 365F (185C) until coating is crisp and food is tender. The trick is to have food cut in a size that cooks before crumbs overbrown. If oil is not hot enough, food will become grease-soaked. Drain deep-fried foods on paper towels before serving. Try deep-fried chicken, fish, seafood, vegetables and appetizers.

Cook's Glossary

Sauté—To sauté meat, heat a small amount of fat in a skillet until a drop of water sizzles on it. Add meat and cook over Medium-High heat. Do not layer meat in skillet. Cook two batches, if necessary. Turn meat over halfway through cooking time and reduce heat to Medium. Spoon off juices as they accumulate because they will inhibit browning. To sauté sliced vegetables, layer and turn them often with a spatula while cooking over Medium heat. Do not cover meats or vegetables, except potatoes, during cooking time.

Pan-fry—Dip cutlets or chops in flour, then in beaten egg and finally in a seasoned crumb mixture. Heat a small amount of fat in a skillet until a drop of water sizzles on it. Cook meat over Medium-High heat until browned, turning once. For fish, dip in milk, then in seasoned-crumb or cornmeal coating. Cook fish in a small amount of hot fat over Medium-High heat. Turn fish and reduce heat to Medium. Cook until fish flakes with a fork. Some high-fat items, such as bacon and sausage, are pan-fried without additional fat.

Oven-fry—Spread fish or chicken with softened butter or margarine. Or, coat fish with lemon juice. Coat fish or chicken with seasoned-cracker-crumb mixture. Gently press crumbs on chicken or fish. Place in a shallow baking pan. Cook chicken in a 400F (205C) oven and fish in a 500F (260C) oven. Chicken is done if juices run clear when chicken is pierced with a fork. Fish is done if flesh barely flakes when tested with a fork. Crumb coating should be browned and crisp.

Bake—Cook food in the oven at a designated temperature. Use very low oven temperatures for food that requires slow cooking and little or no browning, such as meringue shells. Bake food that requires fast cooking and maximum browning, such as oven-fried fish, at very high oven temperatures. Most food is baked between these extremes. Baking may also be called *roasting* when referring to large meat cuts and whole poultry.

Roast—Place large meat cuts or whole poultry on a rack in a shallow baking pan. Do not cover. Cook pork roasts at 350F (175C). Most other meats are roasted at 325F (165C), except some small-diameter roasts that are cooked at a higher temperature. Roast chicken, duckling and Cornish hens at 375F (190C), capons and turkey at 325F (165C). A meat thermometer is the best guide to doneness. Insert in center of largest muscle in a roast, not touching fat or bone. For poultry, insert thermometer in thickest part of thigh. Insert thermometer in roast or poultry 30 minutes before end of cooking.

Broil—Cook food on a rack in a shallow pan, directly under heat. This is usually done in an oven. Adjust oven rack to move food closer or farther from heat. This allows thick foods or foods that need a greater degree of doneness to be cooked on a lower rack so they cook through without burning the outside. Thin foods are broiled close to heat for maximum browning. Foods are often marinated to give more flavor before broiling.

Measurements

3 teaspoons = 1 tablespoon
1/2 tablespoon = 1-1/2 teaspoons
2 tablespoons = 1 fluid ounce
3 tablespoons = 1-1/2 fluid ounces
   or 1 jigger
4 tablespoons = 1/4 cup or 2 fluid ounces
5-1/3 tablespoons = 1/3 cup or
   5 tablespoons + 1 teaspoon
8 tablespoons = 1/2 cup or 4 fluid ounces
10-2/3 tablespoons = 2/3 cup or
   10 tablespoons + 2 teaspoons
12 tablespoons = 3/4 cup or 6 fluid ounces
16 tablespoons = 1 cup or 8 fluid ounces
   or 1/2 pint
1 pint = 2 cups or 16 fluid ounces
1 quart = 4 cups or 2 pints or 32 fluid ounces
1 gallon = 4 quarts or 128 fluid ounces

Metric Equivalents

1/4 teaspoon = 1.25 milliliters
1/2 teaspoon = 2.5 milliliters
3/4 teaspoon = 3.75 milliliters
1 teaspoon = 5 milliliters
1-1/4 teaspoons = 6.25 milliliters
1-1/2 teaspoons = 7.5 milliliters

Metric Equivalents continued

1-3/4 teaspoons = 8.75 milliliters
2 teaspoons = 10 milliliters
1 tablespoon = 15 milliliters
2 tablespoons = 30 milliliters
1/4 cup = 60 milliliters
1/2 cup = 120 milliliters
1 cup = 240 milliliters
2 cups = 480 milliliters
3 cups = 720 milliliters
4 cups = 960 milliliters

Conversion to Metric Measures

When You Know	Multiply By	To Find
teaspoons	5	milliliters
tablespoons	15	milliliters
fluid ounces	30	milliliters
cups	.24	liters
pints	.47	liters
quarts	.95	liters
ounces	28	grams
pounds	.45	kilograms
Fahrenheit	5/9 (after subtracting 32)	Celsius
inches	2.54	centimeters

Appetizers & Beverages

These party-going beverages and appetizers turn any get-together into a special event. Beverages are hot or cold, with spirits or without—and all are delicious! Appetizers include dips and spreads, zesty snacks, flavorful meat and cheese tidbits, and elegant cocktail sandwiches. This is a choice collection of recipes. You will want to try each one.

Basic Danish Cocktail Sandwiches, page 44, and Golden Sangria, page 26.

Appetizers & Beverages

Q. Can you suggest an unusual dip or spread to take to a potluck?

A. Our spectacular layered dip, page 40, is guaranteed to bring raves. Choose the chicken, seafood or Mexican fiesta version, and serve it in an attractive compote or soufflé dish. This beautiful dip features layers of seasoned cream cheese, sauce, chopped fresh vegetables, meat or seafood and cheese. Provide spreaders so guests can dip to the bottom and get a blend of all the complementary flavors.

Q. For large parties I need to make some hors d'oeuvres ahead of time. Can you suggest some?

A. Several appetizers in this chapter can be made 1 to 7 days ahead. Prepare a flavorful cheese spread, page 39, cover tightly and refrigerate up to 1 week. Make crisp filo triangles, page 36, on a leisurely day, and freeze in plastic bags up to 1 week. Snack mixes and spicy nuts, page 46, keep well for several days in airtight containers. Day-before appetizers include layered dips, page 40, and liver pâté, page 42. Zesty cocktail meatballs, page 48, can be refrigerated overnight. At party time, reheat slowly in a covered heavy saucepan.

Q. What foods are appropriate for an antipasto tray?

A. Traditionally, this Italian appetizer course includes salami, thin slices of prosciutto ham wrapped around small wedges of melon, an assortment of cheeses, anchovies or sardines, black and green olives, hard-cooked eggs and fresh or marinated vegetables. It is accompanied by crusty bread. You may want to visit an Italian grocery or delicatessen to look over the fascinating array of delicacies just right for an antipasto tray. For pickled vegetables, choose from mushrooms, artichoke hearts, small green peppers, garbanzo beans, onions, cauliflower or beets. Pickled vegetables are best served in separate small dishes. Fresh vegetables may include tomato slices or cucumber, zucchini and green-pepper sticks. Elsewhere in the book are recipes that would be delicious as part of an antipasto tray: Italian Pasta Salad, page 366; Basic Vegetables Vinaigrette, page 377; Deviled Eggs, page 240; Deviled Eggs Plus, page 240; Dill-Cucumber Relish, page 376; and Fresh-Mushroom Relish, page 376.

Q. What kind of wine should I buy for wine punches or spritzers?

A. Buy good inexpensive wine for these recipes. The other ingredients cover up any difference between this and fine, outstanding wine. Allow time for ingredients to stand several hours or overnight, as directed in the recipes, to blend flavors.

Q. How do I decide how much punch to make for a party?

A. As a rule of thumb, allow 2 (4-ounce) servings for each person. If guests will mingle for an extended time, allow extra punch. Our yields show total servings for each recipe. If the punch recipe yields 50 servings, that means 50 (4-ounce) servings, or 2 servings each for 25 people.

Q. How can I keep punch cold without it becoming diluted as ice cubes melt?

A. Make a fancy ice ring or cubes, page 28, using the same flavor fruit juice as in the punch instead of water. Or, freeze whole fruit, page 28, to keep punch icy cold and provide an attractive floating garnish for the punch bowl.

Q. How do you make a perfect cup of tea?

A. Use freshly drawn cold water. Water aerated from the faucet makes more flavorful tea. Bring water to a full boil. Never reheat the same water for another cup, because aeration is gone. Rinse the serving teapot with hot water to keep tea hot. Use 1 tea bag or 1 teaspoon loose tea per cup of tea. For weaker tea, use 1 tea bag or 1 teaspoon loose tea for each 2 cups of tea. Place loose tea in a tea ball. Place tea bags or tea ball in the heated teapot and pour in boiling water. Cover and steep 3 to 5 minutes or until desired strength. The longer tea is steeped, the stronger it becomes. Remove tea ball or tea bags before serving. Squeeze tea bags gently before removing. Serve hot tea with sugar, lemon or milk.

Q. How do you make a perfect cup of coffee?

A. With so many coffeemakers available that use different brewing methods, it is best to follow the manufacturer's directions. For strong, full-bodied coffee, allow 2 tablespoons coffee for each cup. Vary proportions according to your preference until you find the level that suits you best. Always use cold water and the recommended grind of coffee for your coffeemaker.

How to Make Café au Chocolat

1/Make Spiced Coffee by placing cinnamon sticks, whole nutmeg and whole allspice in the percolator basket with coffee grounds. Or, for a drip coffeemaker, steep brewed coffee with spices.

2/Prepare Hot Cocoa. Pour cocoa and coffee into separate serving pots. Pour coffee and cocoa into a cup at the same time so liquid mixes in the cup.

Café au Chocolat

SERVINGS	16	8
INGREDIENTS		
Spiced Coffee, below	8 servings	4 servings
Hot Cocoa, page 22	8 servings	4 servings
COFFEE CUPS	16 (6-oz.) cups	8 (6-oz.) cups

Prepare Spiced Coffee and Hot Cocoa. To serve, pour Spiced Coffee and Hot Cocoa at the same time into each cup.

Spiced Coffee

SERVINGS	8	4
INGREDIENTS		
drip-grind or regular-grind coffee	3/4 to 1 cup	1/3 to 1/2 cup
stick cinnamon	4 inches in total	2 inches in total
whole nutmeg	1	1
whole allspice	4	2
COFFEEMAKER	8-cup coffeemaker	4-cup coffeemaker

Spoon coffee into the basket of a percolator or a drip coffeemaker. If using percolator, add cinnamon, nutmeg and allspice to percolator basket. If using drip coffeemaker, reserve spices. Add enough water for 4 or 8 cups of coffee. Brew coffee according to manufacturer's directions. For drip coffee, add spices to pot of brewed coffee. Cover; keep warm 5 to 10 minutes. Remove spices with a slotted spoon before serving. Serve coffee with cinnamon-stick stirrers, if desired.

Irish Coffee

SERVINGS	4	2
INGREDIENTS		
Irish whiskey	4 to 6 oz.	2 to 3 oz.
brown sugar	4 teaspoons	2 teaspoons
hot strong coffee	3 to 4 cups	1-1/2 to 2 cups
whipping cream	1/4 cup	2 tablespoons
MUGS OR STEMMED GLASSES	4 (8-oz.) mugs or glasses	2 (8-oz.) mugs or glasses

Pour 1 jigger (1 to 1-1/2 ounces) Irish whiskey into each 8-ounce mug or glass, see number in chart above. Add 1 teaspoon brown sugar to each; stir well. Pour coffee to within 1 inch of top of each; stir well. To float 1 tablespoon whipping cream on each serving, carefully rest a spoon of whipping cream on coffee surface. Gradually tip spoon to pour cream, rotating spoon so cream covers entire surface of coffee. Or, pour cream very slowly over the back of a spoon resting on coffee surface.

Hot Cocoa

SERVINGS	6 to 8	3 or 4
INGREDIENTS		
unsweetened cocoa powder	1/2 cup	1/4 cup
packed brown sugar	1/2 cup	1/4 cup
ground cinnamon	1/2 teaspoon	1/4 teaspoon
hot water	1/2 cup	1/4 cup
milk	7 cups	3-1/2 cups
vanilla extract	1 teaspoon	1/2 teaspoon
marshmallows	to garnish	to garnish
HEAVY SAUCEPAN	3-qt. saucepan	2-qt. saucepan
TIME AT MEDIUM HIGH	14 to 16 minutes	11 to 13 minutes

In a heavy saucepan, see size in chart above, whisk together cocoa powder, brown sugar and cinnamon. Gradually whisk in hot water. Bring to a boil over Medium-High heat, whisking constantly. Gradually whisk in milk. Cook for time in chart above or until very hot but not boiling, stirring often. Whisk in vanilla. Serve in mugs garnished with marshmallows.

Kioka Coffee

SERVINGS	8	4
INGREDIENTS		
coffee liqueur	3/4 cup	6 tablespoons
crème de cacao	1/4 cup	2 tablespoons
orange liqueur	1/4 cup	2 tablespoons
brandy	1/4 cup	2 tablespoons
hot strong coffee	8 cups	4 cups
frozen whipped topping, thawed	1 cup	1/2 cup
shredded orange peel	2 teaspoons	1 teaspoon
MEASURING CUP	2-cup measuring cup	1-cup measuring cup
MUGS	8 (8-oz.) mugs	4 (8-oz.) mugs

In a measuring cup, see size in chart above, combine coffee liqueur, crème de cacao, orange liqueur and brandy. Place 3 tablespoons liqueur mixture in each 8-ounce mug, see number in chart above. Pour coffee to within 1 inch of top of each; mix well. Garnish with whipped topping and orange peel. Cover any remaining liqueur mixture and store at room temperature.

Basic Mulled Fruit Cider

SERVINGS	6	3
INGREDIENTS		
apple cider	4 cups	2 cups
fruit juice or wine	2 cups	1 cup
packed brown sugar	2 tablespoons	1 tablespoon
fruit, cored, cut in wedges	1	1/2
cinnamon sticks	4 inches in total	2 inches in total
whole spice	1 teaspoon	1/2 teaspoon
fruit liqueur or brandy	1/2 cup	1/4 cup
SAUCEPAN	3-qt. saucepan	1-1/2-qt. saucepan
TIME AT MEDIUM LOW	10 to 15 minutes	10 to 15 minutes

In a saucepan, see size in chart above, combine cider, fruit juice or wine, brown sugar and fruit. Tie spices in a piece of cheesecloth or place in a tea ball. Add to saucepan. Bring to a boil over High heat. Reduce heat to Medium Low. Stir in fruit liqueur or brandy; cover. Simmer 10 to 15 minutes or until flavors blend. Remove and discard spices. Serve hot in mugs.

Suggested Combinations
Mulled Holiday Cider: Use cranberry juice for fruit juice. Use pear for fruit. Use whole cloves for spice. Use cranberry liqueur.
Mulled Harvest Cider: Use apple wine for wine. Use apple for fruit. Use whole nutmeg for spice. Use 2 whole nutmeg for large recipe and 1 for small recipe. Use apple brandy.

Basic Spiced Hot Tea

SERVINGS	6	3
INGREDIENTS		
water	6 cups	3 cups
frozen juice concentrate, thawed	1/2 (6-oz.) can (1/3 cup)	3 tablespoons
honey	1/4 cup	2 tablespoons
whole spices, see note below	2 to 4 teaspoons	1 to 2 teaspoons
tea bags	4	2
garnishes, see suggestions below		
SAUCEPAN	3-qt. saucepan	1-1/2-qt. saucepan
TIME AT MEDIUM LOW	10 minutes	10 minutes
STEEPING TIME	3 to 4 minutes	3 to 4 minutes

In a saucepan, see size in chart above, combine water, juice concentrate and honey. Tie spices in a piece of cheesecloth or place in a tea ball. Add to saucepan. Bring to a boil over High heat. Reduce heat to Medium Low. Simmer, uncovered, 10 minutes. Stir in tea bags. Cover and let steep 3 to 4 minutes. Remove and discard spices and tea bags. Garnish according to suggestions below.

Suggested Combinations
Orange Spiced Hot Tea: Use orange-juice concentrate. Use smaller amount of whole allspice and whole cloves for spices. Garnish with orange quarter-slices.
Pineapple Spiced Hot Tea: Use pineapple-juice concentrate. Use whole nutmeg and cinnamon sticks for spice. Garnish with pineapple quarter-slices.

Note: When measuring whole spices, 1 whole nutmeg or 1 (2-inch) cinnamon stick equals 1 teaspoon.

Basic Sparkling-Wine Punch

SERVINGS	20	10
INGREDIENTS		
fruit juice, chilled	2 cups	1 cup
loose-pack frozen fruit	1 (16-oz.) pkg. (4 cups)	1/2 (16-oz.) pkg. (2 cups)
fruit liqueur or brandy	1/2 cup	1/4 cup
lemon juice	1/4 cup	2 tablespoons
sparkling wine, chilled	2 (750-ml.) bottles	1 (750-ml.) bottle
Basic Fancy Ice Ring or Ice Cubes, page 28, if desired	to garnish	to garnish
BOWL	6-qt. bowl	3-qt. bowl

In a bowl, see size in chart above, mix fruit juice, frozen fruit, fruit liqueur or brandy and lemon juice. Immediately before serving, slowly pour in sparkling wine; mix gently. Float ice ring or ice cubes, if desired. Serve in 4-ounce punch cups or fluted champagne glasses.

Suggested Combinations
Sparkling-Wine Wedding Punch: Use white-grape juice. Use frozen raspberries. Use raspberry liqueur or kirsch. Use pink champagne for sparkling wine.
Sparkling-Wine Brunch Punch: Use orange juice. Use frozen melon balls. Use orange liqueur. Omit lemon juice. Use Asti Spumante for sparkling wine.
Sparkling-Wine Celebration Punch: Use apple juice. Use frozen sliced peaches. Use peach brandy. Use sparkling rosé wine.

Basic Punch for a Bunch

SERVINGS	100	50	25
INGREDIENTS			
unsweetened soft-drink powder	4 (.14-oz.) envelopes	2 (.14-oz.) envelopes	1 (.14-oz.) envelope
sugar	3 cups	1-1/2 cups	3/4 cup
water	4 qts.	2 qts.	1 qt.
frozen juice concentrate, thawed	1 (12-oz.) can	1 (6-oz.) can	1/3 cup
water	4 qts.	2 qts.	1 qt.
fruit juice	8 cups	4 cups	2 cups
carbonated beverage, chilled	4 (1-qt.) bottles	2 (1-qt.) bottles	1-qt. bottle
Basic Fancy Ice Ring or Ice Cubes, page 28, if desired	to garnish	to garnish	to garnish
BOWL	4-gallon bowl	2-gallon bowl	5-qt. bowl
REFRIGERATE	8 hours or overnight	8 hours or overnight	8 hours or overnight

In a bowl, see size in chart above, combine soft-drink powder and sugar; mix well. Stir in first amount of water. Stir until powder and sugar dissolve. Stir in juice concentrate, second amount of water and fruit juice. Cover and refrigerate 8 hours or overnight. Immediately before serving, pour in carbonated beverage; mix gently. Float ice ring or ice cubes, if desired. Serve in 4-ounce punch cups.

Suggested Combinations
Prom Punch for a Bunch: Use raspberry soft-drink powder. Use frozen lemonade concentrate. Use cranberry-juice cocktail for fruit juice. Use lemon-lime carbonated beverage.
Reception Punch for a Bunch: Use orange soft-drink powder. Use pineapple-juice concentrate. Use apricot nectar for fruit juice. Use ginger ale for carbonated beverage.

Sparkling-Wine Wedding Punch

Basic Fresh-Fruit Spritzers

SERVINGS	10	5
INGREDIENTS		
fresh fruit, see suggestions below	2 cups	1 cup
fruit liqueur, brandy or wine	2/3 cup	1/3 cup
dry white wine, chilled	1 (750-ml.) bottle (3-1/4 cups)	1-1/2 cups
carbonated beverage, chilled	4 cups	2 cups
PITCHER	3-qt. pitcher	1-1/2-qt. pitcher
STANDING TIME OR	2 hours	2 hours
REFRIGERATE	8 hours or overnight	8 hours or overnight

In a pitcher, see size in chart above, combine fresh fruit and fruit liqueur; mix well. If using peaches or apricots, add a little ascorbic acid color-keeper. Cover and let stand 2 hours at room temperature or refrigerate 8 hours or overnight. Chill 5 or 10 wine glasses. Immediately before serving, pour wine and carbonated beverage into pitcher; mix gently. Pour over ice cubes in chilled glasses. Garnish with marinated fruit.

Suggested Combinations
Rhineland Fruit Spritzer: Use seedless green grapes and small red plums, pitted and quartered, for fruit. Use brandy and plum wine for fruit liqueur. Use Gewürztraminer wine. Use lemon-lime carbonated beverage.
Summertime Fruit Spritzer: Use dark sweet cherries and sliced peeled peaches for fruit. Use peach brandy and cherry brandy for fruit liqueur. Use Vouvray wine. Use plain carbonated soda water.
Honeydew Spritzer: Use honeydew-melon balls and orange sections for fruit. Use melon liqueur and orange liqueur for fruit liqueur. Use Muscadet wine. Use ginger ale for carbonated beverage.

Basic Sangria

SERVINGS	10	5
INGREDIENTS		
water	1-1/2 cups	3/4 cup
sugar	2/3 cup	1/3 cup
whole spices, see note below	4 teaspoons	2 teaspoons
whole fruit, thinly sliced, seeded	4	2
fruit liqueur	1 cup	1/2 cup
wine	2 (750-ml.) bottles	1 (750-ml.) bottle
SAUCEPAN	2-qt. saucepan	1-qt. saucepan
PITCHER	3-qt. pitcher	1-1/2-qt. pitcher
TIME AT MEDIUM LOW	10 minutes	10 minutes
STANDING TIME	1 to 2 hours	1 to 2 hours

In a saucepan, see size in chart above, combine water and sugar. Tie spices in a piece of cheesecloth or place in a tea ball. Add to saucepan. Bring to a boil over High heat, stirring constantly until sugar dissolves. Reduce heat to Medium Low. Simmer, uncovered, 10 minutes. Add fruit and fruit liqueur to sugar syrup in saucepan. Cover and let stand at room temperature 1 to 2 hours, stirring occasionally. Remove and discard spices. In a pitcher, see size in chart above, combine syrup-fruit mixture and wine; mix well. Pour over ice cubes in tall glasses. Garnish with fruit slices.

Suggested Combinations
Traditional Sangria: Use cinnamon sticks and whole allspice for spices. Use oranges and lemons for fruit. Use orange liqueur. Use Burgundy wine.
Golden Sangria, photo on page 18: Use whole nutmeg and whole cloves for spices. Use limes and peaches for fruit. Use peach brandy for fruit liqueur. Use Mosel wine.

Note: When measuring whole spices, 1 whole nutmeg or 1 (2-inch) cinnamon stick equals 1 teaspoon.

How to Make Basic Cocktail Slush

1/In a bowl or large pitcher, mix fruit juice, liquor and liqueur. For Harvey Wallbanger Slush, use orange juice, vodka and Galliano liqueur. For Strawberry Daiquiri Slush, use limeade for fruit juice, rum and strawberry liqueur.

2/Freeze fruit-juice mixtures in loaf pans 6 hours or until slushy. Mixtures will not freeze firm because of the alcohol content. To serve, break up slush with a fork. Spoon into stemmed glasses or layer different colors of slush in glasses.

Basic Cocktail Slush

SERVINGS	6	3
INGREDIENTS		
fruit juice	5 cups	2-1/2 cups
liquor	2/3 cup	1/3 cup
liqueur	6 tablespoons	3 tablespoons
garnishes, see suggestions below		
LOAF PAN	2 (9" x 5" x 3") loaf pans	9" x 5" x 3" loaf pan
FREEZE	6 hours or overnight	6 hours or overnight

In a bowl or large pitcher, combine fruit juice, liquor and liqueur; mix well. Pour into 1 or 2 (9" x 5" x 3") loaf pans; cover. Freeze 6 hours or until slushy. Mixture will not freeze firm. To serve, break up with a fork; spoon into stemmed glasses. Garnish according to suggestions below.

Suggested Combinations
Whiskey Sour Slush: Use lemonade for fruit juice. Use bourbon for liquor. Use bourbon liqueur. Garnish with lemon slices and maraschino cherries.

Strawberry Daiquiri Slush: Use limeade for fruit juice. Use rum for liquor. Use strawberry liqueur. Add 1 or 2 drops red food coloring, if desired. Garnish with fresh strawberries and mint sprigs.

Harvey Wallbanger Slush: Use orange juice. Use vodka for liquor. Use Galliano liqueur. Garnish with orange slices and maraschino cherries.

Margarita Slush: Use limeade for fruit juice. Use tequila for liquor. Use orange liqueur. Dip rims of glasses in lime juice, then in coarse salt, coating rims generously. Garnish with lime slices.

Piña Colada Slush: Use pineapple juice. Use rum for liquor. Use piña colada liqueur. Garnish with pineapple wedges and maraschino cherries.

Basic Fancy Ice Ring or Ice Cubes

YIELD	6-1/2-cup ring	3-1/2-cup ring
INGREDIENTS		
fresh or drained, canned, sliced fruit, whole berries, mint leaves or maraschino cherries	1/2 cup	1/2 cup
water or fruit juice	5-1/2 cups	3 cups
RING MOLD OR ICE-CUBE TRAYS	6-1/2-cup ring mold or ice-cube trays	3-1/2-cup ring mold or ice-cube trays
FREEZE (fruit layer in ring mold)	1-1/2 hours	1-1/2 hours
FREEZE (second amount of liquid added)	1-1/2 to 2 hours	1-1/2 to 2 hours
FREEZE (finished mold or ice cubes)	6 hours or overnight	6 hour or overnight

For ring mold: Arrange fruit and leaves in a design in bottom of a ring mold, see size in chart above. Measure total water or fruit juice. Carefully pour 1/2 cup water or juice into ring mold. Freeze 1-1/2 hours or until firm. Carefully pour 1 cup more water or juice over fruit layer in mold to cover fruit. Freeze 1-1/2 to 2 hours or until firm. Carefully pour in enough remaining water or juice almost to fill mold. Freeze 6 hours or overnight until firm. To unmold, dip mold almost to rim in hot water. Invert. Float ring in a punch bowl.

For ice cubes: Arrange fruit and leaves in each cube portion in ice-cube trays. Fill trays three-fourths full with water or juice. Freeze 6 hours or overnight. Remove cubes from tray according to manufacturer's directions. Float cubes in punch or in individual glasses.

Suggested Combinations
Spring Punch Ice Ring: Use strawberries, mint leaves and canned pineapple slices, quartered, for fruit.
Summer Punch Ice Ring: Use whole, dark, sweet cherries, sliced peaches and green grapes for fruit.
Fancy Iced-Tea Cubes: Use mint leaves and lemon quarter-slices for fruit.

Note: To prevent punch from becoming watery as ice melts, use same fruit juice in ice ring or cubes as in punch. Fruit design is not as visible through ice if you use dark-colored fruit juice instead of water.

Frozen Fruit for Ice

YIELD	for large punch bowl	for small punch bowl
INGREDIENTS		
whole apples, nectarines, oranges, lemons, peaches, pears, plums, grape bunches	6 large or 12 small fruit	3 large or 6 small fruit
OR		
whole strawberries with hulls	1 qt.	1 pint
FREEZE	4 hours or overnight	4 hours or overnight

Wash fruit. Freeze whole fruit 4 hours or overnight. Add whole frozen fruit to punch bowl to keep punch chilled.

How to Make a Basic Fancy Ice Ring

1/Arrange fruit in the bottom of a ring mold. This mold has lemon-slice twists, green-grape clusters and raspberries. Pour 1/2 cup fruit juice or water over fruit. Freeze 1-1/2 hours or until firm. This anchors fruit to bottom of mold.

2/Add 1 cup more fruit juice or water to frozen layer. Freeze 1-1/2 hours or until firm. This prevents fruit from floating. Add enough fruit juice or water almost to fill mold. Freeze 6 hours or until firm. Dip mold almost to rim in hot water and unmold in punch. If using fruit juice, fruit design becomes more visible as frozen juice melts.

Basic Milk Shakes

SERVINGS	4	2
INGREDIENTS		
flavored syrup	1/2 cup	1/4 cup
milk	1/2 cup	1/4 cup
ice cream or sherbet	1 qt.	1 pint
GLASSES	4 (8-oz.) glasses	2 (8-oz.) glasses
BLENDING TIME AT HIGH SPEED (syrup, milk)	5 seconds	5 seconds
BLENDING TIME AT HIGH SPEED (half of ice cream added)	5 to 10 seconds	5 to 10 seconds
BLENDING TIME AT HIGH SPEED (remaining ice cream added)	5 to 10 seconds	5 to 10 seconds

In a blender, combine flavored syrup and milk. Blend at high speed 5 seconds or until well-mixed. Add half of ice cream or sherbet by spoonfuls. Blend at high speed 5 to 10 seconds or until smooth. Add remaining ice cream or sherbet. Blend at high speed 5 to 10 seconds or until ice cream or sherbet is just blended. Stop blender and scrape sides once or twice, if necessary. Pour into 2 or 4 (8-ounce) glasses; serve immediately.

Suggested Combinations
Café au Lait Milk Shake: Use crème de cacao syrup. Use coffee ice cream.
Double-Chocolate Milk Shake: Use chocolate syrup. Use chocolate ice cream.

Variation
Malted Milk: Use 2 tablespoons malted-milk powder for each serving. Blend malt powder with syrup and milk.

Basic Ice-Cream Sodas

SERVINGS	4	2
INGREDIENTS		
flavored syrup or crushed fruit	1/2 cup	1/4 cup
ice cream	1 qt.	1 pint
carbonated beverage	2 cups	1 cup
garnishes, see suggestions below		
GLASSES	4 (12-oz.) glasses	2 (12-oz.) glasses

In each 12-ounce glass, see number in chart above, combine 2 tablespoons flavored syrup or fruit and a little ice cream. Stir until well-mixed. Fill glasses with scoops of ice cream. Slowly pour in some carbonated beverage; stir gently. Add more carbonated beverage to fill glasses; stir gently. Garnish according to suggestions below. Serve immediately with parfait spoons and straws.

Suggested Combinations
Brown Cow: Use root beer instead of flavored syrup. Use vanilla ice cream. Use root beer for carbonated beverage. Garnish with whipped cream and maraschino cherries.
Strawberry-Ice-Cream Soda: Use strawberry syrup or crushed fresh or frozen strawberries. Use strawberry ice cream. Use strawberry carbonated beverage. Garnish with fresh or frozen sliced strawberries.
Mint-Patty Ice-Cream Soda: Use crème de menthe syrup. Use mint-chocolate-chip ice cream. Use plain carbonated soda water. Garnish with mint sprigs.
Peach-Ice-Cream Soda: Use crushed fresh or frozen peaches. Use peach ice cream. Use lemon-lime carbonated beverage. Garnish with fresh or frozen peach slices and lemon balm.
Double-Chocolate Ice-Cream Soda: Use chocolate syrup. Use chocolate ice cream. Use plain carbonated soda water.

Basic Fruit Shakes

SERVINGS	4	2
INGREDIENTS		
loose-pack frozen fruit	1/2 cup	1/4 cup
milk	1 cup	1/2 cup
ice cream or sherbet	1 pint	1 cup
GLASSES	4 (8-oz.) glasses	2 (8-oz.) glasses
BLENDING TIME AT HIGH SPEED (fruit, milk)	5 seconds	5 seconds
BLENDING TIME AT HIGH SPEED (half of ice cream added)	10 to 15 seconds	5 to 10 seconds
BLENDING TIME AT HIGH SPEED (remaining ice cream added)	10 to 15 seconds	5 to 10 seconds

In a blender, combine frozen fruit and milk. Blend at high speed 5 seconds or until pureed. Add half of ice cream or sherbet by spoonfuls. Blend at high speed for time in chart above or until smooth. Add remaining ice cream or sherbet. Blend at high speed for time in chart above or until ice cream is just blended. Stop blender and scrape sides once or twice, if necessary. Pour into 2 or 4 (8-ounce) glasses; serve immediately.

Suggested Combinations
Strawberry Shake: Use frozen strawberries. Use strawberry ice cream. Garnish with strawberries.
Mixed-Fruit Shake: Use frozen mixed fruit. Use orange sherbet. Garnish with peach slices.

Strawberry-Ice-Cream Soda, Mint-Patty Ice-Cream Soda and Mixed-Fruit Shake.

Basic Egg Rolls

YIELD	14 or 15 egg rolls	7 or 8 egg rolls
INGREDIENTS		
drained cooked vegetables	1-1/2 cups	3/4 cup
chopped cooked meat or fish	2 cups	1 cup
shredded cheese	1 cup (4 oz.)	1/2 cup (2 oz.)
chopped fresh vegetable	1/4 cup	2 tablespoons
creamy-style salad dressing	1/2 cup	1/4 cup
herb seed	1 teaspoon	1/2 teaspoon
egg-roll skins, 7" x 6-1/2"	14 or 15 skins, 1 (1-lb.) pkg.	7 or 8 skins, 1/2 (1-lb.) pkg.
vegetable oil for deep-frying	2 qts.	2 qts.
DEEP-FAT FRYER OR HEAVY DUTCH OVEN	5-qt. fryer or Dutch oven	5-qt. fryer or Dutch oven
TIME IN 375F (190C) OIL	2 to 3 minutes	2 to 3 minutes

In a medium bowl, combine cooked vegetables, meat or fish, cheese and fresh vegetable; mix well. Fold in salad dressing and herb seed. Place 1 egg-roll skin in a diamond pattern in front of you. Spread scant 1/4 cup filling in strip across center of egg-roll skin. Fold up bottom corner; fold in corners from each side, envelope-fashion. Fold last corner over and moisten underside of point to seal. Repeat with remaining egg-roll skins and filling. Pour oil into a 5-quart deep-fat fryer or heavy Dutch oven. Fryer should be about half full of oil. Preheat oil to 375F (190C) or until a 1-inch cube of bread turns golden brown in 50 seconds. Fry egg rolls, three at a time, in hot oil 2 to 3 minutes or until browned and crisp. Remove from oil with a slotted spoon and drain on paper towels. Serve hot with a sauce, if desired.

Suggested Combinations

Reuben Egg Rolls: Use snipped, rinsed, drained, canned sauerkraut for cooked vegetable. Use corned beef for meat. Use Swiss cheese. Use chopped green onion for fresh vegetable. Use Thousand Island salad dressing. Use caraway seed for herb seed. Serve with a mustard-type sauce, if desired.

Salmon Egg Rolls: Use peas and carrots for cooked vegetables. Use flaked, drained, canned salmon for fish. Use Cheddar cheese. Use chopped onion for fresh vegetable. Use buttermilk salad dressing. Use celery seed for herb seed. Serve with a sweet-sour sauce, if desired.

Basic Stuffed Mushrooms

YIELD	16 mushroom caps	8 mushroom caps
INGREDIENTS		
cracker crumbs	1/2 cup	1/4 cup
shredded cheese	1/2 cup (2 oz.)	1/4 cup (1 oz.)
chopped cooked meat or seafood	1/2 cup	1/4 cup
chopped vegetables	1/2 cup	1/4 cup
cooking sauce	1/4 cup	2 tablespoons
fresh mushrooms, 1-1/2 to 2 inches in diameter	16	8
butter or margarine, melted	2 tablespoons	1 tablespoon
PIE PLATE	10-inch pie plate	9-inch pie plate
TIME IN 425F (220C) OVEN	20 to 25 minutes	20 to 25 minutes

Do not preheat oven. In a medium bowl, combine cracker crumbs, cheese, meat or seafood and vegetables; toss until well-combined. Add cooking sauce; mix well and set aside. Remove stems from mushrooms and reserve for another use. Wash mushrooms; pat dry on paper towels. Dip mushroom tops in butter or margarine. Fill stem-side with stuffing. Place in a pie plate, see size in chart above, propping up mushrooms along edge of dish, if necessary. Drizzle with any remaining butter or margarine. Bake in a 425F (220C) oven 20 to 25 minutes or until heated through.

Suggested Combinations

Shrimp-Stuffed Mushrooms: Use sesame-cracker crumbs. Use Cheddar cheese. Use chopped cooked shrimp for seafood. Use chopped green onion and chopped pimiento for vegetables. Use cocktail sauce for cooking sauce.

Sausage-Stuffed Mushrooms: Use onion-cracker crumbs. Use mozzarella cheese. Use chopped, fully cooked, smoked sausage for meat. Use chopped green pepper and chopped celery for vegetables. Use pizza sauce for cooking sauce.

How to Make Basic Egg Rolls

1/Place an egg-roll skin with 1 corner toward you. Spread a scant 1/4 cup filling in a strip across center of egg-roll skin.

2/Fold up bottom corner of egg roll over filling. Then fold in corners from each side, envelope-fashion.

3/Fold over top corner, or "flap of the envelope," and moisten underside of point to help seal tip to roll-up.

4/Fry egg rolls, 3 at a time, in deep 375F (190C) oil. Serve Salmon Egg Rolls with bottled sweet-sour sauce, if desired.

Basic Scotch Eggs

SERVINGS	8	4
INGREDIENTS		
ground meat	1 lb.	8 oz.
snipped parsley	2 tablespoons	1 tablespoon
seasoning sauce	2 tablespoons	1 tablespoon
dried leaf herb, ground herb or ground spice	1 teaspoon	1/2 teaspoon
hard-cooked eggs	8	4
vegetable oil for deep-frying	about 2-1/2 qts.	about 2-1/2 qts.
eggs	2	1
milk	2 tablespoons	1 tablespoon
all-purpose flour	to coat lightly	to coat lightly
fine dry breadcrumbs	2/3 cup	1/3 cup
DEEP-FAT FRYER OR HEAVY DUTCH OVEN	5-qt. fryer or Dutch oven	5-qt. fryer or Dutch oven
REFRIGERATE	4 hours	4 hours
TIME IN 350F (175C) OIL:		
ham, sausage	4-1/2 to 5 minutes	4-1/2 to 5 minutes
beef	3-1/2 to 4 minutes	3-1/2 to 4 minutes

In a medium bowl, combine ground meat, parsley, seasoning sauce and herb or spice using a fork; mix well. Using wet hands, shape ground-meat mixture into 4 or 8 patties. Use about 1/4 cup meat mixture to make each patty about 4 inches in diameter. Wrap each hard-cooked egg in meat patty, shaping meat mixture to cover egg completely. Cover and refrigerate at least 4 hours. Pour oil into a 5-quart deep-fat fryer or heavy Dutch oven. Fryer should be about half full of oil. Preheat oil to 350F (175C) or until a 1-inch cube of bread turns brown in 65 seconds. In a pie plate, combine eggs and milk using a fork. Roll meat-covered eggs in flour, then in beaten egg mixture, then in breadcrumbs. Fry, 2 or 3 at a time, in hot oil for time in chart above or until browned and meat is done. Remove from oil with a slotted spoon and drain on paper towels. Serve hot or cold with additional seasoning sauce, if desired.

Suggested Combinations
Scotch Ham & Eggs: Use half ground pork and half ground cooked ham for meat. Use prepared horseradish and prepared mustard for seasoning sauce. Use rubbed sage and thyme for herbs.
Scotch Sausage & Eggs: Use fresh bulk pork sausage for meat. Use bottled sweet-sour sauce for seasoning sauce. Use dry mustard and ginger for spices.
Scotch Steak & Eggs: Use ground beef for meat. Use steak sauce for seasoning sauce. Use rubbed basil and herb pepper for herbs.

Tips for Deep-Fried Appetizers
- Cold Scotch Eggs make a fun lunch-box addition. Eat them within 2 hours or refrigerate until lunch.
- Malakoff is a delightful Swiss dish. After frying cheese-side down, turn French-bread quarters any way you can to make them stay put in bubbling oil. Ours turned themselves crust-side up no matter what we did to turn them over!
- You must freeze Fried Cheese Sticks before frying. If sticks are not frozen, cheese will leak out and leave only a crumb case.
- To clarify oil to reuse for deep-frying, see page 172.

Malakoff

(French-Fried Fondue)

YIELD	64 pieces	32 pieces
INGREDIENTS		
shredded Swiss cheese	2-2/3 cups (about 10-1/2 oz.)	1-1/3 cups (about 5-1/2 oz.)
all-purpose flour	3 tablespoons	4 teaspoons
freshly ground pepper	1/2 teaspoon	1/4 teaspoon
garlic powder	1/8 teaspoon	dash
ground nutmeg	1/8 teaspoon	dash
egg yolks, slightly beaten	4	2
dry white wine	1/3 cup	3 tablespoons
kirsch	1/3 cup	3 tablespoons
egg whites	4	2
small French bread, cut in 1-inch slices	16 slices	8 slices
vegetable oil for deep-frying	2 qts.	2 qts.
MIXER BOWL	1-1/2-qt. bowl	1-1/2-qt. bowl
DEEP-FAT FRYER OR HEAVY DUTCH OVEN	5-qt. fryer or Dutch oven	5-qt. fryer or Dutch oven
BEATING TIME AT HIGH SPEED	1 minute	45 seconds
REFRIGERATE	1 hour	1 hour
TIME IN 365F (185C) OIL (first side)	1 minute	1 minute
TIME IN 365F (185C) OIL (second side)	1 minute	1 minute

In a medium bowl, toss cheese with flour, pepper, garlic powder and nutmeg. Stir in egg yolks; mix well. Stir in wine and kirsch; mix well and set aside. In a 1-1/2-quart mixer bowl, beat egg whites at high speed of an electric mixer for time in chart above or until stiff peaks form. Scrape sides of bowl often. Fold cheese mixture into egg whites. Cut French-bread slices in quarters. Mound cheese mixture on each quarter-piece of bread. Refrigerate in a single layer on a baking sheet 1 hour. Pour oil into a 5-quart deep-fat fryer or heavy Dutch oven. Fryer should be about half full of oil. Preheat oil to 365F (185C) or until a 1-inch cube of bread turns golden brown in 60 seconds. Fry bread quarters, 6 at a time, in hot oil with cheese-side down for 1 minute. Turn crust-side up and fry 1 minute or until golden brown. Remove from oil with a slotted spoon and drain on paper towels. Serve hot.

Fried Cheese Sticks

YIELD	48 sticks	24 sticks
INGREDIENTS		
Cheddar, Swiss, Monterey Jack, caraway, brick, smoked or mozzarella cheese	1-1/2-lb. block	12-oz. block
all-purpose flour	1/2 cup	1/4 cup
eggs, well beaten	2	1
cheese-, saltine-, sesame- or bacon-cracker crumbs	2 cups	1 cup
vegetable oil for deep-frying	2 qts.	2 qts.
DEEP-FAT FRYER OR HEAVY DUTCH OVEN	5-qt. fryer or Dutch oven	5-qt. fryer or Dutch oven
FREEZE	1-1/2 to 2 hours	1-1/2 to 2 hours
TIME IN 375F (190C) OIL	30 to 45 seconds	30 to 45 seconds

Cut cheese in sticks, 1/2 inch thick, 1/2 inch wide and 2 or 3 inches long. Dip each cheese stick in flour, then in egg, then in cracker crumbs, coating all sides. Freeze in a single layer on a baking sheet 1-1/2 to 2 hours. Pour oil into a 5-quart deep-fat fryer or heavy Dutch oven. Fryer should be about half full of oil. Preheat oil to 375F (190C) or until a 1-inch cube of bread turns golden brown in 50 seconds. Fry cheese pieces, 6 at a time, in hot oil 30 to 45 seconds or until browned. Remove from oil with a slotted spoon and drain on paper towels. Serve hot.

Basic Filo Triangles

YIELD	48 triangles	24 triangles
INGREDIENTS		
frozen filo leaves, thawed	8 oz.	4 oz.
ricotta cheese	1/2 cup	1/4 cup
flavored semisoft natural cheese	1 (3-1/2-oz.) carton	1/2 (3-1/2-oz.) carton
egg yolks	2	1
grated Parmesan or Romano cheese	1/4 cup	2 tablespoons
finely chopped vegetables	1/2 cup	1/4 cup
butter or margarine, melted	2/3 cup	1/3 cup
MIXER BOWL	1-1/2-qt. bowl	1-1/2-qt. bowl
BAKING PAN	15" x 10" x 1" baking pan	15" x 10" x 1" baking pan
BEATING TIME AT MEDIUM SPEED (soft cheeses)	30 to 45 seconds	30 to 45 seconds
BEATING TIME AT MEDIUM SPEED (egg yolks added)	30 seconds	30 seconds
TIME IN 375F (190C) OVEN	15 to 18 minutes	15 to 18 minutes

Follow package directions for thawing and using filo dough. In a 1-1/2-quart mixer bowl, beat ricotta cheese and semisoft natural cheese at medium speed of an electric mixer for 30 to 45 seconds or until blended. Scrape sides of bowl often. Beat in egg yolks and Parmesan or Romano cheese for 30 seconds or until blended. By hand, stir in vegetables; set aside. Preheat oven to 375F (190C). Cut filo leaves lengthwise in 2-1/2-inch-wide strips. Stack and place strips between barely dampened cloth towels to prevent drying. Brush first strip of filo with melted butter or margarine. Place 1/2 tablespoon cheese mixture on bottom corner of strip. Fold corner with filling over to top of strip, enclosing filling and forming a triangle. Fold over triangle; continue to fold strip flag-fashion, maintaining triangle shape. Place, seam-side down, on a 15" x 10" x 1" baking pan. Brush with melted butter or margarine. Repeat process with remaining filo strips, butter or margarine and filling. Bake in several batches in preheated oven 15 to 18 minutes or until browned and crisp. Drain on paper towels. Serve hot.

Suggested Combinations
Herb-Garlic Filo Triangles: Use semisoft natural cheese with garlic and herbs. Use Romano cheese. Use snipped parsley and chopped well-drained pimiento for chopped vegetables.

Peppery Filo Triangles: Use semisoft natural cheese with pepper. Use Parmesan and Romano cheeses. Use chopped green onion and chopped, drained, canned mushrooms for vegetables.

Onion Filo Triangles: Use semisoft natural cheese with French onion. Use Parmesan cheese. Use chopped, drained, marinated artichoke hearts for vegetables.

Note: To make triangles ahead, bake, cool on a rack and freeze in plastic bags up to 1 week. To reheat, bake frozen triangles on a baking pan in a preheated 375F (190C) oven 10 minutes.

Tips for Using Filo Dough
- Filo dough, also called *phyllo dough,* is sold in the frozen-food case or the gourmet section of grocery stores or in specialty food shops and delicatessens.
- Very thin, flaky sheets or leaves of filo dough can be cut to make various desserts and appetizers. The filo sheets we used were 18" x 14" in size.
- Most manufacturers recommend thawing unopened dough in the refrigerator 8 hours or overnight, then allowing unopened dough to stand at room temperature 2 hours before using.
- Keep filo dough in original package until filling is made. Filo dough dries out quickly and becomes difficult to handle when exposed to air.
- Cover leaves of filo dough with a slightly damp cloth towel. Use filo leaves as needed, keeping remaining dough covered completely with damp towel.

How to Make Basic Filo Triangles

1/Brush strip of filo dough with melted butter or margarine. Place 1/2 tablespoon cheese filling on bottom corner of dough strip. Fold corner with filling over to top of strip, enclosing filling and forming a triangle.

2/Fold triangle over. Continue to fold strip flag-fashion, maintaining triangle shape. Place, seam-side down, on a baking pan. Brush with melted butter or margarine. Bake in several batches until browned and crisp. Serve filo triangles hot.

Basic Meat & Cheese Puffs

YIELD	20 to 24 puffs	10 to 12 puffs
INGREDIENTS		
mayonnaise or mayonnaise-style salad dressing	1/2 cup	1/4 cup
mustard	1 teaspoon	1/2 teaspoon
prepared horseradish	1 teaspoon	1/2 teaspoon
finely chopped cooked meat	1 cup	1/2 cup
drained pickle relish	1/4 cup	2 tablespoons
hard-cooked eggs, chopped	2	1
snipped parsley	4 teaspoons	2 teaspoons
tiny rye-bread slices	20 to 24	10 to 12
process-cheese slices, quartered	5 to 6	2-1/2 to 3
BAKING PAN	15" x 10" x 1" baking pan	15" x 10" x 1" baking pan
TIME AT BROIL (bread)	1-1/2 to 2-1/2 minutes	1-1/2 to 2-1/2 minutes
TIME AT BROIL (filling added)	30 to 60 seconds	30 to 60 seconds

Preheat an electric broiler. You do not need to preheat a gas broiler. In a medium bowl, combine mayonnaise or salad dressing, mustard and horseradish; mix well. Stir in meat, relish, egg and parsley; set aside. Place bread slices on a 15" x 10" x 1" baking pan. Broil 4 inches from heat 1-1/2 to 2-1/2 minutes or until lightly toasted, turning over once. Spoon about 1 tablespoon meat mixture on each bread round. Top each with a quarter-slice of cheese. Broil 4 inches from heat 30 to 60 seconds or until cheese melts to cover filling.

Suggested Combinations
Corned-Beef & Cheese Puffs: Use prepared mustard. Use corned beef for meat. Use dill-pickle relish. Use Swiss cheese.
Ham & Cheese Puffs: Use Dijon-style mustard. Use ham for meat. Use sweet-pickle relish. Use American cheese.

Basic Appetizer Quiche

SERVINGS	12	6
INGREDIENTS		
pie-crust mix	3 sticks	1-1/2 sticks
finely chopped cooked meat or seafood	2/3 cup	1/3 cup
seasoned dry breadcrumbs	2 tablespoons	1 tablespoon
shredded cheese	1-1/2 cups (6 oz.)	3/4 cup (3 oz.)
chopped, drained, canned vegetables	1/2 cup	1/4 cup
eggs	2	1
half and half	1 cup	1/2 cup
dried leaf herb	1/4 teaspoon	1/8 teaspoon
QUICHE DISHES	12 dishes, 3-1/2 inches in diameter, 5/8 inch deep	6 dishes, 3-1/2 inches in diameter, 5/8 inch deep
BAKING PAN	2 (15" x 10" x 1") baking pans	15" x 10" x 1" baking pan
TIME IN 450F (230C) OVEN	8 to 10 minutes	8 to 10 minutes
TIME IN 375F (190C) OVEN	15 to 16 minutes	15 to 16 minutes
STANDING TIME	5 minutes	5 minutes

Preheat oven to 450F (230C). Prepare pie-crust mix according to package directions. Divide dough for large recipe in 2 portions. On a floured board, roll out each dough portion to a 15" x 10" rectangle, 1/8 inch thick. Cut in 6 or 12 (4-1/2-inch) rounds. Fit dough into 3-1/2-inch quiche dishes; flute edges. Do not prick dough. Fit a 3-1/2-inch piece of foil into bottom and sides of each dough-lined dish; spoon 2 tablespoons dry beans into each. Place on baking pans. Bake in preheated oven 8 to 10 minutes or until lightly browned. Remove foil and beans. Cool shells completely on a rack. Reduce oven temperature to 375F (190C). In a small bowl, combine meat or seafood and breadcrumbs. Carefully spoon into bottom of shells. Top with cheese, then vegetables. In a small bowl, beat eggs, half and half and herb with a fork or whisk until combined but not frothy. Pour over vegetables in pastry shell. Bake in 375F (190C) oven 15 to 16 minutes or until a knife inserted in center comes out clean. Let stand 5 minutes before serving.

Suggested Combinations

Chicken Appetizer Quiche: Use chopped cooked chicken for chopped meat. Use Monterey Jack cheese. Use chopped pimiento and chopped, drained, canned mushrooms for vegetables. Use thyme for herb.

Shrimp Appetizer Quiche: Use chopped cooked shrimp for seafood. Use Cheddar cheese. Use sliced green or black olives and chopped water chestnuts for vegetables. Use dill weed for herb.

Note: If using other small quiche dishes, measure dishes to determine size for rounds of pastry dough. Measure top diameter of dish and depth of dish. Add 1/2 inch to depth of dish. Diameter + depth + 1/2 inch = approximate diameter of pastry round needed to fit quiche dish.

Basic Cheese Spread

YIELD	4 cups	1-3/4 cups
INGREDIENTS		
cream cheese, softened	1 (8-oz.) pkg.	1 (3-oz.) pkg.
shredded cheese, room temperature	4 cups (1 lb.)	2 cups (8 oz.)
ground herb or spice	2 teaspoons	1 teaspoon
seasoning	2 teaspoons	1 teaspoon
wine or cream	5 to 6 tablespoons	2 to 3 tablespoons
chopped additions, see suggestions below	1 cup	1/2 cup
assorted crackers	to accompany	to accompany
MIXER BOWL	3-qt. bowl	1-1/2-qt. bowl
BEATING TIME AT MEDIUM SPEED	3 minutes	2 minutes

In a mixer bowl, see size in chart above, combine cream cheese and shredded cheese. Beat at low speed of an electric mixer to blend. Turn mixer to medium speed. Beat for time in chart above or until smooth. Scrape sides of bowl often. Add herb or spice and seasoning. Beat at low speed of mixer until blended. Blend in enough wine or cream to make of spreading consistency. By hand, stir in chopped additions; mix well. Cover and refrigerate up to 1 week. Serve at room temperature with assorted crackers and sliced firm vegetables or fruit.

Suggested Combinations
Bleu Cheese-Nut Spread: Use Monterey Jack cheese. Omit herb or spice. Use grated lemon peel for seasoning. Use dry white wine. Use crumbled bleu cheese, crumbled cooked bacon and chopped walnuts for chopped additions. Serve with assorted crackers, sliced pears and cauliflowerets.

Cheddar-Burgundy Spread: Use Cheddar cheese. Use dry mustard for spice. Use Worcestershire sauce for seasoning. Use Burgundy wine. Use chopped green olives and chopped green onion for chopped additions. Serve with assorted crackers, sliced apples and celery sticks.

Basic Creamy Dip

YIELD	3-1/2 cups	1-3/4 cups
INGREDIENTS		
dairy sour cream	1 cup	1/2 cup
plain yogurt	1 cup	1/2 cup
dry soup mix	1 (4-serving-size) envelope	1/2 (4-serving-size) envelope
chopped vegetables, meat or seafood	2 cups	1 cup
seasoning	2 tablespoons	1 tablespoon
assorted vegetables, see suggestions below	to accompany	to accompany
REFRIGERATE	2 hours	2 hours

In a medium bowl, stir together sour cream, yogurt and dry soup mix. Stir in vegetables, meat or seafood and seasoning. Cover and refrigerate at least 2 hours or until serving time. Stir before serving. Serve with assorted vegetable dippers.

Suggested Combinations
Creamy Vegetable Dip: Use Swiss-style vegetable dry soup mix. Use thawed, frozen, chopped spinach, pressed in a sieve to remove as much water as possible, chopped water chestnuts, chopped seeded tomatoes and chopped green pepper for vegetables. Use snipped chives for seasoning. Serve with carrot sticks, celery sticks, Chinese pea pods and zucchini rounds as dippers.

Creamy Shrimp Dip: Use tomato-onion dry soup mix. Use chopped cooked shrimp, chopped green onion and chopped pimiento for chopped vegetables and seafood. Use seafood-cocktail sauce for seasoning. Serve with cherry tomatoes, green-pepper strips and cauliflowerets as dippers.

Creamy Ham Dip: Use leek dry soup mix. Use chopped cooked ham, chopped, well-drained, canned artichoke hearts and chopped red pepper for chopped vegetables and meat. Use Dijon-style mustard for seasoning. Serve with red-pepper strips, broccoli flowerets and green onions as dippers.

Basic Layered Dip

YIELD	8 cups	4 cups	2 cups
INGREDIENTS			
cream cheese, softened	2 (8-oz.) pkgs.	1 (8-oz.) pkg.	1/2 (8-oz.) pkg.
cream-style cottage cheese, well-drained	2 cups (1 lb.)	1 cup (8 oz.)	1/2 cup (4 oz.)
dairy sour cream	1/2 cup	1/4 cup	2 tablespoons
seasoning	4 teaspoons	2 teaspoons	1 teaspoon
seasoned sauce	1 cup	1/2 cup	1/4 cup
chopped vegetables	2 cups	1 cup	1/2 cup
chopped cooked meat or seafood	2 cups	1 cup	1/2 cup
small cheese cubes	1/2 cup	1/2 cup	1/4 cup
assorted crackers	to accompany	to accompany	to accompany
MIXER BOWL	1-1/2-qt. bowl	1-1/2-qt. bowl	1-1/2-qt. bowl
SOUFFLE DISH OR COMPOTE	2-1/2-qt. dish	1-1/2-qt. dish	3-cup dish
TIME AT HIGH SPEED	3 minutes	2 minutes	2 minutes
REFRIGERATE	4 hours or overnight	3 hours or overnight	3 hours or overnight

In a 1-1/2-quart mixer bowl, combine cream cheese, cottage cheese, sour cream and seasoning. Beat at low speed of an electric mixer to blend. Turn mixer to high speed. Beat for time in chart above or until fluffy. Scrape sides of bowl occasionally. Pour into a soufflé dish or compote, see size in chart above. Spread evenly with seasoned sauce. Layer in order: vegetables, meat or seafood and cheese cubes. Cover and refrigerate 3 to 4 hours or overnight. Serve with assorted crackers.

Suggested Combinations

Layered Seafood Dip: Use shredded lemon peel and prepared horseradish for seasoning. Use seafood-cocktail sauce for seasoned sauce. Use chopped green onion, sliced ripe olives and chopped green pepper for vegetables. Use chopped cooked shrimp, crab or lobster for seafood. Use Cheddar cheese cubes. Garnish with chopped green onion.

Layered Chicken-Curry Dip: Use curry powder for seasoning. Use chopped chutney for seasoned sauce. Use chopped green onion for part of vegetables; substitute raisins and shredded coconut for remaining chopped vegetables. Use cubed cooked chicken for meat. Use salted peanuts instead of cheese cubes; add immediately before serving. Garnish with chopped green onion.

Layered Fiesta Dip: Use taco seasoning. Use drained mild salsa for seasoned sauce. Use chopped tomatoes, chopped avocado and chopped onion for vegetables. Use chopped, fully cooked, smoked sausage for meat. Use Monterey Jack cheese cubes. Garnish with chopped green chilies. For a variation, substitute bean dip for cream cheese and sour cream. Use 2 (10-1/2-ounce) cans for large recipe, 1 can for medium recipe and 1/2 can for small recipe.

Basic Easy Layered Dip

SERVINGS	8	4
INGREDIENTS		
cream cheese, softened	2 (8-oz.) pkgs.	1 (8-oz.) pkg.
toppings, see suggestions below		
assorted crackers	to accompany	to accompany
PLATE	10-inch plate	8-inch plate

Spread cream cheese in 1-inch-thick circle on a plate, see size in chart above. Spread topping evenly over cream cheese. Surround cheese wheel with crackers. Add additional topping to cream cheese, if necessary, during serving.

Suggested Toppings

Easy Shrimp-Cocktail Dip: Use refrigerated cooked shrimp in cocktail sauce for topping. Use 1 (6-ounce) jar for large recipe and 1/2 jar for small recipe.

Easy Creamy Jalapeño Dip: Use jalapeño jelly for topping. Use 2/3 cup jelly for large recipe and 1/3 cup jelly for small recipe.

Layered Seafood Dip

Guacamole
(Avocado Dip)

YIELD	2 cups	1 cup
INGREDIENTS		
very ripe avocados, peeled, seeded	2 (7- to 8-oz.) avocados	1 (7- to 8-oz.) avocado
lemon juice	1/4 cup	2 tablespoons
garlic salt	1/8 teaspoon	dash
chopped, seeded, peeled tomatoes	1/2 cup	1/4 cup
chopped green onion	2 tablespoons	1 tablespoon
canned chopped green chilies	2 tablespoons	1 tablespoon

In a medium bowl, mash avocado using a pastry blender or fork. Stir in lemon juice and garlic salt; mix well. Fold in tomatoes, green onion and chilies. Place clear plastic wrap directly on entire surface of dip to cover and prevent darkening. Refrigerate until serving time. Serve with corn chips or tortilla chips.

Liver & Bacon Pâté

YIELD	2 cups	1 cup
INGREDIENTS		
bay leaves	4	2
bacon, cut in 1-inch pieces	6 slices	3 slices
bacon drippings	1/4 cup	2 tablespoons
chicken livers	1 lb.	8 oz.
chopped celery	1/4 cup	2 tablespoons
chopped onion	1/4 cup	2 tablespoons
butter or margarine	1/4 cup	2 tablespoons
horseradish sauce	2 tablespoons	1 tablespoon
brandy	2 tablespoons	1 tablespoon
dry mustard	1 teaspoon	1/2 teaspoon
dried leaf thyme	1/2 teaspoon	1/4 teaspoon
hard-cooked-egg yolks	2	1
red caviar, watercress	to garnish	to garnish
MOLD	2-1/2-cup mold	1-1/4-cup mold
HEAVY SKILLET	10-inch skillet	8-inch skillet
TIME AT MEDIUM HIGH	9 to 11 minutes	8 to 10 minutes
TIME AT MEDIUM	12 to 14 minutes	12 to 14 minutes
REFRIGERATE	8 hours or overnight	8 hours or overnight

Oil a mold, see size in chart above. Arrange bay leaves in bottom and up sides of mold; set aside. In a heavy skillet, see size in chart above, cook bacon over Medium-High heat for time in chart above or until crisp, stirring often. Remove bacon with a slotted spoon and drain on paper towels. Reserve in skillet amount of drippings listed in chart above; set aside. In a food processor fitted with a steel blade, process bacon until finely crumbled. Remove bacon and set aside. Cook chicken livers, celery and onion in reserved bacon drippings over Medium heat 12 to 14 minutes or until livers are only slightly pink in center, stirring occasionally. Drain. Process liver mixture in food processor until smooth. Add butter or margarine, horseradish sauce, brandy, dry mustard and thyme to liver mixture. Process until smooth. By hand, stir in crumbled bacon. Spoon liver mixture evenly into mold. Cover mold with foil. Refrigerate 8 hours or overnight. To serve, dip mold quickly in very hot water. To loosen, run a knife around edge of mold and unmold on a serving tray. Sieve egg yolk over mold. Garnish with caviar and watercress. Serve with assorted crackers.

Tips for Chicken Livers
- Chicken livers are very perishable. If purchased fresh, keep only 1 day. Refrigerate until ready to use. Chicken livers are also available frozen in 8-ounce blocks.
- If you do not have a food processor to make pâté, grind bacon, cooked livers and vegetables with the fine blade of a food grinder. By hand, beat in softened butter or margarine and seasonings.
- Chicken livers are done when still slightly pink in center. Overcooked chicken livers become dry and tough.
- For another chicken-liver appetizer, see Bacon-Wrapped Appetizers, page 50.

How to Make Guacamole

1/Use a pastry blender or fork to mash very ripe, peeled avocados in a bowl. If avocados are not ripe enough, they will not mash to a smooth consistency. Add lemon juice and garlic salt, then fold in tomatoes, green onion and chilies.

2/Spoon avocado mixture into a serving bowl. Place clear plastic wrap directly on entire surface of dip. This will prevent dip from darkening. Refrigerate until serving time. Serve with corn chips or tortilla chips.

Basic Quick Hot Dip

YIELD	3 cups	1-1/2 cups
INGREDIENTS		
condensed cream or bean soup	1 (10- to 12-oz.) can	1/2 (10- to 12-oz.) can (2/3 cup)
flavored process cheese spread	1 (5-oz.) jar	1/2 (5-oz.) jar
chopped vegetables, meat or seafood	1/2 cup	1/4 cup
seasoning	2 tablespoons	1 tablespoon
dairy sour cream	1 cup	1/2 cup
potato chips or vegetable dippers	to accompany	to accompany
HEAVY SAUCEPAN	1-1/2-qt. saucepan	1-qt. saucepan
TIME AT MEDIUM HIGH	8 to 10 minutes	4 to 5 minutes
TIME AT MEDIUM LOW	10 to 12 minutes	5 minutes

In a heavy saucepan, see size in chart above, combine soup, cheese spread, vegetables, meat or seafood and seasoning. Cook over Medium-High heat for time in chart above or until cheese melts and mixture is heated through, stirring constantly. Reduce heat to Medium Low. Stir 1/2 cup hot soup mixture into sour cream. Stir sour-cream mixture into soup mixture in saucepan. Cook over Medium-Low heat for time in chart above or until heated through, stirring constantly. Do not boil. Serve hot with potato chips or vegetable dippers.

Suggested Combinations
Quick Hot Chili Dip: Use condensed chili-beef soup. Use process cheese spread with bacon. Use chopped green onion and canned chopped green chilies for chopped vegetables. Use Worcestershire sauce and dry mustard for seasoning.
Quick Hot Shrimp Dip: Use condensed cream of shrimp soup. Use process cheese spread with olives and pimiento. Use chopped celery and chopped cooked shrimp for chopped vegetables and seafood. Use prepared horseradish and prepared mustard for seasoning.

Basic Danish Cocktail Sandwiches   Photo on page 18.

YIELD	40 to 48 sandwiches	20 to 24 sandwiches
INGREDIENTS		
cream cheese, softened	2 (3-oz.) pkgs.	1 (3-oz.) pkg.
mayonnaise or flavored sauce	2 tablespoons	1 tablespoon
finely chopped additions	1 cup	1/2 cup
seasoning	1 teaspoon	1/2 teaspoon
rye-, white- or wheat-bread slices, crusts removed	10 to 12 slices	5 or 6 slices
garnishes, see suggestions below		

In a medium bowl, combine cream cheese and mayonnaise or flavored sauce. Beat with a wooden spoon until smooth. Stir in finely chopped additions and seasoning. Using cookie cutters, cut different shapes from different kinds of bread. Or, cut each bread slice diagonally into 4 triangles. Spread cream-cheese mixture on bread. Garnish according to suggestions below. Cover and refrigerate until serving time or up to 3 or 4 hours.

Suggested Combinations

Danish Cocktail Shrimp Sandwiches: Use seafood-cocktail sauce for flavored sauce. Use finely chopped green onion and finely chopped cooked shrimp for chopped additions. Use grated lemon peel for seasoning. Garnish with whole cooked shrimp, green-pepper strips and capers.

Danish Cocktail Egg Sandwiches: Use mayonnaise. Use chopped hard-cooked egg and chopped well-drained pimiento for chopped additions. Use prepared mustard and herb pepper for seasonings. Garnish with hard-cooked-egg slices, snipped chives and pimiento strips.

Danish Cocktail Corned Beef or Ham Sandwiches: Use horseradish sauce for flavored sauce. Use finely chopped dill pickle and finely chopped cooked corned beef or ham for chopped additions. Use Dijon-style mustard for seasoning. For garnish, roll dill pickle in thin slice of corned beef or ham. Slice in 1/4-inch pieces. Garnish sandwiches with pickle roll-up slice and watercress or parsley.

Danish Cocktail Salmon Sandwiches: Use tartar sauce for flavored sauce. Use finely chopped green pepper and flaked smoked salmon for chopped additions. Use lemon juice for seasoning. Garnish with pieces of smoked salmon, dill weed and avocado slices dipped in lemon juice.

Danish Cocktail Fruit Sandwiches: Use mayonnaise. Use finely chopped pecans and crumbled bleu cheese for chopped additions. Use grated orange peel for seasoning. Garnish with thin apple wedges, dipped in lemon juice, orange quarter-slices and mint sprigs.

Danish Cocktail Vegetable Sandwiches: Use Thousand Island dressing for flavored sauce. Use finely chopped green onion and finely chopped pimiento, drained on paper towels, for chopped additions. Use horseradish mustard for seasoning. Garnish with well-drained, marinated artichoke hearts, quartered, cherry-tomato slices and parsley sprigs.

Tips for Cold Stuffed Appetizers

- Cut cherry tomatoes in an **X**, starting from stem end and cutting two-thirds of the way down tomato. Stuff with smoked salmon, smoked oysters or anchovies. Garnish with watercress sprigs.

- Make small Cream Puffs, page 502, using 1 teaspoon dough for each puff. Remove tops and inside webbing from cooked puffs. Fill with: Basic Egg Salad, page 242; Basic Chicken or Tuna Salad, page 388; or Basic Seafood Salad, page 386.

- Halve small sweet yellow peppers lengthwise. Remove seeds and membrane. Fill with thawed frozen guacamole dip or canned bean dip. Garnish with shredded cheese, chopped tomato or chopped green onion.

- Cut celery in 3-inch lengths. Fill with peanut butter, cheese spread or semisoft natural cheese flavored with garlic and herbs, pepper or French onion.

How to Make Basic Hot Appetizer Dip

1/For Hot Smoky-Beef Dip, snip smoked dried beef into horseradish-cream-cheese base. Fold in chopped tomatoes, chopped hard-cooked eggs and chopped green onion.

2/Spoon dip into a pie plate or small flat casserole. Bake in a 350F (175C) oven until warm, stirring once. Garnish with hard-cooked-egg slices and paprika. Serve with vegetable dippers.

Basic Hot Appetizer Dip

YIELD	2 cups	2/3 cup
INGREDIENTS		
cream cheese, softened	1 (8-oz.) pkg.	1 (3-oz.) pkg.
cooking sauce	3 tablespoons	1 tablespoon
milk	1 tablespoon	1 teaspoon
seasoning	2 teaspoons	1 teaspoon
chopped cooked meat or seafood	1/2 to 1 cup	3 to 5 tablespoons
chopped additions	1/2 cup	3 tablespoons
chopped green onion	2 tablespoons	1 tablespoon
garnish, see suggestions below		
MIXER BOWL	1-1/2-qt. bowl	1-1/2-qt. bowl
PIE PLATE	7-inch pie plate	1-1/2-cup casserole
TIME IN 350F (175C) OVEN	15 to 20 minutes	10 to 15 minutes

Do not preheat oven. In a 1-1/2-quart mixer bowl, beat cream cheese, cooking sauce, milk and seasoning at low speed of an electric mixer about 30 seconds to blend. Turn mixer to medium speed. Beat 1 minute or until smooth and fluffy. By hand, stir in meat or seafood, chopped additions and green onion. Spoon into a pie plate, see size in chart above. Bake in a 350F (175C) oven for time in chart above or until warm, stirring once. Stir before serving. Garnish according to suggestions below. Serve with vegetables or crackers as dippers.

Suggested Combinations
Hot Smoky-Beef Dip: Use horseradish sauce for cooking sauce. Use Worcestershire sauce and Dijon-style mustard for seasoning. Use snipped, sliced, smoked beef for meat. Use finely chopped, seeded, peeled tomatoes and chopped hard-cooked egg for chopped additions. Garnish with hard-cooked eggs.
Hot Reuben Dip: Use Thousand Island dressing for cooking sauce. Use prepared horseradish and prepared mustard for seasoning. Use chopped corned beef for meat. Use finely snipped, rinsed, drained sauerkraut and shredded Swiss cheese for chopped additions. Garnish with chopped, drained, dill pickle.
Hot Clam Dip: Use seafood-cocktail sauce for cooking sauce. Use Worcestershire sauce and grated lemon peel for seasoning. Use chopped, drained, canned clams for seafood. Use chopped ripe olives, chopped pimiento and crumbled bleu cheese for chopped additions. Garnish with snipped parsley.

Basic Snack Mix

YIELD	8 to 10 cups	4 to 5 cups
INGREDIENTS		
small crackers	2 cups	1 cup
chips	2 cups	1 cup
cereal	2 cups	1 cup
pretzels or snack sticks	2 cups	1 cup
nuts	2 cups	1 cup
butter or margarine	1/2 cup	1/4 cup
Worcestershire sauce	2 tablespoons	1 tablespoon
dried ground seasoning	2 teaspoons	1 teaspoon
BAKING PAN	13" x 9" baking pan	9-inch-square baking pan
TIME IN 250F (120C) OVEN	1 hour	1 hour

Do not preheat oven. In a baking pan, see size in chart above, toss together small crackers, chips, cereal, pretzels or snack sticks and nuts; set aside. In a small saucepan, melt butter or margarine. Stir in Worcestershire sauce and seasoning; mix well. Pour over cereal mixture, tossing until well-coated. Bake in a 250F (120C) oven 1 hour or until crisp, stirring occasionally. Cool. Store in airtight containers.

Suggested Combinations
After-School Snack Mix: Use small goldfish crackers, corn chips, wheat squares for cereal and thin pretzels. Use peanuts. Use taco-seasoning mix for seasoning.
Bowl-Game Snack Mix: Use small, square, cheese crackers, pork-rind chips, broken in pieces, round oat cereal and sesame-nut sticks. Use pecans for nuts. Use dry mustard and chili powder for seasoning.

Basic Spicy Toasted Nuts

YIELD	3 cups	1-1/2 cups
INGREDIENTS		
butter or margarine	2 tablespoons	1 tablespoon
herb seed	1/2 teaspoon	1/4 teaspoon
dried ground seasoning	1 teaspoon	1/2 teaspoon
dried ground spice	1 teaspoon	1/2 teaspoon
unsalted nuts, if available, or salted nuts	3 cups (14 oz.)	1-1/2 cups (7 oz.)
BAKING DISH	12" x 7" baking dish	7-inch pie plate
TIME IN 300F (150C) OVEN:		
almonds	30 to 35 minutes	30 to 35 minutes
cashews, macadamia nuts	15 to 20 minutes	15 to 20 minutes

Do not preheat oven. In a small saucepan, melt butter or margarine. Stir in herb seed, seasoning and spice. Spread nuts in a baking dish, see size in chart above. Stir butter mixture and pour over nuts. Toss until well-coated. Bake in a 300F (150C) oven for time in chart above or until crisp and toasted, stirring often. Cool, stirring often. Store in an airtight container.

Suggested Combinations
Spicy Toasted Almonds: Use celery seed for herb seed. Use onion powder for seasoning. Use chili powder for spice. Use whole blanched almonds for nuts.
Spicy Toasted Tropical Nuts: Use sesame seed for herb seed. Use ground dried lemon peel for seasoning. Use ginger for spice. Use whole cashews and whole macadamia nuts for nuts.

Note: If using other nuts, toast in 300F (150C) oven. Stir nuts often; watch closely for doneness after 15 minutes. Nuts toast at very different rates.

How to Make Basic Stuffed Pita Wedges

1/Cut pita bread in half horizontally to make 2 large flat pieces from each round of bread. For Greek-Style Pita Wedges, combine shredded kasseri or mozzarella cheese, green onion, green pepper and ripe olives. Season with oregano and grated lemon peel. Spoon onto bottom half of pita bread.

2/Spread underside of pita-bread top with butter or margarine. Place, buttered-side down, over cheese filling to form a sandwich. Spread more butter or margarine on top crust of sandwich. Sprinkle with sesame seed. Broil 6 inches from heat 3 to 4 minutes or until toasted. Serve hot, cut in wedges.

Basic Stuffed Pita Wedges

YIELD	16 wedges	8 wedges
INGREDIENTS		
pita bread, 8 inches in diameter	2 rounds	1 round
shredded cheese	1 cup (4 oz.)	1/2 cup (2 oz.)
chopped vegetables	1 cup	1/2 cup
seasoning	2 teaspoons	1 teaspoon
butter or margarine, softened	1/4 cup	2 tablespoons
herb seed	2 teaspoons	1 teaspoon
BAKING SHEET	baking sheet	baking sheet
TIME AT BROIL	3 to 4 minutes	3 to 4 minutes

Cut pita bread in half horizontally, making 2 round flat pieces from each one. Place bottom of each round on a baking sheet; set aside. In a medium bowl, combine cheese, vegetables and seasoning; mix well. Spoon onto bottom half of pita bread. Reserve 1 teaspoon butter or margarine for top of each pita bread. Spread remaining butter or margarine on underside of pita-bread top. Place over cheese filling, forming a sandwich. Spread reserved butter or margarine on top crust of each sandwich. Sprinkle with herb seed. Preheat an electric broiler. You do not need to preheat a gas broiler. Broil pita bread 6 inches from heat 3 to 4 minutes or until lightly browned and toasted. Serve hot, cut in wedges.

Suggested Combinations
Greek-Style Pita Wedges: Use kasseri or mozzarella cheese. Use chopped green onion, chopped green pepper and chopped ripe olives for vegetables. Use dried leaf oregano and grated lemon peel for seasoning. Use sesame seed for herb seed.
Smoky Cheddar Pita Wedges: Use smoky Cheddar cheese. Use sliced green olives, chopped onion and chopped celery for vegetables. Use dry mustard and Worcestershire sauce for seasoning. Use poppy seed for herb seed.

Basic Appetizer Meatballs & Franks

YIELD	4 cups	2 cups
INGREDIENTS		
Meatball meat mixture, page 149	medium recipe	small recipe
OR		
cocktail franks	64	32
fruit preserves	1 (10-oz.) jar	1/2 cup
fruit jelly	1 (10-oz.) jar	1/2 cup
dry mustard	2 tablespoons	1 tablespoon
prepared horseradish	2 tablespoons	1 tablespoon
cornstarch	2 tablespoons	1 tablespoon
cold water	2 tablespoons	1 tablespoon
garnishes, see suggestions below		
BAKING PAN	15" x 10" x 1" baking pan	13" x 9" baking pan
HEAVY SAUCEPAN	3-qt. saucepan	1-1/2-qt. saucepan
TIME IN 375F (190C) OVEN	15 to 20 minutes	15 to 20 minutes
TIME AT MEDIUM	10 to 15 minutes	10 to 15 minutes
TIME AT MEDIUM HIGH	3 to 4 minutes	3 to 4 minutes
TIME AT MEDIUM LOW	10 minutes	10 minutes

Do not preheat oven. Prepare Meatball meat mixture. Shape meat mixture into 1-inch meatballs. This will make about 60 tiny meatballs per pound of meat. Place meatballs in a baking pan, see size in chart above. Bake in a 375F (190C) oven 15 to 20 minutes or until no pink remains when beef and sausage meatballs are cut in center. Ham balls should be firm in center and juices should run clear. Drain on paper towels; set aside. In a heavy saucepan, see size in chart above, combine fruit preserves, fruit jelly, dry mustard and horseradish; mix well. Cook over Medium heat 10 to 15 minutes or until jelly melts, stirring often. In a small bowl, combine cornstarch and cold water; mix well. Stir into jelly mixture. Increase heat to Medium High. Cook 3 to 4 minutes or until thickened and bubbly all over, stirring constantly. Stir in meatballs and/or franks. Bring to a boil over Medium-High heat, stirring gently. Reduce heat to Medium Low; cover. Simmer 10 minutes or until heated through, stirring once or twice. Serve with cocktail picks. Garnish according to suggestions below.

Suggested Combinations

Cherry-Ham Appetizer Meatballs: Use ham meatballs. Use cherry preserves. Use cherry jelly. Garnish with drained canned pineapple chunks.

Glazed Sausage Appetizer Meatballs & Franks: Use sausage meatballs and/or cocktail franks. Use pineapple preserves. Use apple jelly. Garnish with large pimiento-stuffed olives.

Sweet-Sour Appetizer Meatballs & Franks: Use beef meatballs and/or cocktail franks. Use orange marmalade for preserves. Use sweet-sour sauce instead of jelly. Garnish with drained canned water chestnuts and mandarin oranges.

Basic Meat Appetizer Kabobs

SERVINGS	4 to 6	2 or 3
INGREDIENTS		
Teriyaki Meat Marinade, page 140, Tangy Meat Marinade, page 139, or Cranberry Meat Marinade, page 138	large recipe	small recipe
boned, skinned chicken breasts OR	1 lb.	8 oz.
pork tenderloin OR	1 lb.	8 oz.
beef sirloin garnishes, see suggestions below	1 lb.	8 oz.
SKEWERS	8 to 12 (4-inch) skewers	4 to 6 (4-inch) skewers
BAKING DISH	9-inch-square baking dish	9" x 5" x 3" loaf dish
BROILER PAN WITH RACK	14" x 10" pan	11" x 7" pan
REFRIGERATE	5 or 6 hours	5 or 6 hours
TIME AT BROIL (first side):		
chicken, pork	3 to 4 minutes	3 to 4 minutes
beef	1 to 2 minutes	1 to 2 minutes
TIME AT BROIL (second side):		
chicken, pork	3 to 5 minutes	3 to 5 minutes
beef	2 to 3 mintues	2 to 3 minutes

Prepare marinade; set aside. Cut chicken or meat in strips, 1 inch wide and 1/4 inch thick. On skewers, thread chicken or meat strips, weaving slices ribbon-fashion onto skewer. Place flat in a baking dish, see size in chart above. Drizzle marinade over skewers, coating chicken or meat well. Cover and refrigerate 5 to 6 hours, turning skewers and spooning marinade over meat or chicken several times. At serving time, drain skewers, reserving marinade. Preheat an electric broiler. You do not need to preheat a gas broiler. Pour water to a depth of 1/4 inch in bottom of a broiler pan, see size in chart above. Place skewers on a rack in broiler pan. Broil on first side 3 inches from heat for time in chart above. Turn skewers over. Broil on second side for time in chart above or until chicken and pork show no pink when cut in center of thickest part and beef is done to your taste. Brush meat with reserved marinade several times while broiling on second side. Garnish according to suggestions below.

Suggested Combinations
Cranberry-Chicken Appetizer Kabobs: Use Cranberry Meat Marinade. Use chicken breasts. Garnish with orange wedge at end of each skewer.
Teriyaki Pork Appetizer Kabobs: Use Teriyaki Meat Marinade. Use pork tenderloin. Garnish with pineapple chunk at end of each skewer.
Tangy Beef Appetizer Kabobs: Use Tangy Meat Marinade. Use beef sirloin. Garnish with cherry tomato at end of each skewer.

Mock Oysters Rockefeller

SERVINGS	4	2
INGREDIENTS		
frozen spinach soufflé, thawed	1 (12-oz.) pkg.	1/2 (12-oz.) pkg.
seasoned dry breadcrumbs	1/3 cup	3 tablespoons
grated Parmesan cheese	1/3 cup	3 tablespoons
prepared horseradish	2 teaspoons	1 teaspoon
grated lemon peel	1 teaspoon	1/2 teaspoon
fresh shucked oysters, drained	16	8
butter or margarine, melted	2 tablespoons	1 tablespoon
lemon slices, quartered	4 slices	2 slices
rock salt	to garnish	to garnish
APPETIZER OR OYSTER SHELLS	16 shells	8 shells
BAKING PAN	15" x 10" x 1" baking pan	12" x 7" baking pan
TIME IN 425F (220C) OVEN	15 to 18 minutes	15 to 18 minutes

Do not preheat oven. In a medium bowl, combine spinach soufflé, breadcrumbs, Parmesan cheese, horse-radish and lemon peel; mix well and set aside. Pat oysters dry on paper towels. Dip oysters in melted butter or margarine and place one in each shell. Top oysters with prepared stuffing. Use about 2 tablespoons stuffing for each oyster. Cover oysters completely with stuffing. Place shells in a baking pan, see size in chart above. Drizzle with any remaining butter or margarine. Bake in a 425F (220C) oven 15 to 18 minutes or until heated through. Serve on a bed of rock salt on serving plates. Garnish each oyster with lemon quarter-slice.

Bacon-Wrapped Appetizers

YIELD	24	12
INGREDIENTS		
bacon slices, cut in half lengthwise, then in thirds crosswise	4	2
chicken livers, quartered OR	6 chicken livers	3 chicken livers
water chestnuts, drained OR	1 (8-oz.) can	1/2 (8-oz.) can
large green olives, stuffed with whole almonds	24	12
BROILER PAN WITH RACK	14" x 10" pan	11" x 7" pan
TIME AT BROIL (first side):		
chicken livers	4 minutes	4 minutes
water chestnuts, olives	3 minutes	3 minutes
TIME AT BROIL (second side):		
chicken livers	1-1/2 minutes	1-1/2 minutes
water chestnuts, olives	45 to 60 seconds	45 to 60 seconds

Wrap 1/6 slice of bacon around each liver, water chestnut or olive; secure with a wooden pick. Place on a broiler pan, see size in chart above, or on a wire rack in a baking pan. Preheat an electric broiler. You do not need to preheat a gas broiler. Broil on first side 4 inches from heat for time in chart above. Turn appetizers over. Broil on second side for time in chart above or until bacon is crisp. Drain on paper towels.

Variations
Bacon-Wrapped Breadsticks: Do not preheat oven. Cut bacon in half lengthwise. Wind half-strips of bacon spiral-fashion around thin, crisp, 6-inch bread sticks. Roll in grated Parmesan cheese. Place on a wire rack in shallow baking pan. Bake in a 400F (205C) oven 22 to 25 minutes or until bacon is crisp, turning over once.
Marinated Bacon-Wrapped Appetizers: Marinate chicken livers and water chestnuts in Teriyaki Meat Marinade, page 140, in the refrigerator 4 hours. Drain. Pat dry on paper towels. Follow directions for broiling, above.

How to Make Mock Oysters Rockefeller

1/To open oysters, place flat-side up on a cloth with hinge of oyster toward your fingertips. Work the tip of an oyster knife into hinge of oyster, pressing against cloth in the palm of your hand.

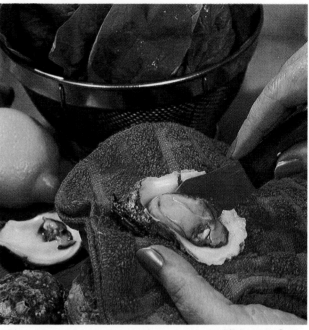

2/Use the notch in oyster knife to pry up top flat shell. Sever muscle attaching meat to the upper shell; remove flat shell. Slide knife under oyster to loosen meat from the round-shaped undershell.

3/Rinse well; pat oysters dry with paper towels. Dip in melted butter or margarine. Then place in small appetizer shells or use flat oyster shells. Cover completely with spinach stuffing.

4/Drizzle with any remaining butter or margarine. Bake in a 425F (220C) oven 15 to 18 minutes or until heated through. Serve on a bed of rock salt. Garnish with lemon slices cut in quarters.

Meats

This chapter will help you in buying, storing and cooking everything from expensive roasts to inexpensive ground beef. We've included basics, plus new ideas for delicious new tastes. Easy-to-read charts give large and small versions of each recipe to help both big families and those who live alone. Color photographs identify standard and lesser-known meat cuts for you.

Pork Rib Crown Roast, page 64.

Meats

Q. When shopping for meat, how do I decide how much to buy?

A. How much meat is left after cooking, and size and number of servings you need, determine how much meat to buy. Whether or not you want leftovers is another factor. General guidelines are:

Boneless meat (ground meat, boneless roasts and steaks, stew meat) — 3 to 4 servings per pound
Bone-in meat (roasts, steaks) — 2 to 3 servings per pound
Bony meat (ribs, short ribs) — 1 to 2 servings per pound

Q. Should I unwrap meat before storing it in the refrigerator?

A. No. Place prepackaged or store-wrapped meat in the refrigerator in the original wrapper. Use within recommended storage time on the chart below. Rehandling meat encourages bacteria growth.

Q. How should I wrap meat for freezing?

A. Wrap meat tightly in moisture-vapor proof wrap to seal out air and lock in moisture. When air enters the package, it draws moisture from the meat surface. *Freezer burn*, a dry meat surface with a white appearance, may result. The meat is safe to eat, but the dry area will be tough and tasteless when cooked. Mark freezing date on packaged meat. Use within recommended storage time on the chart below.

Q. Why do roasting and broiling times sometimes vary from the time charts?

A. Broiling- and roasting-time charts are averages of many tests. Use them as guides. Cooking times can vary considerably due to differences in meats and cooking equipment. Size and shape of meat, amount of fat and bone, and temperature of meat when cooking begins all affect cooking time. Timings in this book are for refrigerated meat.

The best way to tell when a roast is done is to insert a meat thermometer or probe into the center of the largest muscle. For broiled meat, cut a small slit near the center of the meat or along the bone, if present.

Q. Why should I use a rack to roast meat?

A. The rack holds the meat out of the drippings. This allows better heat circulation and more even cooking so true roasting can take place. You do not need a rack for beef rib roast because rib bones generally form a natural rack.

Q. When should I season broiled meats?

A. Season broiled meat after it has browned. Salt may draw juices to the surface and slow the browning process.

Q. Did you use a certain grade of beef for testing?

A. All beef recipes were tested using USDA Choice product.

Storing Meat

TYPE OF MEAT	RECOMMENDED STORAGE TIME IN REFRIGERATOR (36F to 40F, 0C to 5C)	RECOMMENDED STORAGE TIME IN FREEZER (0F, -20C OR COLDER)
roasts (beef)	3 to 5 days	6 to 12 months
roasts (pork, veal, lamb)	3 to 5 days	6 to 9 months
stew meat, ground meat, (beef, lamb, veal)	1 to 2 days	3 to 4 months
stew meat, ground meat (pork)	1 to 2 days	1 to 3 months
variety meats (liver, heart, kidney, tripe)	1 to 2 days	3 to 4 months
bacon, ham, corned beef	1 week	1 to 2 months
hot dogs	4 to 5 days	1 to 2 months
luncheon meats	5 to 7 days	not recommended
sausage (fresh pork)	3 to 5 days	2 months
leftover cooked meat	3 to 4 days	3 months

Note: For unopened packages of processed meat, use by freshness date usually printed on the label. Some refrigerators have meat-storage areas with colder temperatures (29F to 34F, -5C to 0C). These sections may prolong meat-storage times.

Techniques for Roasting Meat

1/For easier carving of loin or rib roasts, ask the butcher to crack chine bone (backbone) and tie roast back together. This is a pork loin roast, but same process is also helpful for veal and lamb loin or rib roasts. For complete carving directions, see page 81.

2/Meats should be roasted on a rack so they do not stew in their own juices. Most roasts require wire or ceramic roasting racks. Loin or rib roasts, such as beef rib roasts, form their own rib rack and do not require additional racks.

3/About 30 minutes before end of roasting time, insert a meat thermometer into roast. Thermometer bulb or tip should be in center of largest muscle. Tip should not touch bone or rest in fat. Measure thermometer halfway down face of roast to determine how far to insert thermometer into center.

4/Seasonings are suggested for beef, page 56, veal, page 60, lamb, page 69, and pork, page 65. This lamb shoulder cushion roast is being seasoned with dried leaf tarragon, paprika and snipped fresh chives before roasting. Seasonings also flavor gravy.

Roast Beef

Beef Round Rump Roast Boneless

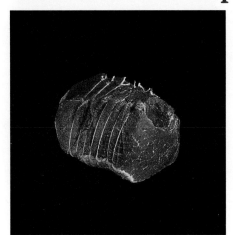

Common Names: Beef Round Rump Roast, Rolled
Servings per Pound: 3
Roasting Method: See opposite.
Buying Tips: For maximum tenderness, select only USDA Choice or Prime roasts. Lower-grade rump roasts should be prepared as pot roasts, page 94.

ROAST	DESIRED DONENESS	TOTAL COOKING TIME IN 325F (165C) OVEN
beef round rump roast boneless, 4 to 6 lbs.	medium (150F, 65C) to well (170F, 75C)	2 to 2-1/2 hours

Beef Rib Eye Roast

Common Names: Delmonico Roast; Beef Rib Eye Pot Roast; Regular Roll Roast
Servings per Pound: 3
Roasting Method: See opposite.

ROAST	DESIRED DONENESS	TOTAL COOKING TIME IN 350F (175C) OVEN
beef rib eye roast, 4 to 6 lbs.	rare (140F, 60C)	1-1/4 to 2 hours
	medium (160F, 70C)	1-1/2 to 2-1/4 hours
	well (170F, 75C)	2 to 2-1/2 hours

Suggested Seasonings for Beef Roasts
- 1 teaspoon dried leaf basil, 1 teaspoon dried leaf rosemary, 1 teaspoon dry mustard and 1/4 teaspoon onion powder.
- 2 teaspoons herb pepper, 1 teaspoon onion salt, 1 teaspoon dried leaf chervil and 1/4 teaspoon garlic powder.

In a small bowl, combine seasonings. Rub mixture over meat before roasting. Double amount of seasonings for roasts larger than 5 pounds.

Beef Loin Tenderloin Roast

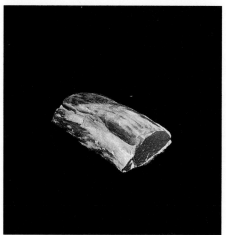

Common Names: Beef Tenderloin Tip Roast; Filet Mignon Roast; Châteaubriand; Beef Tenderloin Roast
Servings per Pound: 3
Roasting Method: See below.
Roasting Tips: Fold narrow end of tenderloin under roast, then tie at 2-inch intervals. In a small bowl, mix 1 tablespoon butter or margarine, 1/4 teaspoon pepper and 1/4 teaspoon garlic salt for each pound of meat. Spread butter or margarine mixture over tenderloin before roasting.

ROAST	DESIRED DONENESS	TOTAL COOKING TIME IN 425F (220C) OVEN
beef loin tenderloin roast, 2 to 4 lbs.	rare (140F, 60C)	45 to 60 minutes

Beef Round Tip Roast

Common Names: Beef Sirloin Tip Roast; Face Round Roast; Tip Sirloin Roast; Round Tip Roast; Crescent Roast
Servings per Pound: 3
Roasting Method: See below.
Buying Tips: For maximum tenderness, select only USDA Choice or Prime roasts.
Carving Tips: Cut roast in half lengthwise. Place each half cut-side down to slice.

ROAST	DESIRED DONENESS	TOTAL COOKING TIME IN 325F (165C) OVEN
beef round tip roast, 6 to 8 lbs.	rare (140F, 60C) to well (170F, 75C)	3-1/2 to 4 hours
beef round tip roast, 3-1/2 to 4 lbs.	rare (140F, 60C) to well (170F, 75C)	2 to 2-1/2 hours

Roasting Method for Beef Roasts

Do not preheat oven. Season roast, if desired; see Suggested Seasonings for Beef Roasts, opposite. Place roast, fat-side up, on a rack in a shallow roasting pan. Roast meat, uncovered, at oven temperature in chart. Use time for desired doneness in chart as guide. About 30 minutes before end of roasting time, insert a meat thermometer with bulb or tip in center of largest muscle of roast. Tip should not touch bone or rest in fat. Continue roasting until thermometer registers about 5F (3C) less than desired temperature. Test temperature in several places in roast. When roast is done, cover with a tent of foil. Let stand 10 to 15 minutes before carving. Internal temperature will rise about 5F (3C) during standing time. Slice and serve.

Beef Rib Roast Small End

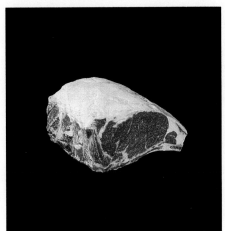

Common Names: Standing Rib Roast; Prime Rib Roast
Servings per Pound: 2
Roasting Method: See page 57.
Roasting Tips: A roast from small end of ribs measures 6 inches from tip of rib to chine or backbone. If rib cut is longer than 6 inches, roast will take less minutes per pound to roast.
Carving Tips: Place roast upright on largest end. Insert a meat fork between top rib and next rib. Carve across face of roast toward rib bone. Cut along rib bone with tip of a knife to remove slice, page 81.

ROAST	DESIRED DONENESS	TOTAL COOKING TIME IN 325F (165C) OVEN
beef rib roast small end, 6 to 8 lbs.	rare (140F, 60C)	2-1/2 to 3 hours
	medium (160F, 70C)	3 to 3-1/2 hours
	well (170F, 75C)	3-1/2 to 4-1/4 hours
beef rib roast small end, 4 to 6 lbs.	rare (140F, 60C)	2-1/4 to 2-3/4 hours
	medium (160F, 70C)	2-1/2 to 3-1/4 hours
	well (170F, 75C)	2-3/4 to 4 hours

Yorkshire Pudding

SERVINGS	8	4
INGREDIENTS		
drippings from beef roast, pages 56 to 58	2/3 cup	1/3 cup
eggs	6	3
milk	2 cups	1 cup
all-purpose flour	2 cups	1 cup
Worcestershire sauce	2 teaspoons	1 teaspoon
onion salt	1 teaspoon	1/2 teaspoon
ROUND PAN	2 (8-inch) round pans	8-inch round pan
TIME IN 425F (220C) OVEN	35 to 40 minutes	35 to 40 minutes

Prepare roast. After removing roast from oven, cover tightly with foil and keep warm. Preheat oven to 425F (220C). Pour 1 tablespoon pan drippings into each round 8-inch pan, see chart above. Place baking pans in oven while it preheats. In a blender, combine remaining drippings, eggs, milk, flour, Worcestershire sauce and onion salt. Cover and process at low speed until smooth. Make large recipe in 2 batches. Or, beat at low speed of an electric mixer until blended. Turn mixer to high speed. Beat 1 minute. Pour into prepared baking pans. Bake in preheated oven 35 to 40 minutes or until puffed and golden brown. Cut pudding into wedges and serve with roast.

Beef Rib Roast Small End and Horseradish-Mustard Sauce, page 76.

Roast Veal
Veal Leg Round Roast

Common Names: Veal Leg Roast; Leg of Veal
Servings per Pound: 2
Roasting Method: See opposite.

ROAST	DESIRED DONENESS	TOTAL COOKING TIME IN 325F (165C) OVEN
veal leg round roast, 5 to 8 lbs., bone-in	well (170F, 75C)	2-3/4 to 3-3/4 hours

Veal Loin Roast

Common Names: Veal Loin Roast
Servings per Pound: 2 or 3
Roasting Method: See opposite.
Carving Tips: Ask butcher to loosen chine bone. Carve down between ribs to serve chops from roast, page 81.

ROAST	DESIRED DONENESS	TOTAL COOKING TIME IN 325F (165C) OVEN
veal loin roast, 4 to 6 lbs., bone-in	well (170F, 75C)	2 to 3 hours

Suggested Seasonings for Veal Roasts
- 1 teaspoon dried dill weed, 1/2 teaspoon celery salt, 1/8 teaspoon onion powder and 1/8 teaspoon paprika.
- 1 tablespoon snipped parsley, 1 teaspoon snipped chives, 1 teaspoon dried leaf savory and 1/4 teaspoon cracked pepper.

In a small bowl, combine seasonings. Rub mixture over meat before roasting. Double amount of seasonings for roasts larger than 5 pounds.

Veal Shoulder Roast Boneless

Common Names: Rolled Veal Shoulder; Veal Rolled Roast
Servings per Pound: 3 or 4
Roasting Method: See below.
Roasting Tips: If desired, place uncooked bacon slices over meat before roasting.

ROAST	DESIRED DONENESS	TOTAL COOKING TIME IN 325F (165C) OVEN
veal shoulder roast boneless, 4 to 6 lbs.	well (170F, 75C)	3 to 4 hours

Veal Rib Roast

Common Names: Rib Veal Roast
Servings per Pound: 2
Roasting Method: See below.
Carving Tips: Ask butcher to loosen chine bone. Carve down between ribs to serve chops from roast, page 81.

ROAST	DESIRED DONENESS	TOTAL COOKING TIME IN 325F (165C) OVEN
veal rib roast, 3 to 5 lbs., bone-in	well (170F, 75C)	2 to 3 hours

Roasting Method for Veal Roasts

Do not preheat oven. Season roast, if desired; see Suggested Seasonings for Veal Roasts, opposite. Place roast, fat-side up, on a rack in a shallow roasting pan. Roast meat, uncovered, in a 325F (165C) oven. Roast to 165F (72C) using time in chart as guide. About 30 minutes before end of roasting time, insert a meat thermometer with bulb or tip in center of largest muscle of roast. Tip should not touch bone or rest in fat. Continue roasting until thermometer registers about 165F (72C). Test temperature in several places in roast. When roast is done, cover with a tent of foil. Let stand 10 to 15 minutes before carving. Internal temperature will rise about 5F (3C) during standing time. Slice and serve.

Roast Pork

Pork Loin Center Loin Roast

Common Names: Center Cut Pork Loin Roast; Pork Roast; Center Cut Loin Roast
Servings per Pound: 2 or 3
Roasting Method: See opposite.
Roasting Tips: To stuff, cut pocket over each rib bone in roast. Starting from fat side, cut through to rib bone. Fill each pocket with about 1/4 cup stuffing. See Sausage-Corn Stuffing, page 67. Tie roast end to end. Shield ends of roast with small pieces of foil if meat becomes too brown.
Carving Tips: Ask butcher to loosen chine bone. Carve down between ribs to serve chops from roast, page 81.

ROAST	DESIRED DONENESS	TOTAL COOKING TIME IN 350F (175C) OVEN
pork loin center loin roast, 3 to 5 lbs., bone-in	well (170F, 75C)	1-3/4 to 3 hours
pork half loin roast, 5 to 7 lbs., bone-in	well (170F, 75C)	3-1/4 to 4 hours

Pork Loin Top Loin Roast Boneless

Common Names: Boneless Roast from Pork Loins; Boneless Pork Loin Roast
Servings per Pound: 3 or 4
Roasting Method: See opposite.

ROAST	DESIRED DONENESS	TOTAL COOKING TIME IN 350F (175C) OVEN
pork loin top loin roast boneless (double loin), 3 to 5 lbs.	well (170F, 75C)	2 to 3-1/4 hours
pork loin top loin roast boneless (single loin), 2 to 4 lbs.	well (170F, 75C)	2 to 3 hours

Pork Loin Blade Roast

Common Names: Pork Loin 7-Rib Roast; Pork Loin 5-Rib Roast; Rib End Roast; Rib Pork Roast; Pork Loin Rib End
Servings per Pound: 2
Roasting Method: See below.

ROAST	DESIRED DONENESS	TOTAL COOKING TIME IN 350F (175C) OVEN
pork loin blade roast, 3 to 4 lbs., bone-in	well (170F, 75C)	2 to 2-1/2 hours
pork loin sirloin roast, 3 to 4 lbs., bone-in	well (170F, 75C)	2 to 2-1/2 hours

Pork Loin Tenderloin Whole

Common Names: Pork Tender; Pork Tenderloin
Servings per Pound: 3 or 4
Roasting Method: See below.
Roasting Tips: With a knife, lightly score (cut shallow lines across) top of roast at 1-inch intervals.

ROAST	DESIRED DONENESS	TOTAL COOKING TIME IN 350F (175C) OVEN
pork loin tenderloin whole, 1 lb.	well (170F, 75C)	60 to 75 minutes

Roasting Method for Pork Roasts

Do not preheat oven. Season roast, if desired; see Suggested Seasonings for Pork Roasts, page 65. Place roast, fat-side up, on a rack in a shallow roasting pan. Roast meat, uncovered, in a 350F (175C) oven. Roast to 165F (72C) using time in chart as guide. About 30 minutes before end of roasting time, insert a meat thermometer with bulb or tip in center of largest muscle of roast. Tip should not touch bone or rest in fat. Continue roasting until thermometer registers 165F (72C). Test temperature in several places in roast. When roast is done, cover with a tent of foil. Let stand 10 to 15 minutes before carving. Internal temperature must read at least 170F (75C) after standing time. Slice and serve.

Pork Rib Crown Roast **Photo on cover and page 52.**

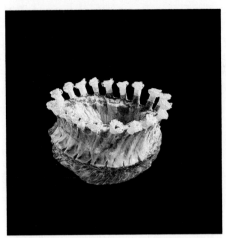

Common Names: Pork Crown Roast; Pork Crown Rib Roast
Servings per Pound: 2 or 3
Roasting Method: See page 63.
Roasting Tips: If roast is stuffed, cover stuffing with a small piece of foil after 30 minutes of roasting time. See Sausage-Corn Stuffing, page 67.
Carving Tips: Carve down between ribs to serve chops from roast, page 81.

ROAST	DESIRED DONENESS	TOTAL COOKING TIME IN 350F (175C) OVEN
pork rib crown roast, 4 to 6 lbs.	well (170F, 75C)	2-3/4 to 3-1/2 hours

Pork Shoulder Arm Picnic

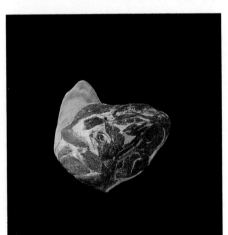

Common Names: Fresh Picnic; Pork Picnic Shoulder; Picnic
Servings per Pound: 2
Roasting Method: See page 63.
Carving Tips: See page 80.

ROAST	DESIRED DONENESS	TOTAL COOKING TIME IN 350F (175C) OVEN
pork shoulder arm picnic, 5 to 8 lbs., bone-in	well (170F, 75C)	3-1/4 to 4-1/2 hours
pork shoulder arm picnic, 3 to 5 lbs., boneless	well (170F, 75C)	2-1/4 to 3-1/2 hours
pork shoulder arm picnic cushion, 3 to 5 lbs., boneless	well (170F, 75C)	2 to 3-1/4 hours

Pork Leg (Fresh Ham) Shank Portion

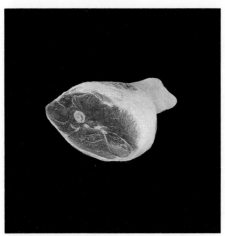

Common Names: Pork Leg Shank Portion; Fresh Ham Shank Portion
Servings per Pound: 2
Roasting Method: See page 63.
Roasting Tips: Trim off skin and some fat before roasting.

ROAST	DESIRED DONENESS	TOTAL COOKING TIME IN 350F (175C) OVEN
fresh ham shank portion, 5 to 10 lbs., bone-in	well (170F, 75C)	3-1/2 to 5-1/4 hours

Pork Shoulder Blade (Boston) Roast

Common Names: Fresh Pork Butt; Pork Butt Roast; Pork Boston Shoulder
Servings per Pound: 2
Roasting Method: See page 63.

ROAST	DESIRED DONENESS	TOTAL COOKING TIME IN 350F (175C) OVEN
pork shoulder blade (Boston) roast, 4 to 6 lbs., bone-in	well (170F, 75C)	2-3/4 to 3-3/4 hours

Suggested Seasonings for Pork Roasts
- 2 teaspoons dried leaf thyme, 1 teaspoon dry mustard, 1 teaspoon celery seed and 1/4 teaspoon garlic powder.
- 2 teaspoons Italian herb seasoning, 1/2 teaspoon garlic salt, 1/4 teaspoon cracked pepper and 1/4 teaspoon ground dried lemon peel.
- 1 teaspoon dried rubbed sage, 1 teaspoon dried leaf rosemary, 1 teaspoon dried leaf marjoram, 1/4 teaspoon garlic salt and 1/4 teaspoon onion salt.

In a small bowl, combine seasonings. Rub mixture over meat before roasting. Double amount of seasonings for roasts larger than 5 pounds.

Spicy Apple Glaze for Meat

YIELD	1 cup	1/2 cup
INGREDIENTS		
cornstarch	4 teaspoons	2 teaspoons
orange liqueur	2 tablespoons	1 tablespoon
syrup from canned spiced crabapples	1 cup	1/2 cup
grated orange peel	1/2 teaspoon	1/4 teaspoon
Kitchen Bouquet	1/2 teaspoon	1/4 teaspoon
SAUCEPAN	1-qt. saucepan	1-qt. saucepan
TIME AT MEDIUM HIGH	4 to 5 minutes	3 to 4 minutes
TIME AT ROASTING TEMPERATURE (glazed on roast)	15 minutes	15 minutes

In a 1-quart saucepan, combine cornstarch and orange liqueur until smooth. Stir in crabapple syrup, orange peel and Kitchen Bouquet. Cook and stir over Medium-High heat for time in chart above or until mixture thickens and bubbles all over. Spoon over pork or veal during last 15 minutes of roasting time. Heat remaining glaze and serve with roast.

Creamy Curry Sauce for Meat

YIELD	1-1/4 cups	2/3 cup
INGREDIENTS		
plain yogurt	1 cup	1/2 cup
chutney, finely chopped	1/4 cup	2 tablespoons
flaked coconut	2 tablespoons	1 tablespoon
finely minced onion	2 tablespoons	1 tablespoon
curry powder	1 to 2 teaspoons	1/2 to 1 teaspoon

In a medium bowl, combine yogurt, chutney, coconut, onion and curry powder; mix well. Refrigerate until serving time. Serve with pork, lamb or beef.

Potatoes Around the Roast

SERVINGS	4 to 6	2 or 3
INGREDIENTS		
baking potatoes	4 medium	2 medium
butter or margarine	1/4 cup	2 tablespoons
dried leaf herbs	1 teaspoon	1/2 teaspoon
celery salt	1/4 teaspoon	1/8 teaspoon
onion salt	1/4 teaspoon	1/8 teaspoon
ROASTING PAN	same as roast	same as roast
TIME AT ROASTING TEMPERATURE (added to roast)	1-1/4 to 2 hours	1-1/4 to 2 hours

Wash and scrub or peel potatoes. Cut each potato lengthwise in 8 wedges. About 1-1/4 to 2 hours before roast is done, place potatoes around roast. Overlap potatoes as little as possible. Dot with butter or margarine. Sprinkle with herb, celery salt and onion salt. Cook at oven temperature for roast 1-1/4 to 2 hours or until tender. Turn and baste with pan drippings once or twice during cooking.

Suggested Herbs: Use same herbs used to season roast. See pages 56, 60, 65 and 69 for suggested seasonings for roasts.

How to Make Stuffed Pork Loin Roast

1/Ask the butcher to crack chine bone of pork loin roast and tie roast back together. Position a sharp knife over each rib bone. Starting from fat side, cut deep pocket through to rib bone. Allow 1 rib bone for each serving.

2/Stuff each pocket with Sausage-Corn Stuffing. Tie roast securely end to end to keep stuffing in pockets during roasting. When done, carve between rib bones so each serving is a stuffed chop.

Sausage-Corn Stuffing

YIELD	5 cups	2-1/2 cups
INGREDIENTS		
fresh bulk pork sausage	8 oz.	4 oz.
chopped green onion	1/4 cup	2 tablespoons
sausage drippings	1/4 cup	2 tablespoons
stuffing mix for pork, saucepan-style	1 (6-oz.) pkg.	1/2 (6-oz.) pkg. (1-1/4 cups crumbs, 2 tablespoons seasonings)
water	1-3/4 cups	3/4 cup
whole-kernel corn, drained	1 (7-oz.) can	1/3 cup
chopped pimiento	1/4 cup	2 tablespoons
SAUCEPAN	2-qt. saucepan	1-qt. saucepan
TIME AT MEDIUM HIGH	15 minutes	10 minutes
TIME AT MEDIUM LOW	6 minutes	6 minutes
STANDING TIME	5 minutes	5 minutes

In a saucepan, see size in chart above, combine sausage and green onion. Cook over Medium-High heat for time in chart above or until sausage is browned, stirring often. Drain sausage mixture, reserving amount of drippings in chart above. Add melted butter or margarine to make enough drippings, if necessary. In same saucepan, combine sausage mixture, reserved drippings, vegetable-seasoning packet from mix and water. Bring to a boil over High heat; cover. Reduce heat to Medium Low and simmer 6 minutes. Add crumbs from mix. Stir to moisten. Stir in corn and pimiento. Cover and let stand 5 minutes. Fluff with a fork. Use to stuff pork rib crown roast or bone-in pork loin roast.

Variation
Casserole Stuffing: Heat any remaining stuffing in a casserole along with roast at oven temperature for roast. Bake for last 30 to 45 minutes of roasting time.

Roast Lamb
Lamb Leg Whole

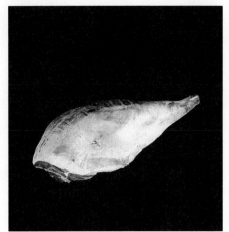

Common Names: Leg of Lamb; Leg, Sirloin On
Servings per Pound: 2
Roasting Method: See opposite.
Carving Tips: Cut 2 or 3 slices of meat from base of leg. Turn roast to rest on this cut surface. Start slicing where shank joins leg. Carve slices at right angles to leg bone. Loosen slices by cutting under them along top of leg bone, page 81.

ROAST	DESIRED DONENESS	TOTAL COOKING TIME IN 325F (165C) OVEN
lamb leg whole, 5 to 9 lbs., bone-in	rare (140F, 60C)	1-3/4 to 3 hours
	medium (160F, 70C)	2 to 3-1/2 hours
	well (170F, 75C)	3 to 4-1/2 hours

Lamb Leg Shank Half

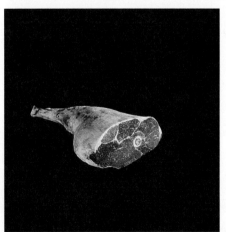

Common Names: Shank Half Leg of Lamb
Servings per Pound: 2 or 3
Roasting Method: See opposite.

ROAST	DESIRED DONENESS	TOTAL COOKING TIME IN 325F (165C) OVEN
lamb leg shank half, 3 to 4 lbs., bone-in	rare (140F, 60C)	1-1/2 to 1-3/4 hours
	medium (160F, 70C)	1-3/4 to 2-1/4 hours
	well (170F, 75C)	2 to 2-1/2 hours
lamb leg sirloin half, 3 to 4 lbs., bone-in	rare (140F, 60C)	1-1/4 to 1-1/2 hours
	medium (160F, 70C)	1-1/2 to 1-3/4 hours
	well (170F, 75C)	1-3/4 to 2 hours

Lamb Leg Roast Boneless

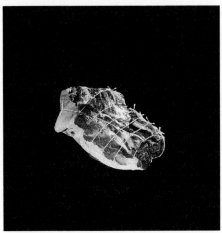

Common Names: Boneless Lamb Leg
Servings per Pound: 3 or 4
Roasting Method: See below.

ROAST	DESIRED DONENESS	TOTAL COOKING TIME IN 325F (165C) OVEN
lamb leg roast boneless, 4 to 7 lbs.	rare (140F, 60C)	2 to 3 hours
	medium (160F, 70C)	2-1/2 to 3-1/2 hours
	well (170F, 75C)	3 to 4 hours

Suggested Seasonings for Lamb Roasts
- 2 teaspoons crumbled dried mint leaves, 1/2 teaspoon lemon pepper and 1/2 teaspoon celery salt.
- 2 teaspoons dried leaf tarragon, 1 teaspoon snipped chives and 1 teaspoon paprika.
- 2 teaspoons dried leaf oregano, 1/2 teaspoon cracked pepper, 1/2 teaspoon garlic salt and 1/4 teaspoon onion powder.

In a small bowl, combine seasonings. Rub mixture over meat before roasting. Double amount of seasonings for roasts larger than 5 pounds.

Roasting Method for Lamb Roasts

Do not preheat oven. Season roast, if desired; see Suggested Seasonings for Lamb Roasts, above. Place roast, fat-side up, on a rack in a shallow roasting pan. Roast meat, uncovered, at oven temperature in chart. Use time for desired doneness in chart as guide. About 30 minutes before end of roasting time, insert a meat thermometer with bulb or tip in center of largest muscle of roast. Tip should not touch bone or rest in fat. Continue roasting until thermometer registers about 5F (3C) less than desired temperature. Test temperature in several places in roast. When roast is done, cover with a tent of foil. Let stand 10 to 15 minutes before carving. Internal temperature will rise about 5F (3C) during standing time. Slice and serve.

Lamb Rib Roast

Common Names: Lamb Rib Rack; Lamb Rack Roast; Hotel Rack
Servings per Pound: 2
Roasting Method: See page 69.
Roasting Tips: Trim off as much fat as possible from roast before cooking. To stuff, cut pocket over each rib bone in roast. Starting from fat side, cut through to rib bone. Fill each pocket with about 2 tablespoons stuffing. See Minted Fruit Stuffing, page 72. Tie roast end to end.
Carving Tips: Carve down between ribs to serve chops from roast, page 81.

ROAST	DESIRED DONENESS	TOTAL COOKING TIME IN 375F (190C) OVEN
lamb rib roast, 2 to 3 lbs., bone-in,	rare (140F, 60C)	1 to 1-1/4 hours
	medium (160F, 70C)	1-1/4 to 1-1/2 hours
	well (170F, 75C)	1-1/2 to 1-3/4 hours
lamb rib roast, 1-1/2 to 2 lbs., bone-in	rare (140F, 60C)	45 to 60 minutes
	medium (160F, 70C)	1 to 1-1/4 hours
	well (170F, 75C)	1-1/4 to 1-1/2 hours

Lamb Rib Crown Roast

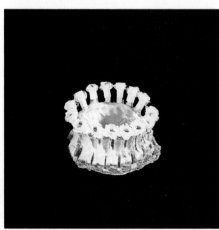

Common Names: Lamb Crown Roast
Servings per Pound: 2 or 3
Roasting Method: See page 69.
Roasting Tips: If roast is stuffed, cover stuffing with a small piece of foil after 30 minutes of roasting time. See Minted Fruit Stuffing, page 72.
Carving Tips: Carve down between ribs to serve chops from roast, page 81.

ROAST	DESIRED DONENESS	TOTAL COOKING TIME IN 325F (165C) OVEN
lamb rib crown roast, 2-1/2 to 4 lbs., bone-in	rare (140F, 60C)	1-1/2 to 2 hours
	medium (160F, 70C)	1-3/4 to 2-1/4 hours
	well (170F, 75C)	2 to 2-1/2 hours

Lamb Shoulder Square Cut Whole

Common Names: Shoulder Block; Shoulder Roast; Square Cut Shoulder
Servings per Pound: 1 or 2
Roasting Method: See page 69.

ROAST	DESIRED DONENESS	TOTAL COOKING TIME IN 325F (165C) OVEN
lamb shoulder square cut, 4 to 6 lbs., bone-in	medium (160F, 70C) well (170F, 75C)	1-3/4 to 2-1/2 hours 2-1/4 to 3 hours

Lamb Shoulder Roast Boneless

Common Names: Boneless Shoulder Netted; Rolled Shoulder Roast
Servings per Pound: 3
Roasting Method: See page 69.
Roasting Tips: To stuff lamb shoulder cushion roast, untie roast and fill with stuffing. Tie roast lengthwise and crosswise. See Minted Fruit Stuffing, page 72.

ROAST	DESIRED DONENESS	TOTAL COOKING TIME IN 325F (165C) OVEN
lamb shoulder roast boneless, 3-1/2 to 5 lbs.	rare (140F, 60C) medium (160F, 70C) well (170F, 75C)	2 to 2-1/2 hours 2-1/4 to 3 hours 2-1/2 to 3-1/2 hours
lamb shoulder cushion roast, boneless, 3-1/2 to 5 lbs. Photo on page 73.	well (170F, 75C)	2 to 2-3/4 hours

Minted Fruit Stuffing

YIELD	2-1/2 cups	1-1/4 cups
INGREDIENTS		
butter or margarine	1/4 cup	2 tablespoons
sliced green onion	1/4 cup	2 tablespoons
sliced celery	1/4 cup	2 tablespoons
chopped walnuts	1/4 cup	2 tablespoons
plain toasted croutons	2 cups	1 cup
chopped mixed dried fruit	1/2 cup	1/4 cup
dried mint leaves, crushed	1/2 teaspoon	1/4 teaspoon
dried leaf marjoram	1/2 teaspoon	1/4 teaspoon
beef broth	1/3 to 1/2 cup	3 to 4 tablespoons
SAUCEPAN	2-qt. saucepan	1-1/2-qt. saucepan
TIME AT MEDIUM HIGH	3 to 4 minutes	3 to 4 minutes

In a saucepan, see size in chart above, melt butter or margarine. Add onion, celery and walnuts. Cook over Medium-High heat 3 to 4 minutes or until onion is tender, stirring frequently. Stir in croutons, dried fruit, mint and marjoram; mix well. Add enough beef broth to moisten. Use to stuff lamb rib roast, lamb shoulder cushion roast or lamb rib crown roast.

Variation
Casserole Stuffing: Heat any remaining stuffing in a casserole at same oven temperature as roast. Bake for last 30 to 40 minutes of roasting time.

Honey-Lime Basting Sauce for Lamb

YIELD	2 cups	1 cup
INGREDIENTS		
cider or apple juice	1-1/2 cups	3/4 cup
honey	1/2 cup	1/4 cup
lime juice	2 tablespoons	1 tablespoon
grated lime peel	1 teaspoon	1/2 teaspoon
dried leaf rosemary	1 teaspoon	1/2 teaspoon
ground ginger	1 teaspoon	1/2 teaspoon
garlic powder	1/8 teaspoon	dash
SAUCEPAN	1-qt. saucepan	1-qt. saucepan
TIME AT MEDIUM HIGH	2 to 3 minutes	1 to 2 minutes

In a 1-quart saucepan, combine cider or apple juice, honey and lime juice; mix well. Cook and stir over Medium-High heat for time in chart above or until honey melts. Stir in lime peel, rosemary, ginger and garlic powder. Spoon over lamb roast about halfway through roasting time. Spoon pan juices over roast several times during roasting. When roast is done, skim fat from pan juices and serve with lamb.

Fresh Mint Sauce for Lamb

YIELD	1 cup
INGREDIENTS	
fresh mint sprigs, 4 inches long	8 sprigs
apple juice	1 cup
green food coloring, if desired	2 drops
cornstarch	1 tablespoon
dry sherry or cold water	1 tablespoon
SAUCEPAN	1-qt. saucepan
TIME AT MEDIUM LOW	15 minutes
TIME AT MEDIUM HIGH	3 minutes

In a 1-quart saucepan, combine mint sprigs and apple juice. Bring to a boil. Reduce heat. Cover and simmer over Medium-Low heat 15 minutes. Remove mint sprigs. Stir in green food coloring, if desired. Mix cornstarch and sherry or water until smooth. Stir into apple-juice mixture. Cook and stir over Medium-High heat 3 minutes or until thickened and bubbly all over. Cool. Serve with roast lamb.

Stuffed Lamb Shoulder Cushion, page 71; with Minted Fruit Stuffing, above; and Herbed Onion Gravy, page 75.

Roast Beef au Jus

YIELD	2 cups	1 cup
INGREDIENTS		
beef roast, pages 56 to 58		
pan drippings from beef roast	all remaining in pan	all remaining in pan
garlic powder	1/8 teaspoon	dash
onion powder	1/8 teaspoon	dash
pepper	1/4 teaspoon	1/8 teaspoon
beef broth	2 cups	1 cup
dry sherry, if desired	1 tablespoon	2 teaspoons
ROASTING PAN	pan from roast	pan from roast
TIME AT MEDIUM HIGH	4 to 5 minutes	3 to 4 minutes

Prepare beef roast. Remove meat from the roasting pan. Cover with foil and keep warm. Remove the rack from pan. Skim fat from pan juices and discard fat. Stir garlic powder, onion powder and pepper into pan juices until well-mixed. Stir in beef broth. If using a large roasting pan, place over 2 burners. Cook and stir over Medium-High heat, scraping up browned particles from bottom of pan. Cook 3 to 5 minutes or until boiling and most of browned particles are mixed into juices. Stir in sherry, if desired. Serve over slices of roast beef or use as dipping sauce for French-dip sandwiches (roast beef on hard rolls).

Basic Gravy for Roasts

YIELD	2 cups	1 cup
INGREDIENTS		
all-purpose flour	1/4 cup	2 tablespoons
beef or chicken broth	2 cups	1 cup
pan drippings from roast	1/4 cup	2 tablespoons
pepper	1/4 teaspoon	1/8 teaspoon
celery salt	1/4 teaspoon	1/8 teaspoon
dried leaf herb, if desired	1/2 teaspoon	1/4 teaspoon
Kitchen Bouquet, if desired	few drops	few drops
ROASTING PAN	pan from roast	pan from roast
TIME AT MEDIUM HIGH	6 to 7 minutes	4 minutes

In a screw-top jar, combine flour and one-fourth of broth. Reserve remaining broth. Shake flour mixture until completely smooth. Place the roasting pan with drippings on a burner over Medium-High heat. If using large roasting pan, place pan on 2 burners over Medium-High heat. Stir flour mixture into drippings, blending well. Quickly stir in remaining broth, pepper, celery salt and herb. Cook and stir over Medium-High heat for time in chart above or until mixture thickens and bubbles all over. Stir in a few drops of Kitchen Bouquet for color, if desired.

Suggested Combinations
Beef or Lamb Gravy: Use beef broth. Use thyme, basil or marjoram for herb.
Pork or Veal Gravy: Use chicken broth. Use rubbed sage or rosemary for herb.

Tips for Gravy

- Add butter, margarine or bacon drippings to pan drippings if there are not enough pan drippings for gravy.
- To prevent lumps in Basic Gravy for Roasts, shake flour and broth together until flour dissolves completely and mixture is smooth. Stir gravy constantly all over roasting pan, scraping up browned bits from bottom.
- If gravy is too thick, add more broth. Bring gravy back to a boil, stirring constantly.
- If gravy is too thin, shake together more flour and broth. Add to gravy. Bring gravy back to a boil, stirring constantly.
- If fat separates from gravy, there is too much fat in proportion to flour. To adjust proportion, shake together more flour and broth, then cook gravy again.

How to Make Roast Beef au Jus

1/Set the roasting pan with meat drippings over 2 burners to heat more evenly. Stir in seasonings and beef broth. Whisk over Medium-High heat, scraping up browned particles from bottom of pan.

2/Serve thin slices of roast beef on hard rolls. Pour natural-juice gravy (au jus) into small serving bowls for each serving. Dip end of sandwich in au jus before each bite. Garnish with pickles and cherry tomatoes.

Basic Soup-Base Gravy for Roasts

YIELD	2-2/3 cups	1-1/3 cups
INGREDIENTS		
pan drippings from roast	1/3 cup	2 tablespoons
all-purpose flour	1/3 cup	2 tablespoons
water	1-1/3 cups	2/3 cup
dried leaf herbs	1 teaspoon	1/2 teaspoon
condensed soup	1 (10- to 11-oz.) can	1/2 (10- to 11-oz.) can (2/3 cup)
ROASTING PAN	pan from roast	pan from roast
TIME AT MEDIUM HIGH (water added)	3 to 4 minutes	2 minutes
TIME AT MEDIUM HIGH (soup added)	2 to 3 minutes	1 to 2 minutes

Measure pan drippings. If necessary, add melted butter or margarine to make amount of drippings listed in chart above. Place the roasting pan with drippings on a burner over Medium-High heat. If using large roasting pan, place pan on 2 burners over Medium-High heat. Stir flour into drippings. Blend well until flour dissolves. Stir in water and herbs. Cook and stir for time in chart above or until mixture thickens and bubbles all over. Whisk in soup. Stir for time in chart above or until heated through.

Suggested Combinations
Creamy Mushroom Gravy: Use pork or veal drippings. Use rubbed sage and rosemary for herbs. Use condensed cream of mushroom soup.
Herbed Onion Gravy, photo on page 73: Use beef or lamb drippings. Use thyme and basil for herbs. Use condensed French onion soup.

Baked Ham
Fully Cooked Ham

TYPE OF HAM	DESIRED DONENESS	TOTAL COOKING TIME IN 325F (165C) OVEN
whole boneless fully cooked ham, 8 to 12 lbs.	140F (60C)	3 to 4 hours
half boneless fully cooked ham, 4 to 7 lbs.	140F (60C)	2 to 3 hours
portion boneless fully cooked ham, 3 to 4 lbs.	140F (60C)	1-1/2 to 2-1/2 hours
whole semiboneless fully cooked ham, 10 to 12 lbs.	140F (60C)	3 to 4 hours
half semiboneless fully cooked ham, 4 to 6 lbs.	140F (60C)	2 to 2-3/4 hours
whole bone-in fully cooked ham, 10 to 14 lbs.	140F (60C)	3 to 4 hours
half bone-in fully cooked ham, 5 to 7 lbs.	140F (60C)	2 to 3 hours
arm picnic shoulder fully cooked ham, 5 to 8 lbs.	140F (60C)	2-1/4 to 3-1/4 hours

Canned Ham

SIZE OF HAM	DESIRED DONENESS	TOTAL COOKING TIME IN 325F (165C) OVEN
canned ham, 5 lbs.	140F (60C)	2 to 2-1/4 hours
canned ham, 3 lbs.	140F (60C)	1-3/4 to 2 hours
canned ham, 1-1/2 lbs.	140F (60C)	1 to 1-1/4 hours

Horseradish-Mustard Sauce   Photo on page 59.

YIELD	2 cups	1 cup
INGREDIENTS		
dairy sour cream	1 cup	1/2 cup
prepared horseradish	3 to 4 tablespoons	1 to 2 tablespoons
Dijon-style mustard	2 teaspoons	1 teaspoon
whipping cream, whipped	1/2 cup	1/4 cup
snipped parsley	to garnish	to garnish

In a medium bowl, combine sour cream, horseradish and mustard; mix well. Fold in whipped cream. Cover and chill. Serve in large mushroom caps or artichoke bottoms garnished with snipped parsley. Serve with roast beef or ham.

Baking Method for Ham

Do not preheat oven. Trim skin and fat from ham, if necessary, so fat layer is only 1/8 inch thick. Score (lightly slit) fat in 1-inch diamonds. Push a whole clove into middle of each diamond, if desired. Place ham, fat-side up, on a rack in a shallow baking pan. Pour enough fruit juice or wine over ham to almost touch bottom of ham on rack. Bake ham, uncovered, in a 325F (165C) oven. Use time in chart as guide. Baste ham with pan juices several times. Add more liquid while baking if liquid evaporates. Cover ham loosely with a tent of foil if outside of ham starts to overbrown. About 30 minutes before end of baking time, insert a meat thermometer with bulb or tip in center of ham. Tip should not touch bone or rest in fat. When thermometer registers 130F (55C), glaze ham, if desired. See glazes, page 78. If using foil tent, replace after glazing. Continue baking ham until thermometer registers 140F (60C). Baste with glaze once or twice while baking. When ham is done, cover loosely with foil. Let stand 10 minutes before carving. Slice and serve.

Cook-Before-Eating Hams

Old-fashioned cook-before-eating hams are available in limited quantities in specialty markets. Follow package directions for cooking ham to internal temperature of 160F (70C).

Tips for Using Ham

- Ham labeled *fully cooked* may be eaten without heating.
- When possible, use same flavor fruit juice to pour over ham for baking as fruit jam you use for glazing, see page 78.
- Keep liquid in the roasting pan to make ham more moist and prevent drippings from burning.
- When ham starts to overbrown during baking, cover brown area with a tent of foil and continue baking.
- Ham that is not glazed may require slightly less cooking time.
- Semiboneless hams have had 2 of the largest bones removed for easier carving.
- To carve ham or smoked arm picnic shoulder, see page 80.
- Butt, rump or sirloin-end portion of half ham has a greater proportion of meat to bone than shank portion of ham.
- Ham *portion* is half ham with some center slices removed.
- Allow following servings for ham:

smoked arm picnic shoulder	1 or 2 servings per pound
whole ham, bone-in	2 or 3 servings per pound
shank half ham	2 servings per pound
rump or butt half ham	2 or 3 servings per pound
boneless ham	3 or 4 servings per pound
semiboneless ham	3 servings per pound

Smoked Ham Whole

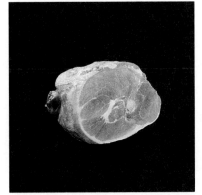

Smoked Ham Shank Portion

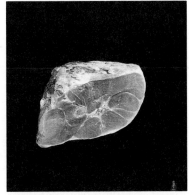

Smoked Ham Rump Portion

Basic Fruit Glaze for Ham

YIELD	1-1/3 cups	2/3 cup
INGREDIENTS		
snipped dried fruit	1/4 cup	2 tablespoons
dry white wine	1/4 cup	2 tablespoons
fruit jam or preserves	1 cup	1/2 cup
ground spice	1/2 teaspoon	1/4 teaspoon
fresh or drained canned fruit	to garnish	to garnish
TIME IN 325F (165C) OVEN (glazed on ham)	20 minutes	20 minutes

In a small bowl, combine dried fruit and wine. Let stand 30 minutes. Stir in jam or preserves and spice. About 20 minutes before end of ham baking time, check meat thermometer. Spread some of glaze over ham when thermometer registers 130F (55C) for fully cooked hams or 150F (65C) for cook-before-eating hams. Arrange fruit garnish over top of ham. Spoon more glaze over fruit and ham. If using a foil tent to keep ham from overbrowning, replace after glazing. Bake remaining 20 minutes or until thermometer registers 140F (60C) for fully cooked hams and 155F (70C) for cook-before-eating hams. Baste ham with glaze once or twice during baking. Cover loosely with foil. Let stand 10 minutes before carving. Serve any remaining glaze with ham. Use small recipe for hams smaller than 4 pounds and large recipe for hams larger than 4 pounds.

Suggested Combinations
Cherry Glaze for Ham: Use dried apples for dried fruit. Use cherry preserves. Use ground dried lemon peel and nutmeg for spice. Garnish with apple slices.
Apricot Glaze for Ham: Use raisins for dried fruit. Use apricot preserves. Use ground dried orange peel and cinnamon for spice. Garnish with apricot halves.
Pineapple Glaze for Ham: Use dried apricots for dried fruit. Use pineapple preserves. Use ginger and ground dried orange peel for spice. Garnish with pineapple rings.
Orange Glaze for Ham: Use golden raisins for dried fruit. Use orange marmalade. Use allspice for spice. Garnish with orange sections or wedges.
Plum Glaze for Ham: Use prunes for dried fruit. Use plum preserves. Use ground dried lemon peel and ginger for spice. Garnish with fresh plum wedges.

Praline Glaze for Ham

YIELD	1/4 cup	2 tablespoons
INGREDIENTS		
packed brown sugar	1/2 cup	1/4 cup
dry mustard	1 teaspoon	1/2 teaspoon
ground allspice	1/2 teaspoon	1/4 teaspoon
praline or orange liqueur	2 tablespoons	1 tablespoon
pecan halves, candied cherries	to garnish	to garnish
TIME IN 325F (165C) OVEN (glazed on ham)	20 minutes	20 minutes

In a small bowl, combine brown sugar, mustard and allspice; mix well. Stir in liqueur. About 20 minutes before end of ham baking time, check meat thermometer. Spread glaze over ham when thermometer registers 130F (55C) for fully cooked hams or 150F (65C) for cook-before-eating hams. If using a foil tent to keep ham from overbrowning, replace after glazing. Bake remaining 20 minutes or until thermometer registers 140F (60C) for fully cooked hams and 160F (70C) for cook-before-eating hams. Garnish with pecan halves and cherries. Cover ham loosely with foil. Let stand 10 minutes before carving. Use small recipe for hams smaller than 4 pounds and large recipe for hams larger than 4 pounds.

How to Make Baked Ham with Fruit Glaze

1/Score (lightly slit) fat on ham in 1-inch diamonds. Stud center of each diamond with a whole clove. Place ham on a rack in a shallow roasting pan. Pour enough fruit juice or wine over ham to almost touch bottom of ham on rack.

2/About 20 minutes before end of baking time, spoon some Plum Glaze or other glaze over ham. Arrange fresh plum or other fruit slices on ham. Spoon more glaze over fruit and ham. Baste ham with glaze once or twice during baking. Serve any remaining glaze with ham.

Mustard Sauce

YIELD	1-1/2 cups	2/3 cup
INGREDIENTS		
egg yolks	2	1
onion salt	1/4 teaspoon	1/8 teaspoon
white pepper	dash	dash
white-wine vinegar	2 teaspoons	1 teaspoon
vegetable oil	1/2 cup	1/4 cup
lemon juice	1 teaspoon	1/2 teaspoon
vegetable oil	1/2 cup	1/4 cup
Dijon-style mustard	1/4 cup	2 tablespoons
honey	2 tablespoons	1 tablespoon
MIXER BOWL	1-1/2-qt. bowl	1-1/2-qt. bowl
BEATING TIME AT HIGH SPEED (first amount of oil)	6 minutes	3 minutes
BEATING TIME AT HIGH SPEED (second amount of oil)	6 minutes	3 minutes

In a 1-1/2-quart mixer bowl, beat egg yolks, onion salt and pepper at medium speed of an electric mixer until blended. Beat in vinegar. Turn mixer to high speed. Add first amount of oil in a thin stream, beating constantly for time in chart above. Oil should be added slowly during entire beating time. Scrape sides of bowl often. Beat in lemon juice. With mixer on high speed, add second amount of oil in a thin stream, beating constantly for time in chart above. Oil should be added slowly during entire beating time. Scrape sides of bowl often. Turn mixer to low speed. Beat in mustard and honey. Cover and refrigerate until serving time. Serve with ham, corned beef or sausage.

Carving Roasts

Note: Carving instructions are for right-handed persons. Left-handed persons should adapt instructions where necessary.

Pork Shoulder Arm Picnic

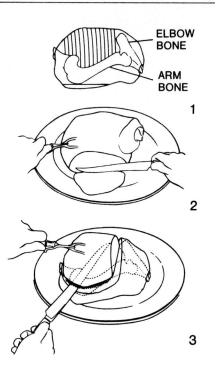

ELBOW BONE

ARM BONE

1

2

3

1. For bone identification and position, refer to illustration number one.

2. With elbow bone to carver's right, cut several slices of meat from base of roast. Turn roast so it rests on cut base.

3. Cut down to arm bone as near elbow bone as possible. Turn the knife and cut horizontally along arm bone to remove boneless portion of arm meat.

4. Set the boneless portion on a cutting surface, then slice.

5. Cut along each side of arm bone to remove 2 more boneless portions. Set these on cutting surface, then slice.

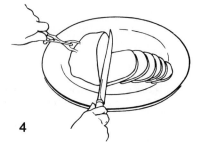

4

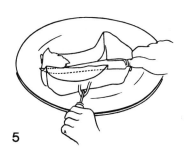

5

Ham Half Shank Portion

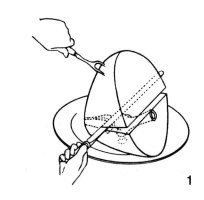

1

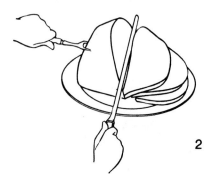

2

1. Place shank end of ham to carver's left with meaty side up. Cut horizontally along top of bone and lift off boneless portion.

2. Set the boneless portion on a cutting surface, then slice.

3. Cut around leg bone to remove second boneless portion from bone. Turn boneless portion so thick side is down; slice. Place remaining ham piece with face-side down. Cut along bone to remove third boneless portion from either right or left side, depending on whether ham was right or left leg. Place boneless portion so slices will be carved across grain.

4. Hold remaining ham piece, face-side down, with a fork. Carve across meat to bone. Cut slice from bone with knife tip.

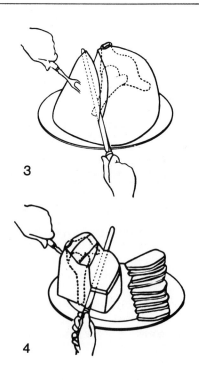

3

4

Lamb Leg Whole

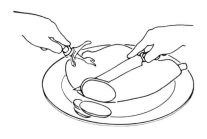

1. Cut several slices of meat from thinnest side of leg to make flat base. Turn roast so it rests on cut base.

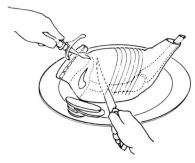

2. Start making vertical slices where shank meets leg bone. Slice down to leg bone.

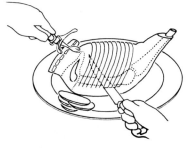

3. Carve horizontally along leg bone to loosen slices.

Beef Rib Roast

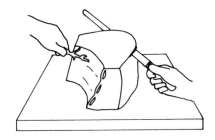

1. If roast is lopsided, remove slice from large end so roast rests flat on cut side. Insert a fork below top rib. Carve across roast toward rib bones.

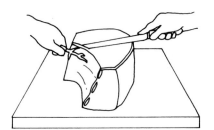

2. Cut along rib bone to remove slices.

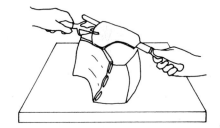

3. Slide a knife under meat slice to place on a serving platter.

Pork, Lamb or Veal Loin or Rib Roast

1

1. Untie roast and remove backbone before bringing roast to the table.

2. Place roast so rib-side faces carver. Insert a fork in top of roast. If roast is stuffed, cut between rib bones so each serving is a stuffed chop. If roast is not stuffed, cut along each side of rib bones. One slice will have rib bone; next slice will be boneless.

2

Pork or Lamb Rib Crown Roast

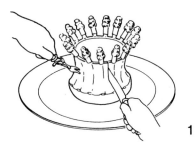

1

1. Remove any stuffing or vegetables from center of roast. Slice down between ribs.

2. Remove and serve chops from roast.

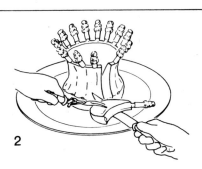

2

Basic Meat & Noodle Casserole

SERVINGS	6 to 8	3 or 4
INGREDIENTS		
medium noodles	4 cups uncooked (6 oz.)	2 cups uncooked (3 oz.)
butter or margarine	2 tablespoons	1 tablespoon
chopped onion	1/2 cup	1/4 cup
tomato-type sauce	1 (15-oz.) can	1 (8-oz.) can
cubed cooked meat	2 cups	1 cup
dried leaf herb	2 teaspoons	1 teaspoon
cream-style cottage cheese	1 (12-oz.) carton (1-1/2 cups)	1/2 (12-oz.) carton (3/4 cup)
semisoft natural cheese or cream cheese	2 (3- or 3-1/2-oz.) pkgs.	1 (3- or 3-1/2-oz.) pkg.
chopped green pepper	1/4 cup	2 tablespoons
chopped green onion	1/4 cup	2 tablespoons
snipped parsley	1/4 cup	2 tablespoons
shredded cheese	1 cup (4 oz.)	1/2 cup (2 oz.)
SKILLET	9-inch skillet	7-inch skillet
BAKING DISH	12" x 7" baking dish	9" x 5" x 3" loaf dish
TIME AT MEDIUM HIGH	3 minutes	3 minutes
TIME IN 350F (175C) OVEN	1 hour	50 minutes
STANDING TIME	10 minutes	10 minutes

Do not preheat oven. Cook noodles according to package directions; drain. In a skillet, see size in chart above, melt butter or margarine. Add onion. Cook over Medium-High heat 3 minutes or until tender. Remove from heat. Stir in tomato-type sauce, meat and herbs; set aside. In a medium bowl, combine cottage cheese, semisoft cheese or cream cheese, green pepper, green onion and parsley; mix well. In a baking dish, see size in chart above, layer in order: half of cooked noodles, half of meat sauce, all cottage-cheese mixture, remaining noodles and remaining meat sauce. Sprinkle with shredded cheese. Bake in a 350F (175C) oven for time in chart above or until heated through. Let stand 10 minutes before serving.

Suggested Combinations
French Meat & Noodle Casserole: Use tomato sauce for tomato-type sauce. Use cubed cooked veal for meat. Use basil for herb. Use semisoft natural cheese with garlic and herbs and shredded Cheddar for cheeses. Use egg noodles.

Italian Meat & Noodle Casserole: Use pizza sauce for tomato-type sauce. Use cubed cooked beef for meat. Use oregano and fennel seed for herbs. Use cream cheese and shredded mozzarella for cheeses. Use green noodles.

Barbecued-Meat Sandwiches

SERVINGS	4	2
INGREDIENTS		
canned spaghetti sauce	1 cup	1/2 cup
brown sugar	2 tablespoons	1 tablespoon
vinegar	2 tablespoons	1 tablespoon
prepared mustard	2 teaspoons	1 teaspoon
prepared horseradish	2 teaspoons	1 teaspoon
Worcestershire sauce	1 tablespoon	1-1/2 teaspoons
cooked meat, thinly sliced	8 oz. (13 slices)	4 oz. (6 or 7 slices)
hamburger buns, split	4	2
SAUCEPAN	2-qt. saucepan	1-qt. saucepan
TIME AT MEDIUM LOW (sauce)	5 minutes	5 minutes
TIME AT MEDIUM LOW (meat added)	5 minutes	5 minutes

In a saucepan, see size in chart above, combine spaghetti sauce, brown sugar, vinegar, mustard, horseradish and Worcestershire sauce. Bring to a boil. Reduce heat; stir. Simmer over Medium-Low heat 5 minutes or until flavors blend. Add meat, turning to coat slices with sauce. Simmer, covered, over Medium-Low heat 5 minutes longer or until heated through. Serve barbecued meat in buns.

How to Make Basic Meat & Noodle Casserole

1/Cook chopped onion in butter or margarine, then stir in tomato-type sauce, cubed cooked meat and seasonings. This Italian casserole has pizza sauce, beef, oregano and fennel seed.

2/Layer half of noodles and half of meat sauce in a baking dish. Spoon in creamy cottage-cheese filling. Top with remaining noodles and meat sauce, then sprinkle with cheese.

Stir-Fried Roast & Rice

SERVINGS	4	2
INGREDIENTS		
cornstarch	1 tablespoon	1-1/2 teaspoons
dry mustard	1 teaspoon	1/2 teaspoon
Worcestershire sauce	2 tablespoons	1 tablespoon
vinegar	4 teaspoons	2 teaspoons
vegetable oil	2 tablespoons	2 tablespoons
fresh mushroom slices	1 cup	1/2 cup
sliced celery	1/2 cup	1/4 cup
sliced green onion	1/4 cup	2 tablespoons
frozen pea pods, thawed	1 (6-oz.) pkg.	1/2 (6-oz.) pkg.
OR		
leftover cooked vegetables	1 cup	1/2 cup
cooked rice	2 cups	1 cup
cooked roast, cut in strips	2 cups	1 cup
beef broth or chicken broth	1 cup	1/2 cup
tomatoes, cut in wedges	2	1
SKILLET OR WOK	12-inch skillet or wok	10-inch skillet or wok
TIME AT MEDIUM HIGH (vegetables)	3 minutes	2 minutes
TIME AT MEDIUM HIGH (thicken sauce)	4 to 5 minutes	4 minutes
TIME AT MEDIUM HIGH (tomatoes added)	1 minute	1 minute

In a small bowl, combine cornstarch and dry mustard; mix well. Stir in Worcestershire sauce and vinegar; set aside. In a skillet or wok, see size in chart above, heat oil over Medium-High heat until a drop of water sizzles on it. Add mushrooms, celery, green onion and pea pods, if using. Toss constantly 2 to 3 minutes or until crisp-tender. Stir in rice, meat, leftover vegetables, if using, cornstarch mixture and broth. Continue tossing 4 to 5 minutes or until thickened and bubbly. Fold in tomato wedges and heat through about 1 minute.

Marinated-Meat Salad

SERVINGS	4 to 6	2 or 3
INGREDIENTS		
cooked meat, thinly sliced	1 lb. (26 slices)	8 oz. (13 slices)
onion, thinly sliced, separated in rings	1 medium	1 small
sliced fresh mushrooms	1 cup	1/2 cup
tomato, peeled, seeded, chopped	1 large	1 small
snipped parsley	1/4 cup	2 tablespoons
capers, drained	2 tablespoons	1 tablespoon
white-wine vinegar	1/2 cup	1/4 cup
dried leaf oregano	1 teaspoon	1/2 teaspoon
dry mustard	1/2 teaspoon	1/4 teaspoon
garlic salt	1/2 teaspoon	1/4 teaspoon
freshly ground pepper	1/2 teaspoon	1/4 teaspoon
fennel seed	1/4 teaspoon	1/8 teaspoon
vegetable oil	1-1/4 cups	2/3 cup
leaf lettuce	8 to 12 leaves	4 to 6 leaves
torn lettuce	4 to 6 cups	2 to 3 cups
BAKING DISH	12" x 7" baking dish	10" x 6" baking dish
REFRIGERATE	8 hours or overnight	8 hours or overnight

In a baking dish, see size in chart above, arrange meat slices. Top with onion rings, mushroom slices, chopped tomato, parsley and capers. In a screw-top jar, combine vinegar, oregano, dry mustard, garlic salt, pepper, fennel seed and oil. Cover and shake well. Pour over meat mixture. Cover and refrigerate several hours or overnight. Line salad plates with leaf lettuce. Top with torn lettuce. Using a slotted spoon, lift meat and vegetables from marinade; place on lettuce. Drizzle with some of marinade.

Variation
Marinated-Meat Sandwiches: Spoon drained marinated-meat mixture onto split, buttered hard rolls lined with leaf lettuce.

Basic Meat & Macaroni Bake

SERVINGS	2 or 3	1 or 2
INGREDIENTS		
frozen macaroni and cheese, thawed OR	1 (12-oz.) pkg.	1 (7-oz.) pkg.
leftover macaroni and cheese	1-1/2 cups	3/4 to 1 cup
milk or cream, if necessary	to moisten	to moisten
chopped pimiento	2 tablespoons	1 tablespoon
chopped green onion	2 tablespoons	1 tablespoon
dried leaf herb	1/4 teaspoon	1/8 teaspoon
cubed cooked meat	1 cup	1/2 cup
leftover or drained canned vegetable	1/2 cup	1/4 cup
tomato slices or green-pepper rings	2 or 3	1 or 2
shredded or crumbled cheese	1/2 cup (2 oz.)	1/4 cup (1 oz.)
dried leaf herb	to garnish	to garnish
CASSEROLE	1-qt. casserole	2-cup casserole
TIME IN 375F (190C) OVEN	35 to 40 minutes	25 to 30 minutes

Do not preheat oven. In a casserole, see size in chart above, combine macaroni and cheese with a little milk or cream, if necessary, to moisten. Stir in pimiento, green onion and first amount of herb; mix well. Fold in meat and vegetable. Top with tomato slices or green-pepper rings. Sprinkle with cheese and additional herb. Bake in a 375F (190C) oven for time in chart above or until heated through.

Suggested Combinations
Italian Meat & Macaroni Bake: Use basil for herb. Use cubed or ground cooked beef for meat. Use Italian green beans for vegetable. Use shredded mozzarella cheese.
Greek Meat & Macaroni Bake: Use oregano for herb. Use cubed cooked lamb for meat. Use peas for vegetable. Use crumbled feta cheese.

Basic Meat Pilaf

SERVINGS	6	3
INGREDIENTS		
bacon	4 slices	2 slices
bacon drippings	1/4 cup	2 tablespoons
chopped onion	1/2 cup	1/4 cup
chopped green pepper	1/2 cup	1/4 cup
long-cooking rice	2 cups uncooked	1 cup uncooked
cubed cooked meat	2 cups	1 cup
beef or chicken broth	1 (14-1/2-oz.) can	1/2 (14-1/2-oz.) can (about 1 cup)
water	1/2 cup	1/4 cup
white wine or soy sauce	1/4 cup	2 tablespoons
drained canned beans	1 (15-oz.) can	1 (8-oz.) can
ground spice	1/2 teaspoon	1/4 teaspoon
canned French-fried onions or chow-mein noodles	1 cup	1/2 cup
SKILLET	9-inch skillet	7-inch skillet
CASSEROLE	2-qt. casserole	1-qt. casserole
TIME AT MEDIUM HIGH (bacon)	8 minutes	4 to 5 minutes
TIME AT MEDIUM HIGH (onion)	4 minutes	4 minutes
TIME IN 350F (175C) OVEN (casserole)	1-1/2 hours	1-1/4 hours
TIME IN 350F (175C) OVEN (onions or noodles added)	5 minutes	5 minutes

Do not preheat oven. In a skillet, see size in chart above, cook bacon over Medium-High heat for time in chart above or until crisp. Drain bacon on paper towels, reserving amount of drippings listed in chart above. Add melted butter or margarine to make enough drippings, if necessary. Crumble bacon and set aside. In same skillet, cook onion and green pepper in reserved drippings 4 minutes or until tender, stirring often. Stir in rice, meat, bacon, broth, water, wine or soy sauce, beans and spice. Spoon into a casserole, see size in chart above. Cover and bake in a 350F (175C) oven for time in chart above or until rice is tender. Fluff with fork. Top with onions or noodles. Bake, uncovered, 5 minutes longer or until topping is warm.

Suggested Combinations
Spanish Meat Pilaf: Use cubed cooked veal for meat. Use chicken broth and white wine. Use garbanzo beans. Use saffron for spice. Use French-fried onions.
Oriental Meat Pilaf: Use cubed cooked pork for meat. Use chicken broth and soy sauce. Use red beans. Use ginger for spice. Use chow-mein noodles.

Tips for Leftover Meat Sauces
For a quick meal, serve hot sliced leftover meats with a sauce.
- Serve beef with: Zesty Horseradish-Mustard Sauce, page 311; Horseradish Bearnaise Sauce, page 304; Caper Hollandaise Sauce, page 306; Beer & Onion-Butter Sauce, page 316; Bordelaise Sauce, page 317; Cumberland Jelly Sauce, page 116; Beef Barbecue Sauce, page 314; or Hollandaise Sauce au Poivre, page 306.

- Accompany leftover roast pork with: Spicy Apple Jelly Sauce, page 116; Zesty Horseradish-Mustard Sauce, page 311; Pork Barbecue Sauce, page 314; or Easy Barbecue Sauce, page 314.

- Try ham with: Cumberland Jelly Sauce, page 116; Spicy Apple Jelly Sauce, page 116; or Pork Barbecue Sauce, page 314.

- Leftover lamb is delicious served with: Lemon-Mint Jelly Sauce, page 116; Minted Hollandaise Sauce, page 306; or Hollandaise Sauce au Poivre, page 306.

- Serve sliced leftover cold meats with: Creamy Tomato Sauce, page 312; or Spanish Sauce, page 312.

Basic Easy Meat Pie

SERVINGS	3 or 4	1 or 2
INGREDIENTS		
condensed cream soup	1 (10- to 11-oz.) can	1/2 (10- to 11-oz.) can (2/3 cup)
Worcestershire sauce	2 teaspoons	1 teaspoon
dried leaf herb or ground spice	1/2 to 1 teaspoon	1/4 to 1/2 teaspoon
dry white wine or water	1/4 cup	2 tablespoons
cubed cooked meat	2 cups	1 cup
leftover or drained canned vegetables	1 cup	1/2 cup
hot instant mashed potatoes OR	4 servings	2 servings
refrigerated biscuits	1 (4.5-oz.) tube (6 biscuits)	1/2 (4.5-oz.) tube (3 biscuits)
shredded cheese	1/2 cup (2 oz.)	1/4 cup (1 oz.)
paprika	to garnish	to garnish
CASSEROLE	2-qt. casserole	1-qt. casserole
TIME IN 425F (220C) OVEN (meat, vegetables)	20 to 25 minutes	15 to 20 minutes
TIME IN 425F (220C) OVEN (potatoes or biscuits added)	12 to 15 minutes	12 to 15 minutes

Do not preheat oven. In a casserole, see size in chart above, whisk together soup, Worcestershire sauce, herb or spice and wine or water. Fold in meat and vegetables. Bake in a 425F (220C) oven for time in chart above or until heated through. Spoon mashed potatoes in serving-size mounds or place biscuits around edge of casserole. Sprinkle potatoes or biscuits with cheese and paprika. Bake 12 to 15 minutes longer or until potatoes are heated through or biscuits are golden brown.

Suggested Combinations

Easy Mexican Meat Pie: Use tomato soup. Use chili powder for spice. Use cubed cooked beef or pork for meat. Use corn and canned chopped green chilies for vegetables. Use refrigerated biscuits and Monterey Jack cheese.

Easy Scottish Shepherd's Pie: Use cream of mushroom soup. Use dill weed for herb. Use cubed cooked lamb or veal for meat. Use carrots and drained canned mushrooms for vegetables. Use mashed potatoes and Cheddar cheese.

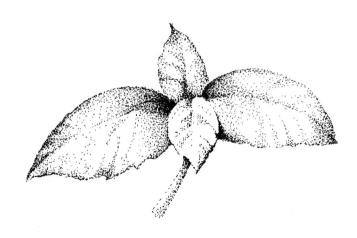

Basic Meat Stew

SERVINGS	8	4	2
INGREDIENTS			
vegetable oil	2 tablespoons	1 tablespoon	1 tablespoon
beef, lamb, pork or veal, cut in 1-inch cubes	2 lbs.	1 lb.	8 oz.
beef or chicken broth	3 cups	2 cups	1 cup
canned tomatoes, cut up OR	1 (28-oz.) can	1 (16-oz.) can	1 (8-oz.) can
cooking sauce	3 cups	1-1/2 cups	3/4 cup
dried leaf herbs or ground spice	4 teaspoons	2 teaspoons	1 teaspoon
bay leaf	1 large	1 medium	1 small
Worcestershire sauce	2 tablespoons	1 tablespoon	2 teaspoons
fresh vegetables	8 cups	4 cups	2 cups
loose-pack frozen vegetables	2 cups	1 cup	1/2 cup
all-purpose flour	1/3 cup	3 tablespoons	1 tablespoon
cold water	2/3 cup	1/3 cup	2 tablespoons
DUTCH OVEN	5-1/2-qt. Dutch oven	4-1/2-qt. Dutch oven	3-qt. saucepan
TIME AT MEDIUM	20 minutes	20 minutes	20 minutes
TOTAL COOKING TIME AT MEDIUM LOW:			
beef, lamb	1-3/4 hours	1-3/4 hours	1-3/4 hours
pork, veal	45 minutes	45 minutes	45 minutes
TIME AT MEDIUM LOW (fresh vegetables added)	last 7 to 45 minutes see timings in Suggested Combinations below	last 7 to 45 minutes	last 7 to 45 minutes
TIME AT MEDIUM LOW (frozen vegetables added)	last 20 minutes	last 20 minutes	last 20 minutes
TIME AT MEDIUM HIGH	1 to 2 minutes	1 to 2 minutes	45 to 60 seconds

In a Dutch oven, see size in chart above, heat oil over Medium heat. Add meat. Cook 20 minutes, turning to brown all sides lightly. Drain off fat. Pour broth and tomatoes or cooking sauce over meat. Stir in herbs or spice. Add bay leaf and Worcestershire sauce. Bring to a boil over High heat. Reduce heat to Medium Low; cover and simmer for time in chart above. Stir in fresh vegetables during last 7 to 45 minutes of meat cooking time, see vegetable time in Suggested Combinations below. Add frozen vegetables during last 20 minutes of meat cooking time. After adding all vegetables, cover and bring stew to a boil over High heat. Reduce heat to Medium Low. Simmer for remainder of meat cooking time or until meat and vegetables are tender. Remove bay leaf. In a screw-top jar, combine flour and cold water; shake well until completely smooth. Stir into stew. Cook, stirring gently, over Medium-High heat for time in chart above or until thickened and bubbly all over.

Suggested Combinations

Old-Fashioned Stew: Use canned tomatoes. Use basil and oregano for herbs. Add potatoes and carrots, cut in 1-inch pieces, and onions, cut in thin wedges, during last 45 minutes of cooking time. Use peas or green beans for frozen vegetable.

Middle Eastern Stew: Use canned tomatoes. Use curry powder for spice. Omit Worcestershire sauce and bay leaf. Add pared butternut squash, cut in 1-inch cubes, onions, cut in thin wedges, and raisins during last 45 minutes of cooking time. Use green beans for frozen vegetable.

Mexican Stew: Use taco sauce for cooking sauce. Use chili powder for spice. Add drained canned pinto beans, corn on the cob, cut in 1-inch pieces, green-pepper strips and zucchini, cut in 1-inch chunks, during last 15 minutes of cooking time. Omit frozen vegetable.

Oriental Stew: Use canned sweet-sour sauce for half of cooking sauce and more broth for remaining half. Use ginger for spice, using half the amount listed. Omit Worcestershire sauce and bay leaf. Add fresh mushroom slices, red-pepper strips, green onions, cut in 1-inch pieces, sliced water chestnuts and thawed frozen pea pods during last 7 minutes of cooking time. Omit frozen vegetable.

How to Make Basic Meat Stew

1/Cut beef, veal, lamb or pork into 1-inch cubes. Make cubes same size for more even cooking. Brown meat cubes in hot oil over Medium heat.

2/Pour broth and tomatoes or cooking sauce over browned meat. For this Mexican Stew, use taco sauce. Stir in seasonings. Simmer on Medium-Low heat. Simmering time varies for different kinds of meat.

3/Add vegetables toward end of cooking time, depending on vegetables used. For this stew, add zucchini chunks, green-pepper strips, corn-on-the-cob chunks and canned pinto beans during last 15 minutes of cooking time.

4/Test meat cubes and vegetables with a fork to be sure they are tender. Add flour and water mixture to thicken stew. Serve stew and juices in bowls.

Basic Oven Stew

SERVINGS	8	4	2
INGREDIENTS			
beef, pork, veal or lamb cut in 1-inch cubes	2 lbs.	1 lb.	8 oz.
beef or chicken broth	2 cups	1 cup	1/2 cup
condensed cream soup	2 (10- to 11-oz.) cans	1 (10- to 11-oz.) can	1/2 (10- to 11-oz.) can (2/3 cup)
dry red or white wine	1/2 cup	1/4 cup	2 tablespoons
dried leaf herb	2 teaspoons	1 teaspoon	1/2 teaspoon
bay leaf	1 large	1 medium	1 small
Worcestershire sauce	2 tablespoons	1 tablespoon	2 teaspoons
frozen stew vegetables	2 (20- to 24-oz.) pkgs.	1 (20- to 24-oz.) pkg.	1/2 (20- to 24-oz.) pkg.
loose-pack frozen peas, beans or corn	2 cups	1 cup	1/2 cup
all-purpose flour	2 to 4 tablespoons	1 to 2 tablespoons	1 tablespoon
cold water	2/3 cup	1/3 cup	3 tablespoons
OVENPROOF DUTCH OVEN	6-qt. Dutch oven	4-1/2-qt. Dutch oven	2-qt. saucepan
TIME IN 325F (165C) OVEN (meat)	1-1/4 to 1-1/2 hours	1 hour	45 to 60 minutes
TIME IN 325F (165C) OVEN (stew vegetables added)	1-3/4 to 2-1/4 hours	1-1/4 to 1-1/2 hours	1 to 1-1/4 hours
TIME IN 325F (165C) OVEN (other frozen vegetables added)	20 minutes	15 minutes	15 minutes
TIME AT MEDIUM HIGH	3 to 4 minutes	1 to 2 minutes	45 to 60 seconds

Do not preheat oven. Place meat in an ovenproof Dutch oven or ovenproof saucepan, see size in chart above. In a medium bowl, whisk together broth, soup and wine. Stir in herb, bay leaf and Worcestershire sauce. Pour over meat. Cover and bake in a 325F (165C) oven for time in chart above or until mixture is bubbling. Stir in frozen stew vegetables. Cover and continue baking for time in chart above or until meat and vegetables are almost tender. Stir in frozen peas, beans or corn. Cover and continue baking for time in chart above or until tender. In a screw-top jar, combine flour and cold water; shake well until completely smooth. Stir into stew. Cook, stirring gently, over Medium-High heat for time in chart above or until thickened and bubbly all over. Remove bay leaf.

Suggested Combinations
Beef Oven Stew: Use beef broth. Use tomato soup and red wine. Use Italian-herb seasoning for herb.
Pork Oven Stew: Use chicken broth. Use cream of celery soup and white wine. Use marjoram and rubbed sage for herbs.
Veal Oven Stew: Use chicken broth. Use creamy chicken-mushroom soup and white wine. Use dill weed for herb.
Lamb Oven Stew: Use beef broth. Use cream of onion soup and red wine. Use thyme and basil for herbs.

Tips for Cooking Stew

- Brown large quantities of meat in two batches. Otherwise, meat will stew in its own juice, which prevents browning.
- When making a range-top stew, bring stew to a full boil so bubbles break all over surface of stew. Reduce heat and simmer so bubbles break just below surface of stew.
- Make sure the lid fits tightly. Loose-fitting lids allow heat and moisture to escape, which alters cooking time and liquid content.
- Size of vegetable and meat cubes affects cooking time. Large pieces or cubes take longer to cook.
- Timings for oven stews may vary, depending on how deep the Dutch oven is. Stew takes longer to heat and cook in a narrow, deep Dutch oven.
- To thicken stew, mix flour and water to a smooth paste by shaking or stirring together. Stir mixture into stew. Stir constantly all over the pan to prevent lumps. Stir gently to avoid breaking vegetable pieces.

Oven Beef Pot Roast

SERVINGS	8	4	2
INGREDIENTS			
vegetable oil	1 tablespoon	1 tablespoon	1 tablespoon
beef chuck roast, 1-1/2 to 1-3/4 inches thick	4 lbs.	2 lbs.	1 lb.
beef broth	1/2 cup	1/2 cup	1/2 cup
onion salt	1/2 teaspoon	1/4 teaspoon	1/8 teaspoon
celery salt	1/2 teaspoon	1/4 teaspoon	1/8 teaspoon
Dijon-style mustard	1 tablespoon	2 teaspoons	1 teaspoon
prepared horseradish	2 tablespoons	1 tablespoon	2 teaspoons
potatoes, cut up	4 medium (1-1/2 lbs.)	2 medium (12 oz.)	1 medium (6 oz.)
carrots, cut up	4 medium (1 lb.)	2 medium (8 oz.)	1 medium (4 oz.)
onions, cut in thin wedges	4 medium (1 lb.)	2 medium (8 oz.)	1 medium (4 oz.)
OVENPROOF DUTCH OVEN	6-qt. Dutch oven	5-qt. Dutch oven	3-qt. saucepan
TIME AT MEDIUM	20 minutes	20 minutes	15 to 20 minutes
TIME IN 325F (165C) OVEN	2-1/4 to 2-1/2 hours	2 to 2-1/4 hours	1-3/4 to 2 hours

Do not preheat oven. In an ovenproof Dutch oven or ovenproof saucepan, see size in chart above, heat oil over Medium heat. Add roast. Brown for time in chart above, turning roast to brown all sides. Drain off fat. Pour broth over roast. Sprinkle roast with onion salt and celery salt. Spread with mustard and horseradish. Arrange vegetables around and on roast. Cover and bake in a 325F (165C) oven for time in chart above or until meat and vegetables are tender. Spoon pan juices over vegetables occasionally during cooking and before serving. Serve with Basic Gravy for Pot Roast, below, if desired.

Basic Gravy for Pot Roast

YIELD	4 cups	2 cups	1 cup
INGREDIENTS			
pan juices from pot roast	2 cups	1 cup	1/2 cup
all-purpose flour	1/2 cup	1/4 cup	2 tablespoons
beef or chicken broth	1 cup	1/2 cup	1/4 cup
wine or juice	1/2 cup	1/4 cup	2 tablespoons
broth or pan juices from pot roast	1/2 cup	1/4 cup	2 tablespoons
DUTCH OVEN OR SKILLET	pan from roast	pan from roast	pan from roast
TIME AT MEDIUM HIGH	12 to 13 minutes	9 to 10 minutes	5 to 6 minutes

Measure pan juices. If necessary, add extra broth to make first amount of juices listed in chart above. In a screw-top jar, combine flour and first amount of broth; shake well until completely smooth. Stir into pan juices in pot-roast pan, see chart above. Add wine or juice and second amount of broth or pan juices. Whisk over Medium-High heat for time in chart above or until thickened and bubbly all over.

Suggested Combinations
Use beef broth for beef and lamb gravy. Use chicken broth for veal and pork gravy. Use dry white wine or juice, such as apple juice or vegetable-tomato juice cocktail, if juice was part of cooking liquid in recipe.

Veal Pot Roast with Vegetables

SERVINGS	6 to 8
INGREDIENTS	
vegetable oil	1 tablespoon
veal shoulder blade roast, about 3-1/4 inches thick	4 lbs.
chicken broth	1/2 cup
onion salt	1/2 teaspoon
celery salt	1/2 teaspoon
pepper	1/4 teaspoon
dried dill weed OR	1 teaspoon
snipped fresh dill weed	1 tablespoon
dried leaf tarragon OR	1 teaspoon
snipped fresh tarragon	1 tablespoon
whole fresh mushrooms	8 oz. (2-1/4 cups)
whole small carrots	12 oz. (3 cups)
whole small onions	8 oz. (about 10)
SKILLET	12-inch skillet
TIME AT MEDIUM (brown meat)	20 minutes
TIME AT MEDIUM LOW (broth added)	1-1/2 hours
TIME AT MEDIUM LOW (vegetables added)	35 to 45 minutes

In a 12-inch skillet, heat oil over Medium heat. Add roast. Brown 20 minutes, turning roast to brown all sides. Drain off fat. Pour chicken broth over roast. Sprinkle roast with onion salt, celery salt, pepper, dill weed and tarragon. Bring to a boil over High heat. Reduce heat to Medium Low; cover. Simmer 1-1/2 hours. Arrange mushrooms, carrots and onions around roast. Spoon pan juices over vegetables. Bring to a boil over High heat. Reduce heat to Medium Low; cover. Simmer 35 to 45 minutes or until meat and vegetables are tender. Rearrange vegetables and spoon pan juices over vegetables once during cooking time. Serve with Basic Gravy for Pot Roast, page 91, if desired.

Tips for Pot Roast

- For large recipes, vegetables above cooking liquid may dry out during cooking. Rearrange vegetables during cooking so all vegetables rest in cooking liquid at some time. After rearranging vegetables, spoon pan juices over vegetables to keep them moist.

- For roasts with generous fat layers, such as lamb, skim off fat periodically during cooking.

- To make gravy, add broth, water or more cooking liquid used in recipe if there are not enough pan juices. Whisk gravy constantly during cooking to prevent lumps.

How to Make Pot Roast with Vegetables

1/Clockwise from front right: Beef chuck blade roast, lamb shoulder cushion roast, veal shoulder blade roast and pork shoulder blade (Boston) roast are all less-tender cuts of meat that make delicious pot roasts.

2/In a large skillet, brown pot roast in hot oil over Medium heat. Turn roast with tongs or a spatula to help retain meat juices. Turn roast to brown all sides. This is veal shoulder blade roast.

3/Pour chicken broth or other cooking liquid over roast. Season veal roast with fresh or dried dill weed and tarragon. Bring to a boil. Cover and simmer over Medium-Low heat 1-1/2 hours. Simmering times vary for different meats.

4/Add whole small carrots, whole fresh mushrooms and whole small onions around veal roast. Continue cooking. Spoon juices over vegetables and rearrange vegetables in skillet once during cooking.

Beef Pot Roast with Vegetables

SERVINGS	8	4	2
INGREDIENTS			
vegetable oil	1 tablespoon	1 tablespoon	1 tablespoon
beef chuck roast, 1-1/2 to 1-3/4 inches thick	4 lbs.	2 lbs.	1 lb.
vegetable-tomato juice cocktail	1/2 cup	1/2 cup	1/2 cup
onion salt	1/2 teaspoon	1/4 teaspoon	1/8 teaspoon
celery salt	1/2 teaspoon	1/4 teaspoon	1/8 teaspoon
pepper	1/4 teaspoon	1/8 teaspoon	dash
dried leaf basil	1 teaspoon	1/2 teaspoon	1/4 teaspoon
dried leaf oregano	1 teaspoon	1/2 teaspoon	1/4 teaspoon
potatoes, cut up	6 medium (2 lbs.)	4 medium (1-1/2 lbs.)	2 medium (12 oz.)
carrots, cut up	4 medium (1 lb.)	2 medium (8 oz.)	1 medium (4 oz.)
onions, cut in thin wedges	4 medium (1 lb.)	2 medium (8 oz.)	1 medium (4 oz.)
SKILLET	12-inch skillet	12-inch skillet	3-qt. saucepan
TIME AT MEDIUM (brown meat)	20 minutes	20 minutes	15 to 20 minutes
TIME AT MEDIUM LOW (liquid added)	1 hour	1 hour	1 hour
TIME AT MEDIUM LOW (vegetables added)	1-1/4 to 1-1/2 hours	1 to 1-1/4 hours	1 to 1-1/4 hours

In a skillet, see size in chart, heat oil over Medium heat. Add roast. Brown for time in chart, turning roast to brown all sides. Drain off fat. Pour cooking liquid over roast. Sprinkle roast with seasonings. Bring to a boil over High heat. Reduce heat to Medium Low; cover. Simmer for time in chart. Arrange vegetables around roast. Spoon pan juices over vegetables. Bring to a boil over High heat. Reduce heat to Medium Low; cover. Simmer for time in chart or until meat and vegetables are tender. Rearrange vegetables and spoon pan juices over vegetables once during cooking time. Skim excess fat from pan juices, if necessary, during cooking. Serve with Basic Gravy for Pot Roast, page 91, if desired.

Variation
Beef Round Rump Pot Roast: Brown and season a 3-1/2- to 4-pound beef round rump roast as above. Brown 20 minutes in hot oil in a 5-1/2-quart Dutch oven. Add cooking liquid and cook over Medium-Low heat 2-1/4 hours. Add vegetables as above and continue cooking for time above.

Beef Chuck Blade Roast

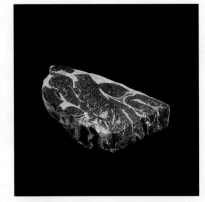

Beef Chuck 7-Bone Pot-Roast

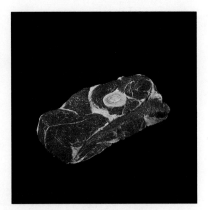

Beef Chuck Arm Pot-Roast

Pork Pot Roast with Vegetables

SERVINGS	4 to 6
INGREDIENTS	
vegetable oil	1 tablespoon
pork shoulder blade (Boston) roast, bone-in, about 3-1/4 inches thick	5 lbs.
apple juice	1/2 cup
onion salt	1/2 teaspoon
celery salt	1/2 teaspoon
pepper	1/4 teaspoon
dried leaf thyme	1 teaspoon
dried rubbed sage	1 teaspoon
sweet potatoes, cut up	1-3/4 lbs. (6 cups)
parsnips, cut up	1 lb. (4 cups)
onions, cut up	1-1/2 lbs. (4 cups)
DUTCH OVEN	5-1/2-qt. Dutch oven
TIME AT MEDIUM (brown meat)	20 minutes
TIME AT MEDIUM LOW (liquid added)	2 hours
TIME AT MEDIUM LOW (vegetables added)	1-1/2 hours

Follow directions for Beef Pot Roast with Vegetables, opposite.

Lamb Pot Roast with Vegetables

SERVINGS	4 to 6
INGREDIENTS	
vegetable oil	1 tablespoon
lamb shoulder cushion roast boneless, about 3-3/4 inches thick	5 lbs.
dry red wine	1/2 cup
onion salt	1/2 teaspoon
celery salt	1/2 teaspoon
pepper	1/4 teaspoon
dried leaf rosemary	1 teaspoon
dried leaf marjoram	1 teaspoon
small new potatoes	2 lbs. (about 16)
turnips or rutabaga, pared, cut up	1-1/2 lbs. (4 cups)
leeks, cut up	6 (2-1/2 cups)
SKILLET	12-inch skillet
TIME AT MEDIUM (brown meat)	20 minutes
TIME AT MEDIUM LOW (liquid added)	1-1/2 hours
TIME AT MEDIUM LOW (vegetables added)	1-1/2 to 2 hours

Follow directions for Beef Pot Roast with Vegetables, opposite.

Oven Swiss Steak Elegante

SERVINGS	8	4	2
INGREDIENTS			
bacon	8 slices	4 slices	2 slices
bacon drippings	1/4 cup	2 tablespoons	1 tablespoon
beef or veal round steak, 1/2 inch thick	2 lbs. (cut in 8 pieces)	1 lb. (cut in 4 pieces)	8 oz. (cut in 2 pieces)
dry white wine	1/2 cup	1/4 cup	1/4 cup
fresh mushroom slices	2 cups	1 cup	1/2 cup
tomatoes, peeled, cut in wedges	4 tomatoes	2 tomatoes	1 tomato
chopped shallots	1/2 cup	1/4 cup	2 tablespoons
dried leaf tarragon	2 teaspoons	1 teaspoon	1/2 teaspoon
snipped parsley	1/4 cup	2 tablespoons	1 tablespoon
OVENPROOF SKILLET	12-inch skillet	10-inch skillet	8-inch skillet
TIME AT MEDIUM HIGH	8 to 9 minutes	6 to 8 minutes	4 to 6 minutes
TIME AT MEDIUM	20 to 25 minutes	15 to 20 minutes	15 to 20 minutes
TIME IN 325F (165C) OVEN	1-3/4 to 2 hours	1-1/2 to 1-3/4 hours	1-1/2 to 1-3/4 hours

Do not preheat oven. In an ovenproof skillet, see size in chart above, cook bacon over Medium-High heat for time in chart above or until crisp, turning once. Drain bacon on paper towels. Reserve in skillet amount of drippings listed in chart above. Crumble bacon and set aside. Cut meat in serving pieces, see number in chart above. Slash fat edges of meat. Cook meat in reserved drippings over Medium heat for time in chart above or until lightly browned, turning once. Do not drain. Pour wine over meat. Top meat with mushrooms, tomatoes and shallots. Sprinkle with tarragon. Cover and bake in a 325F (165C) oven for time in chart above or until tender. Spoon pan juices over meat and vegetables once or twice during cooking. Top with crumbled bacon and snipped parsley. Serve Swiss steak with pan juices.

Tips for Swiss Steak

- Brown large number of meat pieces in 2 batches. Pieces piled on each other will not brown.
- To simmer a large number of pieces, layer meat in the skillet. This increases cooking time. Rearrange top and bottom pieces once during cooking. Spoon pan juices over top pieces occasionally to prevent them from drying out.
- To keep meat warm while making gravy, place it on a warm serving platter and cover with foil.
- Meat will be tough if it has not cooked long enough or has been cooked at too high a temperature. Liquid should barely bubble while meat is simmering. Check periodically during simmering time to be sure liquid is not boiling. If it is boiling, reduce heat slightly.

Basic Swiss Steak

SERVINGS	4 to 6	2 or 3	1 or 2
INGREDIENTS			
beef or veal round steak, 1/2 inch thick	2 lbs. (cut in 6 pieces)	1 lb. (cut in 3 pieces)	8 oz. (cut in 1 or 2 pieces)
OR			
pork or lamb blade steaks, 1/2 inch thick	4 (8- to 10-oz.) steaks	2 (8- to 10-oz.) steaks	1 (8- to 10-oz.) steak
all-purpose flour	1/4 cup	2 tablespoons	1 tablespoon
seasonings	4 teaspoons	2 teaspoons	1 teaspoon
vegetable oil	3 tablespoons	2 tablespoons	1 tablespoon
chopped vegetables	1-1/2 cups	3/4 cup	1/3 cup
canned tomatoes, cut up	1 (28-oz.) can	1 (16-oz.) can	1 (8-oz.) can
chicken or beef bouillon granules	1 tablespoon	1-1/2 teaspoons	3/4 teaspoon
Worcestershire sauce	4 teaspoons	2 teaspoons	1 teaspoon
all-purpose flour	1/4 cup	2 tablespoons	1 tablespoon
cold water	1/2 cup	1/4 cup	2 tablespoons
SKILLET	12-inch skillet	10-inch skillet	8-inch skillet
TIME AT MEDIUM	15 to 20 minutes	15 to 20 minutes	15 to 20 minutes
TIME AT MEDIUM LOW:			
beef	1-1/4 to 1-1/2 hours	1-1/4 to 1-1/2 hours	1 to 1-1/4 hours
veal	45 minutes	45 minutes	30 minutes
pork	1 to 1-1/4 hours	30 to 45 minutes	30 to 45 minutes
lamb	45 to 60 minutes	45 to 60 minutes	45 to 60 minutes
TIME AT MEDIUM HIGH	1 to 2 minutes	1 to 1-1/2 minutes	45 to 60 seconds

Slash fat edges of meat. Cut beef or veal in serving pieces, see number in chart above. In a small bowl, combine first amount of flour and seasonings. Coat meat with flour mixture. With a meat mallet, pound meat on both sides until 1/4 inch thick. Pound around bone in lamb and pork steaks. In a skillet, see size in chart above, heat oil over Medium heat until a drop of water sizzles on it. Add meat. Brown large recipe in 2 batches. Cook meat on both sides 15 to 20 minutes or until lightly browned. Drain off fat. Top meat with chopped vegetables. Combine tomatoes, bouillon granules and Worcestershire sauce. Pour over meat. Bring to a boil over High heat. Reduce heat to Medium Low; cover. Simmer for time in chart above or until meat is tender. Remove meat to a warm serving platter. In a screw-top jar, combine second amount of flour and cold water; shake well until completely smooth. Stir into pan juices. Whisk over Medium-High heat until mixture thickens and bubbles all over. Serve gravy over meat with hot cooked rice, noodles or mashed potatoes, if desired.

Suggested Combinations

Beef Swiss Steak: Use dry mustard and celery salt for seasonings. Use chopped onion and chopped green pepper for vegetables. Use beef bouillon granules.

Veal Swiss Steak: Use fines herbes and onion salt for seasonings. Use sliced mushrooms and sliced leeks for vegetables. Use chicken bouillon granules.

Pork Swiss Steak: Use dried rubbed sage and lemon pepper for seasonings. Use chopped green onion and chopped celery for vegetables. Use chicken bouillon granules.

Lamb Swiss Steak: Use herb pepper and onion salt for seasonings. Use chopped onion and chopped carrot for vegetables. Use beef bouillon granules.

How to Make Basic Swiss Steak

1/Clockwise from center: Pork blade steak, veal round steak, beef round steak and lamb shoulder blade steak are all used for Swiss steak. Slash fat edges of steaks with a knife to prevent curling during cooking.

2/Place meat on a cutting board. Pound mixture of flour and seasonings into meat with a meat mallet. Pound around bone on cuts such as this pork steak. After pounding both sides, meat should be about 1/4 inch thick.

3/Brown meat on both sides in hot oil in a skillet. Meat should lay flat in skillet for browning, so it may be necessary to brown in 2 batches. Top meat with chopped vegetables, canned tomatoes, bouillon granules and Worcestershire sauce.

4/Bring to a boil, then reduce heat to Medium Low. Cover and simmer. When done, meat should be fork-tender and shred easily with a fork. Thicken pan juices to serve with steak.

Basic Pepper Steak

SERVINGS	4	2
INGREDIENTS		
beef round steak or boneless pork loin	1 lb.	8 oz.
vegetable oil	2 tablespoons	1 tablespoon
onions, thinly sliced, separated in rings	2 medium	1 medium
garlic, minced	1 large clove	1 small clove
beef or chicken broth	1-1/2 cups	3/4 cup
dry white or red wine	1/2 cup	1/4 cup
Worcestershire sauce	2 tablespoons	1 tablespoon
dried leaf herb	2 teaspoons	1 teaspoon
black pepper	1/2 teaspoon	1/4 teaspoon
red or green pepper, cut in strips	2 small	1 small
cornstarch	2 tablespoons	1 tablespoon
cold water	1/4 cup	2 tablespoons
tomatoes, cut in wedges	2 tomatoes	1 tomato
hot cooked rice	4 servings	2 servings
SKILLET	12-inch skillet	10-inch skillet
TIME AT MEDIUM HIGH	6 to 7 minutes	5 to 6 minutes
TIME AT MEDIUM LOW (liquid added)	30 minutes	30 minutes
TIME AT MEDIUM LOW (green pepper added)	5 minutes	5 minutes
TIME AT HIGH	3 minutes	1 to 1-1/2 minutes
TIME AT MEDIUM LOW (tomatoes added)	3 to 4 minutes	2 to 3 minutes

Cut meat into thin strips about 1/4 inch wide, 2 to 3 inches long and 1/4 inch thick. Heat oil in a skillet, see size in chart above, over Medium-High heat until a drop of water sizzles on it. Tilt skillet to coat with oil. Add meat, onions and garlic. Cook for time in chart above or until onion is tender, stirring often. Stir in broth, wine, Worcestershire sauce, herb and black pepper. Bring to a boil. Reduce heat to Medium Low; cover. Simmer 30 minutes. Stir in red or green pepper. Cover and simmer 5 minutes or until meat is tender. In a small bowl, combine cornstarch and cold water; mix well until smooth. Stir into meat mixture. Cook and stir over High heat for time in chart above or until mixture thickens and bubbles all over. Reduce heat to Medium Low. Add tomatoes. Cover and heat for time in chart above or until heated through. Serve over hot cooked rice.

Suggested Combinations
Beef Pepper Steak: Use beef broth and red wine. Use basil for herb.
Pork Pepper Steak: Use chicken broth and white wine. Use marjoram for herb.

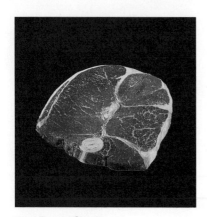

Beef Round Steak

Pork Loin Tenderloin Pieces

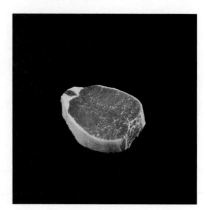

Pork Loin Butterfly Chop

Basic Skillet-Chop Supper

SERVINGS	4	2	1
INGREDIENTS			
pork or veal loin or rib chops, 1/2 inch thick	4 (6-oz.) chops	2 (6-oz.) chops	1 (6-oz.) chop
vegetable oil	1 tablespoon	1 tablespoon	2 teaspoons
onion, cut in thin slices	1 large	1 small	1/2 small
potatoes, cut in 1/4-inch slices	4 small	2 small	1 small
carrots, cut in 1/2-inch slices	4 small	2 small	1 small
condensed beef or chicken broth	1 (10-1/2-oz.) can	1/2 (10-1/2-oz.) can (2/3 cup)	1/4 (10-1/2-oz.) can (1/3 cup)
dried leaf herbs	1 teaspoon	1/2 teaspoon	1/4 teaspoon
all-purpose flour	3 tablespoons	4 to 6 teaspoons	2 to 3 teaspoons
milk	1/3 cup	1/4 cup	2 tablespoons
snipped parsley	2 tablespoons	1 tablespoon	2 teaspoons
SKILLET	12-inch skillet	10-inch skillet	8-inch skillet
TIME AT MEDIUM	15 minutes	15 minutes	15 minutes
TIME AT MEDIUM LOW	35 to 45 minutes	35 to 45 minutes	35 to 45 minutes
TIME AT HIGH	2 to 2-1/2 minutes	1 to 2 minutes	45 to 60 seconds

Slash fat edges of chops. In a skillet, see size in chart above, heat oil over Medium heat. Add chops. Brown 15 minutes or until browned. Drain off fat. Layer onion, potatoes and carrots over chops. Pour broth over all. Sprinkle with herbs. Bring to a boil over High heat. Reduce heat to Medium Low; cover. Simmer 35 to 45 minutes or until vegetables and chops are tender. With a slotted spatula, remove chops and vegetables to a warm serving platter; keep warm. In a screw-top jar, combine flour and milk; shake well until completely smooth. Stir into pan juices in skillet. Cook and stir over High heat for time in chart above or until thickened and bubbly all over. Serve gravy with chops and vegetables. Garnish with snipped parsley.

Suggested Combinations
Pork Skillet-Chop Supper: Use beef broth. Use rubbed sage and thyme for herbs.
Veal Skillet-Chop Supper: Use chicken broth. Use tarragon and Beau Monde for herbs.

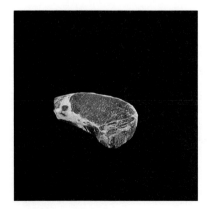

Pork Loin Top Loin Chop

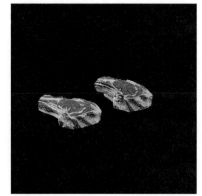

Veal Rib Chops

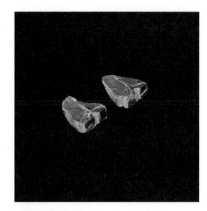

Veal Loin Chops

Onion-Braised Shanks & Noodles

SERVINGS	4 or 5	2 or 3
INGREDIENTS		
vegetable oil	1 tablespoon	1 tablespoon
beef shank cross cuts, 1 to 1-1/2 inches thick	4 lbs.	2 lbs.
OR		
lamb shanks	4 lbs. (4 shanks)	2 lbs. (2 shanks)
condensed French onion soup	2 (10-1/2-oz.) cans	1 (10-1/2-oz.) can
water	2 soup cans	1 soup can
dry white wine	1/4 cup	2 tablespoons
Worcestershire sauce	2 tablespoons	1 tablespoon
chopped carrot	1/2 cup	1/4 cup
chopped celery	1/2 cup	1/4 cup
dried leaf tarragon	2 teaspoons	1 teaspoon
dry mustard	2 teaspoons	1 teaspoon
medium noodles	3 cups uncooked (5 oz.)	1-1/2 cups uncooked (2-1/2 oz.)
all-purpose flour	1/4 cup	2 tablespoons
cold water	1/2 cup	1/4 cup
DUTCH OVEN	6-qt. Dutch oven	4-qt. Dutch oven
TIME AT MEDIUM	15 to 20 minutes	15 to 20 minutes
TIME AT MEDIUM LOW (liquid added)	2 to 2-1/2 hours	1-1/2 to 2 hours
TIME AT MEDIUM LOW (noodles added)	15 minutes	10 to 15 minutes
TIME AT HIGH	45 to 60 seconds	45 to 60 seconds

In a Dutch oven, see size in chart above, heat oil over Medium heat. Add meat. Brown 15 to 20 minutes or until shanks are brown on all sides. It may be necessary to brown 4 shanks in 2 batches. Drain off fat. Pour soup, first amount of water, wine and Worcestershire sauce over meat. Stir in carrot, celery, tarragon and dry mustard. Bring to a boil over High heat. Reduce heat to Medium Low; cover. Simmer for time in chart above or until meat is tender. Stir in noodles and moisten completely. Bring to a boil over High heat. Reduce heat to Medium Low; cover. Simmer for time in chart above or until noodles are tender, stirring once. Remove meat to a warm serving platter. Cover and keep warm. Skim fat from pan juices. In a screw-top jar, combine flour and cold water; shake well until completely smooth. Stir into noodles and broth. Cook over High heat, stirring constantly, 45 to 60 seconds or until thickened and bubbly all over. Serve shanks with noodles and gravy in bowls.

Easy Mustard Sauce

YIELD	3/4 cup	1/3 cup
INGREDIENTS		
mayonnaise or mayonnaise-style salad dressing	1/3 cup	3 tablespoons
dairy sour cream	1/3 cup	3 tablespoons
prepared horseradish	2 tablespoons	1 tablespoon
prepared mustard	2 tablespoons	1 tablespoon

In a small bowl, combine mayonnaise or salad dressing, sour cream, horseradish and mustard. Mix well. Cover and refrigerate until serving time. Serve with corned beef, ham, roast beef, bratwurst or sausage.

How to Make Corned Beef

1/Pour enough beer and water into a Dutch oven to cover corned beef. Add pickling spice, celery leaves, parsley sprigs and cut up onion for flavoring. Bring to a boil and skim off foam. Cover and simmer over Medium-Low heat until tender.

2/After cooking, let meat stand in cooking liquid at room temperature 1 hour. This makes meat more tender. Carve corned beef in thin slices, cutting diagonally across grain of meat. Serve hot corned beef with cabbage wedges and mustard.

Corned Beef

SERVINGS	4 to 6	2 or 3
INGREDIENTS		
corned beef brisket or corned beef round	3 to 4 lbs.	2 lbs.
beer	2 (12-oz.) cans	1 (12-oz.) can
water	to cover	to cover
mixed pickling spice	2 tablespoons	1 tablespoon
celery leaves	2 stalks	1 stalk
parsley	2 sprigs	1 sprig
onion, cut up	1 medium	1 small
DUTCH OVEN	8-qt. Dutch oven	5-qt. Dutch oven
TIME AT MEDIUM LOW:		
brisket	3 hours	2-1/2 hours
round	3-1/2 to 4 hours	
STANDING TIME (in liquid)	1 hour	1 hour
STANDING TIME (before carving)	15 minutes	15 minutes

Place meat in a Dutch oven, see size in chart above. Pour beer over meat. Add enough water to cover meat. Stir in pickling spice, celery leaves, parsley and onion. Bring to a boil over High heat. Skim off foam. Reduce heat to Medium Low; cover. Simmer for time in chart above or until meat is tender. Add more water to cover meat, if necessary, during cooking. After cooking, let meat stand in cooking liquid at room temperature 1 hour. Remove to carving board. Cover tightly with foil and let stand 15 minutes before carving. To serve cold, cover and refrigerate in cooking liquid until serving time. Slice diagonally across grain.

Variation
Corned Beef & Cabbage: While corned beef is standing 15 minutes before carving, add 1 (4-ounce) cabbage wedge for each serving to corned-beef cooking liquid. Bring to a boil over High heat. Reduce heat to Medium Low; cover. Cook 9 to 10 minutes or until cabbage is crisp-tender.

Orange-Glazed Pork Ribs

SERVINGS	3 or 4	1 or 2
INGREDIENTS		
curry powder	2 teaspoons	1 teaspoon
celery seed	2 teaspoons	1 teaspoon
garlic powder	1/8 teaspoon	dash
pork spareribs, loin back ribs or country-style ribs	3 to 4 lbs.	1 to 2 lbs.
orange, sliced	1 medium	1/2 medium
orange marmalade	1 (10-oz.) jar (about 1 cup)	1/2 (10-oz.) jar (about 1/2 cup)
pineapple preserves	1 (10-oz.) jar (about 1 cup)	1/2 (10-oz.) jar (about 1/2 cup)
soy sauce	1/3 cup	3 tablespoons
vinegar	1/3 cup	3 tablespoons
watercress	to garnish	to garnish
ROASTING BAG	23" x 19" bag	16" x 10" bag
ROASTING PAN	14" x 10" pan	12" x 7" pan
TIME IN 350F (175C) OVEN (meat):		
spareribs, loin back ribs	1 to 1-1/4 hours	1 to 1-1/4 hours
country-style ribs	1-1/2 to 2 hours	1-1/2 to 2 hours
TIME IN 350F (175C) OVEN (sauce added)	30 minutes	30 minutes

Do not preheat oven. In a small bowl, combine curry powder, celery seed and garlic powder; mix well. Rub all over ribs. Cut ribs in serving-size pieces. Lightly flour a roasting bag, see size in chart above. Place ribs, bone-side down, in roasting bag set in a roasting pan, see size in chart above. Overlap ribs slightly, if necessary. Top spareribs and loin back ribs with orange slices. Top country-style ribs with orange slices halfway through first baking time. Tie roasting bag closed with an ovenproof twist tie. Make 6 (1/2-inch) slits in roasting bag. Bake ribs in a 350F (175C) oven for time in chart or until almost tender. Carefully open bag and let steam escape. Push orange slices aside. In a medium bowl, combine orange marmalade, pineapple preserves, soy sauce and vinegar; mix well. Spoon over ribs. Tie bag closed. Bake in 350F (175C) oven for time in chart or until ribs show no pink when cut. Arrange ribs on a warm serving platter. Garnish with orange slices and watercress. Skim fat from meat juices. Spoon some juices over ribs. Serve ribs with remaining juices.

Orange-Glazed Beef Ribs

SERVINGS	3 or 4	1 or 2
INGREDIENTS		
beef chuck short ribs	3 to 4 lbs.	1 to 2 lbs.
same ingredients as for Orange-Glazed Pork Ribs, above, except add:	large recipe	small recipe
orange juice	1 cup	1/2 cup
TIME IN 350F (175C) OVEN (meat)	2 to 2-1/2 hours	2 to 2-1/2 hours
TIME IN 350F (175C) OVEN (sauce added)	20 to 30 minutes	20 to 30 minutes

Follow directions for Orange-Glazed Pork Ribs, above. Place beef ribs, bone-side up, in floured roasting bag. Pour orange juice into roasting bag. Before adding sauce, turn ribs bone-side down. Ribs should be tender when done.

How to Make Orange-Glazed Ribs

1/Clockwise from right: Beef chuck short ribs, pork loin back ribs and pork country-style ribs may all be used for this recipe. Rub seasonings of curry powder, celery seed and garlic powder over ribs. Cut pork ribs in serving-size pieces.

2/Place beef ribs, bone-side up, in a floured roasting bag. Arrange pork ribs, bone-side down, in bag. Top with orange slices. Pour orange juice over beef ribs. Pork ribs do not need this additional liquid. Tie roasting bag closed and bake ribs.

3/Partway through baking time, carefully open roasting bag and let steam escape. Turn beef ribs bone-side down. Do not turn pork ribs. Push orange slices aside. Spoon sauce over ribs. Tie roasting bag closed and continue baking beef ribs until fork-tender. Pork ribs are done when they show no pink when cut.

4/When ribs are done, skim fat from meat juices. It's easy to hold roasting bag over a bowl and snip off lower corner. Fat layer floats on top of juices. Remove bag from bowl when fat layer nears bottom of bag. Spoon juices over ribs to serve. Garnish with some of the orange slices and watercress.

Barbecued Pork or Beef Ribs

SERVINGS	3 or 4	1 or 2
INGREDIENTS		
pork spareribs, country-style ribs or loin back ribs	3 to 4 lbs.	1 to 2 lbs.
OR		
beef chuck short ribs	3 to 4 lbs.	1 to 2 lbs.
celery salt	1/2 teaspoon	1/4 teaspoon
garlic salt	1/2 teaspoon	1/4 teaspoon
onion, sliced, separated in rings	1 large	1 small
lemons, sliced	2	1
Honey Barbecue Sauce, below, or bottled barbecue sauce, heated	4 cups	2 cups
BROILER PAN WITH RACK	14" x 10" pan	14" x 10" pan
TIME IN 350F (175C) OVEN (meat):		
pork ribs	2 to 2-1/2 hours	2 to 2-1/2 hours
beef ribs	2-1/2 to 3 hours	2-1/2 to 3 hours
TIME IN 350F (175C) OVEN (sauce added):		
pork ribs	30 minutes	30 minutes
beef ribs	15 minutes	15 minutes

Do not preheat oven. Pour water to a depth of 1/2 inch in a 14" x 10" broiler pan. Place a rack in broiler pan; set aside. Cut pork ribs in serving-size pieces, if desired. Cut whole racks of ribs as necessary to fit broiler pan. Arrange ribs, bone-side down, on rack in broiler pan. Overlap ribs slightly, if necessary. Sprinkle with celery salt and garlic salt. Top with onion rings and lemon slices. Cover tightly with foil. Bake in a 350F (175C) oven for time in chart above or until tender. Uncover. Push lemon and onion slices to center of rack. Spoon half of barbecue sauce evenly over ribs. Bake, uncovered, in 350F (175C) oven for time in chart above or until heated through and glazed. Arrange ribs on a warm serving platter. Spoon more barbecue sauce over ribs. Garnish with some of onion and lemon slices. Serve ribs with remaining sauce.

Honey Barbecue Sauce

YIELD	4 cups	2 cups
INGREDIENTS		
olive oil	1/4 cup	2 tablespoons
chopped onion	2/3 cup	1/3 cup
garlic, minced	1 clove	1/2 clove
honey	1 cup	1/2 cup
ketchup	1 cup	1/2 cup
vinegar	1 cup	1/2 cup
Worcestershire sauce	1/2 cup	1/4 cup
dry mustard	4 teaspoons	2 teaspoons
salt	1-1/2 teaspoons	3/4 teaspoon
dried leaf basil	1 teaspoon	1/2 teaspoon
dried leaf oregano	1 teaspoon	1/2 teaspoon
pepper	1/2 teaspoon	1/4 teaspoon
SAUCEPAN	3-qt. saucepan	2-qt. saucepan
TIME AT MEDIUM HIGH	6 to 7 minutes	5 to 6 minutes
TIME AT MEDIUM	5 minutes	5 minutes

In a saucepan, see size in chart above, combine oil, onion and garlic. Cook over Medium-High heat for time in chart above or until tender, stirring occasionally. Stir in honey, ketchup, vinegar, Worcestershire sauce, dry mustard, salt, basil, oregano and pepper. Bring to a boil over High heat, stirring constantly. Reduce heat to Medium. Simmer, uncovered, 5 minutes.

Barbecued Pork Ribs with Honey Barbecue Sauce

Basic Fruit-Stuffed Chops

SERVINGS	6	4	2
INGREDIENTS			
plain croutons	2 cups	1-1/3 cups	2/3 cup
chopped dried fruit	1/2 cup	1/3 cup	2 tablespoons
dried herbs or ground spices	1 teaspoon	1/2 teaspoon	1/4 teaspoon
fruit juice	1/2 cup	1/3 cup	3 tablespoons
pork or veal loin chops, 1 inch thick	6 (8-oz.) chops	4 (8-oz.) chops	2 (8-oz.) chops
OR			
lamb loin chops, 1 inch thick	12 (4-oz.) chops	8 (4-oz.) chops	4 (4-oz.) chops
fruit juice	1 to 2 teaspoons	1 to 2 teaspoons	1 to 2 teaspoons
fruit jam or jelly	1/2 cup	1/3 cup	3 tablespoons
dry white wine	2 tablespoons	4 teaspoons	2 teaspoons
CASSEROLE	2-cup casserole	2-cup casserole	1-cup casserole
BAKING DISH	13" x 9" baking dish	12" x 7" baking dish	9-inch pie plate
TIME IN 350F (175C) OVEN (meat):			
pork, veal	1 hour	1 hour	1 hour
lamb	45 minutes	45 minutes	45 minutes
TIME IN 350F (175C) OVEN (glaze added)	15 minutes	15 minutes	15 minutes

Do not preheat oven. In a medium bowl, toss together croutons, dried fruit and herbs or spices. Gradually add first amount of fruit juice to moisten stuffing, tossing until juice is absorbed. Set aside. Cut pockets in chops. Starting from fat side, cut through to T-bone. Stuff pockets with some of stuffing. Skewer chops closed with wooden picks. Place remaining stuffing in a casserole, see size in chart above. Drizzle second amount of fruit juice over stuffing; set casserole aside. Place chops on a wire cooling rack in a baking dish, see size in chart above. Pour water to a depth of 1/4 inch in baking dish. Bake, uncovered, in a 350F (175C) oven for time in chart above. In a small bowl, combine fruit jam or jelly and wine; mix well. Spoon glaze over chops. Bake chops and stuffing casserole, uncovered, 15 minutes longer or until lamb and veal are done to your taste. Pork should show no pink when cut in center. Serve extra stuffing with chops.

Suggested Combinations

Fruit-Stuffed Pork Chops: Use snipped dried apples and raisins for dried fruit. Use rubbed sage and thyme for herbs. Use apple juice for fruit juice. Use crabapple jelly for fruit jelly.

Fruit-Stuffed Veal Chops: Use snipped prunes and golden raisins for dried fruit. Use cinnamon and allspice for spices. Use prune juice for fruit juice. Use plum jam for fruit jam.

Fruit-Stuffed Lamb Chops: Use snipped dried apricots and currants for dried fruit. Use crushed mint and nutmeg for herbs and spices. Use apricot nectar for fruit juice. Use apricot preserves for fruit jam.

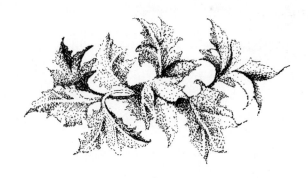

How To Make Basic Fruit-Stuffed Chops

1/Clockwise from top right: Lamb, pork and veal loin chops can all be stuffed. Starting from fat side, cut pocket in each chop, cutting through to T-bone. Allow 2 lamb chops per serving or 1 veal or pork chop per serving.

2/Spoon stuffing of croutons, dried fruit and seasonings into pockets. Lamb chops have dried apricots, currants, mint and nutmeg in fruit stuffing. Secure pockets with wooden picks inserted at an angle.

3/Place chops on a wire rack in a shallow baking dish. Pour water into baking dish to a depth of 1/4 inch. Water should not touch bottom of chops. Bake lamb chops 45 minutes; bake pork or veal chops 1 hour.

4/About 15 minutes before end of cooking time, spoon fruit glaze over chops. Lamb chops are basted with apricot glaze. Continue baking chops, along with casserole of extra stuffing to serve with chops.

Basic Breaded Cutlets

SERVINGS	4	2
INGREDIENTS		
egg	1	1
cooking liquid	1 tablespoon	1 tablespoon
crumb coating	1 cup	1/2 cup
dried leaf herb	1 teaspoon	1/2 teaspoon
all-purpose flour	4 teaspoons	2 teaspoons
pork or veal cutlets	4 (4- to 5-oz.) cutlets	2 (4- to 5-oz.) cutlets
vegetable oil	2 tablespoons	1 tablespoon
SKILLET	12-inch skillet	9- or 10-inch skillet
TIME AT MEDIUM HIGH (first side)	4 to 6 minutes	4 to 6 minutes
TIME AT MEDIUM HIGH (second side)	3 to 5 minutes	3 to 5 minutes

In a pie plate, whisk together egg and cooking liquid until frothy. In another pie plate, mix together crumb coating and herb. Place flour on a piece of waxed paper. Coat cutlets on both sides with flour. Dip both sides in egg mixture, then in crumb mixture, coating generously. In a skillet, see size in chart above, heat oil over Medium-High heat until a drop of water sizzles on it. Add cutlets. Cook, uncovered, on first side 4 to 6 minutes or until cutlets are browned. Carefully turn cutlets over with a wide spatula and rearrange in skillet. Cook, uncovered, on second side 3 to 5 minutes or until veal is done to your taste and pork shows no pink when cut in center.

Suggested Combinations & Variations

Cutlets Parmigiana: Use milk for cooking liquid. Use fine dry breadcrumbs and grated Parmesan cheese for crumb coating; measure 3 parts crumbs to 1 part cheese. Use oregano for herb. When cutlets are cooked, pour 1/4 cup bottled Italian cooking sauce over each one. Top each cutlet with 2 tablespoons shredded mozzarella cheese. Reduce heat to Medium Low. Cover skillet and heat through about 3 minutes.

Wiener Schnitzel: Use lemon juice for cooking liquid. Use fine dry breadcrumbs for crumb coating. Use snipped chives for herb. Serve with lemon wedges.

Herbed-Cutlet Sandwiches: Use milk for cooking liquid. Use finely crushed herb-seasoned stuffing mix for crumb coating. Use marjoram for herb. Serve on hamburger buns with sliced tomatoes, lettuce and Thousand Island dressing.

Breaded Pork Chops

SERVINGS	4	2
INGREDIENTS		
egg	1	1
cooking liquid	1 tablespoon	1 tablespoon
crumb coating	1 cup	1/2 cup
dried leaf herb	1 teaspoon	1/2 teaspoon
all-purpose flour	4 teaspoons	2 teaspoons
pork loin chops, 1/2 inch thick	4 (5- to 7-oz.) chops	2 (5- to 7-oz.) chops
vegetable oil	2 tablespoons	1 tablespoon
SKILLET	12-inch skillet	9- or 10-inch skillet
TIME AT MEDIUM HIGH (first side)	7 to 8 minutes	7 to 8 minutes
TIME AT MEDIUM (second side)	10 to 12 minutes	10 to 12 minutes

Follow directions for Basic Breaded Cutlets, above. Slash fat edges of chops at 1-inch intervals before coating. Reduce heat to Medium to cook second side of chops. Chops are done when no pink shows when cut in center.

How to Make Basic Breaded Cutlets

1/Ask the butcher to put veal or pork pieces through the meat tenderizer to make cubed steaks or cutlets. In a shallow dish, whisk together egg and milk. Lemon juice is used for Wiener Schnitzel.

2/Dip each cutlet on both sides in flour, then in egg mixture and finally in crumb mixture. For Herbed-Cutlet Sandwiches, crumb mixture is herb-seasoned stuffing and marjoram.

3/Heat oil in a skillet over Medium-High heat until a drop of water sizzles on it. Cook cutlets, uncovered, until browned, turning once. Cook pork cutlets until no pink shows when cut in center. Veal cutlets may be cooked to your taste.

4/Serve breaded cutlets on seeded buns for sandwiches. Top with lettuce leaves and tomato slices. Drizzle with Thousand Island dressing. Serve sandwiches with radishes, corn chips and iced tea.

Basic Sautéed Smoked Meats

SERVINGS	4	2
INGREDIENTS		
fully cooked smoked pork chops, 1/2 inch thick	4 (5-oz.) chops	2 (5-oz.) chops
OR		
fully cooked ham slice, 1/2 inch thick	1 (1-1/4-lb.) slice	1/2 slice (10 oz.)
OR		
fully cooked Canadian bacon, 1/4 inch thick	12 (1-1/4-oz.) slices	6 (1-1/4-oz.) slices
butter or margarine	1/4 cup	2 tablespoons
dry mustard	1 teaspoon	1/2 teaspoon
canned sliced or cut-up fruit	1 (16-oz.) can	1 (8-oz.) can
syrup from fruit	1/4 cup	2 tablespoons
packed brown sugar	1/4 cup	2 tablespoons
lemon juice	2 tablespoons	1 tablespoon
ground spice	1 teaspoon	1/2 teaspoon
parsley sprigs	to garnish	to garnish
SKILLET	12-inch skillet	9- or 10-inch skillet
TIME AT MEDIUM HIGH (first side)	4 minutes	3 to 4 minutes
TIME AT MEDIUM (second side)	3 to 4 minutes	3 minutes
TIME AT MEDIUM (sauce)	4 to 5 minutes	2 to 3 minutes

Slash fat edges of meat. In a skillet, see size in chart above, melt butter or margarine over Medium-High heat until a drop of water sizzles on it. Whisk in dry mustard. Add meat. Cook, uncovered, on first side for time in chart above. Spoon off juices as they accumulate; set aside. Reduce heat to Medium. Turn meat over with tongs and rearrange in skillet. Cook, uncovered, on second side for time in chart above. Spoon off juices as they accumulate; set aside. Meat should be heated through and lightly browned. Remove meat from skillet. Cover and keep warm. Return juices to skillet. Drain fruit, reserving amount of syrup listed in chart above. Stir reserved syrup, brown sugar, lemon juice and spice into pan drippings; mix well. Stir in fruit. Cook, stirring often, over Medium heat for time in chart above or until bubbly and heated through. Spoon fruit sauce over meat to serve. Garnish with parsley sprigs.

Suggested Combinations
Sautéed Smoked Pork Chops: Use sliced peaches for fruit and mace for spice.
Sautéed Ham Slice: Use pineapple chunks for fruit and nutmeg for spice.
Sautéed Canadian Bacon: Use apricots for fruit and cinnamon for spice.

Tips for Sautéed Meats

- Sauté meats uncovered for maximum browning. Covering meats during cooking will cause them to steam and not brown.

- Spoon off pan juices as they accumulate. This promotes more browning. Save juices for making a sauce.

- Sauté meats at Medium High on first side. Reduce heat to Medium to cook second side so meat will cook through without overbrowning. Cutlets are the exception. They cook through very quickly and are sautéed at Medium High on both sides.

- Place meat on a warm serving platter and cover with foil to keep warm while making sauce.

How To Make Basic Sautéed Smoked Meats

1/Clockwise from right: Smoked pork loin chops, Canadian bacon and ham slices may all be sautéed with this recipe. Slash fat edges of chops or slices to prevent meat from curling during cooking.

2/In a skillet, brown meat lightly on both sides in hot butter or margarine and dry mustard. To promote browning of meat, spoon off excess juices as they accumulate. Save extra juices for sauce.

3/Prepare sauce using canned peaches, pineapple or apricots. Heat fruit with brown sugar, lemon juice and spice. Cook sauce until it bubbles and fruit is heated through.

4/Spoon hot fruit sauce over smoked chops, Canadian bacon or ham slices on a serving platter. Garnish with parsley sprigs.

Sautéed Minute Steaks

SERVINGS	4	2	1
INGREDIENTS			
butter or margarine	1 tablespoon	2 teaspoons	1 teaspoon
dried leaf herb	1 teaspoon	1/2 teaspoon	1/4 teaspoon
beef cubed steaks (minute steaks)	4 (4-oz.) steaks	2 (4-oz.) steaks	1 (4-oz.) steak
SKILLET	12-inch skillet	9-inch skillet	6-inch skillet
TIME AT MEDIUM HIGH (first side)	2 minutes	2 minutes	2 minutes
TIME AT MEDIUM HIGH (second side)	1-1/2 to 2 minutes	1 minute	1 minute

In a skillet, see size in chart above, heat butter or margarine and herb over Medium-High heat until a drop of water sizzles on it. Add steaks. Cook, uncovered, on first side 2 minutes. Turn steaks over with a spatula and rearrange in skillet. Cook, uncovered, on second side for time in chart above or until done to your taste. These timings are for medium-done steaks.

Suggested Herbs: Use Italian herb seasoning, herb pepper, basil or tarragon for herb.

Sautéed Meat Patties

SERVINGS	4	2	1
INGREDIENTS			
butter or margarine	1 tablespoon	2 teaspoons	1 teaspoon
ground beef, lamb, veal, pork or half ham and half pork	4 (4-oz.) patties, 4 inches in diameter, 1/2 inch thick	2 (4-oz.) patties, 4-inches in diameter, 1/2 inch thick	1 (4-oz.) patty, 4-inches in diameter, 1/2 inch thick
HEAVY SKILLET	11-inch skillet	8-inch skillet	6-inch skillet
TIME AT MEDIUM HIGH (first side):			
beef	2 minutes	2 minutes	2 minutes
lamb, veal	3 minutes	3 minutes	3 minutes
pork, ham	6 minutes	5 minutes	5 minutes
TIME AT MEDIUM (second side):			
beef	2 minutes	2 minutes	2 minutes
lamb, veal	2 to 3 minutes	2 to 3 minutes	2 to 3 minutes
pork, ham	5 to 7 minutes	5 to 7 minutes	5 to 7 minutes

In a heavy skillet, see size in chart above, melt butter or margarine over Medium-High heat until a drop of water sizzles on it. Tilt skillet to coat with butter or margarine. Add patties. Cook, uncovered, on first side for time in chart above. Spoon off excess fat. Reduce heat to Medium. Turn patties over with a spatula and rearrange in skillet. Cook for time in chart above or until beef, lamb and veal are done to your taste. Pork should be well-done and show no pink when cut in center. Ham should be well-done and juices should run clear. Spoon off excess fat as it accumulates in skillet.

Basic Sautéed Steaks & Chops

SERVINGS	4	2
INGREDIENTS		
veal or pork loin chops, 1/2 inch thick	4 (4- to 6-oz.) chops	2 (4- to 6-oz.) chops
OR		
lamb loin chops, 1 inch thick	8 (4-oz.) chops	4 (4-oz.) chops
OR		
beef rib eye steaks, 1 inch thick	4 (8-oz.) steaks	2 (8-oz.) steaks
butter or margarine	1/4 cup	2 tablespoons
butter or margarine	2 tablespoons	1 tablespoon
sliced or chopped fresh vegetables	2 cups	1 cup
wine	1/4 cup	2 to 3 tablespoons
beef or chicken broth	1/4 cup	2 to 3 tablespoons
dried leaf herb	1 teaspoon	1/2 teaspoon
SKILLET	12-inch skillet	9-inch skillet
TIME AT MEDIUM HIGH (first side):		
veal	5 to 6 minutes	5 minutes
pork	6 minutes	5 to 6 minutes
lamb, beef	6 to 7 minutes	6 minutes
TIME AT MEDIUM (second side):		
veal	6 to 7 minutes	5 minutes
pork	7 to 9 minutes	7 to 8 minutes
lamb, beef	6 to 7 minutes	6 minutes
TIME AT MEDIUM HIGH (vegetables)	4 to 6 minutes	4 to 6 minutes
TIME AT MEDIUM HIGH (sauce)	2 to 3 minutes	1 to 2 minutes

Slash fat edges of meat. In a skillet, see size in chart above, melt first amount of butter or margarine over Medium-High heat until a drop of water sizzles on it. Add meat. Cook, uncovered, on first side for time in chart above. Spoon off juices as they accumulate; set aside. Reduce heat to Medium. Turn meat over with tongs and rearrange in skillet. Cook, uncovered, on second side for time in chart above. Spoon off juices as they accumulate; set aside. Cook beef, lamb and veal until done to your taste. Pork should show no pink when cut in center. Remove meat from skillet. Cover and keep warm. Return juices to skillet. Melt second amount of butter or margarine in skillet. Add vegetables. Cook over Medium-High heat 4 to 6 minutes or until almost tender, stirring occasionally. Stir in wine, broth and herb. Cook, uncovered, for time in chart above or until liquid thickens slightly. Stir sauce immediately before serving. Spoon sauce over meat to serve.

Suggested Combinations
Sautéed Beef Steaks: Use sliced fresh mushrooms and chopped shallots for vegetables. Use Madeira wine and beef broth. Use thyme for herb. Stir in a few dashes of Worcestershire sauce.
Sautéed Lamb Chops: Use sliced onion, chopped zucchini and pimiento for vegetables. Use Burgundy wine and beef broth. Use tarragon for herb.
Sautéed Pork Chops: Use sliced celery and sliced leeks for vegetables. Use dry white wine and chicken broth. Use oregano for herb.
Sautéed Veal Chops: Use chopped green pepper and chopped carrots for vegetables. Use dry white wine and chicken broth. Use fines herbes for herb.

Sautéed Calves' Liver

SERVINGS	4	2
INGREDIENTS		
bacon, cut in 1-inch pieces	8 slices	4 slices
bacon drippings	1/4 cup	2 tablespoons
French-fried onions	1 (3-oz.) can	1/2 (3-oz.) can (1 cup)
calves' or baby-beef liver, 1/4 to 1/2 inch thick	1 lb. (4 slices)	8 oz. (2 slices)
snipped parsley	2 tablespoons	1 tablespoon
SKILLET	11-inch skillet	10-inch skillet
TIME AT MEDIUM HIGH (bacon)	9 to 10 minutes	4 to 6 minutes
TIME AT MEDIUM HIGH (onions)	1 to 1-1/2 minutes	1 minute
TIME AT MEDIUM HIGH (liver, first side)	2 to 3 minutes	1 to 2 minutes
TIME AT MEDIUM (liver, second side)	2 to 3 minutes	2 to 3 minutes

In a skillet, see size in chart above, cook bacon, uncovered, over Medium-High heat for time in chart above or until crisp, stirring often. Remove bacon with a slotted spoon and drain on paper towels. Reserve in skillet amount of drippings listed in chart above. Heat reserved drippings over Medium-High heat until a drop of water sizzles on them. Add onions. Cook, uncovered, for time in chart above or until toasted, stirring constantly. Remove onions with slotted spoon and drain on paper towels. Add liver to skillet. Cook, uncovered, over Medium-High heat on first side for time in chart above or until browned. Reduce heat to Medium. Turn liver over with tongs and rearrange in skillet. Cook, uncovered, on second side 2 to 3 minutes. Meat should be brown outside and pink inside when done. Serve liver topped with bacon, French-fried onions and snipped parsley.

Basic Jelly Sauce for Meat

YIELD	1-1/3 cups	2/3 cup
INGREDIENTS		
fruit juice	2/3 cup	1/3 cup
jelly	1/2 cup	1/4 cup
wine	2 tablespoons	1 tablespoon
shredded citrus peel	1 teaspoon	1/2 teaspoon
ground spice	1/4 teaspoon	1/8 teaspoon
cornstarch	4 teaspoons	2 teaspoons
lemon juice	4 teaspoons	2 teaspoons
SAUCEPAN	1-qt. saucepan	1-qt. saucepan
TIME AT MEDIUM	5 to 7 minutes	5 to 7 minutes
TIME AT MEDIUM HIGH	2 to 3 minutes	1 to 2 minutes

In a 1-quart saucepan, combine fruit juice, jelly, wine, citrus peel and spice; mix well. Cook over Medium heat 5 to 7 minutes or until jelly melts, whisking often. In a small bowl, combine cornstarch and lemon juice; mix well. Stir into jelly mixture. Cook over Medium-High heat for time in chart above or until thickened and bubbly all over, whisking constantly. Serve hot or at room temperature.

Suggested Combinations

Cumberland Jelly Sauce: Use orange juice for fruit juice. Use currant jelly. Use port wine. Use orange peel. Use ginger for spice. Serve with ham, game meats, corned beef or tongue.

Lemon-Mint Jelly Sauce: Use apple juice for fruit juice. Use mint jelly. Use white wine. Use lemon peel. Use mace or cardamom for spice. Serve with hot or cold lamb.

Spicy Apple Jelly Sauce: Use apple juice for fruit juice. Use crabapple jelly. Use dry sherry for wine. Use orange peel. Use cinnamon for spice. Serve with pork or ham.

How to Make Sautéed Bratwurst or Hot Dogs

1/Select cook-before-eating bratwurst or fully cooked bratwurst or hot dogs. Simmer meat with onion slices and beer or water.

2/After simmering, drain saucepan or skillet. Brown meat in butter or margarine. Serve in buns with horseradish, ketchup, mustard and relish.

Sautéed Bratwurst or Hot Dogs

SERVINGS	4	2
INGREDIENTS		
cook-before-eating bratwurst or fully cooked hot dogs or bratwurst	4 (2- to 3-oz.) brats or hot dogs	2 (2- to 3-oz.) brats or hot dogs
onion slices	4	2
beer or water	1 (12-oz.) can or bottle (1-1/2 cups)	1/2 (12-oz.) can or bottle (3/4 cup)
butter or margarine	1 tablespoon	2 teaspoons
hot-dog buns, split	4	2
SAUCEPAN (cook-before-eating bratwurst)	3-qt. saucepan	1-1/2-qt. saucepan
SKILLET (fully cooked hot dogs or bratwurst)	8-inch skillet	6-inch skillet
TIME AT MEDIUM LOW:		
cook-before-eating bratwurst	15 to 20 minutes	15 to 20 minutes
fully cooked hot dogs	5 minutes	5 minutes
fully cooked bratwurst	5 minutes	5 minutes
TIME AT MEDIUM HIGH:		
cook-before-eating bratwurst	6 to 8 minutes	6 to 8 minutes
fully cooked hot dogs	4 to 5 minutes	4 to 5 minutes
fully cooked bratwurst	6 to 8 minutes	6 to 8 minutes

Place bratwurst or hot dogs in a saucepan or skillet, see size in chart above. Add onion slices. Pour beer or water over all. Bring to a boil over High heat. Reduce heat to Medium Low; cover. Simmer for time in chart above. Drain well. Remove onion and set aside. Add butter or margarine to same saucepan or skillet with bratwurst or hot dogs. Cook over Medium-High heat for time in chart above or until browned, turning often to brown all sides. Serve in hot-dog buns with reserved onion, horseradish, ketchup, mustard and pickle relish.

Pan-Fried Bacon

SERVINGS	4	2

INGREDIENTS
bacon, regular thickness, 22
  to 25 slices per lb., or
thick sliced, 11 or 12 slices
  per lb.
	8 slices	4 slices

SKILLET	12-inch skillet	10-inch skillet

TIME AT MEDIUM HIGH (first side):
  regular-thickness bacon
  thick-sliced bacon
	4 to 6 minutes
	6 to 8 minutes
		4 to 6 minutes
		6 to 8 minutes

TIME AT MEDIUM (second side):
  regular-thickness bacon
  thick-sliced bacon
	1 to 2 minutes
	3 to 4 minutes
		1 to 2 minutes
		3 to 4 minutes

Place bacon slices flat in a cold skillet, see size in chart above. Cook, uncovered, on first side over Medium-High heat for time in chart above or until bottom is browned. Reduce heat to Medium. Turn bacon over and rearrange slices in skillet. Cook, uncovered, on second side for time in chart above or until bacon is crisp and brown but still juicy. Drain on paper towels. Pour off pan drippings before cooking another batch. To cook additional batches, follow directions above, except cook both sides over Medium heat.

Oven-Fried Bacon

SERVINGS	4	2

INGREDIENTS
bacon, regular thickness, 22
  to 25 slices per lb., or
thick sliced, 11 or 12 slices
  per lb.
	8 slices	4 slices

BROILER PAN WITH RACK	14" x 10" inch pan	14" x 10" pan

TIME IN 425F (220C) OVEN:
  regular-thickness bacon
  thick-sliced bacon
	18 to 20 minutes
	22 to 24 minutes
		18 to 20 minutes
		22 to 24 minutes

Do not preheat oven. Place bacon on a rack in a 14"x 10" broiler pan. Slices should overlap only slightly or bacon will not cook evenly. Bake in a 425F (220C) oven for time in chart above or until bacon is crisp and brown but still juicy. Drain on paper towels.

Pan-Fried Sausage

SERVINGS	4	2

INGREDIENTS
fresh pork link sausage
OR
fresh bulk pork-sausage patties,
  2-3/4 inches in diameter,
  1/2 inch thick
	12 (1-oz.) links
	
	8 (2-oz.) patties
		6 (1-oz.) links
		
		4 (2-oz.) patties

SKILLET	11-inch skillet	8-inch skillet
TIME AT MEDIUM HIGH (first side)	6 to 7 minutes	6 minutes
TIME AT MEDIUM (second side)	6 to 7 minutes	4 minutes

Place sausage links or patties flat in a cold skillet, see size in chart above. Cook, uncovered, on first side over Medium-High heat for time in chart above or until bottoms are well-browned. Reduce heat to Medium. Turn patties over and rearrange in skillet. Continue turning links to brown all sides. Cook, uncovered, on second side for time in chart above or until no pink shows when cut in center.

How to Make Oven-Fried Sausage

1/Arrange sausage links or patties on a rack in a broiler pan. Pour water to a depth of 1/4 inch in broiler pan. Bake in a 425F (220C) oven 30 minutes, turning once.

2/Sausage is done when outside is browned and no pink shows when cut in center. This cooking method prevents spatters and messy cleanup.

Oven-Fried Sausage

SERVINGS	4	2
INGREDIENTS		
fresh pork link sausage	12 (1-oz.) links	6 (1-oz.) links
OR		
fresh bulk pork-sausage patties, 2-3/4 inches in diameter, 1/2 inch thick	8 (2-oz.) patties	4 (2-oz.) patties
BROILER PAN WITH RACK	14" x 10" pan	11" x 7" pan
TIME IN 425F (220C) OVEN (first side)	20 minutes	20 minutes
TIME IN 425F (220C) OVEN (second side)	10 minutes	10 minutes

Do not preheat oven. Pour water to a depth of 1/4 inch in a broiler pan. Place sausage on a rack in broiler pan. Bake in a 425F (220C) oven on first side 20 minutes. Turn sausage over. Bake on second side 10 minutes or until sausage is browned and shows no pink when cut in center. Drain on paper towels.

Basic Beef or Pork Stir-Fry

SERVINGS	4	2	1
INGREDIENTS			
cornstarch	2 tablespoons	1 tablespoon	1 teaspoon
soy sauce	2 tablespoons	1 tablespoon	1 teaspoon
boneless beef sirloin or pork tenderloin	1 lb.	8 oz.	4 oz.
vegetable oil	4 teaspoons	1 tablespoon	2 teaspoons
garlic, minced	1 large clove	1 small clove	1/2 clove
minced gingerroot	4 teaspoons	2 teaspoons	1 teaspoon
vegetable oil	1 to 2 tablespoons	2 to 3 teaspoons	2 to 3 teaspoons
any combination of cut-up vegetables for stir-frying, page 346	4 cups	2 cups	1 cup
chicken or beef broth	1-1/2 cups	3/4 cup	1/3 cup
hot cooked rice or warm chow-mein noodles	4 servings	2 servings	1 serving
WOK OR HEAVY SKILLET	wok or 12-inch skillet	wok or 12-inch skillet	wok or 12-inch skillet
TIME AT 375F (190C) OR MEDIUM HIGH:			
beef	1-1/2 to 2-1/2 minutes	1-1/2 to 2-1/2 minutes	1 to 1-1/2 minutes
pork	8 to 9 minutes	8 to 9 minutes	6 to 8 minutes
TIME AT 375F (190C) OR MEDIUM HIGH (vegetables added)	see timings on page 346		
TIME AT 375F (190C) OR MEDIUM HIGH (broth, soy sauce added)	2 to 3 minutes	1 to 2 minutes	30 to 60 seconds

In a small bowl, combine cornstarch and soy sauce until smooth; set aside. Slice meat in strips 1/4 inch thick, 2 inches long and 1/2 inch wide. In a wok or heavy 12-inch skillet, heat first amount of oil, garlic and gingerroot over Medium-High heat until a drop of water sizzles on it. Use 375F (190C) on an electric wok or skillet. Add meat. Cook over Medium-High heat or at 375F (190C) for time in chart above, stirring and tossing meat constantly. Beef should be medium-done in given time. Cook a little longer for well-done beef. Pork should be cooked until well-done and shows no pink when cut in center. Remove meat with a slotted spatula; set aside. Add remaining oil. Add vegetables, starting with longest-cooking vegetable as directed on page 346. Add other vegetables in decreasing order of cooking time. Cook over Medium-High heat or at 375F (190C) for time on page 346, stirring and tossing constantly. Return meat to wok or skillet. Add broth. Stir in soy-sauce mixture. Cook over Medium-High heat or at 375F (190C) for time in chart above or until thickened and bubbly all over, stirring constantly. Serve over hot cooked rice or warm chow-mein noodles.

Suggested Combinations

Beef Stir-Fry Potpourri: Use boneless beef sirloin. Use sliced zucchini, broccoli flowerets, sliced onions and halved cherry tomatoes for vegetables.

After-Work Pork Stir-Fry: Use pork tenderloin. Use cauliflowerets, green-pepper strips and tomato wedges for vegetables.

Summertime Pork Stir-Fry: Use pork tenderloin. Use yellow crookneck squash, red-pepper strips, bean sprouts and Chinese cabbage for vegetables.

Wintertime Beef Stir-Fry: Use boneless beef sirloin. Use thawed frozen pea pods, green-onion pieces, sliced fresh mushrooms and sliced celery for vegetables.

How to Make Basic Beef or Pork Stir-Fry

1/Slice beef sirloin or pork tenderloin in strips. Strips should be about 1/4 inch thick, 2 inches long and 1/2 inch wide. Meat will slice more easily if it has been partially frozen 1 to 2 hours. Peel gingerroot, then chop in very small pieces.

2/In a wok, heat oil, minced gingerroot and minced garlic until a drop of water sizzles on it. Add meat strips. Cook in hot oil, constantly stirring and tossing meat. Beef should be pink in center when done. Pork should show no pink when cut. Remove meat from wok with a slotted spoon.

3/Add vegetables to wok, starting with longest-cooking vegetable according to chart on page 346. Add other vegetables in their decreasing order of cooking time. In this case, cook onion rings first, then add broccoli, zucchini and cherry tomatoes. Stir and toss vegetables constantly during cooking.

4/Return meat to wok. Add broth and smooth mixture of cornstarch and soy sauce. Cook and stir until mixture thickens and bubbles. Serve over hot cooked rice or warm chow-mein noodles. Warm saki, fried rice, fortune cookies and Chinese tea make pleasing accompaniments.

Meat Fondue

SERVINGS	4	2
INGREDIENTS		
vegetable oil for deep-frying	about 3 cups	about 3 cups
boneless beef sirloin or tenderloin, lamb sirloin or leg, or fully cooked ham, cut in 1-inch cubes	2 to 3 lbs.	1 to 1-1/2 lbs.
OR		
boneless pork loin or tenderloin, cut in 3/4-inch cubes	2 to 3 lbs.	1 to 1-1/2 lbs.
Steak Fondue Sauce, below, Fruited Fondue Sauce, below, Red-Hot Fondue Sauce, below, and Horseradish-Mustard Sauce, page 76	for dipping	for dipping
METAL FONDUE POT	2-qt. pot	2-qt. pot
FRYING TIME AT 400F TO 425F (205C TO 220C):		
beef, lamb	30 to 45 seconds (rare), 1 to 1-1/2 minutes (medium)	30 to 45 seconds (rare), 1 to 1-1/2 minutes (medium)
ham	30 to 45 seconds (hot)	30 to 45 seconds (hot)
pork	2 to 2-1/2 minutes (well)	2 to 2-1/2 minutes (well)

Pour oil to a depth of 2 inches in a 2-quart metal fondue pot. Do not fill fondue pot more than half full with oil. Heat oil over Medium-High heat on the range until a deep-fat or candy thermometer registers 400F to 425F (205C to 220C). Place fondue pot over fondue burner. Spear meat cubes with a fondue fork. Cook for time in chart above or until beef and lamb are done to your taste and ham is heated through. Pork should show no pink when cut in center. Serve with sauces for dipping.

Red-Hot Fondue Sauce

YIELD	2/3 cup	1/3 cup
INGREDIENTS		
hot-style ketchup	1/2 cup	1/4 cup
butter or margarine, melted	1 tablespoon	2 teaspoons
prepared horseradish	1 tablespoon	2 teaspoons
Worcestershire sauce	1-1/2 teaspoons	3/4 teaspoon

In a small bowl, combine all ingredients; mix well. Cover and refrigerate until serving time. Serve with beef, lamb, ham or pork fondue.

Fruited Fondue Sauce

YIELD	2/3 cup	1/3 cup
INGREDIENTS		
pineapple yogurt	1/2 cup	1/4 cup
pineapple jam or chopped chutney	3 tablespoons	4 teaspoons
dry white wine	2 teaspoons	1 teaspoon

In a small bowl, combine all ingredients; mix well. Cover and refrigerate until serving time. Serve with ham or pork fondue.

Steak Fondue Sauce

YIELD	2/3 cup	1/3 cup
INGREDIENTS		
dairy sour cream	1/2 cup	1/4 cup
steak sauce	3 tablespoons	4 teaspoons
chopped green onion	1 tablespoon	2 teaspoons

In a small bowl, combine all ingredients; mix well. Cover and refrigerate until serving time. Serve with beef or lamb fondue.

How to Make Meat Fondue

1/Cut tender cuts of beef, lamb or fully cooked ham in 1-inch cubes. Cut pork in 3/4-inch cubes. Pork must be cooked well-done, so smaller cubes cook more thoroughly. Beef and lamb only need to be cooked to your taste. Fully cooked ham just needs to be heated.

2/Pour cooking oil into a deep fondue pot. Oil should be about 2 inches deep, but pot should be less than half filled with oil. Heat oil on the range until a deep-fat or candy thermometer registers 400F to 425F (205C to 220C).

3/Place fondue pot with oil over the fondue burner. Spear meat cubes with a fondue fork. Cook beef and lamb until rare or medium. Pork should show no pink when cut in center. Ham should be warm in center.

4/Transfer meat to a flatware fork. Eating with the fondue fork may burn your mouth! Serve Steak Fondue Sauce, Horseradish-Mustard Sauce, page 76, or Red-Hot Fondue Sauce as dips for beef or lamb. Serve Fruited Fondue Sauce with pork or ham.

Broiled Beef

Beef Flank Steak

Common Names: Plank Steak; London Broil; Jiffy Steak; Flank Steak Fillet
Servings per Pound: 3
Broiling Method: See opposite.
Broiling Tips: For maximum tenderness, marinate flank steak before broiling. See pages 138 to 140 for marinades. Lightly score (slit) flank steak on both sides in 1-inch diamonds diagonally across grain.
Serving Tips: Carve in thin slices diagonally across grain.

MEAT	DESIRED DONENESS	BROIL FIRST SIDE	BROIL SECOND SIDE
beef flank steak, 1/2 to 3/4 inch thick, 1 to 2 lbs.	rare	2 minutes	2 to 3 minutes
	medium	3 minutes	3 to 4 minutes

Beef Rib Eye Steak

Common Names: Delmonico Steak; Spencer Steak; Beauty Steak; Fillet Steak
Servings per Pound: 2
Broiling Method: See opposite.

STEAK	DESIRED DONENESS	BROIL FIRST SIDE	BROIL SECOND SIDE
beef rib eye steak, 1/2 inch thick, 7 to 8 oz.	rare	2 minutes	2 minutes
	medium	3 minutes	2 minutes
beef rib eye steak, 1 inch thick, 11 to 12 oz.	rare	4 to 5 minutes	4 to 5 minutes
	medium	6 to 7 minutes	6 to 7 minutes
beef rib eye steak, 1-1/2 inches thick, 13 to 16 oz.	rare	5 to 6 minutes	5 to 6 minutes
	medium	7 to 8 minutes	7 to 8 minutes

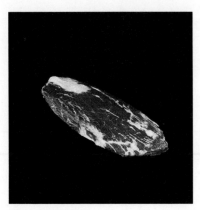

Beef Flank Steak

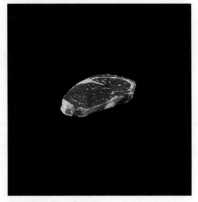

Beef Rib Eye Steak

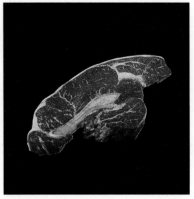

Beef Loin Sirloin Steak

How to Make Beef Flank Steak with Marinade

1/Score flank steak in 1-inch diamonds diagonally across grain of meat. This allows marinade to penetrate more deeply. Scoring tenderizes meat in same manner as pounding Swiss steak.

2/Marinate steak in a heavy plastic bag set in a shallow baking dish so it lies flat. Pour Deviled Meat Marinade, page 138, over steak. Tie bag closed and refrigerate 8 hours or overnight.

Beef Loin Sirloin Steak

Common Names: Round Bone Sirloin Steak; Wedge Bone Sirloin Steak; Flat Bone Sirloin Steak; Pin Bone Sirloin Steak; Shell Sirloin Steak
Servings per Pound: 2
Broiling Method: See below.

STEAK	DESIRED DONENESS	BROIL FIRST SIDE	BROIL SECOND SIDE
beef loin sirloin steak, 1/2 inch thick, 16 to 18 oz.	rare medium	2 minutes 3 minutes	2 minutes 2 minutes
beef loin sirloin steak, 1 inch thick, 2 to 2-1/2 lbs.	rare medium	5 to 6 minutes 7 to 8 minutes	5 to 6 minutes 7 to 8 minutes
beef loin sirloin steak, 1-1/2 inches thick, 3 lbs.	rare medium	8 to 9 minutes 9 to 10 minutes	8 to 9 minutes 9 to 10 minutes

Broiling Method For Meat

Slash fat edges of steaks and chops to prevent curling during cooking. Place meat on a rack in a broiler pan. Place broiler pan on top oven rack. Measure from top surface of meat to the broiler element. Adjust rack so broiler element is 4 to 5 inches away from meats that are 1 to 1-1/2 inches thick. It should be 2 to 3 inches away from cuts that are 1/2 to 3/4 inch thick. Pour water to a depth of 1/4 inch in bottom of broiler pan. Preheat electric broiler. You do not need to preheat a gas broiler. Broil meat on first side for time in chart. Season cooked side of meat with salt and pepper, if desired. Turn meat over with tongs. Broil meat on second side for time in chart or until done to your taste. To check for doneness, cut a small slit along bone or near center of boneless meat. Rare meat has a warm, red center. Medium meat has a hot, pink center. Beef or lamb may be served rare or medium. Well-done meat has no pink in center. Pork *must* be well-done, 170F (75C). Fully cooked ham only needs to be heated through.

Beef Loin T-Bone Steak or Porterhouse Steak

Common Names: T-Bone Steak; Porterhouse Steak
Servings per Pound: 2
Broiling Method: See page 125.
Buying Tip: To identify a porterhouse steak, look for a larger tenderloin muscle than in a T-bone steak.

STEAK	DESIRED DONENESS	BROIL FIRST SIDE	BROIL SECOND SIDE
beef loin T-bone steak, 1/2 inch thick, 8 to 9 oz.	rare medium	2 minutes 3 minutes	2 minutes 2 minutes
beef loin T-bone steak, 1 inch thick, 1-1/4 lbs.	rare medium	5 to 6 minutes 6 to 7 minutes	5 to 6 minutes 6 to 7 minutes
beef loin T-bone steak, 1-1/2 inches thick, 1-3/4 lbs.	rare medium	9 to 10 minutes 10 to 11 minutes	9 to 10 minutes 10 to 11 minutes

Beef Loin Top Loin Steak Boneless

Common Names: Strip Steak; Kansas City Steak; New York Strip Steak; Boneless Club Sirloin Steak
Servings per Pound: 2
Broiling Method: See page 125.

STEAK	DESIRED DONENESS	BROIL FIRST SIDE	BROIL SECOND SIDE
beef loin top loin steak, 1/2 inch thick, 7 to 8 oz.	rare medium	2 minutes 3 minutes	2 minutes 2 minutes
beef loin top loin steak, 1 inch thick, 11 to 12 oz.	rare medium	4 to 5 minutes 6 to 7 minutes	4 to 5 minutes 6 to 7 minutes
beef loin top loin steak, 1-1/2 inches thick, 13 to 16 oz.	rare medium	5 to 6 minutes 7 to 8 minutes	5 to 6 minutes 7 to 8 minutes

Beef Round Top Round Steak

Common Names: Beef Top Round Steak; Beef Top Round Steak, Center Cut
Servings per Pound: 2 or 3
Broiling Method: See page 125.
Broiling Tips: For maximum tenderness, marinate round steak 24 hours before broiling. See pages 138 to 140 for marinades.

STEAK	DESIRED DONENESS	BROIL FIRST SIDE	BROIL SECOND SIDE
beef round top round steak, 1/2 inch thick, 8- to 16-oz. pieces	rare medium	2 minutes 3 minutes	1 to 2 minutes 2 minutes

Beef Loin T-Bone Steak

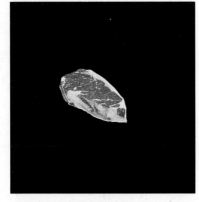

Beef Loin Top Loin Steak

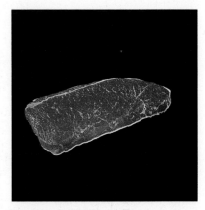

Beef Round Top Round Steak

Broiled Lamb

Lamb Rib Chops

Common Names: Rack Lamb Chops; Rib Lamb Chops
Servings per Pound: 2
Broiling Method: See page 125.

CHOPS	DESIRED DONENESS	BROIL FIRST SIDE	BROIL SECOND SIDE
lamb rib chops, 1/2 inch thick, 2-1/2 oz.	rare	3 minutes	1 minute
	medium	3 minutes	2 minutes
lamb rib chops, 1 inch thick, 3-1/2 oz.	rare	4 minutes	4 to 5 minutes
	medium	5 minutes	5 to 6 minutes
lamb rib chops, 1-1/2 inches thick, 5 oz.	rare	5 minutes	5 minutes
	medium	6 minutes	6 minutes

Lamb Loin Chops

Common Names: Loin Lamb Chops
Servings per Pound: 2
Broiling Method: See page 125.

CHOPS	DESIRED DONENESS	BROIL FIRST SIDE	BROIL SECOND SIDE
lamb loin chops, 1/2 inch thick, 2-1/2 oz.	rare	3 minutes	1 minute
	medium	3 minutes	2 minutes
lamb loin chops, 1 inch thick, 3-1/2 oz.	rare	4 minutes	4 to 5 minutes
	medium	5 minutes	5 to 6 minutes
lamb loin chops, 1-1/2 inches thick, 5 oz.	rare	5 minutes	5 minutes
	medium	6 minutes	6 minutes

Lamb Shoulder Blade Chops

Common Names: Blade Cut Chops; Shoulder Blocks; Shoulder Lamb Chops
Servings per Pound: 2
Broiling Method: See page 125.

CHOPS	DESIRED DONENESS	BROIL FIRST SIDE	BROIL SECOND SIDE
lamb shoulder blade chops, 3/4 inch thick, 8 to 10 oz.	rare	4 minutes	2 minutes
	medium	4 minutes	3 minutes

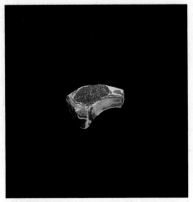

Lamb Rib Chop

Lamb Loin Chop

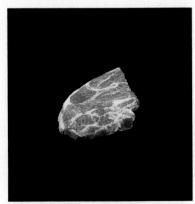

Lamb Shoulder Blade Chop

How to Broil Lamb Chops with Broiler Mates

1/Score fat edges of chops. Place meat on a rack in a broiler pan. Measure distance from the heating element to top of meat. Broiler element should be 4 to 5 inches away from meats that are 1 to 1-1/2 inches thick. It should be 2 to 3 inches away from meats that are 1/2 to 3/4 inch thick.

2/Pour water to a depth of 1/4 inch in bottom of broiler pan. Preheat electric broiler before cooking. You do not need to preheat a gas broiler. Do not salt meat before broiling. Salt draws juices to meat surface and slows browning. Broil meat on first side.

3/Season cooked side of meat, then turn chops over with tongs. Add orange slices topped with mint-jelly mixture during last few minutes of broiling time.

4/To check for doneness, make small cut next to bone in chops. Rare meat is red with warm center. Medium-done meat is pink with hot center.

Broiled Pork

Pork Loin Rib Chops or Loin Chops

Common Names: Rib Cut Chops; Pork Chops End Cut; Rib Pork Chops; Center Cut Chops; Center Loin Chops; Loin End Chops; Pork Chops
Servings per Pound: 3
Broiling Method: See page 125.
Broiling Tips: For maximum juiciness, marinate 1/2- to 1-inch pork chops before broiling. See marinades, pages 138 to 140. Do not marinate 1-1/2-inch pork chops before broiling because outside will char before chops are cooked through.

CHOPS	DESIRED DONENESS	BROIL FIRST SIDE	BROIL SECOND SIDE
pork rib or loin chops, 1/2 inch thick, 4 oz.	well	6 to 7 minutes	7 to 8 minutes
pork rib or loin chops, 1 inch thick, 9 oz.	well	10 minutes	10 to 11 minutes
pork rib or loin chops, 1-1/2 inches thick, 14 oz.	well	13 minutes	13 minutes

Pork Shoulder Blade Steak

Common Names: Pork Loin 7-Rib Cut; Pork Steak
Servings per Pound: 2
Broiling Method: See page 125.

STEAK	DESIRED DONENESS	BROIL FIRST SIDE	BROIL SECOND SIDE
pork shoulder blade steak, 1/2 inch thick, 12 oz.	well	6 to 7 minutes	7 to 8 minutes

Tips for Marinating Meats

- Do not save and reuse marinades once they have been used on meats. Cover and refrigerate extra marinade that was not poured over meat. Most marinades keep up to 1 week.

- Marinated meat may cook a little more quickly than usual guidelines indicate.

- Less-tender cuts, such as beef round steak and beef flank steak, require 18 to 24 hours of marinating for maximum tenderness. Beef steaks, such as rib eyes, are already tender and will absorb desired marinade flavor in about 8 hours.

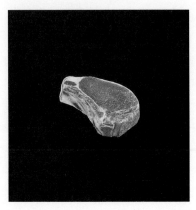
Pork Loin Rib Chop

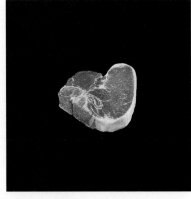
Pork Loin Chop

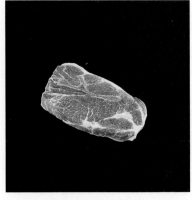
Pork Shoulder Blade Steak

Smoked Pork Loin Chops

Common Names: Smoked Pork Chops; Center Cut Pork Chops Smoked
Servings per Pound: 3
Broiling Method: See page 125.

CHOPS	DESIRED DONENESS	BROIL FIRST SIDE	BROIL SECOND SIDE
fully cooked smoked pork loin chops, 3/4 inch thick, 6 to 8 oz.	heated through	4 to 5 minutes	4 to 5 minutes

Smoked Pork Loin Canadian-Style Bacon

Common Names: Canadian Bacon; Back Bacon
Servings per Pound: 3 or 4
Broiling Method: See page 125.

BACON	DESIRED DONENESS	BROIL FIRST SIDE	BROIL SECOND SIDE
fully cooked Canadian-bacon slices, 1/8 inch thick, 1/2 oz.	heated through	2 minutes	1 to 1-1/2 minutes
fully cooked Canadian-bacon slices, 1/4 inch thick, 1-1/4 oz.	heated through	3 minutes	1-1/2 to 2 minutes
fully cooked Canadian-bacon slices, 1/2 inch thick, 2-1/2 oz.	heated through	4 minutes	2 to 3 minutes

Smoked Ham Center Slice

Common Names: Ham Center Slice
Servings per Pound: 3
Broiling Method: See page 125.

HAM	DESIRED DONENESS	BROIL FIRST SIDE	BROIL SECOND SIDE
fully cooked ham center slice, 1/2 inch thick, 1 to 1-1/4 lbs.	heated through	4 to 5 minutes	3 to 4 minutes
fully cooked ham center slice, 1 inch thick, 2-1/4 to 2-1/2 lbs.	heated through	7 to 8 minutes	7 to 8 minutes

Smoked Pork Loin Chop

Smoked Pork Loin Canadian-Style Bacon

Smoked Ham Center Slice

Regular-Sliced Bacon

Servings per Pound: 6
Broiling Method: See page 125.

BACON	DESIRED DONENESS	BROIL FIRST SIDE	BROIL SECOND SIDE
regular-sliced bacon, 22 slices per lb.	crisp	2 to 2-1/2 minutes	1 minute

Note: Thick-sliced bacon does not broil satisfactorily.

Sausage Links

Servings per Pound: 4
Broiling Method: See page 125.

SAUSAGE	DESIRED DONENESS	BROIL FIRST SIDE	BROIL SECOND SIDE
fresh pork-sausage links, 1-1/4 oz.	well	4 minutes	2 minutes

Pork-Sausage Patties

Servings per Pound: 4
Broiling Method: See page 125.

PATTIES	DESIRED DONENESS	BROIL FIRST SIDE	BROIL SECOND SIDE
fresh bulk pork-sausage patties, 1/2 inch thick, 4 inches in diameter, 4 oz.	well	5 minutes	4 minutes
fresh bulk pork-sausage patties, 1/2 inch thick, 2-3/4 inches in diameter, 2 oz.	well	5 minutes	3 minutes

Tips for Broiling Meat

- Broiling time is affected more by meat thickness than by weight. Broil 1/2- to 3/4-inch cuts 2 to 3 inches from heat. Broil 1- to 1-1/2-inch cuts 4 to 5 inches from heat. If meat is closer to the broiler element, broiling times will be shorter than those given in the chart. If meat is farther away from the broiler element, broiling times will be longer.
- Slash fat edges of steaks and chops to prevent meat from curling as it broils.
- Pour water to a depth of 1/4 inch in the bottom of broiler pan to prevent spatters during broiling and make cleanup easier. It also helps keep drier meats moist. If you don't use water in bottom of broiler pan, decrease cooking times slightly.
- To tenderize less-tender cuts of meat, such as beef round steak and beef flank steak, marinate before broiling. Lightly score flank steak on both sides in 1-inch diamonds diagonally across grain before marinating. See marinades on pages 138 to 140.
- Pork chops are juicier if you marinate them before broiling. However, do not marinate 1-1/2-inch-thick chops or they will char on outside before center is cooked.
- Marinate tender steaks to add flavor. Cooking time for marinated steaks may be slightly less.
- Beef chuck steak may be broiled with marginal success. Marinate beef chuck steak at least 24 hours. Use timings for sirloin steak as guide.
- Marinate steaks and chops in a heavy plastic bag set in a shallow baking dish so they lie flat in single layer.
- Pull out oven rack to check meat for doneness. Do not reach in under the broiler element to pull out broiler pan.
- Broiled meats will continue to cook some after you remove them from broiler.

Broiled Ground Meats

Ground-Pork Patties

Servings per Pound: 4
Broiling Method: See page 125.

PATTIES	DESIRED DONENESS	BROIL FIRST SIDE	BROIL SECOND SIDE
ground-pork patties, 1/2 inch thick, 4 inches in diameter, 4 oz.	well	5 minutes	4 minutes

Ham Patties

Servings per Pound: 4
Broiling Method: See page 125.

PATTIES	DESIRED DONENESS	BROIL FIRST SIDE	BROIL SECOND SIDE
ham patties, half ground ham and half ground pork, 1/2 inch thick, 4 inches in diameter, 4 oz.	well	5 minutes	5 minutes

Ground-Beef Patties

Common Names: Ground Chuck; Ground Round; Ground Sirloin; Hamburger
Servings per Pound: 4
Broiling Method: See page 125.

PATTIES	DESIRED DONENESS	BROIL FIRST SIDE	BROIL SECOND SIDE
ground-beef patties, 1/2 inch thick, 4 inches in diameter, 4 oz.	rare medium well	3 minutes 4 minutes 4 minutes	2 to 3 minutes 3 minutes 4 to 5 minutes

Ground-Veal Patties

Servings per Pound: 4
Broiling Method: See page 125.

PATTIES	DESIRED DONENESS	BROIL FIRST SIDE	BROIL SECOND SIDE
ground-veal patties, 1/2 inch thick, 4 inches in diameter, 4 oz.	medium well	4 minutes 4 minutes	3 minutes 4 minutes

Ground-Lamb Patties

Servings per Pound: 4
Broiling Method: See page 125.

PATTIES	DESIRED DONENESS	BROIL FIRST SIDE	BROIL SECOND SIDE
ground-lamb patties, 1/2 inch thick, 4 inches in diameter, 4 oz.	rare medium well	3 minutes 3 minutes 4 minutes	2 minutes 3 minutes 3 minutes

Basic Stuffed Hot Dogs

SERVINGS	4	2
INGREDIENTS		
chopped vegetables	1/4 cup	2 tablespoons
shredded cheese	1/4 cup (1 oz.)	2 tablespoons
cooking sauce	2 tablespoons	1 tablespoon
regular-sliced bacon	4 slices	2 slices
fully cooked hot dogs	4	2
hot-dog buns, split, pita-bread halves or taco shells	4	2
guacamole dip, deli coleslaw or deli three-bean salad	to accompany	to accompany
BROILER PAN WITH RACK	11" x 7" pan	11" x 7" pan
TIME AT BROIL (bacon, first side)	2 minutes	2 minutes
TIME AT BROIL (bacon, second side)	1 minute	1 minute
TIME AT BROIL (hot dogs, first side)	2-1/2 to 3 minutes	2-1/2 to 3 minutes
TIME AT BROIL (hot dogs, second side)	1-1/2 to 2 minutes	1-1/2 to 2 minutes

Preheat an electric broiler. You do not need to preheat a gas broiler. In a small bowl, combine vegetables, cheese and cooking sauce; mix well. Set aside. Place bacon on a rack in an 11" x 7" broiler pan. Broil 4 to 5 inches from heat 2 minutes. Turn bacon over. Broil 1 minute. Drain on paper towels. Bacon should be only partially cooked and still pliable. Slit hot dogs lengthwise, cutting to, but not through, other side or ends. Stuff vegetable mixture into slits in hot dogs. Wind partially cooked bacon spiral fashion around hot dogs, covering filling as much as possible. Secure with wooden picks inserted at a slant. Place hot dogs, stuffed-side down, on rack in broiler pan. Broil 4 to 5 inches from heat 2-1/2 to 3 minutes. Turn hot dogs over. Broil 1-1/2 to 2 minutes or until bacon is crisp. Serve and garnish using suggestions below.

Suggested Combinations

Mexicali Hot Dogs: Use canned chopped green chilies and chopped black olives for vegetables. Use Monterey Jack cheese. Use taco sauce for cooking sauce. Serve in taco shells with guacamole dip.

International Hot Dogs: Use chopped sweet pickle and chopped tomato for vegetables. Use Cheddar cheese. Use horseradish sauce for cooking sauce. Serve in pita bread with drained deli coleslaw. Garnish with paprika.

Barbecued Hot Dogs: Use chopped onion and chopped green pepper for vegetables. Use Swiss cheese. Use barbecue sauce for cooking sauce. Serve in hot-dog buns with drained, deli three-bean salad.

How to Make Basic Stuffed Hot Dogs

1/Broil bacon on both sides until partially cooked but still pliable. Slit hot dogs lengthwise, cutting to, but not through, other side or ends.

2/For International Hot Dogs, combine chopped sweet pickle, chopped tomato, shredded Cheddar cheese and horseradish sauce. Spoon pickle mixture into slits in hot dogs.

3/Wind partially cooked bacon spiral fashion around hot dogs, covering filling as much as possible. Secure with wooden picks inserted at a slant. Place, filling-side down, on same broiler pan.

4/Broil until bacon is crisp, turning once. Serve International Hot Dogs in pita-bread halves with coleslaw, Barbecued Hot Dogs in buns with three-bean salad and Mexicali Hot Dogs in taco shells with guacamole dip.

Basic Marinated Meat Kabobs

SERVINGS	4	2
INGREDIENTS		
meat marinade, pages 138 to 140	large recipe	small recipe
boneless beef sirloin, lamb leg, pork loin or fully cooked ham, cut in 1-inch cubes	1-1/2 lbs.	12 oz.
water	2 cups	1 cup
vegetables and fruit	4 or 5 pieces per skewer	4 or 5 pieces per skewer
cherry tomatoes, if desired	8 to 10	4 or 5
hot cooked rice	4 servings	2 servings
SAUCEPAN	2-qt. saucepan	1-qt. saucepan
BROILER PAN WITH RACK	14" x 10" pan	14" x 10" pan
METAL SKEWERS	4 to 6	2 or 3
REFRIGERATE	8 hours or overnight	8 hours or overnight
TIME AT BROIL (first side):		
beef, lamb	2 minutes (rare), 3 minutes (medium)	2 minutes (rare), 3 minutes (medium)
pork	5 minutes (well)	5 minutes (well)
ham	3 minutes	3 minutes
TIME AT BROIL (second side):		
beef, lamb	2 to 3 minutes (rare), 3 to 4 minutes (medium)	2 to 3 minutes (rare), 3 to 4 minutes (medium)
pork	4 to 5 minutes (well)	4 to 5 minutes (well)
ham	3 minutes	3 minutes
TIME AT BROIL (cherry tomatoes)	2 to 3 minutes	2 to 3 minutes

Prepare marinade. Refrigerate meat in marinade according to marinade recipe, 8 hours or overnight. Drain meat, reserving marinade. If using onion or green or red pepper, bring water to a boil in a saucepan, see size in chart above. Add green or red pepper and onion wedges. Remove from heat and let stand 5 minutes. Drain. Preheat an electric broiler. You do not need to preheat a gas broiler. Pour water to a depth of 1/4 inch in a 14" x 10" broiler pan. On metal skewers, thread drained marinated meat, alternating with vegetables or fruit, except cherry tomatoes. Leave small spaces between meat, vegetables and fruit on each skewer. Place skewers on a rack in broiler pan. Place broiler pan on an oven rack so the broiler element is 4 to 5 inches away from top of meat. Brush with some of reserved marinade. Broil on first side for time in chart above. Using hot pads, turn skewers over. Brush with some of reserved marinade. Broil meat and vegetables or fruit on second side for time in chart above or until beef and lamb are done to your taste and ham is heated through. Pork should show no pink when cut in center. Add skewer of cherry tomatoes to broiler pan during last 2 to 3 minutes of broiling time, if desired. Before serving, brush meat, vegetables and fruit with some of reserved marinade. Serve on hot cooked rice.

Suggested Combinations
Marinated Beef Kabobs: Use Mediterranean Marinade, page 138, or Teriyaki Meat Marinade, page 140. Use onion and green or red pepper, cut in 1-inch wedges, and fresh mushroom caps for vegetables.

Marinated Lamb Kabobs: Use Mediterranean Marinade, page 138, or Teriyaki Meat Marinade, page 140. Use zucchini, cut in 1-inch chunks, drained marinated artichoke hearts and large pimiento-stuffed green olives for vegetables.

Marinated Ham Kabobs: Use Cranberry Meat Marinade, page 138. Use unpared avocado, cut in 1-inch wedges, orange or cantaloupe, cut in 1-inch wedges or chunks, and quartered fresh pineapple slices for fruit.

Marinated Pork Kabobs: Use Teriyaki Meat Marinade, page 140, or Easy Meat Marinade, page 139. Use red or green apples, cut in 1-inch wedges, yellow crookneck squash, cut in 1-inch chunks, and whole water chestnuts for fruit and vegetables.

Cranberry Meat Marinade

YIELD	1-1/3 cups	2/3 cup
INGREDIENTS		
vegetable oil	1/2 cup	1/4 cup
cranberry-juice cocktail	1/2 cup	1/4 cup
honey	2 tablespoons	1 tablespoon
port wine	2 tablespoons	1 tablespoon
ground cinnamon	1/2 teaspoon	1/4 teaspoon
ground cloves	1/4 teaspoon	1/8 teaspoon
ham or pork	4 to 6 servings	2 or 3 servings
REFRIGERATE	8 hours or overnight	8 hours or overnight

In a screw-top jar, combine oil, cranberry juice, honey, port wine, cinnamon and cloves. Cover and shake well. Follow directions for Deviled Meat Marinade, below. Use to marinate ham or pork.

Mediterranean Meat Marinade

YIELD	1-1/3 cups	2/3 cup
INGREDIENTS		
olive oil	1/2 cup	1/4 cup
dry red wine	1/2 cup	1/4 cup
lemon juice	2 tablespoons	1 tablespoon
chopped green onion	1/4 cup	2 tablespoons
snipped parsley	1/4 cup	2 tablespoons
dried leaf oregano	1/2 teaspoon	1/4 teaspoon
dried leaf rosemary	1/2 teaspoon	1/4 teaspoon
dried leaf basil	1/2 teaspoon	1/4 teaspoon
garlic powder	1/8 teaspoon	dash
beef, lamb or pork	4 to 6 servings	2 or 3 servings
REFRIGERATE	8 hours or overnight	8 hours or overnight

In a screw-top jar, combine oil, wine, lemon juice, green onion, parsley, oregano, rosemary, basil and garlic powder. Cover and shake well. Follow directions for Deviled Meat Marinade, below. Use to marinate beef, lamb or pork.

Deviled Meat Marinade   Photo on page 125.

YIELD	1 cup	1/2 cup
INGREDIENTS		
vegetable oil	2/3 cup	1/3 cup
lemon juice	1/4 cup	2 tablespoons
chopped green onion	1/4 cup	2 tablespoons
snipped parsley	2 tablespoons	1 tablespoon
Dijon-style mustard	2 tablespoons	1 tablespoon
dried leaf thyme	1 teaspoon	1/2 teaspoon
garlic powder	1/4 teaspoon	1/8 teaspoon
beef, lamb or pork	4 to 6 servings	2 or 3 servings
REFRIGERATE	8 hours or overnight	8 hours or overnight

In a screw-top jar, combine oil, lemon juice, green onion, parsley, Dijon-style mustard, thyme and garlic powder. Cover and shake well. Place meat cubes or roast in a heavy plastic bag set in a deep bowl. Or, place steaks and chops in a single layer in a heavy plastic bag set in a shallow baking dish. Pour marinade over meat. Tie bag tightly closed. Refrigerate 8 hours or overnight, rearranging meat in bag or turning bag over occasionally. Drain meat, reserving marinade. Broil steaks, chops or cubes on skewers according to directions on pages 124 to 136. Baste meat with reserved marinade during last 2 minutes of broiling time. Or, roast meat according to directions on pages 55 to 71. Use some marinade as part of gravy liquid, if desired.

How to Make Marinated Pork Roast

1/Use a funnel to avoid spills when pouring oil and cranberry juice into a jar for Cranberry Meat Marinade. Marinating helps tenderize less-tender cuts of meat and enhances flavor of tender cuts. If desired, reserve some marinade to use for part of gravy liquid.

2/Marinate roasts, such as this pork loin roast, in a heavy plastic bag set in a pitcher or deep bowl. Select a bowl that closely conforms to shape and size of meat to keep meat submerged in marinade. Pour marinade over meat. Tie bag closed. Refrigerate 8 hours or overnight.

Tangy Meat Marinade

YIELD	1-1/2 cups	3/4 cup
INGREDIENTS		
vegetable oil	2/3 cup	1/3 cup
steak sauce	1/4 cup	2 tablespoons
dry sherry	1/4 cup	2 tablespoons
red-wine vinegar	1/4 cup	2 tablespoons
Worcestershire sauce	1 tablespoon	2 teaspoons
beef, lamb or pork	4 to 6 servings	2 or 3 servings
REFRIGERATE	8 hours or overnight	8 hours or overnight

In a screw-top jar, combine oil, steak sauce, sherry, vinegar and Worcestershire sauce. Cover and shake well. Follow directions for Deviled Meat Marinade, opposite. Use to marinate beef, lamb or pork.

Easy Meat Marinade

YIELD	1-1/3 cups	2/3 cup
INGREDIENTS		
red-wine-vinegar salad dressing	1 (8-oz.) bottle (1 cup)	1/2 cup
apple juice	1/4 cup	2 tablespoons
dried leaf oregano	2 teaspoons	1 teaspoon
dried leaf basil	2 teaspoons	1 teaspoon
prepared horseradish	2 teaspoons	1 teaspoon
lamb, beef or pork	4 to 6 servings	2 or 3 servings
REFRIGERATE	8 hours or overnight	8 hours or overnight

In a screw-top jar, combine salad dressing, apple juice, oregano, basil and horseradish. Cover and shake well. Follow directions for Deviled Meat Marinade, opposite. Use to marinate lamb, beef or pork.

Teriyaki Meat Marinade

YIELD	1-1/2 cups	3/4 cup
INGREDIENTS		
soy sauce	1/2 cup	1/4 cup
dry sherry	1/2 cup	1/4 cup
white vinegar	1/4 cup	2 tablespoons
water	1/4 cup	2 tablespoons
ground ginger	1/2 teaspoon	1/4 teaspoon
garlic powder	1/8 teaspoon	dash
beef, lamb or pork	4 to 6 servings	2 or 3 servings
REFRIGERATE	8 hours or overnight	8 hours or overnight

In a screw-top jar, combine soy sauce, sherry, vinegar, water, ginger and garlic powder. Cover and shake well. Follow directions for Deviled Meat Marinade, page 138. Use to marinate beef, lamb or pork.

Basic Fruit & Jam Broiler Mates

SERVINGS	4	2
INGREDIENTS		
fruit jam or jelly	2 tablespoons	1 tablespoon
cream sherry	1 teaspoon	1/2 teaspoon
ground spice	1/4 teaspoon	1/8 teaspoon
fruit, see suggestions below		
shredded coconut or chopped nuts	4 teaspoons	2 teaspoons
BROILER PAN WITH RACK	same as meat	same as meat
TIME AT BROIL:		
broiler pan 2 to 3 inches from heat	2 minutes	2 minutes
broiler pan 4 to 5 inches from heat	4 minutes	4 minutes

Place meat to be broiled to 1 side or end of the rack in the broiler pan. Broil according to directions for meat recipe. In a small bowl, combine jam or jelly, cream sherry and spice. Spread jam mixture on fruit slices. Add fruit slices to broiler pan with meat during last 2 to 4 minutes of broiling time, see distance from broiler element in chart above. Sprinkle fruit with coconut or nuts before serving.

Suggested Combinations

Apple Broiler Mate: Use crabapple jelly. Use cinnamon for spice. Cut unpeeled apple crosswise in 1/2-inch slices. Use 1 slice per serving. Sprinkle with chopped pecans. Serve with pork.

Orange Broiler Mate, photo on page 129: Use mint jelly. Use mace for spice. Cut unpeeled orange crosswise in 1/2-inch slices. Use 1 slice per serving. Sprinkle with almonds. Serve with lamb.

Papaya or Cantaloupe Broiler Mate: Use currant jelly. Use nutmeg for spice. Cut unpeeled papaya or cantaloupe crosswise in 1/2-inch slices. Remove seeds and halve slices. Use 1/2 slice per serving. Sprinkle with coconut. Serve with veal.

Pineapple Broiler Mate: Use orange marmalade. Use allspice for spice. Cut fresh pineapple crosswise in 1/2-inch slices. Quarter slices. Use 1/4 slice per serving. Sprinkle with coconut. Serve with ham.

How to Make Herbed Vegetable Broiler Mates

1/Cut tomatoes in slices about 1/2 inch thick. Top with generous spoonful of breadcrumb topping mixed with basil and mozzarella cheese. Mushrooms, artichoke bottoms and avocado wedges may also be stuffed with interesting cheese mixtures.

2/Place crumb-topped broiler mates at 1 end of the broiler pan 3 to 4 minutes before meat is done. Time depends on how far meat is from broiler element. Broil vegetables with meat until meat is cooked and vegetables are heated through.

Basic Herbed Vegetable Broiler Mates

SERVINGS	6	3
INGREDIENTS		
butter or margarine, softened	1 tablespoon	1-1/2 teaspoons
seasoned dry breadcrumbs	2 tablespoons	1 tablespoon
shredded or crumbled cheese	2 tablespoons	1 tablespoon
dried leaf herb	1/2 teaspoon	1/4 teaspoon
vegetables, see suggestions below		
BROILER PAN WITH RACK	same as meat	same as meat
TIME AT BROIL:		
broiler pan 2 to 3 inches from heat	3 minutes	3 minutes
broiler pan 4 to 5 inches from heat	4 minutes	4 minutes

Place meat to be broiled to 1 side or end of the rack in the broiler pan. Broil according to directions for meat recipe. In a small bowl, combine butter or margarine, dry breadcrumbs, cheese and herb. Spread about 2 teaspoons over each vegetable serving. Add vegetables to broiler pan with meat during last 3 to 4 minutes of broiling time, see distance from broiler element in chart above.

Suggested Combinations
Tomato Broiler Mate: Use mozzarella cheese. Use basil for herb. Cut tomatoes crosswise in 1/2-inch slices. Use 1 slice per serving. Serve with pork.
Avocado Broiler Mate, photo on page 127: Use bleu cheese. Use tarragon for herb. Cut unpeeled avocado lengthwise in wedges. Use 1 wedge per serving. Serve with beef.
Mushroom Broiler Mate: Use Swiss cheese. Use dill weed for herb. Use mushroom caps 1-1/2 to 2 inches in diameter. Use 1 cap per serving. Serve with veal.
Artichoke Broiler Mate: Use Cheddar cheese. Use thyme for herb. Use canned artichoke bottoms. Use 1 artichoke bottom per serving. Serve with lamb.

Curried Chutney Topper for Lamb

YIELD	1/3 cup	3 tablespoons
INGREDIENTS		
chopped peach or mango chutney	1/3 cup	3 tablespoons
chopped green onion	2 tablespoons	1 tablespoon
dry white wine	2 teaspoons	1 teaspoon
curry powder	1/2 teaspoon	1/4 teaspoon
broiled lamb chops	8 chops	4 chops
BROILER PAN WITH RACK	14" x 10" pan	11" x 7" pan
TIME AT BROIL	1 minute	1 minute

In a small bowl, combine chutney, green onion, wine and curry powder; mix well. Spread chutney mixture on each hot broiled lamb chop. Return to broiler and broil 1 minute or until topper is heated through.

Spiced-Cheese Steak Topper   Photo on page 127.

YIELD	1/2 cup	1/4 cup
INGREDIENTS		
semisoft natural cheese with garlic and herbs or with pepper	1 (3-1/2-oz.) carton	1/2 (3-1/2-oz.) carton
chopped green onion	2 tablespoons	1 tablespoon
chopped pimiento	2 tablespoons	1 tablespoon
chopped green olives	2 tablespoons	1 tablespoon
cooked steaks	4 steaks	2 steaks

In a small bowl, combine cheese, green onion, pimiento and olives; mix well. Cover and refrigerate until serving time. Immediately before serving, spoon about 1 tablespoon cheese mixture on each hot cooked steak. Spread over steak to melt. Serve remaining cheese topper with steaks.

Green-Peppercorn Steak Topper

YIELD	1/2 cup	1/4 cup
INGREDIENTS		
butter or margarine, softened	1/2 cup	1/4 cup
green peppercorns, drained, rinsed	4 teaspoons	2 teaspoons
capers, drained	2 teaspoons	1 teaspoon
garlic, minced	1 large clove	1 small clove
brandy	2 tablespoons	1 tablespoon
cooked steaks	4 steaks	2 steaks

In a small mixer bowl, beat butter or margarine, green peppercorns, capers, garlic and brandy at high speed of an electric mixer until well-combined and fluffy. Immediately before serving, spoon about 1 tablespoon peppercorn-butter mixture on each hot cooked steak. Spread over steak to melt. Serve remaining butter with steaks.

How to Make Zesty Fruit Topper for Meat

1/Mix lemon juice, mustard and horseradish into apricot-, pineapple- or peach-pie filling for a quick topper.

2/Spread fruit topper on hot broiled ham slice, pork chops or lamb chops. Broil 1 minute or until topper is heated through.

Zesty Fruit Topper for Meat

YIELD	1/3 cup	3 tablespoons
INGREDIENTS		
apricot-, pineapple- or peach-pie filling	1/3 cup	3 tablespoons
lemon juice	1 tablespoon	1-1/2 teaspoons
prepared mustard	2 teaspoons	1 teaspoon
prepared horseradish	1 teaspoon	1/2 teaspoon
broiled ham slice	1 inch thick	1/2 inch thick
OR		
broiled pork chops	4 chops	2 chops
OR		
broiled lamb chops	8 chops	4 chops
BROILER PAN WITH RACK	14" x 10" pan	11" x 7" pan
TIME AT BROIL	1 minute	1 minute

In a small bowl, combine pie filling, lemon juice, mustard and horseradish; mix well. Spread on hot broiled ham slice, pork chops or lamb chops. Return to broiler. Broil 1 minute or until topper is heated through.

Basic Relish Burger Topper

YIELD	2/3 cup	1/3 cup
INGREDIENTS		
chopped or sliced vegetables	1/2 cup	1/4 cup
chopped green onion	2 tablespoons	1 tablespoon
chopped green or red pepper	2 tablespoons	1 tablespoon
flavored salad dressing	2 tablespoons	1 tablespoon
herb seed	1/4 teaspoon	1/8 teaspoon
shredded or crumbled cheese	1/4 cup (1 oz.)	2 tablespoons
cooked burgers	4 burgers	2 burgers

In a small bowl, combine chopped or sliced vegetables, green onion, green or red pepper, flavored salad dressing and herb seed; mix well. Cover and refrigerate until serving time. Immediately before serving, fold in cheese. Spoon on hot cooked burgers.

Suggested Combinations
Tomato-Relish Burger Topper: Use chopped tomato and chopped zucchini for vegetables. Use Italian salad dressing. Use celery seed for herb seed. Use shredded Cheddar cheese. Serve with beef, lamb or pork burgers.
Pickle-Relish Burger Topper: Use chopped dill pickle and chopped cauliflower for vegetables. Use herb-and-spice salad dressing. Use dill seed for herb seed. Use crumbled feta cheese. Serve with beef or lamb burgers.
Onion-Relish Burger Topper: Use thinly sliced onion, separated in rings, for vegetable. Use bleu-cheese salad dressing. Use mustard seed for herb seed. Use crumbled bleu cheese. Serve with beef, lamb or pork burgers.

Basic Creamy Burger Topper

YIELD	2/3 cup	1/3 cup
INGREDIENTS		
flavored sour-cream dip	1/2 cup	1/4 cup
chopped vegetables or meat	1/3 cup	3 tablespoons
prepared mustard	1 teaspoon	1/2 teaspoon
dried leaf herb	1/4 teaspoon	1/8 teaspoon
broiled burgers	4 burgers	2 burgers
BROILER PAN WITH RACK	14" x 10" pan	11" x 7" pan
TIME AT BROIL	15 to 30 seconds	15 to 30 seconds

In a small bowl, combine sour-cream dip, vegetables or meat, mustard and herb; mix well. Refrigerate until serving time. Spoon 1 tablespoon topper on each hot broiled burger. Return to broiler and broil 15 to 30 seconds or until topper is heated through. Serve remaining topper with burgers.

Suggested Combinations
Creamy-Onion Burger Topper: Use toasted-onion sour-cream dip. Use chopped avocado and chopped tomato for vegetables. Use basil for herb. Serve with beef, lamb or pork burgers.
Creamy-Bacon Burger Topper: Use horseradish-and-bacon sour-cream dip. Use crumbled cooked bacon for meat. Use tarragon for herb. Serve with beef, lamb or pork burgers.

Broiled Ground-Beef Patty, page 133, with Tomato-Relish Burger Topper.

Basic Meat Loaf

SERVINGS	6	4	2
INGREDIENTS			
ground meat	1-1/2 lbs.	1 lb.	8 oz.
eggs	2	1	1
quick-cooking oats	1/3 cup	1/4 cup	2 tablespoons
chopped vegetables	1/2 cup	1/3 cup	3 tablespoons
cooking liquid	1/2 cup	1/3 cup	3 tablespoons
dried leaf herbs	3/4 teaspoon	1/2 teaspoon	1/4 teaspoon
OR			
ground spices	1/2 teaspoon	1/4 teaspoon	1/8 teaspoon
celery salt	3/4 teaspoon	1/2 teaspoon	1/4 teaspoon
(omit for ham loaf)			
cooking liquid	1/2 cup	1/3 cup	2 tablespoons
dry white wine	2 tablespoons	1 tablespoon	2 teaspoons
dried leaf herbs	3/4 teaspoon	1/2 teaspoon	1/4 teaspoon
OR			
ground spices	1/2 teaspoon	1/4 teaspoon	1/8 teaspoon
BAKING DISH	9" x 5" x 3" loaf dish	9" x 5" x 3" loaf dish	7-inch pie plate
TIME IN 350F (175C) OVEN:			
beef loaf, ham loaf	1 hour 15 minutes to 1 hour 20 minutes	1 hour to 1 hour 10 minutes	40 to 45 minutes
pork loaf	1 hour 35 minutes to 1 hour 40 minutes	1 hour 10 minutes to 1 hour 15 minutes	40 to 45 minutes
STANDING TIME	5 minutes	5 minutes	5 minutes

Do not preheat oven. In a medium bowl, combine ground meat, eggs, oats, vegetables, first amount of cooking liquid, first amount of herbs or spices and celery salt; mix well. Shape into loaf in a baking dish, see size in chart above. Shape loaf so meat does not touch sides of dish. In a small bowl, combine second amount of cooking liquid, wine and second amount of herbs or spices. Spoon over loaf. Bake in a 350F (175C) oven for time in chart above or until beef and pork do not show pink when cut in center. Juices should run clear in center of ham loaf. A meat thermometer inserted in center of beef, ham or pork loaf should register 170F (75C). Let meat loaf stand, covered, 5 minutes before slicing.

Suggested Combinations

Beef Loaf: Use lean ground beef. Use chopped green pepper and chopped onion for vegetables. Use bottled barbecue sauce for cooking liquid. Use basil and thyme for herbs.

Pork Loaf: Use ground pork. Use chopped celery and sliced green olives for vegetables. Use pizza sauce for cooking liquid. Use oregano and basil for herbs.

Ham Loaf: Use half ground ham and half ground pork. Use chopped water chestnuts and chopped green onion for vegetables. Use pineapple ice-cream topping for cooking liquid. Use cinnamon and nutmeg for spices. Omit celery salt.

How to Make Basic Meat Loaf

1/Clockwise from right: Ground beef, ground pork and ground ham may all be used for meat loaf. Combine ground meat with chopped vegetables, oats, eggs, herbs or spices and cooking liquid. Thoroughly mix meat mixture. For Ham Loaf, use half ground ham and half ground pork with chopped water chestnuts and green onions.

2/Form meat into a firm loaf shape in a baking dish. Smooth out cracks in meat because they will widen during baking. Shape loaf so sides do not touch baking dish. This allows fat to drain more easily.

3/Mix together more cooking liquid, wine and herbs or spices to spoon over loaf before baking. Ham Loaf is glazed with pineapple ice-cream topping, cinnamon and nutmeg.

4/Bake beef and pork loaves until no pink shows when cut in center. Juices should run clear in center of ham loaf. Let loaf stand, covered, 5 minutes; then cut in thick slices. Garnish with pineapple wedges.

Cheesy Meatball Supper

SERVINGS	6	3
INGREDIENTS		
Meatballs, opposite	24	12
butter or margarine	2 tablespoons	1 tablespoon
chopped onion	2/3 cup	1/3 cup
all-purpose flour	2 tablespoons	1 tablespoon
milk	2 cups	1 cup
frozen Welsh rarebit, thawed	2 (12-oz.) pkgs.	1 (12-oz.) pkg.
dry white wine	1/4 cup	2 tablespoons
prepared mustard	2 teaspooons	1 teaspoon
chopped zucchini	2/3 cup	1/3 cup
chopped pimiento	1/4 cup	2 tablespoons
hot cooked noodles	4 servings	2 servings
snipped parsley	to garnish	to garnish
SAUCEPAN	3-qt. saucepan	2-qt. saucepan
TIME AT MEDIUM HIGH (onion)	5 minutes	4 minutes
TIME AT MEDIUM HIGH (flour added)	1 minute	1 minute
TIME AT MEDIUM HIGH (milk added)	8 to 9 minutes	5 to 6 minutes
TIME AT MEDIUM HIGH (rarebit, vegetables added)	4 minutes	2 minutes
TIME AT MEDIUM LOW	5 to 10 minutes	5 to 10 minutes

Prepare Meatballs; keep warm. In a saucepan, see size in chart above, melt butter or margarine over Medium-High heat. Add onion. Cook for time in chart above or until tender, stirring occasionally. Stir in flour. Cook and stir 1 minute. Whisk in milk. Cook and stir for time in chart above or until thickened and bubbly all over. Whisk in rarebit, wine and mustard. Stir in zucchini and pimiento. Cook and stir until just boiling. Reduce heat to Medium Low. Gently stir in meatballs. Cover and simmer 5 to 10 minutes or until heated through, stirring occasionally. Serve over hot cooked noodles. Garnish with snipped parsley.

Note: If chilled meatballs are used, allow 20 to 25 minutes for meatballs to heat through.

Chili-Meatball Stew

SERVINGS	4	2
INGREDIENTS		
Meatballs, opposite	16	8
chili with beans	1 (25-oz.) can	1 (15-oz.) can
whole-kernel corn, drained	1 (16-oz.) can	1 (8-oz.) can
instant minced onion	1 teaspoon	1/2 teaspoon
bacon-horseradish sour-cream dip	1 cup	1/2 cup
HEAVY SAUCEPAN	3-qt. saucepan	1-1/2-qt. saucepan
TIME AT MEDIUM	4 to 6 minutes	4 to 6 minutes

Prepare Meatballs. In a heavy saucepan, see size in chart above, bring chili with beans to a boil over Medium-High heat, stirring occasionally. Fold in Meatballs, corn and instant minced onion. Bring to a boil. Reduce heat to Medium. Place sour-cream dip in a small bowl. Stir 1/2 cup hot chili mixture into sour-cream dip. Fold dip mixture into meatball mixture in saucepan. Cook over Medium heat 4 to 6 minutes or until heated through, stirring often.

How to Make Meatballs

1/Ground beef, pork sausage or half ham and half pork may be used for meatballs. Mix meat thoroughly with oats, ketchup, eggs and seasonings. Divide meat mixture in bowl into quarters. Shape each quarter into one-fourth number of meatballs for recipe.

2/Bake in a baking dish in a 375F (190C) oven. When done, beef and sausage meatballs should show no pink when cut in center. Ham meatballs should be firm in center and juices should run clear. Drain meatballs on paper towels before serving.

Meatballs

SERVINGS	6 to 8 (36 meatballs)	4 to 6 (24 meatballs)	2 or 3 (12 meatballs)
INGREDIENTS			
ground beef, fresh bulk pork sausage, or half ground ham and half ground pork	1-1/2 lbs.	1 lb.	8 oz.
quick-cooking oats	1/3 cup	1/4 cup	3 tablespoons
ketchup	3 tablespoons	2 tablespoons	1 tablespoon
eggs	2	1	1
Worcestershire sauce	2 tablespoons	4 teaspoons	2 teaspoons
instant minced onion	1 tablespoon	2 teaspoons	1 teaspoon
dried parsley flakes	1-1/2 teaspoons	1 teaspoon	1/2 teaspoon
dry mustard	1-1/2 teaspoons	1 teaspoon	1/2 teaspoon
celery salt (omit for sausage or ham balls)	3/4 teaspoon	1/2 teaspoon	1/4 teaspoon
BAKING PAN	15" x 10" x 1" baking pan	13" x 9" baking dish	8-inch-square baking dish
TIME IN 375F (190C) OVEN:			
beef meatballs	20 to 25 minutes	20 to 25 minutes	20 to 25 minutes
sausage meatballs	25 to 30 minutes	25 to 30 minutes	25 to 30 minutes
ham meatballs	25 to 30 minutes	25 to 30 minutes	25 to 30 minutes

Do not preheat oven. In a medium bowl, combine ground meat, oats, ketchup, eggs, Worcestershire sauce, onion, parsley, dry mustard and celery salt, if using; mix well. Shape into 1-1/2-inch meatballs, see number in chart above. Place in a baking pan, see size in chart above. Bake in a 375F (190C) oven for time in chart above or until no pink shows when beef or sausage meatballs are cut in center. Ham balls should be firm in center and juices should run clear. Remove from pan and drain on paper towels. Use for Cheesy Meatball Supper, opposite, Chili-Meatball Stew, opposite, or Spaghetti & Meatballs, page 150.

Note: For cocktail meatballs, see Basic Appetizer Meatballs & Franks, page 48.

Spaghetti & Meatballs

SERVINGS	8	4	2
INGREDIENTS			
onion, cut up	1 large	1 medium	1 small
celery, cut up	2 stalks	1 stalk	1/2 stalk
green pepper, cut up	1 medium	1/2 medium	1/4 medium
olive oil	2 tablespoons	1 tablespoon	1 tablespoon
canned tomatoes, cut up	2 (28-oz.) cans	1 (28-oz.) can	1 (16-oz.) can
dried leaf oregano	4 teaspoons	2 teaspoons	1 teaspoon
dried leaf basil	2 teaspoons	1 teaspoon	1/2 teaspoon
bay leaf	1 large	1 medium	1 small
tomato sauce	1 (15-oz.) can	1 (8-oz.) can	1 (8-oz.) can
water	2 cups	1 cup	1/2 cup
dry red wine or beef broth	1 cup	1/2 cup	1/4 cup
Worcestershire sauce	2 tablespoons	1 tablespoon	2 teaspoons
Meatballs, page 149	36	24	12
hot cooked spaghetti	8 servings	4 servings	2 servings
grated Parmesan cheese	to garnish	to garnish	to garnish
DUTCH OVEN	6-qt. Dutch oven	3-qt. saucepan	2-qt. saucepan
TIME AT MEDIUM HIGH	12 minutes	10 minutes	8 minutes
TIME AT MEDIUM LOW (sauce)	4 hours	3 hours	2-1/2 hours
TIME AT MEDIUM LOW (meatballs added)	10 to 15 minutes	10 minutes	10 minutes

In a blender or a food processor fitted with a steel blade, process onion, celery and green pepper until very finely chopped. Place olive oil and chopped vegetables in a Dutch oven, see size in chart above. Cook over Medium-High heat for time in chart above or until tender, stirring occasionally. In blender or food processor, process canned tomatoes and herbs until smooth. Process tomatoes for large recipe in 2 batches. Pour into Dutch oven. Stir in tomato sauce, water, wine or broth and Worcestershire sauce; mix well. Bring to a boil. Reduce heat to Medium Low. Simmer, uncovered, for time in chart above or until thick, stirring occasionally. Meanwhile, prepare Meatballs; keep warm. Gently stir into sauce. Cover and simmer for time in chart above or until meatballs are heated through. Serve sauce and meatballs over hot cooked spaghetti. Sprinkle with Parmesan cheese.

Note: If chilled meatballs are used, allow 20 to 25 minutes for meatballs to heat through.

Porcupine Meatballs

SERVINGS	4	2
INGREDIENTS		
ground beef	1 lb.	8 oz.
long-cooking rice	1/4 cup uncooked	2 tablespoons uncooked
finely chopped vegetables	1/4 cup	2 tablespoons
egg	1	1
dried leaf herb	1 teaspoon	1/2 teaspoon
beef broth	1/4 cup	2 tablespoons
condensed tomato soup	1 (10-3/4-oz.) can	1/2 (10-3/4-oz.) can (2/3 cup)
beef broth	1/2 cup	1/4 cup
Worcestershire sauce	2 teaspoons	1 teaspoon
SKILLET	10-inch skillet	8-inch skillet
TIME AT MEDIUM LOW	35 to 40 minutes	35 to 40 minutes

In a medium bowl, combine ground beef, rice, chopped vegetables, egg, herb and first amount of beef broth; mix well. Shape into 1-1/2-inch meatballs. Place in a skillet, see size in chart above. In same bowl, whisk together tomato soup, second amount of beef broth and Worcestershire sauce. Pour over meatballs. Bring to a boil over High heat. Reduce heat to Medium Low. Cover and simmer 35 to 40 minutes or until rice is tender, stirring often. Skim fat from pan juices. Serve pan juices over meatballs.

Suggested Vegetables: chopped onion, chopped celery, chopped green pepper, chopped carrot.
Suggested Herbs: basil, oregano, thyme.

Basic Ground-Meat Sandwiches   Photo on page 9.

SERVINGS	8	4
INGREDIENTS		
ground meat	1 lb.	8 oz.
chopped vegetables	1 cup	1/2 cup
cooking sauce	1 cup	1/2 cup
Worcestershire sauce	2 teaspoons	1 teaspoon
dried leaf herb or ground spice	1 teaspoon	1/2 teaspoon
dry mustard	1 teaspoon	1/2 teaspoon
taco shells or hamburger buns, split	8	4
shredded cheese	1/2 cup (2 oz.)	1/4 cup (1 oz.)
toppings, see suggestions below	to garnish	to garnish
SKILLET	11-inch skillet	8-inch skillet
TIME AT MEDIUM HIGH	9 to 10 minutes	6 to 7 minutes
TIME AT MEDIUM LOW	10 minutes	10 minutes

Crumble ground meat into a skillet, see size in chart above. Add chopped vegetables. Cook over Medium-High heat for time in chart above or until meat is browned and vegetables are tender, stirring often. Drain off fat. Stir in cooking sauce, Worcestershire sauce, herb or spice and dry mustard; mix well. Bring to a boil. Reduce heat to Medium Low. Simmer, uncovered, 10 minutes or until flavors blend and meat mixture is thick, stirring occasionally. Spoon into taco shells or hamburger buns. Sprinkle with cheese. Garnish with toppings according to suggestions below.

Suggested Combinations
Tacos: Use ground beef or fresh bulk pork sausage. Use chopped onion and canned chopped green chilies for vegetables. Use taco sauce for cooking sauce. Use chili powder for spice. Serve in taco shells. Use Cheddar cheese. Garnish with shredded lettuce, chopped tomatoes and guacamole dip.
Sloppy Joes: Use ground beef. Use chopped onion and chopped celery for vegetables. Use barbecue sauce for cooking sauce. Use oregano for herb. Serve in hamburger buns. Use mozzarella cheese. Garnish with chopped tomatoes and sliced black or green olives.

Spanish-Style Baked Beans

SERVINGS	6 to 8	3 or 4
INGREDIENTS		
Cooked Dried Beans, page 350	large recipe	small recipe
reserved bean liquid or beef or chicken broth	3 cups	1-1/2 cups
fresh bulk pork sausage	1 lb.	8 oz.
chopped green pepper	1 cup	1/2 cup
chopped onion	1 cup	1/2 cup
chopped tomatoes	3 cups	1-1/2 cups
chopped zucchini	1 cup	1/2 cup
sliced green olives	1/2 cup	1/4 cup
Worcestershire sauce	2 tablespoons	1 tablespoon
dried leaf basil	2 teaspooons	1 teaspoon
dried leaf thyme	1 teaspoon	1/2 teaspoon
bay leaf	1 large	1 small
black pepper	1/2 teaspoon	1/4 teaspoon
OVENPROOF DUTCH OVEN	5-qt. Dutch oven	3-qt. saucepan
TIME AT MEDIUM HIGH	18 to 20 minutes	12 minutes
TIME IN 350F (175C) OVEN	2 hours	1-1/2 hours

Prepare Cooked Dried Beans. Drain, reserving amount of liquid listed in chart above. Do not preheat oven. In an ovenproof Dutch oven or ovenproof saucepan, see size in chart above, combine sausage, green pepper and onion. Cook over Medium-High heat for time in chart above or until meat is browned and vegetables are tender, stirring often. Drain off fat. Stir in beans, tomatoes, zucchini, reserved bean liquid or broth, olives, Worcestershire sauce, basil, thyme, bay leaf and black pepper. Bake, covered, in a 350F (175C) oven for time in chart above or until thickened and flavors blended, stirring occasionally. Remove bay leaf before serving. Serve in bowls.

How to Make Ranch-Style Chili

1/In a skillet, brown ground beef or sausage with onion and green pepper over Medium-High heat. Drain off fat. Stir in tomatoes, seasonings and red beans.

2/Simmer chili until vegetables are tender and flavors blend. Serve in bowls topped with chopped onion, chopped green chilies and shredded Cheddar cheese.

Ranch-Style Chili

SERVINGS	4	2
INGREDIENTS		
celery salt (omit for sausage)	1/2 teaspoon	1/4 teaspoon
ground beef or fresh bulk pork sausage	1 lb.	8 oz.
chopped onion	1/2 cup	1/4 cup
chopped green pepper	1/2 cup	1/4 cup
canned tomatoes, cut up	1 (16-oz.) can	1 (8-oz.) can
tomato sauce	1 (8-oz.) can	1/2 (8-oz.) can
Worcestershire sauce	2 tablespoons	1 tablespoon
dried leaf oregano	2 teaspoons	1 teaspoon
bay leaf	1 large	1 small
chili powder	2 teaspoons	1 teaspoon
bottled hot-pepper sauce	1/4 teaspoon	1/8 teaspoon
red beans, drained, rinsed	1 (16-oz.) can	1 (8-oz.) can
oyster crackers, canned chopped green chilies, shredded cheese, chopped onion	to garnish	to garnish
SKILLET	11-inch skillet	8-inch skillet
TIME AT MEDIUM HIGH	9 to 10 minutes	6 to 7 minutes
TIME AT MEDIUM LOW	45 minutes	45 minutes

If using ground beef, sprinkle celery salt in a skillet, see size in chart above. Crumble ground beef or sausage into skillet. Add onion and green pepper. Cook over Medium-High heat for time in chart above or until meat is browned, stirring frequently. Drain off fat. Stir in tomatoes, tomato sauce, Worcestershire sauce, oregano, bay leaf, chili powder and hot-pepper sauce. Gently stir in beans. Bring to a boil over High heat. Reduce heat to Medium Low; cover. Cook 45 minutes or until vegetables are tender and flavors blend, stirring occasionally. Remove bay leaf. Serve in bowls topped with oyster crackers, chilies, cheese and onion.

Variation
Substitute 3 cups peeled, quartered, fresh tomatoes for 16-ounce can of tomatoes or 1-1/2 cups peeled, quartered, fresh tomatoes for 8-ounce can of tomatoes.

Lasagne

SERVINGS	8 to 10	4 or 5
INGREDIENTS		
fresh bulk pork sausage	1 lb.	8 oz.
chopped onion	1/2 cup	1/4 cup
chopped green pepper	1/2 cup	1/4 cup
garlic, minced	1 large clove	1 small clove
canned tomatoes, cut up	1 (16-oz.) can	1 (8-oz.) can
tomato sauce	1 (16-oz.) can	1 (8-oz.) can
tomato paste	1 (6-oz.) can	1/2 (6-oz.) can (1/4 cup)
dried leaf basil	2 teaspoons	1 teaspoon
dried leaf oregano	2 teaspoons	1 teaspoon
eggs	2	1
all-purpose flour	2 tablespoons	1 tablespoon
cream-style cottage cheese	2 cups (1 lb.)	1 cup (8 oz.)
grated Parmesan cheese	1/2 cup	1/4 cup
snipped parsley	1/4 cup	2 tablespoons
chopped green onion	1/4 cup	2 tablespoons
frozen chopped spinach, cooked	1 (10-oz.) pkg.	1/2 (10-oz.) pkg.
lasagne noodles, cooked, well-drained	10 (about 6 oz. uncooked)	6 (about 4 oz. uncooked)
sliced mozzarella cheese	12 oz.	6 oz.
SKILLET	11-inch skillet	10-inch skillet
BAKING DISH	13" x 9" baking dish	8-inch-square baking dish
TIME AT MEDIUM HIGH	9 to 10 minutes	9 to 10 minutes
TIME AT MEDIUM LOW	30 minutes	25 minutes
TIME IN 375F (190C) OVEN	50 to 60 minutes	45 to 50 minutes
STANDING TIME	10 minutes	10 minutes

Do not preheat oven. Grease a baking dish, see size in chart above; set aside. Crumble sausage into a skillet, see size in chart above. Add onion, green pepper and garlic. Cook over Medium-High heat 9 to 10 minutes or until meat is browned and vegetables are tender, stirring often. Drain off fat. Stir in tomatoes, tomato sauce, tomato paste, basil and oregano. Bring to a boil over High heat. Reduce heat to Medium Low. Simmer, uncovered, for time in chart above or until sauce is very thick, stirring occasionally. In a medium bowl, beat eggs. Whisk in flour until well-blended. Stir in cottage cheese, Parmesan cheese, parsley and green onion. Press cooked spinach in a sieve to remove as much water as possible. Stir spinach into cottage-cheese mixture. In prepared baking dish, layer in order: half each of noodles, cottage-cheese mixture, mozzarella cheese and meat sauce. Repeat layers. Bake, uncovered, in a 375F (190C) oven for time in chart above or until heated through. Let stand 10 minutes before cutting in squares to serve.

Choucroute

(Sauerkraut & Pork-Sausage Stew)

SERVINGS	6 to 8	3 or 4
INGREDIENTS		
fresh bulk pork sausage	1 lb.	8 oz.
chopped onion	1 cup	1/2 cup
chopped carrot	1 cup	1/2 cup
chopped celery	1 cup	1/2 cup
garlic, minced	1 large clove	1 small clove
sauerkraut, drained, rinsed	2 (16-oz.) cans	1 (16-oz.) can
apple juice	2 cups	1 cup
dry white wine	1/2 cup	1/4 cup
freshly ground pepper	1/2 teaspoon	1/4 teaspoon
parsley	4 sprigs	2 sprigs
bay leaf	1 large	1 small
juniper berries	10	5
fully cooked Polish sausage, halved	8 oz.	4 oz.
fully cooked smoked sausage, cut in 1-inch pieces	8 oz.	4 oz.
fully cooked smoked cocktail-sausage links	5 oz.	2-1/2 oz.
canned small, new potatoes, drained	2 (16-oz.) cans	1 (16-oz.) can
apples, cored, cut in wedges	2	1
OVENPROOF DUTCH OVEN	6-qt. Dutch oven	3-qt. saucepan
TIME AT MEDIUM HIGH	20 to 22 minutes	15 minutes
TIME AT MEDIUM LOW	15 minutes	15 minutes
TIME IN 350F (175C) OVEN	1 hour	45 minutes

Do not preheat oven. In an ovenproof Dutch oven or ovenproof saucepan, see size in chart above, combine sausage, onion, carrot, celery and garlic. Cook over Medium-High heat for time in chart above or until meat is browned and vegetables are tender, stirring often. Drain off fat. Stir in sauerkraut, apple juice, wine and pepper. Tie parsley, bay leaf and juniper berries in a piece of cheesecloth. Add to sauerkraut mixture. Bring to a boil over High heat. Reduce heat to Medium Low; cover. Simmer 15 minutes. Stir in sausages, potatoes and apples. Cover and bake in a 350F (175C) oven for time in chart above or until flavors blend and stew is heated through. Remove cheesecloth bag.

Note: Juniper berries are available dried in the spice sections of large supermarkets.

Tips for Making Crisp Pizza Crust (See pages 156 and 157.)

- Sprinkle cheese on bottom crust to help seal out juices. Use freshly shredded cheese. It forms a more leakproof coating than prepackaged shredded cheese.
- Bake pizza on bottom oven rack for crisper bottom crust.
- Avoid watery vegetables, such as fresh tomatoes and zucchini, that release water during baking and make crust soggy.
- Use as little of second amount of flour as possible when making dough. This will make crisper crust.
- Spoon pizza sauce *over* meat and vegetables to help prevent a soggy crust.

Basic Pizza

YIELD	2 (12-inch) pizzas (4 servings)	1 (12-inch) pizza (2 servings)
INGREDIENTS		
Pizza Crust, below	large recipe	small recipe
olive oil	2 teaspoons	1 teaspoon
shredded cheese	2 cups (8 oz.)	1 cup (4 oz.)
chopped, sliced or ground cooked meat	1 lb.	8 oz.
chopped vegetables	2 cups	1 cup
thick pizza sauce	1 (16-oz.) can (2 cups)	1 (8-oz.) can (1 cup)
dried leaf herbs or seed	4 teaspoons	2 teaspoons
shredded cheese	2 cups (8 oz.)	1 cup (4 oz.)
grated Parmesan cheese	1/4 cup	2 tablespoons
PIZZA PAN	2 (12-inch) pans	1 (12-inch) pan
TIME IN 450F (230C) OVEN	25 to 30 minutes	25 to 30 minutes

Preheat oven to 450F (230C). Oil 1 or 2 (12-inch) pizza pans; set aside. Prepare Pizza Crust. Fit dough into prepared pizza pans. Brush dough with olive oil. Sprinkle crusts with first amount of shredded cheese. Top with cooked meat and chopped vegetables. Spoon pizza sauce evenly over meat and vegetables. Sprinkle with herbs or seed, then with second amount of shredded cheese and Parmesan cheese. Place on bottom rack of oven. Bake 25 to 30 minutes or until crust is browned and filling is bubbly. Cut in serving-size wedges with a pizza-cutting wheel or kitchen shears.

Suggested Combinations
Sausage Pizza: Use mozzarella cheese. Use drained, cooked, fresh bulk pork sausage for meat. Use chopped green onion, chopped red pepper and avocado slices for vegetables. Use fennel seed for herb seed.

Hamburger Pizza: Use Monterey Jack cheese. Use drained, cooked, ground beef for meat. Use sliced mushrooms, sliced green olives and chopped onion for vegetables. Use oregano and basil for herbs.

Canadian-Bacon Pizza: Use Swiss cheese. Use diced, cooked Canadian bacon for meat. Use chopped green pepper, chopped pimiento and fresh broccoli flowerets for vegetables. Use Italian herb seasoning for herbs.

Pizza Crust

YIELD	Crust for 2 (12-inch) pizzas	Crust for 1 (12-inch) pizza
INGREDIENTS		
all-purpose flour	1-1/2 cups	3/4 cup
active dry yeast	1 envelope	1/2 envelope (1 teaspoon)
onion salt	1/2 teaspoon	1/4 teaspoon
milk	1 cup	1/2 cup
vegetable shortening	1/3 cup	3 tablespoons
all-purpose flour	1 to 1-1/4 cups	1/2 to 2/3 cup
PIZZA PAN	2 (12-inch) pans	1 (12-inch) pan
MIXER BOWL	1-1/2-qt. bowl	1-1/2-qt. bowl
SAUCEPAN	1-qt. saucepan	1-qt. saucepan
BEATING TIME AT MEDIUM SPEED	4 minutes	4 minutes
STANDING TIME	20 minutes	20 minutes

Oil 1 or 2 (12-inch) pizza pans; set aside. In a 1-1/2-quart mixer bowl, combine first amount of flour, yeast and onion salt; mix well and set aside. In a 1-quart saucepan, heat milk and shortening only until warm (120F, 50C). Shortening does not need to melt. Add warm milk mixture to flour mixture. Beat at medium speed of an electric mixer 4 minutes. Scrape sides of bowl often. By hand, gradually stir in just enough of second amount of flour to make soft dough that leaves the side of the bowl and forms a smooth ball. Cover and let stand about 20 minutes while preparing topping. For large recipe, divide dough into 2 portions. With oiled fingers, pat dough evenly over bottom of oiled pizza pans, building up edge slightly. Follow directions for Basic Pizza, above.

How to Make Basic Pizza

1/Pizza dough is easy to make with an electric mixer. The secret to a crisp crust is to use as little flour as possible in the dough. With oiled fingers, pat pizza dough evenly over bottom of an oiled pizza pan, building up edge slightly to form crust.

2/Brush circle of dough with olive oil. Sprinkle with some shredded cheese. Top with cooked meat and chopped vegetables. This Canadian-Bacon Pizza has Swiss cheese with chopped Canadian bacon, green pepper, pimiento and broccoli flowerets.

3/Spoon thick canned pizza sauce over meat and vegetables. Sprinkle with herbs. Add more shredded cheese and a light dusting of Parmesan cheese.

4/Use a pizza-cutting wheel or kitchen shears to cut cooked pizza into serving wedges. Serve with frosty mugs of beer or soft drinks.

Poultry

Easy and economical, elegant or everyday—poultry is an excellent main-dish choice. Use it for special company meals or family-night suppers. Versatile poultry adapts to almost any seasoning or cooking method. You can depend on it to please your family's tastes.

Roast Turkey Breast, page 191; with Mediterranean Rice Stuffing, page 190; and Herb-Butter Basting Sauce for Poultry, page 182.

Poultry

Q. How do I decide how much turkey to buy?

A. For turkeys 12 pounds or smaller, allow about 1 pound per person. Larger birds have a higher proportion of meat to bone weight. For a 12- to 24-pound turkey, allow about 3/4 pound per person. If you want leftovers, allow 2 pounds per person when buying a turkey 12 pounds or smaller. Allow 1-1/2 pounds per person for 12- to 24-pound birds.

Q. Is it necessary to wash poultry before cooking?

A. Yes. Thoroughly rinse poultry pieces or whole poultry, including neck and body cavities, in cold tap water. Pat dry with paper towels. Wash your hands and utensils thoroughly in hot soapy water after preparing raw poultry.

Q. For a holiday dinner, may I partially cook the turkey the day before, refrigerate it and finish cooking it the next day?

A. No. Poultry must be cooked completely at one time to kill bacteria. Always cook poultry to well-done stage. Never eat it rare or undercooked.

Thawing Poultry

- Thaw poultry using one of these methods:

  Refrigerator defrosting: Leave poultry in original bag or wrapping. Do not puncture or open wrapping. Place bird on a tray in the refrigerator. Bird will defrost in 1 to 4 days, depending on size. Allow 24 hours for every 3 to 5 pounds of poultry. If not completely defrosted, unwrap and finish thawing in cold water.

  Room-temperature defrosting: Leave poultry in original bag or wrapping. Do not puncture or open wrapping. Place bird in double paper bags or wrap in 10 layers of newspaper. Close tightly and place on a tray. Thaw at cool room temperature away from heat just until thawed. For birds larger than 12 pounds, allow 1 hour for each pound, plus 3 hours. For medium birds smaller than 12 pounds, allow 1 hour for each pound, plus 6 hours. For small birds such as chickens or Cornish hens, allow 8 to 10 hours. If not completely defrosted, unwrap and finish thawing in cold water.

  Cold-water defrosting: Cover wrapped poultry with cold water. Change water occasionally. Allow 30 minutes for each pound of poultry, plus 2 hours.

- Thawed poultry should be cold to the touch, but completely defrosted in cavity. Birds frozen with giblets in body cavity take longer to thaw.

- Thawed poultry must be refrigerated or cooked immediately.

- Do not refreeze thawed poultry.

- Commercially frozen stuffed turkeys must not be thawed before roasting. Follow label directions.

Storing Poultry

- Promptly place prepackaged or store-wrapped poultry in the refrigerator in original wrapper. Do not allow thawed frozen or fresh poultry to stand at room temperature. Refrigerate fresh poultry in coldest part of refrigerator and use within 1 to 2 days. Cooking times in this book are for refrigerated birds.

- Never stuff poultry with dressing before refrigerating or freezing.

- To freeze poultry, wrap tightly in moisture-vapor proof wrap and store at 0F (-20C) or colder. Commercially frozen poultry may be kept frozen in original wrapping.

- Wrap cooked poultry in moisture-vapor proof wrap and freeze up to 4 to 6 weeks. Longer storage may cause dryness.

- Store frozen whole uncooked turkey or chicken up to 12 months.

- Store frozen whole uncooked goose or duckling up to 6 months.

- To store leftover poultry, see tips, page 190.

How to Make Steamed Chicken

1/Pour water to a depth of 1/2 inch in a Dutch oven. Place a steamer basket in Dutch oven and make sure water level is below basket. Cover bottom of basket with fresh sage, parsley, thyme and lemon slices. Arrange chicken pieces over herbs and lemon. If you must stack pieces, leave some air space between them.

2/Bring water to a boil over High heat. Cover tightly and reduce heat to Medium. Do not lift the lid for 25 minutes. Water should simmer enough to make steam escape from under lid. To check for doneness, cut a small slit in center of thickest piece of chicken. Dark meat usually takes longest to cook.

Steamed Chicken

SERVINGS	4	2
INGREDIENTS		
parsley	8 sprigs	4 sprigs
sage, if desired	2 sprigs	1 sprig
thyme, if desired	2 sprigs	1 sprig
lemon	4 slices	2 slices
broiler-fryer chicken, cut up	1 (3-lb.) chicken	1/2 (3-lb.) chicken
OR		
whole chicken breasts, split lengthwise	2 (1-lb.) breasts	1 (1-lb.) breast
DUTCH OVEN	4-qt. Dutch oven	3-qt. saucepan
TIME AT MEDIUM	25 to 30 minutes	25 to 30 minutes

Pour water to a depth of 1/2 inch in a Dutch oven, see size in chart above. Place a steamer basket in Dutch oven. Water level should be below steamer basket. Place herbs and lemon slices in bottom of basket. Arrange chicken pieces over herbs and lemon. Choose the burner closest in size to diameter of Dutch oven. Bring water to a boil over High heat. Cover tightly. Reduce heat to Medium. Cook 25 minutes without lifting lid to check for doneness. Water should simmer enough to make steam escape from under lid. Cook until largest chicken piece shows no pink when cut at thickest part.

How to Test Chicken for Doneness

- Whole chicken—Insert a meat thermometer between leg and thigh 30 minutes before end of roasting time. Thermometer should register 185F (85C) in thickest part of thigh when done. Check temperature in both thighs. Cut between leg and thigh. Juices should run clear. Use a paper towel to grasp drumstick. Drumstick should move easily when you "shake hands."
- Chicken pieces—Cook chicken pieces until tender when pierced with a fork. Clear juices and no pink color indicate doneness. Chicken should show no pink when cut in thickest part.

Poached Chicken

SERVINGS	4	2
INGREDIENTS		
celery, cut up	2 stalks	1 stalk
carrot, cut up	1 medium	1 small
onion, cut up	1 medium	1 small
parsley	2 sprigs	1 sprig
peppercorns	6	3
sage, if desired	2 sprigs	1 sprig
lemon balm, if desired	2 sprigs	1 sprig
broiler-fryer chicken, cut up	1 (3-lb.) chicken	1/2 (3-lb.) chicken
OR		
whole chicken breasts, split lengthwise	2 (1-lb.) breasts	1 (1-lb.) breast
condensed chicken broth	2 (10-3/4-oz.) cans	1 (10-3/4-oz.) can
dry white wine	1/2 cup	1/4 cup
SKILLET	12-inch skillet	10-inch skillet
TIME AT MEDIUM LOW:		
broiler-fryer chicken	45 minutes	35 to 40 minutes
chicken breasts	50 to 60 minutes	50 to 60 minutes
YIELD	2-2/3 cups chicken-breast pieces or 2 cups broiler-fryer pieces, 3-1/2 to 4 cups broth	1-1/3 cups chicken-breast pieces or 1 cup broiler-fryer pieces, 1-3/4 to 2 cups broth

In a skillet, see size in chart above, combine celery, carrot, onion, parsley, peppercorns and sage, and lemon balm, if desired. Arrange chicken, meaty-side down, over vegetable mixture. Pour broth and wine over all. Bring to a boil over High heat. Reduce heat to Medium Low; cover. Simmer for time in chart above or until tender.

To chill chicken: Remove chicken from broth. Remove and discard skin and bones. Cover or wrap chicken tightly with plastic wrap; refrigerate. When needed, cut chicken into small cubes or 2-inch pieces. Strain broth. Skim off fat if necessary. Cover; refrigerate until required. Use for Chicken & Noodles, opposite, or for chicken casseroles, pages 163 to 167.

Poached Giblets

YIELD	from 1 turkey	from 1 chicken
INGREDIENTS		
giblets, including neck	12 oz. from 1 (12-lb.) turkey	5 oz. from 1 (3-lb.) chicken
celery, cut up	2 stalks	1 stalk
carrot, cut up	2 small	1 small
onion, cut up	1 medium	1 small
parsley	2 sprigs	1 sprig
bay leaf	1 large	1 small
chicken broth	2 cups	1 cup
SAUCEPAN	2-qt. saucepan	1-qt. saucepan
TIME AT MEDIUM LOW (without liver)	1 to 1-1/4 hours	35 to 45 minutes
TIME AT MEDIUM LOW (liver added)	10 minutes	5 minutes

Remove skin from neck. Set liver aside. In a saucepan, see size in chart above, combine celery, carrot, onion, parsley and bay leaf. Arrange neck, heart and gizzard over vegetable mixture. Pour broth over all. Bring to a boil over High heat. Reduce heat to Medium Low; cover. Simmer for time in chart above or until tender. Add liver; cover. Cook over Medium-Low heat for time in chart above or until liver is tender. Discard neck. Chop giblets to use in stuffing, pages 186 to 188, or Gravy for Roast Poultry, page 184. Strain broth; use for gravy or soup.

How to Make Chicken & Noodles

1/Bring poaching liquid from chicken to a boil over High heat. Stir in chicken and medium noodles or corkscrew macaroni. Add chopped fresh vegetables, such as carrots, celery, zucchini and broccoli. Season with marjoram, thyme, rubbed sage or a combination of these.

2/Bring mixture to a boil. Cover and simmer over Medium-Low heat 15 minutes, stirring once or twice. When noodles are tender, stir in flour mixture. Stir over Medium-High heat until thickened. Serve garnished with paprika and parsley.

Chicken & Noodles

SERVINGS	4	2
INGREDIENTS		
strained poaching broth, from Poached Chicken, opposite	3 cups	1-1/2 cups
medium noodles or corkscrew macaroni	2 cups uncooked	1 cup uncooked
Poached Chicken, boned, skinned, cut in 2-inch pieces	1 broiler fryer or 1 or 2 whole breasts	1/2 broiler fryer or 1 whole breast
chopped vegetables	2 cups	1 cup
dried leaf herb	1-1/2 teaspoons	3/4 teaspoon
all-purpose flour	2 tablespoons	1 tablespoon
cold water	1/4 cup	2 tablespoons
paprika, snipped parsley	to garnish	to garnish
SKILLET	12-inch skillet	10-inch skillet
TIME AT MEDIUM LOW	15 minutes	15 minutes
TIME AT MEDIUM HIGH	3 to 3-1/2 minutes	1 to 1-1/2 minutes

In a skillet, see size in chart above, bring poaching broth to a boil over High heat. Stir in uncooked noodles or macaroni, chicken, vegetables and herb. Bring to a boil. Reduce heat to Medium Low; cover. Simmer 15 minutes or until noodles are tender, stirring once or twice. In a screw-top jar, combine flour and cold water; shake well until completely smooth. Stir into chicken mixture. Cook and stir over Medium-High heat for time in chart above or until thickened and bubbly all over. Garnish with paprika and snipped parsley.

Suggested Vegetables: chopped onion, chopped carrot, chopped celery, chopped zucchini, chopped broccoli.

Suggested Herbs: rubbed sage, marjoram, thyme.

Creamed Chicken

SERVINGS	4 (4 cups)	2 (2 cups)
INGREDIENTS		
butter or margarine	1/4 cup	2 tablespoons
shredded carrot	1/4 cup	2 tablespoons
finely chopped celery	1/4 cup	2 tablespoons
chopped green onion	1/4 cup	2 tablespoons
all-purpose flour	1/4 cup	2 tablespoons
celery salt	1/2 teaspoon	1/4 teaspoon
chicken broth	1 cup	1/2 cup
milk	1 cup	1/2 cup
cubed cooked chicken or turkey	2 cups	1 cup
sliced mushrooms, drained	1 (2-1/2-oz.) jar	1/2 (2-1/2-oz.) jar
chopped pimiento	1/4 cup	2 tablespoons
SAUCEPAN	2-qt. saucepan	1-qt. saucepan
TIME AT MEDIUM HIGH (butter, vegetables)	7 minutes	4 minutes
TIME AT MEDIUM HIGH (flour added)	1 minute	1 minute
TIME AT MEDIUM HIGH (broth, milk added)	9 to 11 minutes	5 to 7 minutes

In a saucepan, see size in chart above, melt butter or margarine over Medium-High heat. Add carrot, celery and green onion. Cook for time in chart above or until tender, stirring occasionally. Stir in flour and celery salt until smooth. Cook and stir 1 minute. Whisk in chicken broth and milk. Cook for time in chart above or until thickened and bubbly all over, whisking constantly. Stir in chicken or turkey, mushrooms and pimiento. Use for Chicken a la King, below; Chicken & Stuffing Casserole, opposite; Chicken Pot Pies, page 166; or Creamy Chicken & Macaroni Casserole, page 166.

Chicken a la King

SERVINGS	4	2
INGREDIENTS		
Creamed Chicken, above	large recipe	small recipe
baked patty shells, popovers, waffles or toast triangles	4 servings	2 servings
chopped toasted almonds	1/4 cup	2 tablespoons
paprika	to garnish	to garnish
SAUCEPAN	2-qt. saucepan	1-qt. saucepan
TIME AT MEDIUM LOW	20 to 22 minutes	8 to 10 minutes

Prepare Creamed Chicken. After stirring in chicken or turkey, mushrooms and pimiento, reduce heat to Medium Low; cover. Cook for time in chart above or until heated through, stirring occasionally. Serve over patty shells, popovers, waffles or toast triangles. Garnish with almonds and paprika.

Tips for Cubing Chicken

- Chicken is easier to cut into cubes after chilling because cubes retain their shape better.
- A 1-pound whole chicken breast yields about 1 cup chicken cubes.
- A 3-pound whole chicken yields about 2 cups chicken cubes.

How to Make Chicken & Stuffing Casserole

1/Stir drained cooked vegetables, such as green beans and corn, into hot Creamed Chicken. This is a good way to use leftover vegetables. Pour chicken mixture into a casserole.

2/Prepare instant mashed potatoes. Fold in herb-seasoned stuffing mix and dairy sour cream. Spoon potato mixture in mounds on casserole. Sprinkle with paprika. Bake until heated through.

Chicken & Stuffing Casserole

SERVINGS	4	2
INGREDIENTS		
Creamed Chicken, opposite	large recipe	small recipe
drained cooked vegetables	2 cups	1 cup
packaged instant mashed-potato buds	4 servings	2 servings
herb-seasoned stuffing mix	1 cup	1/2 cup
dairy sour cream	1/2 cup	1/4 cup
paprika, snipped parsley	to garnish	to garnish
CASSEROLE	2-qt. casserole	1-qt. casserole
TIME IN 375F (190C) OVEN	35 to 40 minutes	25 to 30 minutes

Do not preheat oven. Prepare Creamed Chicken. Stir in vegetables. Pour into a casserole, see size in chart above; set aside. Prepare potatoes according to package directions. Fold in stuffing mix and sour cream. Spoon potato mixture in mounds on casserole. Sprinkle potatoes with paprika. Bake, uncovered, in a 375F (190C) oven for time in chart above or until heated through. Sprinkle with parsley.

Suggested Vegetables: whole-kernel corn, cut green beans, peas, carrot slices, broccoli flowerets, cut asparagus.

Chicken Pot Pies

SERVINGS	4	2
INGREDIENTS		
Creamed Chicken, page 164	large recipe	small recipe
drained cooked vegetables	1 cup	1/2 cup
dried leaf marjoram	1/2 teaspoon	1/4 teaspoon
dried rubbed sage	1/2 teaspoon	1/4 teaspoon
pie-crust mix	3 sticks	1-1/2 sticks
CASSEROLE	4 (10- to 12-oz.) casseroles	2 (10- to 12-oz.) casseroles
TIME IN 425F (220C) OVEN	30 to 35 minutes	30 to 35 minutes

Preheat oven to 425F (220C). Prepare Creamed Chicken. Stir in vegetables, marjoram and sage. Cover and set aside. Prepare pie-crust mix according to package directions. Divide into 2 or 4 equal portions according to number of casseroles in chart above. On a lightly floured surface, roll out two-thirds of each dough portion large enough to line inside of each casserole. Fit dough into bottom and up sides of each casserole. Spoon 1-1/4 cups chicken mixture into each casserole. Roll out remaining one-third of each dough portion to fit top of each casserole. Place dough on casseroles. Trim and flute edges. Cut vents for steam to escape. Bake in preheated oven 30 to 35 minutes or until crust is browned and filling is bubbly. Serve pot pies in casseroles.

Suggested Vegetables: peas, cut green beans, chopped broccoli, sliced carrots, chopped cauliflower, mixed vegetables, whole-kernel corn.

Creamy Chicken & Macaroni Casserole

SERVINGS	4	2
INGREDIENTS		
macaroni	1/2 cup uncooked	1/4 cup uncooked
Creamed Chicken, page 164	large recipe	small recipe
shredded American cheese	1 cup (4 oz.)	1/2 cup (2 oz.)
drained, cooked, whole-kernel corn	1/2 cup	1/4 cup
dried leaf savory	1/2 teaspoon	1/4 teaspoon
dried leaf thyme	1/2 teaspoon	1/4 teaspoon
herb-seasoned croutons	1 cup	1/2 cup
butter or margarine, melted	2 tablespoons	1 tablespoon
grated Parmesan cheese	1 tablespoon	2 teaspoons
CASSEROLE	1-1/2-qt. casserole	1-qt. casserole
TIME IN 375F (190C) OVEN	35 to 40 minutes	25 to 30 minutes

Do not preheat oven. Cook macaroni according to package directions; drain. Prepare Creamed Chicken. Fold in cooked macaroni, American cheese, corn, savory and thyme. Pour into a casserole, see size in chart above. In a small saucepan, toss together croutons and melted butter or margarine. Spoon over casserole. Sprinkle with Parmesan cheese. Bake, uncovered, in a 375F (190C) oven for time in chart above or until heated through.

Basic Chicken Stew

SERVINGS	4	2
INGREDIENTS		
vegetable oil	3 tablespoons	2 tablespoons
broiler-fryer chicken, cut up	1 (3-lb.) chicken	1/2 (3-lb.) chicken
chopped or sliced fresh vegetables	4 cups	2 cups
condensed soup	1 (10- to 11-oz.) can	1/2 (10- to 11-oz.) can
cooking liquid	1/2 cup	1/4 cup
dried leaf herbs	2 teaspoons	1 teaspoon
SKILLET	12-inch skillet	10-inch skillet
TIME AT MEDIUM (chicken)	15 to 20 minutes	15 to 20 minutes
TIME AT MEDIUM (vegetables added)	2 to 3 minutes	1 to 2 minutes
TIME AT MEDIUM LOW	30 to 40 minutes	30 to 40 minutes

In a skillet, see size in chart above, heat oil over Medium heat until a drop of water sizzles on it. Add chicken pieces, skin-side down. Cook 15 to 20 minutes or until browned, turning once. Drain off fat. Arrange vegetables around chicken. In a small bowl, whisk together soup, cooking liquid and herbs; mix well. Spoon over chicken and vegetables. Cook over Medium heat for time in chart above. Reduce heat to Medium Low; cover. Simmer 30 to 40 minutes or until chicken is tender. Serve vegetables and pan juices with chicken.

Suggested Combinations

Chicken Stew Italiano: Use chopped onion, chopped green pepper, drained canned garbanzo beans and peeled, quartered, fresh tomatoes for vegetables. Use oregano and basil for herbs. Use tomato bisque for soup. Use dry white wine for cooking liquid.

Autumn Chicken Stew: Use carrots, cut in 1/2-inch pieces, onions, cut in thin wedges, chopped celery, and winter squash, cut in 1/2-inch cubes, for vegetables. Use rubbed sage and thyme for herbs. Use cream of chicken soup. Use chicken broth for cooking liquid.

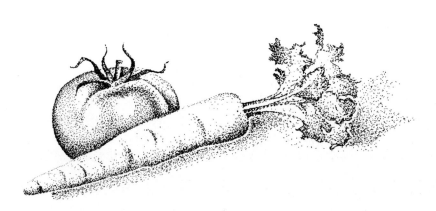

Tips for Using Chicken Broth

- There are several products you may use when recipes call for chicken broth.

  Ready-to-use canned chicken broth: This usually comes in a 14-1/2-ounce can and does not need diluting.

  Chicken bouillon granules or cubes: To use, dissolve 1 teaspoon granules or 1 cube per 1 cup boiling water.

  Canned condensed chicken broth: To use, dilute with 1 soup can of water. Mix well.

- If recipe specifies *condensed* chicken broth, do not dilute broth according to label directions. Recipe allows for necessary dilution.

How to Make Basic Chicken Stew

1/Brown chicken pieces in a skillet, turning once. Drain off fat. Arrange vegetables around chicken. For Chicken Stew Italiano, use chopped onion, chopped green pepper, drained canned garbanzo beans and peeled, quartered, fresh tomatoes.

2/Whisk together condensed soup and wine or broth with complementary herbs. For this stew, use tomato bisque soup and white wine with oregano and basil for herbs. Spoon over chicken and vegetables. Cover and simmer until chicken is tender when pierced with a fork.

Basic Oven-Braised Chicken

SERVINGS	3 or 4	1 or 2
INGREDIENTS		
herb or spice	2 teaspoons	1 teaspoon
garlic powder	1/8 teaspoon	dash
onion salt	1/8 teaspoon	dash
broiler-fryer chicken, cut up	1 (3-lb.) chicken	1/2 (3-lb.) chicken
sliced or chopped fruit, vegetables	1 cup	1/2 cup
cooking sauce	1 cup	1/2 cup
BAKING DISH	13" x 9" baking dish	8-inch-square baking dish
TIME IN 375F (190C) OVEN (chicken)	30 minutes	30 minutes
TIME IN 375F (190C) OVEN (sauce added)	30 minutes	30 minutes

Do not preheat oven. In a small bowl, combine herb or spice, garlic powder and onion salt; mix well. Rub on skin side of chicken pieces. Place chicken, bone-side down, in a baking dish, see size in chart above. Bake chicken in a 375F (190C) oven 30 minutes. Arrange fruit and vegetables around chicken. Spoon cooking sauce evenly over chicken, fruit and vegetables. Bake 30 minutes longer or until chicken is tender, spooning sauce over once or twice. Arrange chicken on a warm serving platter. Spoon sauce and fruit and vegetables over chicken to serve.

Suggested Combinations
Oven-Barbecued Chicken: Use celery seed for herb. Use sliced onion, chopped green pepper and sliced lemon for vegetables and fruit. Use barbecue sauce for cooking sauce.
Mexicali Oven-Braised Chicken: Use ground cumin for spice. Use sliced green olives, chopped green chilies and chopped green onion for vegetables. Use taco sauce for cooking sauce.

Basic Stuffed Chicken Breasts

SERVINGS	8	4
INGREDIENTS		
chopped vegetables, meat	1/2 cup	1/4 cup
shredded cheese	1/2 cup (2 oz.)	1/4 cup (1 oz.)
snipped chives	1 teaspoon	1/2 teaspoon
dried leaf herb	1/2 teaspoon	1/4 teaspoon
whole chicken breasts, boned, skinned, split lengthwise	4 (8-oz.) breasts (after boning)	2 (8-oz.) breasts (after boning)
butter or margarine	1/4 cup	2 tablespoons
fine dry breadcrumbs	1/3 cup	3 tablespoons
grated Parmesan cheese	2 tablespoons	1 tablespoon
all-purpose flour	1/4 cup	2 tablespoons
BAKING DISH	13" x 9" baking dish	10" x 6" baking dish
TIME IN 400F (205C) OVEN	40 to 45 minutes	40 to 45 minutes

Preheat oven to 400F (205C). In a medium bowl, combine chopped vegetables and meat, cheese, chives and herb; mix well and set aside. Lay chicken-breast halves, boned-side up, on a cutting board. Using small end of a meat mallet, pound this side until 1/4 inch thick. Divide stuffing evenly among chicken breasts. Spread stuffing over middle third of each chicken breast. Roll up chicken breasts. Start from narrow end, tucking in sides envelope-fashion. Secure ends with wooden picks. Melt butter or margarine in a baking dish, see size in chart above, in oven. On a piece of waxed paper, combine breadcrumbs and Parmesan cheese. Roll stuffed breasts in flour, then in melted butter or margarine, then in crumb mixture. Pat crumbs gently onto all sides of rolled breasts. Place rolls, seam-side down, in baking dish. Bake in preheated oven, uncovered, 40 to 45 minutes or until browned and tender. Remove picks before serving.

Suggested Combinations
California Stuffed Chicken Breasts: Use chopped avocado and chopped tomatoes for vegetables. Omit meat. Use Monterey Jack cheese. Use rubbed sage for herb.
Stuffed Chicken Breasts Cordon Bleu: Use drained, canned, mushroom pieces and chopped cooked ham for vegetables and meat. Use Swiss cheese. Use dill weed for herb.
Stuffed Chicken Breasts Florentine: Use cooked chopped spinach, pressed in a sieve to remove as much water as possible, and chopped pimiento for vegetables. Omit meat. Use Cheddar cheese. Use thyme for herb.

Steps in Boning Chicken Breasts

1. Place whole chicken breast, skin-side down, on a cutting board with narrow end of breast away from you.
2. Cut through white cartilage at **V** of neck to breast bone.
3. Grasp small bones on either side of breast bone. Bend each side of breast back toward cutting board. Push up with your fingers to snap out breast bone.
4. Use a sharp narrow-blade knife to remove small bones or cartilage. Cut as close to bone as possible.
5. Turn chicken breast over. Grasp loose end of skin and peel away from chicken breast, if desired.

How to Make Basic Stuffed Chicken Breasts

1/For filling, combine chopped vegetables and meat, shredded cheese, chives and herb. This Florentine filling is spinach, pimiento, Cheddar cheese, chives and thyme. Cut boned and skinned chicken breasts in half lengthwise. Place, boned-side up, on a cutting board. Pound with small end of a meat mallet until 1/4 inch thick. Do not pound other side.

2/Spread filling over middle third of chicken breast. Starting from narrow end, roll up envelope-fashion, tucking in sides. Secure with a wooden pick inserted like a straight pin at end of roll. Coat with flour, melted butter or margarine and bread-crumb mixture. Place, seam-side down, in a baking dish. Bake at 400F (205C) 40 to 45 minutes or until tender.

Chicken Divan Supreme

SERVINGS	8	4
INGREDIENTS		
frozen broccoli spears or asparagus spears	2 (10-oz.) pkgs.	1 (10-oz.) pkg.
whole chicken breasts, boned, skinned, split lengthwise	4 (8-oz.) breasts (after boning)	2 (8-oz.) breasts (after boning)
bacon, halved crosswise	8 slices	4 slices
smoked sliced beef	1 (2-1/2-oz.) pkg.	1/2 (2-1/2-oz.) pkg.
cooked rice	3 cups	1-1/2 cups
condensed creamy chicken-mushroom soup	2 (10-3/4-oz.) cans	1 (10-3/4-oz.) can
dairy sour cream	1 cup	1/2 cup
sliced mushrooms, drained	2 (2-1/2-oz.) jars	1 (2-1/2-oz.) jar
snipped chives	2 tablespoons	1 tablespoon
SAUCEPAN	3-qt. saucepan	1-1/2-qt. saucepan
BAKING DISH	13" x 9" baking dish	10" x 6" baking dish
TIME AT MEDIUM LOW	2 minutes	2 minutes
TIME IN 375F (190C) OVEN (without sauce)	40 minutes	40 minutes
TIME IN 375F (190C) OVEN (sauce added)	35 minutes	30 minutes

Do not preheat oven. In a saucepan, see size in chart above, combine frozen vegetable and water according to package directions. Bring to a boil over High heat. Reduce heat to Medium Low; cover. Simmer 2 minutes. Drain and set aside. Place chicken breasts in a baking dish, see size in chart above. Place 2 bacon pieces lengthwise on each chicken breast. Bake, uncovered, in a 375F (190C) oven 40 minutes. With a spatula, remove bacon-topped chicken. Drain baking dish. In same baking dish, layer in order: smoked beef, rice, broccoli or asparagus and chicken breasts topped with bacon. In a medium bowl, stir together soup and sour cream. Stir in mushrooms. Spoon soup mixture evenly over casserole. Bake, uncovered, for time in chart above or until bubbly and heated through. Garnish with snipped chives.

Deep-Fried Chicken

SERVINGS	4	2
INGREDIENTS		
broiler-fryer chicken, cut up OR	1 (3-lb.) chicken	1/2 (3-lb.) chicken
whole chicken breasts, split lengthwise OR	2 (1-lb.) breasts	1 (1-lb.) breast

chicken drumsticks, wings or
  thighs
	8 (3- or 4-oz.)
	  pieces
		4 (3- or 4-oz.)
		  pieces

vegetable-juice cocktail or cranberry-juice cocktail	1 cup	1/2 cup
egg or egg yolk	1 egg	1 egg yolk
milk	2 tablespoons	1 tablespoon
fine dry breadcrumbs	1/4 cup	2 tablespoons
cornstarch	1/4 cup	2 tablespoons
all-purpose flour	1/4 cup	2 tablespoons
dry mustard	1 teaspoon	1/2 teaspoon
herb pepper	1 teaspoon	1/2 teaspoon
vegetable oil for deep-fat frying	about 2-1/2 qts.	about 2-1/2 qts.
SKILLET	12-inch skillet	10-inch skillet
DEEP-FAT FRYER OR HEAVY DUTCH OVEN	5-qt. fryer or Dutch oven	5-qt. fryer or Dutch oven
TIME AT MEDIUM LOW	30 minutes	30 minutes
TIME IN 365F (185C) OIL	2 to 2-1/2 minutes	2 to 2-1/2 minutes

Place chicken, skin-side down, in a skillet, see size in chart above. Pour juice over chicken. Bring to a boil over High heat. Reduce heat to Medium Low; cover. Simmer 30 minutes or until tender. Drain chicken. In a pie plate, whisk together egg or egg yolk and milk. On a piece of waxed paper, combine breadcrumbs, cornstarch, flour, dry mustard and herb pepper; mix well. Dip chicken pieces in egg mixture, then in crumb mixture. Pour oil into a 5-quart deep-fat fryer or Dutch oven. Fryer should be about half full of oil. Preheat oil to 365F (185C) or until a 1-inch cube of bread turns golden brown in 50 seconds. Fry chicken pieces, 2 or 3 at a time, in 365F (185C) oil 2 to 2-1/2 minutes or until browned, turning once. Remove chicken with tongs or a slotted spoon and drain on paper towels. Keep warm in a 175F (80C) oven only while frying remaining chicken or coating will lose crispness.

Tips for Deep-Fat Frying

- Use soybean, peanut, cottonseed, safflower or corn oil for deep-fat frying.
- Oil absorbs flavors of fried food, so fry mild-tasting foods before strong-tasting ones. For example, fry potatoes before fish.
- After cooking, let oil cool completely before straining into a heatproof container.
- To store, cover and refrigerate oil. Do not use this oil for anything except frying.
- To clarify oil to use another time: Add several potato slices for each cup of oil to absorb residual food flavors. Heat oil slowly. When potatoes have browned, strain warm oil through several layers of cheesecloth set in a strainer. Clarify and reuse oil only once or twice to avoid "greasy-spoon restaurant" taste.

How to Make Deep-Fried Chicken

1/Place chicken, skin-side down, in a skillet. Pour vegetable-juice cocktail or cranberry-juice cocktail over chicken. Bring to a boil. Cover and simmer over Medium-Low heat 30 minutes or until tender.

2/Drain chicken. Dip in egg mixture and then in crumb mixture on waxed paper. Bring waxed paper up around chicken to coat.

3/Fill a deep-fat fryer about half full of oil. Heat oil to 365F (185C). Crumbs will be grease-soaked if oil is not hot enough, and will burn if oil is too hot.

4/Fry 2 or 3 chicken pieces at a time in hot oil 2 to 2-1/2 minutes or until browned, turning once. Remove chicken with tongs or a slotted spoon and drain on paper towels.

Skillet-Fried Chicken

SERVINGS	2 to 4	1 or 2
INGREDIENTS		
all-purpose flour	2/3 cup	1/3 cup
paprika	1 tablespoon	2 teaspoons
celery salt	1 teaspoon	1/2 teaspoon
pepper	1/2 teaspoon	1/4 teaspoon
broiler-fryer chicken, cut up	1/2 (3-lb.) chicken	1/4 (3-lb.) chicken
OR		
whole chicken breasts, split lengthwise	2 (1-lb.) breasts	1 (1-lb.) breast
OR		
chicken drumsticks, wings or thighs	8 (3- or 4-oz.) pieces	4 (3- or 4-oz.) pieces
vegetable oil for deep-fat frying	about 3 cups	about 2 cups
ELECTRIC SKILLET OR HEAVY SKILLET	12-inch skillet	10-inch skillet
TIME AT 340F (170C) OR MEDIUM	15 minutes	15 minutes
TIME AT 300F (150C) OR MEDIUM LOW (covered)	10 minutes	10 minutes
TIME AT 300F (150C) OR MEDIUM LOW (uncovered)	5 to 10 minutes	5 to 10 minutes

In a plastic bag, combine flour, paprika, celery salt and pepper. Shake chicken pieces, a few at a time, in flour mixture. Pour oil to a depth of 1/2 inch in a skillet, see size in chart above. Preheat oil over Medium heat until a 1-inch cube of bread turns golden brown in 65 seconds. Use 340F (170C) on an electric skillet. Add chicken pieces, skin-side up. Do not crowd pieces in skillet. Cook, uncovered, 15 minutes, turning once when well browned. Reduce heat to Medium Low or 300F (150C). Turn chicken skin-side up. Cover and cook 10 minutes. Turn chicken skin-side down. Cook, uncovered, 5 to 10 minutes or until tender and juices run clear. Drain on paper towels.

Tips for Frying Safety

- Occasionally, oil overheats and catches fire. To extinguish fire:

  Do not use water. Water spreads flames.

  Immediately cover fryer with metal lid or baking sheet. This cuts off fire's oxygen.

  Or, douse flames with a box of baking soda or an ABC or BC dry chemical fire extinguisher.

  Think ahead. Fire can occur whenever hot oil is used. Get out baking soda along with food to be fried.

- To avoid burns, use hot pads or oven mitts when working with hot oil.

- Dry fryer thoroughly before using. Water drops make hot oil spatter.

- Use a wire basket to lower and raise food from fat.

Basic Oven-Fried Chicken

SERVINGS	4	2
INGREDIENTS		
butter or margarine, softened	1/4 cup	2 tablespoons
mustard	1 teaspoon	1/2 teaspoon
dried leaf herb	2 teaspoons	1 teaspoon
celery salt	1/4 teaspoon	1/8 teaspoon
onion salt	1/4 teaspoon	1/8 teaspoon
broiler-fryer chicken, cut up, halved lengthwise or quartered	1 (3-lb.) chicken	1/2 (3-lb.) chicken
OR		
whole chicken breasts, split lengthwise	2 (1-lb.) breasts	1 (1-lb.) breast
OR		
chicken drumsticks, thighs or wings	8 (3- or 4-oz.) pieces	4 (3- or 4-oz.) pieces
fine cracker or stuffing crumbs	1 cup	1/2 cup
herb seed	2 teaspoons	1 teaspoon
BAKING PAN	15" x 10" jelly-roll pan	9-inch-square baking pan
TIME IN 400F (205C) OVEN:		
broiler fryer, cut up	50 to 55 minutes	50 to 55 minutes
broiler fryer, halved	55 to 60 minutes	55 to 60 minutes
broiler fryer, quartered	50 to 55 minutes	50 to 55 minutes
chicken breasts	50 to 55 minutes	50 to 55 minutes
chicken drumsticks, thighs	45 to 50 minutes	45 to 50 minutes
chicken wings	35 to 40 minutes	35 to 40 minutes

Preheat oven to 400F (205C). In a small bowl, combine butter or margarine, mustard, leaf herb, celery salt and onion salt; mix well. Wash chicken pieces. Dry skin side with paper towels. Spread butter or margarine mixture on skin side of chicken pieces. On a piece of waxed paper, combine crumbs and herb seed. Roll chicken in crumb mixture. Pat crumbs gently onto all sides of chicken. Place chicken, skin-side up, in a baking pan, see size in chart above. Bake in preheated oven for time in chart above. When done, chicken should be browned and tender. Juices should run clear.

Suggested Combinations
Old-Fashioned Oven-Fried Chicken: Use prepared mustard. Use thyme and rubbed sage for herbs. Use saltine-cracker crumbs. Use celery seed for herb seed.
Cheesy Oven-Fried Chicken: Use Dijon-style mustard. Use tarragon and chives for herbs. Use cheese-cracker crumbs. Use poppy seed for herb seed.
Herbed Oven-Fried Chicken: Use prepared mustard. Use marjoram for herb. Use herb-seasoned-stuffing crumbs. Use sesame seed for herb seed.
Bacon Oven-Fried Chicken: Use stone-ground mustard. Use dill weed and chervil for herbs. Use bacon-cracker crumbs. Use sesame seed for herb seed.

Tips for Making Gravy

- **If gravy is too thick:** Whisk in more broth or water. Cook until heated through.

- **If gravy is too thin:** In a screw-top jar, combine 1 to 2 tablespoons all-purpose flour and 2 to 4 tablespoons cold water or broth; shake well until completely smooth. Whisk flour mixture into gravy. Cook over Medium-High heat until thickened and bubbly, whisking constantly.

How to Make Basic Oven-Fried Chicken

1/Combine butter or margarine with special mustard, herb, celery salt and onion salt. For Cheesy Oven-Fried Chicken, use Dijon-style mustard with tarragon and chives for herbs. Wash chicken pieces and pat dry with paper towels. Spread butter mixture on chicken pieces. Butter mixture will be difficult to spread if chicken pieces are moist.

2/Combine cracker crumbs and herb seed. Cheesy Oven-Fried Chicken has cheese-cracker crumbs and poppy seed. Roll chicken in crumbs. Pat crumbs into butter mixture on chicken. Place, skin-side up, in a shallow baking pan. Bake at 400F (205C) 35 to 60 minutes depending on type of chicken pieces.

Cream Gravy for Basic Oven-Fried Chicken

YIELD	2-1/4 cups	1-1/8 cups
INGREDIENTS		
drippings from chicken	1/4 cup (from 4 servings)	2 tablespoons (from 2 servings)
butter or margarine	2 tablespoons	1 tablespoon
all-purpose flour	1/4 cup	2 tablespoons
chicken bouillon granules	2 teaspoons	1 teaspoon
dry mustard	1 teaspoon	1/2 teaspoon
herb pepper	1 teaspoon	1/2 teaspoon
milk	2 cups	1 cup
SAUCEPAN	1-1/2-qt. saucepan	1-qt. saucepan
TIME AT MEDIUM HIGH (flour)	1 minute	1 minute
TIME AT MEDIUM HIGH (milk added)	8 to 10 minutes	6 to 8 minutes

Place cooked chicken on an ovenproof platter. Turn off oven. Keep uncovered chicken warm in oven with door ajar. Scrape chicken drippings from baking pan into a saucepan, see size in chart above. Melt butter or margarine with chicken drippings over Medium-High heat. Whisk in flour until blended. Cook and stir 1 minute. Whisk in bouillon granules, dry mustard and herb pepper; mix well. Whisk in milk. Cook for time in chart above or until thickened and bubbly all over, whisking constantly. Serve with chicken and mashed potatoes, rice or noodles, if desired.

Chicken & Vegetable Stir-Fry

SERVINGS	4	2	1
INGREDIENTS			
cornstarch	2 tablespoons	1 tablespoon	1 teaspoon
dry mustard	2 teaspoons	1 teaspoon	1/2 teaspoon
soy sauce	2 tablespoons	1 tablespoon	1 teaspoon
chicken breasts, boned, skinned	2 (8-oz.) breasts (after boning)	1 (8-oz.) breast (after boning)	1/2 (8-oz.) breast (after boning)
vegetable oil	4 teaspoons	1 tablespoon	2 teaspoons
almonds or cashews	1/2 cup	1/4 cup	2 tablespoons
vegetable oil	1 tablespoon	2 teaspoons	1 teaspoon
vegetable oil	2 tablespoons	1 tablespoon	2 teaspoons
any combination of cut-up vegetables for stir-frying, page 346	4 cups	2 cups	1 cup
chicken broth	1-1/4 cups	2/3 cup	1/3 cup
dry sherry	1/4 cup	2 tablespoons	1 tablespoon
hot cooked rice or warm chow-mein noodles	4 servings	2 servings	1 serving
WOK OR HEAVY SKILLET	wok or 12-inch skillet	wok or 12-inch skillet	wok or 12-inch skillet
TIME AT 375F (190C) OR MEDIUM HIGH (nuts)	1 to 1-1/2 minutes	15 to 30 seconds	15 to 30 seconds
TIME AT 375F (190C) OR MEDIUM HIGH (chicken)	4 to 5 minutes	2 to 3 minutes	1-1/2 to 2-1/2 minutes
TIME AT 375F (190C) OR MEDIUM HIGH (vegetables)	see timings on page 346		
TIME AT 375F (190C) OR MEDIUM HIGH (thicken sauce)	3 to 4 minutes	45 to 60 seconds	15 to 30 seconds

In a small bowl, combine cornstarch and dry mustard; mix well. Stir in soy sauce until smooth; set aside. Slice chicken in strips, 1/4 inch thick, 2 inches long and 1/2 inch wide. In a wok or heavy 12-inch skillet, heat first amount of oil over Medium-High heat until a drop of water sizzles on it. Use 375F (190C) on an electric wok or skillet. Add nuts. Cook for time in chart above, stirring and tossing nuts constantly until toasted. Remove nuts with a slotted spoon; set aside. Add second amount of oil. Add chicken. Cook over Medium High or at 375F (190C) for time in chart above, stirring and tossing chicken constantly. Chicken should be cooked until firm and white. Remove chicken with slotted spoon; set aside. Add remaining oil. Add vegetables, starting with longest-cooking vegetable as directed on page 346. Add other vegetables in decreasing order of cooking time. Cook over Medium-High heat or at 375F (190C) for time on page 346, stirring and tossing constantly. Return chicken to wok or skillet. Add broth and dry sherry. Stir in soy-sauce mixture. Cook over Medium-High heat or at 375F (190C) for time in chart above or until thickened and bubbly all over, stirring constantly. Stir in nuts. Serve over hot cooked rice or warm chow-mein noodles.

Broiled Chicken

SERVINGS	4	2
INGREDIENTS		
broiler-fryer chicken, split lengthwise	1 (3-lb.) chicken	1/2 (3-lb.) chicken
OR		
whole chicken breasts, split lengthwise	2 (1-lb.) breasts	1 (1-lb.) breast
Basic Basting Sauce for Broiled Poultry, below, or Herb-Butter Basting Sauce, page 182	large recipe	small recipe
BROILER PAN WITH RACK	14" x 10" pan	14" x 10" pan
TIME AT BROIL (first side):		
broiler-fryer halves	25 minutes	25 minutes
chicken breasts	15 minutes	15 minutes
TIME AT BROIL (second side, without sauce):		
broiler-fryer halves	8 to 10 minutes	8 to 10 minutes
chicken breasts	5 to 6 minutes	5 to 6 minutes
TIME AT BROIL (second side, sauce added):		
broiler-fryer halves	30 to 90 seconds	30 to 90 seconds
chicken breasts	30 to 45 seconds	30 to 45 seconds

Place chicken, skin-side down, on a rack in a 14" x 10" broiler pan. Place broiler pan on an oven rack so the broiler element is 5 to 6 inches away for chicken halves and 4 to 5 inches away for chicken breasts. Measure from top of chicken to broiler element. Pour water to a depth of 1/4 inch in bottom of broiler pan. Preheat electric broiler. You do not need to preheat a gas broiler. Broil chicken on first side for time in chart above. Turn chicken over with tongs. Broil chicken on second side for time in chart above or until tender and juices run clear. For another doneness test, cut a small slit in thickest part of chicken. Meat should not be pink. Brush chicken with basting sauce. Broil for time in chart above or until sauce is bubbly.

Basic Basting Sauce for Broiled Poultry

YIELD	2/3 cup	1/3 cup
INGREDIENTS		
butter or margarine	1/4 cup	2 tablespoons
fruit jam or jelly	1/3 cup	3 tablespoons
fruit liqueur, wine or fruit juice	1 tablespoon	2 teaspoons
ground spice	1/8 teaspoon	dash
SAUCEPAN	1-qt. saucepan	1-qt. saucepan
TIME AT MEDIUM	4 minutes	3 minutes
TIME AT BROIL (basted on poultry)	30 to 90 seconds	30 to 90 seconds

In a 1-quart saucepan, melt butter or margarine over Medium heat. Stir in jam or jelly, liqueur, wine or fruit juice and spice. Cook and stir for time in chart above or until bubbly and blended. Brush on skin side of broiled chicken during last 30 to 90 seconds of broiling time. Keep remaining sauce warm and serve with chicken.

Suggested Combinations
Plum Basting Sauce for Broiled Poultry: Use plum jam. Use plum wine. Use ginger for spice.
Currant Basting Sauce for Broiled Poultry: Use currant jelly. Use crème de cassis for liqueur. Use cinnamon for spice.

How to Broil Chicken with Basting Sauce

1/Place chicken halves or split breasts on a rack in a broiler pan. Measure from highest point of chicken to the broiler element. Arrange oven rack so chicken halves are 5 to 6 inches away from element or breast halves are 4 to 5 inches away from element.

2/Pour water to a depth of 1/4 inch in bottom of broiler pan. Water helps prevent splatters, keeps chicken moist and makes clean-up easier. Place chicken, skin-side down, on rack. Preheat an electric broiler. You do not need to preheat a gas broiler.

3/Broil chicken, skin-side down, 25 minutes for halves or 15 minutes for breasts. Using oven mitts or hot pads, pull out oven rack and remove chicken from broiler. To preserve juices, turn chicken over with tongs instead of a fork.

4/Broil chicken, skin-side up, 8 to 10 minutes for halves or 5 to 6 minutes for breasts. When done, juices should run clear when chicken is pierced with a fork. Brush with sauce, such as Plum Basting Sauce. Broil 30 to 90 seconds. Do not let sauce burn.

Basic Fruit Glaze for Roast Poultry

YIELD	2-2/3 cups	1-1/3 cups
INGREDIENTS		
thin orange-peel slivers	from 1/4 orange	from 1/8 orange
chicken broth	1 cup	1/2 cup
dry white wine	1/2 cup	1/4 cup
cooking liquid from peel	3/4 cup	1/3 cup
sugar	1/4 cup	2 tablespoons
cornstarch	2 tablespoons	1 tablespoon
fruit juice	1 cup	1/2 cup
fruit liqueur	1/4 cup	2 tablespoons
fruit sections or slices, well-drained	1 cup	1/2 cup
SAUCEPAN	1-1/2-qt. saucepan	1-qt. saucepan
TIME AT MEDIUM	10 minutes	10 minutes
TIME AT MEDIUM HIGH	5 to 6 minutes	4 to 5 minutes
TIME AT ROASTING TEMPERATURE (glazed on poultry)	20 to 30 minutes	20 to 30 minutes

In a saucepan, see size in chart above, combine slivered peel, chicken broth and wine. Bring to a boil over High heat. Reduce heat to Medium. Simmer, uncovered, 10 minutes or until peel is tender. Drain, reserving peel and amount of cooking liquid listed in chart above. In same saucepan, combine sugar and cornstarch; mix well. Whisk in fruit juice, cooking liquid from peel, orange peel and liqueur. Cook over Medium-High heat for time in chart above or until thickened and bubbly all over, whisking constantly. Stir in fruit. Spoon over poultry during last 20 to 30 minutes of roasting time. Heat remaining glaze and serve with poultry.

Suggested Combinations
Glaze à l'Orange for Roast Poultry: Use orange juice and orange liqueur. Use orange sections for fruit.
Glaze à l'Apricot for Roast Poultry: Use apricot nectar for juice and apricot brandy for liqueur. Use apricot halves, cut in half, for fruit.

Herb-Butter Basting Sauce for Poultry

Photo on page 158.

YIELD	1/2 cup	1/4 cup
INGREDIENTS		
butter or margarine	1/2 cup	1/4 cup
dried leaf herbs	2 teaspoons	1 teaspoon
celery salt	1/2 teaspoon	1/4 teaspoon
onion salt	1/2 teaspoon	1/4 teaspoon
SAUCEPAN	1-qt. saucepan	1-qt. saucepan
TIME AT MEDIUM HIGH	3-1/2 minutes	2-1/2 minutes

In a 1-quart saucepan, heat butter or margarine over Medium-High heat for time in chart above or until melted, stirring once or twice. Stir in herbs, celery salt and onion salt; mix well. Stir before brushing on poultry.

Suggested Herbs: tarragon, rubbed sage, thyme, rosemary, marjoram, savory.

How to Make Basic Fruit Glaze for Roast Poultry

1/Score orange to remove peel in sections. Scrape off white membrane inside peel as much as possible. Using a small sharp knife, cut peel into thin slivers. Simmer peel in chicken broth and wine until tender.

2/Mix cooking liquid and peel with fruit juice and fruit liqueur. Thicken this mixture with cornstarch mixed with sugar to prevent lumping. Stir in apricots or orange sections. Spoon glaze over roast capon or other poultry 20 to 30 minutes before poultry is done.

Basic Cranberry Glaze for Roast Poultry

YIELD	1 cup	1/2 cup
INGREDIENTS		
cranberry-orange relish	1/2 cup	1/4 cup
fruit jam or preserves	1/2 cup	1/4 cup
fruit liqueur or fruit juice	2 tablespoons	1 tablespoon
ground spice	1/2 teaspoon	1/4 teaspoon
TIME AT ROASTING TEMPERATURE (glazed on poultry)	20 to 30 minutes	20 to 30 minutes

In a medium bowl, stir together cranberry relish, jam or preserves, liqueur or fruit juice and spice; mix well. Spoon over poultry during last 20 to 30 minutes of roasting time. Heat remaining glaze and serve with poultry.

Suggested Combinations
Cranberry-Orange Glaze for Roast Poultry, photo on page 189: Use orange marmalade for jam. Use orange liqueur or orange juice. Use allspice for spice.
Cranberry-Apricot Glaze for Roast Poultry: Use apricot jam. Use apricot brandy or apricot nectar for juice. Use cardamom for spice.
Cranberry-Pineapple Glaze for Roast Poultry: Use pineapple preserves. Use cranberry liqueur or cranberry-juice cocktail for juice. Use ginger for spice.

Gravy for Roast Poultry

YIELD	3-1/2 cups	1-3/4 cups
INGREDIENTS		
pan drippings from poultry	2/3 cup	1/3 cup
all-purpose flour	2/3 cup	1/3 cup
chicken broth	1-1/3 cups	2/3 cup
chicken broth	1-1/3 cups	2/3 cup
dried rubbed sage	1/2 teaspoon	1/4 teaspoon
dried leaf thyme	1/2 teaspoon	1/4 teaspoon
onion salt	1/4 teaspoon	1/8 teaspoon
pepper	1/4 teaspoon	1/8 teaspoon
Kitchen Bouquet, if desired	few drops	few drops
ROASTING PAN	roasting pan from poultry	roasting pan from poultry
TIME AT MEDIUM HIGH	5 to 7 minutes	4 to 5 minutes

Measure pan drippings. If necessary, add melted butter or margarine to make amount of drippings listed in chart above. In a screw-top jar, combine flour and first amount of broth; shake well until completely smooth. Place the roasting pan with drippings on a burner over Medium-High heat. If using large roasting pan, place pan on 2 burners over Medium-High heat. Stir flour mixture into pan drippings, blending well. Quickly stir in second amount of broth, sage, thyme, onion salt and pepper. Cook for time in chart above or until thickened and bubbly all over, stirring constantly. Stir in a few drops of Kitchen Bouquet for color, if desired.

Variation
Giblet Gravy: Prepare Poached Giblets, page 162, while poultry is roasting. Use poaching broth instead of chicken broth in gravy. Chop giblets. Add to thickened gravy and heat through.

Easy Gravy for Roast Poultry

YIELD	3-1/3 cups	1-2/3 cups
INGREDIENTS		
pan drippings from poultry	1/3 cup	2 tablespoons
all-purpose flour	1/4 cup	2 tablespoons
water	1-1/3 cups	2/3 cup
dry white wine	1/3 cup	2 tablespoons
poultry seasoning	1/2 teaspoon	1/4 teaspoon
herb pepper	1/2 teaspoon	1/4 teaspoon
condensed creamy chicken-mushroom soup	1 (10-3/4-oz.) can	1/2 (10-3/4-oz.) can (2/3 cup)
sliced mushrooms, drained	1 (2-1/2-oz.) jar	1/2 (2-1/2-oz.) jar
ROASTING PAN	roasting pan from poultry	roasting pan from poultry
TIME AT MEDIUM HIGH (water, wine added)	4 to 5 minutes	2 minutes
TIME AT MEDIUM HIGH (soup added)	2 to 3 minutes	1 minute

Measure pan drippings. If necessary, add melted butter or margarine to make amount of drippings listed in chart above. Place the roasting pan with drippings on a burner over Medium-High heat. If using large roasting pan, place pan with drippings on 2 burners over Medium-High heat. Stir flour into drippings. Blend well until flour is dissolved and bubbly. Stir in water, wine, poultry seasoning and herb pepper. Cook and stir for time in chart above or until thickened and bubbly all over. Whisk in soup and mushrooms. Cook and stir for time in chart above or until heated through.

How to Make Basic Cranberry Sauce

1/Make a syrup of sugar, spice, fruit juice and fruit liqueur or wine. Cranberry-Raspberry Sauce has cinnamon, raspberry syrup and white wine. When syrup boils, stir in cranberries and other fruit, such as raspberries and dried apricots.

2/Cook over Medium-High heat until cranberry skins pop, indicating cranberries are tender. Cranberries will look deflated instead of plump. Reduce heat to Medium and boil gently until sauce is slightly thickened.

Basic Cranberry Sauce

YIELD	2-2/3 cups	1-1/3 cups
INGREDIENTS		
sugar	1 cup	1/2 cup
ground spice	1/2 teaspoon	1/4 teaspoon
fruit juice	2/3 cup	1/3 cup
fruit liqueur or wine	1/3 cup	2 tablespoons
fresh or frozen cranberries	2 cups	1 cup
chopped fresh fruit, thawed frozen fruit or dried fruit	1 cup	1/2 cup
SAUCEPAN	3-qt. saucepan	1-1/2-qt. saucepan
TIME AT MEDIUM HIGH	9 to 10 minutes	7 to 8 minutes
TIME AT MEDIUM	10 minutes	8 minutes

In a saucepan, see size in chart above, combine sugar, spice, fruit juice and fruit liqueur or wine; mix well. Bring to a boil over Medium-High heat, stirring occasionally to dissolve sugar. When mixture boils, stir in cranberries and other fruit. Cook, uncovered, for time in chart above or until cranberry skins pop. Reduce heat to Medium. Boil gently for time in chart above or until slightly thickened, stirring occasionally. Cover and refrigerate.

Suggested Combinations

Cranberry-Orange Sauce: Use ginger for spice. Use orange juice and orange liqueur. Use chopped orange sections or mandarin oranges and golden raisins for fruit.

Cranberry-Raspberry Sauce: Use cinnamon for spice. Use syrup from thawed frozen raspberries for fruit juice and white wine. Use raspberries and snipped dried apricots for fruit.

Double-Cranberry Sauce: Use allspice or nutmeg for spice. Use cranberry-juice cocktail for fruit juice and cranberry liqueur. Use chopped peeled apple and raisins for fruit.

Basic Cornbread Stuffing

YIELD	9 cups	4-1/2 cups	2-1/4 cups
INGREDIENTS			
chopped green onion	1 cup	1/2 cup	1/4 cup
butter or margarine	1 cup	1/2 cup	1/4 cup
coarse cornbread crumbs	4 cups	2 cups	1 cup
fruited granola	4 cups	2 cups	1 cup
chopped cooked meat or cooked ground meat	1 cup	1/2 cup	1/4 cup
chopped fruit	1-1/3 cups	2/3 cup	1/3 cup
ground spices	2 teaspoons	1 teaspoon	1/2 teaspoon
SAUCEPAN	4-qt. saucepan	2-qt. saucepan	1-qt. saucepan
TIME AT MEDIUM HIGH	5 minutes	4 to 5 minutes	3 minutes

In a saucepan, see size in chart above, cook green onion in butter or margarine over Medium-High heat for time in chart above or until tender, stirring occasionally. Add cornbread crumbs, granola, meat, fruit and spices. Toss gently until moistened. Use 8 to 9 cups to stuff a 20- to 24-pound turkey, 4 to 4-1/2 cups to stuff a 10- to 12-pound turkey and 2 cups to stuff a 3- to 4-pound chicken or 4 (20-ounce) Cornish hens.

Suggested Combinations
Pineapple-Ham Cornbread Stuffing: Use chopped ham for meat. Use drained, canned, crushed pineapple for fruit. Use allspice and cloves for spices.
Apple-Sausage Cornbread Stuffing: Use drained, cooked, fresh bulk pork sausage for meat. Use chopped fresh apple for fruit. Use cinnamon and nutmeg for spices.
Pear-Bacon Cornbread Stuffing: Use crumbled cooked bacon for meat. Use bacon drippings instead of butter or margarine, if desired. Use chopped fresh pear for fruit. Use ground dried lemon peel and ginger for spices.

Basic Bread Stuffing

YIELD	10 cups	5 cups	2-1/2 cups
INGREDIENTS			
sliced bread	1 (1-lb.) loaf	1/2 (1-lb.) loaf	1/4 (1-lb.) loaf
flavoring ingredient	1 cup	1/2 cup	1/4 cup
finely chopped onion	1 cup	1/2 cup	1/4 cup
finely chopped celery	1 cup	1/2 cup	1/4 cup
dried leaf herbs	4 teaspoons	2 teaspoons	1 teaspoon
butter or margarine, softened	3/4 cup	6 tablespoons	3 tablespoons
cooking liquid	1/2 to 3/4 cup	1/4 to 1/2 cup	2 to 4 tablespoons
ROASTING PAN	8-qt. roasting pan	4-qt. roasting pan	2-qt. roasting pan
TIME IN 325F (165C) OVEN	30 minutes	20 minutes	15 to 20 minutes

Do not preheat oven. Stand bread slices on edge around inside of a roasting pan, see size in chart above. Overlap slices as little as possible. Bake in a 325F (165C) oven for time in chart above or until bread is dry. Turn and rearrange slices several times to dry evenly. Tear bread into small pieces in roasting pan. Add flavoring ingredient, onion, celery and herbs. Toss until well-combined. Add butter or margarine. Knead butter or margarine with bread mixture until butter is absorbed. Add just enough cooking liquid to moisten. Use 8 to 9 cups to stuff a 20- to 24-pound turkey, 4 to 4-1/2 cups to stuff a 10- to 12- pound turkey and 2 cups to stuff a 3- to 4- pound chicken or 4 (20-ounce) Cornish hens.

Suggested Combinations
Oyster Bread Stuffing: Use white bread. Use chopped, drained, fresh oysters for flavoring ingredient. Use oyster liquor for cooking liquid. Use marjoram, thyme and rubbed sage for herbs.
Giblet Bread Stuffing: Use white bread. Use chopped, drained, poached giblets, page 162, for flavoring ingredient. Use giblet poaching broth for cooking liquid. Use rubbed sage, rosemary and thyme for herbs.
Grandma's Bread Stuffing: Use raisin bread. Use chopped roasted chestnuts, see page 188, or toasted walnuts for flavoring ingredient. Use chicken broth for cooking liquid. Use parsley flakes, rubbed sage and rosemary for herbs.

How to Stuff Poultry

1/Remove giblets. Run cold water into body cavity of bird several times. Pat bird dry with paper towels. Turn bird, breast-side down, on a board. Twist wing-tips behind back. Fill neck cavity with Pineapple-Ham Cornbread Stuffing or other stuffing.

2/Skewer flap of skin at neck end over stuffing and wing-tips if flap is long enough. Skewer neck skin closed with a metal skewer inserted like a straight pin. If skin flap is too short to skewer, hold skin over stuffing and carefully turn bird over.

3/Stand bird upright in a bowl with neck-end down. Spoon stuffing loosely into body cavity. Do not pack stuffing into bird. Bake extra stuffing in a separate casserole, see Extra-Stuffing Casserole, page 188.

4/If you plan to serve whole bird at table, tie legs together with string so bird retains attractive shape. If bird is served in kitchen, it is not necessary to tie legs. Thighs cook more evenly when not tied.

Basic Crouton Stuffing

YIELD	9 cups	4-1/2 cups	2 cups
INGREDIENTS			
chopped or sliced vegetables, fruit, meat	3 cups	1-1/2 cups	3/4 cup
butter, margarine or bacon drippings	1/2 cup	1/4 cup	2 tablespoons
toasted croutons	7 cups	3-1/2 cups	1-3/4 cups
chicken broth	2/3 cup	1/3 cup	3 tablespoons
dried leaf herbs or spice	4 teaspoons	2 teaspoons	1 teaspoon
seasoning liquid	2 teaspoons	1 teaspoon	1/2 teaspoon
SKILLET	11-inch skillet	9-inch skillet	8-inch skillet
TIME AT MEDIUM HIGH	8 to 9 minutes	6 to 8 minutes	4 to 5 minutes

In a skillet, see size in chart above, cook vegetables, fruit and meat in butter, margarine or bacon drippings over Medium-High heat for time in chart above or until tender, stirring often. Add croutons, broth, herbs or spice and seasoning liquid. Toss gently until moistened. Use 8 to 9 cups to stuff a 20- to 24-pound turkey, 4 to 4-1/2 cups to stuff a 10- to 12-pound turkey and 2 cups to stuff a 3- to 4-pound chicken or 4 (20-ounce) Cornish hens.

Suggested Combinations
Oriental Crouton Stuffing: Use butter or margarine. Use sliced water chestnuts, chopped green pepper, bean sprouts and drained, canned, mandarin oranges for vegetables and fruit. Use plain croutons. Use minced fresh gingerroot for spice and cook with vegetables and fruit. Use soy sauce as seasoning liquid.
Italian Crouton Stuffing: Use butter or margarine. Use sliced mushrooms, chopped onion, chopped red pepper and chopped pepperoni for vegetables and meat. Use garlic croutons. Use oregano and basil for herbs. Use Worcestershire sauce for seasoning liquid.
Pilgrim Crouton Stuffing, photo on page 193: Use bacon drippings. Use cubed, peeled butternut or acorn squash, chopped apple, raisins and chopped celery for vegetables and fruit. Use herb-seasoned croutons. Use rubbed sage and thyme for herbs. Use port wine for seasoning liquid.

Extra-Stuffing Casserole

SERVINGS	4 or 5	1 or 2
INGREDIENTS		
refrigerated, unbaked poultry stuffing, pages 186 to 190	3 to 4 cups	1 to 2 cups
chicken broth	3 to 4 tablespoons	1 to 2 tablespoons
CASSEROLE	1-qt. casserole	2-cup casserole
TIME AT ROASTING TEMPERATURE (same temperature as poultry)	20 to 30 minutes	15 to 20 minutes

Spoon stuffing that would not fit into bird into a casserole, see size in chart above. Or, make a second kind of stuffing to accompany bird. Cover and refrigerate. Twenty to 30 minutes before bird is done, add to stuffing 1 tablespoon broth per cup of stuffing. Toss to mix well. Cover and bake at same temperature as bird. Bake for time in chart above or until stuffing is heated through.

Tips for Roasting Chestnuts
- Pierce shells of fresh chestnuts several times with a large fork, or make small slits in each chestnut with a sharp knife. This allows steam to escape.
- Place chestnuts in a single layer on a baking sheet. Bake in a preheated 400F (205C) oven 20 to 25 minutes. Cool until easily handled. Peel off shell with a small knife.
- To use for stuffing, follow directions for Grandma's Bread Stuffing, page 186.

Roast Cornish Hens, page 194; with Oriental Crouton Stuffing, above; and Cranberry-Orange Glaze for Roast Poultry, page 183.

Basic Rice Stuffing

YIELD	8 cups	4 cups	2 cups
INGREDIENTS			
chopped or sliced vegetables	3-1/3 cups	1-2/3 cups	3/4 cup
butter or margarine	3/4 cup	6 tablespoons	3 tablespoons
cooked rice	6 cups	3 cups	1-1/2 cups
chopped nuts or seeds	2/3 cup	1/3 cup	2 tablespoons
broth or dry white wine	2/3 cup	1/3 cup	2 tablespoons
dried leaf herbs OR	4 teaspoons	2 teaspoons	1 teaspoon
ground spices	2 teaspoons	1 teaspoon	1/2 teaspoon
SKILLET	11-inch skillet	9-inch skillet	8-inch skillet
TIME AT MEDIUM HIGH	7 to 9 minutes	6 to 7 minutes	3 to 4 minutes

In a skillet, see size in chart above, cook vegetables in butter or margarine over Medium-High heat for time in chart above or until tender, stirring often. Stir in rice, nuts or seeds, broth or wine and herbs or spices. Toss gently until moistened. Use 8 cups to stuff a 20- to 24-pound turkey, 4 cups to stuff a 10- to 12-pound turkey and 2 cups to stuff a 3- to 4-pound chicken or 4 (20-ounce) Cornish hens.

Suggested Combinations

Herbed Brown-Rice Stuffing: Use chopped celery, chopped onion, chopped carrot and chopped green pepper for vegetables. Use cooked brown rice. Use sunflower kernels for seeds. Use chicken broth. Use savory and tarragon for herbs.

Elegant Wild-Rice Stuffing: Use sliced mushrooms, chopped green onion, drained, quartered, canned artichoke hearts and chopped pimiento for vegetables. Use cooked wild rice. Use toasted pecans for nuts. Use dry white wine. Use thyme and marjoram for herbs.

Mediterranean Rice Stuffing, photo on page 158: Use thawed frozen peas, chopped onion, chopped red pepper and sliced green olives for vegetables. Use cooked white rice. Use toasted almonds for nuts. Use chicken broth. Use saffron and chili powder for spices.

Tips for Keeping Leftover Poultry

- Remove stuffing from bird while still hot. Spoon into a refrigerator container or casserole. Cover and refrigerate. Use within 1 to 2 days.

- Refrigerate extra gravy in a closed container. Use within 2 to 3 days. Gravy does not freeze well if it has been thickened.

- Leave uncarved meat on bird. It will stay more moist. Wrap bird in enough foil to seal. Place in a large plastic bag. Refrigerate. Use within 4 to 5 days.

Roast Poultry

Roasting Method for Turkey————————

Do not preheat oven. Prepare butter-type basting sauce or sweet-type glaze, pages 182 and 183; set aside. Remove giblets from bird; poach for stuffing or gravy, page 162, if desired. Remove excess fat from body cavity. Rinse cavity of bird. Pat bird dry with paper towels. Twist wing-tips behind back. Loosely pack stuffing, see amount in chart, into body and neck cavities, if desired. See stuffing recipes on pages 186 to 190. Skewer neck cavity closed, if necessary, to hold in stuffing. Tie legs together or tuck under band of skin or wire clip, if present. Place bird, breast-side up, on a rack in a shallow roasting pan. Brush with butter-type basting sauce, if desired. Roast in 325F (165C) oven for time in chart. Insert a meat thermometer between leg and thigh 30 minutes before end of roasting time. Meat thermometer should register 185F (85C) in thickest part of thigh when done. Juices should run clear when bird is pierced with a fork between leg and thigh. Baste bird with sweet glaze, if desired, 20 to 30 minutes before end of roasting time. If bird begins to overbrown during roasting, cover bird with a tent of foil. If stuffed, roast until a thermometer inserted in center of stuffing registers 165F (72C). When done, cover birds larger than 5 pounds with foil; let stand 10 to 15 minutes before carving, see pages 196 and 197. Prepare gravy, page 184, if desired.

Roast Turkey Breast (Medium)   Photo on page 158.

INGREDIENTS	Stuffed	Unstuffed
whole turkey breast	1 (5- to 7-lb.) breast	1 (5- to 7-lb.) breast
stuffing	3 cups	omit
butter-type basting sauce	1/2 cup	1/2 cup
sweet-type glaze	1 cup	1 cup
TIME IN 325F (165C) OVEN	3 to 3-1/2 hours	2-3/4 to 3-1/4 hours

Follow directions for Roasting Method for Turkey, above, except: Lightly pack stuffing into rib cavity. Tie rib cavity closed to hold in stuffing. Insert a meat thermometer in thickest part of breast to check for doneness. If stuffed, spoon off and reserve for gravy all but 2 to 3 tablespoons drippings about 30 minutes before end of cooking time. Spoon any extra stuffing around breast and continue roasting.

Roast Turkey Breast (Small)

INGREDIENTS	Stuffed	Unstuffed
whole turkey breast	1 (2- to 5-lb.) breast	1 (2- to 5-lb.) breast
stuffing	2 cups	omit
butter-type basting sauce	1/4 cup	1/4 cup
sweet-type glaze	1/2 cup	1/2 cup
TIME IN 325F (165C) OVEN	2-1/2 to 3 hours	2-1/4 to 2-3/4 hours

Follow directions for Roasting Method for Turkey, above, and special instructions above for Medium Turkey Breast.

Roast Turkey Hindquarter

INGREDIENTS	Stuffed	Unstuffed
turkey hindquarter (leg and thigh)		1 (2- to 3-lb.) hindquarter
stuffing	do not stuff	
butter-type basting sauce		1/4 cup
sweet-type glaze		1/2 cup
TIME IN 325F (165C) OVEN		2-3/4 to 3-1/2 hours

Follow directions for Roasting Method for Turkey, above, except: Place hindquarter, meaty-side up, on a rack in a shallow roasting pan.

Roast Turkey (Extra Large)

INGREDIENTS	Stuffed	Unstuffed
turkey (with giblets)	1 (20- to 24-lb.) turkey	1 (20- to 24-lb.) turkey
stuffing	8 to 9 cups	omit
butter-type basting sauce	1/2 cup	1/2 cup
TIME IN 325F (165C) OVEN	6-1/2 to 7-1/2 hours	5-1/2 to 6-1/2 hours

Follow directions for Roasting Method for Turkey, page 191.

Roast Turkey (Large)

INGREDIENTS	Stuffed	Unstuffed
turkey (with giblets)	1 (16- to 20-lb.) turkey	1 (16- to 20-lb.) turkey
stuffing	8 cups	omit
butter-type basting sauce	1/2 cup	1/2 cup
TIME IN 325F (165C) OVEN	5-1/2 to 7 hours	4-1/2 to 6 hours

Follow directions for Roasting Method for Turkey, page 191.

Roast Turkey (Medium)

INGREDIENTS	Stuffed	Unstuffed
turkey (with giblets)	1 (12- to 16-lb.) turkey	1 (12- to 16-lb.) turkey
stuffing	6 cups	omit
butter-type basting sauce	1/2 cup	1/2 cup
TIME IN 325F (165C) OVEN	4-1/2 to 6 hours	3-1/2 to 5 hours

Follow directions for Roasting Method for Turkey, page 191.

Roast Turkey (Small)

INGREDIENTS	Stuffed	Unstuffed
turkey (with giblets)	1 (8- to 12-lb.) turkey	1 (8- to 12-lb.) turkey
stuffing	3-1/2 to 4-1/2 cups	omit
butter-type basting sauce	1/4 cup	1/4 cup
TIME IN 325F (165C) OVEN	4 to 5 hours	3 to 4 hours

Follow directions for Roasting Method for Turkey, page 191.

Tips for Roasting Poultry

- Use a shallow roasting pan. Deep, old-fashioned roasters may slow cooking time.
- Place bird on a roasting rack so it does not stew in its own juice. A rack also helps distribute heat more evenly.
- Use cooking times for whole poultry only as guidelines. Factors that affect cooking time are:

Stuffing—Unstuffed birds cook more quickly than stuffed birds.

Meatiness—Meaty birds cook more slowly than bony birds.

Temperature—Refrigerated birds cook more slowly than birds at room temperature. Cooking times in this book are for refrigerated birds. Poultry is extremely perishable. Do not keep it at room temperature for any period of time.

How to Know When Roast Poultry is Done

1/Insert a quick-registering thermometer in center of stuffing in body cavity. This is Pilgrim Crouton Stuffing, page 188. Thermometer must register 165F (72C). If temperature is lower, continue roasting bird until temperature is reached. Stuffing that has not reached 165F (72C) is not safe to eat.

2/Insert a meat thermometer in thickest part of thigh 30 minutes before end of roasting time. Most thermometers register more accurately if not left in bird for entire roasting time. Thermometer should register 185F (85C). If temperature is lower, continue roasting until temperature is reached. Check temperature of both thighs.

3/To check accuracy of thermometer test, cut between leg and thigh of bird. Juices should run clear. Red or pink juice indicates bird is not done. If juices are not clear, continue roasting until they are.

4/For another doneness test, use a paper towel or napkin to grasp end of drumstick. When bird is done, drumstick should move easily in socket when you "shake hands." Cover birds larger than 5 pounds with foil. Let stand 10 to 15 minutes before carving.

Roasting Method for Poultry

Do not preheat oven. Prepare butter-type basting sauce or sweet-type glaze, pages 182 and 183; set aside. Remove giblets from bird; poach for stuffing or gravy, page 162, if desired. Remove excess fat from body cavity. Rinse cavity of bird. Pat bird dry with paper towels. Twist wing-tips behind back. Loosely pack stuffing, see amount in chart, into body and neck cavities, if desired. See stuffing recipes on pages 186 to 190. Skewer neck cavity closed, if necessary, to hold in stuffing. Tie legs together or tuck under band of skin or wire clip, if present. Place bird, breast-side up, on a rack in a shallow roasting pan. Brush with butter-type basting sauce, if desired. Roast at oven temperature in chart for time in chart. Insert a meat thermometer between leg and thigh 30 minutes before end of roasting time. Meat thermometer should register 185F (85C) in thickest part of thigh when done. Juices should run clear when bird is pierced with a fork between leg and thigh. Baste bird with sweet glaze, if desired, 20 to 30 minutes before end of roasting time. If bird begins to overbrown during roasting, cover bird with a tent of foil. If stuffed, roast until a thermometer inserted in center of stuffing registers 165F (72C). When done, cover birds larger than 5 pounds with foil; let stand 10 to 15 minutes before carving. Prepare gravy, page 184, if desired.

Roast Capon

INGREDIENTS	Stuffed	Unstuffed
capon (with giblets)	1 (6- to 8-1/2-lb.) capon	1 (6- to 8-1/2-lb.) capon
stuffing	4 to 5 cups	omit
butter-type basting sauce	1/4 cup	1/4 cup
sweet-type glaze	2/3 cup	2/3 cup
TIME IN 325F (165C) OVEN	3-1/4 to 4 hours	3-1/4 to 3-3/4 hours

Follow directions for Roasting Method for Poultry, above.

Roast Chicken

INGREDIENTS	Stuffed	Unstuffed
broiler-fryer or roasting chicken (with giblets)	1 (3- to 4-lb.) chicken	1 (3- to 4-lb.) chicken
stuffing	1-1/2 to 2 cups	omit
butter-type basting sauce	1/4 cup	1/4 cup
sweet-type glaze	1/2 cup	1/2 cup
TIME IN 375F (190C) OVEN	1-1/2 to 2 hours	1-1/2 to 1-3/4 hours

Follow directions for Roasting Method for Poultry, above.

Roast Cornish Hens

INGREDIENTS	Stuffed	Unstuffed
Cornish hens (with giblets)	20-oz. hens	20-oz. hens
stuffing	1/2 cup per hen	omit
butter-type basting sauce	2 tablespoons per hen	2 tablespoons per hen
sweet-type glaze	1/4 cup per hen	1/4 cup per hen
TIME IN 375F (190C) OVEN	1-1/4 to 1-1/2 hours	1 to 1-1/4 hours

Follow directions for Roasting Method for Poultry, above.

How to Make Roast Duckling

1/Remove as much fat as possible from body cavity. Rub skin all over with a mixture of rosemary, fennel seed, celery seed and onion salt. Using the tip of a sharp knife, pierce skin all over so fat can escape during roasting.

2/Place duckling on a rack in a shallow roasting pan. Roast at 375F (190C). Use a baster or large spoon to remove fat from pan several times during roasting. If desired, spoon Glaze à l'Orange, page 182, over duckling during last 20 to 30 minutes of roasting time.

Roast Duckling

INGREDIENTS	Stuffed	Unstuffed
domestic duckling (with giblets)	1 (4- to 5- lb.) duckling	1 (4- to 5- lb.) duckling
stuffing	2 cups	omit
butter-type basting sauce	do not use	do not use
sweet-type glaze	2/3 cup	2/3 cup
TIME IN 375F (190C) OVEN	2-1/2 to 3 hours	2-1/4 to 2-3/4 hours

Follow directions for Roasting Method for Poultry, opposite, except: Rub skin with mixture of 1 teaspoon dried leaf rosemary, 1 teaspoon fennel seed, 1 teaspoon celery seed and 1/2 teaspoon onion salt. Before roasting, pierce skin all over with the tip of a sharp knife. Remove fat from roasting pan several times during roasting.

Carving a Turkey

Traditional Carving Method at the Table

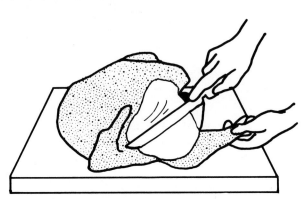

1. Remove drumstick and thigh from 1 side of bird. Grasp drumstick and pull away from bird as far as possible. Joint connecting leg to body may snap free. If not, sever joint with a knife. Cut thigh from bird by cutting along body contour.

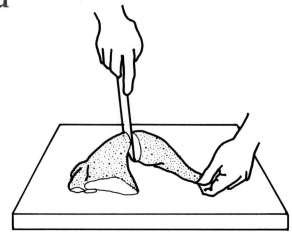

2. Place drumstick and thigh on a cutting surface. Cut through connecting joint.

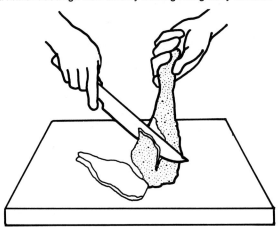

3. Grasp end of drumstick and tilt to convenient angle. Slice meat down drumstick on all sides.

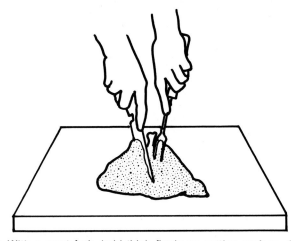

4. With a meat fork, hold thigh firmly on cutting surface. Cut even slices parallel to bone.

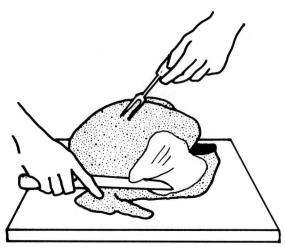

5. To carve breast, place knife parallel to cutting surface. Cut into breast through to bone. Make cut as close to wing as possible. This is base cut. All breast slices will end at this cut.

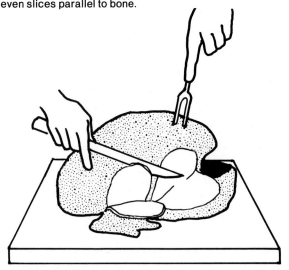

6. Carve downward on breast, ending at base cut. Start each new slice slightly higher on breast. Keep slices thin and even. When needed, repeat for other side of bird.

Carving Method in the Kitchen

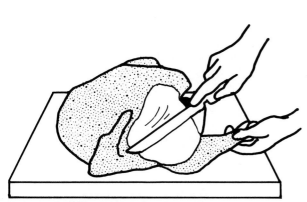

1. Remove drumstick and thigh from 1 side of bird. Grasp drumstick and pull away from bird as far as possible. Joint connecting leg to body may snap free. If not, sever joint with a knife. Cut thigh from bird by cutting along body contour.

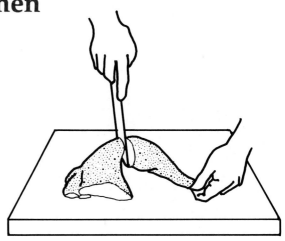

2. Place drumstick and thigh on a cutting surface. Cut through connecting joint.

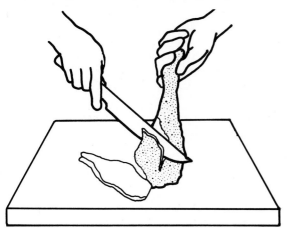

3. Grasp end of drumstick and tilt to convenient angle. Slice meat down drumstick on all sides.

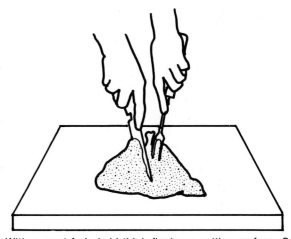

4. With a meat fork, hold thigh firmly on cutting surface. Cut even slices parallel to bone.

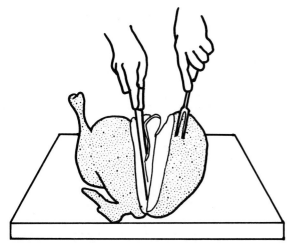

5. Remove half of breast by cutting along breast bone and rib cage with sharp knife.

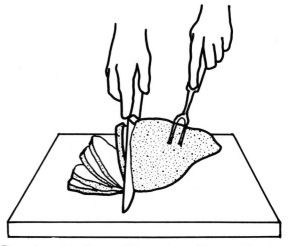

6. Place breast half on cutting surface. Slice evenly across grain of meat. When needed, repeat for other side of bird.

Fish
& Seafood

The delicacies of the sea are worthy of sharp-eyed shopping and your best cooking efforts. Two rules are vital in buying and preparing seafood: Buy only the *freshest* fish and shellfish, and cook it just until done—do not overcook. The recipes in this chapter will help you master the fine art of fish cookery.

Steamed Mussels or Clams Deluxe, page 225.

Fish & Seafood

Q. How can I be sure the fish or shellfish I buy is fresh?

A. Buying the freshest fish available is an important first step toward preparing fish. Fresh fish has a mild, sweet smell. Do not buy fish that has a fishy odor. Fresh whole fish has firm, elastic flesh that springs back when you touch it. The eyes should protrude and be clear with black pupils. Gills should appear bright red. Scales, if present, should be shiny and adhere tightly to the fish. Look for a moist, translucent appearance on fish fillets and steaks.

When selecting frozen fish, avoid fish with a white, cottony appearance, brownish tinge or discoloration. These indicate poor quality. Do not buy fish with spots of blood on it or icy edges on the packaging. These may indicate the fish has been thawed and refrozen. It is not necessarily spoiled, but it is likely to be dry and tasteless after cooking.

Oysters, mussels and clams in the shell must be live when purchased. They usually keep their shells tightly closed. Discard unusually light or heavy shells, as they are probably not alive. Live shellfish snap their shells shut if tapped. Shucked shellfish should be plump, sweet-smelling and even in color.

Q. Should I cook fish and seafood the same day I purchase it?

A. Fresh fish is best if prepared and eaten immediately. If that is not possible, wrap it in clear plastic wrap and store in the coldest part of the refrigerator no longer than 2 days. Prepackaged fish may be stored in the original wrapping. Shellfish bought from a market must be refrigerated promptly and used within 24 hours. Cover live shellfish with a loosely closed paper bag or a plastic bag with many small breathing holes in the top. If shellfish are stored in water, use salt water; fresh water will kill shellfish. Store shucked shellfish in tightly covered containers.

Refrigerate cooked seafood in covered containers up to 3 days.

Q. How can I freeze fish for longer storage?

A. To freeze fish, check at the market to be sure the fish or shellfish is "fresh" and was not frozen for shipping. Wrap fish in clear plastic wrap or foil. Seal, label and freeze. Pack shrimp or shucked oysters, clams, scallops or mussels in freezer containers, leaving a 1/2-inch space at the top. Seafood that is purchased frozen should be stored in its original package.

Store uncooked seafood or fat fish in the freezer at 0F (-20C) up to 3 months. Store lean fish up to 6 months. Wrap cooked seafood tightly in clear plastic wrap or foil; store in the freezer at 0F (-20C) up to 2 to 3 months.

Q. How do I estimate how much shrimp to buy?

A. Shrimp are sold fresh and uncooked as *green shrimp,* frozen in the shell or frozen peeled. If you buy large shrimp in the shell, expect 16 to 20 shrimp per pound. Medium shrimp are usually 26 to 30 per pound, and small shrimp are 43 to 50 per pound. Shrimp size and number per pound may vary in some markets. We used these guides in recipe-testing.

One pound of frozen shrimp in the shell yields 1-3/4 to 2 cups cut-up cooked shrimp. Eight ounces of cooked, peeled, medium shrimp makes three shrimp cocktails.

Q. What is the difference between hard-shell and soft-shell clams?

A. Hard-shell clams have hard shells, usually round, that are difficult to break with your hands. The smaller hard-shell clams are often called *littlenecks* or *cherrystones,* and the larger ones are called *quahogs.* Soft-shell clams are oval with light, brittle shells that can be broken easily. These clams are often called *steamers.*

Q. What are the differences among whole cleaned fish, pan-dressed fish, fillets and steaks?

A. When whole fish is available, it is generally sold scaled and gutted; you only need to remove the fins. Pan-dressed fish is whole, cleaned fish with head and tail removed. Fillets are boneless, skinless pieces of fish. They are the most fragile fish cut. Steaks are cross sections from larger, round-shaped fish. They are generally 1 inch thick, contain some backbone and are surrounded by skin.

Allow 12 to 16 ounces of whole cleaned fish for each serving. Allow 8 ounces of pan-dressed fish for each serving. Because fish steaks and fillets are almost all edible, allow 3 to 4 ounces for each serving.

Q. You have included marinades in this chapter. Marinating fish is new to me.

A. Marinating fish adds delicious flavor and helps keep the fish moist during cooking. Tangy Beer Marinade, page 226, is wonderful on broiled fish or shellfish. Deviled Meat Marinade, page 138, is another good choice for broiled fish. Or, try Mediterranean Meat Marinade, page 138, substituting dry white wine for the red wine in the recipe. All of these marinades enhance the natural flavor of fish or shellfish.

Q. It is so easy to overcook fish. Is there a general timing guide for perfectly cooked fish?

A. In our testing, we found the timing method developed by the Canadian Department of Fisheries to be a useful guide. Measure the fish at its thickest point, and allow 10 minutes cooking time for each inch. If your fish fillet measures 1/2 inch at its thickest point, it should require about 5 minutes cooking time. This rule of thumb applies generally to steaming, poaching, broiling and pan-frying fish.

Watch fish carefully as it cooks. Because fish is delicate and varies a great deal, always test fish and shellfish for doneness. Use a timer and check fish after the minimum cooking time given in the recipe. When done, the thickest portion of the fish should just begin to flake when tested with a fork. Cooked shellfish should be opaque when cut in center of thickest part.

Q. What is a good method for baking whole fish?

A. Using a roasting bag is a wonderful way to bake whole fish. It is simple, the fish is moist and flavorful, and the cleanup is minimal. For directions, see page 207.

Q. What sauces go well with fish?

A. The right sauce adds the perfect finishing touch to fish. We have included several. Try a zesty Seafood-Cocktail Sauce, page 232; a best-ever Tartar Sauce, page 234; Cucumber-Dill Sauce, page 212; or several savory butters, pages 202 and 235. Also, the Soups & Sauces chapter contains a number of sauces that are wonderful with fish and shellfish. See the listings on pages 222 and 224.

Techniques for Cooking Fish

1/To skin fish fillets before cooking, place fillets skin-side down on a board. Holding 1 end of skin firmly against board, run the blade of a sharp knife at an angle between fillet and skin. Skinning prevents fillets from curling during cooking.

2/Use a ruler to measure thickness of fish before cooking. Measure at thickest point of fillet, whole fish or steak. As a rule of thumb, allow 10 minutes cooking time per inch of thickness when you broil, poach, steam or pan-fry fish.

Basic Baked Fish Fillets or Steaks

SERVINGS	4	2	1
INGREDIENTS			
flavored semisoft natural cheese	1/4 cup	2 tablespoons	1 tablespoon
cooking sauce	2 tablespoons	1 tablespoon	1 teaspoon
skinned fish fillets, 1/4 to 3/4 inch thick	4 (4-oz.) fillets	2 (4-oz.) fillets	1 (4-oz.) fillet
OR			
fish steaks, 3/4 to 1 inch thick	4 (5-oz.) steaks	2 (5-oz.) steaks	1 (5-oz.) steak
dry breadcrumbs	1/4 cup	2 tablespoons	1 tablespoon
vegetable slices	8 to 12	4 to 6	2 or 3
shredded cheese	1/2 cup (2 oz.)	1/4 cup (1 oz.)	2 tablespoons
snipped parsley, chives or other fresh herb	4 teaspoons	2 teaspoons	1 teaspoon
BAKING DISH	12" x 7" baking dish	8-inch-square baking dish	7-inch pie plate
TIME IN 350F (175C) OVEN:			
fillets	15 to 20 minutes	15 to 20 minutes	15 to 20 minutes
steaks	19 to 21 minutes	19 to 21 minutes	19 to 21 minutes
garnish added (fillets, steaks)	2 to 3 minutes	2 to 3 minutes	2 to 3 minutes

Do not preheat oven. In a small bowl, combine semisoft cheese and cooking sauce; mix well. If necessary, cut large fillets into 4- or 5-ounce serving pieces. Arrange fillets or steaks in a baking dish, see size in chart above. Generously spread with cheese mixture. Sprinkle with breadcrumbs. Bake in a 350F (175C) oven for time in chart above or until center of fish is beginning to flake when tested with a fork. Arrange vegetable slices on fish. Sprinkle with cheese and parsley, chives or other fresh herb. Bake 2 to 3 minutes longer or until cheese melts.

Suggested Combinations
French-Onion Baked Fish Fillets: Use semisoft natural cheese with French onion. Use mayonnaise or mayonnaise-style salad dressing for cooking sauce. Use zucchini slices for vegetable. Use Colby cheese. Use snipped dill weed for fresh herb.
Salmon Steaks au Poivre (Salmon Steaks with Pepper): Use semisoft natural cheese with pepper. Use tartar sauce for cooking sauce. Use halved tomato slices for vegetable. Use Monterey Jack cheese with pepper. Use snipped parsley.
Herbed Baked Fish Fillets: Use semisoft natural cheese with garlic and herbs. Use seafood-cocktail sauce for cooking sauce. Use green-pepper rings for vegetable. Use Cheddar cheese. Use snipped chives.

Lemon-Butter Sauce

YIELD	2/3 cup	1/3 cup
INGREDIENTS		
butter or margarine, melted	1/2 cup	1/4 cup
lemon juice	1/4 cup	2 tablespoons
grated lemon peel	1 teaspoon	1/2 teaspoon
dried leaf herb	1/4 teaspoon	1/8 teaspoon
onion powder	1/8 teaspoon	dash
garlic powder	1/8 teaspoon	dash
cayenne pepper	dash	dash

In a small bowl, combine all ingredients; mix well. Serve with fish or seafood. Or, use to baste fish or seafood during broiling or baking.

Suggested Herbs: thyme, dill weed, tarragon, basil, oregano.

How to Make Basic Baked Fish Fillets

1/To make the creamy topping, mix together flavored semisoft cheese with some cooking sauce. For Herbed Baked Fish Fillets, use semisoft cheese with garlic and herbs and seafood-cocktail sauce. Generously spread cheese mixture over fillets in a baking dish. Sprinkle fillets with dry breadcrumbs.

2/Bake in a 350F (175C) oven until thickest part of fillet is beginning to flake when tested with a fork. Arrange vegetable slices, such as green-pepper rings, on fish. Sprinkle with shredded cheese and garnish with snipped herb. These fillets have Cheddar cheese and snipped chives.

Butter-Baked Fish Fillets or Steaks

SERVINGS	4	2	1
INGREDIENTS			
skinned fish fillets, 1/4 to 1/2 inch thick	4 (4-oz.) fillets	2 (4-oz.) fillets	1 (4-oz.) fillet
OR			
fish steaks, 3/4 to 1 inch thick	4 (5-oz.) steaks	2 (5-oz.) steaks	1 (5-oz.) steak
butter or margarine, melted	1/4 cup	2 tablespoons	1 tablespoon
lemon juice	2 tablespoons	1 tablespoon	1 teaspoon
dried leaf herb	1/2 teaspoon	1/4 teaspoon	1/8 teaspoon
snipped parsley, paprika	to garnish	to garnish	to garnish
BAKING DISH	12" x 7" baking dish	8-inch-square baking dish	7-inch pie plate
TIME IN 350F (175C) OVEN:			
fillets	18 to 20 minutes	18 to 20 minutes	18 to 20 minutes
steaks	20 to 23 minutes	20 to 23 minutes	20 to 23 minutes

Do not preheat oven. If necessary, cut large fillets into 4- or 5-ounce serving pieces. Arrange fillets or steaks in a baking dish, see size in chart above. In a small bowl, combine butter or margarine, lemon juice and herb. Spoon over fish. Bake in a 350F (175C) oven for time in chart above or until center of fish is beginning to flake when tested with a fork. Sprinkle with parsley and paprika before serving.

Suggested Herbs: thyme, dill weed, tarragon, basil, oregano.

Stuffed Fish Fillets

SERVINGS	8	4
INGREDIENTS		
Florentine Rice Stuffing, below, or Wine-Mushroom Stuffing, page 206	large recipe	small recipe
skinned flounder or sole fillets, 1/4 inch thick	8 (5- to 6-oz.) fillets	4 (5- to 6-oz.) fillets
butter or margarine, melted	1/2 cup	1/4 cup
dry white wine	2 tablespoons	1 tablespoon
lemon juice	2 tablespoons	1 tablespoon
shredded lemon peel	1 teaspoon	1/2 teaspoon
dry mustard	1 teaspoon	1/2 teaspoon
toasted sliced almonds	1/2 cup	1/4 cup
snipped parsley	2 tablespoons	1 tablespoon
BAKING DISH	13" x 9" baking dish	10" x 6" baking dish
TIME IN 350F (175C) OVEN	30 to 35 minutes	30 to 35 minutes

Do not preheat oven. Prepare Florentine Rice Stuffing or Wine-Mushroom Stuffing. Spread about 1/4 cup stuffing over each fillet. Cover and refrigerate any remaining stuffing. Roll up, jelly-roll style, starting at narrow end. Secure with wooden picks or tie with string. Place, seam-side down, in a baking dish, see size in chart above. In a small bowl, whisk together butter or margarine, wine, lemon juice, lemon peel and dry mustard. Spoon over fillets. Bake, uncovered, in a 350F (175C) oven 30 to 35 minutes or until center of fish is beginning to flake when tested with a fork. Spoon any remaining stuffing around fish in baking dish during last 10 minutes of cooking time. Remove picks or string from fish. Spoon some pan juices over fish. Sprinkle with toasted almonds and parsley before serving.

Florentine Rice Stuffing

YIELD	2-1/2 cups	1-1/4 cups
INGREDIENTS		
bacon, cut in 1-inch pieces	6 slices	3 slices
bacon drippings	1/4 cup	2 tablespoons
chopped onion	1/2 cup	1/4 cup
chopped celery	1/2 cup	1/4 cup
chopped carrot	1/2 cup	1/4 cup
frozen chopped spinach, cooked, well-drained	1 (10-oz.) pkg.	1/2 (10-oz.) pkg.
cooked rice	1 cup	1/2 cup
shredded lemon peel	2 teaspoons	1 teaspoon
plain yogurt	1/2 cup	1/4 cup
SKILLET	11-inch skillet	9-inch skillet
TIME AT MEDIUM HIGH (bacon)	8 to 10 minutes	7 to 9 minutes
TIME AT MEDIUM HIGH (vegetables)	5 to 6 minutes	4 to 5 minutes

In a skillet, see size in chart above, cook bacon over Medium-High heat for time in chart above or until crisp, stirring often. Remove bacon with a slotted spoon and drain on paper towels; set aside. Reserve in skillet amount of drippings listed in chart above. Cook onion, celery and carrot in reserved drippings over Medium-High heat for time in chart above or until tender, stirring often. Press spinach in a sieve to remove as much water as possible. Stir bacon, spinach, rice, and lemon peel into skillet; mix well. Stir in yogurt. Use as stuffing for Stuffed Whole Fish, page 206, or Stuffed Fish Fillets, above.

Stuffed Fish Fillets with Florentine Rice Stuffing

Stuffed Whole Fish

SERVINGS	4 to 6	2 or 3
INGREDIENTS		
Florentine Rice Stuffing, page 204, or Wine-Mushroom Stuffing, below	small recipe for large fish or large recipe for 4 small fish	small recipe
cleaned, whole, large fish, 2 to 2-1/2 inches thick OR	1 (3- to 4-lb.) fish with head and tail	1 (1-1/2- to 2-lb.) fish with head and tail
cleaned whole trout or other small whole fish	4 (12-oz.) fish with heads and tails	2 (12-oz.) fish with heads and tails
butter or margarine, melted	2 tablespoons	1 tablespoon
dried leaf herb	1 teaspoon	1/2 teaspoon
lemon or lime slices	8	4
BAKING PAN	15" x 10" x 2" baking pan	13" x 9" baking pan
TIME IN 350F (175C) OVEN:		
large fish	45 to 60 minutes	40 to 50 minutes
small fish	35 to 40 minutes	35 to 40 minutes

Do not preheat oven. Prepare Florentine Rice Stuffing or Wine-Mushroom Stuffing. Remove head, tail and fins from fish, if desired. Fill cavity of cleaned fish with stuffing. Cover and refrigerate any remaining stuffing. Tie fish cavity closed in several places with string so fish holds its shape. Place fish in a baking pan, see size in chart above. In a small bowl, combine butter or margarine and herb. Brush butter or margarine mixture over fish. Top with lemon or lime slices. Bake in a 350F (175C) oven for time in chart above or until center of thickest part of fish is beginning to flake when tested with a fork. Spoon any extra stuffing around fish in baking pan during last 10 minutes of cooking time.

Suggested Herbs: thyme, dill weed, tarragon, basil, oregano.

Wine-Mushroom Stuffing

YIELD	2 cups	1 cup
INGREDIENTS		
sliced fresh mushrooms	4 cups	2 cups
sliced leeks	1/2 cup	1/4 cup
chopped celery	1/2 cup	1/4 cup
dry white wine	1/2 cup	1/4 cup
snipped parsley	1/4 cup	2 tablespoons
Worcestershire sauce	2 teaspoons	1 teaspoon
lemon juice	2 teaspoons	1 teaspoon
dried leaf tarragon	1 teaspoon	1/2 teaspoon
garlic salt	1/4 teaspoon	1/8 teaspoon
freshly ground pepper	1/4 teaspoon	1/8 teaspoon
SKILLET	12-inch skillet	10-inch skillet
TIME AT MEDIUM	23 to 25 minutes	10 to 12 minutes

In a skillet, see size in chart above, combine all ingredients; mix well. Bring to a boil over High heat. Reduce heat to Medium. Simmer, uncovered, for time in chart above or until most of wine and juices evaporate, stirring occasionally. Use as stuffing for Stuffed Whole Fish, above, or Stuffed Fish Fillets, page 204.

Tips for Preparing Whole Fish for Cooking

- Ask someone at the market to scale the fish; it is a messy job. Otherwise, scrape off scales with a sharp knife.
- Rinse fish inside and out under cold water, removing stray scales. Pat dry on paper towels.

How to Make Oven-Braised Whole Fish

1/Fill cavity of cleaned fish with chopped vegetables. This red snapper is stuffed with mushrooms, leeks and zucchini. Tie cavity closed in several places with string so fish holds its shape during cooking.

2/Place sliced vegetables evenly in bottom of a floured roasting bag set in a baking pan. Sliced carrots, celery and onion are in this roasting bag. Place fish on vegetables. Spoon a wine-butter sauce over fish. Top with sliced tomato and lime; close bag. Make slits in bag; bake.

Oven-Braised Whole Fish

SERVINGS	4 to 6	2 or 3
INGREDIENTS		
cleaned, whole, large fish,	1 (3- to 4-lb.) fish	1 (1-1/2- to 2-lb.) fish
2 to 2-1/2 inches thick	with head and tail	with head and tail
chopped vegetables	2/3 cup	1/3 cup
sliced vegetables	2 cups	1 cup
butter or margarine, melted	1/4 cup	2 tablespoons
dry white wine	1/4 cup	2 tablespoons
tomato, lemon, lime slices	8	4
ROASTING BAG	20" x 14" bag	16" x 10" bag
BAKING PAN	15" x 10" x 2" baking pan	13" x 9" baking pan
TIME IN 350F (175C) OVEN	45 to 50 minutes	35 to 40 minutes

Do not preheat oven. Remove head, tail and fins from fish, if desired. Fill cavity of cleaned fish with chopped vegetables. Tie fish cavity closed in several places with string so fish holds its shape. Lightly flour a roasting bag, see size in chart above. Set bag in a baking pan, see size in chart above. Arrange sliced vegetables evenly in bottom of floured bag. Place fish on vegetables in bag. In a small bowl, combine butter or margarine and wine. Spoon over fish. Arrange tomato, lemon or lime slices on fish. Close bag with an ovenproof twist tie. Make 6 (1/2-inch) slits in top of bag. Bake in a 350F (175C) oven for time in chart above or until center of thickest part of fish is beginning to flake when tested with a fork inserted through slit in roasting bag. Carefully open bag and let steam escape. Serve fish with vegetables.

Suggested Chopped Vegetables (to stuff fish): mushrooms, green onion, fennel, leeks, zucchini, yellow crookneck squash.
Suggested Sliced Vegetables (in roasting bag): onions, green or red pepper, carrots, celery.

Fancy Fish en Coquilles

(Fancy Fish in Shells)

SERVINGS	6	3
INGREDIENTS		
Caper Sauce, page 310	medium recipe	small recipe
boned, drained, cooked fish, broken in chunks or cubed	2 cups (about 1 lb.)	1 cup (about 8 oz.)
drained cooked peas and carrots	1/2 cup	1/4 cup
dry breadcrumbs	2 tablespoons	1 tablespoon
grated Parmesan cheese	2 tablespoons	1 tablespoon
snipped parsley	2 teaspoons	1 teaspoon
butter or margarine, melted	2 teaspoons	1 teaspoon
BAKING SHELLS	6 (4-1/2 " x 4-3/4 ") shells	3 (4-1/2" x 4-3/4 ") shells
TIME IN 425F (220C) OVEN	20 to 25 minutes	20 to 25 minutes

Do not preheat oven. Prepare Caper Sauce. Fold in cooked fish and peas and carrots. Spoon into 3 or 6 (4-1/2 " x 4-3/4 ") baking shells. In a small bowl, combine breadcrumbs, Parmesan cheese, parsley and butter or margarine; mix well. Sprinkle on fish mixture. Place shells on a baking sheet. Bake in a 425F (220C) oven 20 to 25 minutes or until heated through.

Seafood Shells au Gratin

SERVINGS	4	2
INGREDIENTS		
deveined, peeled, cooked shrimp, lump crabmeat or lobster, cut in 1/2-inch pieces	2 cups	1 cup
finely chopped green onion	1/4 cup	2 tablespoons
finely chopped pimiento	1/4 cup	2 tablespoons
coarse saltine-cracker crumbs	2/3 cup	1/3 cup
snipped parsley	2 tablespoons	1 tablespoon
dried leaf tarragon	1 teaspoon	1/2 teaspoon
dry white wine	about 2 tablespoons	about 1 tablespoon
conchiglioni (jumbo pasta sea shells), cooked, drained, rinsed, patted dry	12 (about 4 oz.)	6 (about 2 oz.)
Mornay Sauce, page 310	large recipe	medium recipe
paprika	to garnish	to garnish
BAKING DISH	13" x 9" baking dish	10" x 6" baking dish
TIME IN 375F (190C) OVEN	25 to 30 minutes	25 to 30 minutes

Do not preheat oven. In a medium bowl, toss together cooked shrimp, crabmeat or lobster, green onion, pimiento, cracker crumbs, parsley and tarragon; mix well. Add enough white wine to moisten. Stuff about 1/4 cup seafood mixture into each cooked pasta shell. Arrange shells, filling-side up, in a baking dish, see size in chart above. Leave some space between shells. Spoon Mornay Sauce over shells, coating pasta completely. Cover tightly with foil. Bake in a 375F (190C) oven 25 to 30 minutes or until heated through. To serve, stir sauce in baking dish and spoon over shells. Sprinkle with paprika.

How to Make Fancy Fish en Coquilles

1/Prepare Caper Sauce. Break cooked, boned fish in chunks, or cube fish if flesh is firm enough. Fold fish and cooked peas and carrots into Caper Sauce.

2/Spoon fish mixture into large baking shells. Sprinkle with a mixture of breadcrumbs, Parmesan cheese, parsley and butter or margarine. Place on a baking sheet and bake.

Scalloped Oysters

SERVINGS	6 to 8	3 or 4
INGREDIENTS		
butter or margarine, melted	1/2 cup	1/4 cup
coarse saltine-cracker crumbs	3 cups	1-1/2 cups
snipped parsley	2 tablespoons	1 tablespoon
finely chopped green onion	2 tablespoons	1 tablespoon
paprika	1/4 teaspoon	1/8 teaspoon
shucked oysters, drained	1 qt. (2 lbs., about 44)	1 pint (1 lb., about 22)
whipping cream	1/4 cup	2 tablespoons
Worcestershire sauce	2 teaspoons	1 teaspoon
bottled hot-pepper sauce	1/4 teaspoon	1/8 teaspoon
freshly ground pepper	1/4 teaspoon	1/8 teaspoon
PIE PLATE	10-inch pie plate	7-inch pie plate
TIME IN 350F (175C) OVEN	55 to 60 minutes	35 to 40 minutes
STANDING TIME	5 minutes	5 minutes

Do not preheat oven. In a large bowl, combine butter or margarine, cracker crumbs, parsley, green onion and paprika. Reserve 1-1/3 cups cracker mixture for large recipe topping or 2/3 cup for small recipe; set aside. Add oysters to remaining cracker mixture. Toss gently to mix. In a small bowl, combine whipping cream, Worcestershire sauce, hot-pepper sauce and pepper; mix well. Stir into oyster mixture. Spoon into a pie plate, see size in chart above. Sprinkle with reserved crumbs. Bake in a 350F (175C) oven for time in chart above or until edges of oysters in center of pie plate have started to curl and crumbs are browned. Let stand, uncovered, 5 minutes before serving.

Basic Tuna-Noodle Casserole

SERVINGS	4 to 6	2 or 3
INGREDIENTS		
medium noodles	3 cups uncooked (4 oz.)	1-1/2 cups uncooked (2 oz.)
tuna, drained, broken in chunks	1 (6-1/2-oz.) can	1 (3-1/4-oz.) can
chopped vegetables	2 cups	1 cup
mayonnaise or tartar sauce	1/2 cup	1/4 cup
condensed cream soup	1 (10- to 11-oz.) can	1/2 (10- to 11-oz.) can (2/3 cup)
milk	1/2 cup	1/4 cup
seasoning	2 teaspoons	1 teaspoon
shredded cheese	1 cup (4 oz.)	1/2 cup (2 oz.)
nuts	1/2 cup	1/4 cup
snipped parsley	to garnish	to garnish
CASSEROLE	2-qt. casserole	1-qt. casserole
TIME IN 375F (190C) OVEN	50 to 55 minutes	35 to 40 minutes

Do not preheat oven. Cook noodles according to package directions; drain. In a casserole, see size in chart above, combine tuna, vegetables and mayonnaise or tartar sauce; mix well. Fold in cooked noodles. In a medium bowl, whisk together soup, milk and seasoning until blended. Stir in cheese. Fold soup mixture into tuna mixture. Sprinkle with nuts. Bake in a 375F (190C) oven for time in chart above or until heated through. Garnish with parsley.

Suggested Combinations

Swiss Tuna-Noodle Casserole: Use sliced green olives, chopped onion, chopped green pepper and shredded carrot for vegetables. Use mayonnaise. Use cream of onion soup. Use dried leaf basil and dry mustard for seasoning. Use Swiss cheese. Use slivered almonds for nuts.

Cheddar Tuna-Noodle Casserole: Use sliced celery, chopped pimiento, chopped green onion and thawed frozen peas for vegetables. Use tartar sauce. Use creamy chicken-mushroom soup. Use celery seed and Dijon-style mustard for seasoning. Use Cheddar cheese. Use chopped pecans for nuts.

Tips for Using Tuna & Salmon in Casseroles

- For casseroles, use chunk-style tuna instead of the more expensive solid-pack variety. Save more by buying light tuna rather than fancy white albacore tuna. To reduce calories, choose water-pack tuna.

- For casseroles, use pink salmon rather than more expensive red salmon. Pink salmon also flakes more easily.

- To make casseroles on pages 212 and 213 even better, substitute leftover cooked salmon for canned salmon.

How to Make Baked Tuna-Salad Casserole

1/Drain and flake tuna. In a baking dish, toss tuna with celery, fresh fruit, toasted nuts and green onion. This casserole has pears and seedless red grapes for fruit and toasted pecans for nuts.

2/Whisk together mayonnaise and lemon juice. Fold in shredded cheese—in this case, Cheddar. Fold into tuna mixture. Sprinkle with lightly crushed potato chips. Bake in a 425F (220C) oven.

Baked Tuna-Salad Casserole

SERVINGS	5 or 6	2 or 3
INGREDIENTS		
tuna, drained, flaked	2 (6-1/2-oz.) cans	1 (6-1/2-oz.) can
chopped celery	1 cup	1/2 cup
chopped fresh fruit	1 cup	1/2 cup
toasted nuts	1/2 cup	1/4 cup
chopped green onion	1/4 cup	2 tablespoons
mayonnaise or mayonnaise-style salad dressing	2/3 cup	1/3 cup
lemon juice	2 tablespoons	1 tablespoon
shredded cheese	1 cup (4 oz.)	1/2 cup (2 oz.)
potato chips, lightly crushed	to garnish	to garnish
BAKING DISH	8-inch-square baking dish	7-inch pie plate
TIME IN 425F (220C) OVEN	25 minutes	20 minutes

Do not preheat oven. In a baking dish, see size in chart above, combine tuna, celery, fruit, nuts and green onion. In a small bowl, whisk together mayonnaise or salad dressing and lemon juice. Fold in cheese. Fold cheese mixture into tuna mixture. Sprinkle chips on casserole. Bake in a 425F (220C) oven for time in chart above or until heated through.

Suggested Fruit: apples, pears, well-drained mandarin-orange sections, seedless grapes.
Suggested Nuts: slivered almonds, pecan halves, cashews, halved macadamia nuts.
Suggested Cheese: Cheddar, Swiss, Monterey Jack.

Basic Salmon- or Tuna-Rice Squares Photo on page 317.

SERVINGS	8	4
INGREDIENTS		
eggs	4	2
milk	2 cups	1 cup
shredded cheese	1 cup (4 oz.)	1/2 cup (2 oz.)
chopped vegetables	2/3 cup	1/3 cup
seasoning	2 teaspoons	1 teaspoon
hot cooked rice	3 cups	1-1/2 cups
salmon, drained, broken in chunks, bones and skin removed OR	1 (16-oz.) can	1 (7-3/4-oz.) can
tuna, drained, broken in chunks	2 (6-1/2-oz.) cans	1 (6-1/2-oz.) can
paprika	to garnish	to garnish
sauce, see suggestions below		
BAKING DISH	12" x 7" baking dish	9" x 5" x 3" loaf dish
TIME IN 325F (165C) OVEN	55 to 60 minutes	45 to 50 minutes
STANDING TIME	10 minutes	5 minutes

Preheat oven to 325F (165C). In a large bowl, beat eggs slightly with a fork or whisk. Stir in milk, cheese, vegetables and seasoning; mix well. Fold in rice and salmon or tuna. Pour evenly into a baking dish, see size in chart above. Sprinkle with paprika. Bake in a 325F (165C) oven for time in chart above or until a knife inserted off-center comes out clean. Cover with foil and let stand for time in chart above before serving. To serve, cut in squares. Ladle sauce over squares.

Suggested Combinations
Salmon-Rice Squares: Use Cheddar cheese. Use sliced ripe olives, sliced green onion and chopped pimiento for vegetables. Use Worcestershire sauce for seasoning. Use white rice. Use salmon. Serve with Zucchini Cream Sauce, page 316.
Italian Tuna-Rice Squares: Use mozzarella cheese. Use chopped, seeded, peeled tomatoes, chopped green pepper and chopped onion for vegetables. Use dried leaf oregano and dry mustard for seasoning. Use brown rice. Use tuna. Serve with Spanish Sauce, page 312.

Cucumber-Dill Sauce

YIELD	2/3 cup	1/3 cup
INGREDIENTS		
cucumber-sour-cream dip	1/2 cup	1/4 cup
finely chopped, seeded, peeled cucumber	1/4 cup	2 tablespoons
chopped green onion	2 tablespoons	1 tablespoon
prepared horseradish	1 teaspoon	1/2 teaspoon
dried dill weed	1/8 teaspoon	dash

In a small bowl, combine all ingredients; mix well. Cover and refrigerate until serving time. Serve with hot or cold fish.

How to Make Basic Tuna- or Salmon-Loaf Pie

1/Combine flaked tuna or salmon with cracker crumbs and chopped fruit and vegetables. Apple-Tuna-Loaf Pie has onion-cracker crumbs, chopped celery and chopped apple. Add eggs, cooking sauce, mustard and lemon juice. Mix until thoroughly combined.

2/Grease a baking dish. Pat fish mixture gently into baking dish. Bake in a 350F (175C) oven 25 to 30 minutes or until firm and set in center. Cover with foil and let stand 5 minutes. Cut in wedges to serve. Serve tuna loaf with warmed applesauce.

Basic Tuna- or Salmon-Loaf Pie

SERVINGS	4 to 6	2 or 3
INGREDIENTS		
salmon, drained, flaked, bones and skin removed	1 (16-oz.) can	1 (7-3/4-oz.) can
OR		
tuna, drained, flaked	2 (6-1/2-oz.) cans	1 (6-1/2-oz.) can
crushed-cracker crumbs	1 cup	1/2 cup
chopped vegetables, fruit	1/2 cup	1/4 cup
eggs, slightly beaten	2	1
cooking sauce	1/2 cup	1/4 cup
prepared mustard	2 teaspoons	1 teaspoon
lemon juice	2 teaspoons	1 teaspoon
sauce, see suggestions below		
BAKING DISH	9-inch pie plate	6-inch ovenproof skillet
TIME IN 350F (175C) OVEN	25 to 30 minutes	25 to 30 minutes
STANDING TIME	5 minutes	5 minutes

Do not preheat oven. Grease a baking dish, see size in chart above. In a medium bowl, combine salmon or tuna, cracker crumbs and chopped fruit and vegetables; mix well. Add eggs, cooking sauce, mustard and lemon juice; mix well. Pat gently into greased baking dish. Bake in a 350F (175C) oven 25 to 30 minutes or until firm and set in center. Cover with foil and let stand 5 minutes. To serve, cut in wedges. Serve sauce with wedges.

Suggested Combinations
Pacific-Salmon-Loaf Pie: Use salmon. Use sesame-cracker crumbs. Use finely chopped onion and green pepper for vegetables. Use chili sauce for cooking sauce. Serve with tartar sauce for sauce.
Apple-Tuna-Loaf Pie: Use tuna. Use onion-cracker crumbs. Use finely chopped celery and chopped peeled apple for vegetables and fruit. Use mayonnaise for cooking sauce. Serve with warmed applesauce for sauce.

Poaching Liquid for Fish

YIELD	4 cups	2 cups	1 cup
INGREDIENTS			
water	2 cups	1 cup	1/2 cup
dry white wine	1 cup	1/2 cup	1/4 cup
sliced vegetables	1-1/2 cups	3/4 cup	1/3 cup
parsley	6 sprigs	3 sprigs	1 sprig
lemon slices	4	2	1
bay leaf	1 large	1 small	1/2 small
peppercorns	16	8	4
flavored salt	1/2 teaspoon	1/4 teaspoon	1/8 teaspoon
SKILLET	see size in recipes for poached fillets or steaks, below, whole fish, opposite, or scallops, page 216		
COOKING TIME	see timings in recipes for poached fillets or steaks, below, whole fish, opposite, or scallops, page 216		

In a skillet, see size in chart, combine all ingredients. Bring to a boil over High heat. Follow directions for Poached Fish Fillets or Steaks, below, Poached Whole Fish, opposite, or Poached Scallops, page 216.

Suggested Vegetables: sliced onion, sliced carrots, sliced leeks, sliced celery, sliced parsley root, sliced green onion, sliced mushrooms.
Suggested Flavored Salt: celery salt, onion salt, garlic salt.

Poached Fish Fillets or Steaks

SERVINGS	6 to 8	3 or 4	1 or 2
INGREDIENTS			
Poaching Liquid for Fish, above	large recipe	medium recipe	small recipe
fish fillets, 1/2 to 3/4 inch thick	8 (4-oz.) fillets	4 (4-oz.) fillets	2 (4-oz.) fillets
OR			
fish steaks, 3/4 to 1 inch thick	6 (5-oz.) steaks	3 (5-oz.) steaks	1 (5-oz.) steak
SKILLET	12-inch skillet	10-inch skillet	8-inch skillet
TIME AT MEDIUM LOW:			
fillets	5 to 7-1/2 minutes	5 to 7-1/2 minutes	5 to 7-1/2 minutes
steaks	7-1/2 to 10 minutes	7-1/2 to 10 minutes	7-1/2 to 10 minutes

In a skillet, see size in chart above, prepare Poaching Liquid for Fish. Add fish fillets or steaks to hot poaching liquid. Bring to a boil over High heat. Reduce heat to Medium Low; cover. Simmer for time in chart above. If steaks are not immersed in poaching liquid, turn steaks over halfway through cooking time. Fish is done when center is beginning to flake when tested with a fork. Remove fish from liquid with a slotted spatula. Serve poached fish hot or cold with fish sauces, see page 222. Or, use for cooked fish in Basic Fish en Papillote, page 216, or Fancy Fish en Coquilles, page 208. To use poaching liquid as stock, strain through cheesecloth.

How to Make Poached Whole Fish

1/For a pan-dressed fish, cut off tail with a sharp knife. With knife at an angle, cut down on both sides of fin on back of fish, cutting as close to bone as possible. Remove fin on underside of fish in the same way. Remove head by cutting just behind fin on side of fish.

2/Tie fish cavity closed in several places. Add fish to hot poaching liquid in a skillet or roasting pan, depending on size of fish. If necessary, add enough water to poaching liquid so liquid comes halfway up fish. When done, thickest part of fish will begin to flake when tested with a fork.

Poached Whole Fish

SERVINGS	3 to 6	1 or 2
Poaching Liquid for Fish, opposite	large recipe	medium recipe
cleaned, whole, large fish, 1-1/2 to 2-3/4 inches thick OR	1 (3- to 4-lb.) fish with head and tail	1 (1-1/2-lb.) fish with head and tail
cleaned whole trout or other small whole fish, 1 to 1-1/4 inches thick	2 (12-oz.) fish with heads and tails	1 (12-oz.) fish with head and tail
DEEP ROASTING PAN OR SKILLET (large fish) OR	15" x 9" roasting pan	10- to 12-inch skillet
SKILLET (small fish)	12-inch skillet	12-inch skillet
TIME AT MEDIUM LOW: large fish small fish	20 to 30 minutes 10 to 12-1/2 minutes	15 to 20 minutes 10 to 12-1/2 minutes

In a roasting pan or skillet, see size in chart above, prepare Poaching Liquid for Fish. Remove head, tail and fins from fish, if desired. If using large whole fish, tie fish cavity closed in several places with string so fish holds its shape. If using small fish, wrap each fish in a piece of cheesecloth. Add fish to hot poaching liquid. If necessary, add water to poaching liquid so liquid comes halfway up fish. Bring to a boil over High heat. Reduce heat to Medium Low; cover. Simmer for time in chart above. Turn fish over with large slotted spatulas halfway through cooking time. Fish is done when center or thickest part of fish is beginning to flake when tested with a fork. Remove fish from liquid with slotted spatulas. Remove string or cheesecloth. Serve poached fish hot or cold with fish sauces, see page 222. To use poaching liquid as stock, strain through cheesecloth.

Basic Fish en Papillote

(Basic Fish in Parchment)

SERVINGS	6	3
INGREDIENTS		
Poached Fish Fillets or Steaks, page 214	6 steaks or fillets	3 steaks or fillets
large-size frozen vegetables, cooked, drained	2 (10-oz.) pkgs.	1 (10-oz.) pkg.
chopped vegetable	1/4 cup	2 tablespoons
condensed cream soup	2 (10- to 11-oz.) cans	1 (10- to 11-oz.) can
cooking sauce	2/3 cup	1/3 cup
all-purpose flour	2 tablespoons	1 tablespoon
dried leaf herb	1 teaspoon	1/2 teaspoon
lemon juice	4 teaspoons	2 teaspoons
garnish, see suggestions below		
BAKING PARCHMENT	6 (12-inch) squares	3 (12-inch) squares
BAKING DISH	15" x 10" x 1" baking pan	12" x 7" baking dish
TIME IN 425F (220C) OVEN	25 to 30 minutes	25 to 30 minutes

Prepare Poached Fish Fillets or Steaks. Preheat oven to 425F (220C). Butter 1 side of 3 or 6 (12-inch) baking-parchment squares. Place squares buttered-side up. Place cooked frozen vegetables and chopped vegetable in 1 corner of each square, leaving 1-1/2-inch border on each side. Top with cooked fish. In a medium bowl, whisk together soup, cooking sauce, flour, herb and lemon juice. Spoon over fish. Fold half of each parchment square over fish to make a triangle; fold edges to seal. Place packets, folded edges up, in a baking dish, see size in chart above. Bake in preheated oven 25 to 30 minutes or until fish is heated through. Slit open packets. Garnish according to suggestions below.

Suggested Combinations

Zesty Snapper en Papillote: Use red-snapper fillets for poached fish. Use broccoli spears for frozen vegetables. Use chopped celery for chopped vegetable. Use cream of shrimp soup. Use seafood-cocktail sauce for cooking sauce. Use thyme for herb. Garnish each packet with several cooked, whole, small shrimp and snipped chives.

Sophisticated Salmon en Papillote: Use salmon steaks for poached fish. Use asparagus spears for frozen vegetables. Use chopped pimiento for chopped vegetable. Use cream of onion soup. Use tartar sauce for cooking sauce. Use dill weed for herb. Garnish each packet with several hard-cooked-egg slices and sprigs of dill weed.

Poached Scallops

SERVINGS	4	2
INGREDIENTS		
Poaching Liquid for Fish, page 214	large recipe	medium recipe
fresh, small bay scallops or frozen, large sea scallops	2 lbs.	1 lb.
SKILLET	12-inch skillet	10-inch skillet
TIME AT MEDIUM LOW (small bay scallops)	1-1/2 minutes	1-1/2 minutes
TIME AT MEDIUM (large sea scallops)	5 minutes	5 minutes

In a skillet, see size in chart above, prepare Poaching Liquid for Fish. Add scallops to hot poaching liquid. Bring to a boil over High heat. Reduce heat to Medium Low for bay scallops or Medium for frozen sea scallops; cover. Simmer for time in chart above or until scallops are opaque when cut in center. Remove scallops with a slotted spoon. Serve with fish sauces, see page 222, or use for cooked scallops in recipes. To use poaching liquid as stock, strain through cheesecloth.

Sophisticated Salmon en Papillote

Boiled Whole Lobster

SERVINGS	4	2
INGREDIENTS		
water	4 gallons	2 gallons
live whole lobster	4 (1-lb.) lobsters	2 (1-lb.) lobsters
Lemon-Butter Sauce, melted, page 202	large recipe	small recipe
CANNING KETTLE	6-gallon canner	6-gallon canner
TIME AT MEDIUM LOW	20 minutes	20 minutes

In a 6-gallon canning kettle, bring water to a boil over High heat. Using large tongs, plunge lobsters head first into boiling water. Bring to a boil over High heat. Reduce heat to Medium Low; cover. Simmer 20 minutes or until one of small legs on side of lobster twists out easily. With large tongs, remove lobsters from water.

To serve lobster: Place lobster on its back on a large cutting board. Place a dish towel over claws. With a meat mallet, crack lobster claws. With a sharp knife, cut down center of tail section, cutting to, but not through, bottom shell. Repeat with remaining lobsters. Arrange each lobster on a serving platter. Serve lobster with Lemon-Butter Sauce or melted butter or margarine.

To eat lobster: Pull off tail flippers and suck out meat. Break small legs at joints and remove meat with picks or suck out meat. Twist off claws. Use nut crackers to crack claw enough to remove meat. Twist tail section off body. Bend shell backward to expose meat.

Boiled Shrimp

SERVINGS	4	2
INGREDIENTS		
beer	2 (12-oz.) cans	1 (12-oz.) can
water	3 cups	1-1/2 cups
onion slices	4	2
celery leaves	2 branch ends	1 branch end
parsley	4 sprigs	2 sprigs
bay leaf	1 large	1 small
mixed pickling spice	2 teaspoons	1 teaspoon
vegetable oil	2 teaspoons	1 teaspoon
fresh or frozen large (16 to 20 per lb.), medium (26 to 30 per lb.), or small (43 to 50 per lb.) shrimp in the shell	2 lbs.	1 lb.
DUTCH OVEN	5-qt. Dutch oven	3-qt. saucepan
TIME AT MEDIUM HIGH:		
large or medium shrimp	3 to 4 minutes	3 to 4 minutes
small shrimp	1-1/2 to 2 minutes	1-1/2 to 2 minutes

In a Dutch oven, see size in chart above, combine beer, water, onion, celery leaves, parsley, bay leaf, pickling spice and oil. Bring to a boil over High heat. Mixture will foam. Quickly stir in shrimp. If using frozen shrimp, break apart with a large fork. Bring to a boil over High heat. Reduce heat to Medium High. Simmer, uncovered, for time in chart above, stirring often. Shrimp are done when shells turn pink and shrimp meat is opaque when cut in center. Drain. Serve hot in the shell with Spicy Seafood Butter, page 235, if desired. Or, remove shell and sand vein; rinse and refrigerate. Serve as an appetizer with Seafood-Cocktail Sauce, page 232, or use in salads or casseroles.

How to Serve and Eat Whole Lobster

1/Place hot lobster on its back on a large board. Place a dish towel over claws. Pound each claw several times with a meat mallet.

2/With a sharp knife, split tail section of lobster lengthwise. Arrange each lobster on a serving platter.

3/Pull off tail flippers and suck out meat. Break small legs at joints and suck out meat or remove meat with picks. Dip meat in Lemon-Butter Sauce or melted butter or margarine.

4/Twist off claws. Use a nut cracker to finish cracking claw enough to remove meat. Many people consider this meat the "tenderloin" of lobster. Twist off tail section. Bend shell back to expose meat.

Seafood Newburg

SERVINGS	4	2
INGREDIENTS		
deveined, peeled, cooked shrimp, lump crabmeat or lobster, cut up	2 cups	1 cup
dry sherry	1/4 cup	2 tablespoons
butter or margarine	1/4 cup	2 tablespoons
all-purpose flour	1/4 cup	2 tablespoons
paprika	1/2 teaspoon	1/4 teaspoon
celery salt	1/4 teaspoon	1/8 teaspoon
freshly ground pepper	1/4 teaspoon	1/8 teaspoon
milk	2 cups	1 cup
baked patty shells	4	2
HEAVY SAUCEPAN	2-qt. saucepan	1-qt. saucepan
TIME AT MEDIUM HIGH (flour)	1 minute	1 minute
TIME AT MEDIUM HIGH (milk added)	8 to 10 minutes	4 to 5 minutes
TIME AT MEDIUM	5 to 7 minutes	3 to 5 minutes

In a medium bowl, combine shrimp, crabmeat or lobster and sherry; set aside. In a saucepan, see size in chart above, melt butter or margarine over Medium-High heat. Whisk in flour, paprika, celery salt and pepper. Cook 1 minute, whisking constantly. Whisk in milk. Cook for time in chart above or until thickened and bubbly all over, whisking constantly. Reduce heat to Medium. Stir in seafood mixture. Cover and cook for time in chart above or until heated through, stirring occasionally. Serve in patty shells.

Seafood Cocktail

SERVINGS	6	3
INGREDIENTS		
shredded lettuce or crushed ice	2 to 3 cups	1 to 1-1/2 cups
deveined, peeled, cooked shrimp, lump crabmeat or lobster, chilled	1 lb.	8 oz.
OR		
fresh oysters or cherrystone or littleneck clams on-the-half-shell	30 to 36	15 to 18
Seafood-Cocktail Sauce, page 232	1-1/2 cups	3/4 cup
lemon wedges	to garnish	to garnish
SHERBET GLASSES OR SMALL PLATES	6	3

Arrange lettuce or ice in 3 or 6 sherbet glasses or small plates. Arrange shrimp, crabmeat, lobster, oysters or clams on lettuce or ice. Serve with small cups of Seafood-Cocktail Sauce. Allow 1/4 cup sauce for each serving. Garnish with lemon wedges.

How to Make Shrimp Tostada

1/To peel shrimp, hold shrimp with legs up. Remove legs on underside of shrimp. Grasp shell on each side and peel off. With a sharp knife, make a shallow slit along top of shrimp, opposite the side where legs were removed. Remove sand vein. Wash shrimp under cold running water.

2/Toss together shredded lettuce, beets, carrot, corn and beans; cover and refrigerate. Fry flour tortillas in hot oil until puffed and crisp; drain on paper towels. Top tortillas with lettuce mixture and shrimp. Garnish with shredded cheese, chilies, tomato wedges and ripe olives. Drizzle with dressing.

Shrimp Tostada

SERVINGS	4	2
INGREDIENTS		
shredded lettuce	2 cups	1 cup
sliced or chopped vegetables	2 cups	1 cup
Thousand Island dressing	1 cup	1/2 cup
picante sauce	1/2 cup	1/4 cup
vegetable oil for frying	about 1 cup	about 1 cup
flour tortillas	4 (8-inch) tortillas	2 (8-inch) tortillas
shrimp, cooked, peeled, deveined, chilled	2 lbs.	1 lb.
shredded Cheddar cheese	1 cup (4 oz.)	1/2 cup (2 oz.)
canned chopped green chilies	1 to 2 tablespoons	1 to 2 teaspoons
tomato wedges, large ripe olives	to garnish	to garnish
SKILLET	10-inch skillet	10-inch skillet
TIME AT MEDIUM HIGH	1 to 1-1/4 minutes for each side	1 to 1-1/4 minutes for each side

In a large bowl, toss together lettuce and vegetables. Cover and refrigerate. In a small bowl, stir together Thousand Island dressing and picante sauce; refrigerate. Pour oil to a depth of 1/4 inch in a 10-inch skillet. Heat over Medium-High heat until a drop of water sizzles on it. Cook flour tortillas in oil, one at a time, 1 to 1-1/4 minutes on each side or until puffed and crisp. Drain on paper towels. To serve, top tortillas with lettuce mixture. Arrange shrimp on lettuce. Sprinkle with cheese and green chilies. Garnish with tomato wedges and ripe olives. Drizzle with some dressing mixture. Serve with remaining dressing mixture.

Suggested Vegetables: chopped green onion, sliced mushrooms, chopped zucchini, chopped carrot, diced cooked beets, cooked whole-kernel corn, cooked beans.

Steamed Whole Fish

SERVINGS	2 to 4	1 or 2
INGREDIENTS		
parsley	8 sprigs	4 sprigs
burnet, if desired	4 sprigs	2 sprigs
thyme, if desired	2 sprigs	1 sprig
lemon slices	4	2
cleaned, whole, large fish, 1-1/2 to 2-3/4 inches thick	1 (3- to 4-lb.) fish with head and tail	1 (1-1/2- to 2-lb.) fish with head and tail
OR		
cleaned whole trout or other small whole fish, 1-1/4 to 1-1/2 inches thick	2 (12-oz.) fish with heads and tails	1 (12-oz.) fish with head and tail
DEEP ROASTING PAN OR SKILLET (large fish)	15" x 9" roasting pan	12-inch skillet
OR		
SKILLET (small fish)	12-inch skillet	12-inch skillet
TIME AT MEDIUM:		
large fish	20 to 30 minutes	15 to 20 minutes
small fish	10 to 12 minutes	10 to 12 minutes

Pour water to a depth of 1/2 inch in a roasting pan or skillet, see size in chart above. Place a cooking or cooling rack in bottom of pan. Water level should be below rack. Arrange herbs and lemon slices on rack. Remove head, tail and fins from fish, if desired. Tie fish cavity closed with string in several places so fish holds its shape. Place fish on herbs and lemon slices. Choose the burner closest in size to the diameter of skillet or place roasting pan over 2 burners. Bring water in roasting pan or skillet to a boil over High heat; cover tightly. Reduce heat to Medium. Cook for minimum time in chart above without lifting lid to check for doneness. Water should simmer enough to make steam escape from under lid. Cook until center or thickest part of fish is beginning to flake when tested with a fork. Serve steamed fish hot or cold with fish sauces, see below.

Tips for Sauces to Accompany Fish

- For delicious fish accompaniments in this chapter, see: Lemon-Butter Sauce, page 202; Cucumber-Dill Sauce, page 212; Tartar Sauce, page 234; and Zesty Fish Butter, page 235.

- Sauce recipes in other chapters that complement fish are: Caper Sauce, page 310; Fresh-Herb Sauce, page 311; Curried Onion-Butter Sauce, page 316; Hollandaise Sauce, page 306; Maltaise Sauce, page 306; Dill Hollandaise Sauce, page 306; Spanish Sauce, page 312; Creamy Tomato Sauce, page 312, Fish Barbecue Sauce, page 314; Easy Barbecue Sauce, page 314; and Velouté Sauce, page 310. Velouté Sauce is a tasty way to use strained stock from poached fish.

How to Make Steamed Fish Steaks

1/Pour water to a depth of 1/2 inch in a skillet. Place a cooling rack in skillet. Water level should be below rack. Arrange lemon slices and parsley, burnet and thyme sprigs on rack. Place 3/4- to 1-inch-thick fish steaks over herbs on rack.

2/Bring to a boil over High heat; cover tightly. Reduce heat to Medium. Cook 7-1/2 minutes before lifting lid to see if fish flakes when tested with a fork. Serve with Tartar Sauce, page 234. Garnish with lemon, cherry tomatoes and burnet, if desired.

Steamed Fish Fillets & Steaks

SERVINGS	4	2
INGREDIENTS		
lemon slices	4	2
parsley	8 sprigs	4 sprigs
burnet, if desired	4 sprigs	2 sprigs
thyme, if desired	2 sprigs	1 sprig
fish fillets, 1/4 to 3/4 inch thick	4 (4-oz.) fillets	2 (4-oz.) fillets
OR		
fish steaks, 3/4 to 1 inch thick	4 (5-oz.) steaks	2 (5-oz.) steaks
SKILLET	12-inch skillet	10- or 12-inch skillet
TIME AT MEDIUM:		
fillets, 1/4 inch thick	2-1/2 to 3 minutes	2-1/2 to 3 minutes
fillets, 1/2 to 3/4 inch thick	5 to 7 minutes	5 to 7 minutes
steaks	7-1/2 to 10 minutes	7-1/2 to 10 minutes

Pour water to a depth of 1/2 inch in a skillet, see size in chart above. Place a cooling rack in skillet. Water level should be below cooling rack. Arrange lemon slices and herbs on rack. If necessary, cut large fillets into 4- or 5-ounce serving pieces. Arrange fish evenly over herbs and lemon. Choose the burner closest in size to the diameter of skillet. Bring water in skillet to a boil over High heat; cover tightly. Reduce heat to Medium. Cook for minimum time in chart above without lifting lid to check for doneness. Water should simmer enough to make steam escape from under lid. Cook until center or thickest part of fish is beginning to flake when tested with a fork. Serve steamed fish hot or cold with fish sauces, see opposite.

Steamed Mussels, Clams, Shrimp or Crab

SERVINGS	3 or 4	1 or 2
INGREDIENTS		
fresh mussels or cherrystone, littleneck or steamer clams, in the shell	48	24
OR		
frozen cooked Alaskan king-crab legs	4 (8-oz.) legs	2 (8-oz.) legs
OR		
fresh medium shrimp (26 to 30 per lb.) in the shell	2 lbs.	1 lb.
lemon, sliced	1	1/2
parsley	6 sprigs	3 sprigs
mixed pickling spice	2 teaspoons	1 teaspoon
butter or margarine (clams, mussels only)	2 teaspoons	1 teaspoon
butter or margarine, melted	1/2 cup	1/4 cup
DUTCH OVEN	6-qt. Dutch oven	4-qt. Dutch oven
TIME AT MEDIUM HIGH:		
clams, mussels	5 to 7 minutes	5 to 7 minutes
shrimp	3 to 5 minutes	3 to 5 minutes
frozen crab legs	8 to 10 minutes	8 to 10 minutes

If using mussels or clams, scrub thoroughly. Remove beards from mussels. Discard extra-heavy mussels. Place mussels or clams in a sink or large bowl. Cover with a salt-water solution of 1/3 cup salt to 1 gallon water. Soak 15 minutes. Rinse. Repeat soaking and rinsing twice. Drain. If using crab legs, break each crab leg in half at center joint, using paper towels to protect your hands. Place lemon slices, parsley, pickling spice and first amount of butter or margarine (for clams or mussels only) in a Dutch oven, see size in chart above. Add water to a depth of 1/4 inch. Choose the burner closest in size to the diameter of Dutch oven. Bring to a boil over High heat. Add seafood. Bring to a boil over High heat; cover tightly. Reduce heat to Medium High. Cook for minimum time in chart above without lifting lid to check for doneness. Shake pan often. Water should simmer enough to make steam escape from under lid. Cook mussels or clams until shells just begin to open. Cook crab legs until hot in center. Cook shrimp until meat is opaque when cut in center. Discard unopened mussels or clams. Drain, reserving mussel or clam broth for dipping mussels or clams, if desired. Serve with small bowls of melted butter or margarine.

Tips for Sauces to Accompany Seafood
- See page 232 for Seafood-Cocktail Sauce.
- Other sauces that are delicious served with seafood are: Zesty Horseradish-Mustard Sauce, page 311; Horseradish Béarnaise Sauce, page 304; and Caper Hollandaise Sauce, page 306.
- Excellent bottled seafood-cocktail sauces are sold in the refrigerated section of the grocery store along with items such as prepared horseradish.

Steamed Mussels or Clams Deluxe   Photo on page 198.

SERVINGS	3 or 4	1 or 2
INGREDIENTS		
fresh mussels or cherrystone, littleneck or steamer clams, in the shells	48	24
chopped vegetables	3 cups	1-1/2 cups
olive oil	1/4 cup	2 tablespoons
chopped seeded tomatoes	2 cups	1 cup
dry white wine	1 cup	1/2 cup
dried leaf herb	2 teaspoons	1 teaspoon
DUTCH OVEN	6-qt. Dutch oven	4-qt. Dutch oven
TIME AT MEDIUM HIGH (vegetables)	9 to 11 minutes	5 to 7 minutes
TIME AT MEDIUM HIGH (clams or mussels added)	5 to 7 minutes	5 to 7 minutes

Clean and soak mussels and clams according to directions for Steamed Mussels, Clams, Shrimp or Crab, opposite. Choose the burner closest in size to the diameter of the Dutch oven, see size in chart above. In Dutch oven, cook chopped vegetables in olive oil over Medium-High heat for time in chart above or until tender, stirring occasionally. Stir in tomatoes, wine and herb. Bring to a boil over High heat. Add mussels or clams. Bring to a boil over High heat; cover tightly. Reduce heat to Medium High. Cook for minimum time in chart above without lifting lid to check for doneness. Shake pan often. Cook until shells just begin to open. Discard unopened mussels or clams. Serve mussels or clams, vegetables and cooking broth in soup bowls.

Suggested Vegetables: onion, celery, green pepper, carrot.
Suggested Herbs: thyme, marjoram.

Steamed Whole Lobster

SERVINGS	4	2
INGREDIENTS		
lemon, sliced	1	1/2
parsley	6 sprigs	3 sprigs
live whole lobster	4 (1- to 1-1/4-lb.) lobsters	2 (1- to 1-1/4-lb.) lobsters
butter or margarine, melted	1/2 cup	1/4 cup
DEEP ROASTING PAN WITH LID	17" x 12" roasting pan	15" x 9" roasting pan
TIME AT MEDIUM	20 to 25 minutes	20 to 25 minutes

Place lemon slices and parsley sprigs in a roasting pan, see size in chart above. Set pan over 2 burners. Add water to a depth of 1 inch. Bring to a boil over High heat. Add lobsters. Quickly cover pan tightly. Place a brick or other heavy object on the lid. Make sure vent in roasting-pan lid is closed. When steam is escaping from under lid of roasting pan, reduce heat to Medium. Cook for minimum time in chart above without lifting lid to check for doneness. Water should simmer enough to make steam escape from under lid. Cook until one of small legs on side of lobster twists out easily. Serve with small cups of melted butter or margarine. Follow directions for Boiled Whole Lobster, pages 218 and 219, to serve and eat lobster.

Marinated Scallop Kabobs

SERVINGS	3 or 4	1 or 2
INGREDIENTS		
Tangy Beer Marinade, below	small recipe	small recipe
medium sea scallops, about 1 inch in diameter	1 lb. (about 36)	8 oz. (about 18)
bacon slices, cut in half lengthwise, then in thirds crosswise	6 slices	3 slices
lemon wedges, halved	4	2
fresh mushroom caps	14 to 16	7 or 8
zucchini or yellow crookneck squash, cut in 1/2-inch slices, halved crosswise	1/2 medium	1/4 medium
cherry tomatoes	7 or 8	3 or 4
hot cooked rice	3 or 4 servings	1 or 2 servings
SKEWERS	8 (12-inch) skewers	4 (12-inch) skewers
BROILER PAN WITH RACK	15" x 15" pan	14" x 10" pan
REFRIGERATE	2 hours	2 hours
TIME AT BROIL (first side)	3 to 4 minutes	3 to 4 minutes
TIME AT BROIL (second side)	1-1/2 to 2 minutes	1-1/2 to 2 minutes

Prepare Tangy Beer Marinade. Refrigerate scallops in marinade according to marinade recipe, about 2 hours. Drain scallops, reserving marinade. Pat scallops dry on paper towels. Wrap 1/6 slice of bacon around each scallop, securing bacon around scallop as each is threaded on a skewer. Dip lemon wedges and vegetables in marinade. On 4 or 8 (12-inch) skewers, thread bacon-wrapped scallops, alternating with lemon wedges, mushroom caps and squash slices. Leave small spaces between scallops and vegetables on each skewer. Leave room at end of each skewer for cherry tomatoes to be added later. Preheat an electric broiler. You do not need to preheat a gas broiler. Place skewers on a rack in a broiler pan, see size in chart above. Turn each scallop bacon-side up. Place broiler pan on an oven rack so the broiler element is 2 to 3 inches away from top of food on skewer. Broil on first side 3 to 4 minutes. Using hot pads, turn skewers over. Add 1 cherry tomato to end of each skewer. Brush vegetables only with reserved marinade. Do not brush scallops or bacon will not cook. Broil on second side 1-1/2 to 2 minutes or until bacon is brown. Serve kabobs on hot cooked rice.

Tangy Beer Marinade

YIELD	1-1/3 cups	2/3 cup
INGREDIENTS		
vegetable oil	1/2 cup	1/4 cup
beer	1/2 cup	1/4 cup
steak sauce	2 tablespoons	1 tablespoon
vinegar	2 tablespoons	1 tablespoon
Worcestershire sauce	4 teaspoons	2 teaspoons
garlic powder	1/4 teaspoon	1/8 teaspoon
REFRIGERATE	2 hours	2 hours

In a screw-top jar, combine all ingredients. Cover and shake well. To marinate shrimp or scallops, place in a heavy plastic bag set in a deep bowl. To marinate fish fillets or steaks, place in a single layer in a heavy plastic bag set in a shallow baking dish. Pour marinade over seafood or fish. Tie bag tightly closed. Refrigerate 2 hours, rearranging seafood or fish in bag or turning bag over once. Drain, reserving marinade. Use for Broiled Shrimp, opposite, Marinated Scallop Kabobs, above, or Marinated Broiled Fish, page 228. Baste seafood or fish with reserved marinade during broiling time.

How to Make Marinated Scallop Kabobs

1/Leave a small space between items on the skewer. Broil scallop kabob with bacon-side of scallops toward broiler element. After broiling on first side, turn skewers over and add cherry tomatoes to end of each skewer. Brush vegetables with reserved marinade. Do not brush scallops or bacon will not cook.

2/Broil on second side until bacon is brown. Spoon hot cooked rice onto serving plates. Sprinkle with snipped parsley. Using a hot pad, hold a skewer at an angle on plate. Slip scallops and vegetables off skewer with a large meat fork. Or, serve skewers on a serving platter on parsleyed rice.

Broiled Shrimp

SERVINGS	4	2
INGREDIENTS		
Deviled Meat Marinade, page 138, or Tangy Beer Marinade, opposite	small recipe	small recipe
fresh or thawed, frozen, medium shrimp in the shell (26 to 30 per lb.)	2 lbs.	1 lb.
BROILER PAN WITH RACK	15" x 15" pan	14" x 10" pan
REFRIGERATE	2 hours	2 hours
TIME AT BROIL (first side)	2-1/2 to 3-1/2 minutes	2-1/2 to 3-1/2 minutes
TIME AT BROIL (second side)	1-1/2 to 2 minutes	1-1/2 to 2 minutes

Prepare Deviled Meat Marinade or Tangy Beer Marinade. Peel raw shrimp, leaving tails intact. Remove sand vein. Refrigerate shrimp in marinade according to marinade recipe, about 2 hours. Drain shrimp, reserving marinade. Preheat an electric broiler. You do not need to preheat a gas broiler. Pour water to a depth of 1/4 inch in bottom of a broiler pan, see size in chart above. Place shrimp on a rack in broiler pan. Brush with reserved marinade. Place broiler pan on an oven rack so the broiler element is 2 to 3 inches away from top of shrimp. Broil on first side 2-1/2 to 3-1/2 minutes. Turn shrimp over. Brush with reserved marinade. Broil on second side 1-1/2 to 2 minutes or until shrimp are opaque when cut in center. Brush with marinade before serving.

Broiled Fish

SERVINGS	4	2
INGREDIENTS		
Lemon-Butter Sauce, page 202, or Zesty Fish Butter, page 235	1/4 cup	2 tablespoons
lemon slices, parsley sprigs, if desired		
skinned fish fillets, 1/4 to 1/2 inch thick	4 (4-oz.) fillets	2 (4-oz.) fillets
OR		
fish steaks or skinned fillets, 3/4 to 1 inch thick	4 (5-oz.) fillets or steaks	2 (5-oz.) fillets or steaks
OR		
cleaned whole trout or other small whole fish	4 (12-oz.) fish with heads and tails	2 (12-oz.) fish with heads and tails
lemon wedges, snipped parsley	to garnish	to garnish
BROILER PAN WITH RACK	14" x 10" pan	11" x 7" pan
TIME AT BROIL (first side):		
fillets, 1/4 to 1/2 inch thick	2 to 3 minutes	2 to 3 minutes
fillets or steaks, 3/4 to 1 inch thick	4 to 5 minutes	4 to 5 minutes
small whole fish	6 to 7 minutes	6 to 7 minutes
TIME AT BROIL (second side):		
fillets, 1/4 to 1/2 inch thick	1 to 2 minutes	1 to 2 minutes
fillets or steaks, 3/4 to 1 inch thick	4 to 5 minutes	4 to 5 minutes
small whole fish	5 to 6 minutes	5 to 6 minutes

Prepare Lemon-Butter Sauce or Zesty Fish Butter. Preheat an electric broiler. You do not need to preheat a gas broiler. Pour water to a depth of 1/4 inch in bottom of a broiler pan, see size in chart above. Add several lemon slices and parsley sprigs to water in pan, if desired. If necessary, cut large fillets into 4- or 5-ounce serving pieces. Lightly score (make shallow slits in) whole fish diagonally 3 times on each side. Place fish on a rack in broiler pan. Brush with some butter sauce. Place broiler pan on an oven rack so the broiler element is 3 to 4 inches from fillets and steaks or 4 to 5 inches from small whole fish. Measure from top of fish to broiler element. Broil fish on first side for time in chart above. Turn fish over with a spatula. Brush with more butter sauce. Broil fish on second side for time in chart above or until thickest part of whole fish or center of fillets and steaks is beginning to flake when tested with a fork. Brush with more butter sauce before serving. Garnish with lemon wedges and parsley.

Variations

Marinated Broiled Fish: Marinate fish in Tangy Beer Marinade, page 226, before cooking. Baste with reserved marinade instead of butter sauce during broiling. Use large recipe of marinade for 4 servings; use small recipe for 2 servings.

Crumb-Topped Broiled Fish: Brush fish with butter sauce; then sprinkle each serving with 1 to 2 teaspoons fine dry breadcrumbs before last 30 seconds of broiling time. Do not allow crumbs to burn. This is recommended for thin fillets because they broil too quickly to brown.

How to Make Broiled Lobster Tails Deluxe

1/Using sharp scissors, split soft-shell undersides of lobster tails lengthwise in center. Fold back shell. Insert wooden skewers lengthwise so tails will lie flat during cooking. Pour water to a depth of 1/4 inch in bottom of a broiler pan with a rack.

2/Broil, hard-shell sides up. Turn lobster tails over. Cover tail and soft shells that have been folded back with small pieces of foil to prevent scorching. Brush lobster meat with Spicy Seafood Butter, page 235. Broil on second side until lobster meat is opaque when cut in center of thickest part.

Broiled Lobster Tails Deluxe

SERVINGS	4 to 8	2 to 4
INGREDIENTS		
Spicy Seafood Butter, page 235, melted	large recipe	small recipe
lobster tails	4 (6-oz., 10-oz. or 16-oz.) tails	2 (6-oz., 10-oz. or 16-oz.) tails
BROILER PAN WITH RACK	14" x 10" pan	11" x 7" pan
TIME AT BROIL (first side):		
6-oz. tails	8 to 10 minutes	8 to 10 minutes
10-oz. tails	10 to 12 minutes	10 to 12 minutes
16-oz. tails	13 to 15 minutes	13 to 15 minutes
TIME AT BROIL (second side):		
6-oz. tails	5 to 7 minutes	5 to 7 minutes
10-oz. tails	5 to 7 minutes	5 to 7 minutes
16-oz. tails	8 to 10 minutes	8 to 10 minutes

Prepare Spicy Seafood Butter; set aside. Preheat an electric broiler. You do not need to preheat a gas broiler. Using sharp scissors, split soft-shell undersides of lobster tails lengthwise in center. Fold back shell. In each shell, insert a wooden skewer lengthwise so tails will lie flat during cooking. Pour water to a depth of 1/4 inch in bottom of a broiler pan, see size in chart above. Place lobster tails, hard-shell sides up, on a rack in broiler pan. Place broiler pan on an oven rack so the broiler element is 4 to 5 inches from tops of lobster tails. Broil on first side for time in chart above. Turn lobster tails over. Using small pieces of foil, cover tails and soft shells that have been folded back along sides of lobster tails. This prevents scorching. Brush lobster meat with some Spicy Seafood Butter. Broil on second side for time in chart above or until lobster meat is opaque when cut in center of thickest part. Brush with Spicy Seafood Butter twice during broiling time. Remove skewers. Serve with small cups of Spicy Seafood Butter.

Fish & Seafood 229

Stir-Fried Sweet & Sour Shrimp

SERVINGS	4	2
INGREDIENTS		
packed brown sugar	1/2 cup	1/4 cup
cornstarch	2 tablespoons	1 tablespoon
tomato sauce	1 (8-oz.) can	1/2 (8-oz.) can (1/2 cup)
red-wine vinegar	1/2 cup	1/4 cup
vegetable oil	2 tablespoons	1 tablespoon
fresh medium shrimp (26 to 30 per lb.), peeled, deveined	1 lb.	8 oz.
vegetable oil	2 tablespoons	1 tablespoon
red or green pepper, cut in 1/8-inch strips	1 large	1 small
green onions, cut in 1-inch pieces	8	4
pineapple chunks, drained	1 (8-oz.) can	1/2 (8-oz.) can
sliced water chestnuts, drained	1 (8-oz.) can	1/2 (8-oz.) can
hot cooked rice	4 servings	2 servings
WOK OR HEAVY SKILLET	wok or 12-inch skillet	wok or 10-inch skillet
TIME AT 375F (190C) OR MEDIUM HIGH (shrimp)	6-1/2 to 7-1/2 minutes	6-1/2 to 7-1/2 minutes
TIME AT 375F (190C) OR MEDIUM HIGH (vegetables)	3 to 4 minutes	3 to 4 minutes
TIME AT 375F (190C) OR MEDIUM HIGH (thicken sauce)	3 to 4 minutes	45 to 60 seconds

In a small bowl, combine brown sugar and cornstarch; mix well. Whisk in tomato sauce and red-wine vinegar until smooth; set aside. In a wok or heavy skillet, see size in chart above, heat first amount of oil over Medium-High heat until a drop of water sizzles on it. Use 375F (190C) on an electric wok or skillet. Add shrimp. Cook 6-1/2 to 7-1/2 minutes, stirring and tossing shrimp constantly until shrimp is opaque when cut in center. Remove shrimp with a slotted spoon; set aside. Add second amount of oil. Add red or green pepper and green onion. Cook over Medium-High heat or at 375F (190C) 3 to 4 minutes or until vegetables are crisp-tender, stirring and tossing constantly. Return shrimp to wok. Add pineapple and water chestnuts. Stir in tomato-sauce mixture. Cook over Medium-High heat or at 375F (190C) for time in chart above or until thickened and bubbly all over, stirring constantly. Serve over hot cooked rice.

Tips for Cleaning Shrimp

- Shrimp can be cleaned raw or cooked. It is easier to peel and devein shrimp under cold running water.
- To peel shrimp, remove shell, starting from underside where small legs are located. Begin peeling off shell at head end, and work toward tail. Leave tail section intact as a handle if shrimp will be served whole, either fried or in a chilled cocktail.
- To devein peeled shrimp, use a small sharp knife to score (lightly slit) along back of shrimp, opposite from where legs were. Remove small black sand vein that runs along back of shrimp just under the surface.

How to Make Stir-Fried Sweet & Sour Shrimp

1/In a wok or heavy skillet, heat oil until a drop of water sizzles on it. Add deveined, peeled, raw shrimp. Cook at 375F (190C) or over Medium-High heat 6-1/2 to 7-1/2 minutes, stirring and tossing shrimp constantly. Cook until shrimp is opaque when cut in center.

2/Remove shrimp. Add more oil and stir-fry red or green pepper and green onion until crisp-tender, stirring and tossing constantly. Add shrimp, pineapple chunks and water chestnuts. Stir in sweet-sour tomato-sauce mixture. Cook and stir until thickened and bubbly all over.

Basic Oven-Fried Fish

SERVINGS	4	2
INGREDIENTS		
flavored cracker crumbs	1/2 cup	1/4 cup
dried leaf herb	1/2 teaspoon	1/4 teaspoon
poppy or sesame seed	1/4 teaspoon	1/8 teaspoon
skinned fish fillets, 1/2 to 3/4 inch thick	4 (4-oz.) fillets	2 (4-oz.) fillets
lemon juice or creamy salad dressing	4 teaspoons	2 teaspoons
butter or margarine, melted	2 tablespoons	1 tablespoon
snipped parsley, lime wedges	to garnish	to garnish
BAKING DISH	12" x 7" baking dish	8-inch-square baking dish
TIME IN 500F (260C) OVEN	10 to 12 minutes	10 to 12 minutes

Preheat oven to 500F (260C). On a piece of waxed paper, combine cracker crumbs, herb and herb seed; mix well. Place fillets, former skin-side down, on another piece of waxed paper. Drizzle with lemon juice or spread with salad dressing. Sprinkle with crumb mixture. With a spatula, carefully place fillets, crumb-side up, in a baking dish, see size in chart above. Drizzle evenly with butter or margarine. Bake in preheated oven 10 to 12 minutes or until fish is beginning to flake in center when tested with a fork. Garnish with snipped parsley and lime wedges.

Suggested Crackers: cheese crackers, onion crackers, saltines.
Suggested Herbs: oregano, basil, dill weed, thyme.
Suggested Salad Dressings: creamy cucumber dressing, creamy onion dressing, creamy Italian dressing, buttermilk dressing.

Deep-Fried Fish & Seafood

SERVINGS	2 to 4	1 or 2
INGREDIENTS		
skinned fish fillets, 1/4 to 3/4 inch thick, cut in half crosswise	4 (4-oz.) fillets	2 (4-oz.) fillets
OR		
peeled, raw, medium shrimp or large sea scallops	1 lb. (about 30 to 40)	8 oz. (about 15 to 20)
OR		
shucked oysters or clams, drained	1 pint (about 20 to 24)	1/2 pint (about 10 to 12)
egg	1	1
water	2 tablespoons	2 tablespoons
all-purpose flour	1/4 to 1/2 cup	2 to 4 tablespoons
seasoned dry breadcrumbs	1 to 1-1/3 cups	1/2 to 2/3 cup
vegetable oil for deep-frying	2 qts.	2 qts.
DEEP-FAT FRYER OR HEAVY DUTCH OVEN	5-qt. fryer or Dutch oven	5-qt. fryer or Dutch oven
FRYING TIME AT 350F (175C):		
fillets, 1/4 inch thick	2 to 3 minutes	2 to 3 minutes
fillets, 1/2 to 3/4 inch thick	4-1/2 to 5-1/2 minutes	4-1/2 to 5-1/2 minutes
shrimp	3-1/2 to 4-1/2 minutes	3-1/2 to 4-1/2 minutes
scallops	2-1/2 to 3-1/2 minutes	2-1/2 to 3-1/2 minutes
oysters	2-1/2 to 3 minutes	2-1/2 to 3 minutes
clams	2 to 2-1/2 minutes	2 to 2-1/2 minutes

Rinse fish or seafood. Pat dry on paper towels. In a pie plate, whisk together egg and water. Place flour on a piece of waxed paper. Place breadcrumbs on another piece of waxed paper. Coat fish or seafood with flour. Dip in egg mixture, then in crumb mixture, coating all sides well. Place breaded fish on a rack; set aside. Pour oil into a 5-quart deep-fat fryer or Dutch oven. Fryer should be about half full of oil. Preheat oil to 350F (175C) or until a 1-inch cube of bread turns golden brown in 65 seconds. Fry fish or seafood, several pieces at a time, in hot oil for time in chart above or until browned. Fish is done when it flakes in center when tested with a fork. Seafood is done when it is opaque when cut in center. Remove with a slotted spoon and drain on paper towels. Keep warm in a 250F (120C) oven while frying remaining fish or seafood. Do not keep warm more than 20 minutes or coating will lose crispness.

Seafood-Cocktail Sauce

YIELD	3-1/3 cups	1-2/3 cups
INGREDIENTS		
chili sauce	2 cups	1 cup
prepared horseradish	2/3 cup	1/3 cup
coarsely chopped onion	1/2 cup	1/4 cup
lemon juice	1/4 cup	2 tablespoons
Worcestershire sauce	4 teaspoons	2 teaspoons
bottled hot-pepper sauce	1 teaspoon	1/2 teaspoon
grated lemon peel	1 teaspoon	1/2 teaspoon
PROCESSING TIME	45 to 60 seconds	45 to 60 seconds

In a blender or food processor fitted with a steel blade, combine all ingredients. Process 45 to 60 seconds or until blended. Cover and refrigerate until serving time. Serve with seafood dishes.

Deep-Fried Shrimp with Seafood-Cocktail Sauce

Pan-Fried Fish

SERVINGS	2 to 4	1 or 2
INGREDIENTS		
milk	2 tablespoons	1 tablespoon
yellow cornmeal	2 tablespoons	1 tablespoon
packaged biscuit mix	2 tablespoons	1 tablespoon
all-purpose flour	2 tablespoons	1 tablespoon
sesame seed	1 teaspoon	1/2 teaspoon
paprika	1/4 teaspoon	1/8 teaspoon
celery salt	1/4 teaspoon	1/8 teaspoon
onion powder	dash	dash
skinned fish fillets, 1/4 to 3/4 inch thick	1 lb.	8 oz.
OR		
cleaned whole trout or other small whole fish	2 (12-oz.) fish with heads and tails	1 (12-oz.) fish with head and tail
vegetable oil for frying	about 1-1/3 cups	about 1 cup
SKILLET	12-inch skillet	10- to 12-inch skillet
TIME AT MEDIUM HIGH (first side):		
fillets, 1/4 inch thick	3 minutes	3 minutes
fillets, 1/2 to 3/4 inch thick	4 minutes	4 minutes
whole trout	5 to 6 minutes	5 to 6 minutes
TIME AT MEDIUM (second side):		
fillets, 1/4 inch thick	1-1/2 to 2 minutes	1-1/2 to 2 minutes
fillets, 1/2 to 3/4 inch thick	3 to 4 minutes	3 to 4 minutes
whole trout	6 to 7 minutes	6 to 7 minutes

Pour milk into a pie plate. In another pie plate, combine cornmeal, biscuit mix, flour, sesame seed, paprika, celery salt and onion powder. Dip fish in milk; shake off excess milk. Dip in cornmeal mixture, pressing mixture gently onto all sides. Place breaded fish on a rack; set aside. Pour oil to a depth of 1/4 inch in a skillet, see size in chart above. Heat oil over Medium-High heat until a drop of water sizzles on it. Add fish in a single layer. Cook on first side for time in chart above. Turn fish over. Reduce heat to Medium. Cook on second side for time in chart above or until fish flakes in center when tested with a fork. Drain on paper towels.

Tartar Sauce

YIELD	1-1/2 cups	3/4 cup
INGREDIENTS		
plain yogurt	1/2 cup	1/4 cup
mayonnaise or mayonnaise-style salad dressing	1/2 cup	1/4 cup
chopped dill pickle	1/2 cup	1/4 cup
sliced green olives	1/2 cup	1/4 cup
onion powder	1/4 teaspoon	1/8 teaspoon
freshly ground pepper	1/4 teaspoon	1/8 teaspoon

In a medium bowl, combine all ingredients; mix well. Cover and refrigerate until serving time. Serve with hot or cold fish.

Zesty Fish Butter

YIELD	1-1/2 cups	3/4 cup
INGREDIENTS		
onion, cut up	1/2 small	1/4 small
Dijon-style mustard	4 teaspoons	2 teaspoons
Worcestershire sauce	2 teaspoons	1 teaspoon
bottled hot-pepper sauce	1/4 teaspoon	1/8 teaspoon
dry white wine	2 tablespoons	1 tablespoon
lemon juice	2 tablespoons	1 tablespoon
butter or margarine, softened	1 cup	1/2 cup
PROCESSING TIME (seasonings, liquid)	30 seconds	30 seconds
PROCESSING TIME (butter added)	2 minutes	2 minutes

In a food processor fitted with a steel blade, process onion, Dijon-style mustard, Worcestershire sauce, hot-pepper sauce, wine and lemon juice 30 seconds or until smooth. Stop processor and scrape down sides 3 times. Add butter or margarine. Process 2 minutes longer or until well-mixed. Stop processor and scrape down sides 3 times. Serve on hot cooked fish. Or, melt Zesty Fish Butter and use to baste fish during broiling or baking. Keeps, covered, in the refrigerator up to several weeks.

Spicy Seafood Butter

YIELD	1-1/2 cups	3/4 cup
INGREDIENTS		
onion, cut up	1/2 small	1/4 small
garlic	1 small clove	1/2 small clove
celery seed	1 teaspoon	1/2 teaspoon
dried leaf tarragon	1 teaspoon	1/2 teaspoon
white pepper	1/8 teaspoon	dash
dry white wine	2 tablespoons	1 tablespoon
lemon juice	2 tablespoons	1 tablespoon
butter or margarine, softened	1 cup	1/2 cup
drained capers	2 teaspoons	1 teaspoon
prepared horseradish	1 teaspoon	1/2 teaspoon
PROCESSING TIME (seasonings, liquid)	30 seconds	30 seconds
PROCESSING TIME (butter added)	2 minutes	2 minutes

In a food processor fitted with a steel blade, process onion, garlic, celery seed, tarragon, white pepper, wine and lemon juice 30 seconds or until smooth. Stop processor and scrape down sides 3 times. Add butter or margarine. Process 2 minutes longer or until well-mixed. Stop processor and scrape down sides 3 times. By hand, stir in capers and horseradish. Serve on shrimp, scallops, clams or oysters. Melt Spicy Seafood Butter over Low heat before serving, if desired. Stir well before serving. Keeps, covered, in the refrigerator up to several weeks.

Eggs & Cheese

For low cost, high nutrition and versatility, eggs and cheese are hard to match. You will find egg and cheese classics in this chapter, plus new ways to serve this ever-popular combination.

Springtime Mock Quiche, page 263.

Eggs & Cheese

Q. What do egg sizes mean?

A. Egg size is based on weight per dozen. A dozen extra-large eggs weigh at least 27 ounces. Large eggs weigh at least 24 ounces. Medium eggs weigh at least 21 ounces.

Q. Which eggs are the best buy?

A. The best buy varies according to the cost per ounce (unit cost). To determine unit cost for each size, divide the price of the eggs by the approximate ounces in a carton. Divide the price of extra-large eggs by 27; divide the price of large eggs by 24; divide the price of medium eggs by 21. This allows you to determine the best buy.

Q. Do egg sizes make a difference in cooking?

A. In our test kitchens, we used refrigerated extra-large eggs for testing recipes in this book. In most recipes, you may use any egg size. If the amount of egg is critical, we include a cup measure as a guide.

Q. What is the best way to store eggs?

A. Eggs must be refrigerated. Warm temperatures cause rapid loss of quality and spoilage. Eggs keep up to 5 weeks in the refrigerator. Store eggs in the carton with the large end up to help keep the yolk centered. Do not use cracked or checked eggs because of possible salmonella contamination.

Refrigerate hard-cooked eggs promptly after cooking, and use within 1 week. Refrigerate leftover whites in a covered jar up to 7 days. Cover leftover yolks with water; cover container and refrigerate. Use within 2 days.

Q. Can eggs be frozen successfully?

A. Clean, fresh, separated eggs freeze very well. Leftover egg whites can be frozen easily. Pour into freezer containers, seal tightly, label and freeze. Thaw frozen egg whites in containers overnight in the refrigerator or under cold running water. Use thawed whites just as you would fresh, substituting 2 tablespoons thawed egg white for 1 large fresh egg white. The whites will beat to better volume if you let them stand at room temperature 30 minutes before beating.

You can also freeze egg yolks or whole eggs, but you need to give them special treatment. Mix yolks or whole eggs thoroughly but do not whip in air. Eggs should not be frothy. Pour into freezer containers. For every 4 egg yolks or every 2 whole eggs, add one of the following: 1/8 teaspoon salt, 1-1/2 teaspoons sugar or 1-1/2 teaspoons corn syrup. Seal tightly; label with the number of yolks or eggs, and the seasoning added (salt for main dishes, sweetening for desserts). Substitute 3 tablespoons thawed whole egg for 1 large fresh whole egg, or 1 tablespoon thawed egg yolk for 1 large fresh egg yolk. Use thawed frozen eggs only in dishes that will be well-cooked. Eggs, egg whites or egg yolks may be stored in the freezer 8 to 10 months.

Q. Are there any secrets for making perfect hard-cooked eggs?

A. Follow directions on page 240 for cooking eggs. Plunge eggs into cold water immediately after cooking. This stops the cooking process and helps prevent a dark ring from forming around the yolk. This ring is harmless, but not very attractive. Generally, very fresh eggs are more difficult to peel because they have a smaller air pocket.

If you mix up hard-cooked and fresh eggs in the shell, spin the eggs on their side. Hard-cooked eggs spin evenly like a top. Fresh eggs wobble as they spin.

Q. Are there some tips for getting the most volume when whipping egg whites?

A. Start with room-temperature egg whites. Separate eggs carefully. Even a tiny speck of yolk will prevent whites from whipping properly. This is because of the fat in the egg yolk. Use bowls and beaters that have no grease film. Do not use plastic bowls because they often have a grease film—even when clean. Follow recipe directions for adding sugar. If sugar is added too quickly or not quickly enough, egg whites will not reach their maximum volume. The tips of stiff-beaten egg whites stand straight up when the beaters are lifted from the bowl. The tips of egg whites beaten to soft peaks curl over when beaters are lifted.

Q. Is there any difference between white-shelled eggs and brown-shelled eggs?

A. No. The breed of hen determines egg-shell color. Yolks from brown eggs are often a deeper yellow and add pleasing color to cakes and omelets.

Q. Can I use an egg that has a blood spot?

A. Yes. These eggs are safe to eat, but you may want to remove the spot with the tip of a knife.

How to Separate & Beat Eggs

1/To separate egg yolk from white, crack egg in center. Gently separate egg shell into halves. Working over a custard cup, let yolk drop gently from 1 egg-shell half to other while egg white slips down sides into custard cup. Put egg yolk and egg white into separate bowls. Separate each additional egg over custard cup. If 1 yolk breaks during separation, it destroys the whipping properties of only 1 egg white—not the whole bowl of whites. Whites with any amount of yolk in them will not whip.

2/The whisk is being lifted from egg yolks that have been beaten until thick and lemon-colored. Notice lighter color and thick consistency of these yolks. What is the difference between slightly beaten and well-beaten eggs? In the foreground, frothy eggs have been well-beaten with a whisk or beater. Yolk and white are completely combined, forming homogeneous mixture. At left, slightly beaten eggs have broken yolks, but whites and yolks are not completely combined. Eggs can be slightly beaten with a fork.

Q. How long can cheese be refrigerated?

A. Hard cheese, such as Cheddar, Swiss and Parmesan, can be kept several weeks. Soft cheese, such as cream, cottage, Neufchâtel, ricotta, Brie and Camembert, is very perishable. Use it within a few days after purchase. Refrigerate cheese in the original wrapper. After opening, cover cut surfaces tightly with foil or plastic wrap to keep surfaces from drying out. Store strong-smelling cheese in tightly covered refrigerator dishes. Wrap and refrigerate process cheese after opening.

Q. What if mold develops on cheese?

A. Natural cheese sometimes develops mold spots when stored under moist conditions or when improperly wrapped. The mold is harmless and can usually be scraped off easily. If mold has deeply penetrated cheese, cut off moldy portion and discard it. Cheese that has dried out from long storage can be grated and kept in a covered container or plastic bag in the refrigerator.

Q. Should cheese be frozen?

A. You may freeze most natural cheese, up to 1 pound in size, for 6 weeks to 2 months if the original package is unopened. Freeze opened and resealed cheese packages only 6 weeks. Pasteurized process cheese can be frozen 4 months, but the texture may be affected. To freeze, limit cheese to 1 pound or less in size and no more than 1 inch in thickness. Wrap tightly in moisture-proof wrap. Seal, label and freeze. Thaw wrapped cheese in the refrigerator 24 hours. Use soon after thawing.

Cottage cheese and Neufchâtel cheese do not freeze well.

Q. What do the terms mild and sharp indicate?

A. Mild cheese is cured or ripened 2 to 3 months and has little flavor development. It is fairly soft and has a more open texture. Medium-aged cheese is cured up to 6 months. It is mellow, has a smoother texture and some of the nutty flavor of aged cheese. Sharp cheese is cured more than 6 months and has richer flavor. In cooking, sharp cheese melts more easily and blends well with other ingredients.

Hard-Cooked Eggs

SERVINGS	4 to 8	2 to 4
INGREDIENTS		
eggs	8	4
cold water	about 7 cups	about 4 cups
salt	2-1/2 teaspoons	1-1/2 teaspoons
SAUCEPAN	3-qt. saucepan	1-1/2-qt. saucepan
TIME AT LOW	20 minutes	20 minutes
STANDING TIME (in cold water)	5 minutes	5 minutes

Place eggs in a saucepan, see size in chart above. Add cold water. Allow 2 cups for first egg and about 2/3 cup for each additional egg. Water should be about 1 inch above eggs. Add salt. Use 1 teaspoon salt for each 3 cups water. Bring to a boil over High heat. Reduce heat to Low; cover. Simmer 20 minutes. Drain. Run cold water over eggs in saucepan until water remains cold in pan. Let eggs stand in cold water 5 minutes. Tap egg gently to crack shell all over. Peel under cold running water, starting at large end of egg. Use for garnishes or for Deviled Eggs, below, Deviled-Egg Rolls Cordon Bleu, opposite, Basic Egg-Salad Sandwiches, page 242, or Basic Creamed Eggs, page 242.

Variation

Soft-Cooked Eggs: To help prevent food poisoning from soft-cooked eggs, use clean, uncracked eggs. To cook, bring water to a boil over High heat. With a slotted spoon, lower eggs into boiling water. Reduce heat to Low. Cook, covered, 4 to 6 minutes, depending on desired softness of egg. Serve immediately.

Deviled Eggs

YIELD	16 egg halves	8 egg halves
INGREDIENTS		
Hard-Cooked Eggs, above	8	4
mayonnaise or mayonnaise-style salad dressing	1/3 cup	3 tablespoons
prepared mustard	2 teaspoons	1 teaspoon
celery salt	1/4 teaspoon	1/8 teaspoon
pepper	1/4 teaspoon	1/8 teaspoon
paprika, snipped chives or snipped parsley	to garnish	to garnish

Prepare Hard-Cooked Eggs. Cut hard-cooked eggs in half lengthwise. Place yolks in a small bowl; mash thoroughly with a fork. Stir in mayonnaise or salad dressing, mustard, celery salt and pepper. Using a spoon or pastry tube, fill egg whites with yolk mixture. Cover and refrigerate until serving time. Sprinkle with paprika, snipped chives or snipped parsley before serving. Or, use for Deviled-Egg Rolls Cordon Bleu, opposite.

Deviled Eggs Plus

YIELD	16 egg halves	8 egg halves
INGREDIENTS		
Same ingredients as for Deviled Eggs, above, except add:	large recipe	small recipe
chopped olives	1/4 cup	2 tablespoons
OR		
chopped pickle	1/4 cup	2 tablespoons
OR		
finely chopped green onion	2 tablespoons	1 tablespoon
OR		
chopped green chilies	2 tablespoons	1 tablespoon

Stir olives, pickle, green onion or chilies into egg-yolk mixture for Deviled Eggs. Continue following directions for Deviled Eggs.

How to Make Deviled-Egg Rolls Cordon Bleu

1/Fold rectangular slices of boiled ham in half lengthwise and place on sorrel or large spinach leaf. Place deviled-egg half near tip of leaf. Roll up leaf jelly-roll style, starting at tip end. Place, seam-side down, in au gratin or casserole dish.

2/Place 2 deviled-egg rolls in each dish. Sprinkle with chopped tomatoes, chopped onion, chopped green pepper, chopped celery, basil and shredded Swiss cheese. Bake in a 350F (175C) oven 40 to 45 minutes or until heated through.

Deviled-Egg Rolls Cordon Bleu

SERVINGS	4	2
INGREDIENTS		
Deviled Eggs, opposite	8 halves	4 halves
thinly sliced boiled ham	8 slices	4 slices
sorrel or large spinach leaves	8	4
chopped tomatoes	2 cups	1 cup
chopped onion	1/4 cup	2 tablespoons
chopped green pepper	1/4 cup	2 tablespoons
chopped celery	1/4 cup	2 tablespoons
dried leaf basil	1 teaspoon	1/2 teaspoon
shredded Swiss cheese	1/2 cup (2 oz.)	1/4 cup (1 oz.)
AU GRATIN DISHES OR INDIVIDUAL CASSEROLES	4 (8-oz.) dishes	2 (8-oz.) dishes
TIME IN 350F (175C) OVEN	40 to 45 minutes	40 to 45 minutes

Do not preheat oven. Prepare Deviled Eggs. Fold ham slices in half lengthwise. Place folded ham slice on sorrel or spinach leaf. Place 1 egg half on tip end of leaf. Roll up, jelly-roll style, starting at tip end. Place, seam-side down, in an 8-ounce au gratin or casserole dish. Repeat with remaining eggs, ham and sorrel or spinach leaves, placing 2 rolls in each dish. Sprinkle tomatoes, onion, green pepper, celery and basil evenly on rolls. Top with Swiss cheese. Bake, uncovered, in a 350F (175C) oven 40 to 45 minutes or until heated through.

Basic Egg-Salad Sandwiches

SERVINGS	4 sandwiches (2 cups filling)	2 sandwiches (1 cup filling)
INGREDIENTS		
Hard-Cooked Eggs, page 240, chopped	6	3
mayonnaise or mayonnaise-style salad dressing	1/4 cup	2 tablespoons
pickle relish	2 tablespoons	1 tablespoon
seasonings	2 teaspoons	1 teaspoon
pita-bread halves or hamburger buns, split	4	2
chopped or sliced vegetables	to garnish	to garnish
shredded or crumbled cheese	1/4 cup	2 tablespoons

Prepare Hard-Cooked Eggs. In a medium bowl, combine eggs, mayonnaise or salad dressing, pickle relish and seasonings; mix well. Cover and refrigerate until serving time. To serve, spoon into pita-bread halves or split hamburger buns. Top with vegetable garnish and cheese.

Suggested Combinations
All-American Egg-Salad Buns: Use dill-pickle relish. Use prepared mustard for seasoning. Serve in buns. Top with shredded carrot, chopped green onion and alfalfa sprouts. Use shredded Colby cheese.
Mediterranean Egg-Salad Pockets: Use sweet-pickle relish. Use dry mustard and herb pepper for seasonings. Serve in pita-bread halves. Top with sliced olives, chopped green onion, chopped tomatoes and chopped green pepper. Use crumbled feta cheese.

Basic Creamed Eggs

SERVINGS	6	3
INGREDIENTS		
Hard-Cooked Eggs, page 240, quartered	6	3
butter or margarine	1/4 cup	2 tablespoons
chopped vegetables	1 cup	1/2 cup
all-purpose flour	1/4 cup	2 tablespoons
dried leaf herb	1/2 to 1 teaspoon	1/4 to 1/2 teaspoon
pepper	1/4 teaspoon	1/8 teaspoon
milk	1 cup	1/2 cup
chicken broth	1 cup	1/2 cup
cubed cooked meat or seafood	1 cup	1/2 cup
chopped pimiento	1/4 cup	2 tablespoons
cornbread squares or patty shells	6	3
SAUCEPAN	2-qt. saucepan	1-qt. saucepan
TIME AT MEDIUM HIGH (vegetables)	4 to 5 minutes	4 to 5 minutes
TIME AT MEDIUM HIGH (flour added)	1 minute	1 minute
TIME AT MEDIUM HIGH (milk, broth added)	7 minutes	6 minutes
TIME AT MEDIUM LOW	15 to 20 minutes	15 to 20 minutes

Prepare Hard-Cooked Eggs. In a saucepan, see size in chart above, combine butter or margarine and vegetables. Cook over Medium-High heat 4 to 5 minutes or until vegetables are almost tender, stirring occasionally. Whisk in flour, herb and pepper. Cook and stir 1 minute. Whisk in milk and broth. Cook for time in chart above or until thickened and bubbly all over, stirring constantly. Fold in eggs, meat or seafood and pimiento. Reduce heat to Medium Low; cover. Cook 15 to 20 minutes or until heated through, stirring occasionally. Allow 5 to 10 minutes longer to heat if hard-cooked eggs have been refrigerated. Serve on hot cornbread squares or in baked patty shells.

Suggested Combinations
Plantation Creamed Eggs: Use chopped onion and chopped zucchini for vegetables. Use thyme in larger amount for herb. Use cubed ham for meat. Serve on cornbread squares.
Gloucester Creamed Eggs: Use chopped green onion and chopped fresh mushrooms for vegetables. Use dill weed in smaller amount for herb. Use drained cooked shrimp for seafood. Serve in patty shells.

Mediterranean Egg-Salad Pockets

Florentine Egg Ring

SERVINGS	6	4
INGREDIENTS		
frozen chopped spinach, cooked	1-1/2 (10-oz.) pkgs.	1 (10-oz.) pkg.
semisoft natural cheese with garlic and herbs	1-1/2 (3-1/2-oz.) cartons	1 (3-1/2-oz.) carton
hot cooked rice	3 cups	2 cups
chopped pimiento	3 tablespoons	2 tablespoons
eggs	6	4
shredded Cheddar cheese	6 tablespoons (1-1/2 oz.)	1/4 cup (1 oz.)
paprika	to garnish	to garnish
GLASS RING MOLD	8-cup ring mold	5-cup ring mold
TIME IN 350F (175C) OVEN	25 to 30 minutes	25 to 30 minutes
STANDING TIME	5 minutes	5 minutes

Preheat oven to 350F (175C). Butter a ring mold, see size in chart above. Press spinach in a sieve to remove as much water as possible. In a large bowl, combine hot spinach and semisoft cheese. Stir until cheese melts. Stir in rice and pimiento. Spoon into buttered ring mold. Gently press in mold. With a spoon or small measuring cup, make 1 depression in top of rice ring for each egg. Break 1 egg into each depression. Sprinkle 1 tablespoon cheese on each egg, covering yolk. Bake in preheated oven 25 to 30 minutes or until eggs are set. Let stand 5 minutes before serving. To loosen, run a knife around edges of mold. Cut between eggs. With a spatula, lift out wedges to serve. Sprinkle with paprika.

Variation
Florentine Egg Cups: For each serving, gently press 1/2 cup rice mixture into a buttered 6-ounce custard cup. Break 1 egg into center of each cup. Top with cheese as above. Bake as above.

Basic Shirred (Baked) Eggs

SERVINGS	4	2
INGREDIENTS		
cooking sauce	1/4 cup	2 tablespoons
eggs	4	2
flavored salt, pepper	to taste	to taste
dried leaf herb	1 teaspoon	1/2 teaspoon
butter or margarine	4 teaspoons	2 teaspoons
shredded cheese	1/4 cup (1 oz.)	2 tablespoons
CUSTARD CUPS	4 (6-oz.) custard cups	2 (6-oz.) custard cups
TIME IN 350F (175C) OVEN	20 to 23 minutes	20 to 23 minutes
STANDING TIME	2 minutes	2 minutes

Preheat oven to 350F (175C). Butter 2 or 4 (6-ounce) custard cups. Spoon 1 tablespoon cooking sauce into each custard cup. Break 1 egg into each cup. Sprinkle with flavored salt, pepper and herb. Cut up 1 teaspoon butter or margarine; place on each egg. Sprinkle 1 tablespoon cheese on each egg, covering yolk. Bake in preheated oven 20 to 23 minutes or until eggs are cooked to your taste. After 20 minutes, yolks will be soft. After 23 minutes, yolks will be set. Let stand 2 minutes before serving. Serve in custard cups.

Suggested Combinations
Mexican Shirred Eggs: Use taco or enchilada sauce for cooking sauce. Use celery salt for flavored salt. Use basil for herb. Use Monterey Jack cheese.
Italian Shirred Eggs: Use pizza sauce or spaghetti sauce for cooking sauce. Use onion salt for flavored salt. Use oregano for herb. Use mozzarella cheese.

How to Make Florentine Egg Ring

1/Press spinach in a sieve to remove as much water as possible. Combine spinach with semisoft cheese, hot cooked rice and pimiento.

2/Spoon spinach-rice mixture into a buttered ring mold, pressing gently so mixture will hold together.

3/Using a spoon or small measuring cup, make 1 depression in top of rice ring for each egg. Space eggs evenly around top of mold.

4/Gently slip 1 egg into each depression. Sprinkle eggs with shredded Cheddar cheese, covering yolks. Bake until set.

Poached Eggs

SERVINGS	2 to 4	1 or 2
INGREDIENTS		
white vinegar	2 tablespoons	1 tablespoon
eggs	4	2
salt and pepper	to taste	to taste
HEAVY SKILLET	10-inch skillet	8-inch skillet
TIME AT MEDIUM LOW	4 to 6 minutes	4 to 6 minutes

Pour water to a depth of 1 inch in a heavy skillet, see size in chart above. Stir in vinegar. Bring to a boil over High heat. Reduce heat to Medium Low. Break eggs, 1 at a time, into a custard cup or sauce dish. Slip eggs into water, 1 at a time, toward edge of skillet rather than toward center. Space eggs as evenly as possible in skillet. Cover and cook 4 to 6 minutes or until done to your taste. With a slotted spoon, remove eggs. Season to taste with salt and pepper; serve immediately. Or, use for Basic Poached Eggs Deluxe, below.

Note: To poach more than 1 batch of eggs, use fresh water for each batch. Otherwise, egg white from previous batch will make liquid boil over.

Basic Poached Eggs Deluxe

SERVINGS	4	2
INGREDIENTS		
hot Poached Eggs, above	4	2
hot cooked meat	8 bacon slices or 8 oz. sausage	4 bacon slices or 4 oz. sausage
tostada shells	4	2
OR		
croissants or English muffins, split, buttered, toasted	4	2
hot cooked sauce	1/2 to 1 cup	1/4 to 1/2 cup
garnish, see suggestions below		

Prepare Poached Eggs. Place each serving of meat on tostada shell or half of croissant or English muffin. Top with poached egg. Spoon sauce over eggs. Garnish according to suggestions below. Serve egg-topped croissant or muffin half with other half on the side.

Suggested Combinations
Huevos Rancheros: Use drained, cooked, fresh bulk pork sausage for meat. Use tostada shells. Use bottled taco sauce or enchilada sauce for cooked sauce. Garnish with canned chopped green chilies and shredded Cheddar cheese.

Gold Coast Eggs: Use drained crisp-cooked bacon for meat. Use croissants. Use Cheddar-Cheese Sauce, page 311, for sauce. Garnish with snipped chives and chopped pimiento.

Eggs Benedict: Use broiled Canadian-bacon slices, page 131, for meat. Use English muffins. Use Hollandaise Sauce, page 306, for cooked sauce. Garnish with sliced truffles or rolled anchovy fillets.

How to Make Poached Eggs

1/Pour water to a depth of 1 inch in a heavy skillet. It is essential to use a heavy skillet. Stir in white vinegar to help set up eggs. Bring water to a boil.

2/Break each egg into a custard cup. Slip egg into water toward edge of skillet instead of toward center. This helps center yolk.

3/Space eggs evenly in skillet. Cover and cook over Medium-Low heat 4 to 6 minutes or until done to your taste. With a slotted spoon, remove eggs from skillet.

4/For Huevos Rancheros, serve eggs over cooked sausage on tostada shells. Top with heated taco or enchilada sauce, chopped chilies and shredded cheese.

Fried Eggs

SERVINGS	2 to 4	1 or 2
INGREDIENTS		
butter, margarine, bacon drippings or sausage drippings	1/4 cup	2 tablespoons
eggs	4	2
salt and pepper	to taste	to taste
SKILLET	10-inch skillet	8-inch skillet
TIME AT MEDIUM (before basting)	30 seconds	30 seconds
TIME AT MEDIUM (basting eggs)	5 to 6 minutes	4 to 5 minutes

In a skillet, see size in chart above, heat butter, margarine, bacon drippings or sausage drippings over Medium heat until a drop of water sizzles on it. Break eggs, 1 at a time, into a custard cup or sauce dish. Slip eggs into hot fat, 1 at a time, without breaking yolks. Cook 30 seconds until whites start to set. Tilt skillet so fat runs to the side. Spoon hot fat quickly and continuously over eggs. Keeping skillet tilted, baste eggs with hot fat for time in chart above or until done to your taste. Season with salt and pepper.

Variations
Over-Easy Fried Eggs: When eggs are cooked, use a spatula to separate eggs into individual portions. Gently turn eggs over without breaking yolks. Cook over Medium heat 20 to 30 seconds.

Well-Done Fried Eggs: After first 30 seconds of cooking time, gently break yolks with a spatula. This prevents runny yolks. Continue cooking and basting until whites are cooked and yolks are firm.

Butter-Steamed Eggs

SERVINGS	2 to 4	1 or 2
INGREDIENTS		
butter or margarine	4 teaspoons	2 teaspoons
eggs	4	2
water	2 teaspoons	2 teaspoons
salt and pepper	to taste	to taste
SKILLET	10-inch skillet	8-inch skillet
TIME AT MEDIUM (without water)	1 minute	1 minute
TIME AT MEDIUM (water added)	2-1/2 to 3-1/2 minutes	1-1/2 to 2 minutes

In a skillet, see size in chart above, melt butter or margarine over Medium heat until a drop of water sizzles on it. Break eggs, 1 at time, into a custard cup or sauce dish. Slip eggs into hot fat, 1 at a time, without breaking yolks. Cover and cook 1 minute. Quickly add water around eggs. Cover and cook for time in chart above or until done to your taste. Season to taste with salt and pepper.

Variation
Over-Easy Steamed Eggs: When eggs are cooked, gently turn eggs over without breaking yolks. Cook, uncovered, over Medium heat 20 to 30 seconds.

How to Make Fried Eggs

1/Gently slip eggs, 1 at a time, into hot fat in a skillet. Cook over Medium heat 30 seconds to set white. Tilt skillet so fat runs to the side. Spoon hot fat quickly and continuously over eggs. Baste eggs with fat until white film forms over yolks and whites are set. Shake skillet to judge firmness of yolks.

2/When eggs are done, gently turn them over and cook 20 to 30 seconds if you like them "over easy." For Fried-Egg Sandwich, serve egg on whole-wheat toast topped with bacon slices. Garnish sandwich with herb pepper, grated Parmesan cheese and snipped chives.

Fried-Egg Sandwich

SERVINGS	4	2
INGREDIENTS		
hot buttered wheat toast	4 slices	2 slices
hot crisp-cooked bacon	8 slices	4 slices
hot Fried Eggs, opposite	4	2
herb pepper	1/2 teaspoon	1/4 teaspoon
grated Parmesan cheese	4 teaspoons	2 teaspoons
snipped chives	1 teaspoon	1/2 teaspoon

Place toast on hot serving plates. Top each slice of toast with 2 bacon slices and 1 fried egg. Sprinkle with herb pepper, cheese and chives.

Tips for Fried Eggs

● Use very fresh eggs for fried eggs. Yolks of eggs that have been stored a while break more easily.

● Brown crispy edge around fried egg means skillet is too hot. Reduce heat.

● For low-calorie fried egg, omit butter or margarine in Butter-Steamed Eggs, opposite, and use a non-stick skillet.

Basic Scrambled-Egg Casserole

SERVINGS	6 to 8	3 or 4
INGREDIENTS		
condensed cream soup	1 (10- to 11-oz.) can	1/2 (10- to 11-oz.) can (2/3 cup)
shredded cheese	1-1/2 cups (6 oz.)	3/4 cup (3 oz.)
dried leaf herb, ground herb or herb seed	2 teaspoons	1 teaspoon
butter or margarine	2 tablespoons	1 tablespoon
slightly beaten eggs	12	6
chopped or sliced vegetables	2 cups	1 cup
cubed or crumbled cooked meat	1 cup	1/2 cup
snipped chives	2 teaspoons	1 teaspoon
cashews or canned French-fried onions	1 cup	1/2 cup
snipped parsley	2 tablespoons	1 tablespoon
SKILLET	12-inch skillet	10-inch skillet
BAKING DISH	12" x 7" baking dish	9" x 5" x 3" loaf dish
TIME AT MEDIUM	14 to 15 minutes	5 to 6 minutes
REFRIGERATE	2 to 24 hours	2 to 24 hours
TIME IN 350F (175C) OVEN (casserole)	40 minutes	30 minutes
TIME IN 350F (175C) OVEN (topping added)	5 to 10 minutes	5 to 10 minutes

Do not preheat oven. In a medium bowl, stir together soup, cheese and herb; set aside. In a skillet, see size in chart above, melt butter or margarine over Medium heat until a drop of water sizzles on it. Add eggs, vegetables, meat and chives. Cook for time in chart above or until eggs are set, but still glossy, stirring gently so uncooked egg flows underneath. Fold in soup mixture. Spoon evenly into a baking dish, see size in chart above. Cover and refrigerate 2 to 24 hours. Uncover and bake in a 350F (175C) oven for time in chart above or until heated through. Sprinkle with cashews or French-fried onions and parsley. Bake 5 to 10 minutes longer or until topping is hot.

Suggested Combinations

Chicken-&-Scrambled-Egg Casserole: Use creamy chicken-mushroom soup. Use Swiss cheese. Use rubbed sage and thyme for herbs. Use sliced fresh mushrooms, chopped pimiento, sliced water chestnuts and thawed frozen pea pods for vegetables. Pat pea pods dry on paper towel before using. Use cubed cooked chicken or turkey for meat. Use cashews for topping.

Smoked-Sausage-&-Scrambled Egg Casserole: Use cream of onion soup. Use brick cheese. Use celery seed and dry mustard for herbs. Use cubed cooked potatoes, chopped green pepper and chopped onion for vegetables. Use cubed, fully cooked, smoked sausage for meat. Use French-fried onions for topping.

Scrambled Eggs

SERVINGS	3 or 4	1 or 2	1
INGREDIENTS			
eggs	4	2	1
milk	1/4 cup	2 tablespoons	1 tablespoon
baking powder	1/4 teaspoon	1/8 teaspoon	dash
salt and pepper	to taste	to taste	to taste
butter or margarine	2 teaspoons	1 teaspoon	1/2 teaspoon
SKILLET	10-inch skillet	8-inch skillet	6-inch skillet
TIME AT MEDIUM	3 to 3-1/2 minutes	2 to 2-1/2 minutes	1-1/2 to 2 minutes

In a small bowl, whisk together eggs, milk, baking powder, salt and pepper. In a skillet, see size in chart above, melt butter or margarine over Medium heat until a drop of water sizzles on it. Add egg mixture. Cook for time in chart above, stirring gently with a spatula so uncooked egg flows underneath. Eggs are done when set but still glossy.

How to Make Scrambled Eggs Plus

1/Sauté chopped green pepper, chopped celery and sliced mushrooms in butter or margarine called for in Scrambled Eggs. When vegetables are tender, pour in eggs whisked with milk, baking powder, salt and pepper. Stir eggs gently so uncooked egg flows underneath during cooking.

2/When eggs are almost set, stir in halved cherry tomatoes. Add sour cream, if desired. Gently lift and cook eggs until set but still glossy. Sprinkle eggs with shredded cheese, if desired. Remove skillet from heat and cover 1 minute to melt cheese.

Scrambled Eggs Plus

SERVINGS	3 or 4	1 or 2	1
INGREDIENTS			
Same ingredients as for Scrambled Eggs, opposite, except add:	large recipe	medium recipe	small recipe
chopped vegetables AND/OR	1/2 cup	1/4 cup	2 tablespoons
flavored dairy sour cream or yogurt OR	1/4 cup	2 tablespoons	1 tablespoon
cream-style cottage cheese AND/OR	1/4 cup	2 tablespoons	1 tablespoon
shredded Cheddar, Swiss or other cheese	1/4 cup	2 tablespoons	1 tablespoon

Prepare Scrambled Eggs, except:

For Scrambled Eggs with Chopped Vegetables: Use onion, green pepper, celery or sliced mushrooms. Cook vegetables in butter or margarine called for in Scrambled Eggs. Cook over Medium heat until almost tender before adding eggs to same skillet. Or, stir in halved cherry tomatoes just before eggs are done.

For Scrambled Eggs with Sour Cream or Yogurt: Stir sour cream or yogurt into eggs when eggs are almost done.

For Scrambled Eggs with Cottage Cheese: Substitute cottage cheese for milk.

For Scrambled Eggs with Shredded Cheese: Sprinkle cheese on eggs when almost done. Remove skillet from heat and cover about 1 minute to melt cheese.

French Omelet

SERVINGS	4	2	1
INGREDIENTS			
eggs	8	4	2
milk	1/4 cup	2 tablespoons	1 tablespoon
salt	1/2 teaspoon	1/4 teaspoon	1/8 teaspoon
pepper	1/4 teaspoon	1/8 teaspoon	dash
butter or margarine	8 teaspoons	4 teaspoons	2 teaspoons
Basic Omelet Filling, below OR	large recipe	medium recipe	small recipe
shredded cheese	1 cup (4 oz.)	1/2 cup (2 oz.)	1/4 cup (1 oz.)
SKILLET	8-inch skillet	8-inch skillet	8-inch skillet
TIME AT MEDIUM HIGH (each omelet)	2 to 3 minutes	2 to 3 minutes	2 to 3 minutes

In a medium bowl, combine eggs, milk, salt and pepper. Beat with a fork or whisk until well-mixed but not frothy. In an 8-inch skillet, melt 2 teaspoons butter or margarine over Medium-High heat until a drop of water sizzles on it. Pour in about 1/2 cup egg mixture. Cook 2 to 3 minutes, gently lifting edges so uncooked egg flows underneath until eggs are set. Spoon 1/4 to 1/3 cup filling or cheese across center third of omelet. Fold sides over filling. With 2 spatulas, lift omelet onto serving plate. To make additional omelets, repeat process with remaining butter or margarine, egg mixture and filling.

Basic Omelet Filling

YIELD	1 to 1-1/3 cups	1/2 to 2/3 cup	1/4 to 1/3 cup
INGREDIENTS			
butter, margarine or bacon drippings	1 tablespoon	2 teaspoons	1 teaspoon
chopped vegetables, fruit	2 cups	1 cup	1/2 cup
dried leaf herb, ground herb or ground spice	1/2 teaspoon	1/4 teaspoon	1/8 teaspoon
sour-cream dip	1/2 cup	1/4 cup	2 tablespoons
garnish, see suggestions below			
SKILLET	8-inch skillet	8-inch skillet	6-inch skillet
TIME AT MEDIUM HIGH	7 to 10 minutes	5 to 7 minutes	5 to 7 minutes

In a skillet, see size in chart above, combine butter, margarine or bacon drippings, vegetables and fruit, and herb or spice. Cook over Medium-High heat for time in chart above or until barely tender, stirring often. Stir in sour-cream dip. Cover and keep warm while making omelets.

Suggested Combinations
Mushroom Omelet Filling: Use bacon drippings. Use sliced fresh mushrooms, chopped shallots or green onion and snipped parsley for vegetables. Use fines herbes for herb. Use horseradish-and-bacon sour-cream dip. Garnish with crumbled cooked bacon and snipped parsley.

Apple-Raisin Omelet Filling: Use butter or margarine. Use chopped celery, chopped apple and raisins for vegetables and fruit. Use cinnamon for spice. Use plain dairy sour cream for dip. Garnish with chopped pecans, shredded orange peel and powdered sugar.

Spanish Omelet Filling: Use butter or margarine. Use chopped green pepper, chopped tomatoes and chopped onion for vegetables. Use chili powder for spice. Use toasted-onion sour-cream dip. Garnish with shredded Cheddar cheese and chili peppers.

How to Make French Omelet

1/Cook egg mixture in hot butter or margarine, gently lifting cooked portion with a spatula so uncooked egg flows underneath. Cook until eggs are set.

2/Spoon Basic Omelet Filling or shredded cheese across center third of omelet. This filling is for Apple-Raisin Omelet.

3/Fold sides of omelet over filling. With 2 spatulas, lift omelet onto a serving plate.

4/Garnish Apple-Raisin Omelet with chopped pecans, shredded orange peel and a dusting of powdered sugar.

Basic American Breakfast Pies

SERVINGS	6	3
INGREDIENTS		
butter or margarine	2 tablespoons	1 tablespoon
loose-pack, frozen, hash-brown potatoes	4 cups	2 cups
chopped green onion	1/2 cup	1/4 cup
dried leaf herb or ground spice	1 teaspoon	1/2 teaspoon
celery salt	1/2 teaspoon	1/4 teaspoon
butter or margarine	2 tablespoons	1 tablespoon
chopped vegetables, meat	2 cups	1 cup
milk	1-1/3 cups	2/3 cup
eggs	4	2
shredded cheese	1 cup (4-oz.)	1/2 cup (2-oz.)
CUSTARD CUPS	6 (10-oz.) custard cups	3 (10-oz.) custard cups
SKILLET	10-inch skillet	8-inch skillet
TIME AT MEDIUM HIGH (potatoes)	10 minutes	7 minutes
TIME IN 400F (205C) OVEN (potato crust)	15 minutes	15 minutes
TIME AT MEDIUM HIGH (vegetables, meat)	6 to 7 minutes	5 to 6 minutes
TIME IN 400F (205C) OVEN (pies)	20 to 25 minutes	20 to 25 minutes
STANDING TIME	5 minutes	5 minutes

Preheat oven to 400F (205C). Grease 3 or 6 (10-ounce) custard cups. In a skillet, see size in chart above, combine first amount of butter or margarine, potatoes, green onion, herb or spice and celery salt. Cook over Medium-High heat for time in chart above or until potatoes are thawed and soft, stirring often. Gently press into greased custard cups, forming crust that comes within 1/2 inch of top of cups. Place on a baking sheet. Bake in preheated oven 15 minutes. In same skillet, combine second amount of butter or margarine, vegetables and meat. Cook over Medium-High heat for time in chart above or until tender. Spoon into potato crusts. In a medium bowl, whisk together milk and eggs until smooth. Pour over vegetable mixture in crusts. Sprinkle with cheese. Bake in preheated oven 20 to 25 minutes or until puffed and set in center. Let stand 5 minutes before serving.

Suggested Combinations
Denver Breakfast Pie: Use savory for herb. Use chopped onion, chopped green pepper and chopped pimiento for vegetables. Use Cheddar cheese.

Iowa Breakfast Pie: Use basil for herb. Use diced cooked ham, cooked, drained, whole-kernel corn and chopped celery for vegetables and meat. Use caraway cheese.

Texas Breakfast Pie: Use chili powder for spice. Use canned, drained kidney beans, chopped onion and diced cooked beef for vegetables and meat. Use Longhorn cheese.

Iowa Breakfast Pie

Fluffy Omelet

SERVINGS	2 or 3	1 or 2
INGREDIENTS		
eggs, separated	4	2
water	2 tablespoons	1 tablespoon
salt	1/8 teaspoon	dash
butter or margarine	1 tablespoon	2 teaspoons
Basic Creamed Vegetables, page 355, if desired	about 1-1/2 cups	about 1 cup
OR		
Quick Cheese Sauce, below, if desired	about 2 cups	about 1 cup
MIXER BOWL (egg whites)	1-1/2-qt. bowl	1-1/2-qt. bowl
HEAVY OVENPROOF SKILLET	10- to 11-inch skillet	8- to 9-inch skillet
BEATING TIME AT HIGH SPEED (egg whites)	45 seconds	45 seconds
BEATING TIME AT HIGH SPEED (egg yolks)	4 to 5 minutes	4 to 5 minutes
TIME AT MEDIUM	7 to 8 minutes	7 to 8 minutes
TIME IN 325F (165C) OVEN	10 minutes	10 minutes

Preheat oven to 325F (165C). In a 1-1/2-quart mixer bowl, beat egg whites, water and salt at high speed of an electric mixer for 45 seconds or until stiff peaks form. Scrape sides of bowl often. In another bowl, beat egg yolks at high speed of mixer for 4 to 5 minutes or until thick and lemon-colored. Scrape sides of bowl often. Slowly pour egg yolks over egg whites and gently fold together. Some fluffs of egg white should remain. In a heavy ovenproof skillet, see size in chart above, melt butter or margarine over Medium-High heat until a drop of water sizzles on it. Gently spread egg mixture evenly in skillet. Reduce heat to Medium. Cook 7 to 8 minutes or until omelet is puffed and bottom is golden brown. Place skillet in oven. Bake in preheated oven 10 minutes or until top springs back when touched and a knife inserted in center comes out clean. To loosen omelet, run a spatula around edge of skillet. Crease center of omelet with edge of spatula. Fold omelet in half and gently roll out onto a warm platter. Serve with Basic Creamed Vegetables or Quick Cheese Sauce, if desired.

Quick Cheese Sauce

YIELD	2 cups	1 cup
INGREDIENTS		
white-sauce mix	1 (1-3/4-oz.) envelope	1 (1-oz.) envelope
milk	see amount listed on sauce package	
shredded cheese	1 cup (4 oz.)	1/2 cup (2 oz.)
SAUCEPAN	1-1/2-qt. saucepan	1-qt. saucepan

In a saucepan, see size in chart above, prepare white-sauce mix with milk according to package directions. When white sauce is thickened and bubbly all over, add cheese and stir until melted.

Tips for Omelet Sauces

- Other sauces that are good served over omelets are: Hollandaise Sauce, page 306; Cheese Sauce, page 311; Mushroom Cream Sauce, page 316; Zucchini Cream Sauce, page 316; and Spanish Sauce, page 312.
- For a do-it-yourself party, let guests make their own omelets and choose from a selection of prepared fillings and sauces.

How to Make Fluffy Omelet

1/In a heavy ovenproof skillet, cook egg mixture in hot butter or margarine over Medium heat 7 to 8 minutes. Omelet should be puffed and golden-brown on bottom.

2/Bake omelet in preheated 325F (165C) oven 10 minutes or until top springs back when touched and a knife inserted in center comes out clean. Crease center of omelet with a spatula.

3/Fold over omelet using the crease as guide for outside edge. Gently roll omelet out onto warm serving platter.

4/To serve, divide omelet into portions by using 2 forks placed back-to-back. Serve with Basic Creamed Vegetables, page 355, or Quick Cheese Sauce, opposite, if desired.

Basic Soufflé

SERVINGS	6 to 8	4 or 5	2
INGREDIENTS			
butter or margarine	6 tablespoons	1/4 cup	2 tablespoons
chopped vegetable	1/4 cup	2 tablespoons	1 tablespoon
all-purpose flour	6 tablespoons	1/4 cup	2 tablespoons
seasoning	1-1/2 teaspoons	1 teaspoon	1/2 teaspoon
milk	1-1/2 cups	1 cup	1/2 cup
crumbled or shredded cheese	2 cups	1-1/3 cups	2/3 cup
chopped vegetables, cooked meat or seafood	2 cups	1-1/3 cups	2/3 cup
eggs, separated	6	4	2
cream of tartar	3/4 teaspoon	1/2 teaspoon	1/4 teaspoon
sauce, if desired, see suggestions below	about 2 cups	about 1 cup	about 1/2 cup
SAUCEPAN	2-qt. saucepan	1-1/2-qt. saucepan	1-qt. saucepan
MIXER BOWL (egg whites)	3-qt. bowl	3-qt. bowl	1-1/2-qt. bowl
MIXER BOWL (egg yolks)	1-1/2-qt. bowl	1-1/2-qt. bowl	1-1/2-qt. bowl
SOUFFLÉ DISH	2-1/2-qt. soufflé dish	1-1/2-qt. soufflé dish	3-cup soufflé dish
TIME AT MEDIUM HIGH (vegetable)	5 minutes	3 minutes	2 minutes
TIME AT MEDIUM HIGH (flour added)	1 minute	1 minute	30 seconds
TIME AT MEDIUM HIGH (milk added)	4-1/2 to 5 minutes	4 minutes	2 minutes
BEATING TIME AT HIGH SPEED (egg whites)	1-1/2 to 2 minutes	1-1/2 to 2 minutes	45 to 60 seconds
BEATING TIME AT HIGH SPEED (egg yolks)	5 minutes	5 minutes	4 minutes
TIME IN 300F (150C) OVEN	70 to 75 minutes	70 to 75 minutes	65 to 70 minutes

Preheat oven to 300F (150C). In a saucepan, see size in chart above, melt butter or margarine. Add first amount of chopped vegetable. Cook over Medium-High heat for time in chart above or until tender, stirring occasionally. Stir in flour and seasoning. Cook and stir for time in chart above. Whisk in milk. Cook for time in chart above or until thickened and bubbly all over, whisking constantly. Remove from heat. Add cheese and stir until melted. Stir in second amount of vegetables and meat or seafood. In a mixer bowl, see size in chart above, beat egg whites and cream of tartar at high speed of an electric mixer for time in chart above or until stiff peaks form. Scrape sides of bowl often. Set aside. In a 1-1/2-quart mixer bowl, beat egg yolks at high speed of mixer for time in chart above or until thick and lemon-colored. Scrape sides of bowl often. Fold in cheese-sauce mixture. Slowly pour egg-yolk mixture over egg whites and gently fold together. Pour into ungreased soufflé dish, see size in chart above. Bake in preheated oven for time in chart above or until a knife inserted at a slant toward center comes out clean. Serve immediately with sauce, if desired.

Suggested Combinations
Seafood Soufflé: Use chopped green onion for first vegetable. Use Dijon-style mustard for seasoning. Use crumbled bleu cheese. Use chopped, drained, canned, marinated artichoke hearts and flaked, drained, canned crabmeat or lobster or drained, cooked, small shrimp for vegetables and seafood. Serve with Mushroom Cream Sauce, page 316.

Ham Soufflé: Use chopped green pepper for first vegetable. Use prepared horseradish for seasoning. Use shredded Swiss cheese. Use drained, thawed, frozen, chopped broccoli or asparagus and finely cubed cooked ham for vegetables and meat. Gently press broccoli or asparagus in a sieve to remove as much water as possible. Serve with Béchamel Sauce, page 310.

Cheese Soufflé: Use chopped onion for first vegetable. Use dry mustard for seasoning. Use Cheddar or other cheese. Omit vegetables and meat. Serve with Spanish Sauce, page 312.

How to Make Basic Soufflé

1/Beat egg whites and cream of tartar at high speed of an electric mixer until stiff peaks form. When beaters are lifted, peaks stand straight up and do not fall over.

2/Pour egg-yolk mixture over beaten egg whites. Using a rubber spatula, gently fold in yolk mixture with a circular under-and-over motion.

Basic Cheese & Crouton Strata

SERVINGS	6 to 8	3 or 4
INGREDIENTS		
flavored croutons	2 cups	1 cup
cooked ground meat or flaked cooked fish	2 cups	1 cup
chopped vegetables	2 cups	1 cup
seasoning sauce	2/3 cup	1/3 cup
seasoning	2 teaspoons	1 teaspoon
shredded cheese	1 cup (4 oz.)	1/2 cup (2 oz.)
flavored croutons	2 cups	1 cup
eggs	4	2
milk	2 cups	1 cup
BAKING DISH	12" x 7" baking dish	9" x 5" x 3" loaf dish
REFRIGERATE	2 to 24 hours	2 to 24 hours
TIME IN 350F (175C) OVEN	50 to 60 minutes	45 to 50 minutes
STANDING TIME	10 minutes	10 minutes

Do not preheat oven. Place first amount of croutons in a baking dish, see size in chart above; set aside. In a medium bowl, combine meat or fish and vegetables. Fold in seasoning sauce and seasoning. Spoon vegetable mixture evenly over croutons in baking dish. Top with cheese and second amount of croutons. In a medium bowl, whisk together eggs and milk until blended. Pour evenly over croutons in baking dish. Cover and refrigerate 2 to 24 hours. Bake, uncovered, in a 350F (175C) oven for time in chart above or until set in center. Let stand 10 minutes before serving.

Suggested Combinations
Tuna, Cheese & Crouton Strata: Use Cheddar croutons. Use flaked drained tuna for fish. Use peas, chopped green onion, chopped dill pickle and sliced olives for vegetables. Use bottled tartar sauce for seasoning sauce. Use lemon juice for seasoning. Use Cheddar cheese.
Sausage, Cheese & Crouton Strata: Use seasoned croutons. Use drained, cooked, fresh bulk pork sausage for meat. Use drained, whole-kernel corn, canned chopped green chilies and chopped onion for vegetables. Use chili sauce for seasoning sauce. Use chili powder for seasoning. Use Monterey Jack cheese.

Basic Quiche

YIELD	10-inch quiche (8 wedges)	9-inch quiche (6 wedges)	7-inch quiche (4 wedges)
INGREDIENTS			
shredded cheese	1 cup (4 oz.)	3/4 cup (3 oz.)	1/3 cup (1-1/3 oz.)
prebaked quiche shell, page 467	10-inch quiche shell	9-inch quiche shell	7-inch quiche shell
Corned-Beef, Sausage or Bacon Quiche Filling, page 262	large recipe	medium recipe	small recipe
eggs	4	3	2
half and half	2 cups	1-1/2 cups	3/4 cup
seasoning	1 teaspoon	3/4 teaspoon	1/4 teaspoon
shredded cheese	1 cup (4 oz.)	3/4 cup (3 oz.)	1/3 cup (1-1/3 oz.)
garnishes, see suggestions below			
BAKING DISH	10-inch quiche dish	9-inch pie plate	7-inch pie plate
TIME IN 375F (190C) OVEN	45 to 55 minutes	40 to 45 minutes	30 to 35 minutes
STANDING TIME	10 minutes	10 minutes	10 minutes

Preheat oven to 375F (190C). Sprinkle first amount of cheese in prebaked quiche shell. Spoon filling over cheese. In a medium bowl, combine eggs, half and half and seasoning. Beat with a whisk or fork until well-mixed but not frothy. Pour into pastry shell. Sprinkle with second amount of cheese. Bake in preheated oven for time in chart above or until a knife inserted off-center comes out clean. Let stand 10 minutes before serving. Garnish according to suggestions below.

Suggested Combinations
Reuben Quiche: Use Swiss cheese. Use Corned-Beef Quiche Filling. Use caraway seed as seasoning. Garnish each serving with shredded lettuce and Thousand Island dressing.
Sausage-Spinach Quiche: Use Cheddar cheese. Use Sausage Quiche Filling. Use thyme for seasoning. Garnish with 1 to 2 tablespoons crushed herb-seasoned stuffing before baking.
Quiche Lorraine: Use Gruyère cheese. Use Bacon Quiche Filling. Use dry mustard for seasoning. Garnish with bacon curls.

Note: For quiche shell, prepare pastry dough. Fit pastry into baking dish, see size in chart above. Flute edge, but do not prick pastry. With a piece of foil, line unbaked pastry shell. Add 1-1/2 cups dry beans. Bake in a preheated 450F (230C) oven 10 minutes. Remove foil and beans. Cool pastry shell on a rack. Reserve these beans for baking other pie shells.

Tips for Quiche

- Prebake quiche shell without pricking dough first. This helps to prevent a soggy crust. For the same reason, sprinkle crust with cheese as first layer in quiche.

- Check a basic quiche for doneness by inserting a knife *off-center* in filling. If quiche is done, knife will come out clean. Quiche will continue to cook through to center during 10-minute standing time. Cooking until quiche is set in center will cause overbaking during standing time. This may cause quiche to water. However, Basic Mock Quiche, page 263, must be cooked until a knife inserted in *center* comes out clean. If center is not set when this type of quiche is removed from the oven, it will not set up during standing time.

- Don't cut quiche straight from the oven. The 10-minute standing time is essential to allow quiche structure to set up before cutting.

- Serve very thin slices of quiche for an appetizer. Or, to make miniature quiches, see Basic Appetizer Quiche, page 38.

How to Make Basic Quiche

1/Prepare pastry shell, but do not prick shell. Line unbaked shell with foil, then add dry beans. Bake in a 450F (230C) oven 10 minutes. Remove foil and beans. Cool pastry shell on a rack.

2/Sprinkle some shredded cheese in cooled prebaked pastry shell. Spoon quiche filling over cheese. This is Corned-Beef Quiche Filling, page 262.

3/Combine eggs, half and half and seasonings until well-mixed but not frothy. Pour egg mixture into pastry shell. Sprinkle with more shredded cheese. Swiss cheese is used for Reuben Quiche.

4/When done, a knife inserted off-center in quiche will come out clean. Let quiche stand 10 minutes to firm up before serving. Garnish this quiche with shredded lettuce and Thousand Island dressing.

Bacon Quiche Filling

YIELD	1-1/3 cups	1 cup	1/2 cup
INGREDIENTS			
bacon, cut in 1-inch pieces	12 slices	9 slices	5 slices
chopped onion	1/2 cup	1/3 cup	3 tablespoons
SKILLET	10-inch skillet	8-inch skillet	6-inch skillet
TIME AT MEDIUM HIGH	14 to 15 minutes	14 to 15 minutes	14 to 15 minutes

In a skillet, see size in chart above, combine bacon and onion. Cook over Medium-High heat 14 to 15 minutes or until bacon is crisp and onion is tender, stirring often. Drain thoroughly. Use in Basic Quiche, page 260.

Sausage Quiche Filling

YIELD	2-1/4 cups	1-1/2 cups	1 cup
INGREDIENTS			
chopped cooked spinach, drained	1/2 cup	1/3 cup	3 tablespoons
fresh bulk pork sausage	12 oz.	8 oz.	4 oz.
SKILLET	10-inch skillet	8-inch skillet	6-inch skillet
TIME AT MEDIUM HIGH	8 to 9 minutes	7 to 8 minutes	7 to 8 minutes

Press spinach in a sieve to remove as much water as possible. In a skillet, see size in chart above, combine spinach and sausage. Cook over Medium-High heat for time in chart above or until sausage is browned, stirring often. Drain thoroughly. Use in Basic Quiche, page 260.

Corned-Beef Quiche Filling

YIELD	1-1/3 cups	1 cup	1/2 cup
INGREDIENTS			
butter or margarine	1 tablespoon	2 teaspoons	1 teaspoon
chopped cooked corned beef	1 cup	3/4 cup	1/3 cup
chopped green pepper	1/4 cup	2 tablespoons	1 tablespoon
drained canned sauerkraut, rinsed	1/4 cup	3 tablespoons	2 tablespoons
SKILLET	10-inch skillet	8-inch skillet	6-inch skillet
TIME AT MEDIUM HIGH	4 to 5 minutes	4 to 5 minutes	4 to 5 minutes

In a skillet, see size in chart above, combine all ingredients. Cook over Medium-High heat 4 to 5 minutes or until green pepper is tender, stirring often. Drain thoroughly. Use in Basic Quiche, page 260.

Basic Mock Quiche

SERVINGS	6 to 8	3 or 4
INGREDIENTS		
butter or margarine	2 tablespoons	1 tablespoon
sliced or chopped vegetables, meat	3 cups	1-1/2 cups
shredded cheese	1 cup (4 oz.)	1/2 cup (2 oz.)
milk	2 cups	1 cup
eggs	4	2
packaged biscuit mix	1 cup	1/2 cup
dried leaf herb	1 teaspoon	1/2 teaspoon
PIE PLATE	10-inch pie plate	7-inch pie plate
SKILLET	10-inch skillet	8-inch skillet
MIXER BOWL	1-1/2-qt. bowl	1-1/2-qt. bowl
TIME AT MEDIUM HIGH	6 to 9 minutes	5 to 7 minutes
BEATING TIME AT MEDIUM SPEED	1 minute	1 minute
TIME IN 400F (205C) OVEN	40 to 45 minutes	30 to 35 minutes
STANDING TIME	5 minutes	5 minutes

Preheat oven to 400F (205C). Grease a pie plate, see size in chart above. In a skillet, see size in chart above, combine butter or margarine, vegetables and meat. Cook over Medium-High heat for time in chart above or until tender, stirring often. Drain thoroughly. In greased pie plate, combine cooked vegetables, meat and cheese; set aside. In a 1-1/2-quart mixer bowl, combine milk, eggs, biscuit mix and herb. Beat at medium speed of an electric mixer for 1 minute or until well-combined. Place pie plate on an oven rack. Carefully pour batter over vegetable mixture in pie plate. Bake in preheated oven for time in chart above or until a knife inserted in center comes out clean. Let stand 5 minutes before serving. Garnish as desired.

Suggested Combinations
Springtime Mock Quiche, photo on page 236: Use thawed, frozen, cut asparagus, snipped chives and chopped pimiento for vegetables. Omit meat. Use brick cheese. Use dill weed for herb.

Farmer's Breakfast Mock Quiche: Use diced cooked ham, diced cooked potatoes, chopped green pepper and chopped onion for vegetables and meat. Use Cheddar cheese. Use thyme for herb.

Italian Mock Quiche: Use diced salami or pepperoni, drained, canned, sliced mushrooms and chopped green onion for vegetables and meat. Use mozzarella cheese. Use oregano for herb.

Cheese Fondue

SERVINGS	4 (2-2/3 cups)	2 (1-1/3 cups)
INGREDIENTS		
process Swiss-cheese slices, diced	8 oz.	4 oz.
process Gruyère cheese, diced	8 oz.	4 oz.
all-purpose flour	2 tablespoons	1 tablespoon
garlic powder	1/8 teaspoon	dash
ground nutmeg	1/8 teaspoon	dash
freshly ground pepper	1/4 teaspoon	1/8 teaspoon
dry white wine	1-1/2 cups	3/4 cup
French-bread chunks		
kirsch		
HEAVY SAUCEPAN	2-qt. saucepan	1-1/2-qt. saucepan
TIME AT MEDIUM	18 to 20 minutes	12 to 14 minutes

In a medium bowl, toss together Swiss cheese, Gruyère cheese, flour, garlic powder, nutmeg and pepper; set aside. In a heavy saucepan, see size in chart above, bring wine to a boil over Medium-High heat. Reduce heat to Medium. Gradually add cheese and flour mixture, a small amount at a time, for time in chart above, whisking constantly. Allow each addition of cheese to melt before adding more cheese. Mixture should be thick and smooth when done. Pour into a ceramic fondue pot. Keep warm over fondue burner. Dip chunks of French bread in small bowls of kirsch, then swirl in hot cheese mixture. If mixture becomes too thick, stir in a little more warmed dry white wine.

Old-English Cheese Rarebit

SERVINGS	4 or 5 (2-1/2 cups)	2 or 3 (1-1/4 cups)
INGREDIENTS		
all-purpose flour	2 tablespoons	1 tablespoon
dry mustard	2 teaspoons	1 teaspoon
milk	1-1/2 cups	3/4 cup
Worcestershire sauce	4 teaspoons	2 teaspoons
egg yolks, beaten	2	1
cubed, sharp, process American cheese	2 cups (8 oz.)	1 cup (4 oz.)
English muffins or croissants, split, buttered, toasted	4 or 5	2 or 3
SAUCEPAN	2-qt. saucepan	1-1/2-qt. saucepan
TIME AT MEDIUM HIGH	7 to 8 minutes	7 to 8 minutes
TIME AT MEDIUM (egg yolks added)	1 to 3 minutes	1 to 3 minutes
TIME AT MEDIUM (cheese added)	6 to 8 minutes	5 to 6 minutes

In a saucepan, see size in chart above, combine flour and dry mustard. Whisk in 1/4 cup milk until smooth. Whisk in remaining milk and Worcestershire sauce. Cook over Medium-High heat 7 to 8 minutes or until slightly thickened and bubbly all over, whisking constantly. Reduce heat to Medium. Gradually stir half of hot sauce into egg yolks. Return yolk mixture to saucepan. Cook over Medium heat 1 to 3 minutes or until mixture thickens slightly more and is heated through, whisking constantly. Gradually stir in cheese, whisking constantly for time in chart above or until cheese melts and rarebit is hot. Serve over English muffins or croissants.

Creamy Pasta Casserole

INGREDIENTS	6	3
SERVINGS	**6**	**3**
INGREDIENTS		
rigatoni	4 cups uncooked (8 oz.)	2 cups uncooked (4 oz.)
sliced ripe olives	1/4 cup	2 tablespoons
chopped pimiento	1/4 cup	2 tablespoons
snipped parsley	1/4 cup	2 tablespoons
snipped chives	2 tablespoons	1 tablespoon
herb pepper	2 teaspoons	1 teaspoon
dairy sour cream	1 cup	1/2 cup
all-purpose flour	2 tablespoons	1 tablespoon
cream-style cottage cheese	2 cups (1 lb.)	1 cup (8 oz.)
milk	2/3 cup	1/3 cup
prepared horseradish	2 teaspoons	1 teaspoon
Dijon-style mustard	2 teaspoons	1 teaspoon
chopped pecans	1/2 cup	1/4 cup
grated Parmesan cheese	1/4 cup (3/4 oz.)	2 tablespoons
snipped parsley	2 tablespoons	1 tablespoon
CASSEROLE	deep 2-qt. casserole	deep 1-qt. casserole
TIME IN 375F (190C) OVEN (casserole)	45 to 50 minutes	25 to 30 minutes
TIME IN 375F (190C) OVEN (topping added)	10 to 15 minutes	10 to 15 minutes

Do not preheat oven. Cook rigatoni according to package directions; drain. In a casserole, see size in chart above, gently toss together cooked rigatoni, olives, pimiento, first amount of parsley, chives and herb pepper. Set aside. In a medium bowl, whisk together sour cream and flour. Whisk in cottage cheese, milk, horseradish and Dijon-style mustard until blended. Pour over rigatoni mixture; mix well. Cover and bake in a 375F (190C) oven for time in chart above. In a small bowl, combine pecans, Parmesan cheese and second amount of parsley; mix well. Stir pasta mixture in casserole. Sprinkle nut mixture over casserole. Bake, uncovered, 10 to 15 minutes longer or until heated through.

Tips for Using Shredded Cheese

- Four ounces of hard cheese yields 1 cup shredded cheese. Cheese shredded with a food processor, rather than by hand, is fluffier and does not conform to this cup-measure formula. If using a food processor, estimate weight of cheese instead of using cup measure.

- Use fresh-shredded cheese whenever possible. Preshredded cheese may have had mold-inhibiting ingredients, anti-caking agents, spice or flavoring added. Moisture is sometimes removed, so preshredded cheese may be partly dehydrated. Most preshredded cheese does not melt evenly in sauces and may give sauce a curdled appearance.

How to Make Cheese-Stuffed Manicotti

1/To make filling, combine eggs, ricotta cheese or cottage cheese, Parmesan and Romano cheese, green onion, parsley, basil and mozzarella cheese. Stuff cheese mixture into cooked manicotti shells.

2/Spoon half of Italian-sauce mixture into bottom of casserole. Place stuffed manicotti shells on sauce, then pour rest of sauce over shells. Sprinkle with more mozzarella cheese and bake.

Cheese-Stuffed Manicotti

SERVINGS	4 to 6	2 or 3
INGREDIENTS		
Italian cooking sauce	3 cups	1-1/2 cups
dry red wine	1/2 cup	1/4 cup
dried leaf oregano	2 teaspoons	1 teaspoon
eggs	2	1
ricotta cheese or drained cottage cheese	1 cup (8 oz.)	1/2 cup (4 oz.)
grated Parmesan cheese and Romano cheese	1/2 cup (1-1/2 oz.)	1/4 cup (3/4 oz.)
chopped green onion	1/4 cup	2 tablespoons
snipped parsley	1/4 cup	2 tablespoons
dried leaf basil	1 teaspoon	1/2 teaspoon
shredded mozzarella cheese	2 cups (8 oz.)	1 cup (4 oz.)
manicotti shells, cooked, drained	8	4
shredded mozzarella cheese	1 cup (4 oz.)	1/2 cup (2 oz.)
BAKING DISH	12" x 7" baking dish	10" x 6" baking dish
TIME IN 350F (175C) OVEN	40 to 45 minutes	35 to 40 minutes
STANDING TIME	5 minutes	5 minutes

Do not preheat oven. In a medium bowl, combine cooking sauce, wine and oregano; mix well. Pour half of sauce into a baking dish, see size in chart above; set aside. In another medium bowl, beat eggs. Stir in ricotta or cottage cheese, grated Parmesan and Romano cheese, green onion, parsley and basil; mix well. Fold in first amount of mozzarella cheese. Stuff about 1/3 cup cheese mixture into each cooked manicotti shell. Place manicotti on sauce in baking dish. Pour remaining Italian-sauce mixture over manicotti, coating all pasta. Sprinkle with second amount of mozzarella cheese. Bake in a 350F (175C) oven for time in chart above or until filling is heated through. Let stand 5 minutes before serving. To serve, spoon sauce over manicotti.

Basic Macaroni & Cheese

SERVINGS	4	2
INGREDIENTS		
macaroni	1-1/2 cups uncooked (about 6 oz.)	3/4 cup uncooked (about 3 oz.)
butter, margarine or bacon drippings	3 tablespoons	2 tablespoons
chopped green onion	1/4 cup	2 tablespoons
all-purpose flour	3 tablespoons	4 teaspoons
dried leaf herb	1 teaspoon	1/2 teaspoon
pepper	1/4 teaspoon	1/8 teaspoon
milk	1-1/2 cups	3/4 cup
cooking liquid	1/2 cup	1/4 cup
shredded cheese	2 cups (8 oz.)	1 cup (4 oz.)
chopped or sliced cooked vegetables	1/2 cup	1/4 cup
vegetable garnish, see suggestions below		
dry breadcrumbs	1/2 cup	1/4 cup
dried leaf herb	1/2 teaspoon	1/4 teaspoon
butter or margarine, melted	2 tablespoons	1 tablespoon
SAUCEPAN	2-qt. saucepan	1-qt. saucepan
CASSEROLE	deep 2-qt. casserole	deep 1-qt. casserole
TIME AT MEDIUM HIGH (onion)	4 to 5 minutes	4 minutes
TIME AT MEDIUM HIGH (flour added)	1 minute	1 minute
TIME AT MEDIUM HIGH (milk, liquid added)	7 to 8 minutes	4 to 5 minutes
TIME IN 350F (175C) OVEN	40 to 45 minutes	30 to 35 minutes

Do not preheat oven. Cook macaroni according to package directions; drain. In a saucepan, see size in chart above, combine butter, margarine or bacon drippings and green onion. Cook over Medium-High heat for time in chart above or until onion is tender, stirring often. Stir in flour, first amount of herb and pepper until smooth. Cook and stir 1 minute. Stir in milk and cooking liquid. Cook for time in chart above or until thickened and bubbly all over, whisking constantly. Add cheese and stir until melted. In a casserole, see size in chart above, toss together cooked macaroni and cooked vegetables. Pour cheese sauce over macaroni mixture; mix gently. Top with vegetable garnish. In a small bowl, combine breadcrumbs, second amount of herb and melted butter or margarine. Sprinkle on casserole. Bake, uncovered, in a 350F (175C) oven for time in chart above or until bubbly and heated through.

Suggested Combinations

Family Macaroni & Cheese: Use butter or margarine. Use thyme for herb. Use chicken broth for cooking liquid. Use Cheddar cheese. Use elbow macaroni. Use cooked diced carrots and chopped pimiento for vegetables. Garnish with green-pepper rings.

Alpine Macaroni & Cheese: Use butter or margarine. Use dill weed for herb. Use dry white wine for cooking liquid. Use Swiss cheese. Use shell macaroni. Use drained, canned, sliced mushrooms and sliced pimiento-stuffed olives for vegetables. Garnish with sliced dill pickles.

Pennsylvania Dutch Macaroni & Cheese: Use bacon drippings. Use basil for herb. Use milk for cooking liquid. Use Edam cheese. Use corkscrew macaroni. Use cooked chopped spinach, pressed in a sieve to remove as much water as possible, for vegetable. Garnish with sliced pickled beets and crumbled cooked bacon.

How to Make Basic Macaroni & Cheese

1/In a casserole, toss together cooked macaroni and cooked vegetables. Pour hot cheese sauce over macaroni mixture and stir gently. This Family Macaroni & Cheese includes cooked carrots and pimiento.

2/Top casserole with a vegetable garnish, such as green-pepper rings, and a sprinkling of buttered breadcrumbs. Jar shows layered corkscrew macaroni, elbow macaroni and shell macaroni. All can be used for this recipe.

Basic Quick Macaroni & Cheese

SERVINGS	4 to 6	2 or 3
INGREDIENTS		
macaroni	2 cups uncooked (about 8 oz.)	1 cup uncooked (about 4 oz.)
condensed cream soup	1 (10- to 11-oz.) can	1/2 (10- to 11-oz.) can (2/3 cup)
cooking liquid	1 cup	1/2 cup
milk	1/2 cup	1/4 cup
dried leaf herb	1/2 teaspoon	1/4 teaspoon
process cheese-food slices, torn in small pieces	8 oz.	4 oz.
CASSEROLE	deep 2-qt. casserole	deep 1-qt. casserole
TIME IN 350F (175C) OVEN	50 to 55 minutes	30 to 35 minutes

Do not preheat oven. Cook macaroni according to package directions; drain. In a casserole, see size in chart above, whisk together soup, cooking liquid, milk and herb until well-blended. Stir in cooked macaroni and cheese; mix well. Cover and bake in a 350F (175C) oven for time in chart above or until bubbly and heated through. Stir before serving.

Suggested Combinations
Quick American Macaroni & Cheese: Use cream of tomato soup. Use tomato sauce for cooking liquid. Use basil for herb. Use bacon-flavored process cheese food.
Quick Swiss Macaroni & Cheese: Use cream of onion soup. Use cream-style corn for cooking liquid. Use savory for herb. Use Swiss process cheese food.
Quick Home-Style Macaroni & Cheese: Use cream of celery soup. Use cut-up stewed tomatoes with juice for cooking liquid. Use thyme for herb. Use pimiento-flavored process cheese food.

Basic Cheesy Stuffed Peppers

SERVINGS	4	2
INGREDIENTS		
large green or red peppers	4 (5- to 7-oz.) peppers	2 (5- to 7-oz.) peppers
bacon, cut in 1-inch pieces	4 slices	2 slices
bacon drippings	2 tablespoons	1 tablespoon
chopped vegetables	2 cups	1 cup
cooked rice	2 cups	1 cup
toasted nuts	1/4 cup	2 tablespoons
OR		
toasted seeds	2 tablespoons	1 tablespoon
dried leaf herb	1 teaspoon	1/2 teaspoon
plain yogurt	1 cup	1/2 cup
shredded cheese	1 cup (4 oz.)	1/2 cup (2 oz.)
BAKING DISH	13" x 9" baking dish	8-inch-square baking dish
SKILLET	10-inch skillet	8-inch skillet
TIME AT MEDIUM HIGH (bacon)	6 to 9 minutes	6 to 9 minutes
TIME AT MEDIUM HIGH (vegetables)	6 to 7 minutes	4 to 5 minutes
TIME IN 350F (175C) OVEN	50 minutes	50 minutes

Do not preheat oven. Cut peppers in half lengthwise. Remove seeds and membrane. Place, cut-side up, in a baking dish, see size in chart above; set aside. In a skillet, see size in chart above, cook bacon over Medium-High heat 6 to 9 minutes or until crisp. Remove bacon with a slotted spoon and drain on paper towels; set aside. Reserve in skillet amount of drippings listed in chart above. Add chopped vegetables to skillet. Cook over Medium-High heat for time in chart above or until vegetables are tender, stirring often. Stir in bacon, rice, nuts or seeds and herb; mix well. Fold in yogurt and cheese. Spoon rice mixture into peppers. Bake in a 350F (175C) oven 50 minutes or until heated through.

Suggested Combinations

Cheddar-Stuffed Peppers: Use drained, cooked, whole-kernel corn, pimiento and chopped green onion for vegetables. Use white rice. Use peanuts for nuts. Use thyme for herb. Use Cheddar cheese.

Swiss-Stuffed Peppers: Use chopped carrot, chopped celery, chopped onion and chopped mushrooms for vegetables. Use brown rice. Use sunflower kernels. Use savory for herb. Use Swiss cheese.

Mozzarella-Stuffed Peppers: Use chopped onion, chopped zucchini, chopped tomatoes and sliced olives for vegetables. Use saffron-rice mix. Use pecans for nuts. Use oregano for herb. Use mozzarella cheese.

Tips for Identifying Cheese

- Natural cheese is milk curd separated from whey. Coagulation is caused by the action of extra lactic acid, the addition of rennet or both. Natural cheese is either fresh or aged.

- Pasteurized process cheese is a blend of fresh and aged natural cheese that has been shredded, mixed with an emulsifier and heated. Heating stops the ripening. This stabilizes flavor and keeping quality, and produces a smooth texture. Pasteurized process cheese slices easily and melts evenly. The percentage of cheese ingredient in process cheese generally equals the percentage of cheese ingredient found in the natural cheese from which it is made.

- Pasteurized process cheese food is prepared like process cheese, but it contains less cheese. It has a slightly higher moisture content and lower milk-fat content. At least 51 percent of the finished weight must consist of the cheese ingredient.

Cheese, Wine & Fruit Guide

CHEESE	WINE	FRUIT
Bel Paese	Full-bodied red wine, tawny port, Madeira, cream sherry, heavy white wine.	Pineapple, honeydew melon, pears, green grapes, apples.
bleu or blue	Robust red wine.	Pears, apples, plums.
brick	Semidry or semisweet white wine, rosé or light red wine.	Pineapple, apples, pears, green grapes.
Brie	Premium or vintage full-bodied red wine; soft or fruity white wine with more-bland Brie.	Plums, peaches, red grapes, pineapple, honeydew melon.
Camembert	Red wine, dry or semidry white wine, dessert wine, champagne.	Apples, pineapple, plums, pears, green grapes.
Cheddar	Full-bodied red wine; white or rosé wines with mild Cheddar.	Apples, pears, red grapes, pineapple, honeydew melon.
Colby	Versatile, but best with white or rosé wine.	Pineapple, apples, green grapes, plums.
cream	Sparkling, sweet white and rosé wine.	Strawberries, plums, peaches, watermelon.
Edam	White, rosé or dry red wine, dry to sweet sherry, port, Madeira, dessert wine.	Apples, pineapple, pears, plums, red grapes.
fontina	White or rosé wine; dry red wine with strong fontina.	Cantaloupe, pineapple, apples, pears, grapes.
Gorgonzola	Robust red wine.	Pears, apples, plums.
Gouda	White, rosé or dry red wine, dry to sweet sherry, port, Madeira, dessert wine.	Apples, pineapple, pears, plums, red grapes.
Limburger	Dry red wine.	Pears, grapes, melons.
Monterey Jack	White, rosé or red wine, dry to semidry sherry, vermouth, sparkling wine.	Pineapple, red grapes, apples, pears.
Muenster	White wine, preferably fruity or spicy type.	Apples, pears, cantaloupe, grapes, pineapple.
Neufchâtel	Wine punch, semisweet white wine, rosé.	Grapes, strawberries, peaches, plums, melons.
Port du Salut	White or red wine.	Plums, pears, melons.
provolone	Red wine.	Apples, pears, plums.
Swiss	White wine, champagne, light red wine.	Apples, grapes, melons, pears, plums.

Cheese Serving Guide

CHEESE	CHARACTERISTICS	SERVING SUGGESTIONS
American process	Semisoft to soft; smooth body; light-yellow to orange color; mild flavor.	Sandwiches; casseroles; salads.
Bel Paese	Soft; smooth waxy body; creamy yellow color; mild to moderately robust flavor.	With fresh fruit and crackers for dessert.
bleu or blue	Semisoft; white color, marbled with blue-green mold; piquant, spicy flavor.	With fresh fruit and crackers for dessert; sandwiches; egg dishes; vegetables; salads and dressings.
brick	Semisoft; smooth open texture; numerous eyes; light to deep-yellow color; mild and sweet flavor becoming pungent as it ages.	Sandwiches; salads; casseroles.
Brie	Soft; thin edible crust, creamy white interior; mild to pungent flavor.	With fresh fruit and crackers for dessert.

Cheese Serving Guide Continued

CHEESE	CHARACTERISTICS	SERVING SUGGESTIONS
Camembert	Soft, almost fluid; thin edible crust, creamy interior; mild to pungent flavor.	With fresh fruit and crackers for dessert.
Cheddar	Hard; nearly white to orange color; mild to sharp flavor.	Sandwiches; salads; casseroles; snacks.
Colby	Hard, but softer than Cheddar; white to light-yellow or orange color; mild to mellow flavor.	Sandwiches; appetizers; salads; casseroles.
cottage, Dutch, farmers or pot	Soft; moist, delicate, large or small curds; white color; mild but slightly acid flavor.	Sandwiches; salads; egg dishes; casseroles.
cream	Soft; smooth, buttery texture; white color; mild, slightly acid flavor.	Salads; sandwiches; cheesecake; as spread for fruit breads.
Edam	Semisoft to hard; creamy yellow interior with natural paraffin coating; mild, nutlike flavor.	Salads; sandwiches; with fresh fruit and crackers for dessert.
feta	White; crumbly and grainy; strong, salty, sour flavor; sometimes packed in brine; cooking cheese of Greece.	Salads; sauces; casseroles.
fontina	Semisoft to hard; granular; may have small round eyes; pale yellow color; robust, salty flavor.	Appetizers; casseroles; with fresh fruit and crackers for dessert.
Gorgonzola	See bleu cheese.	
Gouda	Hard, but softer than Cheddar; creamy yellow, with or without red-wax coating; mild, nutlike flavor.	Casseroles; sandwiches; with fresh fruit and crackers for dessert.
Limburger	Soft; smooth waxy body; creamy white interior, brownish exterior; strong, robust, highly aromatic flavor.	Sandwiches; with fresh fruit and crackers for dessert.
Monterey Jack	Semisoft; small openings throughout; creamy, white color; mild to mellow flavor.	Sandwiches; Mexican dishes; salads; egg dishes.
mozzarella	Semisoft; smooth body; creamy white color, mild to mellow flavor.	Italian dishes such as pizza, lasagne.
Muenster	Semisoft; smooth waxy body with many small openings; creamy white interior; mild to mellow flavor.	Sandwiches; casseroles.
Neufchâtel	Soft; smooth, creamy white texture; mild flavor.	Sandwiches; dips; spreads.
Parmesan	Very hard; granular; light-yellow color with brown or black coating; piquant flavor.	Grated in Italian dishes, breads, soups, salads.
Port du Salut	Semisoft; smooth, buttery texture; creamy white interior; mellow or mild to robust flavor.	With fresh fruit and crackers for dessert.
provolone	Hard; stringy texture; yellowish white interior; mellow to sharp flavor with smoky tang.	Appetizers; casseroles.
ricotta	Soft; moist and grainy or dry; white color; bland semisweet flavor.	Salads; dips; Italian dishes.
Romano	Very hard; granular; sharp, piquant flavor.	Grated in Italian dishes, breads, soups, salads.
scamorze	See mozzarella.	
Swiss	Hard; smooth with large eyes; pale-yellow color; mild, sweet, nut like flavor.	Fondue; salads; sandwiches; casseroles.

Selection of Cheeses

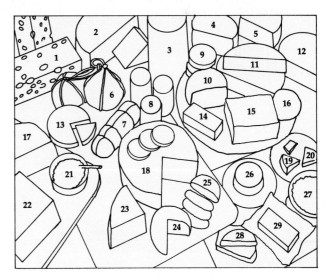

1. Swiss
2. white Cheddar
3. Colby (Longhorn)
4. Muenster
5. bleu
6. provolone
7. provolone
8. Colby (midget)
9. Monterey Jack
10. caraway
11. Port du Salut
12. Gorgonzola
13. fontina
14. Limburger
15. brick
16. scamorze
17. Romano
18. Cheddar
19. Brie
20. Camembert
21. Parmesan (grated)
22. Parmesan
23. Cheddar wedge
24. Edam
25. Gouda
26. ricotta
27. cottage
28. Bel Paese
29. cream

Soups
& Sauces

This chapter presents a marvelous collection of soups and sauces. You will find shortcut soups that go together in minutes, as well as flavorful blends that simmer an hour or two. Choose the recipe that fits your schedule and ingredients at hand.

To add a finishing touch to meat, chicken, fish and vegetables, try one of our well-seasoned sauces.

Cheddar-Cheese Soup, page 281.

Soups & Sauces

Q. What sauces go with what foods?

A. A sauce should complement—not mask—the food it accompanies. Select sauces with compatible seasonings for the food you are serving. The list below will help you find the right sauce for your menu.

Chicken: Caper Sauce, page 310; Fresh-Herb Sauce, page 311; Curried Onion-Butter Sauce, page 316; Chicken Barbecue Sauce, page 314; Easy Barbecue Sauce, page 314.

Fish: Caper Sauce, page 310; Fresh-Herb Sauce, page 311; Curried Onion-Butter Sauce, page 316; Hollandaise Sauce, page 306; Maltaise Sauce, page 306; Dill Hollandaise Sauce, page 306; Spanish Sauce, page 312; Creamy Tomato Sauce, page 312; Fish Barbecue Sauce, page 314; Easy Barbecue Sauce, page 314.

Seafood: Zesty Horseradish-Mustard Sauce, page 311; Horseradish Béarnaise Sauce, page 304; Caper Hollandaise Sauce, page 306.

Beef: Zesty Horseradish-Mustard Sauce, page 311; Horseradish Béarnaise Sauce, page 304; Béarnaise Sauce, page 304; Caper Hollandaise Sauce, page 306; Beer & Onion-Butter Sauce, page 316; Bordelaise Sauce, page 317; Cumberland Jelly Sauce, page 116; Choron Sauce, page 312; Beef Barbecue Sauce, page 314; Easy Barbecue Sauce, page 314; Hollandaise Sauce au Poivre, page 306.

Pork: Spicy Apple Jelly Sauce, page 116; Zesty Horseradish-Mustard Sauce, page 311; Béarnaise Sauce, page 304; Pork Barbecue Sauce, page 314; Easy Barbecue Sauce, page 314.

Ham: Cumberland Jelly Sauce, page 116; Spicy Apple Jelly Sauce, page 116; Pork Barbecue Sauce, page 314.

Lamb: Lemon-Mint Jelly Sauce, page 116; Minted Hollandaise Sauce, page 306; Hollandaise Sauce au Poivre, page 306.

Game Meats: Cumberland Jelly Sauce, page 116; Beef Barbecue Sauce, page 314; Easy Barbecue Sauce, page 314.

Cold Meats or Sausage: Spanish Sauce, page 312; Creamy Tomato Sauce, page 312.

Egg Dishes: Hollandaise Sauce, page 306; Cheese Sauce, page 311; Mushroom Cream Sauce, page 316; Zucchini Cream Sauce, page 316; Spanish Sauce, page 312.

Vegetables: Cheese Sauce, page 311; Hollandaise Sauce, page 306; Maltaise Sauce, page 306; Dill Hollandaise Sauce, page 306; Herbed Fresh-Tomato Sauce, page 313; Creamy Tomato Sauce, page 312.

Q. How should I store leftover soups and sauces?

A. Pour soups into refrigerator containers; cover and refrigerate. Most meat or vegetable soups keep 3 to 4 days. Seafood soups spoil easily, so keep them only 1 to 2 days. For longer storage, some soups can be frozen. Thickened soups and sauces do not freeze well. The thickening breaks down and the mixture will appear curdled when thawed. Broth soups, bean, pea or lentil soups and unthickened vegetable or meat soups may be frozen up to 6 months.

Cover and refrigerate leftover thickened sauces up to 3 to 4 days. They will become very thick after chilling. Acid sauces, such as tomato-based barbecue sauces or Spanish sauces, may be refrigerated up to 1 week.

Q. Can soups and sauces be reheated successfully?

A. Yes. After refrigerating, thickened sauce or soup will be much thicker. Spoon the soup or sauce into a heavy saucepan. Whisk in a little of the same liquid used in the original recipe. Cover and cook over Medium-Low heat, stirring often. Add more liquid, if necessary, to regain original consistency.

To reheat Hollandaise or Béarnaise Sauce, see page 304. Broth soups made with soup bones will thicken or gel after chilling. Heat these soups before adding additional liquid. Most will return to the original consistency after heating; if not, add a little broth.

Q. Can a novice cook make Hollandaise Sauce?

A. Yes. Let your blender do the work. Once you discover this no-fail method of preparing Hollandaise Sauce and Béarnaise Sauce, you will make them often. For an added bonus, you can make the sauce 30 minutes before mealtime and keep it warm. Or, make it hours ahead and then reheat it. This can be a real plus on a busy day.

How to Make Basic Cold Vegetable Bisque

1/Cold Curried Broccoli Bisque is an elegant first course. Place cooked vegetables in a blender container. Use 1/2 cup cooking liquid to blend vegetables until pureed.

2/Whisk some of pureed vegetables into sour-cream dip to heat-shock cream so it will not curdle. Combine with remaining vegetable mixture. Serve thoroughly chilled.

Basic Cold Vegetable Bisque

SERVINGS	6 to 8	3 or 4
INGREDIENTS		
chopped vegetable	1/2 cup	1/4 cup
butter or margarine	1/4 cup	2 tablespoons
seasoning	1 teaspoon	1/2 teaspoon
condensed chicken broth	2 (10-3/4-oz.) cans	1 (10-3/4-oz.) can
frozen vegetable	2 (8- to 10-oz.) pkgs.	1 (8- to 10-oz.) pkg.
lemon juice	4 teaspoons	2 teaspoons
sour-cream dip	1 (8-oz.) carton	1/2 cup
garnishes, see suggestions below		
SAUCEPAN	3-qt. saucepan	2-qt. saucepan
TIME AT MEDIUM HIGH	6 to 7 minutes	4 to 5 minutes
TIME AT MEDIUM LOW	6 to 8 minutes	6 to 8 minutes
REFRIGERATE	8 hours or overnight	5 hours or overnight

In a saucepan, see size in chart above, cook chopped vegetable in butter or margarine over Medium-High heat for time in chart above or until tender, stirring occasionally. Whisk in seasoning and broth. Add frozen vegetable. Bring to a boil over High heat. Reduce heat to Medium Low. Break up vegetable pieces with a large fork; cover. Simmer over Medium-Low heat 6 to 8 minutes or until tender. Stir in lemon juice. Remove vegetables with a slotted spoon; place in a blender or food processor fitted with a steel blade. Add 1/2 cup cooking liquid to vegetables. Reserve remaining cooking liquid in saucepan. Process vegetable mixture until pureed. Process large recipe in 2 batches. In a large bowl, whisk together sour-cream dip and reserved cooking liquid. Gradually whisk in pureed vegetable mixture. Cover and refrigerate for time in chart above or until cold. Serve cold. Garnish according to suggestions below.

Suggested Combinations
Cold Curried Broccoli Bisque: Use chopped onion for chopped vegetable. Use curry powder for seasoning. Use chopped broccoli for frozen vegetable. Use onion-sour-cream dip. Garnish with spoonful of onion-sour-cream dip, watercress and shredded lemon peel.
Cold Cucumber-Asparagus Bisque: Use chopped celery for chopped vegetable. Use dried leaf tarragon for seasoning. Use cut asparagus for frozen vegetable. Use cucumber-sour-cream dip. Garnish with spoonful of cucumber-sour-cream dip and snipped chives.

Basic Gazpacho

SERVINGS	8 to 12	4 to 6
INGREDIENTS		
finely chopped, seeded, peeled tomatoes	1 cup	1/2 cup
chopped or sliced vegetables	3 cups	1-1/2 cups
tomato-based juice	3 cups	1-1/2 cups
condensed broth	1 (10- to 11-oz.) can	2/3 cup
wine	1/2 cup	1/4 cup
vinegar	2 tablespoons	1 tablespoon
seasoning	1/2 teaspoon	1/4 teaspoon
garnishes, see suggestions below		
BOWL	3-qt. bowl	1-1/2-qt. bowl
REFRIGERATE	5 hours or overnight	3 hours or overnight

In a bowl, see size in chart above, combine tomatoes, vegetables, tomato-based juice, condensed broth, wine, vinegar and seasoning; mix well. Cover and refrigerate for time in chart above or until thoroughly chilled. Serve cold. Garnish according to suggestions below.

Suggested Combinations
Spanish-Style Gazpacho: Use chopped seeded cucumber, chopped green onion, chopped celery and sliced ripe olives for vegetables. Use tomato-vegetable-juice cocktail. Use beef broth. Use dry white wine. Use red-wine vinegar. Use garlic powder and hot-pepper sauce for seasoning. Garnish with cucumber twists and celery leaves.

Monterey-Style Gazpacho: Use chopped peeled avocado, chopped, drained, canned artichoke hearts, chopped onion and canned chopped green chilies for vegetables. Use clam-tomato juice. Use chicken broth. Use dry sherry for wine. Use white-wine vinegar. Use dried leaf tarragon for seasoning. Garnish with avocado slices and cilantro sprigs.

Vichyssoise Deluxe

SERVINGS	8 to 12	4 to 6
INGREDIENTS		
chopped seeded zucchini or chopped carrot	1 cup	1/2 cup
loose-pack, frozen, hash-brown potatoes, thawed	1 lb. (4 cups)	8 oz. (2 cups)
chopped onion	1 cup	1/2 cup
sliced leeks	2/3 cup	1/3 cup
chicken broth	2 (14-1/2-oz.) cans	1 (14-1/2-oz.) can
chicken-bouillon granules	2 teaspoons	1 teaspoon
half and half	2 cups	1 cup
dairy sour cream	1 cup	1/2 cup
snipped chives	to garnish	to garnish
SAUCEPAN	3-qt. saucepan	1-1/2-qt. saucepan
TIME AT MEDIUM LOW	15 to 18 minutes	12 to 15 minutes
REFRIGERATE	8 hours or overnight	8 hours or overnight

To seed zucchini, cut in half lengthwise with a knife; cut out seeds in a lengthwise **V** shape. In a saucepan, see size in chart above, combine zucchini or carrot, potatoes, onion, leeks, broth and bouillon granules. Bring to a boil over High heat. Reduce heat to Medium Low; cover. Simmer for time in chart above or until vegetables are tender, stirring occasionally. Remove vegetables with a slotted spoon; place in a blender or food processor fitted with a steel blade. Add 1/2 cup cooking liquid to vegetables. Reserve remaining cooking liquid in saucepan. Process vegetable mixture in blender or food processor until pureed. Process large recipe in 2 batches. Pour pureed mixture into a large bowl. Add reserved cooking liquid. Gradually whisk in half and half and sour cream. Cover and refrigerate 8 hours or overnight. Serve cold. Garnish with chives.

Monterey-Style Gazpacho

Basic Fruit Soup

SERVINGS	8	4
INGREDIENTS		
dried fruit	2 cups (about 12 oz.)	1 cup (about 6 oz.)
water	2 cups	1 cup
wine	1 cup	1/2 cup
cinnamon sticks	4 inches in total	2 inches in total
whole spices	2 teaspoons	1 teaspoon
sliced fresh fruit	1 cup	1/2 cup
fruit juice	2 cups	1 cup
jelly	1/2 cup	1/4 cup
packed brown sugar	1/4 cup	2 tablespoons
cornstarch	2 teaspoons	1 teaspoon
cold water	1 tablespoon	1 tablespoon
HEAVY SAUCEPAN	3-qt. saucepan	1-1/2-qt. saucepan
TIME AT MEDIUM LOW (dried fruit)	20 minutes	20 minutes
TIME AT MEDIUM LOW (fresh fruit added)	10 to 15 minutes	10 to 15 minutes
TIME AT MEDIUM HIGH	8 minutes	5 minutes
COOLING TIME	30 minutes	30 minutes

In a heavy saucepan, see size in chart above, combine dried fruit, water and wine. Tie cinnamon sticks and whole spices in a piece of cheesecloth; add to fruit mixture. Bring to a boil over High heat. Reduce heat to Medium Low; cover. Simmer 20 minutes or until fruit is tender. Stir in fresh fruit, fruit juice, jelly and brown sugar; mix well. Bring to a boil over High heat. Reduce heat to Medium Low; cover. Simmer 10 to 15 minutes or until fruit is tender. Remove and discard spice bag. In a small bowl, thoroughly combine cornstarch and cold water. Stir into fruit mixture. Cook over Medium-High heat for time in chart above or until thickened and bubbly all over, stirring gently. Cool at room temperature 30 minutes. Serve warm. Or, cover and refrigerate to serve cold.

Suggested Combinations

Amber Harvest Fruit Soup: Use dried apricots and golden raisins for dried fruit. Use red port wine. Use whole allspice and whole nutmeg for spices. Use peeled pineapple, cut in 1-inch pieces, for fresh fruit. Use pineapple juice. Use currant jelly.

Figgy Fruit Soup: Use dried figs, stemmed and snipped lengthwise, and dried apple chunks for dried fruit. Use cream sherry for wine. Use whole cardamom and whole cloves for spices. Use unpeeled orange, cut in slices and quartered, for fresh fruit. Use apple juice. Use apple jelly.

Note: When measuring whole spices, 1 whole nutmeg equals 1 teaspoon.

Tips for Cold Soup

- Garnish cold cream soups with snipped chives, snipped fresh herbs or snipped parsley. Or, top with coarsely chopped raw vegetables, such as green onions, carrots or celery. Or, sprinkle with toasted chopped nuts, croutons or paprika.
- Garnish broth-type cold soups with very thin lemon slices, watercress sprigs or green-onion fans.
- If you do not have icers to serve cold soup, improvise and make your own. Set custard cups in ice-filled fruit dishes. Or, nestle small glasses in large ice-filled goblets. For a luncheon, chilled consommé looks special served in dainty tea cups.
- Serve cold soups with assorted crackers, melba toast or Bacon-Wrapped Breadsticks, page 50.

Basic Cheese Soup

SERVINGS	3 or 4	1 or 2
INGREDIENTS		
chopped vegetables	1-1/2 cups	3/4 cup
butter, margarine or bacon drippings	1/4 cup	2 tablespoons
all-purpose flour	1/4 cup	2 tablespoons
paprika	1 teaspoon	1/2 teaspoon
dry mustard	1 teaspoon	1/2 teaspoon
chicken broth	1 (14-1/2-oz.) can (about 2 cups)	1 cup
milk	1 cup	1/2 cup
Worcestershire sauce	2 teaspoons	1 teaspoon
shredded cheese	2 cups (8 oz.)	1 cup (4 oz.)
garnishes, see suggestions below		
HEAVY SAUCEPAN	2-qt. saucepan	1-1/2-qt. saucepan
TIME AT MEDIUM HIGH (vegetables)	10 to 12 minutes	8 to 10 minutes
TIME AT MEDIUM HIGH (flour added)	1 minute	1 minute
TIME AT MEDIUM HIGH (broth, milk added)	12 to 14 minutes	6 to 8 minutes
TIME AT MEDIUM LOW	10 minutes	10 minutes

In a heavy saucepan, see size in chart above, cook vegetables in butter, margarine or bacon drippings over Medium-High heat for time in chart above or until tender, stirring often. Whisk in flour, paprika and dry mustard. Cook and stir 1 minute. Whisk in broth, milk and Worcestershire sauce. Cook for time in chart above or until thickened and bubbly all over, whisking constantly. Reduce heat to Medium Low. Whisk in cheese until melted; cover. Simmer 10 minutes or until heated through and flavors blend, stirring occasionally.

Suggested Combinations
Cheddar-Cheese Soup, photo on page 274: Use chopped onion, chopped celery and chopped carrot for vegetables. Use Cheddar cheese. Garnish with hot buttered popcorn, grated Parmesan cheese and herb pepper.

California Cheese Soup: Use chopped green onion, chopped seeded tomatoes and canned chopped green chilies for vegetables. Use Monterey Jack cheese. Garnish with corn chips and additional chopped green chilies.

Tips for Cheese Soup
- Process cheese melts more easily and produces a smooth finished soup.
- Natural cheese provides better soup flavor but more granular texture than process cheese.
- Packaged, shredded natural cheese does not melt evenly in soup. Instead, use a block of natural cheese and shred it yourself. To prevent lumping, add natural cheese in small portions to hot soup. Whisk each addition until it melts before adding more cheese.

Basic Beef Soup

SERVINGS	4	2
INGREDIENTS		
beef chuck short ribs, 1 inch thick	2 lbs.	1 lb.
water	5 cups	3 cups
chopped vegetables	2 cups	1 cup
beef-bouillon granules	4 teaspoons	2 teaspoons
dried leaf herbs or ground herbs	2 teaspoons	1 teaspoon
bay leaf	1 large	1 small
Worcestershire sauce	1 tablespoon	2 teaspoons
quick-cooking barley	1/2 cup	1/4 cup
OR		
potatoes, cut in 1/2-inch cubes	2 large	1 large
DUTCH OVEN	4-qt. Dutch oven	3-qt. saucepan
TIME AT MEDIUM LOW (ribs)	2-1/2 to 3 hours	2-1/2 to 3 hours
TIME AT MEDIUM LOW (barley or potatoes added)	30 to 35 minutes	30 to 35 minutes

In a Dutch oven, see size in chart above, place short ribs meaty-side down. Add water, vegetables, bouillon granules, herbs, bay leaf and Worcestershire sauce; mix well. Bring to a boil over High heat. Reduce heat to Medium Low; cover. Simmer 2-1/2 to 3 hours or until meat is tender. Remove beef from soup. Remove and discard bones from beef. Cut up beef. Return beef to soup. Add barley or potatoes. Bring to a boil over High heat. Reduce heat to Medium Low; cover. Simmer 30 to 35 minutes or until barley or potatoes are tender. Remove bay leaf. Skim off excess fat.

Suggested Combinations
Beef-Barley Soup: Use chopped onion, chopped celery and chopped tomatoes for vegetables. Use basil and dry mustard for herbs. Use barley.

Potato-Beef Soup: Use chopped green onion, chopped cabbage and chopped carrot for vegetables. Use thyme and marjoram for herbs. Use potatoes.

Basic Consommé Plus

SERVINGS	4 to 6	2 or 3
INGREDIENTS		
canned broth	2 (14-1/2-oz.) cans	1 (14-1/2-oz.) can
cooking liquid	1 cup	1/2 cup
wine	2 tablespoons	1 tablespoon
seasoning	1 to 2 teaspoons	1/2 to 1 teaspoon
dried leaf herb or ground spice	1/2 teaspoon	1/4 teaspoon
thinly sliced vegetables	2 cups	1 cup
SAUCEPAN	3-qt. saucepan	1-1/2-qt. saucepan
TIME AT MEDIUM LOW	5 to 8 minutes	5 to 8 minutes

In a saucepan, see size in chart above, combine broth, cooking liquid, wine, seasoning and herb or spice; mix well. Add vegetables. Bring to a boil over High heat. Reduce heat to Medium Low; cover. Simmer 5 to 8 minutes or until vegetables are crisp-tender.

Suggested Combinations
Zesty Beef Consommé: Use beef broth. Use non-alcoholic Bloody-Mary mix for cooking liquid. Use dry white wine. Use prepared horseradish for seasoning. Use basil for herb. Use thinly sliced celery, leeks and mushrooms for vegetables.

Oriental Chicken Consommé: Use chicken broth. Use apple juice for cooking liquid. Use dry sherry for wine. Use lemon juice for seasoning. Use ginger for spice. Use thinly sliced spinach, green onion, water chestnuts and bean sprouts for vegetables.

How to Make Basic Beef Soup

1/Place short ribs, meaty-side down, in a pot. Add water, chopped onion, chopped celery, chopped tomatoes and beef-bouillon granules to make Beef-Barley Soup. Use basil, dry mustard, bay leaf and Worcestershire sauce for seasonings.

2/Bring mixture to a boil. Cover and simmer over Medium-Low heat 2-1/2 to 3 hours. To check for doneness, use a fork to check tenderness of meat in thickest part.

3/Cut meat off bones and return meat to soup. Add quick-cooking barley. Bring mixture to a boil. Cover and simmer over Medium-Low heat 30 to 35 minutes or until barley is tender.

4/Use a large spoon to skim off fat layer on top of soup. Or, refrigerate soup and lift off fat layer after it solidifies. Serve soup piping hot with crisp crackers.

Basic Lamb Soup

SERVINGS	4	2
INGREDIENTS		
lamb shanks	2 (1-lb.) shanks	1 (1-lb.) shank
OR		
meaty leg-of-lamb bone	1 leg-of-lamb bone	1/2 leg-of-lamb bone
water	8 cups	4 cups
chopped vegetables	3 cups	1-1/2 cups
beef-bouillon granules	4 teaspoons	2 teaspoons
dried leaf herbs	2 teaspoons	1 teaspoon
bay leaf	1 large leaf	1 small leaf
Worcestershire sauce	4 teaspoons	2 teaspoons
quick-cooking barley or quick-cooking brown rice	2/3 cup	1/3 cup
DUTCH OVEN	5-qt. Dutch oven	3-qt. saucepan
TIME AT MEDIUM LOW (shanks)	1-1/2 to 2 hours	1-1/2 to 2 hours
TIME AT MEDIUM LOW (barley or brown rice added)	30 to 35 minutes	30 to 35 minutes

In a Dutch oven, see size in chart above, combine lamb shanks or leg-of-lamb bone, water, vegetables, bouillon granules, herbs, bay leaf and Worcestershire sauce. Bring to a boil over High heat. Reduce heat to Medium Low; cover. Simmer 1-1/2 to 2 hours or until meat is tender, turning meat over halfway through cooking time. Remove lamb from soup. Remove and discard bones from lamb. Cut up lamb. Return lamb to soup. Add barley or brown rice. Bring to a boil over High heat. Reduce heat to Medium Low; cover. Simmer 30 to 35 minutes or until barley or rice is tender. Remove bay leaf. Skim off excess fat.

Suggested Combinations
Mediterranean Lamb Soup: Use chopped onion, chopped green pepper, sliced green olives and chopped tomatoes for vegetables. Use mint and shredded lemon peel for herbs. Use brown rice.
Scotch Broth: Use chopped onion, chopped carrot, chopped celery and chopped turnip for vegetables. Use tarragon and parsley flakes for herbs. Use barley.

Note: For small recipe, ask butcher to cut shank in half crosswise so it will lie flat in pan.

Cooking Times for Soup Ingredients

	amount added to 6 cups soup liquid	simmering time at Medium Low
INGREDIENT		
quick-cooking barley	1/2 cup uncooked	30 to 35 minutes
potatoes, cut in 1/2-inch cubes	2 large	30 to 35 minutes
quick-cooking brown rice	1/2 cup uncooked	30 to 35 minutes
medium noodles	1-1/2 cups uncooked (2 oz.)	20 to 25 minutes
Minute rice	1/2 cup uncooked	20 to 25 minutes
vegetables, see preparation on page 300	4 cups	15 to 25 minutes (at Medium)

Add ingredient toward end of soup cooking time after meat is cooked and tender. Stir ingredient into simmering soup liquid. Bring to a boil over High heat. Reduce heat to Medium Low for all ingredients except vegetables. Reduce heat to Medium for vegetables. Cover and simmer for time in chart above or until tender.

Note: If cooking vegetables *and* grains, potatoes, rice or pasta in same soup, use Medium heat. Cook vegetables for time in chart above; reduce cooking time 5 to 10 minutes for other ingredients.

How to Make Basic Lamb Soup

1/For the small recipe, ask the butcher to cut lamb shank in half crosswise. This allows the bone to lie flat in the pot. For Mediterranean Lamb Soup, combine with water, onion, green pepper, tomato and green olives for vegetables.

2/If using fresh mint, snip about four times the amount of dried mint into the soup. Add shredded lemon peel, bouillon granules, bay leaf and Worcestershire sauce for seasonings. Bring soup to a boil. Cover and simmer over Medium-Low heat.

3/Halfway through cooking time, use tongs to turn lamb shanks over for more even cooking. When done, lamb meat should be tender when tested with a fork. Cut meat in pieces. Discard fat and bones.

4/Add quick-cooking brown rice. Bring to a boil, then cover and simmer until rice is tender. Use a spoon to skim fat layer off top of soup before serving. Lay spoon flat on surface of soup; then gently depress it to collect fat.

Basic Chicken Soup

SERVINGS	4	2
INGREDIENTS		
broiler-fryer chicken, cut up	1/2 (3-lb.) chicken	1/4 (3-lb.) chicken
water	6 cups	3 cups
chopped vegetables	2 cups	1 cup
chicken-bouillon granules	2 tablespoons	1 tablespoon
dried leaf herb	2 teaspoons	1 teaspoon
peppercorns	16	8
medium noodles	1-1/2 cups uncooked (2 oz.)	3/4 cup uncooked (1 oz.)
OR		
Minute rice	1/2 cup uncooked	1/4 cup uncooked
DUTCH OVEN	4-qt. Dutch oven	3-qt. saucepan
TIME AT MEDIUM LOW (chicken)	45 minutes	45 minutes
TIME AT MEDIUM LOW (noodles or rice added)	20 to 25 minutes	20 to 25 minutes

In a Dutch oven, see size in chart above, combine chicken, water, vegetables, bouillon granules and herb. Tie peppercorns in a piece of cheesecloth or place in a tea ball. Add to soup. Bring to a boil over High heat. Reduce heat to Medium Low; cover. Simmer 45 minutes or until chicken is tender. Remove peppercorns and chicken from soup. Discard peppercorns. Remove and discard bones and skin from chicken. Cut up chicken. Return chicken to soup. Add noodles or rice. Bring to a boil over High heat. Reduce heat to Medium Low; cover. Simmer 20 to 25 minutes or until rice or noodles are tender. Skim off excess fat.

Suggested Combinations
Chicken-Noodle Soup: Use chopped celery, chopped carrot and chopped onion for vegetables. Use thyme and rubbed sage for herbs. Use noodles.
Chicken-Rice Soup: Use chopped zucchini, chopped green onion and chopped mushrooms for vegetables. Use tarragon for herb. Use Minute rice.

Cream of Chicken Soup

SERVINGS	4 to 6	2 or 3
INGREDIENTS		
Same ingredients as for Basic Chicken Soup, above, except omit rice or noodles and add:	large recipe	small recipe
all-purpose flour	2/3 cup	1/3 cup
milk	1 cup	1/2 cup
whipping cream	1 cup	1/2 cup
TIME AT MEDIUM HIGH	13 to 15 minutes	11 to 13 minutes
TIME AT MEDIUM LOW	3 to 5 minutes	6 to 8 minutes

Prepare Basic Chicken Soup, following recipe directions through cutting up cooked chicken. Remove vegetables from broth with a slotted spoon. Place in a blender or food processor fitted with a steel blade. Add 1/2 cup broth. Reserve remaining broth in Dutch oven. Process broth and vegetables until pureed. Return pureed mixture to Dutch oven. In a screw-top jar, combine flour and milk; shake well until completely smooth. Stir into pureed mixture. Cook over Medium-High heat for time in chart above or until thickened and bubbly all over, whisking constantly. Reduce heat to Medium Low. Stir in chicken. Gradually whisk in cream. Cover and cook for time in chart above or until heated through, stirring occasionally. Do not boil.

How to Make Basic Canned Chicken Soup Plus

1/For Far Eastern Chicken Soup, cook frozen Chinese-style vegetables with sauce cubes in canned chicken-rice soup and chicken broth. Add soy sauce for a flavor boost. Stir in cubes of chicken or turkey.

2/Bring to a boil. Cover and simmer over Medium-Low heat until vegetables are tender, stirring to dissolve sauce cubes. Serve soup in small bowls with additional soy sauce.

Basic Canned Chicken Soup Plus

SERVINGS	4	2
INGREDIENTS		
condensed soup	2 (10- to 11-oz.) cans	1 (10- to 11-oz.) can
chicken broth	2-1/2 cups	1-1/4 cups
water	1-1/4 cups	2/3 cup
seasoning	2 teaspoons	1 teaspoon
frozen vegetables with sauce cubes	1 (10-oz.) pkg.	1/2 (10-oz.) pkg.
cubed cooked chicken or turkey	2 cups	1 cup
SAUCEPAN	4-qt. saucepan	2-qt. saucepan
TIME AT MEDIUM LOW	5 to 8 minutes	5 to 7 minutes

In a saucepan, see size in chart above, combine soup, broth, water and seasoning. Stir in frozen vegetables and chicken or turkey. Bring to a boil over High heat, stirring occasionally. Reduce heat to Medium Low; cover. Simmer for time in chart above or until vegetables are tender, stirring occasionally to dissolve sauce cubes.

Suggested Combinations
Italian Chicken Soup: Use chicken broth with noodles. Use Worcestershire sauce for seasoning. Use frozen Italian-style vegetables.
Far Eastern Chicken Soup: Use chicken-rice soup. Use soy sauce for seasoning. Use frozen Chinese-style vegetables.

Basic Bean Soup

SERVINGS	5 or 6	2 or 3
INGREDIENTS		
dried beans	12 oz. (about 1-2/3 cups uncooked)	6 oz. (about 3/4 cup uncooked)
water	6 cups	3 cups
baking soda	1/4 teaspoon	1/8 teaspoon
smoked ham hocks, cut in 2-inch pieces, or meaty ham bone	2 lbs.	1 lb.
chopped vegetables	1-1/3 cups	2/3 cup
water	5 cups	3 cups
dried leaf herb, herb seed or ground spice	2 teaspoons	1 teaspoon
Worcestershire sauce	4 teaspoons	2 teaspoons
cooking sauce	2 cups	1 cup
garnishes, see suggestions below		
HEAVY DUTCH OVEN	5-qt. Dutch oven	3-qt. saucepan
SOAKING TIME	8 hours or overnight	8 hours or overnight
TIME AT MEDIUM LOW (beans, vegetables)	1-1/2 to 2 hours	1-1/2 to 2 hours
TIME AT MEDIUM LOW (cooking sauce added)	20 to 30 minutes	20 to 30 minutes

Sort and rinse beans. In a heavy Dutch oven, see size in chart above, combine beans, first amount of water and baking soda; mix well. Cover and soak 8 hours or overnight. Drain and rinse beans. Return beans to Dutch oven. Add ham hocks, vegetables, second amount of water, herb, seed or spice and Worcestershire sauce; mix well. Bring to a boil over High heat. Reduce heat to Medium Low. Skim off foam. Cover and simmer 1-1/2 to 2 hours or until beans are tender, stirring occasionally. Remove ham hocks from soup. Remove and discard bones. Cut up ham. Return ham to soup. Skim off excess fat. Stir in cooking sauce. Bring to a boil over High heat. Reduce heat to Medium Low; cover. Simmer 20 to 30 minutes or until flavors blend. Garnish each serving according to suggestions below.

Suggested Combinations
Garbanzo-Bean Soup: Use dried garbanzo beans. Use chopped green pepper, chopped onion and chopped green olives for vegetables. Use fennel seed for herb seed and ground cumin for spice. Use taco sauce for cooking sauce. Garnish with canned chopped green chilies and corn chips.

Navy-Bean Soup: Use dried pea beans or navy beans. Use chopped onion, chopped celery and chopped carrot for vegetables. Use thyme and basil for dried leaf herbs. Use applesauce for cooking sauce. Garnish with apple slices.

Tips for Soup Courses

- For first-course soups, choose light soups, such as Fruit Soup, page 280, Zesty Beef or Oriental Chicken Consomme, page 282, Gazpacho, page 278, Vichyssoise Deluxe, page 278, or Cold Vegetable Bisque, page 277. French Onion Soup, page 302, with its broiled two-cheese topper, is a special first course that is worth a little extra effort.

- Main-dish soups include Cream of Chicken and Basic Chicken Soup, page 286, full-bodied beef and lamb soups, pages 282 to 285, slow-simmered bean soups, page 288, thick lentil and split-pea soups, pages 190 and 191, fish and seafood chowders, pages 292 to 296, and Basic Cheese Soup, page 281. Each of these delicious soups can be the star of your menu. You only need to add bread, a simple salad or relish and a light dessert.

- Vegetable soups of all kinds are an excellent choice for sandwich partners. The start-from-scratch vegetable soup, page 300, can be adapted for any season. Creamy vegetable soups, page 298, taste extra rich without cream. Puree half the vegetable mixture in a blender or food processor for a velvety soup with no extra calories. Also, we have included two wonderful versions of potato soup, page 297.

Navy-Bean Soup

Basic Lentil Soup

SERVINGS	4	2
INGREDIENTS		
dried lentils	8 oz. (1-1/3 cups uncooked)	4 oz. (2/3 cup uncooked)
fully cooked sausage links, cut in 1/2-inch pieces	1 lb.	8 oz.
chopped vegetables	1-1/2 cups	3/4 cup
water	5 cups	3 cups
Worcestershire sauce	4 teaspoons	2 teaspoons
bay leaf	1 large	1 small
flavored salt	1 teaspoon	1/2 teaspoon
dried leaf herbs	2 teaspoons	1 teaspoon
pepper	1/4 teaspoon	1/8 teaspoon
garnishes, see suggestions below		
DUTCH OVEN	5-qt. Dutch oven	3-qt. saucepan
TIME AT MEDIUM LOW	1-1/4 to 1-1/2 hours	1-1/4 to 1-1/2 hours

Rinse and drain lentils. In a Dutch oven, see size in chart above, combine lentils, sausage, vegetables, water, Worcestershire sauce, bay leaf, flavored salt, herbs and pepper; mix well. Bring to a boil over High heat. Reduce heat to Medium Low; cover. Simmer 1-1/4 to 1-1/2 hours or until lentils are tender, stirring occasionally. Remove bay leaf. Skim off excess fat. Garnish each serving according to suggestions below.

Suggested Combinations
Spicy Lentil Soup: Use hot smoked Italian sausage. Use chopped onion and chopped green pepper for vegetables. Use onion salt for flavored salt. Use marjoram and basil for herbs. Use crushed red pepper for pepper. Garnish with chopped green pepper and chopped radishes.
Mushroom-Lentil Soup: Use sliced smoked bratwurst for sausage. Use sliced mushrooms and chopped green onion for vegetables. Use celery salt for flavored salt. Use fines herbes and grated lemon peel for herb. Use white pepper. Garnish with plain yogurt and sliced green olives.

Tips for Using Dried Beans, Lentils & Split Peas
- If you do not have time to soak beans overnight, omit baking soda. Bring beans and soaking water to a boil over High heat. Boil 2 minutes. Turn off heat. Cover and let stand 1 hour. Drain. Follow recipe directions for cooking beans.

- Do not use acid ingredients, such as fruit juices or tomatoes, for initial cooking of soaked beans. Acid prevents beans from becoming tender. First, cook beans in water or non-acid liquid until tender; then add acid ingredients.

- For thicker bean soup, remove about half of cooked beans with a slotted spoon. Mash beans and stir back into soup.

- Lentils are legumes. The seeds of the plant are used in soups, stews and salads. Egyptian lentils, the most common variety, were used in Basic Lentil Soup, above. These lentils are small, reddish, lens-shaped seeds. Buy the variety that does not require soaking.

- Split peas are available in two varieties. Green split peas come from dried green peas. Yellow split peas come from yellow field peas. Buy the variety that does not require soaking.

- Store lentils or split peas in a tightly covered container or sealed plastic bag.

How to Make Basic Split-Pea Soup

1/Two varieties of split peas, yellow and green, are layered in the jar in background. For Ham & Split-Pea Soup, stir green split peas into ground ham that has been cooked with green onion and celery. Add chicken broth and water. Use marjoram and mustard seed for seasonings.

2/Bring to a boil, then cover and simmer over Medium-Low heat 1-1/2 to 1-3/4 hours or until peas are tender. Soup mixture will become very thick. Serve soup in bowls, garnished with herbed croutons and small cubes of cooked ham.

Basic Split-Pea Soup

SERVINGS	4	2
INGREDIENTS		
dried split peas	8 oz. (1-1/3 cups uncooked)	4 oz. (2/3 cup uncooked)
ground meat	8 oz.	4 oz.
chopped vegetables	1 cup	1/2 cup
broth	2 (14-1/2-oz.) cans	1 (14-1/2-oz.) can
water	1-1/2 cups	1 cup
herb or herb seed	2 teaspoons	1 teaspoon
flavored croutons	to garnish	to garnish
DUTCH OVEN	4-qt. Dutch oven	3-qt. saucepan
TIME AT MEDIUM HIGH	6 to 7 minutes	6 to 7 minutes
TIME AT MEDIUM LOW	1-1/2 to 1-3/4 hours	1-1/2 to 1-3/4 hours

Rinse and drain split peas. In a Dutch oven, see size in chart above, cook meat and vegetables over Medium-High heat 6 to 7 minutes or until meat is cooked and vegetables are tender, stirring often. Drain well. Stir in peas, broth, water and herb or seed; mix well. Bring to a boil over High heat. Reduce heat to Medium Low; cover. Simmer 1-1/2 to 1-3/4 hours or until peas are tender, stirring occasionally. Garnish with croutons.

Suggested Combinations
Beefy Split-Pea Soup: Use ground beef for meat. Use chopped onion and chopped carrot for vegetables. Use beef broth. Use dried leaf thyme and dry mustard for herbs. Garnish with Cheddar croutons.
Ham & Split-Pea Soup: Use ground ham for meat. Use chopped green onion and chopped celery for vegetables. Use chicken broth. Use dried leaf marjoram for herb and mustard seed for herb seed. Garnish with herbed croutons.

Zesty Fish Chowder

SERVINGS	6	3
INGREDIENTS		
bacon, cut in 1-inch pieces	6 slices	3 slices
bacon drippings	1/4 cup	2 tablespoons
chopped celery	1/2 cup	1/4 cup
chopped green onion	1/4 cup	2 tablespoons
shredded carrot	1/4 cup	2 tablespoons
prepared horseradish	2 teaspoons	1 teaspoon
dry mustard	1 teaspoon	1/2 teaspoon
grated lemon peel	1 teaspoon	1/2 teaspoon
pepper	1/4 teaspoon	1/8 teaspoon
potatoes, peeled, cut in 1/2-inch cubes	2 large	1 large
chicken broth or clam juice	2 cups	1 cup
milk	3 cups	1-1/2 cups
fish fillets, cut in 1/2-inch pieces	1 lb.	8 oz.
frozen chopped spinach, thawed, well-drained	1 (10-oz.) pkg.	1/2 (10-oz.) pkg.
chopped pimiento	1/4 cup	2 tablespoons
all-purpose flour	1/4 cup	2 tablespoons
milk	1/2 cup	1/4 cup
DUTCH OVEN	4-qt. Dutch oven	2-qt. saucepan
TIME AT MEDIUM HIGH (bacon)	6 to 8 minutes	8 to 10 minutes
TIME AT MEDIUM HIGH (vegetables)	5 to 6 minutes	4 to 5 minutes
TIME AT MEDIUM LOW (potatoes, broth added)	8 minutes	8 minutes
TIME AT MEDIUM LOW (milk, fish added)	2-1/2 to 3-1/2 minutes	2-1/2 to 3-1/2 minutes
TIME AT MEDIUM HIGH (flour, milk added)	3 to 4 minutes	3 to 4 minutes

In a Dutch oven, see size in chart above, cook bacon over Medium-High heat for time in chart above or until crisp, stirring occasionally. Remove with a slotted spoon and drain on paper towels; set aside. Reserve in pan amount of bacon drippings listed in chart above. Cook celery, green onion and carrot in reserved drippings over Medium-High heat for time in chart above or until tender, stirring occasionally. Stir in horseradish, dry mustard, lemon peel and pepper; mix well. Stir in potatoes and broth or clam juice. Bring to a boil over High heat. Reduce heat to Medium Low; cover. Simmer 8 minutes or until potatoes are almost tender. Stir in first amount of milk and fish. Bring to a boil over High heat. Reduce heat to Medium Low; cover. Simmer 2-1/2 to 3-1/2 minutes or until fish flakes when tested with a fork. Press spinach in a sieve to remove as much water as possible. Stir spinach and pimiento into soup. In a screw-top jar, combine flour and second amount of milk; shake well until completely smooth. Stir into soup. Cook over Medium-High heat 3 to 4 minutes or until thickened and bubbly all over, stirring constantly. Garnish each serving with cooked bacon pieces.

Note: When cutting fish into pieces, be sure to remove any bones.

How to Make Zesty Fish Chowder

1/Sauté celery, green onion and carrot in bacon drippings. Add horseradish, dry mustard and lemon peel for seasonings. Simmer potato cubes and broth or clam juice with vegetables until tender. Stir in 1/2-inch pieces of fish fillets.

2/Bring soup to a boil. Cover and simmer 2-1/2 to 3-1/2 minutes or until fish flakes. It cooks very quickly. Add chopped spinach and pimiento to soup. Shake together flour and milk until completely smooth, then stir into soup and cook until thickened.

Basic Quick Seafood Chowder

SERVINGS	6	3
INGREDIENTS		
condensed cream soup	2 (10-3/4-oz.) cans	1 (10-3/4-oz.) can
milk	3 soup cans	1-1/2 soup cans
seasoning	4 teaspoons	2 teaspoons
loose-pack, frozen, combination vegetables	4 cups	2 cups
cooked seafood or fish	2 cups	1 cup
shredded cheese	1 cup (4 oz.)	1/2 cup (2 oz.)
garnishes, see suggestions below		
HEAVY SAUCEPAN	4-qt. saucepan	2-qt. saucepan
TIME AT MEDIUM LOW	4 to 8 minutes	4 to 8 minutes

In a heavy saucepan, see size in chart above, whisk together cream soup, milk and seasoning. Add frozen vegetables and seafood or fish. Bring to a boil over High heat, stirring often. Reduce heat to Medium Low; cover. Simmer 4 to 8 minutes or until vegetables are tender, stirring occasionally. Remove from heat. Stir in cheese until melted. Garnish according to suggestions below.

Suggested Combinations
Quick Shrimp Chowder: Use cream of shrimp soup. Use prepared horseradish for seasoning. Use broccoli, corn and red pepper for frozen vegetables. Use cooked shrimp for seafood. Use process Swiss cheese. Garnish with herb pepper.

Quick Tuna Chowder: Use creamy chicken-mushroom soup. Use prepared mustard for seasoning. Use broccoli, small whole carrots and water chestnuts for frozen vegetables. Use drained canned tuna, broken in chunks, for fish. Use process American cheese. Garnish with chopped hard-cooked egg and paprika.

New England Clam Chowder

SERVINGS	4	2
INGREDIENTS		
salt pork, rind removed, cut in 1/4-inch cubes	4 oz.	2 oz.
salt-pork drippings	1/4 cup	2 tablespoons
frozen O'Brien potatoes, thawed, see note below	2 cups	1 cup
all-purpose flour	2 tablespoons	1 tablespoon
celery salt	1/2 teaspoon	1/4 teaspoon
pepper	1/4 teaspoon	1/8 teaspoon
half and half	4 cups	2 cups
clam juice	1/2 cup	1/4 cup
chopped steamed clams or drained canned clams	1 cup	1/2 cup
snipped parsley	to garnish	to garnish
HEAVY SAUCEPAN	3-qt. saucepan	1-1/2-qt. saucepan
TIME AT MEDIUM HIGH (salt pork)	9 to 11 minutes	9 to 11 minutes
TIME AT MEDIUM HIGH (potatoes)	7 to 9 minutes	7 to 9 minutes
TIME AT MEDIUM HIGH (flour added)	1 minute	1 minute
TIME AT MEDIUM HIGH (liquid added)	14 to 16 minutes	10 to 12 minutes
TIME AT MEDIUM LOW	5 minutes	5 minutes

In a heavy saucepan, see size in chart above, cook salt pork over Medium-High heat 9 to 11 minutes or until crisp. Remove with a slotted spoon and drain on paper towels; set aside. Reserve in saucepan amount of drippings listed in chart above. Add butter or margarine to make enough drippings, if necessary. Cook potatoes in reserved drippings over Medium-High heat 7 to 9 minutes or until tender, stirring often. Stir in flour, celery salt and pepper; mix well. Cook and stir 1 minute. Stir in half and half and clam juice. Cook for time in chart above or until thickened and bubbly all over, stirring constantly. Reduce heat to Medium Low. Stir in clams; cover. Cook over Medium-Low heat 5 minutes or until heated through. Garnish with cooked salt pork and parsley.

Note: Frozen O'Brien potatoes are shredded potatoes with chopped onion, chopped green pepper and chopped red pepper added.

Tips for Clam Chowder

- If you use canned clams, 1 (6-1/2-ounce) can of chopped clams yields about 1/2 cup clams and 1/2 cup juice.
- If you want to steam fresh clams, see page 224.
- Supplement with bottled clam juice if canned clams or steamed fresh clams do not have enough juice.

How to Make Manhattan Seafood Chowder

1/Use scissors to cut up canned stewed tomatoes quickly. These tomatoes are canned with celery, green pepper and onion. Combine stewed tomatoes with water, Bloody-Mary mix, chili powder, sautéed onion, sautéed green pepper and frozen mixed vegetables.

2/Simmer soup mixture until frozen vegetables are tender. Stir in cooked clams, shrimp or tuna chunks. Cover and cook over Medium-Low heat until seafood is heated through. Serve in bowls with oyster crackers.

Manhattan Seafood Chowder

SERVINGS	4	2
INGREDIENTS		
butter or margarine	2 tablespoons	1 tablespoon
chopped onion	1/2 cup	1/4 cup
chopped green pepper	1/2 cup	1/4 cup
stewed tomatoes, cut up	2 (16-oz.) cans	1 (16-oz.) can
water	2 cups	1 cup
non-alcoholic Bloody-Mary mix	1 cup	1/2 cup
chili powder	2 teaspoons	1 teaspoon
frozen mixed vegetables	1 cup	1/2 cup
chopped cooked clams, cooked, whole, tiny shrimp or tuna chunks	1-1/2 to 2 cups	3/4 to 1 cup
SAUCEPAN	3-qt. saucepan	2-qt. saucepan
TIME AT MEDIUM HIGH	6 to 8 minutes	4 to 5 minutes
TIME AT MEDIUM LOW (vegetable mixture)	15 minutes	10 minutes
TIME AT MEDIUM LOW (seafood added)	5 minutes	5 minutes

In a saucepan, see size in chart above, combine butter or margarine, onion and green pepper. Cook over Medium-High heat for time in chart above or until tender, stirring occasionally. Stir in stewed tomatoes, water, Bloody-Mary mix, chili powder and frozen vegetables. Bring to a boil over High heat. Reduce heat to Medium Low; cover. Simmer for time in chart above or until vegetables are tender. Stir in clams, shrimp or tuna. Cover and cook 5 minutes or until heated through.

Oyster Stew

SERVINGS	4	2
INGREDIENTS		
fresh-shucked oysters with liquor	1 pint (24 to 30 oysters)	1/2 pint (12 to 15 oysters)
reserved oyster liquor	1/3 to 1/2 cup	3 to 4 tablespoons
milk	3 cups	1-1/2 cups
chopped celery	1/2 cup	1/4 cup
chopped green onion	1/4 cup	2 tablespoons
butter or margarine	1/4 cup	2 tablespoons
celery salt	1/2 teaspoon	1/4 teaspoon
dried leaf thyme	1/2 teaspoon	1/4 teaspoon
dry mustard	1/2 teaspoon	1/4 teaspoon
pepper	1/4 teaspoon	1/8 teaspoon
hot-pepper sauce	1/4 teaspoon	1/8 teaspoon
whipped cream, snipped chives	to garnish	to garnish
SAUCEPAN (milk, liquor)	1-1/2-qt. saucepan	1-qt. saucepan
HEAVY SAUCEPAN (vegetables, oysters)	2-qt. saucepan	1-1/2-qt. saucepan
TIME AT MEDIUM HIGH (milk, liquor)	8 to 10 minutes	5 to 6 minutes
TIME AT MEDIUM HIGH (celery, onion)	8 to 9 minutes	6 to 7 minutes
TIME AT MEDIUM (oysters added)	6 to 7 minutes	5 to 6 minutes
TIME AT MEDIUM (milk added)	8 to 12 minutes	3 to 5 minutes

Drain oysters, reserving amount of liquor listed in chart above. Set oysters aside. In a saucepan, see size in chart above, combine oyster liquor and milk. Cook, uncovered, over Medium-High heat for time in chart above or until very hot. Do not boil. Remove from heat. Cover and set aside. In a heavy saucepan, see size in chart above, cook celery and green onion in butter or margarine over Medium-High heat for time in chart above or until tender, stirring occasionally. Reduce heat to Medium. Stir in celery salt, thyme, dry mustard, pepper and pepper sauce; mix well. Add oysters. Cook for time in chart above or until edges of oysters just start to curl, stirring often. Stir in hot milk mixture. Cover and cook for time in chart above or until heated through, stirring occasionally. Serve in bowls. Garnish each serving with whipped cream and chives.

Tips for Oyster Stew

- Use small, tender stewing oysters for oyster stew rather than large frying oysters. One pint contains about 24 to 30 small oysters and about 1/3 to 1/2 cup oyster liquor.

- To open fresh oysters in the shell, follow directions for How to Make Mock Oysters Rockefeller, page 51.

- Oysters become tough if overcooked. Cook oysters in butter only until edges start to curl. Heat milk separately and then add to oysters to prevent oysters from overcooking while milk heats.

Basic Potato Soup

SERVINGS	5 or 6	2 or 3
INGREDIENTS		
potatoes, peeled, cut in 1/2-inch cubes	2 large (3 cups cubed)	1 large (1-1/2 cups cubed)
chicken broth	2 cups	1 cup
sliced or chopped vegetables	2 cups	1 cup
bacon drippings, butter or margarine	1/4 cup	2 tablespoons
all-purpose flour	1/4 cup	2 tablespoons
dried leaf herb	1 teaspoon	1/2 teaspoon
milk	2 cups	1 cup
plain yogurt	1 cup	1/2 cup
garnishes, see suggestions below		
SAUCEPAN (potatoes)	1-1/2-qt. saucepan	1-qt. saucepan
SAUCEPAN (vegetables)	3-qt. saucepan	2-qt. saucepan
TIME AT MEDIUM LOW	8 minutes	8 minutes
TIME AT MEDIUM HIGH (vegetables)	8 to 10 minutes	6 to 8 minutes
TIME AT MEDIUM HIGH (flour added)	1 minute	1 minute
TIME AT MEDIUM HIGH (milk added)	6 to 8 minutes	4 to 5 minutes
TIME AT MEDIUM	11 to 13 minutes	8 to 10 minutes

In a saucepan, see size in chart above, bring potatoes and broth to a boil over High heat. Reduce heat to Medium Low; cover. Cook 8 minutes or until tender. Do not drain. With a slotted spoon, remove half of potatoes; mash. Return to saucepan and set aside. In another saucepan, see size in chart above, cook vegetables in bacon drippings, butter or margarine over Medium-High heat for time in chart above or until tender, stirring occasionally. Whisk in flour and herb. Cook and stir 1 minute. Whisk in milk. Cook for time in chart above or until thickened and bubbly all over, stirring constantly with a whisk. Remove from heat. Gradually whisk half of hot milk mixture into yogurt. Return milk-yogurt mixture to saucepan, whisking well. Stir in potato mixture. Reduce heat to Medium; cover. Simmer for time in chart above or until heated through, stirring occasionally. Garnish each serving according to suggestions below.

Suggested Combinations

Potato Soup Florentine: Use chopped onions, sliced water chestnuts and thawed, frozen, chopped spinach, pressed in a sieve to remove as much water as possible, for vegetables. Use bacon drippings. Use thyme for herb. Garnish with spoonfuls of plain yogurt and crumbled cooked bacon.

Creamy Mushroom-Potato Soup: Use sliced fresh mushrooms, sliced leeks and sliced celery for vegetables. Use butter or margarine. Use tarragon for herb. Garnish with a wedge of semisoft natural cheese with garlic and herbs, snipped chives and paprika.

Tips for Hot Soups

- Serve hot soups in a variety of ways. Use large mugs for smooth cream soups. Serve appetizer broth soups in small glass bowls or wine glasses. Pour hot soup over the back of a metal spoon set in the glass to prevent the glass from cracking. Serve hearty chunky soups in low flat bowls for easier eating.

- Keep broth-based soups hot by leaving the pot covered over Low heat. Stir creamed soups occasionally while keeping them warm over Low heat. Watch creamed soups so they do not scorch on the bottom, separate or curdle from overheating.

Basic Creamy Vegetable Soup

SERVINGS	6	4	2
INGREDIENTS			
cubed or sliced vegetables, see suggestions below	3 cups	2 cups	1 cup
butter, margarine or bacon drippings	3 tablespoons	2 tablespoons	1 tablespoon
milk	3 cups	2 cups	1 cup
all-purpose flour	3 tablespoons	2 tablespoons	1 tablespoon
broth	2 cups	1 cup	1/2 cup
dried leaf herb or ground spice	3/4 to 1-1/2 teaspoons	1/2 to 1 teaspoon	1/4 to 1/2 teaspoon
grated Parmesan cheese	6 tablespoons	1/4 cup	2 tablespoons
butter or margarine	6 pats	4 pats	2 pats
snipped parsley or chives	to garnish	to garnish	to garnish
HEAVY SAUCEPAN	3-qt. saucepan	2-qt. saucepan	1-1/2-qt. saucepan
TIME AT MEDIUM HIGH (vegetables)	see timings in suggestions below		
TIME AT MEDIUM HIGH (flour, broth added)	23 to 25 minutes	21 to 23 minutes	12 to 14 minutes

In a heavy saucepan, see size in chart above, cook vegetables in first amount of butter, margarine or bacon drippings over Medium-High heat for time in suggestions below or until tender, stirring occasionally. Stir in milk. In a blender or food processor fitted with a steel blade, puree half of vegetable mixture until smooth. Return vegetable mixture to saucepan. In a screw-top jar, combine flour and 1/2 cup broth; shake well until completely smooth. Stir into vegetable mixture. Stir in any remaining broth and herb or spice. Cook over Medium-High heat for time in chart above or until thickened and bubbly all over, stirring constantly. Stir in cheese. Garnish each serving with 1 butter or margarine pat and fresh herbs or slices of appropriate vegetable.

Suggested Combinations
Creamy Carrot-Parsnip Soup: Use chopped carrots and chopped parsnips for vegetables. Cook in fat 18 to 20 minutes. Use beef broth. Use basil for herb.
Creamy Butternut-Onion Soup: Use peeled butternut or acorn squash, cut in 1/2-inch cubes, and onion, cut in thin slices, for vegetables. Cook in fat 8 to 10 minutes. Use chicken broth. Use smaller amount of cinnamon and nutmeg for spices.
Creamy Artichoke-Leek Soup: Use canned artichoke hearts, quartered and drained, and leeks, sliced 1/4 inch thick, for vegetables. Cook in fat 8 to 10 minutes. Use chicken broth. Use tarragon for herb.
Creamy Asparagus-Mushroom Soup: Use frozen cut asparagus, thawed, and fresh mushrooms, sliced 1/4 inch thick, for vegetables. Cook in fat 8 to 10 minutes. Use chicken broth. Use smaller amount of dill weed for herb.

Tips for Garnishing Hot Canned Soups

- Sprinkle tomato soup with buttered popcorn, grated Parmesan cheese and snipped parsley.
- Top creamy chicken-mushroom soup with herb-seasoned croutons, dried leaf thyme and chopped pimiento.
- Garnish split-pea soup with cubed cooked ham, chopped green onion and chopped carrot.
- Sprinkle chili-beef soup with shredded Cheddar cheese, chopped onion and canned chopped green chilies.
- Top cream of asparagus soup with chopped hard-cooked eggs, sunflower kernels and snipped watercress.
- Garnish cheese soup with chopped toasted pecans, snipped chives and chopped, seeded, peeled tomato.
- Sprinkle bean soup with crumbled cooked bacon, chopped green onion and crushed corn chips.

Creamy Carrot-Parsnip Soup

Basic Vegetable Soup

SERVINGS	8	4
INGREDIENTS		
soup bones	2 lbs.	1 lb.
canned tomatoes, cut up	1 (28-oz.) can	1 (16-oz.) can
vegetable-juice cocktail	2 (12-oz.) cans	1 (12-oz.) can
water	3 cups	1-1/2 cups
chopped onion	1 cup	1/2 cup
celery leaves	4 branch ends	2 branch ends
parsley	6 sprigs	3 sprigs
dried leaf herb	2 teaspoons	1 teaspoon
bay leaf	1 large	1 small
Worcestershire sauce	1 tablespoon	2 teaspoons
any combination of fresh or thawed frozen vegetables, see chart below	4 cups	2 cups
DUTCH OVEN	6-qt. Dutch oven	4-qt. Dutch oven
TIME AT MEDIUM LOW	1 hour	1 hour
TIME AT MEDIUM	15 to 25 minutes	15 to 25 minutes

In a Dutch oven, see size in chart above, combine soup bones, tomatoes, vegetable-juice cocktail, water, onion, celery leaves, parsley, herb, bay leaf and Worcestershire sauce; mix well. Bring to a boil over High heat. Reduce heat to Medium Low; cover. Simmer 1 hour. Remove and discard bones, celery branches, parsley sprigs and bay leaf. Add vegetables. Bring to a boil over High heat. Reduce heat to Medium; cover. Boil gently 15 to 25 minutes or until vegetables are tender. Skim off excess fat.

Suggested Combinations
Harvest Vegetable Soup: Use parsnips, winter squash and broccoli for vegetables. Use basil for herb.
Spring Vegetable Soup: Use asparagus, mushrooms and leeks for vegetables. Use dill weed for herb.
Summer Vegetable Soup: Use zucchini, corn on the cob and green beans for vegetables. Use oregano for herb.
Winter Vegetable Soup: Use carrots, potatoes and cabbage for vegetables. Use marjoram for herb.

Suggested Vegetables for Basic Vegetable Soup

VEGETABLE	PREPARATION
asparagus	cut in 1-inch lengths
broccoli flowerets	cut in 1-inch chunks
cabbage	cut in 1/8-inch slices
carrots	cut in 1/8-inch slices
cauliflowerets	cut in 1-inch chunks
celery	cut in 1/8-inch slices
corn on the cob	cut in 1-inch chunks
fennel	cut in 1/8-inch slices
green beans	cut in 1-inch lengths
kohlrabi	cut in 1/8-inch slices
leeks	cut in 1/8-inch slices
mushrooms, large	cut in 1/8-inch slices
mushrooms, small	leave whole
parsnips	cut in 1/8-inch slices
peas	leave whole
potatoes	cut in 1/2-inch cubes
rutabagas	cut in 1/2-inch cubes
sorrel	cut in 1/8-inch slices
spinach	cut in 1/8-inch slices
squash, winter	cut in 1/2-inch cubes
sweet potatoes	cut in 1/2-inch cubes
turnips	cut in 1/2-inch cubes
zucchini	cut in 1-inch chunks

How to Make Basic Vegetable Soup

1/Vegetables are cut into different-sized pieces according to their cooking times. Acorn squash is cut in 1/2-inch cubes, while more-tender zucchini squash is cut in 1-inch chunks. In background, bulb-shaped green roots are kohlrabi; long slender onions are leeks.

2/For a flavorful soup base, use inexpensive soup bones with little or no meat, canned tomatoes, vegetable-juice cocktail and water. Chopped onion, celery leaves, parsley sprigs, herb, bay leaf and Worcestershire sauce are also used as basic seasonings.

3/Simmer bone mixture 1 hour to develop flavors. Remove bones and celery, parsley and bay leaf. Vary vegetable soup by seasons. Spring Vegetable Soup features fresh asparagus, cut in 1-inch lengths, small whole mushrooms, and leeks, cut in 1/8-inch slices.

4/Add vegetables and bring to a boil. Cover and boil gently over Medium heat 15 to 25 minutes until vegetables are tender. Skim off fat from top of soup. Serve in bowls, accompanied by crisp bread sticks.

French Onion Soup

SERVINGS	4	2
INGREDIENTS		
French bread, sliced 1/2 inch thick	4 slices	2 slices
butter or margarine	6 tablespoons	3 tablespoons
onions, thinly sliced	4 medium (4 to 5 cups)	2 medium (2 to 2-1/2 cups)
sugar	1 tablespoon	2 teaspoons
all-purpose flour	2 teaspoons	1 teaspoon
dry mustard	1 teaspoon	1/2 teaspoon
condensed chicken broth	2 (10-3/4-oz.) cans	1 (10-3/4-oz.) can
dry white wine	1/4 cup	2 tablespoons
Worcestershire sauce	2 teaspoons	1 teaspoon
grated Parmesan cheese	1/4 cup (3/4 oz.)	2 tablespoons
shredded Gruyère cheese	1 cup (4 oz.)	1/2 cup (2 oz.)
BAKING SHEET	baking sheet	baking sheet
HEAVY SKILLET	11-inch skillet	10-inch skillet
SOUP BOWLS	4 (1-1/2-cup) ovenproof bowls	2 (1-1/2-cup) ovenproof bowls
TIME AT BROIL (bread)	2 minutes	2 minutes
TIME IN 250F (120C) OVEN	dry bread in oven until soup is done	
TIME AT MEDIUM (onions)	30 to 35 minutes	20 to 25 minutes
TIME AT MEDIUM (sugar, flour added)	1 minute	1 minute
TIME AT MEDIUM LOW	10 to 15 minutes	10 minutes
TIME AT BROIL (finished soup)	2 to 2-1/2 minutes	2 to 2-1/2 minutes

Place French bread on a baking sheet. Preheat an electric broiler. You do not need to preheat a gas broiler. Broil bread 4 inches from the heating element 2 minutes or until toasted, turning bread over once. Move baking sheet to middle oven rack. Dry bread in a 250F (120C) oven until soup is done. In a heavy skillet, see size in chart above, melt butter or margarine over Medium heat. Add onions. Cook for time in chart above or until onions are very tender and light golden brown, stirring often. In a small bowl, stir together sugar, flour and dry mustard. Stir into onions over Medium heat 1 minute or until blended. Stir in broth, wine and Worcestershire sauce; mix well. Bring to a boil over Medium-High heat. Reduce heat to Medium Low; cover. Simmer for time in chart above. Ladle soup into 2 or 4 (1-1/2-cup) ovenproof bowls. Set bowls on a baking sheet. Top each serving with 1 slice dried French bread. Sprinkle with Parmesan cheese, then Gruyère cheese. Broil soup 4 inches from heat 2 to 2-1/2 minutes or until cheese is bubbly and melted.

Tips for Using Broth in Soup

Use the type of broth specified in each recipe.

- Condensed beef broth or bouillon is available in 10-1/2-ounce cans. Condensed chicken broth or bouillon is available in 10-3/4-ounce cans. This broth is concentrated and provides more flavor. If the recipe calls for *condensed* broth, do not dilute it. The recipe allows for necessary dilution. If the recipe calls only for chicken or beef *broth,* dilute *condensed* broth with 1 can water.

- Ready-to-serve beef or chicken broth is available in 14-1/2-ounce cans. If the recipe calls for chicken or beef broth, use this broth *without* diluting.

- Beef- or chicken-bouillon *granules* may be used to make broth. Use 1 teaspoon bouillon granules in 1 cup boiling water. Stir until dissolved. Or, sprinkle bouillon granules into soups to give stock more flavor.

- Vegetable, beef or chicken bouillon *cubes* may be used to make broth. Use 1 bouillon cube in 1 cup boiling water. Stir until dissolved.

- For homemade broth, save pan juices from poached or braised meat or poultry. Cover and refrigerate, or freeze in airtight containers for longer storage. Keep separate freezer containers for beef and chicken broth. Add pan juices to frozen broth as they become available.

How to Make French Onion Soup

1/In a heavy skillet, cook thinly sliced onions in butter or margarine until onions are light golden brown. Stir often to keep onions on bottom of skillet from overbrowning.

2/Stir sugar, flour and dry mustard into onions. Cook 1 minute. Stir in chicken broth, white wine and Worcestershire sauce. Bring to a boil, then simmer soup 10 to 15 minutes to blend flavors.

3/Ladle soup into ovenproof serving bowls. Top each serving with a toasted French-bread slice, grated Parmesan cheese and shredded Gruyère cheese.

4/Place bowls on a baking sheet. Place on the oven rack so cheese is 4 inches from the heating element. Broil 2 to 2-1/2 minutes or until cheese melts.

Béarnaise Sauce

YIELD	2-2/3 cups	1-1/3 cups
INGREDIENTS		
dry white wine	1/3 cup	3 tablespoons
white-wine vinegar	1/3 cup	3 tablespoons
chopped onion	2 tablespoons	1 tablespoon
dried leaf tarragon	2 teaspoons	1 teaspoon
dried leaf chervil	2 teaspoons	1 teaspoon
reserved wine mixture	1/3 cup	3 tablespoons
egg yolks	6	3
salt	1/8 teaspoon	dash
white pepper	1/8 teaspoon	dash
butter or margarine, melted	1-1/2 cups	3/4 cup
dried leaf tarragon	1/2 teaspoon	1/4 teaspoon
dried leaf chervil	1/2 teaspoon	1/4 teaspoon
SAUCEPAN	1-qt. saucepan	1-qt. saucepan
TIME AT MEDIUM HIGH	6 to 8 minutes	4 to 6 minutes
BLENDING TIME AT LOW SPEED	30 seconds	30 seconds
BLENDING TIME AT HIGH SPEED (while adding butter)	3 to 3-1/2 minutes	1-1/2 to 1-3/4 minutes
BLENDING TIME AT HIGH SPEED (after adding butter)	1 to 1-1/2 minutes	45 to 60 seconds

In a 1-quart saucepan, combine wine, vinegar, onion, first amount of tarragon and first amount of chervil. Bring to a boil over High heat. Reduce heat to Medium High. Continue boiling for time in chart above or until liquid is reduced by one-half. Strain wine mixture, reserving amount listed in chart above. Cool to lukewarm. Discard herbs and onion. In a blender, combine reserved wine mixture, egg yolks, salt and pepper. Cover and blend at low speed 30 seconds or until frothy. Turn blender to high speed. Slowly pour in hot melted butter or margarine, blending constantly for time in chart above. After adding butter or margarine, continue blending for time in chart above. Scrape sides of blender often. Stir in second amounts of tarragon and chervil. Stir before using. Serve with meats.

Horseradish Béarnaise Sauce

YIELD	2-2/3 cups	1-1/3 cups
INGREDIENTS		
Same ingredients as for Béarnaise Sauce, above, except omit second amounts of tarragon and chervil and add:	large recipe	small recipe
prepared horseradish	4 to 6 teaspoons	2 to 3 teaspoons

Prepare Béarnaise Sauce, omitting second amounts of tarragon and chervil. Stir horseradish into finished sauce; mix well. Serve with beef or seafood.

Tips for Warming Hollandaise or Béarnaise Sauces

- To keep sauce warm before serving, pour sauce into a large measuring cup. Set cup in a pan of very hot tap water. Water level should be same as sauce level in cup. Stir sauce frequently. Sauce will remain warm about 30 minutes.
- To reheat 1 cup refrigerated sauce, place sauce in a 1-cup measuring cup. Set cup in a 2-quart saucepan of boiling water set away from heat. Water level should be same as sauce level in cup. Stir sauce frequently. Sauce will be warm in 7 to 10 minutes.

How to Make Béarnaise Sauce

1/In a small saucepan, combine white wine, vinegar, chopped onion, tarragon and chervil. Measure depth of liquid. Boil until liquid is reduced by one-half. Measure again with ruler to determine when half of liquid has evaporated.

2/Strain cooked wine mixture; cool to lukewarm. In a blender, combine cooled liquid, egg yolks, salt and pepper. Cover and blend at low speed 30 seconds or until mixture is frothy.

3/With blender at high speed, slowly pour melted butter into funnel formed in blender by egg mixture. Add butter very slowly during blending time.

4/Continue blending mixture 45 to 90 seconds after adding butter. Mixture will be thick. Stir in more tarragon and chervil. Serve in small individual sauce dishes as an accompaniment to meats.

Hollandaise Sauce

YIELD	2 cups	1 cup
INGREDIENTS		
egg yolks	6	3
lemon juice	1/4 cup	2 tablespoons
salt	1/8 teaspoon	dash
white pepper	1/8 teaspoon	dash
butter or margarine, melted	1 cup	1/2 cup
grated lemon peel	1/2 teaspoon	1/4 teaspoon
BLENDING TIME AT LOW SPEED	30 seconds	30 seconds
BLENDING TIME AT HIGH SPEED (while adding butter)	3 to 3-1/2 minutes	1-1/2 to 1-3/4 minutes
BLENDING TIME AT HIGH SPEED (after adding butter)	1 to 1-1/2 minutes	30 to 60 seconds

In a blender, combine egg yolks, lemon juice, salt and pepper. Cover and blend at low speed 30 seconds or until frothy. Turn blender to high speed. Slowly pour in hot melted butter or margarine, blending constantly for time in chart above. After adding butter or margarine, continue blending for time in chart above. Scrape sides of blender often. Stir in peel. Stir before serving. Serve with egg dishes, vegetables or fish.

Basic Herbed Hollandaise Sauce

YIELD	2 cups	1 cup
INGREDIENTS		
Hollandaise Sauce, above	large recipe	small recipe
dried leaf herb	1/2 teaspoon	1/4 teaspoon
OR		
snipped fresh herb	2 teaspoons	1 teaspoon
OR		
drained, rinsed, green peppercorns or capers	2 tablespoons	1 tablespoon

Prepare Hollandaise Sauce. After blending, stir herb, peppercorns or capers into finished sauce.

Suggested Combinations
Minted Hollandaise Sauce: Use dried or fresh mint leaves for herb. Serve with lamb.
Hollandaise Sauce au Poivre: Use green peppercorns. Serve with beef steaks or lamb chops.
Dill Hollandaise Sauce: Use dried or fresh dill weed for herb. Serve with fish or vegetables.
Caper Hollandaise Sauce: Use capers. Serve with seafood.

Maltaise Sauce

YIELD	2 cups	1 cup
INGREDIENTS		
Same ingredients as for Hollandaise Sauce, above, except reduce lemon juice by one-half and add:	large recipe	small recipe
frozen orange-juice concentrate, thawed	2 tablespoons	1 tablespoon

Prepare Hollandaise Sauce, adding orange-juice concentrate with lemon juice. Serve with vegetables or fish.

White Sauce—Thin

YIELD	2 cups	1-1/4 cups	1/2 cup
INGREDIENTS			
butter or margarine	2 tablespoons	1 tablespoon	1-1/2 teaspoons
all-purpose flour	2 tablespoons	1 tablespoon	1-1/2 teaspoons
salt or flavored salt	1/2 teaspoon	1/4 teaspoon	1/8 teaspoon
pepper	1/8 teaspoon	dash	dash
milk	2 cups	1 cup	1/2 cup
SAUCEPAN	1-1/2-qt. saucepan	1-qt. saucepan	1-qt. saucepan
TIME AT MEDIUM HIGH (flour added)	1 minute	30 seconds	30 seconds
TIME AT MEDIUM HIGH (milk added)	6-1/2 to 8-1/2 minutes	5 to 7 minutes	3 to 4 minutes

In a saucepan, see size in chart above, melt butter or margarine over Medium-High heat. Whisk in flour, salt and pepper. Cook and stir for time in chart above. Whisk in milk. Cook for time in chart above or until thickened and bubbly all over, whisking constantly. Sauce should be thickened and smooth.

White Sauce—Thick

YIELD	2-1/2 cups	1-1/4 cups	2/3 cup
INGREDIENTS			
butter or margarine	1/2 cup	1/4 cup	2 tablespoons
all-purpose flour	1/2 cup	1/4 cup	2 tablespoons
salt or flavored salt	1/2 teaspoon	1/4 teaspoon	1/8 teaspoon
pepper	1/8 teaspoon	dash	dash
milk	2 cups	1 cup	1/2 cup
SAUCEPAN	1-1/2-qt. saucepan	1-qt. saucepan	1-qt. saucepan
TIME AT MEDIUM HIGH (flour added)	1 minute	1 minute	1 minute
TIME AT MEDIUM HIGH (milk added)	6-1/2 to 8-1/2 minutes	5 to 7 minutes	3 to 4 minutes

In a saucepan, see size in chart above, melt butter or margarine over Medium-High heat. Whisk in flour, salt and pepper. Cook and stir 1 minute. Whisk in milk. Cook for time in chart above or until thickened and bubbly all over, whisking constantly. Sauce should be thickened and smooth.

Tips for Making & Using White Sauce

- When making White Sauce, butter or margarine and flour are cooked together to maximize thickening effect of flour. This butter-flour mixture is called *roux*.
- Whisking roux and milk mixture during cooking prevents flour from lumping in sauce. Do not whisk rapidly or sauce will break down. Whisk at about the same rate as you would stir with a spoon.
- White Sauce thickens more as it cools.
- White sauces are used in many recipes. Thin White Sauce is used as a base for cream soup. Medium White Sauce is the most versatile of white sauces. It is used as a base for many flavored sauces and is the right consistency to serve over meat, poultry, fish or vegetables. Thick White Sauce is usually used to bind ingredients together, such as in croquettes.

How to Make White Sauce

1/White Sauce is the foundation for many other sauces, so it is worth mastering. Whisk flour, salt and pepper into melted butter or margarine until mixture is smooth. Cook and stir flour mixture 30 to 60 seconds. This ensures proper thickening.

2/Whisk cold milk into cooked flour mixture. Whisk sauce continuously as it cooks to prevent flour mixture from lumping. Not only do lumps create undesirable texture, they also prevent sauce from thickening properly.

3/To make Cheese Sauce, page 311, gradually whisk shredded or cubed cheese into hot thickened sauce over Medium-Low heat until cheese melts. Cheddar, Swiss, Monterey Jack, Gruyère, brick and American are all good choices for Cheese Sauce.

4/To make Fresh-Herb Sauce, page 311, snip fresh herbs, parsley and chives into hot thickened White Sauce. Use basil, tarragon, oregano, dill weed or thyme for herbs. If fresh herbs are not available, substitute about one-fourth as much dried herb for fresh.

White Sauce—Medium
(Béchamel Sauce)

YIELD	2-1/4 cups	1-1/4 cups	2/3 cup
INGREDIENTS			
butter or margarine	1/4 cup	2 tablespoons	1 tablespoon
all-purpose flour	1/4 cup	2 tablespoons	1 tablespoon
salt or flavored salt	1/2 teaspoon	1/4 teaspoon	1/8 teaspoon
pepper	1/8 teaspoon	dash	dash
milk	2 cups	1 cup	1/2 cup
SAUCEPAN	1-1/2-qt. saucepan	1-qt. saucepan	1-qt. saucepan
TIME AT MEDIUM HIGH (flour added)	1 minute	1 minute	30 seconds
TIME AT MEDIUM HIGH (milk added)	6-1/2 to 8-1/2 minutes	5 to 7 minutes	3 to 4 minutes

In a saucepan, see size in chart above, melt butter or margarine over Medium-High heat. Whisk in flour, salt and pepper. Cook and stir for time in chart above. Whisk in milk. Cook for time in chart above or until thickened and bubbly all over, whisking constantly. Sauce should be thickened and smooth.

Variations
Veloute Sauce: Same ingredients as for White Sauce—Medium, above, except use chicken broth or fish stock instead of milk.
Mornay Sauce: Same ingredients as for White Sauce—Medium, above, except use half chicken broth and half milk for liquid. Stir 2 tablespoons shredded Gruyère cheese and 2 tablespoons grated Parmesan cheese into each cup hot sauce.

Caper Sauce

YIELD	2-1/2 cups	1-1/3 cups	2/3 cup
INGREDIENTS			
White Sauce—Medium, above	large recipe	medium recipe	small recipe
dry mustard	1 teaspoon	1/2 teaspoon	1/4 teaspoon
drained capers	2 tablespoons	4 teaspoons	2 teaspoons
snipped parsley	2 tablespoons	4 teaspoons	2 teaspoons
chopped pimiento	2 tablespoons	4 teaspoons	2 teaspoons
snipped chives	1 tablespoon	2 teaspoons	1 teaspoon
grated lemon peel	1 teaspoon	1/2 teaspoon	1/4 teaspoon
TIME AT MEDIUM LOW	1 to 2 minutes	1 to 2 minutes	1 to 2 minutes

Prepare White Sauce—Medium, adding dry mustard to butter with flour. Stir capers, parsley, pimiento, chives and lemon peel into hot sauce. Stir over Medium-Low heat 1 to 2 minutes or until heated through. Serve with chicken or fish.

Zesty Horseradish-Mustard Sauce

YIELD	2-1/3 cups	1-1/4 cups	2/3 cup
INGREDIENTS			
White Sauce—Medium, opposite	large recipe	medium recipe	small recipe
prepared horseradish	1-1/2 teaspoons	1 teaspoon	1/2 teaspoon
prepared or Dijon-style mustard	1-1/2 teaspoons	1 teaspoon	1/2 teaspoon

Prepare White Sauce—Medium. Stir horseradish and mustard into hot sauce. Serve with meat or seafood.

Cheese Sauce

YIELD	2-3/4 cups	1-1/2 cups	3/4 cup
INGREDIENTS			
White Sauce—Medium, opposite	large recipe	medium recipe	small recipe
dry mustard	1-1/2 teaspoons	1 teaspoon	1/2 teaspoon
shredded or cubed cheese	1-1/2 cups (6 oz.)	1 cup (4 oz.)	1/2 cup (2 oz.)
TIME AT MEDIUM LOW	3 to 4 minutes	2 to 3 minutes	30 to 60 seconds

Prepare White Sauce—Medium, adding dry mustard to butter or margarine with flour. Gradually whisk cheese into hot sauce over Medium-Low heat for time in chart above or until cheese melts. Whisk until smooth.

Suggested Cheeses: Cheddar, Swiss, Gruyère, brick, Monterey Jack, American.

Fresh-Herb Sauce

YIELD	2-1/2 cups	1-1/2 cups	2/3 cup
INGREDIENTS			
White Sauce—Medium, opposite	large recipe	medium recipe	small recipe
fresh snipped herbs	2 to 4 tablespoons	1 to 2 tablespoons	2 to 3 teaspoons
snipped parsley	2 tablespoons	1 tablespoon	2 teaspoons
snipped chives	1 tablespoon	2 teaspoons	1 teaspoon

Prepare White Sauce—Medium. Stir fresh herbs, parsley and chives into hot sauce. Serve with chicken or fish.

Suggested Herbs: basil, tarragon, oregano, dill weed, thyme.

Variation
Substitute dried leaf herbs for fresh herbs. Use 1 to 2 teaspoons for large recipe, 1/2 to 1 teaspoon for medium recipe and 1/4 to 1/2 teaspoon for small recipe. Yield will be slightly less.

Creamy Tomato Sauce

YIELD	2-1/4 cups	1 cup
INGREDIENTS		
chopped, seeded, peeled tomatoes	1-1/2 cups	3/4 cup
plain yogurt	1 cup	1/2 cup
snipped parsley	1/4 cup	2 tablespoons
chopped green onion	2 tablespoons	1 tablespoon
snipped fresh herb OR	2 tablespoons	1 tablespoon
dried leaf herb	1 to 2 teaspoons	1/2 to 1 teaspoon
white-wine vinegar	2 teaspoons	1 teaspoon
drained capers	2 teaspoons	1 teaspoon
freshly ground pepper	1/4 teaspoon	1/8 teaspoon
REFRIGERATE	3 hours or overnight	3 hours or overnight

In a medium bowl, combine tomatoes, yogurt, parsley, green onion and herb; mix well. Stir in vinegar, capers and pepper. Cover and refrigerate 3 hours or overnight. Serve as relish with cold-vegetable platters, cold fish or cold meats.

Suggested Herbs: basil, oregano, thyme, dill weed, burnet.

Spanish Sauce

YIELD	3 cups	1-1/2 cups
INGREDIENTS		
olive oil	1/4 cup	2 tablespoons
chopped onion	1/2 cup	1/4 cup
chopped green pepper	1/2 cup	1/4 cup
chopped celery	1/2 cup	1/4 cup
canned tomatoes, drained, cut up	2 (28-oz.) cans	1 (28-oz.) can
packed brown sugar	4 teaspoons	2 teaspoons
garlic salt	1/2 teaspoon	1/4 teaspoon
dried leaf oregano	1 teaspoon	1/2 teaspoon
dried leaf basil	1 teaspoon	1/2 teaspoon
HEAVY SAUCEPAN	2-qt. saucepan	1-1/2-qt. saucepan
TIME AT MEDIUM HIGH	10 to 12 minutes	6 to 8 minutes
TIME AT MEDIUM LOW	30 to 45 minutes	30 to 45 minutes

In a heavy saucepan, see size in chart above, combine olive oil, onion, green pepper and celery. Cook over Medium-High heat for time in chart above or until tender, stirring often. Stir in tomatoes, brown sugar, garlic salt, oregano and basil; mix well. Bring to a boil over High heat. Reduce heat to Medium Low. Simmer, uncovered, 30 to 45 minutes or until very thick, stirring occasionally. Serve hot with omelets, sausage or fish. Or, chill and serve with cold cuts for sandwiches.

Choron Sauce

YIELD	2-2/3 cups	1-1/3 cups
INGREDIENTS		
Same ingredients as for Béarnaise Sauce, page 304, except omit second amounts of tarragon and chervil and add:	large recipe	small recipe
tomato paste	2 tablespoons	1 tablespoon

Prepare Béarnaise Sauce, omitting second amounts of tarragon and chervil. Stir tomato paste into finished sauce; whisk well. Serve with beef.

How to Make Creamy Tomato Sauce

1/Tomatoes are easier to peel if they have been blanched first. Plunge tomatoes into boiling water 30 to 60 seconds, then place in cold water. Peels will slip off easily with a small knife.

2/Cut tomatoes in wedges, then seed and chop. Combine with yogurt, parsley, green onion, herbs, vinegar, capers and pepper. Serve with cold meat and relish tray.

Herbed Fresh-Tomato Sauce

YIELD	3-1/2 cups	1-3/4 cups
INGREDIENTS		
tomatoes, peeled, cored, quartered	6	3
celery, cut up	1 stalk	1/2 stalk
green pepper, cut up	1 small	1/2 small
onion, cut up	1/2 small	1/4 small
fresh herb leaves	1/4 cup	2 tablespoons
OR		
dried leaf herbs	4 teaspoons	2 teaspoons
parsley	4 sprigs	2 sprigs
SAUCEPAN	2-qt. saucepan	1-qt. saucepan
TIME AT MEDIUM LOW	15 to 20 minutes	15 to 20 minutes

In a blender or food processor fitted with a steel blade, combine tomatoes, celery, green pepper, onion, herbs and parsley. Process until smooth. Process large recipe in 2 or 3 batches. Pour into a saucepan, see size in chart above. Bring to a boil over Medium-High heat, stirring often. Reduce heat to Medium Low; cover. Simmer 15 to 20 minutes or until flavors blend, stirring occasionally. Serve on vegetables or pasta. Or, use instead of tomato sauce in recipes.

Suggested Herbs: oregano, basil, thyme, marjoram.

Note: To peel tomatoes easily, plunge tomatoes into boiling water 30 to 60 seconds, then plunge into cold water.

Basic Barbecue Sauce

YIELD	4-1/3 cups	2-1/4 cups
INGREDIENTS		
vegetable oil	1/4 cup	2 tablespoons
chopped vegetables	2 cups	1 cup
ketchup	2 cups	1 cup
water	1 cup	1/2 cup
cooking liquid	1 cup	1/2 cup
packed brown sugar	1/4 cup	2 tablespoons
vinegar	1/4 cup	2 tablespoons
seasoning	2 tablespoons	1 tablespoon
dried leaf herbs or herb seed	2 teaspoons	1 teaspoon
OR		
ground spices	1 teaspoon	1/2 teaspoon
HEAVY SAUCEPAN	3-qt. saucepan	1-1/2-qt. saucepan
TIME AT MEDIUM HIGH	8 to 10 minutes	6 to 9 minutes
TIME AT MEDIUM LOW	2 hours	1-1/2 hours

In a heavy saucepan, see size in chart above, cook oil and vegetables over Medium-High heat for time in chart above or until tender, stirring often. Stir in ketchup, water, cooking liquid, brown sugar, vinegar, seasoning and herbs, seed or spices. Bring to a boil over High heat. Reduce heat to Medium Low. Simmer, uncovered, for time in chart above or until slightly thickened, stirring occasionally. Brush on broiled or grilled meats, fish or poultry during last 1 to 2 minutes cooking time. Heat and serve remaining sauce.

Suggested Combinations
Beef Barbecue Sauce: Use chopped onion and chopped mushrooms for vegetables. Use red wine for cooking liquid. Use red-wine vinegar. Use Worcestershire sauce for seasoning. Use mustard seed.
Chicken Barbecue Sauce: Use chopped green onion and chopped celery for vegetables. Use cranberry-juice cocktail for cooking liquid. Use white vinegar. Use Worcestershire sauce for seasoning. Use thyme and marjoram for herbs.
Pork Barbecue Sauce: Use chopped onion for vegetable and chopped apple instead of second vegetable. Use apple juice for cooking liquid. Use cider vinegar. Use Worcestershire sauce for seasoning. Use cinnamon and nutmeg for spices.
Fish Barbecue Sauce: Use chopped green onion and chopped green pepper for vegetables. Use beer for cooking liquid. Use white-wine vinegar. Use prepared horseradish for seasoning. Use celery seed.

Easy Barbecue Sauce

YIELD	2-1/2 cups	1-1/4 cups
INGREDIENTS		
chili sauce	1 (12-oz.) bottle (1 cup)	1/2 (12-oz.) bottle (1/2 cup)
cranberry-orange relish	1 cup	1/2 cup
packed brown sugar	1/4 cup	2 tablespoons
vinegar	2 tablespoons	1 tablespoon
Worcestershire sauce	4 teaspoons	2 teaspoons
celery seed	1 teaspoon	1/2 teaspoon
dry mustard	1 teaspoon	1/2 teaspoon
liquid smoke	1/2 teaspoon	1/4 teaspoon
SAUCEPAN	1-qt. saucepan	1-qt. saucepan
TIME AT MEDIUM LOW	5 minutes	5 minutes

In a 1-quart saucepan, combine all ingredients; mix well. Bring to a boil over High heat, stirring often. Reduce heat to Medium Low. Simmer, uncovered, 5 minutes, stirring often. Serve with ribs, chicken, fish or hamburgers.

Chicken Barbecue Sauce

Basic Vegetable Cream Sauce

YIELD	3 cups	1-1/2 cups	3/4 cup
INGREDIENTS			
butter, margarine or bacon drippings	1/4 cup	2 tablespoons	1 tablespoon
chopped or sliced vegetables	3 cups	1-1/2 cups	3/4 cup
all-purpose flour	6 tablespoons	3 tablespoons	4 teaspoons
dried leaf herb	1 teaspoon	1/2 teaspoon	1/4 teaspoon
flavored salt	1/2 teaspoon	1/4 teaspoon	1/8 teaspoon
pepper	1/4 teaspoon	1/8 teaspoon	dash
milk	1 cup	1/2 cup	1/4 cup
chicken broth	1 cup	1/2 cup	1/4 cup
snipped watercress or chives	to garnish	to garnish	to garnish
HEAVY SAUCEPAN	3-qt. saucepan	1-1/2-qt. saucepan	1-qt. saucepan
TIME AT MEDIUM HIGH (vegetables)	9 to 11 minutes	7 to 9 minutes	5 to 7 minutes
TIME AT MEDIUM HIGH (flour added)	1 minute	1 minute	30 seconds
TIME AT MEDIUM HIGH (milk, broth added)	11 to 13 minutes	4 to 6 minutes	2 to 3 minutes

In a heavy saucepan, see size in chart above, combine butter, margarine or bacon drippings and vegetables. Cook over Medium-High heat for time in chart above or until tender, stirring often. Stir in flour, herb, flavored salt and pepper. Cook and stir for time in chart above. Whisk in milk and chicken broth. Cook for time in chart above or until thickened and bubbly all over, whisking constantly. Serve with soufflés, omelets or crepes. Garnish with watercress or chives.

Suggested Combinations
Mushroom Cream Sauce: Use sliced fresh mushrooms, sliced leeks and chopped celery for vegetables. Use tarragon for herb. Use celery salt for flavored salt. Garnish with watercress.
Zucchini Cream Sauce: Use chopped zucchini, chopped green onion and chopped pimiento for vegetables. Use basil for herb. Use onion salt for flavored salt. Garnish with chives.

Basic Onion-Butter Sauce

YIELD	1-1/3 cups	2/3 cup
INGREDIENTS		
butter or margarine	1/4 cup	2 tablespoons
onions, thinly sliced, separated in rings	2 medium (2 cups sliced)	1 medium (1 cup sliced)
cooking liquid	1/2 cup	1/4 cup
seasoning	2 teaspoons	1 teaspoon
whole or ground spice	1 teaspoon	1/2 teaspoon
snipped parsley or chives	to garnish	to garnish
SKILLET	10-inch skillet	8-inch skillet
TIME AT MEDIUM HIGH (onions)	8 to 10 minutes	8 to 10 minutes
TIME AT MEDIUM HIGH (liquid, seasoning added)	1 to 2 minutes	1 to 2 minutes

In a skillet, see size in chart above, cook butter or margarine and onions over Medium-High heat 8 to 10 minutes or until tender, stirring often. Stir in cooking liquid, seasoning and herb or spice. Cook and stir 1 to 2 minutes or until heated through. Serve with meats, chicken or fish. Garnish with parsley or chives.

Suggested Combinations
Beer & Onion-Butter Sauce: Use beer for cooking liquid. Use Worcestershire sauce for seasoning. Use drained, rinsed, green peppercorns for spice. Serve on steak or burgers. Garnish with parsley.
Curried Onion-Butter Sauce: Use dry white wine for cooking liquid. Use Dijon-style mustard for seasoning. Use curry powder for spice. Serve on chicken or fish. Garnish with chives.

How to Make Basic Vegetable Cream Sauce

1/To make a creamed vegetable sauce, sauté vegetables in butter, then follow photo directions for White Sauce, page 309. This Zucchini Cream Sauce has chopped zucchini, chopped green onion and pimiento for vegetables.

2/Whisk sauce constantly until mixture is thickened and bubbly. Serve vegetable cream sauces over soufflés, omelets or crepes. Zucchini Cream Sauce is ladled over Salmon-Rice Squares, page 212.

Bordelaise Sauce

YIELD	1-1/2 cups	3/4 cup
INGREDIENTS		
sliced fresh mushrooms	1 cup	1/2 cup
chopped shallots	1/4 cup	2 tablespoons
butter or margarine	1/4 cup	2 tablespoons
dried leaf thyme	1/4 teaspoon	1/8 teaspoon
bay leaf	1 small	1/2 small
dry red wine	1/2 cup	1/4 cup
cornstarch	4 teaspoons	2 teaspoons
beef broth	1 cup	1/2 cup
snipped parsley	to garnish	to garnish
SKILLET	10-inch skillet	8-inch skillet
TIME AT MEDIUM HIGH (vegetables)	6 to 7 minutes	4 to 5 minutes
TIME AT MEDIUM LOW	12 to 14 minutes	7 to 9 minutes
TIME AT MEDIUM HIGH (broth added)	2 to 3 minutes	1-1/2 to 2-1/2 minutes

In a skillet, see size in chart above, cook mushrooms and shallots in butter or margarine over Medium-High heat for time in chart above or until tender, stirring often. Stir in thyme, bay leaf and wine. Bring to a boil. Reduce heat to Medium Low. Cook, uncovered, for time in chart above or until wine is absorbed, stirring often. In a small bowl, combine cornstarch and a little broth; mix well. Stir into mushroom mixture. Stir in remaining broth. Cook over Medium-High heat for time in chart above or until thickened and bubbly all over, stirring constantly. Remove bay leaf. Serve with beef or pork. Garnish with snipped parsley.

Vegetables & Salads

We see an ever-increasing variety of vegetables and fruit in our grocery stores. This is due partly to improved transportation and handling techniques. It is also due to increased consumer awareness and expectations. With public interest high in health and nutrition, fresh vegetables and fruit are enjoying new-found popularity. Also, public acceptance of ethnic cuisines of all kinds has encouraged the introduction of formerly exotic vegetables to our grocery shelves. With the excellent recipes and ideas in this chapter, you will never run out of interesting ways to serve vegetables.

Shown starting from the top: Fresh-Mushroom Relish, Chow-Chow Relish and Dill-Cucumber Relish, page 376.

Vegetables & Salads

Q. What do I look for when buying vegetables and fruit?

A. There are several guidelines for you to keep in mind when selecting fresh produce. For best quality and lowest cost, buy vegetables and fruit at the peak of their season. Check vegetables and fruit for blemishes, wilted leaves or dried stems. Fresh produce should be firm, crisp and bright in color. Handle with care! Bruises increase spoilage.

Q. How should I ripen produce that is sold hard and unripe, such as avocados, tomatoes, pears, peaches and nectarines?

A. Place unripe vegetables and fruit in a paper bag. Let stand at room temperature. Ripen until they yield to light pressure. Then refrigerate until ready to use.

Q. What are the differences in potatoes?

A. The oblong russet Burbanks, commonly called *Idaho* potatoes, are ideal for baking. Good baking potatoes are fully mature and brown, with a slightly rough skin. They are fluffy and mealy when cooked. New potatoes are ideal for boiling. Choose new potatoes that feel smooth and almost silky. When boiled, they have a smooth, waxy texture. They hold their shape well when cubed for salads or casseroles.

Q. Should I wash vegetables before storing in the refrigerator?

A. Most vegetables and fruit should not be washed; moisture speeds deterioration. However, greens should be washed promptly after purchase to bring out their freshest, crispest best. Shake off excess water, then spread on paper towels. Place in plastic bags in the refrigerator. Use within 1 to 2 days.

Q. How can I serve a really crisp tossed salad?

A. Chill salad plates and forks ahead of time. Prepare a salad bowl with a variety of washed chilled greens. Cover and place in the freezer for a few minutes to give the salad a super chill. Add the dressing, toss and serve immediately.

How to Store Lettuce

1/With a small knife, remove core from iceberg lettuce. Run cold water into core hole. Drain upside down in the sink 10 minutes. For leaf-type lettuce, remove each leaf from core and swish up and down in a sink of cold water. If leaves are muddy, dunk several times in fresh water. Drain in a colander 10 minutes.

2/Place head lettuce, cored-end down, on a folded paper towel. Refrigerate in the vegetable crisper in a plastic bag. Wrap leaf lettuce in a paper towel and refrigerate the same way. Other greens shown include: escarole in the foreground; Boston lettuce and red-tipped leaf lettuce on the board; tiny-leafed Bibb lettuce, crinkly leafed curly endive, and big-leafed romaine in the colander.

Q. Is there an easy way to keep fruit, such as apples, bananas or peaches, from darkening when I cut them for salad?

A. Yes. Brush cut edges with lemon juice. Or, dip in ascorbic acid color-keeper, prepared according to package directions. Use either method with any fruit that darkens easily.

Q. How are vegetable and salad recipes organized in this chapter?

A. Vegetable recipes are arranged by cooking method: steamed, boiled, baked, sautéed, stir-fried and deep-fried. Directions and cooking times accompany each method. Following these, you'll learn how to cook dried beans and make vegetables au gratin, vegetable casseroles and fast fix-ups for plain vegetables. Next come recipes for potatoes, hot and chilled vegetable salads, relishes, fruit salads, and seafood and chicken salads. Finally, you will discover a collection of wonderful dressings.

Storing Fresh Vegetables

VEGETABLE	HOW TO STORE	STORAGE TIME
artichokes, beets, cauliflower, cucumbers, eggplant, green onions, okra, peppers, summer squash, zucchini	Do not wash. Store in original wrapping or plastic bag in refrigerator crisper.	3 to 4 days
asparagus	Do not wash. Wrap stems in damp paper towels. Place in plastic bag in refrigerator crisper.	1 to 2 days
avocados, tomatoes	Store ripe avocados or tomatoes uncovered in refrigerator crisper. Let unripe ones stand in paper bag at room temperature until ripened.	1 to 2 days
broccoli, Brussels sprouts, lima beans, peas	Do not wash. Place in plastic bag in refrigerator crisper.	1 to 2 days
cabbage, carrots, celery, parsnips, radishes, rutabagas, turnips	Do not wash. Cover or store in original wrapping in refrigerator crisper.	1 week or more
corn on the cob, in husks	Do not wash. Store uncovered in refrigerator crisper.	Use as soon as possible.
corn on the cob, husks removed	Do not wash. Place in plastic bag in refrigerator crisper.	Use as soon as possible.
green or wax beans	Wash; place in plastic bag in refrigerator crisper.	1 to 2 days
greens for salads, beet greens, collard greens, kale, mustard greens, spinach, turnip greens	Wash immediately after purchase; shake off excess water. Pat with paper towels; place in plastic bag in refrigerator crisper.	1 to 2 days
head lettuce (for prompt use)	Remove core; wash, allowing water to run between leaves. Drain well, cored-end down. Place in plastic bag in refrigerator crisper.	3 to 4 days
head lettuce (for longer storage)	Do not wash. Store in original wrapping or plastic bag in refrigerator crisper.	1 week
sweet potatoes	Store in cool, dark, dry, well-ventilated area. Do not store in refrigerator.	1 to 2 weeks
white potatoes, dry onions, winter squash	Store in cool, dark, dry, well-ventilated area. Do not store in refrigerator.	several weeks

Steamed Vegetables

Steaming Method for Vegetables

Prepare fresh vegetables according to directions in chart. Pour water to a depth of 1/2 inch in a saucepan, see size in chart. Place a steamer basket in saucepan. Water level should be below steamer basket. Spread vegetables evenly in basket. Choose the burner closest in size to diameter of saucepan. Bring to a boil over High heat. Cover tightly. Reduce heat to Medium. Cook over Medium heat for minimum time in chart. Do not lift the lid before end of minimum cooking time. Water should simmer enough to make steam escapes from under lid. Cook until vegetables are crisp-tender. Cook potatoes, beets and acorn squash until tender.

Steamed Artichokes

SERVINGS	4	2	1
VEGETABLE fresh artichokes	4 (11- to 14-oz.) artichokes	2 (11- to 14-oz.) artichokes	1 (11- to 14-oz.) artichoke
DUTCH OVEN	7-qt. Dutch oven	4-qt. Dutch oven	3-qt. saucepan
TIME AT MEDIUM	45 to 55 minutes	25 to 30 minutes	25 to 30 minutes

Wash artichokes under cold water. Cut off stem and 1 inch from top of each artichoke. With scissors, snip off tips of leaves. Brush cut edges with lemon juice to prevent darkening. To cook, see Steaming Method for Vegetables, above.

Steamed Asparagus

SERVINGS	3 or 4	2	1
VEGETABLE fresh asparagus	1 lb. (14 medium stalks)	8 oz. (8 medium stalks)	4 oz. (4 medium stalks)
SAUCEPAN	3-qt. saucepan	3-qt. saucepan	3-qt. saucepan
TIME AT MEDIUM	6 to 7 minutes	6 to 7 minutes	6 to 7 minutes

Wash asparagus. Grasp each stalk at both ends and bend in a bow shape. Stalk will break where tender part begins. Discard tough part of stalk. Cut on the diagonal in 1-inch pieces. To cook, see Steaming Method for Vegetables, above.

Steamed Beans

SERVINGS	6	3	1 or 2
VEGETABLE fresh green or wax beans	1 lb. (4 cups)	8 oz. (2 cups)	4 oz. (1 cup)
SAUCEPAN	3-qt. saucepan	3-qt. saucepan	3-qt. saucepan
TIME AT MEDIUM	19 to 21 minutes	14 to 16 minutes	11 to 12 minutes

Wash beans and trim ends. Cut in 1- or 2-inch pieces or leave whole. To cook, see Steaming Method for Vegetables, above.

How to Steam Vegetables

1/Pour water to a depth of 1/2 inch in a saucepan large enough to hold the steamer basket and a tight-fitted saucepan lid. Water level should be below steamer basket.

2/Spread vegetables evenly in steamer basket. You may make several layers of vegetables. Bring to a boil. Cover tightly. Steam over Medium heat until crisp-tender.

Steamed Beets

SERVINGS	4	2	1
VEGETABLE fresh beets	3 lbs. (9 beets)	1-1/2 lbs. (4 or 5 beets)	12 oz. (2 or 3 beets)
SAUCEPAN	3-qt. saucepan	3-qt. saucepan	3-qt. saucepan
TIME AT MEDIUM	50 to 60 minutes	50 to 60 minutes	50 to 60 minutes

Select small or medium beets. Wash beets. Cut off all but 1 inch of stem and root. Do not peel. To cook, see Steaming Method for Vegetables, opposite. Peel after cooking. Slice or dice medium beets; serve small beets whole.

Steamed Broccoli

SERVINGS	6	3	1 or 2
VEGETABLE fresh broccoli	1 lb.	8 oz.	4 oz.
SAUCEPAN	3-qt. saucepan	3-qt. saucepan	3-qt. saucepan
TIME AT MEDIUM	5 to 7 minutes	4 to 5 minutes	3 to 4 minutes

Wash broccoli. Cut into flowerets with 2 inches of stalk. Slice lengthwise 1/4 inch thick. Slice remaining stalk into 1/8-inch-thick slices. Place sliced stalk in bottom of steamer basket with flowerets on top. To cook, see Steaming Method for Vegetables, opposite.

Steamed Brussels Sprouts

SERVINGS	4	2	1
VEGETABLE fresh Brussels sprouts	1 lb. (20 sprouts)	8 oz. (10 sprouts)	4 oz. (5 sprouts)
SAUCEPAN	3-qt. saucepan	3-qt. saucepan	3-qt. saucepan
TIME AT MEDIUM	15 to 17 minutes	12 to 14 minutes	12 to 14 minutes

Trim off wilted outer leaves and excess stems from sprouts. Wash sprouts. Halve large sprouts. To cook, see Steaming Method for Vegetables, page 322.

Steamed Cabbage

SERVINGS	4	2	1
VEGETABLE fresh cabbage, cut in wedges	1/2 head (4 wedges)	1/4 head (2 wedges)	1/8 head (1 wedge)
SAUCEPAN	3-qt. saucepan	3-qt. saucepan	3-qt. saucepan
TIME AT MEDIUM	13 to 15 minutes	13 to 15 minutes	12 to 14 minutes

Cut cabbage in wedges, allowing 1 wedge per serving. Remove outer leaves, but do not core. For red cabbage, add 1 tablespoon vinegar to each cup of cooking water. To cook, see Steaming Method for Vegetables, page 322.

Steamed Carrots

SERVINGS	4	2	1
VEGETABLE fresh carrots, sliced	1 lb. (2-2/3 cups)	8 oz. (1-1/3 cups)	4 oz. (2/3 cup)
SAUCEPAN	3-qt. saucepan	3-qt. saucepan	3-qt. saucepan
TIME AT MEDIUM	10 to 11 minutes	8 to 9 minutes	6 to 7 minutes

Wash, trim and peel carrots. Slice on the diagonal in 1/4-inch slices. To cook, see Steaming Method for Vegetables, page 322.

Steamed Cauliflower

SERVINGS	6 to 8	3 or 4	1 or 2
VEGETABLE fresh cauliflower, sliced	1 head (2 lbs.)	1/2 head (1 lb.)	1/4 head (8 oz.)
DUTCH OVEN	4-qt. Dutch oven	4-qt. Dutch oven	4-qt. Dutch oven
TIME AT MEDIUM	7 to 9 minutes	7 to 8 minutes	7 to 8 minutes

Wash and trim cauliflower. Remove core and all but 1 inch of stalk. Cut lengthwise in 1/2-inch-thick slices. To cook, see Steaming Method for Vegetables, page 322.

Steamed Corn

SERVINGS	6	4	2
VEGETABLE fresh corn on the cob	6 (12-oz.) ears	4 (12-oz.) ears	2 (12-oz.) ears
DUTCH OVEN	7-qt. Dutch oven	4-qt. Dutch oven	4-qt. Dutch oven
TIME AT MEDIUM	13 to 15 minutes	11 to 13 minutes	10 to 12 minutes

Husk corn and remove corn silk. To cook, see Steaming Method for Vegetables, page 322.

Steamed Spinach

SERVINGS	3 or 4	2	1
VEGETABLE fresh spinach	1 lb. (12 to 16 cups)	8 oz. (6 to 8 cups)	4 oz. (3 to 4 cups)
DUTCH OVEN	4-qt. Dutch oven	4-qt. Dutch oven	4-qt. Dutch oven
TIME AT MEDIUM	4 to 6 minutes	4 to 5 minutes	4 to 5 minutes

Wash and drain spinach. Trim off tough stem ends. Gently pack spinach in a steamer basket. To cook, see Steaming Method for Vegetables, page 322.

Steamed Squash (Acorn)

SERVINGS	6	3
VEGETABLE fresh acorn squash	2 (1-lb.) squash	1 (1-lb.) squash
DUTCH OVEN	7-qt. Dutch oven	4-qt. Dutch oven
TIME AT MEDIUM (whole)	3 minutes	3 minutes
TIME AT MEDIUM (slices)	11 to 13 minutes	10 to 11 minutes

Place whole squash in a steamer basket. Bring to a boil over High heat. Reduce heat to Medium; cover. Simmer 3 minutes. Remove squash. Trim ends. Slice crosswise in 1/2-inch rings; remove seeds. Place slices in steamer basket. To cook, see Steaming Method for Vegetables, page 322.

Steamed Squash (Crookneck or Zucchini)

SERVINGS	4	3	1
VEGETABLE fresh yellow crookneck or zucchini squash, sliced	1 lb. (4 cups)	12 oz. (3 cups)	4 oz. (1 cup)
SAUCEPAN	3-qt. saucepan	3-qt. saucepan	3-qt. saucepan
TIME AT MEDIUM	9 to 11 minutes	8 to 9 minutes	4 to 5 minutes

Wash squash. Cut on the diagonal in 1/4-inch slices. To cook, see Steaming Method for Vegetables, page 322.

Boiled Fresh Vegetables

Boiling Method for Fresh Vegetables ⎯⎯⎯⎯⎯

Prepare vegetables according to directions in chart. In a saucepan, see size in chart, combine with enough water to barely cover vegetables. Bring to a boil over High heat. Reduce heat to Medium Low; cover. Simmer for time in chart or until tender when pierced with a fork. Drain.

Boiled Artichokes

SERVINGS	4	2	1
VEGETABLE fresh artichokes	4 (11- to 14-oz.) artichokes	2 (11- to 14-oz.) artichokes	1 (11- to 14-oz.) artichoke
DUTCH OVEN	8-qt. Dutch oven	4-qt. Dutch oven	3-qt. saucepan
TIME AT MEDIUM LOW	20 to 30 minutes	20 to 30 minutes	20 to 30 minutes

Wash artichokes under cold water. Cut off stem and 1 inch from top of each artichoke. With scissors, snip off tips of leaves. Brush cut edges with lemon juice to prevent darkening. Place artichokes, base-side down, in Dutch oven, see size in chart above. To cook, see Boiling Method for Fresh Vegetables, above. Drain upside down after cooking.

Boiled Asparagus

SERVINGS	8	4	2
VEGETABLE fresh asparagus	2 lbs. (50 slender stalks)	1 lb. (25 slender stalks)	8 oz. (12 slender stalks)
SKILLET	10-inch skillet	8-inch skillet	8-inch skillet
TIME AT MEDIUM LOW	5 to 6 minutes	5 to 6 minutes	5 to 6 minutes

Wash asparagus. Grasp each stalk at both ends and bend in a bow shape. Stalk will break where tender part begins. Discard tough part of stalk. To cook, see Boiling Method for Fresh Vegetables, above.

Boiled Beans

SERVINGS	6	3	1 or 2
VEGETABLE fresh green or wax beans	1 lb. (4 cups)	8 oz. (2 cups)	4 oz. (1 cup)
SAUCEPAN	2-qt. saucepan	1-1/2-qt. saucepan	1-qt. saucepan
TIME AT MEDIUM LOW	14 minutes	12 minutes	12 minutes

Wash beans and trim ends. Cut in 1- or 2-inch pieces or leave whole. To cook, see Boiling Method for Fresh Vegetables, above.

How to Boil Fresh Artichokes

1/Wash artichokes under cold water. With a sharp knife, cut off stem at base of artichoke so artichoke stands upright easily. Cut off about 1 inch from top of artichoke.

2/With scissors, snip off prickly tip of each leaf on each layer of leaves. Brush cut edges with lemon juice to prevent edges from turning dark.

3/Place artichokes, base-side down, in a saucepan. Cover with water. Bring to a boil. Cover and simmer over Medium-Low heat until leaves pull out easily. Drain artichokes upside down on a rack. Artichokes may be served hot or chilled.

4/Using a grapefruit spoon and paring knife, remove fuzzy choke from artichoke center. Serve hot artichokes with melted butter and lemon wedges. To eat, pull off individual leaves and scrape off meat at base of leaf with your teeth.

Boiled Beet Greens

SERVINGS	4	2	1
VEGETABLE fresh beet greens	1 lb. (10 to 12 cups)	8 oz. (5 to 6 cups)	4 oz. (2-1/2 to 3 cups)
SAUCEPAN	6-qt. saucepan	3-qt. saucepan	1-1/2-qt. saucepan
TIME AT MEDIUM LOW	11 minutes	11 minutes	10 minutes

Wash greens. Cut stems in 3- to 4-inch lengths. Place greens and stems with water that clings to leaves in a saucepan, see size in chart above. Cook over High heat until steam forms. Reduce heat to Medium Low; cover. Simmer for time in chart above or until tender. Drain.

Boiled Beets

SERVINGS	4	2	1
VEGETABLE fresh beets	3 lbs. (about 9 beets)	1-1/2 lbs. (4 or 5 beets)	12 oz. (2 or 3 beets)
SAUCEPAN	3-qt. saucepan	2-qt. saucepan	1-qt. saucepan
TIME AT MEDIUM LOW (small or medium beets)	20 to 30 minutes	20 to 30 minutes	20 to 30 minutes
TIME AT MEDIUM LOW (large beets)	35 to 45 minutes	35 to 45 minutes	35 to 45 minutes

Select small or medium beets, if available. Wash beets. Cut off all but 1 inch of stem and root. Do not peel. To cook, see Boiling Method for Fresh Vegetables, page 326. Peel after cooking. Slice or dice medium or large beets; serve small beets whole.

Boiled Broccoli

SERVINGS	8	4	2
VEGETABLE fresh broccoli	1-1/2 lbs. (7 cups)	12 oz. (3-1/2 cups)	6 oz. (1-1/2 cups)
SAUCEPAN	3-qt. saucepan	2-qt. saucepan	1-1/2-qt. saucepan
TIME AT MEDIUM LOW	9 minutes	5-1/2 minutes	4 minutes

Wash broccoli. Cut into flowerets with 2 inches of stalk. To cook, see Boiling Method for Fresh Vegetables, page 326. Cooking water should barely cover stalks, not flowerets.

Boiled Brussels Sprouts

SERVINGS	6	4	2
VEGETABLE fresh Brussels sprouts	1-1/2 lbs. (30 sprouts)	1 lb. (20 sprouts)	8 oz. (10 sprouts)
SAUCEPAN	2-qt. saucepan	1-1/2-qt. saucepan	1-qt. saucepan
TIME AT MEDIUM LOW	13 minutes	13 minutes	12 minutes

Trim off wilted outer leaves and excess stems from sprouts. Wash sprouts. Halve large sprouts. To cook, see Boiling Method for Fresh Vegetables, page 326.

Piquant-Glazed Beets and Sweet-Glazed Acorn Squash, page 356.

Boiled Cabbage (Shredded)

SERVINGS	3 or 4	2	1
VEGETABLE fresh cabbage, shredded	1/3 head (4 cups)	1/6 head (2 cups)	1/12 head (1 cup)
SAUCEPAN	3-qt. saucepan	1-1/2-qt. saucepan	1-qt. saucepan
TIME AT MEDIUM LOW	8 minutes	8 minutes	8 minutes

Cut cabbage in 1/4-inch shreds. To cook, see Boiling Method for Fresh Vegetables, page 326.

Boiled Cabbage (Wedges)

SERVINGS	4	2	1
VEGETABLE fresh cabbage, cut in wedges	1/2 head (4 wedges)	1/4 head (2 wedges)	1/8 head (1 wedge)
SAUCEPAN	3-qt. saucepan	2-qt. saucepan	1-qt. saucepan
TIME AT MEDIUM LOW	9 minutes	8 minutes	7 minutes

Cut cabbage in wedges, allowing 1 wedge per serving. Remove outer leaves, but do not core. To cook, see Boiling Method for Fresh Vegetables, page 326.

Boiled Carrots (Sliced)

SERVINGS	4	2	1
VEGETABLE fresh carrots, sliced	1 lb. (2-2/3 cups)	8 oz. (1-1/3 cups)	4 oz. (2/3 cup)
SAUCEPAN	1-1/2-qt. saucepan	1-qt. saucepan	1-qt. saucepan
TIME AT MEDIUM LOW	9 minutes	9 minutes	9 minutes

Wash, trim and peel carrots. Halve thick portion of carrots lengthwise. Slice 1/2 inch thick. To cook, see Boiling Method for Fresh Vegetables, page 326.

Boiled Carrots (Whole)

SERVINGS	6	3
VEGETABLE fresh carrots, small whole	1-1/2 lbs. (6 cups)	12 oz. (3 cups)
SAUCEPAN	2-qt. saucepan	1-1/2-qt. saucepan
TIME AT MEDIUM LOW	12 minutes	12 minutes

Wash, trim and peel carrots. To cook, see Boiling Method for Fresh Vegetables, page 326.

Boiled Cauliflower (Whole)

SERVINGS	6 to 8	3 or 4
VEGETABLE fresh cauliflower, whole	1 head (2 lbs.)	1/2 head (1 lb.)
DUTCH OVEN	6-qt. Dutch oven	2-qt. saucepan
TIME AT MEDIUM LOW	8 minutes	6 minutes

Wash and trim cauliflower. Remove some core, leaving enough to hold head intact. Place head, cored-side down, in a saucepan, see size in chart above. To cook, see Boiling Method for Fresh Vegetables, page 326.

Boiled Cauliflowerets

SERVINGS	6 to 8	3 or 4	1 or 2
VEGETABLE fresh cauliflower, cut in flowerets	1 head (2 lbs.)	1/2 head (1 lb.)	1/4 head (8 oz.)
SAUCEPAN	3-qt. saucepan	1-1/2-qt. saucepan	1-1/2-qt. saucepan
TIME AT MEDIUM LOW	7 minutes	6 minutes	6 minutes

Wash and trim cauliflower. Remove core. Cut into flowerets with 1 inch of stalk. To cook, see Boiling Method for Fresh Vegetables, page 326.

Boiled Collard Greens

SERVINGS	4	2
VEGETABLE fresh collard greens, shredded	1-1/2 lbs. (12 cups)	12 oz. (6 cups)
DUTCH OVEN	6-qt. Dutch oven	4-qt. Dutch oven
TIME AT MEDIUM LOW	30 to 35 minutes	30 to 35 minutes

Wash and trim collards, discarding yellow leaves. Cut collards in 1/4-inch shreds. Use 4 cups cooking water for large recipe and 2 cups cooking water for small recipe. To cook, see Boiling Method for Fresh Vegetables, page 326. Stir occasionally while cooking.

Boiled Corn on the Cob

SERVINGS	6	4	2
VEGETABLE fresh corn on the cob	6 (12-oz.) ears	4 (12-oz.) ears	2 (12-oz.) ears
DUTCH OVEN	6-qt. Dutch oven	6-qt. Dutch oven	6-qt. Dutch oven
TIME AT MEDIUM LOW	6 to 8 minutes	6 to 8 minutes	6 to 8 minutes

Husk corn and remove corn silk. To cook, see Boiling Method for Fresh Vegetables, page 326.

Boiled Eggplant

SERVINGS	2	1
VEGETABLE fresh eggplant, cubed	1/2 small (1-1/2 cups)	1/4 small (3/4 cup)
SAUCEPAN	1-1/2-qt. saucepan	1-qt. saucepan
TIME AT MEDIUM LOW	4 to 5 minutes	4 to 5 minutes

Wash, trim and peel eggplant. Cut in 1-inch cubes. To cook, see Boiling Method for Fresh Vegetables, page 326.

Boiled Fennel

SERVINGS	8	4
VEGETABLE fresh fennel	4 (1-1/4 to 1-1/2 lb.) stalks	2 (1-1/4 to 1-1/2 lb.) stalks
SKILLET	11-inch skillet	9-inch skillet
TIME AT MEDIUM LOW	20 to 22 minutes	18 to 20 minutes

Wash fennel; cut off tops. Reserve a few feathery leaves for garnish. Cut off bottoms. Quarter fennel lengthwise. Remove and discard tough outer portion, leaving hearts. To cook, see Boiling Method for Fresh Vegetables, page 326.

Boiled Kohlrabi

SERVINGS	6 to 8	3 or 4	1 or 2
VEGETABLE fresh kohlrabi, sliced	4 (8-oz.) kohlrabi (4-1/2 cups)	2 (8-oz.) kohlrabi (2-1/3 cups)	1 (8-oz.) kohlrabi (1-1/4 cups)
SAUCEPAN	3-qt. saucepan	1-1/2-qt. saucepan	1-qt. saucepan
TIME AT MEDIUM LOW	8 to 9 minutes	8 to 9 minutes	8 to 9 minutes

Wash and peel kohlrabi. Cut in 3/8-inch slices. To cook, see Boiling Method for Fresh Vegetables, page 326.

Boiled Leeks

SERVINGS	2	1
VEGETABLE fresh leeks, sliced	4 (3- to 4-oz.) leeks (2 cups)	2 (3- to 4-oz.) leeks (1 cup)
SAUCEPAN	1-1/2-qt. saucepan	1-qt. saucepan
TIME AT MEDIUM LOW	5 minutes	5 minutes

Cut tops off leeks to within 1 to 2 inches of white part. Remove and discard outer leaves. To wash leeks, cut lengthwise through to center. Run water between leaves to remove sand. Slice 1/4 inch thick. Cut large leeks in half lengthwise, then in 1/4-inch slices. To cook, see Boiling Method for Fresh Vegetables, page 326.

How to Boil Greens

1/Roll large leaves, such as collards, and snip into strips. Tender leaves, such as spinach in the wire colander and beet greens in the red colander, may be cooked whole. Beet greens and spinach are cooked only with water that clings to leaves after washing.

2/Collards in the foreground, crinkly leafed mustard in the red colander and darker green crinkly leafed turnip greens in the wire colander, are tougher. These are cooked a long time in 1 cup water for each 3 to 4 cups greens. You may flavor these greens during cooking with bacon pieces or ham cubes.

Boiled Mustard Greens

SERVINGS	4	2
VEGETABLE fresh mustard greens	2 lbs. (16 cups)	1 lb. (8 cups)
DUTCH OVEN	5-qt. Dutch oven	5-qt. Dutch oven
TIME AT MEDIUM LOW	35 to 40 minutes	35 to 40 minutes

Wash and trim greens, discarding yellow leaves. Use 4 cups cooking water for large recipe and 2 cups cooking water for small recipe. To cook, see Boiling Method for Fresh Vegetables, page 326. Stir occasionally while cooking.

Boiled Okra

SERVINGS	4	2
VEGETABLE fresh okra, sliced	1 lb. (4 cups)	8 oz. (2 cups)
SAUCEPAN	2-qt. saucepan	1-1/2-qt. saucepan
TIME AT MEDIUM LOW	5 minutes	5 minutes

Wash okra and trim ends. Cut in 1/2-inch slices. To cook, see Boiling Method for Fresh Vegetables, page 326.

Boiled Onions

SERVINGS	4 to 6	2 or 3
VEGETABLE fresh onions, tiny whole	1 lb. (46 onions)	8 oz. (23 onions)
SAUCEPAN	2-qt. saucepan	1-1/2-qt. saucepan
TIME AT MEDIUM LOW	14 to 16 minutes	14 to 16 minutes

Peel onions. To cook, see Boiling Method for Fresh Vegetables, page 326.

Boiled Parsnips

SERVINGS	8	4	2
VEGETABLE fresh parsnips, sliced	2 lbs. (6 cups)	1 lb. (3 cups)	8 oz. (1-1/2 cups)
SAUCEPAN	3-qt. saucepan	2-qt. saucepan	1-qt. saucepan
TIME AT MEDIUM LOW	4 to 6 minutes	4 to 6 minutes	4 to 6 minutes

Wash, trim and peel parsnips. Remove core of large parsnips. Halve thick portion of parsnips lengthwise. Slice 1/2 inch thick. To cook, see Boiling Method for Fresh Vegetables, page 326.

Boiled Peas

SERVINGS	4	2	1
VEGETABLE fresh peas	2 lbs. (2-2/3 cups)	1 lb. (1-1/3 cups)	8 oz. (2/3 cup)
SAUCEPAN	1-1/2-qt. saucepan	1-1/2-qt. saucepan	1-qt. saucepan
TIME AT MEDIUM LOW	5 to 7 minutes	5 to 7 minutes	5 to 7 minutes

Shell and wash peas. To cook, see Boiling Method for Fresh Vegetables, page 326.

Boiled New Potatoes

SERVINGS	4	2	1
VEGETABLE fresh, small, new potatoes	2 lbs. (16 potatoes)	1 lb. (8 potatoes)	8 oz. (4 potatoes)
SAUCEPAN	3-qt. saucepan	1-1/2-qt. saucepan	1-qt. saucepan
TIME AT MEDIUM LOW	18 minutes	18 minutes	18 minutes

Wash potatoes. Halve large potatoes so all potatoes are about same size. Peel small strip around center of whole potatoes. To cook, see Boiling Method for Fresh Vegetables, page 326.

Boiled Potatoes (Cubed)

SERVINGS	4	2
VEGETABLE fresh potatoes, cubed	4 potatoes (4 cups)	2 potatoes (2 cups)
SAUCEPAN	2-qt. saucepan	1-1/2-qt. saucepan
TIME AT MEDIUM LOW	9 to 10 minutes	9 to 10 minutes

Wash, peel and cut potatoes in 3/4-inch cubes. To cook, see Boiling Method for Fresh Vegetables, page 326.

How to Boil Turnips, Rutabagas & Parsnips

1/Halve thick portion of parsnips lengthwise before slicing. This makes all slices more equal in size. Peel and cube purple-tinged turnips, shown in the wire basket, or rutabagas, in front of the saucepan.

2/Place vegetables in a saucepan with barely enough water to cover. Bring to a boil over High heat. Reduce heat to Medium Low; cover. Simmer vegetables until tender when pierced with a fork. Drain. Mature vegetables require more time to cook.

Boiled Potatoes (Halved)

SERVINGS	6	3	2
VEGETABLE fresh potatoes, halved	6 medium	3 medium	2 medium
SAUCEPAN	3-qt. saucepan	2-qt. saucepan	1-1/2-qt. saucepan
TIME AT MEDIUM LOW	19 minutes	18 minutes	15 minutes

Wash and halve potatoes. Peel if desired. To cook, see Boiling Method for Fresh Vegetables, page 326.

Boiled Rutabagas

SERVINGS	4 to 6	2 or 3	1 or 2
VEGETABLE fresh rutabagas, cubed	1-3/4 lbs. (5 cups)	12 oz. (2-1/2 cups)	6 oz. (1-1/4 cups)
SAUCEPAN	2-qt. saucepan	1-1/2-qt. saucepan	1-qt. saucepan
TIME AT MEDIUM LOW	13 to 15 minutes	13 to 15 minutes	13 to 15 minutes

Wash, trim and peel rutabaga. Cut in 1-inch cubes. To cook, see Boiling Method for Fresh Vegetables, page 326.

Boiled Spinach

SERVINGS	3 or 4	2	1
VEGETABLE fresh spinach	1 lb. (12 to 16 cups)	8 oz. (6 to 8 cups)	4 oz. (3 to 4 cups)
DUTCH OVEN	5-qt. Dutch oven	3-qt. saucepan	1-1/2-qt. saucepan
TIME AT MEDIUM LOW	6 minutes	4 minutes	4 minutes

Wash spinach. Trim off tough stem ends. Place spinach with water that clings to leaves in a saucepan, see size in chart above. Cook over High heat until steam forms. Reduce heat to Medium Low; cover. Simmer for time in chart above or until tender, stirring once. Drain.

Boiled Squash (Butternut)

SERVINGS	4	2	1
VEGETABLE fresh butternut squash, cubed	2/3 medium (4 cups)	1/3 medium (2 cups)	1/6 medium (1 cup)
SAUCEPAN	2-qt. saucepan	1-1/2-qt. saucepan	1-qt. saucepan
TIME AT MEDIUM LOW	8 to 9 minutes	8 to 9 minutes	8 to 9 minutes

Trim and peel squash. Cut in 1-inch cubes. To cook, see Boiling Method for Fresh Vegetables, page 326.

Boiled Squash (Spaghetti)

SERVINGS	4 to 6	2 or 3
VEGETABLE fresh spaghetti squash, halved	1 (4-lb.) squash	1 (2-lb.) squash
SKILLET	12-inch skillet	12-inch skillet
TIME AT MEDIUM LOW	20 to 30 minutes	20 to 30 minutes

Halve squash lengthwise. Remove seeds. Place, cut-side down, in a 12-inch skillet. Pour water to a depth of 2 inches in skillet. Bring to a boil over High heat. Reduce heat to Medium Low; cover. Simmer 20 to 30 minutes or until tender. Drain. To serve, loosen squash from shell and separate into strands with a fork.

Boiled Squash (Crookneck or Zucchini)

SERVINGS	4	3	1
VEGETABLE fresh yellow crookneck or zucchini squash, sliced	1 lb. (4 cups)	12 oz. (3 cups)	4 oz. (1 cup)
SAUCEPAN	2-qt. saucepan	2-qt. saucepan	1-qt. saucepan
TIME AT MEDIUM LOW	4 minutes	4 minutes	3 minutes

Wash squash. Cut in 1/4-inch slices. To cook, see Boiling Method for Fresh Vegetables, page 326.

How to Boil Spaghetti Squash

1/Halve spaghetti squash lengthwise and remove seeds. Place, cut-side down, in a large skillet. Add water to a depth of 2 inches. On the board, amber-skinned butternut squash is peeled and cubed, ready to boil. Green-skinned acorn squash can be steamed, page 325, or baked, page 338.

2/Simmer spaghetti squash 20 to 30 minutes or until tender. Remove squash halves from skillet. Using a fork, pull strands of squash into "spaghetti." Work from the center toward the skin. Serve with spaghetti sauce and grated Parmesan cheese.

Boiled Turnip Greens

SERVINGS	4	2
VEGETABLE fresh turnip greens	2 lbs. (8 cups)	1 lb. (4 cups)
DUTCH OVEN	5-qt. Dutch oven	4-qt. Dutch oven
TIME AT MEDIUM LOW	25 to 30 minutes	25 to 30 minutes

Wash and trim greens, discarding yellow leaves and stems. Tear into pieces. Use 4 cups cooking water for large recipe and 2 cups cooking water for small recipe. To cook, see Boiling Method for Fresh Vegetables, page 326. Stir occasionally while cooking.

Boiled Turnips

SERVINGS	3 or 4	1 or 2
VEGETABLE fresh turnips, cubed	1 lb. (3 cups)	8 oz. (1-1/2 cups)
SAUCEPAN	2-qt. saucepan	1-qt. saucepan
TIME AT MEDIUM LOW	7 to 9 minutes	7 to 9 minutes

Wash, trim and peel turnips. Cut in 1-inch cubes. To cook, see Boiling Method for Fresh Vegetables, page 326.

Baked Fresh Whole Vegetables

Baked Corn on the Cob

VEGETABLE	TIME IN 425F (220C) OVEN	TIME IN 375F (190C) OVEN	TIME IN 325F (165C) OVEN
fresh corn on the cob, 12-oz. ears	30 to 35 minutes	35 to 40 minutes	55 to 60 minutes

Do not preheat oven. Husk corn and remove corn silk. Spread each ear with about 2 teaspoons Herbed Vegetable Butter, page 340. Roll each ear in foil, twisting ends to seal. Place in a baking dish in single layer. Bake at desired temperature for time in chart above or until kernels are tender.

Baked Onions

VEGETABLE	TIME IN 425F (220C) OVEN	TIME IN 375F (190C) OVEN	TIME IN 325F (165C) OVEN
fresh onions, 6 oz. each	40 to 50 minutes	50 to 60 minutes	60 to 70 minutes

Do not preheat oven. Wash onions. Trim off ends but do not peel. Spread top of each onion with Herbed Vegetable Butter, page 340. Place each onion on a piece of foil. Bring ends of foil up over onion; twist top to seal. Place in a baking dish in single layer. Bake at desired temperature for time in chart above or until tender.

Baked Potatoes

VEGETABLE	TIME IN 425F (220C) OVEN	TIME IN 375F (190C) OVEN	TIME IN 325F (165C) OVEN
fresh baking potatoes, 8 oz. each	55 to 70 minutes	60 to 75 minutes	75 to 90 minutes

Do not preheat oven. Scrub potatoes under running water. Pierce potatoes several times on all sides with a large fork to vent steam. For soft skins after baking, brush skins with shortening or oil or wrap each potato in foil. Bake at desired temperature for time in chart above or until tender when pierced in center with large fork. Serve with Herbed Vegetable Butter, page 340.

Baked Squash (Acorn)

VEGETABLE	TIME IN 425F (220C) OVEN	TIME IN 375F (190C) OVEN	TIME IN 325F (165C) OVEN
fresh acorn squash, 1 to 2 lbs. each	10 minutes (whole squash)	10 minutes (whole squash)	10 minutes (whole squash)
	20 to 30 minutes (cut squash)	30 to 40 minutes (cut squash)	35 to 45 minutes (cut squash)
	5 to 10 minutes (glaze added)	10 minutes (glaze added)	10 minutes (glaze added)

Do not preheat oven. Place whole squash in a shallow baking dish. Bake 10 minutes at desired oven temperature. Cut squash in 1-inch rings or halve squash. Remove seeds. Place squash halves, cut-side down, in baking dish. Or, overlap rings in baking dish. Cover with foil. Bake at desired oven temperature for time in chart above or until almost tender. Turn squash halves cut-side up. Spoon glaze from Basic Sweet-Glazed Vegetables, page 356, into squash halves or over squash rings. Bake, uncovered, at desired temperature for time in chart above or until tender. Spoon glaze over rings before serving. Or, serve plain baked squash with Herbed Vegetable Butter, page 340.

How to Bake Fresh Whole Vegetables

1/Whole vegetables may be baked at 425F (220C), 375F (190C) or 325F (165C). Select oven temperature that matches rest of meal.

2/To prepare onions, trim off ends but do not peel. Spread top of each onion with Herbed Vegetable Butter, page 340. Wrap each onion in foil; place in a baking dish to cook.

3/To prepare sweet potatoes, scrub potatoes under running water. Pierce potatoes several times on all sides with a large fork to vent steam. For soft skins after baking, brush skins with shortening or oil, or wrap each potato in foil. Bake until potatoes are tender when pierced in center with a fork.

4/To prepare acorn squash, bake whole squash 10 minutes to soften skin. Cut squash in half. Remove seeds. Cover and bake, cut-side down, until almost tender. Turn cut-side up. Spoon glaze from Basic Sweet-Glazed Vegetables, page 356, into center of squash. Continue baking until squash is tender when pierced with a fork.

Vegetables & Salads 339

Baked Sweet Potatoes

	TIME IN 425F (220C) OVEN	TIME IN 375F (190C) OVEN	TIME IN 325F (165C) OVEN
VEGETABLE fresh sweet potatoes, 8 oz. each	45 to 60 minutes	70 to 85 minutes	80 to 95 minutes

Do not preheat oven. Scrub potatoes under running water. Pierce potatoes several times on all sides with a large fork to vent steam. For soft skins after baking, brush skins with shortening or oil or wrap each potato in foil. Bake at desired temperature for time in chart above or until tender when pierced in center with large fork. Serve with Herbed Vegetable Butter, below.

Baked Tomatoes

	TIME IN 425F (220C) OVEN	TIME IN 375F (190C) OVEN	TIME IN 325F (165C) OVEN
VEGETABLE fresh tomatoes, 5 to 6 oz. each	20 to 25 minutes	25 to 30 minutes	30 to 35 minutes

Do not preheat oven. Wash and core tomatoes. Cut thin slice from top and bottom of each tomato. Place, cored-side up, in a shallow baking dish. Top each tomato with about 2 teaspoons Herbed Vegetable Butter, below. Bake at desired temperature for time in chart above or until barely heated through. Spoon juices over tomatoes to serve. Top with spoonfuls of plain yogurt; sprinkle with chives and paprika.

Herbed Vegetable Butter

YIELD	3/4 cup	1/2 cup	1/4 cup
INGREDIENTS			
butter or margarine, softened	3/4 cup	1/2 cup	1/4 cup
dried leaf herb	1-1/2 teaspoons	1 teaspoon	1/2 teaspoon
celery salt or onion salt	3/4 teaspoon	1/2 teaspoon	1/4 teaspoon
dried parsley flakes or dried snipped chives	3/4 teaspoon	1/2 teaspoon	1/4 teaspoon

In a small bowl, combine all ingredients; mix well. Serve on hot cooked vegetables. Cover leftover butter; store in refrigerator.

Suggested Herbs: tarragon, dill weed, oregano, Italian herb seasoning, basil, thyme, marjoram, savory.

Twice-Baked Potatoes, page 361; Baked Tomatoes; Baked Corn on the Cob, page 338; and Herbed Vegetable Butter.

Baked Frozen Vegetables

SERVINGS	6 to 8	3 or 4	1 or 2
INGREDIENTS			
loose-pack frozen vegetables	4 cups	2 cups	1 cup
any combination of chopped green onion, zucchini, tomatoes, celery or green pepper	1/2 cup	1/4 cup	2 tablespoons
dried leaf herb	1/2 teaspoon	1/4 teaspoon	1/8 teaspoon
onion salt	1/4 teaspoon	1/8 teaspoon	dash
butter or margarine	2 tablespoons	1 tablespoon	2 teaspoons
CASSEROLE	1-1/2-qt. casserole	1-qt. casserole	1-1/2- to 2-cup casserole
TIME IN 350F (175C) OVEN	see timings for vegetables in chart below		

Do not preheat oven. In a casserole, see size in chart above, break up frozen vegetables as much as possible with a large fork. Toss with chopped fresh vegetables, herb and onion salt. Cut butter or margarine in small pieces; distribute on vegetable mixture. Cover and bake in a 350F (175C) oven for time in chart below or until tender, stirring twice during baking.

Suggested Herbs: basil, oregano, tarragon, fennel, dill weed, rubbed sage, thyme, parsley, chives, Italian herb seasoning, herb pepper, marjoram, caraway.

Suggested Frozen Vegetables for Baking

AMOUNT	4 cups	2 cups	1 cup
	COOKING TIME IN 350F (175C) OVEN		
VEGETABLE			
cut asparagus	40 to 45 minutes	35 to 40 minutes	30 to 35 minutes
beans, cut green	65 to 75 minutes	45 to 50 minutes	35 to 40 minutes
beans, large lima	55 to 65 minutes	40 to 50 minutes	35 to 40 minutes
broccoli cuts	45 to 55 minutes	30 to 40 minutes	25 to 30 minutes
Brussels sprouts	55 to 65 minutes	45 to 50 minutes	45 to 50 minutes
carrot slices	50 to 60 minutes	40 to 45 minutes	35 to 40 minutes
cauliflower cuts	50 to 55 minutes	40 to 45 minutes	40 to 45 minutes
corn, whole kernel	40 to 50 minutes	35 to 40 minutes	30 to 35 minutes
onions, tiny whole	50 to 60 minutes	40 to 50 minutes	40 to 45 minutes
peas	40 to 50 minutes	35 to 40 minutes	30 to 35 minutes
vegetable combinations	50 to 60 minutes	35 to 45 minutes	25 to 30 minutes

How to Bake Frozen Vegetables

1/Most loose-pack frozen vegetables in plastic pour bags can be baked without defrosting first. Combine with chopped fresh vegetables and seasonings. Toss tiny whole frozen onions with tomatoes, celery and green pepper. Sprinkle with tarragon and onion salt.

2/Cut butter or margarine in small pieces; distribute on vegetable mixture. To speed cooking time, bake vegetables in several individual casseroles instead of a large one. Cover and bake until vegetables are tender, stirring twice for even cooking.

Basic Combination-Vegetable Casserole

SERVINGS	4 to 6	2 or 3
INGREDIENTS		
frozen, loose-pack, combination vegetables	1 (16-oz.) bag (4 to 5 cups)	1/2 (16-oz.) bag (2 to 2-1/2 cups)
toasted slivered almonds	1/2 cup	1/4 cup
powdered, non-dairy coffee creamer	1/2 cup	1/4 cup
all-purpose flour	2 tablespoons	1 tablespoon
dried leaf herb	1/2 teaspoon	1/4 teaspoon
butter or margarine	1 tablespoon	2 teaspoons
boiling chicken broth	1 cup	1/2 cup
CASSEROLE	1-1/2-qt. casserole	1-qt. casserole
TIME IN 350F (175C) OVEN	45 to 50 minutes	35 to 40 minutes
STANDING TIME	10 minutes	10 minutes

Do not preheat oven. Place frozen vegetables and almonds in a casserole, see size in chart above. Sprinkle with non-dairy creamer, flour and herb. Cut butter or margarine in small pieces; distribute on casserole. Pour hot broth evenly over vegetables; cover. Bake in a 350F (175C) oven for time in chart above or until vegetables are tender, stirring once halfway through baking time. Stir again when done. Let stand, covered, 10 minutes before serving.

Suggested Combinations
Italian Combination-Vegetable Casserole: Use green beans, cauliflower and carrots for frozen-vegetable combination. Use Italian herb seasoning.
Golden Combination-Vegetable Casserole: Use corn, carrots and onions for frozen-vegetable combination. Use marjoram for herb.
Red & Green Combination-Vegetable Casserole: Use broccoli, green beans, pearl onions and red pepper for frozen-vegetable combination. Use dill weed for herb.

Basic Sautéed Vegetables

SERVINGS	3 or 4	1 or 2
INGREDIENTS		
butter or margarine	2 tablespoons	1 tablespoon
sliced vegetable, see chart below	4 cups	2 cups
any combination of chopped green pepper, celery, onion, chilies, carrot or pimiento	1/2 cup	1/4 cup
celery salt	1/4 teaspoon	1/8 teaspoon
onion salt	1/4 teaspoon	1/8 teaspoon
dried leaf herbs, herb seed or ground spice	1 teaspoon	1/2 teaspoon
shredded cheese, if desired OR	1/2 cup (2 oz.)	1/4 cup (1 oz.)
grated Parmesan cheese, if desired	1/4 cup	2 tablespoons
SKILLET	10- or 11-inch skillet	8-inch skillet
TIME AT MEDIUM (vegetables)	see timings for vegetables in chart below	
TIME AT MEDIUM (cheese added)	1 to 2 minutes	1 to 2 minutes

In a skillet, see size in chart above, melt butter or margarine. Add vegetables. Sprinkle with celery salt, onion salt and herbs. Cook mushrooms, onions, tomatoes, zucchini or yellow summer squash, *uncovered,* over Medium heat for time in chart below or until tender. Cook potatoes, *covered,* over Medium heat 15 minutes. Uncover potatoes and cook over Medium heat for time in chart below. With a wide spatula, carefully lift and turn vegetable slices occasionally. Sprinkle with cheese, if desired. Cook over Medium heat 1 to 2 minutes or until cheese melts.

Suggested Combinations

Sautéed Mushrooms: Use chopped onion and chopped celery for vegetable combination. Use tarragon and basil for herbs. Use grated Parmesan cheese, if desired.

Sautéed Onions: Use chopped celery and chopped pimiento for vegetable combination. Use Italian herb seasoning for herbs. Use shredded Cheddar cheese, if desired.

Sautéed Potatoes: Use chopped pimiento, chopped green onion and chopped celery for vegetable combination. Use dill weed and caraway seed for herb and herb seed. Use shredded Swiss cheese, if desired.

Sautéed Tomatoes: Use chopped green pepper, chopped celery and chopped green onion for vegetable combination. Use basil and thyme for herbs. Use shredded mozzarella cheese, if desired.

Sautéed Zucchini or Yellow Summer Squash: Use chopped carrot and chopped green pepper or chopped chilies for vegetable combination. Use fennel seed and cumin for herb seed and spice. Use Monterey Jack cheese, if desired.

Suggested Vegetables for Sautéing

AMOUNT	4 cups	2 cups
	COOKING TIME AT MEDIUM, UNCOVERED	
VEGETABLE		
mushrooms, cut in 1/4-inch slices	7 to 9 minutes	7 to 9 minutes
onions, cut in 1/4-inch slices	20 to 25 minutes	20 to 25 minutes
tomatoes, cut in 1-inch wedges	4 to 6 minutes	4 to 6 minutes
zucchini or yellow summer squash, cut in 1/4-inch slices	9 to 11 minutes	9 to 11 minutes
	COOKING TIME AT MEDIUM	
potatoes, cut in 1/4-inch slices	15 minutes (covered) 10 minutes (uncovered)	15 minutes (covered) 3 to 4 minutes (uncovered)

How to Make Basic Sautéed Vegetables

1/For sautéed vegetables, slice zucchini, yellow summer squash, mushrooms, onions or potatoes in 1-inch-thick slices. Cut tomatoes in 1-inch wedges.

2/Add sliced vegetables to melted butter or margarine in a skillet. Top with chopped green pepper, celery, onion, chilies, carrot or pimiento. Sprinkle with onion salt, celery salt and herbs.

3/Cook all vegetables except potatoes uncovered. Potatoes must be covered for part of sautéing time to cook through before overbrowning. Turn vegetables occasionally during cooking.

4/When vegetables are tender, sprinkle with shredded or grated cheese such as Monterey Jack, Cheddar, Swiss, mozzarella or Parmesan. Heat 1 to 2 minutes or until cheese melts.

Basic Stir-Fried Vegetables

SERVINGS	4	2	1
INGREDIENTS			
vegetable oil	2 tablespoons	1 tablespoon	2 teaspoons
garlic, minced	1 large clove	1 small clove	1/2 small clove
minced fresh gingerroot	4 teaspoons	2 teaspoons	1 teaspoon
vegetables, see chart below	4 cups	2 cups	1 cup
soy sauce, teriyaki sauce or bottled sweet-sour sauce, if desired	2 tablespoons	1 tablespoon	2 teaspoons
OR			
oyster sauce or fish sauce, if desired	1/2 teaspoon	1/4 teaspoon	1/8 teaspoon
WOK OR HEAVY SKILLET	wok or 11-inch skillet	wok or 11-inch skillet	wok or 11-inch skillet
TIME AT 375F (190C) OR MEDIUM HIGH	see timings for vegetables in chart below		

In a wok or heavy 11-inch skillet, heat oil, garlic and gingerroot over Medium-High heat until a drop of water sizzles on it. Use 375F (190C) on an electric wok or skillet. Quickly add vegetables. Cook, stirring and tossing constantly, for time in chart below or until vegetables are hot and crisp-tender. To stir-fry a combination of vegetables, add vegetable with longest cooking time first. Add other vegetables in decreasing order of cooking times. Add sauce during last 30 seconds of cooking time, if desired.

Suggested Vegetables for Stir-Frying

AMOUNT	4 cups	2 cups	1 cup
	COOKING TIME AT 375F (190C) OR MEDIUM-HIGH HEAT		
VEGETABLE			
bean sprouts	2-1/2 to 3 minutes	2 to 2-1/2 minutes	1-1/2 to 2 minutes
broccoli, cut in 1/8-inch-thick flowerets	5 to 6 minutes	5 to 6 minutes	4 to 5 minutes
cauliflower, cut in 1/8-inch-thick flowerets	5-1/2 to 6 minutes	4-1/2 to 5 minutes	3-1/2 to 4 minutes
celery, cut in 1/8-inch slices	7 to 7-1/2 minutes	6 to 6-1/2 minutes	5 to 5-1/2 minutes
Chinese cabbage, shredded	2 to 2-1/2 minutes	1-1/2 to 2 minutes	1 to 1-1/2 minutes
green onions, cut in 1-inch lengths	7-1/2 to 8 minutes	5 to 5-1/2 minutes	3 to 3-1/2 minutes
green or red pepper, cut in 1/8-inch strips	5 to 5-1/2 minutes	3-1/2 to 4 minutes	2 to 2-1/2 minutes
mushrooms, cut in 1/8-inch slices	1-1/2 to 2 minutes	1 to 1-1/2 minutes	1 to 1-1/2 minutes
onions, cut in 1/8-inch slices	8 to 8-1/2 minutes	5 to 5-1/2 minutes	4 to 4-1/2 minutes
pea pods, frozen, thawed	3-1/2 to 4 minutes	2 to 2-1/2 minutes	1-1/2 to 2 minutes
tomatoes, cut in 8 wedges	1-1/2 to 2 minutes	1-1/2 to 2 minutes	1-1/2 to 2 minutes
tomatoes, cherry, halved	2 to 3 minutes	1-1/2 to 2 minutes	1-1/2 to 2 minutes
yellow crookneck squash, cut in 1/8-inch slices	4-1/2 to 5 minutes	3 to 3-1/2 minutes	2-1/2 to 3 minutes
zucchini, cut in 1/8-inch slices	4-1/2 to 5 minutes	3 to 3-1/2 minutes	2-1/2 to 3 minutes

How to Make Basic Stir-Fried Vegetables

1/Peel gingerroot with a small knife, then mince into very small pieces. Refrigerate extra gingerroot in a covered jar of dry sherry.

2/Shred Chinese cabbage by slicing across head. Cut mushrooms in 1/8-inch slices and red pepper in 1/8-inch strips. Rinse bean sprouts. Remove ends from pea pods.

3/Heat oil, garlic and gingerroot in a wok or skillet until a drop of water sizzles on it. Add longest-cooking vegetable first, then add other vegetables in decreasing order of cooking times.

4/Toss and stir vegetables constantly during cooking. When vegetables are crisp-tender, add bottled sweet-sour sauce, if desired, and heat through before serving.

Basic Deep-Fried Vegetables

BATTER YIELD	1 cup batter	1/2 cup batter
INGREDIENTS		
all-purpose flour	1/2 cup	1/4 cup
milk	1/2 cup	1/4 cup
egg white	1 white	1 tablespoon
celery salt	1/4 teaspoon	1/8 teaspoon
vegetables, see chart below		
seasoned dry breadcrumbs	1 to 2 cups	1/2 to 1 cup
vegetable oil for deep-fat frying	about 2-1/2 qts.	about 2-1/2 qts.
salt	to taste	to taste
DEEP-FAT FRYER OR HEAVY DUTCH OVEN	5-qt. fryer or Dutch oven	5-qt. fryer or Dutch oven
TIME IN 365F (185C) OIL	1-1/2 to 2 minutes	1-1/2 to 2 minutes

In a medium bowl, whisk together flour, milk, egg white and celery salt until smooth. Dip vegetable pieces in batter, then roll in crumbs. Pour oil into a 5-quart deep-fat fryer or heavy Dutch oven. Fryer should be about half full of oil. Preheat oil to 365F (185C) or until a 1-inch cube of bread turns golden brown in 50 seconds. Fry vegetable pieces, a few at a time, in 365F (185C) oil 1-1/2 to 2 minutes or until browned. Turn once, if necessary, for pieces to brown evenly. Remove vegetables from oil with a slotted spoon and drain on paper towels. Keep deep-fried pieces warm in a 175F (80C) oven while frying remaining pieces. Deep-fried vegetables may be kept in warm oven up to 2 hours. Sprinkle with salt to taste.

Suggested Vegetables for Deep-Frying

	amount for 1 cup batter	amount for 1/2 cup batter
VEGETABLE		
broccoli, broken in small flowerets	2 (4-oz.) stalks	1 (4-oz.) stalk
cauliflower, broken in small flowerets	1 small head	1/2 small head
eggplant, cut in sticks, 1/2 inch thick, 2-1/2 to 3 inches long	1/2 medium	1/4 medium
green or red pepper, cut in 1/4-inch strips	2 large	1 large
mushrooms, 1 inch in diameter	36	18
onion, sliced 1/4 inch thick, separated in rings	1 medium	1/2 medium
zucchini, cut in sticks, 1/4 inch thick, 2-1/2 to 3 inches long	2 medium	1 medium

How to Make Basic Deep-Fried Vegetables

1/To deep-fry vegetables, cut green or red pepper in strips, eggplant and zucchini in sticks, onions in rings and cauliflower or broccoli in small flowerets. Leave mushrooms whole. For batter, whisk together flour, milk, egg white and celery salt until smooth.

2/Dip vegetables in batter, then roll in seasoned dry bread-crumbs on a piece of waxed paper. Lift waxed paper up around vegetables to help coat with crumbs. Coat only a few vegetables at a time with crumbs.

3/Pour cooking oil into a deep-fat fryer or heavy Dutch oven. Fill fryer about half full. Heat oil to 365F (185C) or until a 1-inch cube of bread turns golden brown in 50 seconds.

4/Cook vegetables, a few at a time, in hot oil 1-1/2 to 2 minutes or until brown. Remove from oil with a slotted spoon. Drain on paper towels. Sprinkle with salt to taste.

Cooked Dried Beans

YIELD	6 to 7 cups (6 to 8 servings)	3 to 3-1/2 cups (3 or 4 servings)
INGREDIENTS		
dried navy, kidney, pinto, baby lima or garbanzo beans or black-eyed peas	1 lb. (about 2-1/2 cups uncooked)	8 oz. (about 1-1/4 cups uncooked)
water	8 cups	4 cups
baking soda	1/4 teaspoon	1/8 teaspoon
water	6 cups	3 cups
salt	1 teaspoon	1/2 teaspoon
DUTCH OVEN	5-qt. Dutch oven	3-qt. saucepan
SOAKING TIME	8 hours or overnight	8 hours or overnight
TIME AT MEDIUM LOW:		
navy, garbanzo, pinto beans	55 to 65 minutes	55 to 65 minutes
kidney beans, baby lima beans, black-eyed peas	35 to 45 minutes	35 to 45 minutes

Sort and rinse beans. In a Dutch oven, see size in chart above, combine beans, first amount of water and baking soda; mix well. Cover and let stand 8 hours or overnight. Drain and rinse beans. Return beans to Dutch oven. Add second amount of water and salt. Bring to a boil over High heat. Skim off foam. Reduce heat to Medium Low; cover. Simmer for time in chart above or until tender. Use for Ginger-Honey Baked Beans, opposite, or Spanish-Style Baked Beans, page 152.

Note: As a rule, use 8 cups *soaking* water for 1 pound beans. Use 6 cups *cooking* water for 1 pound beans.

Easy Baked Beans

SERVINGS	6 to 8	3 or 4
INGREDIENTS		
bacon, cut in 1-inch pieces	6 slices	3 slices
reserved bacon drippings	2 tablespoons	1 tablespoon
chopped onion	1/2 cup	1/4 cup
baked beans in brown-sugar sauce	2 (16- to 18-oz.) cans or jars	1 (16- to 18-oz.) can or jar
packed brown sugar	1/4 cup	2 tablespoons
barbecue sauce	1/4 cup	2 tablespoons
Worcestershire sauce	2 tablespoons	1 tablespoon
prepared mustard	1 teaspoon	1/2 teaspoon
SKILLET	8-inch skillet	6-inch skillet
CASSEROLE	2-qt. casserole	1-qt. casserole
TIME AT MEDIUM HIGH (bacon)	7 to 8 minutes	6 to 7 minutes
TIME AT MEDIUM HIGH (onion)	4 minutes	3 minutes
TIME IN 350F (175C) OVEN	1-1/4 hours	1 hour

Do not preheat oven. In a skillet, see size in chart above, cook bacon over Medium-High heat for time in chart above or until crisp, stirring often. Remove bacon with a slotted spoon and drain on paper towels. Reserve in skillet amount of drippings listed in chart above. Add onion to skillet. Cook over Medium-High heat for time in chart above or until tender, stirring occasionally. In a casserole, see size in chart above, combine bacon, onion, beans, brown sugar, barbecue sauce, Worcestershire sauce and mustard; mix well. Bake, uncovered, in a 350F (175C) oven for time in chart above or until heated through.

How to Make Ginger-Honey Baked Beans

1/Layered in the jar from bottom are navy, garbanzo, kidney and pinto beans. All may be used for this recipe. Soak beans overnight in water and baking soda mixture. Drain and rinse beans. Bring beans and water to a boil in a Dutch oven. Skim off foam.

2/Simmer beans over Medium-Low heat until tender. Drain beans, reserving cooking liquid. In a casserole, combine cooked beans, crushed pineapple, cooked bacon, honey, molasses, onion, dry mustard and ginger. Cover and bake in a slow oven, stirring occasionally.

Ginger-Honey Baked Beans

SERVINGS	8 to 10	4 or 5
INGREDIENTS		
prepared navy, kidney, pinto or garbanzo beans, see Cooked Dried Beans, opposite	6 to 7 cups	3 to 3-1/2 cups
crushed pineapple	1 (8-oz.) can	1/2 (8-oz.) can
bacon, cooked, crumbled	8 slices	4 slices
honey	1/2 cup	1/4 cup
molasses	1/2 cup	1/4 cup
chopped onion	1 cup	1/2 cup
dry mustard	2 teaspoons	1 teaspoon
ground ginger	1 teaspoon	1/2 teaspoon
reserved cooking liquid	1-1/2 cups	3/4 cup
BEANPOT OR CASSEROLE	3-qt. beanpot	1-1/2-qt. beanpot
TIME IN 300F (150C) OVEN	3 hours	3 hours

Prepare navy, kidney, pinto or garbanzo beans according to directions for Cooked Dried Beans. Drain, reserving all cooking liquid. Do not preheat oven. In a beanpot or casserole, see size in chart above, combine beans, crushed pineapple with juice, bacon, honey, molasses, onion, dry mustard and ginger. Stir in amount of reserved cooking liquid listed in chart above. Cover and bake in a 300F (150C) oven 3 hours or until flavors blend and bean mixture is slightly thick, stirring occasionally. Add additional reserved cooking liquid if beans become too dry during baking. Navy beans especially may require up to 1 cup more liquid.

Basic Vegetables au Gratin

SERVINGS	8 to 10	4 or 5	2 or 3
INGREDIENTS			
butter or margarine	1/4 cup	2 tablespoons	1 tablespoon
chopped green onion	1/4 cup	2 tablespoons	1 tablespoon
all-purpose flour	1/4 cup	2 tablespoons	1 tablespoon
celery salt	1/2 teaspoon	1/4 teaspoon	1/8 teaspoon
dried leaf herb	1/2 teaspoon	1/4 teaspoon	1/8 teaspoon
milk	1 cup	1/2 cup	1/4 cup
chicken broth	1 cup	1/2 cup	1/4 cup
lemon juice	2 teaspoons	1 teaspoon	1/2 teaspoon
shredded cheese	1 cup (4 oz.)	1/2 cup (2 oz.)	1/4 cup (1 oz.)
hot, drained, cooked vegetables	8 cups	4 cups	2 cups
chopped pimiento	1/4 cup	2 tablespoons	1 tablespoon
butter or margarine, melted	2 tablespoons	1 tablespoon	2 teaspoons
dry breadcrumbs	1/4 cup	2 tablespoons	1 tablespoon
grated Parmesan cheese	2 tablespoons	1 tablespoon	2 teaspoons
snipped parsley	2 tablespoons	1 tablespoon	1 teaspoon
SAUCEPAN	3-qt. saucepan	1-1/2-qt. saucepan	1-qt. saucepan
CASSEROLE	deep 2-qt. casserole	deep 1-qt. casserole	deep 2-cup casserole
TIME AT MEDIUM HIGH (green onion)	2 minutes	2 minutes	1 minute
TIME AT MEDIUM HIGH (flour added)	1 minute	1 minute	1 minute
TIME AT MEDIUM HIGH (milk, broth added)	6 to 7 minutes	4 to 5 minutes	3 minutes
TIME IN 350F (175C) OVEN	40 to 45 minutes	25 to 30 minutes	15 to 20 minutes

Do not preheat oven. In a saucepan, see size in chart above, melt first amount of butter or margarine. Add green onion. Cook over Medium-High heat for time in chart above or until tender, stirring occasionally. Whisk in flour, celery salt and herb. Cook and stir 1 minute. Add milk, broth and lemon juice. Cook and whisk for time in chart above or until thickened and bubbly all over. Stir in shredded cheese until melted. Stir in hot vegetables and pimiento. Pour into a casserole, see size in chart above. In a small bowl, combine second amount of butter or margarine, breadcrumbs, Parmesan cheese and parsley. Sprinkle on casserole or around edge. Bake, uncovered, in a 350F (175C) oven for time in chart above or until heated through.

Suggested Combinations
Swiss Vegetables au Gratin: Use savory for herb. Use Swiss cheese. Use broccoli flowerets, small whole carrots and small whole onions for vegetables.
Cheddar Vegetables au Gratin: Use basil for herb. Use Cheddar cheese. Use cauliflowerets, Brussels sprouts and crinkle-cut carrots for vegetables.

Swiss Vegetables au Gratin

Basic Quick Vegetables au Gratin

SERVINGS	8 to 10	4 or 5
INGREDIENTS		
condensed cream soup	1 (10- to 11-oz.) can	1/2 (10- to 11-oz.) can (2/3 cup)
shredded cheese	1 cup (4 oz.)	1/2 cup (2 oz.)
milk	1/3 cup	3 tablespoons
dry mustard	1 teaspoon	1/2 teaspoon
chili powder	1/2 teaspoon	1/4 teaspoon
hot, drained, cooked vegetables	4 cups	2 cups
sliced water chestnuts, drained	1 (8-oz.) can	1/2 (8-oz.) can
sliced mushrooms, drained	2 (2-1/2-oz.) cans	1 (2-1/2-oz.) can
cracker crumbs	1/2 cup	1/4 cup
butter or margarine, melted	2 tablespoons	1 tablespoon
CASSEROLE	2-qt. casserole	1-qt. casserole
TIME IN 350F (175C) OVEN	50 to 60 minutes	45 to 50 minutes

Do not preheat oven. In a casserole, see size in chart above, whisk together soup, cheese, milk, dry mustard and chili powder. Fold in hot vegetables, water chestnuts and mushrooms. Toss cracker crumbs with melted butter or margarine. Sprinkle on vegetable mixture. Bake, uncovered, in a 350F (175C) oven for time in chart above or until heated through.

Suggested Combinations
Quick Sprouts & Kohlrabi au Gratin: Use creamy chicken-mushroom soup and Cheddar cheese. Use Brussels sprouts and kohlrabi for vegetables. Use soda-cracker crumbs.
Quick New Potatoes au Gratin: Use cream of onion soup and Swiss cheese. Use small new potatoes for vegetable. Use sesame-cracker crumbs.
Quick Winter Vegetables au Gratin: Use cream of celery soup and Monterey Jack cheese. Use broccoli, cauliflower and carrots for vegetables. Use cheese-cracker crumbs.

Basic Scalloped-Vegetable Casserole

SERVINGS	8	4
INGREDIENTS		
condensed cream of onion soup	1 (10-3/4-oz.) can	1/2 (10-3/4-oz.) can
plain yogurt	1 cup	1/2 cup
milk	1/2 cup	1/4 cup
butter or margarine	2 tablespoons	1 tablespoon
shredded carrot	1 cup	1/2 cup
chopped green onion or celery	1/2 cup	1/4 cup
hot, drained, cooked vegetables	4 cups	2 cups
herb-stuffing mix	2 cups	1 cup
SAUCEPAN	3-qt. saucepan	2-qt. saucepan
BAKING DISH	12" x 7" baking dish	9" x 5" x 3" loaf dish
TIME AT MEDIUM HIGH	6 minutes	5 minutes
TIME IN 350F (175C) OVEN	35 to 40 minutes	30 to 35 minutes

Do not preheat oven. In a medium bowl, whisk together soup, yogurt and milk; set aside. In a saucepan, see size in chart above, melt butter or margarine. Add carrot and green onion or celery. Cook over Medium-High heat for time in chart above or until tender, stirring often. Add soup mixture and hot vegetables; mix well. Place half of vegetable mixture in a baking dish, see size in chart above. Top with two-thirds of dry stuffing mix. Add remaining vegetable mixture and top with remaining stuffing mix. Bake, uncovered, in a 350F (175C) oven for time in chart above or until heated through.

Suggested Combinations
Scalloped-Corn Casserole: Use cooked whole-kernel corn for vegetable.
Scalloped-Cabbage Casserole: Use cooked shredded cabbage for vegetable.
Scalloped-Zucchini Casserole: Use cooked sliced zucchini for vegetable.
Scalloped-Broccoli-Cauliflower Casserole: Use cooked chopped broccoli and cooked cauliflowerets for vegetables.

Basic Creamed Vegetables

SERVINGS	6 to 8	3 or 4	1 or 2
INGREDIENTS			
butter or margarine	2 tablespoons	1 tablespoon	1 teaspoon
all-purpose flour	2 tablespoons	1 tablespoon	1 teaspoon
celery salt	1/4 teaspoon	1/8 teaspoon	dash
pepper	1/8 teaspoon	dash	dash
dried leaf herb	1/2 teaspoon	1/4 teaspoon	1/8 teaspoon
milk	1-1/2 cups	3/4 cup	1/3 cup
hot, drained, cooked vegetables	4 cups	2 cups	1 cup
SAUCEPAN	1-1/2-qt. saucepan	1-qt. saucepan	1-qt. saucepan
TIME AT MEDIUM HIGH (butter, flour)	1 minute	1 minute	30 seconds
TIME AT MEDIUM HIGH (milk added)	7 to 8 minutes	5 to 6 minutes	2 to 3 minutes
TIME AT MEDIUM	2 to 3 minutes	2 minutes	1 to 2 minutes

In a saucepan, see size in chart above, melt butter or margarine. Whisk in flour, celery salt, pepper and herb. Whisk over Medium-High heat for time in chart above. Whisk in milk. Cook for time in chart above or until thickened and bubbly all over, whisking constantly. Reduce heat to Medium. Stir in hot vegetables; cover. Cook for time in chart above or until heated through, stirring occasionally.

Suggested Combinations
Creamed Peas & New Potatoes: Use dill weed for herb. Use cooked peas and cooked, small, new potatoes for vegetables.
Creamed Carrots & Onions: Use summer savory for herb. Use cooked, small, whole carrots and cooked, tiny, whole onions for vegetables.
Creamed Succotash: Use basil for herb. Use cooked whole-kernel corn and cooked lima beans for vegetables.
Creamed Asparagus Deluxe: Use tarragon for herb. Use cooked asparagus cuts for vegetable and substitute hard-cooked-egg slices for second vegetable.
Creamed Vegetables Elegante: Use fines herbes for herb. Use cooked sliced leeks and cooked sliced mushrooms for vegetables.

Basic Creamy Vegetable Casserole

SERVINGS	6 to 8	3 or 4
INGREDIENTS		
condensed cream soup	1 (10- to 11-oz.) can	1/2 (10- to 11-oz.) can
milk	2/3 cup	1/3 cup
mayonnaise or mayonnaise-style salad dressing	1/4 cup	2 tablespoons
hot, well-drained, cooked vegetable	4 cups	2 cups
chopped celery or water chestnuts	1/2 cup	1/4 cup
chopped pimiento	1/4 cup	2 tablespoons
snipped parsley	1/4 cup	2 tablespoons
French-fried onions	1 (3-oz.) can	1/2 (3-oz.) can
CASSEROLE	1-1/2-qt. casserole	1-qt. casserole
TIME IN 350F (175C) OVEN (casserole)	35 to 40 minutes	25 to 30 minutes
TIME IN 350F (175C) OVEN (topping added)	5 minutes	5 minutes

Do not preheat oven. In a casserole, see size in chart above, whisk together soup, milk and mayonnaise or salad dressing. Fold in hot vegetable, celery or water chestnuts, pimiento, parsley and one-fourth French-fried onions. Cover and bake in a 350F (175C) oven for time in chart above or until heated through. Uncover. Top with remaining French-fried onions. Bake 5 minutes longer.

Suggested Soups: cream of mushroom, creamy chicken-mushroom, cream of celery or cream of onion.
Suggested Vegetables: cut green beans, cauliflowerets, sliced carrots, broccoli flowerets, whole-kernel corn.

Basic Piquant-Glazed Vegetables

Photo on pages 2 and 329.

SERVINGS	6 to 8	3 or 4	1 or 2
INGREDIENTS			
hot, cooked, cubed or sliced vegetable	4 cups	2 cups	1 cup
butter or margarine	2 tablespoons	1 tablespoon	2 teaspoons
packed brown sugar	2 tablespoons	1 tablespoon	2 teaspoons
cornstarch	1 tablespoon	1-1/2 teaspoons	3/4 teaspoon
beef or chicken broth	1/2 cup	1/4 cup	2 tablespoons
vinegar	1/4 cup	2 tablespoons	1 tablespoon
dried leaf herb	1 teaspooon	1/2 teaspoon	1/4 teaspoon
SAUCEPAN	2- to 3-qt. saucepan	1-1/2- to 2-qt. saucepan	1-qt. saucepan
TIME AT MEDIUM HIGH	11 to 13 minutes	7 to 9 minutes	4 to 5 minutes

Drain vegetable. Return to same saucepan, see size in chart above. Add butter or margarine to vegetable. In a small bowl, combine brown sugar and cornstarch; mix well. Stir in broth and vinegar. Blend until smooth. Gently stir vinegar mixture into vegetable. Add herb. Cook and stir gently over Medium-High heat for time in chart above or until glaze is thickened and bubbly all over and vegetable is hot.

Suggested Vegetables: beets, broccoli, cauliflower, cabbage or spinach.
Suggested Herbs: tarragon, basil, oregano, marjoram or thyme.

Basic Sweet-Glazed Vegetables

SERVINGS	6 to 8	3 or 4	1 or 2
INGREDIENTS			
hot, cooked, cubed or sliced vegetable	4 cups	2 cups	1 cup
butter or margarine	1/4 cup	2 tablespoons	1 tablespoon
maple-flavored syrup or honey	1/4 cup	2 tablespoons	1 tablespoon
grated lemon or orange peel	1/2 teaspoon	1/4 teaspoon	1/8 teaspoon
ground spice	1/4 teaspoon	1/8 teaspoon	dash
SAUCEPAN	2- to 3-qt. saucepan	1-1/2- to 2-qt. saucepan	1-qt. saucepan
TIME AT MEDIUM LOW	3 to 4 minutes	2 to 3 minutes	1 to 2 minutes

Drain vegetable. Return to same saucepan, see size in chart above. Add butter or margarine. Stir over Medium-Low heat until melted. In a small bowl, combine syrup or honey, lemon or orange peel, and spice. Pour over vegetable. Cook, stirring gently, for time in chart above or until vegetable is heated through and lightly glazed.

Suggested Vegetables: butternut squash, carrots, beets or sweet potatoes.
Suggested Spices: cinnamon, nutmeg, mace, allspice or cloves.

Variation
Sweet-Glazed Acorn Squash, photo on pages 2 and 329: Melt butter or margarine in a small saucepan. Stir in syrup or honey, lemon or orange peel and spice. Spoon glaze over cooked squash rings or into center of cooked squash halves in a baking dish. Bake at desired oven temperature according to directions on page 338.

How to Make Basic Buttery Vegetable Toss

1/Lima beans, green beans, carrots, peas, cut asparagus, broccoli and cauliflower are all good choices for this recipe. Toast almonds, pecans, walnuts, peanuts or cashews in butter, margarine or bacon drippings.

2/Pour toasted nut mixture over hot cooked vegetable. Toss nuts and vegetable with cheese-, herb-, rye- or onion-flavored croutons. Sprinkle with tarragon, dill weed, basil, oregano, thyme or savory. Add snipped parsley and chives and toss gently.

Basic Buttery Vegetable Toss

SERVINGS	6 to 8	3 or 4	1 or 2
INGREDIENTS			
butter, margarine or bacon drippings	1/4 cup	2 tablespoons	1 tablespoon
nut pieces	1/2 cup	1/4 cup	2 tablespoons
hot, cooked, cubed or sliced vegetable	4 cups	2 cups	1 cup
flavored croutons	1 cup	1/2 cup	1/4 cup
dried leaf herb	1 teaspoon	1/2 teaspoon	1/4 teaspoon
pepper	1/4 teaspoon	1/8 teaspoon	dash
snipped chives	1 tablespoon	2 teaspoons	1 teaspoon
snipped parsley	1 tablespoon	2 teaspoons	1 teaspoon
bacon, cooked, crumbled, if desired	6 slices	3 slices	1 slice
SKILLET	8-inch skillet	6-inch skillet	6-inch skillet
TIME AT MEDIUM HIGH	2 to 2-1/2 minutes	1-1/2 to 2 minutes	1 to 1-1/2 minutes

In a skillet, see size in chart above, melt butter, margarine or bacon drippings over Medium-High heat. Stir in nuts. Toss and stir for time in chart above or until nuts are toasted. Pour over hot vegetable. Toss with croutons, herb, pepper, chives, parsley and bacon, if desired.

Suggested Nuts: almonds, pecans, walnuts, peanuts or cashews.
Suggested Croutons: herb-, cheese-, rye- or onion-flavored.
Suggested Vegetables: green beans, carrots, peas, asparagus, broccoli, lima beans or cauliflower.
Suggested Herbs: tarragon, dill weed, basil, oregano, thyme or savory.

Easy Scalloped Potatoes

SERVINGS	8	4
INGREDIENTS		
frozen potato thins with skins, thawed	1 (24-oz.) pkg. (6 cups)	1/2 (24-oz.) pkg. (3 cups)
chopped green pepper	1/4 cup	2 tablespoons
chopped green onion	1/4 cup	2 tablespoons
chopped pimiento	1/4 cup	2 tablespoons
shredded Swiss or Cheddar cheese	1 cup (4 oz.)	1/2 cup (2 oz.)
condensed cream of potato soup	2 (10-3/4-oz.) cans	1 (10-3/4-oz.) can
chicken broth	1 (14-1/2-oz.) can	1 cup
prepared mustard	2 teaspoons	1 teaspoon
prepared horseradish	2 teaspoons	1 teaspoon
dried leaf Italian herbs	2 teaspoons	1 teaspoon
snipped parsley	1/4 cup	2 tablespoons
BAKING DISH	12" x 7" baking dish	9" x 5" x 3" loaf dish
TIME IN 375F (190C) OVEN	50 to 60 minutes	45 to 50 minutes

Do not preheat oven. In a baking dish, see size in chart above, layer half of potatoes, green pepper, green onion, pimiento and cheese. In a medium bowl, whisk together soup, broth, mustard, horseradish and Italian herbs. Pour half of soup mixture over potato mixture. Repeat layers. Bake, uncovered, in a 375F (190C) oven for time in chart above or until potatoes are tender. Sprinkle with parsley.

Scalloped Potatoes Deluxe

SERVINGS	6	3
INGREDIENTS		
butter or margarine	2 tablespoons	1 tablespoon
all-purpose flour	2 tablespoons	1 tablespoon
celery salt	1/2 teaspoon	1/4 teaspoon
herb pepper	1/2 teaspoon	1/4 teaspoon
all-purpose flour	2 tablespoons	1 tablespoon
milk	2 cups	1 cup
chicken broth, fat skimmed off	1 cup	1/2 cup
snipped parsley	1/4 cup	2 tablespoons
snipped chives	2 tablespoons	1 tablespoon
potatoes, peeled, sliced 1/8 inch thick	6 medium (2 lbs., 5 cups sliced)	3 medium (1 lb., 2-1/2 cups sliced)
paprika	to garnish	to garnish
SAUCEPAN	2-qt. saucepan	1-qt. saucepan
CASSEROLE	deep 2-qt. casserole	deep 1-qt. casserole
TIME AT MEDIUM HIGH (flour)	1 minute	1 minute
TIME AT MEDIUM HIGH (milk, broth added)	14 to 15 minutes	9 minutes
TIME IN 350F (175C) OVEN (covered)	45 minutes	40 minutes
TIME IN 350F (175C) OVEN (uncovered)	25 minutes	20 minutes
STANDING TIME	10 minutes	10 minutes

Do not preheat oven. In a saucepan, see size in chart above, melt butter or margarine. Whisk in first amount of flour, celery salt and herb pepper. Whisk over Medium-High heat 1 minute. In a screw-top jar, combine second amount of flour and milk; shake well until completely smooth. Whisk milk mixture and broth into butter or margarine mixture. Cook, whisking constantly, for time in chart above or until thickened and bubbly all over. Stir in parsley and chives. In a casserole, see size in chart above, arrange half of potatoes. Pour half of sauce over potatoes. Repeat layers. Cover and bake in a 350F (175C) oven for time in chart above. Uncover and stir gently. Bake, uncovered, for time in chart above or until potatoes are tender. Stir gently. Sprinkle with paprika. Let stand, covered, 10 minutes before serving.

How to Make Easy Scalloped Potatoes

1/In a casserole, layer frozen potato thins, thawed, with chopped green pepper, green onion, pimiento and shredded cheese.

2/Whisk together condensed cream of potato soup, chicken broth and seasonings until smooth. Pour over vegetable mixture in alternate layers and bake.

Basic Sweet-Potato Casserole

SERVINGS	8	4
INGREDIENTS		
canned cut fruit	1 (16-oz.) can	1 (8-oz.) can
canned fruit syrup or fruit juice	1/4 cup	2 tablespoons
butter or margarine, melted	1/4 cup	2 tablespoons
packed brown sugar	1/4 cup	2 tablespoons
ground spice	1 teaspoon	1/2 teaspoon
vacuum-packed sweet potatoes, drained	2 (18-oz.) cans	1 (18-oz.) can
chopped nuts	1/2 cup	1/4 cup
miniature marshmallows	2 cups	1 cup
BAKING DISH	13" x 9" baking dish	10" x 6" baking dish
TIME IN 375F (190C) OVEN	35 to 40 minutes	25 to 30 minutes

Do not preheat oven. Drain fruit. If using syrup from canned fruit, reserve amount listed in chart above. In a baking dish, see size in chart above, combine reserved syrup or fruit juice, butter or margarine, brown sugar and spice. Mix well. Add sweet potatoes, turning to coat with juice mixture. Arrange fruit over sweet potatoes. Sprinkle with nuts and marshmallows. Bake in a 375F (190C) oven for time in chart above or until marshmallows are golden and casserole is heated through.

Suggested Fruit: sliced peaches, apricot halves or pineapple chunks.
Suggested Spices: cinnamon, nutmeg, allspice, cloves or mace.
Suggested Nuts: walnuts, pecans, cashews or hazelnuts.

Mashed Potatoes

SERVINGS	12 to 16	6 to 8	3 or 4
INGREDIENTS			
Idaho or russet potatoes, cut in 3/4-inch cubes	4 lbs. (12 potatoes)	2 lbs. (6 potatoes)	1 lb. (3 potatoes)
milk	2/3 to 1 cup	1/3 to 2/3 cup	3 to 5 tablespoons
butter or margarine	1/4 cup	2 tablespoons	1 tablespoon
onion salt	1 teaspoon	1/2 teaspoon	1/4 teaspoon
herb pepper	1 teaspoon	1/2 teaspoon	1/4 teaspoon
SAUCEPAN	4-qt. saucepan	2-qt. saucepan	1-qt. saucepan
TIME AT MEDIUM LOW (boil potatoes)	12 minutes	11 minutes	10 minutes
TIME AT MEDIUM LOW (heat mashed potatoes)	10 minutes	10 minutes	7 minutes

In a saucepan, see size in chart above, combine potatoes and enough water to cover. Bring to a boil over High heat. Reduce heat to Medium Low; cover. Cook for time in chart above or until potatoes are tender, stirring twice. Drain well. Place potatoes in a mixer bowl. Add smaller amount of milk, butter or margarine, onion salt and herb pepper. Beat at low speed of an electric mixer until potatoes are broken up. Turn mixer to high speed. Beat just until fluffy. Do not overbeat. Add more milk, if necessary, in small amounts. Return potatoes to saucepan. Cover and place over Medium-Low heat for time in chart above or until heated through, stirring once or twice.

Buffet Potato Casserole

SERVINGS	12 to 16	6 to 8
INGREDIENTS		
semisoft natural cheese with herbs and spices	2 (3-1/2-oz.) cartons	1 (3-1/2-oz.) carton
hot cooked mashed potatoes or hot instant mashed-potato buds	16 servings (8 cups)	8 servings (4 cups)
chopped green onion	1/2 cup	1/4 cup
snipped parsley	1/4 cup	2 tablespoons
paprika	to garnish	to garnish
CASSEROLE	2-qt. casserole	1-qt. casserole
REFRIGERATE	2 to 24 hours	2 to 24 hours
TIME IN 350F (175C) OVEN	1 hour and 30 to 40 minutes	55 to 65 minutes

Do not preheat oven. Stir cheese into hot potatoes until melted. Stir in green onion and parsley. Spoon into a casserole, see size in chart above. Sprinkle with paprika. Cover and refrigerate up to 24 hours. Bake, uncovered, in a 350F (175C) oven for time in chart above or until heated through.

Parsley Buttered Steamed New Potatoes

SERVINGS	4	2	1
INGREDIENTS			
fresh, small, new potatoes	2 lbs. (16 potatoes)	1 lb. (8 potatoes)	8 oz. (4 potatoes)
butter or margarine	2 tablespoons	1 tablespoon	2 teaspoons
snipped parsley	1/4 cup	2 tablespoons	1 tablespoon
SAUCEPAN	3-qt. saucepan	3-qt. saucepan	3-qt. saucepan
TIME AT MEDIUM	18 to 20 minutes	18 to 20 minutes	18 to 20 minutes

Wash potatoes. Halve large potatoes so all potatoes are about the same size. Peel small strip around center of whole potatoes. Pour water to a depth of 1/2 inch in a saucepan, see size in chart above. Place a steamer basket in saucepan. Water level should be below steamer basket. Spread potatoes evenly in basket. Choose the burner closest in size to diameter of saucepan. Bring to a boil over High heat. Cover tightly. Reduce heat to Medium. Cook over Medium heat for minimum time in chart above. Do not lift the lid before end of minimum cooking time. Water should simmer enough to make steam escape from under lid. Cook until potatoes are tender. Toss potatoes, butter or margarine and parsley in a serving dish.

Twice-Baked Potatoes

SERVINGS	6	4	2
INGREDIENTS			
hot baked potatoes	6 large	4 large	2 large
onion sour-cream dip	1 cup	1/2 cup	1/4 cup
milk	6 to 8 tablespoons	4 to 6 tablespoons	2 to 3 tablespoons
celery salt	1/2 teaspoon	1/4 teaspoon	1/8 teaspoon
pepper	1/4 teaspoon	1/8 teaspoon	dash
shredded Cheddar cheese	2 cups (8 oz.)	1 cup (4 oz.)	1/2 cup (2 oz.)
chopped green onion	2 tablespoons	4 teaspoons	2 teaspoons
cooked crumbled bacon	2 tablespoons	4 teaspoons	2 teaspoons
BAKING DISH	13" x 9" baking dish	12" x 7" baking dish	10" x 6" baking dish
MIXER BOWL	3-qt. bowl	3-qt. bowl	1-1/2-qt. bowl
TIME IN 325F (165C) OVEN **OR**	35 to 40 minutes	35 to 40 minutes	35 to 40 minutes
TIME IN 375F (190C) OVEN **OR**	25 to 30 minutes	25 to 30 minutes	25 to 30 minutes
TIME IN 425F (220C) OVEN	15 to 20 minutes	15 to 20 minutes	15 to 20 minutes

After baking potatoes, leave oven preheated to desired oven temperature, see choices in chart above. Cut hot potatoes in half lengthwise. Scoop out potato pulp into a mixer bowl, see size in chart above. Keep shells intact. Add sour-cream dip, milk, celery salt, pepper and half of cheese to potatoes. Beat at low speed of an electric mixer until blended. Turn mixer to high speed. Beat just until fluffy. Do not overbeat. Spoon potato mixture back into shells. Place in a baking dish, see size in chart above. Sprinkle with remaining cheese, green onion and bacon. Bake at desired oven temperature for time in chart above or until heated through.

Buttery Oven-Browned Potatoes

SERVINGS	4 or 5	2 or 3	1
INGREDIENTS			
butter or margarine	1/4 cup	2 tablespoons	1 tablespoon
baking potatoes	4 (8- to 9-oz.) potatoes	2 (8- to 9-oz.) potatoes	1 (8- to 9-oz.) potato
celery salt	1/2 teaspoon	1/4 teaspoon	1/8 teaspoon
onion salt	1/2 teaspoon	1/4 teaspoon	1/8 teaspoon
paprika	1/2 teaspoon	1/4 teaspoon	1/8 teaspoon
BAKING DISH	14" x 10" baking dish	12" x 7" baking dish	9-inch pie plate
TIME IN 350F (175C) OVEN **(melt butter)**	6 minutes	6 minutes	5 minutes
TIME IN 350F (175C) OVEN:			
potato slices	35 to 40 minutes	35 to 40 minutes	35 to 40 minutes
potato wedges	25 to 30 minutes	25 to 30 minutes	25 to 30 minutes

Do not preheat oven. Place butter or margarine in a baking dish, see size in chart above. Place baking dish in a 350F (175C) oven for time in chart above or until butter or margarine melts. Meanwhile, scrub potatoes. Slice potatoes, lengthwise, in thirds. Or, cut potatoes in 8 lengthwise wedges. Turn potatoes in melted butter or margarine in baking dish, coating all sides. Place potatoes, cut-side up, in baking dish. Sprinkle with celery salt, onion salt and paprika. Bake in 350F (175C) oven for time in chart above or until potatoes are browned and tender.

Basic Hot German Vegetable Salad

SERVINGS	8	4
INGREDIENTS		
bacon, cut in 1-inch pieces	6 slices	3 slices
reserved bacon drippings	1/4 cup	2 tablespoons
onion, sliced, separated in rings	1 small	1/2 small
green pepper, cut in strips	1 small	1/2 small
all-purpose flour	2 tablespoons	1 tablespoon
sugar	2 tablespoons	1 tablespoon
pepper	1/4 teaspoon	1/8 teaspoon
chicken broth	1 cup	1/2 cup
vinegar	1/2 cup	1/4 cup
cooked or canned drained vegetables	4 cups	2 cups
sliced fresh vegetable	1 cup	1/2 cup
pimiento strips	1/4 cup	2 tablespoons
snipped parsley	1/4 cup	2 tablespoons
SKILLET	11-inch skillet	8-inch skillet
TIME AT MEDIUM HIGH (bacon)	10 minutes	7 minutes
TIME AT MEDIUM HIGH (onion, green pepper)	3 minutes	2 to 3 minutes
TIME AT MEDIUM HIGH (flour, sugar added)	1 minute	1 minute
TIME AT MEDIUM HIGH (broth, vinegar added)	3 minutes	1 to 2 minutes
TIME AT MEDIUM LOW	8 to 10 minutes	6 to 8 minutes

In a skillet, see size in chart above, cook bacon over Medium-High heat for time in chart above or until crisp, stirring frequently. Remove bacon with a slotted spoon and drain on paper towels; set aside. Reserve in skillet amount of drippings listed in chart above. Add onion and green pepper to skillet. Cook over Medium-High heat for time in chart above or until crisp-tender, stirring occasionally. Stir in flour, sugar and pepper. Cook and stir 1 minute. Stir in broth and vinegar. Cook and stir for time in chart above or until thickened and bubbly all over. Reduce heat to Medium Low. Fold in cooked vegetables, fresh vegetable and pimiento; mix gently. Cover and cook for time in chart above or until heated through, stirring occasionally. Top with bacon and parsley before serving.

Suggested Combinations

Hot German Potato Salad: Use white vinegar. Use cubed cooked or canned potatoes for cooked vegetable. Use sliced zucchini for fresh vegetable.

Hot Three-Bean Salad: Use red-wine vinegar. Use cooked or canned cut green beans, wax beans and kidney beans for cooked vegetable. Use sliced mushrooms for fresh vegetable.

Hot Three-Bean Salad

Basic Rice Salad

SERVINGS	6	3
INGREDIENTS		
hot cooked rice	3 cups	1-1/2 cups
flavored salad dressing	1/4 cup	2 tablespoons
sliced or chopped vegetables	2 cups	1 cup
cubed cooked meat or seafood	1-1/2 cups	3/4 cup
chopped toasted almonds	1/2 cup	1/4 cup
chopped green onion	1/4 cup	2 tablespoons
sliced pimiento-stuffed green olives	1/4 cup	2 tablespoons
mayonnaise or mayonnaise-style salad dressing	1/2 cup	1/4 cup
flavored salad dressing	2 tablespoons	1 tablespoon
dried leaf herb or ground spice	1 teaspoon	1/2 teaspoon
SERVING BOWL	3-qt. bowl	1-1/2-qt. bowl
REFRIGERATE	4 hours	4 hours

In a serving bowl, see size in chart above, combine hot cooked rice and first amount of flavored salad dressing. Cool at room temperature 1 hour. Fold in vegetables, meat or seafood, almonds, green onion and olives. Toss lightly to mix. In a small bowl, combine mayonnaise or salad dressing, second amount of flavored salad dressing and herb or spice; mix well. Fold into salad. Toss gently to mix well. Cover and refrigerate 4 hours.

Suggested Combinations
Curried Rice Salad: Use long-grain white rice and creamy onion-and-chive dressing for flavored salad dressing. Use chopped, drained, marinated artichoke hearts for vegetable. Use ham for meat. Use curry for spice.

Wild-Rice & Shrimp Salad: Use wild rice and bleu-cheese dressing for flavored salad dressing. Use sliced hearts of palm and sliced fresh mushrooms for vegetables. Use cooked shelled shrimp for seafood. Use tarragon for herb.

Tabbouleh

SERVINGS	8	4
INGREDIENTS		
finely chopped fresh parsley	3 cups	1-1/2 cups
finely chopped peeled tomatoes	2 cups	1 cup
finely chopped green onion	1 cup	1/2 cup
fine bulgur (precooked cracked wheat)	1/2 cup	1/4 cup
olive oil	2/3 cup	1/3 cup
lemon juice	1/4 cup	2 tablespoons
dried leaf mint	1 teaspoon	1/2 teaspoon
salt	1/2 teaspoon	1/4 teaspoon
coarsely ground pepper	1/4 teaspoon	1/8 teaspoon
romaine lettuce, coarsely chopped tomatoes	to garnish	to garnish
REFRIGERATE	2 to 3 hours	2 to 3 hours

In a medium bowl, mix parsley, finely chopped tomatoes, green onion and dry bulgur; set aside. In a screw-top jar, combine olive oil, lemon juice, mint, salt and pepper. Cover and shake well. Pour over parsley mixture. Toss gently to mix well. Cover and refrigerate 2 to 3 hours. To serve, arrange romaine leaves on a serving platter. Mound parsley mixture in center of platter. Top with coarsely chopped tomatoes. Arrange smaller romaine leaves around edge of platter. Use small romaine leaves as dippers for Tabbouleh, if desired.

How to Make Basic Potato Salad

1/Pour flavored salad dressing, such as buttermilk, over hot cooked potatoes. Marinate at room temperature 30 minutes, stirring occasionally. When new potatoes are in season, use quartered tiny new potatoes instead of cubed potatoes.

2/Gently fold in chopped vegetables and slices of hard-cooked eggs. Scandinavian Potato Salad includes pickled beets, onion and dill pickle for vegetables. Fold in a mayonnaise-based dressing laced with herb seed, such as caraway seed. Cover and refrigerate several hours or overnight.

Basic Potato Salad

SERVINGS	9	6
INGREDIENTS		
hot cooked potatoes, cubed	9 medium (6 cups)	6 medium (4 cups)
flavored salad dressing	1/2 cup	1/3 cup
chopped vegetables	1-1/2 cups	1 cup
hard-cooked eggs, sliced	6	4
mayonnaise or mayonnaise-style salad dressing	1/2 cup	1/3 cup
mustard	1-1/2 teaspoons	1 teaspoon
herb seed or ground spice	1-1/2 teaspoons	1 teaspoon
salt	1/2 teaspoon	1/4 teaspoon
SERVING BOWL	4-qt. bowl	3-qt. bowl
REFRIGERATE	6 hours or overnight	4 hours or overnight

In a serving bowl, see size in chart above, combine hot potatoes and flavored salad dressing. Cool at room temperature 30 minutes, stirring occasionally. Fold in vegetables and eggs. In a small bowl, combine mayonnaise or salad dressing, mustard, herb seed or spice, and salt; mix well. Fold into potato mixture. Cover and refrigerate 4 to 6 hours or overnight.

Suggested Combinations

Mexicali Potato Salad: Use Green Goddess dressing for flavored salad dressing. Use cooked whole-kernel corn, canned chopped green chilies and chopped green onion for vegetables. Use prepared mustard. Use chili powder for spice.

Farm-Style Potato Salad: Use French dressing for flavored salad dressing. Use chopped green onion, chopped celery and sliced pimiento-stuffed green olives for vegetables. Use horseradish mustard. Use celery seed for herb seed.

Scandinavian Potato Salad: Use buttermilk dressing for flavored salad dressing. Use chopped pickled beets, chopped onion and chopped dill pickle for vegetables. Use Dijon-style mustard. Use caraway seed for herb seed.

Basic Sweet-Sour Pasta Salad

SERVINGS	12 to 16	6 to 8
INGREDIENTS		
pasta	1 lb. (5 cups uncooked)	8 oz. (2-1/2 cups uncooked)
vinegar	1-1/2 cups	3/4 cup
sugar	1-1/2 cups	3/4 cup
vegetable oil	1/4 cup	2 tablespoons
prepared mustard	2 tablespoons	1 tablespoon
dried leaf herb	1 teaspoon	1/2 teaspoon
celery salt	1/2 teaspoon	1/4 teaspoon
coarsely ground pepper	1/2 teaspoon	1/4 teaspoon
garlic powder	1/4 teaspoon	1/8 teaspoon
chopped vegetables	4 cups	2 cups
snipped parsley	2 tablespoons	1 tablespoon
SAUCEPAN	2-qt. saucepan	1-qt. saucepan
SERVING BOWL	4-qt. bowl	2-qt. bowl
TIME AT MEDIUM	1 minute	1 minute
REFRIGERATE	4 hours or overnight	4 hours or overnight

Cook pasta according to package directions; drain. In a saucepan, see size in chart above, combine vinegar, sugar and oil. Bring to a boil over High heat. Reduce heat to Medium. Boil 1 minute or until sugar dissolves, stirring often. Whisk in mustard, herb, celery salt, pepper and garlic powder. Pour over hot pasta in a serving bowl, see size in chart above. Cool to room temperature, stirring occasionally. Fold in vegetables and parsley. Toss to mix well. Cover and refrigerate 4 hours or overnight.

Suggested Combinations
Italian Pasta Salad: Use white-wine vinegar. Use oregano for herb. Use mostaccioli for pasta. Use drained, canned, garbanzo beans, chopped zucchini, pimiento and chopped green onion for vegetables.
French Pasta Salad: Use tarragon vinegar. Use dill weed for herb. Use shell macaroni for pasta. Use sliced mushrooms, chopped shallots, chopped carrot and chopped celery for vegetables.

Basic Macaroni & Cheese Salad

SERVINGS	8	4
INGREDIENTS		
macaroni	8 oz. (2-1/2 cups uncooked)	4 oz. (1-1/4 cups uncooked)
flavored salad dressing	1/2 cup	1/4 cup
chopped vegetables	1-1/2 cups	3/4 cup
shredded or crumbled cheese	2 cups (8 oz.)	1 cup (4 oz.)
mayonnaise or mayonnaise-style salad dressing	1/2 cup	1/4 cup
mustard	1 teaspoon	1/2 teaspoon
dried leaf herb	1 teaspoon	1/2 teaspoon
SERVING BOWL	3-qt. bowl	1-1/2-qt. bowl
REFRIGERATE	4 hours or overnight	4 hours or overnight

Cook macaroni according to package directions; drain. In a serving bowl, see size in chart above, combine hot macaroni and flavored salad dressing; mix well. Cool at room temperature 30 minutes, stirring occasionally. Fold in vegetables and cheese. In a small bowl, combine mayonnaise or salad dressing, mustard and herb. Fold into macaroni mixture. Cover and refrigerate 4 hours or overnight.

Suggested Combinations
Greek Macaroni & Cheese Salad: Use shell macaroni. Use vinegar-and-oil dressing with spices and herbs for flavored salad dressing. Use chopped green pepper, chopped celery, sliced ripe olives, chopped green onion and chopped tomatoes for vegetables. Use feta cheese. Use Dijon-style mustard. Use oregano for herb.
All-American Macaroni & Cheese Salad: Use elbow macaroni. Use creamy Italian dressing for flavored salad dressing. Use chopped onion, chopped pimiento, chopped celery and shredded carrot for vegetables. Use shredded Cheddar cheese. Use prepared mustard. Use basil for herb.

Greek Macaroni & Cheese Salad

Wilted Garden Salad

SERVINGS	6	3
INGREDIENTS		
torn leaf lettuce	12 cups	6 cups
thinly sliced fresh mushrooms	1 cup	1/2 cup
fresh herb leaves	1/4 cup	2 tablespoons
chive-blossom petals, if desired	6 blossoms	3 blossoms
chopped leek or green onion	1/4 cup	2 tablespoons
vegetable oil	1/3 cup	3 tablespoons
raspberry vinegar	1/2 cup	1/4 cup
lemon juice	2 tablespoons	1 tablespoon
shredded lemon peel	1/2 teaspoon	1/4 teaspoon
toasted sliced almonds	1/4 cup	2 tablespoons
SERVING BOWL	4-qt. bowl	2-qt. bowl
SAUCEPAN	1-qt. saucepan	1-qt. saucepan
TIME AT MEDIUM HIGH (onion)	4 minutes	3 minutes
TIME AT MEDIUM HIGH (vinegar, lemon juice added)	2 to 2-1/2 minutes	1-1/2 to 2 minutes

In a serving bowl, see size in chart above, combine lettuce, mushrooms, herb leaves and chive blossoms, if desired. Cover and refrigerate. Immediately before serving time, place leek or green onion and oil in a 1-quart saucepan. Cook over Medium-High heat for time in chart above or until tender. Stir in raspberry vinegar, lemon juice and lemon peel. Cook and stir for time in chart above or until boiling. Pour over lettuce mixture. Toss until well-coated. Sprinkle with toasted almonds. Serve immediately.

Suggested Herb Leaves: basil, oregano, savory, tarragon, marjoram, parsley or dill.

Hot Spinach Salad

SERVINGS	6 to 8	3 or 4
INGREDIENTS		
torn spinach	1 (10-oz.) bunch (16 cups)	1/2 (10-oz.) bunch (8 cups)
hard-cooked eggs, sliced	4	2
chopped radishes	1/4 cup	2 tablespoons
bacon, cut in 1-inch pieces	8 slices	4 slices
reserved bacon drippings	1/3 cup	3 tablespoons
chopped green onion	1/4 cup	2 tablespoons
all-purpose flour	4 teaspoons	2 teaspoons
celery seed	1/2 teaspoon	1/4 teaspoon
chicken broth	1/2 cup	1/4 cup
lemon juice	3 tablespoons	4 teaspoons
prepared horseradish	1 tablespoon	1-1/2 teaspoons
Worcestershire sauce	1 tablespoon	1-1/2 teaspoons
SERVING BOWL	6-qt. bowl	3-qt. bowl
SKILLET	11-inch skillet	8-inch skillet
TIME AT MEDIUM HIGH (bacon)	10 minutes	6 minutes
TIME AT MEDIUM HIGH (onion)	2 minutes	1 minute
TIME AT MEDIUM HIGH (flour added)	1 minute	1 minute
TIME AT MEDIUM HIGH (seasonings, broth added)	30 to 60 seconds	30 to 60 seconds

In a serving bowl, see size in chart above, combine spinach, eggs and radishes. Cover and refrigerate. Immediately before serving time, place bacon in a skillet, see size in chart above. Cook over Medium-High heat for time in chart above or until crisp, stirring often. Remove bacon with a slotted spoon and drain on paper towels; set aside. Reserve in skillet amount of bacon drippings listed in chart above. Add green onion to skillet. Cook and stir over Medium-High heat for time in chart above or until tender. Whisk in flour. Cook and stir 1 minute. Stir in celery seed, chicken broth, lemon juice, horseradish and Worcestershire sauce. Cook and stir 30 to 60 seconds or until thickened and bubbly all over. Stir bacon into sauce. Pour over spinach mixture. Toss until well-coated. Serve immediately.

How to Make Wilted Garden Salad

1/Toss together leaf lettuce, fresh mushroom slices and fresh herb leaves in a salad bowl. This is red and green leaf lettuce with basil, oregano and tarragon leaves. Pull apart purple-blossomed chives into individual petals, if desired.

2/Immediately before serving, make hot dressing. Sauté leeks or green onion in oil. Stir in raspberry vinegar, lemon juice and lemon peel. Cook and stir until boiling. Raspberry vinegar is available at gourmet shops or in gourmet sections of supermarkets.

3/Pour boiling dressing over chilled lettuce mixture. Toss lightly until leaves are well-coated.

4/Quickly dish hot salad onto serving plates. Garnish with a sprinkle of toasted almond slices.

Basic Overnight Tossed Salad

SERVINGS	12	6
INGREDIENTS		
torn salad greens	12 cups	6 cups
hard-cooked eggs, sliced	6	3
dried leaf herb or herb seed	1 teaspoon	1/2 teaspoon
bacon, crisp-cooked, drained, crumbled	10 slices	5 slices
sliced or chopped fresh fruit, vegetables	4 cups	2 cups
shredded or crumbled cheese	2 cups (8 oz.)	1 cup (4 oz.)
plain or flavored yogurt	2/3 cup	1/3 cup
creamy flavored salad dressing	2/3 cup	1/3 cup
chopped green onion, paprika, toasted walnuts or sliced truffles	to garnish	to garnish
SERVING BOWL	5-qt. bowl	3-qt. bowl
REFRIGERATE	4 hours or overnight	4 hours or overnight

In a serving bowl, see size in chart above, layer in order: half the salad greens, egg slices, herb or herb seed, bacon, fruit or vegetables and remaining salad greens. Sprinkle with cheese. In a small bowl, combine yogurt and flavored salad dressing; mix well. Spread evenly over top of salad, sealing to edges of bowl. Cover and refrigerate 4 hours or overnight. Garnish and toss salad immediately before serving.

Suggested Combinations

Everyday Tossed Salad: Use iceberg lettuce for salad greens. Use salad seasoning for herb. Use thawed frozen peas, chopped green onion and chopped pimiento for vegetables. Use shredded Cheddar cheese. Use plain yogurt with creamy onion-and-chive salad dressing. Garnish with chopped green onion and paprika.

California Tossed Salad: Use romaine for salad greens. Use celery seed for herb seed. Use orange sections, sliced avocado, red-onion rings and chopped green pepper for fruit and vegetables. Use shredded Monterey Jack cheese. Use orange yogurt with creamy French salad dressing. Garnish with toasted walnuts.

Riviera Tossed Salad: Use endive, escarole and sorrel for salad greens. Use tarragon for herb. Use thinly sliced broccoli flowerets, sliced radishes, sliced zucchini and chopped shallots for vegetables. Use crumbled bleu cheese. Use plain yogurt with creamy bleu-cheese salad dressing. Garnish with sliced truffles.

Herb-French Salad Dressing

YIELD	2-1/4 cups	1 cup
INGREDIENTS		
French Salad Dressing, page 390, made with red-wine vinegar	2-1/4 cups	1 cup
dried leaf tarragon	2 teaspoons	1 teaspoon
dried leaf basil	1 teaspoon	1/2 teaspoon
dried dill weed	1 teaspoon	1/2 teaspoon
SCREW-TOP JAR	1-qt. jar	1-pint jar

Prepare French Salad Dressing, using red-wine vinegar and adding tarragon, basil and dill weed. Serve on fresh cauliflower, zucchini and tomato salad. Or, use for Basic Vegetables Vinaigrette, page 377.

How to Make California Tossed Salad

1/Remove hard center rib from romaine leaves by tearing off tender leaf portion along sides of rib. Slice hard-cooked eggs, red onion and avocado. Chop green pepper.

2/Use a serrated knife to section orange. Peel orange, removing all white membrane. Cut down along membrane of 1 orange section to center of orange.

3/To loosen orange section, turn knife blade upward and slide along opposite membrane. Repeat with each orange section. First section is most difficult to remove.

4/Layer half of romaine, hard-cooked egg slices, celery seed, cooked crumbled bacon, orange sections, avocado slices, red-onion rings, chopped green pepper and remaining romaine. Top with shredded Monterey Jack cheese. Spread dressing on top, sealing to edges of bowl. Refrigerate 4 hours or overnight.

Basic Tossed Salad

SERVINGS	6	3
INGREDIENTS		
torn salad greens	6 cups	3 cups
chopped or sliced vegetables, meat	2 cups	1 cup
shredded or crumbled cheese	1/2 cup (2 oz.)	1/4 cup (1 oz.)
nuts or croutons	1/2 cup	1/4 cup
Easy Salad-Dressing Combination, below	1/2 to 3/4 cup	1/4 to 1/3 cup
SERVING BOWL	4-qt. bowl	2-qt. bowl

Place greens in a serving bowl, see size in chart above. Arrange chopped or sliced vegetables and meat on greens. Cover and refrigerate until serving time. Immediately before serving, sprinkle with cheese and nuts or croutons. Drizzle with dressing. Toss gently until well-coated.

Suggested Combinations

Spinach-Cheddar Salad: Use spinach for salad greens. Use cauliflowerets, sliced radishes, sliced mushrooms, cooked crumbled bacon and red-onion rings for vegetables and meat. Use shredded Cheddar cheese. Use sliced almonds for nuts. Use Springtime Dressing.

Boston Bleu-Cheese Salad: Use Boston lettuce for salad greens. Use halved, drained, canned artichoke hearts, avocado slices, yellow plum or cherry tomatoes and chopped green onion for vegetables. Use crumbled bleu cheese. Use toasted pecans for nuts. Use Special Goddess Dressing.

Romaine Caesar Salad: Use romaine for salad greens. Use chopped onion, chopped red pepper, chopped celery and sliced zucchini for vegetables. Use grated Parmesan cheese. Use toasted garlic croutons. Use Roman-Holiday Dressing.

Greek-Isle Salad: Use leaf lettuce for salad greens. Use chopped green pepper, chopped green onion, thin tomato wedges and ripe olives for vegetables. Use crumbled feta cheese. Use herb croutons. Use Italian Dressing Special.

Easy Salad-Dressing Combinations

DRESSING	1/2 cup bottled salad dressing +	1/2 cup bottled salad dressing +	1/4 cup other ingredient
Special Goddess Dressing	Green Goddess salad dressing	creamy bleu-cheese salad dressing	chopped pimiento
Springtime Dressing	creamy onion-and-chive salad dressing	creamy cucumber salad dressing	cooked crumbled bacon
Roman-Holiday Dressing	creamy Caesar salad dressing	creamy garlic-French salad dressing	grated Parmesan cheese
Italian Dressing Special	non-creamy Italian salad dressing	non-creamy Caesar salad dressing	snipped parsley
BLT Dressing	creamy bacon-and-tomato salad dressing	Russian salad dressing	finely chopped onion
Islander Dressing	Thousand Island salad dressing	buttermilk salad dressing	chopped hard-cooked egg
Napoleon Dressing	creamy Italian salad dressing	creamy French salad dressing	crumbled bleu cheese

In a medium bowl, combine 1/2 cup of each bottled salad dressing. Whisk until blended. Stir in 1/4 cup of additional ingredient. Cover and refrigerate until serving time. Stir again before serving. Makes 1 to 1-1/4 cups.

Note: Use a 2-cup screw-top jar to shake together ingredients for Italian Dressing Special.

Spinach-Cheddar Salad and Springtime Dressing

Sweet Coleslaw

SERVINGS	8	4
INGREDIENTS		
shredded cabbage	8 cups	4 cups
shredded carrot	1 cup	1/2 cup
chopped green pepper	1 cup	1/2 cup
sugar	1/2 cup	1/4 cup
vinegar	1/2 cup	1/4 cup
water	2 tablespoons	1 tablespoon
celery seed	1 teaspoon	1/2 teaspoon
mustard seed	1 teaspoon	1/2 teaspoon
onion salt	1/4 teaspoon	1/8 teaspoon
SERVING BOWL	4-qt. bowl	2-qt. bowl
SAUCEPAN	1-qt. saucepan	1-qt. saucepan
TIME AT MEDIUM	1 minute	1 minute
REFRIGERATE	4 hours	4 hours

In a serving bowl, see size in chart above, combine cabbage, carrot and green pepper; refrigerate. In a 1-quart saucepan, combine sugar, vinegar, water, celery seed, mustard seed and onion salt. Bring to a boil over High heat. Reduce heat to Medium; cook 1 minute. Cool to room temperature. Pour vinegar mixture over cabbage mixture. Toss until well-coated. Cover and refrigerate 4 hours, tossing occasionally. Toss again immediately before serving.

Creamy Fruited Coleslaw

SERVINGS	6	3
INGREDIENTS		
frozen whipped topping, thawed	1/2 cup	1/4 cup
pineapple yogurt	1/2 cup	1/4 cup
ground cinnamon	1/2 teaspoon	1/4 teaspoon
miniature marshmallows	1 cup	1/2 cup
crushed pineapple, drained	1 (8-oz.) can	1/2 (8-oz.) can
chopped orange sections	1/2 cup	1/4 cup
snipped dried apricots	1/2 cup	1/4 cup
raisins	1/4 cup	2 tablespoons
flaked coconut	1/4 cup	2 tablespoons
shredded cabbage	4 cups	2 cups
SERVING BOWL	3-qt. bowl	1-1/2-qt. bowl
REFRIGERATE	2 to 3 hours	2 to 3 hours

In a serving bowl, see size in chart above, combine whipped topping, pineapple yogurt and cinnamon. Stir in marshmallows, pineapple, orange, apricots, raisins and coconut. Fold in cabbage. Cover and refrigerate 2 to 3 hours.

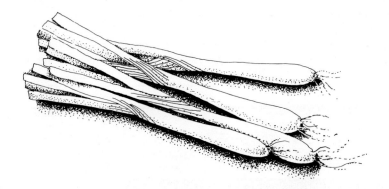

How to Make Basic Marinated Vegetable Salad

1/Canned or frozen peas, canned kidney beans or frozen combination vegetables are all good bases for this salad. Toss cooked or canned vegetables with celery, green onion, pimiento and pickle relish. Pour creamy dressing mix over vegetables. This Marinated Confetti Salad has frozen broccoli, corn and red pepper with creamy Italian-dressing mix.

2/Refrigerate to marinate until serving time. Immediately before serving, fold in hard-cooked-egg slices, cheese cubes and chow-mein noodles, French-fried onions or croutons. Cheddar cheese and chow-mein noodles complement this salad.

Basic Marinated Vegetable Salad

SERVINGS	8	4
INGREDIENTS		
frozen vegetables, cooked, drained	1 (20-oz.) bag (4 to 5 cups)	1 (10-oz.) pkg. or 1/2 (20-oz.) bag (2 to 2-1/2 cups)
OR		
canned vegetable, drained	2 (16-oz.) cans	1 (16-oz.) can
chopped celery	1/2 cup	1/4 cup
chopped green onion	1/4 cup	2 tablespoons
chopped pimiento	1/4 cup	2 tablespoons
pickle relish	1/4 cup	2 tablespoons
dressing mix made with milk and mayonnaise	1 cup	1/2 cup
cubed cheese	2 cups (8 oz.)	1 cup (4 oz.)
hard-cooked eggs, sliced	2	1
croutons, canned French-fried onions or chow-mein noodles	1 cup	1/2 cup
REFRIGERATE	3 hours or overnight	3 hours or overnight

In a serving bowl, combine cooked or canned vegetables, celery, green onion, pimiento and relish. Fold dressing into vegetable mixture. Cover and refrigerate 3 hours or overnight. Immediately before serving, fold in cheese, eggs and croutons, French-fried onions or chow-mein noodles.

Suggested Combinations
Marinated Pea Salad: Use frozen or canned peas for vegetable. Use caraway cheese and cheese croutons. Use herb-dressing mix.

Marinated Kidney-Bean Salad: Use canned kidney beans, drained and rinsed, for vegetable. Use pepper cheese and French-fried onions. Use onion-dressing mix.

Marinated Confetti Salad: Use frozen combination vegetables for vegetables. Use Cheddar cheese and chow-mein noodles. Use creamy Italian-dressing mix.

Spiced Fruit

YIELD	3-1/2 cups	1-3/4 cups
INGREDIENTS		
canned peach halves, pear halves or whole apricots	1 (29-oz.) can	1 (16-oz.) can
reserved fruit syrup	1 cup	1/2 cup
whole cloves	1 tablespoon	1-1/2 teaspoons
sugar	1/2 cup	1/4 cup
cinnamon stick	1 (4-inch) stick	1 (2-inch) stick
white-wine vinegar, fruit wine or fruit liqueur	1/2 cup	1/4 cup
SERVING BOWL	2-qt. bowl	1-qt. bowl
SAUCEPAN	1-1/2-qt. saucepan	1-qt. saucepan
TIME AT MEDIUM	1 minute	30 to 60 seconds
REFRIGERATE	8 hours or overnight	8 hours or overnight

Drain fruit, reserving amount of syrup listed in chart above; set aside. Cut peach and pear halves in half again. Push several cloves into each piece of fruit. Place fruit in a serving bowl, see size in chart above; set aside. In a saucepan, see size in chart above, combine reserved syrup and sugar. Add cinnamon stick. Bring to a boil over High heat, stirring occasionally. Reduce heat to Medium. Cook, uncovered, for time in chart above or until sugar dissolves. Stir in vinegar, wine or liqueur. Pour syrup over fruit. Cover and refrigerate 8 hours or overnight. Before serving, remove cinnamon stick. Keeps for several weeks.

Basic Vegetable Relish   Photo on page 318.

YIELD	1 quart	1 pint
INGREDIENTS		
vinegar	1/2 cup	1/4 cup
water	1/2 cup	1/4 cup
sugar	2 tablespoons	1 tablespoon
herb seed	1 teaspoon	1/2 teaspoon
pickling salt	1 teaspoon	1/2 teaspoon
celery seed	1/2 teaspoon	1/4 teaspoon
mustard seed	1/2 teaspoon	1/4 teaspoon
garlic, minced	1 large clove	1 small clove
sliced or coarsely chopped vegetables	4 cups	2 cups
SAUCEPAN	1-qt. saucepan	1-qt. saucepan
GLASS BAKING DISH	12" x 7" baking dish	9" x 5" x 3" loaf dish
TIME AT MEDIUM	1 minute	1 minute
REFRIGERATE	8 hours or overnight	8 hours or overnight

In a 1-quart saucepan, combine vinegar, water, sugar, herb seed, pickling salt, celery seed, mustard seed and garlic. Bring to a boil over High heat, stirring occasionally. Reduce heat to Medium. Simmer, uncovered, 1 minute or until sugar dissolves. Combine vegetables in a glass baking dish, see size in chart above. Pour vinegar mixture over vegetables. Stir gently. Cover and refrigerate 8 hours or overnight, stirring occasionally. To serve, use a slotted spoon. Reserve marinade to store leftover vegetables. Keeps for several weeks.

Suggested Combinations
Dill-Cucumber Relish: Use tarragon wine vinegar. Use cucumber slices, red-pepper sticks, thin onion slices and 1/4-inch-thick broccoli-floweret slices for vegetables. Use dill seed for herb seed.
Chow-Chow Relish: Use cider vinegar. Use shredded cabbage, drained, cooked, whole-kernel corn, chopped carrot, chopped green pepper and chopped onion for vegetables. Use caraway seed for herb seed.
Fresh-Mushroom Relish: Use white-wine vinegar. Use sliced fresh mushrooms, whole pitted ripe olives, sliced green onion, snipped parsley and halved cherry tomatoes for vegetables. Use fennel seed for herb seed. To store more than a few days, add cherry tomatoes immediately before serving

How to Make Spiced Fruit

1/Drain canned peach halves, pear halves or whole apricots. Cut peach and pear halves in half again. Stud fruit pieces with whole cloves. Place fruit in a serving bowl.

2/Simmer canned fruit syrup with sugar and cinnamon sticks. Add wine vinegar, fruit wine or fruit liqueur; pour over fruit. Refrigerate up to several weeks.

Basic Vegetables Vinaigrette

SERVINGS	6 to 8	3 or 4
INGREDIENTS		
sliced or chopped vegetables	6 cups	3 cups
salad dressing, see suggestions below	2 cups	1 cup
leaf lettuce	to garnish	to garnish
hard-cooked-egg slices, fresh herbs or tomato wedges	to garnish	to garnish
BOWL	2-qt. bowl	1-qt. bowl
REFRIGERATE	3 hours	2 hours

In a bowl, see size in chart above, combine vegetables. Pour dressing over vegetables; mix gently. Cover and refrigerate 2 to 3 hours, stirring occasionally. To serve, arrange leaf lettuce on a serving platter or individual salad plates. With a slotted spoon, lift vegetables from marinade and place on leaf lettuce. Garnish according to suggestions below.

Suggested Combinations
Asparagus-Salad Vinaigrette: Use cooked fresh or frozen asparagus spears, chopped radish, chopped tomatoes, chopped onion and snipped parsley for vegetables. Use Italian Salad Dressing, page 391. Garnish with hard-cooked-egg slices.

Cabbage-Patch-Salad Vinaigrette: Use cooked broccoli flowerets, cooked cauliflowerets, halved cherry tomatoes and chopped green onion for vegetables. Use Herb-French Salad Dressing, page 370. Garnish with fresh basil leaves, fresh dill-seed heads or parsley sprigs.

Mushroom-Salad Vinaigrette: Use thinly sliced raw mushrooms, snipped chives, snipped parsley and chopped pimiento for vegetables. Use Vinaigrette Salad Dressing, page 391. Garnish with tomato wedges.

Striped Gelatin Salad

SERVINGS	12 to 15	6 to 8
INGREDIENTS		
cherry-flavored gelatin	1 (3-oz.) pkg.	1 (3-oz.) pkg.
boiling water	3/4 cup	3/4 cup
cold water	3/4 cup	3/4 cup
lemon-flavored gelatin	1 (3-oz.) pkg.	omit
boiling water	3/4 cup	omit
cold water	3/4 cup	omit
orange-flavored gelatin	1 (3-oz.) pkg.	omit
boiling water	3/4 cup	omit
cold water	3/4 cup	omit
lime-flavored gelatin	1 (3-oz.) pkg.	1 (3-oz.) pkg.
boiling water	3/4 cup	3/4 cup
cold water	3/4 cup	3/4 cup
sugar	2/3 cup	1/3 cup
unflavored gelatin	2 (1/4-oz.) envelopes	1 (1/4-oz.) envelope
milk	2 cups	1 cup
lemon or orange yogurt	1 cup	1/2 cup
BOWLS	5 medium bowls	3 medium bowls
BAKING DISH	13" x 9" baking dish	10" x 6" baking dish
SAUCEPAN	2-qt. saucepan	1-qt. saucepan
TIME AT MEDIUM LOW	15 to 18 minutes	15 to 18 minutes
REFRIGERATE (each colored gelatin layer)	25 to 40 minutes	25 to 40 minutes
REFRIGERATE (yogurt layers)	10 minutes	10 minutes
REFRIGERATE (finished salad)	4 hours or overnight	4 hours or overnight

For 12 to 15 servings: In each of 4 medium bowls, combine 1 package flavored gelatin and 3/4 cup boiling water. Stir until gelatin is completely dissolved. Stir 3/4 cup cold water into each bowl. Pour first flavored-gelatin mixture into a 13" x 9" baking dish. Refrigerate 25 to 40 minutes or until set but not firm. Reserve other gelatin flavors at room temperature. Meanwhile, in a 2-quart saucepan, combine sugar and unflavored gelatin. Gradually add milk. Heat and stir over Medium-Low heat 15 to 18 minutes or until gelatin is completely dissolved. Place yogurt in a medium bowl. Stir half the hot gelatin mixture into yogurt. Whisk yogurt mixture into remaining gelatin mixture in saucepan until smooth. Spoon one-third of yogurt mixture over first set gelatin layer. Gently spread yogurt mixture over gelatin. Refrigerate 10 minutes or until set. Repeat layering process, alternating colored gelatin and yogurt layers. After adding each layer, refrigerate until set. Each layer will set a few minutes faster than last layer. Finished salad will have 4 colored-gelatin layers and 3 yogurt layers. Cover and refrigerate finished salad 4 hours or overnight until firm. To serve, cut in squares or ribbon strips.

For 6 to 8 servings: Follow directions for 12 to 15 servings except use half of each colored gelatin for each layer. Use a 10" x 6" baking dish and a 1-quart saucepan. Alternate red and green gelatin layers with yogurt layers.

Note: Use different gelatin colors for different occasions. Or, substitute flavors of same color. Apricot or peach flavors substitute for orange colors. Strawberry or raspberry flavors substitute for red colors.

How to Make Striped Gelatin Salad

1/For the holidays, use cherry and lime gelatin. Substitute colors for other occasions. Stir gelatin in boiling water until completely dissolved. When dissolved, gelatin mixture will be clear like red gelatin, not cloudy like green gelatin.

2/For 6 to 8 servings, pour half of red gelatin into a 10" x 6" baking dish. Refrigerate until set but not firm. Gelatin is ready for next layer if it sticks to your finger when lightly touched.

3/When first red layer is set, ladle yogurt filling over gelatin and spread gently. As before, refrigerate until set but not firm. Continue layering salad, alternating green gelatin, yogurt gelatin, red gelatin, yogurt gelatin and green gelatin.

4/Refrigerate finished salad until firm. It will have 2 red layers, 2 green layers and 3 white layers. To serve, cut gelatin in squares. Or, make holiday bows by arranging 3 (2-inch) strips of salad on each serving plate. Garnish with cherry and lettuce in each center.

Gazpacho-Guacamole Mold

SERVINGS	16	8
INGREDIENTS		
lemon-flavored gelatin	2 (3-oz.) pkgs.	1 (3-oz.) pkg.
boiling water	2 cups	1 cup
Spanish-style vegetable soup	2 (10-1/2-oz.) cans	1 (10-1/2-oz.) can
sliced pimiento-stuffed green olives	2/3 cup	1/3 cup
chopped zucchini	2/3 cup	1/3 cup
unflavored gelatin	3 (1/4-oz.) envelopes	1-1/2 (1/4-oz.) envelopes (3-3/4 teaspoons)
cold water	2 cups	1 cup
non-creamy Italian salad dressing	1 cup	1/2 cup
plain yogurt	1 cup	1/2 cup
frozen spicy guacamole dip, thawed	2 (6-oz.) containers	1 (6-oz.) container
chopped green onion	1/4 cup	2 tablespoons
chopped pimiento	1/4 cup	2 tablespoons
lettuce leaves, chilies, olives	to garnish	to garnish
BOWL	2-qt. bowl	1-qt. bowl
MOLD	12-cup fluted tube pan	6-1/2-cup ring mold
SAUCEPAN	2-qt. saucepan	1-qt. saucepan
REFRIGERATE (soup mixture, partially set)	1-1/2 hours	1-1/4 hours
REFRIGERATE (olives, zucchini added)	30 minutes	30 minutes
TIME AT MEDIUM	5 minutes	3 minutes
REFRIGERATE (guacamole mixture, partially set)	20 to 30 minutes	20 to 30 minutes
REFRIGERATE (finished mold)	8 hours or overnight	8 hours or overnight

In a bowl, see size in chart above, combine lemon-flavored gelatin and boiling water. Stir until gelatin is completely dissolved. Stir in soup. Refrigerate in bowl for time in chart above or until partially set. Fold in olive slices and zucchini. Lightly oil a mold, see size in chart above. Pour gelatin mixture into mold. Refrigerate 30 minutes or until set but not firm. Meanwhile, in a saucepan, see size in chart above, mix unflavored gelatin with cold water. Let stand 1 minute to soften. Stir over Medium heat for time in chart above or until gelatin is completely dissolved. Remove from heat. Whisk in salad dressing, yogurt and guacamole dip. Refrigerate 20 to 30 minutes or until partially set. Fold in green onion and pimiento. Let stand at room temperature until gazpacho layer is set but not firm. Pour guacamole mixture over gazpacho layer in mold. Smooth top of guacamole layer. Cover and refrigerate 8 hours or overnight until firm. To serve, arrange lettuce leaves on a serving plate. Unmold salad in center and garnish with chilies and olives.

Tips for Gelatin Salads

- Do not use fresh or frozen pineapple, kiwifruit, papaya, fresh figs or prickly pears in gelatin salads. Enzymes in these fruits prevent gelatin from setting.

- To layer gelatin, refrigerate each layer until set but not firm before adding next layer. When the set gelatin sticks to your finger when touched, it is ready for next layer. If gelatin is too firm, next layer will slip off.

- Before adding fruit, vegetables, nuts or other solid ingredients to gelatin, refrigerate gelatin until partially set. Gelatin should resemble thick syrup. Solid ingredients can then be distributed without floating to top of gelatin. If gelatin is too firm when ingredients are folded in, mixture will have lumpy texture.

- Use gelatin salads within 24 hours. Gelatin will start to lose liquid and break down after this time.

- Lightly oil the mold, especially a mold with an intricate design. This simplifies removal.

- To unmold gelatin, dip mold in warm water up to rim 10 to 15 seconds. Lift mold from water. Run a knife around edge of mold. Shake gently to loosen gelatin from edges. Place a wet plate on top of mold. Turn plate and mold over together. Shake gelatin onto plate and lift off mold. If mold does not come off, repeat procedure with warm water.

Basic Fruit-Sauce Mold

SERVINGS	8 to 10	4 or 5
INGREDIENTS		
fruit-flavored gelatin	2 (3-oz.) pkgs.	1 (3-oz.) pkg.
boiling water	2 cups	1 cup
fruit sauce	1 (16-oz.) can	1 (8-oz.) can
dry wine or fruit juice	1/2 cup	1/4 cup
chopped fruit or vegetables	1 cup	1/2 cup
chopped pecans or toasted slivered almonds	1/2 cup	1/4 cup
MOLD	6-cup mold	3-1/2-cup mold
REFRIGERATE (partially set)	1-3/4 hours	1-3/4 hours
REFRIGERATE (finished salad)	8 hours or overnight	8 hours or overnight

In a large bowl, combine gelatin and boiling water. Stir until gelatin is completely dissolved. Stir in fruit sauce and wine or juice; mix well. Refrigerate 1-3/4 hours or until partially set. Fold in fruit or vegetables and nuts. Lightly oil a mold, see size in chart above. Pour gelatin mixture into mold. Cover and refrigerate 8 hours or overnight until firm. To serve, unmold salad.

Suggested Combinations
Cranberry-Sauce Mold: Use raspberry-flavored gelatin. Use canned whole-cranberry sauce for fruit sauce. Use dry red wine. Use chopped apple and chopped celery for fruit and vegetables. Use pecans for nuts.
Applesauce Mold: Use lemon-flavored gelatin. Use chunky-style applesauce for fruit sauce. Use apple juice. Use chopped apple and raisins or snipped dates for fruit. Use pecans for nuts.
Crushed-Pineapple Mold: Use orange-flavored gelatin. Use canned crushed pineapple with juice for fruit sauce. Use dry white wine or orange juice. Use orange sections or drained canned mandarin oranges, shredded carrot and sliced green olives for fruit and vegetables. Use almonds for nuts.

Basic Fruit-Salad Mold

SERVINGS	8 to 10	4 or 5
INGREDIENTS		
fruit-flavored gelatin	2 (3-oz.) pkgs.	1 (3-oz.) pkg.
boiling water	2 cups	1 cup
cold liquid	1-1/2 cups	3/4 cup
chopped or sliced fruit	1-1/2 to 2-1/2 cups	3/4 to 1-1/4 cups
toasted slivered almonds, toasted coconut or toasted chopped pecans	1/2 cup	1/4 cup
BAKING DISH OR	12" x 7" baking dish	9" x 5" x 3" loaf dish
MOLD	6-cup mold	3-cup mold
REFRIGERATE (partially set)	1-3/4 hours	1 hour 10 minutes
REFRIGERATE (finished salad)	8 hours or overnight	8 hours or overnight

In a medium bowl, see size in chart above, combine gelatin and boiling water. Stir until gelatin is completely dissolved. Stir in cold liquid. Refrigerate for time in chart above or until partially set, stirring occasionally. Skim foam from top of partially set gelatin, if necessary. Fold in fruit and nuts or coconut. Lightly oil a baking dish or mold, see size in chart above. Pour gelatin mixture into dish or mold. Cover and refrigerate 8 hours or overnight until firm. To serve, unmold or cut in squares.

Suggested Combinations
Peach-Grape Salad Mold: Use peach-flavored gelatin. Use ginger ale for cold liquid. Use chopped fresh or cut-up, drained, canned peaches and halved grapes for fruit. Use almonds and coconut.
Strawberry-Banana Salad Mold: Use strawberry-banana-flavored gelatin. Use strawberry carbonated beverage for cold liquid. Use chopped fresh pear or apple and sliced bananas for fruit. Use pecans for nuts.

Basic Frozen Yogurt-Salad Cups

SERVINGS	12	6
INGREDIENTS		
flavored yogurt	2 cups	1 cup
packed brown sugar	1/4 cup	2 tablespoons
canned fruit, drained, chopped	1 (16-oz.) can	1 (8-oz.) can
OR		
cranberry-orange relish	1 cup	1/2 cup
miniature marshmallows	1/2 cup	1/4 cup
chopped nuts	1/4 cup	2 tablespoons
flaked coconut	1/4 cup	2 tablespoons
MUFFIN PAN	12 (2-1/2 inch) muffin cups	6 (2-1/2 inch) muffin cups
FREEZE	4 hours or overnight	4 hours or overnight
STANDING TIME	10 to 15 minutes	10 to 15 minutes

In a medium bowl, combine yogurt and brown sugar; mix well. Fold in fruit or relish, marshmallows, nuts and coconut. Line muffin pan, see size in chart above, with paper bake cups. Spoon yogurt mixture into bake cups. Cover and freeze 4 hours or overnight until firm. Let salads stand 10 to 15 minutes at room temperature before serving. To store leftover salads, seal in a plastic bag and put in the freezer.

Suggested Combinations
Frozen Orange-Cranberry Yogurt-Salad Cups: Use orange yogurt. Use cranberry-orange relish.
Frozen Lemon-Peach Yogurt-Salad Cups: Use lemon yogurt. Use canned peaches for fruit.
Frozen Pineapple-Apricot Yogurt-Salad Cups: Use pineapple yogurt. Use canned apricots for fruit.

Basic Frozen-Fruit Gelatin Salad

SERVINGS	8 to 10	4 or 5
INGREDIENTS		
fruit-flavored gelatin	2 (3-oz.) pkgs.	1 (3-oz.) pkg.
boiling water	1-1/2 cups	3/4 cup
frozen fruit in syrup	2 (10-oz.) pkgs.	1 (10-oz.) pkg.
cold liquid	1/2 cup	1/4 cup
toasted slivered almonds or chopped pecans	1/2 cup	1/4 cup
BAKING DISH	12" x 7" baking dish	9" x 5" x 3" loaf dish
REFRIGERATE	8 hours or overnight	8 hours or overnight

In a medium bowl, combine gelatin and boiling water. Stir until gelatin is completely dissolved. Add frozen fruit. Quickly stir to thaw fruit, using a large meat fork to break up fruit. Stir in cold liquid. Fold in nuts. Pour into a baking dish, see size in chart above. Cover and refrigerate 8 hours or overnight until firm. To serve, cut in squares.

Note: Do not attempt to pour this salad into a mold. It is a soft gel that may break when turned out of mold.

Suggested Combinations
Strawberry-Almond Gelatin Salad: Use strawberry-flavored gelatin. Use frozen sliced strawberries in syrup. Use white grape juice or pineapple juice for cold liquid. Use almonds for nuts.
Raspberry-Pecan Gelatin Salad: Use raspberry-flavored gelatin. Use frozen raspberries in syrup. Use Burgundy or rosé wine for cold liquid. Use pecans for nuts.

Basic Creamy Fruit Salad

SERVINGS	12 to 16	6 to 8
INGREDIENTS		
instant cream-pudding mix	1 (3-3/4-oz.) pkg.	1/2 (3-3/4-oz.) pkg. (1/3 cup)
milk	1 cup	1/2 cup
frozen juice concentrate, thawed	1/2 (6-oz.) can (1/3 cup)	3 tablespoons
flavored yogurt	1 cup	1/2 cup
any combination of cut-up fresh or drained canned fruit: bananas, apples, pears, apricots, pineapple chunks, oranges, cherries, kiwifruit or peaches	10 to 12 cups	5 to 6 cups
MIXER BOWL	1-1/2-qt. bowl	1-1/2-qt. bowl
SERVING BOWL	4-qt. bowl	2-qt. bowl
REFRIGERATE	2 to 24 hours	2 to 24 hours

In a 1-1/2-quart mixer bowl, beat pudding mix, milk and juice concentrate at low speed of an electric mixer for 2 minutes. By hand, stir in yogurt. Combine fruit in a serving bowl, see size in chart above. Fold pudding mixture into fruit. Cover and refrigerate at least 2 hours, but no longer than 24 hours, or mixture may become soupy. Stir gently before serving.

Suggested Combinations
Creamy Tropicale Salad: Use banana-cream-pudding mix, limeade concentrate and banana yogurt.
Creamy Hawaiian Salad: Use pineapple-cream-pudding mix, pineapple-juice concentrate and pineapple yogurt.
Creamy Coconut Salad: Use coconut-cream-pudding mix, lemonade concentrate and lemon yogurt.
Kids' Favorite Creamy Fruit Salad: Use vanilla-cream-pudding mix, orange-juice concentrate and orange yogurt.

Basic Waldorf Salad

SERVINGS	6 to 8	3 or 4
INGREDIENTS		
frozen whipped topping, thawed	1/2 cup	1/4 cup
mayonnaise or mayonnaise-style salad dressing	1/2 cup	1/4 cup
white port wine or apple juice	2 tablespoons	1 tablespoon
grated citrus peel	1 teaspoon	1/2 teaspoon
spice	1/2 teaspoon	1/4 teaspoon
cored and cubed apples	4 cups	2 cups
other sliced or cubed fruit	2 cups	1 cup
chopped celery	1/2 cup	1/4 cup
chopped toasted nuts	1/2 cup	1/4 cup
SERVING BOWL	3-qt. bowl	1-1/2-qt. bowl
REFRIGERATE	3 to 4 hours	2 to 3 hours

In a serving bowl, see size in chart above, combine whipped topping, mayonnaise or salad dressing, port wine or apple juice, citrus peel and spice. Mix well. Fold in apples, other fruit, celery and nuts. Cover and refrigerate for time in chart above.

Suggested Combinations
Tropical Waldorf Salad: Use lime peel for citrus peel and curry powder for spice. Use drained pineapple chunks, papaya chunks and quartered kiwifruit slices for other fruit. Use macadamia nuts.
Buffet Waldorf Salad: Use grated orange peel for citrus peel and freshly grated nutmeg for spice. Use seeded halved grapes, raisins, banana slices and drained mandarin oranges for other fruit. Use pecans for nuts.

How to Make Easy Frozen Salad

1/Cherry-, apricot- or strawberry-pie filling provides base for this easy salad. Stir sweetened condensed milk, crushed pineapple, nuts and lemon or lime juice together. Fold in whipped topping; freeze in a pie plate.

2/With a sharp knife, cut frozen salad without defrosting. Serve wedges on leaf lettuce, garnished with strawberries, cherries or apricot slices.

Easy Frozen Salad

SERVINGS	8	4
INGREDIENTS		
cherry-, apricot- or strawberry-pie filling	1 (21-oz.) can	1/2 (21-oz.) can (1-1/4 cups)
sweetened condensed milk	1 (14-oz.) can (1-1/3 cups)	1/2 (14-oz.) can (2/3 cup)
crushed pineapple, drained	1 (8-1/4-oz.) can	1/2 (8-1/4-oz.) can (1/3 cup)
chopped pecans or walnuts	1/2 cup	1/4 cup
lemon or lime juice	1/4 cup	2 tablespoons
red or yellow food coloring, if desired	few drops	few drops
frozen whipped topping, thawed	1 (4-oz.) carton	1 cup
cherries, apricot slices or strawberries	to garnish	to garnish
PIE PLATE	10-inch pie plate	7-inch pie plate
FREEZE	4 hours or overnight	4 hours or overnight

In a medium bowl, combine pie filling, sweetened condensed milk, pineapple, nuts and lemon or lime juice. Add red food coloring to cherry or strawberry salad, or yellow food coloring to apricot salad, if desired. Mix well. Fold in whipped topping. Turn into a pie plate, see size in chart above. Cover and freeze 4 hours or overnight until firm. With a serrated knife, slice frozen salad in wedges to serve. Garnish with appropriate fruit.

Basic Seafood Salad

SERVINGS	6 to 8	3 or 4
INGREDIENTS		
mayonnaise or mayonnaise-style salad dressing	1/2 cup	1/4 cup
flavoring sauce	1/2 cup	1/4 cup
lemon juice	2 teaspoons	1 teaspoon
mustard	2 teaspoons	1 teaspoon
Worcestershire sauce	1 teaspoon	1/2 teaspoon
chopped celery	1/4 cup	2 tablespoons
drained capers	2 tablespoons	1 tablespoon
chopped pimiento	2 tablespoons	1 tablespoon
snipped parsley	2 tablespoons	1 tablespoon
dried leaf herb	1 teaspoon	1/2 teaspoon
cooked seafood	2 lbs.	1 lb.
OR		
canned tuna	4 (7-oz.) cans	2 (7-oz.) cans
chopped or sliced vegetables	2 cups	1 cup
hard-cooked eggs, cut in wedges	4	2
lettuce and vegetables or fruit	to garnish	to garnish
SERVING BOWL	3-qt. bowl	1-1/2-qt. bowl
REFRIGERATE	4 hours	3 hours

In a small bowl, combine mayonnaise or salad dressing, flavoring sauce, lemon juice, mustard, Worcestershire sauce, celery, capers, pimiento, parsley and herb. Mix well. In a serving bowl, see size in chart above, combine seafood, chopped or sliced vegetables and hard-cooked eggs. Fold dressing into seafood mixture; toss gently to mix. Cover and refrigerate 3 to 4 hours. Serve and garnish according to suggestions below.

Suggested Combinations

Shrimp Salad Elegante: Use cocktail sauce for flavoring sauce. Use horseradish mustard. Use dill weed for herb. Use deveined peeled shrimp for seafood. Use thawed frozen pea pods, chopped green onion and sliced water chestnuts for vegetables. Serve on Boston lettuce, garnished with cherry tomatoes and avocado slices.

Crab or Lobster Salad Deluxe: Use sour cream for flavoring sauce. Use Dijon-style mustard. Use herb pepper for herb. Use lump crabmeat or lobster, broken in large chunks, for seafood. Use quartered canned artichoke hearts, chopped shallots and sliced fresh mushrooms for vegetables. Serve on Bibb lettuce, garnished with ripe olives and tomato wedges.

Tuna Salad Supreme: Use tartar sauce for flavoring sauce. Use stone-ground mustard. Use tarragon for herb. Use solid-pack tuna, drained and broken in large chunks. Use sliced canned hearts of palm, chopped green onion and avocado slices for vegetables. Serve on red-tipped leaf lettuce, garnished with cooked asparagus spears and sliced papaya or mango.

Creamy Seafood-Salad Dressing

YIELD	1-1/2 cups	3/4 cup
INGREDIENTS		
Mayonnaise Dressing, page 394	3/4 cup	1/3 cup
chopped cooked shrimp	1/2 cup	1/4 cup
prepared horseradish	2 tablespoons	1 tablespoon
drained capers	2 tablespoons	1 tablespoon
lemon juice	2 teaspoons	1 teaspoon
grated lemon peel	1 teaspoon	1/2 teaspoon

Prepare Mayonnaise Dressing. In a medium bowl, combine shrimp, horseradish, capers, lemon juice, peel and Mayonnaise Dressing; mix well. Cover and refrigerate until serving time. Serve on seafood salads.

Shrimp Salad Elegante

Basic Chicken or Tuna Salad

SERVINGS	6	3
INGREDIENTS		
cubed cooked chicken	3 cups	1-1/2 cups
OR		
tuna, drained, broken in chunks	3 (6-1/2-oz.) cans	1 (10-oz.) can
chopped celery	1/2 cup	1/4 cup
chopped nuts	1/2 cup	1/4 cup
chopped onion	2 tablespoons	1 tablespoon
sliced or chopped fruit or vegetables	2 cups	1 cup
mayonnaise or mayonnaise-style salad dressing	1/3 cup	3 tablespoons
yogurt	1/3 cup	3 tablespoons
dry white wine or fruit juice	2 tablespoons	1 tablespoon
Dijon-style mustard	1 teaspoon	1/2 teaspoon
celery salt	1/4 teaspoon	1/8 teaspoon
dried leaf herb	1 teaspoon	1/2 teaspoon
OR		
ground spice	1/2 teaspoon	1/4 teaspoon
grape clusters, chutney or cooked crumbled bacon	to garnish	to garnish
SERVING BOWL	3-qt. bowl	1-1/2-qt. bowl
REFRIGERATE	2 to 3 hours	2 to 3 hours

In a serving bowl, see size in chart above, combine chicken or tuna, celery, nuts, onion and fruit or vegetables. In a small bowl, whisk together mayonnaise or salad dressing, yogurt, white wine or fruit juice, Dijon-style mustard, celery salt and herb or spice. Mix well. Fold into chicken or tuna mixture, tossing gently to mix. Cover and refrigerate until serving time. Stir before serving. Garnish according to suggestions below.

Suggested Combinations

Fruited Chicken or Tuna Salad: Use toasted slivered almonds for nuts. Use halved seedless green grapes, chopped apple and orange sections for fruit. Use orange or lemon yogurt. Use marjoram for herb. Garnish with grape clusters.

Far Eastern Chicken or Tuna Salad: Use salted peanuts for nuts. Use raisins, sliced bananas, pineapple chunks and flaked coconut for fruit. Use banana yogurt. Use curry powder or ginger for spice. Garnish with chutney.

Mom's Old-Fashioned Chicken or Tuna Salad: Use walnuts for nuts. Use chopped hard-cooked eggs with sliced avocado, sliced olives, chopped sweet pickle and capers for vegetables. Use plain yogurt. Use tarragon for herb. Garnish with cooked crumbled bacon.

Buttermilk Dressing

YIELD	3/4 cup	1/3 cup
INGREDIENTS		
mayonnaise or mayonnaise-style salad dressing	1/2 cup	1/4 cup
buttermilk	1/2 cup	1/4 cup

In a medium bowl, combine mayonnaise or salad dressing and buttermilk. Whisk well. Cover and refrigerate until serving time. Serve on tossed vegetable salads. Or, use as a base for Creamy Cucumber Salad Dressing, opposite, Creamy Curry Salad Dressing, opposite, Creamy Bacon Salad Dressing, page 394, and Creamy Bleu-Cheese Salad Dressing, page 395.

How to Make Far Eastern Chicken Salad

1/In a large bowl, toss together cubed cooked chicken, celery, peanuts, onion, raisins, bananas, pineapple and flaked coconut.

2/Fold banana-yogurt dressing into salad. Refrigerate. Serve on leaf lettuce, garnished with a spoonful of chutney.

Creamy Cucumber Salad Dressing

YIELD	1-1/3 cups	2/3 cup
INGREDIENTS		
Buttermilk Dressing, opposite	3/4 cup	1/3 cup
cucumber	1/2 medium	1/4 medium
finely chopped green onion	2 tablespoons	1 tablespoon
dried dill weed	1/2 teaspoon	1/4 teaspoon

Prepare Buttermilk Dressing. Peel cucumber and cut in half lengthwise. Scoop out seeds and pulp. Finely chop remaining firm white flesh of cucumber. In a medium bowl, combine cucumber, green onion, dill weed and Buttermilk Dressing; mix well. Cover and refrigerate until serving time. Serve on chef's salad or seafood salads.

Creamy Curry Salad Dressing

YIELD	1 cup	1/2 cup
INGREDIENTS		
Buttermilk Dressing, opposite	3/4 cup	1/3 cup
snipped chives	2 tablespoons	1 tablespoon
finely chopped onion	2 tablespoons	1 tablespoon
curry powder	1/2 teaspoon	1/4 teaspoon

Prepare Buttermilk Dressing. In a medium bowl, combine Buttermilk Dressing, chives, chopped onion and curry powder; mix well. Cover and refrigerate until serving time. Serve on chilled asparagus spears on Boston lettuce, garnished with hard-cooked-egg slices.

Basic Taco Salad

SERVINGS	6	3
INGREDIENTS		
mixed torn salad greens	6 cups	3 cups
chopped or sliced vegetables	4 cups	2 cups
sliced ripe olives	1/2 cup	1/4 cup
ground meat	1 lb.	8 oz.
chopped green onion	1/4 cup	2 tablespoons
cooking sauce	1 cup	1/2 cup
beef or chicken broth	1/2 cup	1/4 cup
dry red or white wine	2 tablespoons	1 tablespoon
ground spice	1 teaspoon	1/2 teaspoon
shredded Cheddar cheese	1 cup (4 oz.)	1/2 cup (2 oz.)
avocado, peeled, sliced	1	1/2
corn chips or canned chow-mein noodles	to garnish	to garnish
SERVING BOWL	4-qt. bowl	2-qt. bowl
SKILLET	10-inch skillet	8-inch skillet
TIME AT MEDIUM HIGH	10 to 12 minutes	7 to 9 minutes
TIME AT MEDIUM	6 to 8 minutes	6 to 8 minutes

In a serving bowl, see size in chart above, combine salad greens, vegetables and olives. Cover and refrigerate until serving time. At serving time, in a skillet, see size in chart above, combine ground meat and green onion. Cook, uncovered, over Medium-High heat for time in chart above or until meat is browned and onion is tender. Drain off fat. Stir in cooking sauce, broth, wine and spice. Bring to a boil; reduce heat to Medium. Cook, uncovered, 6 to 8 minutes or until thick, stirring occasionally. Skim off excess fat. Spoon meat sauce over salad. Top with cheese, avocado slices and corn chips or chow-mein noodles. Toss and serve immediately.

Suggested Combinations

Chili-Style Taco Salad: Use drained, rinsed, canned red beans, fresh tomato wedges and canned chopped green chilies for vegetables. Use ground beef for meat and taco sauce for cooking sauce. Use beef broth and red wine. Use chili powder for spice. Garnish with avocado and corn chips.

Sweet & Sour Taco Salad: Use shredded Chinese cabbage for part of salad greens. Use sliced water chestnuts, bean sprouts and bamboo shoots for vegetables. Use ground pork for meat and sweet-sour sauce for cooking sauce. Use chicken broth and white wine. Use ginger and dry mustard for spice. Omit cheese and avocado. Garnish with chow-mein noodles. Serve with soy sauce, if desired.

French Salad Dressing

YIELD	2-1/4 cups	1 cup
INGREDIENTS		
vegetable oil or olive oil	1-1/2 cups	3/4 cup
red- or white-wine vinegar	1/3 cup	3 tablespoons
dry white wine	2 tablespoons	1 tablespoon
beaten egg	2 tablespoons	1 tablespoon
sugar	4 teaspoons	2 teaspoons
lemon juice	4 teaspoons	2 teaspoons
finely chopped onion	2 teaspoons	1 teaspoon
dry mustard	1 teaspoon	1/2 teaspoon
salt	1/4 teaspoon	1/8 teaspoon
minced garlic	large clove	small clove
white pepper	1/8 teaspoon	dash
SCREW-TOP JAR	1-qt. jar	1-pint jar

In a screw-top jar, see size in chart above, combine all ingredients. Cover and shake well until blended. Refrigerate until serving time. Shake well before serving. Serve on leaf lettuce, then sprinkle with grated Parmesan cheese. Or, use as base for Herb-French Salad Dressing, page 370, Italian Salad Dressing, opposite, or Vinaigrette Salad Dressing, opposite. Keeps 2 to 3 days.

How to Make Italian Salad Dressing

1/In a screw-top jar, combine oil, white-wine vinegar, white wine, egg, sugar, lemon juice, onion and seasonings. Stir in oregano and pimiento. Cover and shake well. Refrigerate until ready to use.

2/For Asparagus-Salad Vinaigrette, page 377, sprinkle cooked asparagus spears with chopped radish, tomatoes, onion and parsley. Pour Italian Salad Dressing over vegetables. Refrigerate several hours. Serve on leaf lettuce garnished with hard-cooked-egg slices.

Italian Salad Dressing

YIELD	2-1/2 cups	1-1/4 cups
INGREDIENTS		
Same ingredients as for French Salad Dressing, opposite, but use:	large recipe	small recipe
white-wine vinegar	1/2 cup	1/4 cup
finely chopped pimiento	2 teaspoons	1 teaspoon
dried leaf oregano	1 teaspoon	1/2 teaspoon

Follow directions for French Salad Dressing, increasing white-wine vinegar to amount given above and adding oregano and pimiento. Serve on tossed leaf lettuce. Or, use for Vegetables Vinaigrette, page 377.

Vinaigrette Salad Dressing

YIELD	2-2/3 cups	1-1/3 cups
INGREDIENTS		
Same ingredients as for French Salad Dressing, opposite, but use:	large recipe	small recipe
white-wine vinegar	2/3 cup	1/3 cup

Follow directions for French Salad Dressing, increasing white-wine vinegar to amount given above. Serve on tossed vegetable salads. Or, use for Vegetables Vinaigrette, page 377.

Celery-Seed Fruit Dressing

YIELD	2-1/3 cups	1-1/4 cups
INGREDIENTS		
sugar	1/2 cup	1/4 cup
paprika	4 teaspoons	2 teaspoons
celery seed	1 teaspoon	1/2 teaspoon
dry mustard	1 teaspoon	1/2 teaspoon
onion powder	1/8 teaspoon	dash
honey	1/2 cup	1/4 cup
lime juice	1/2 cup	1/4 cup
vegetable oil	1 cup	1/2 cup
MIXER BOWL	1-1/2-qt. bowl	1-1/2-qt. bowl
BEATING TIME AT HIGH SPEED	5 minutes	2 minutes

In a 1-1/2-quart mixer bowl, combine sugar, paprika, celery seed, dry mustard and onion powder; mix well. With an electric mixer at low speed, beat in honey and lime juice. Turn mixer to high speed. Add oil in a thin stream, beating constantly for time in chart above. Oil should be added slowly during entire beating time. Cover and refrigerate. Serve on chilled fruit on lettuce-lined plates.

To use a blender or food processor: Combine all ingredients except oil in blender or food processor fitted with a steel blade. Process 10 to 15 seconds. Scrape down sides of bowl. With blender or processor running at high speed, gradually add oil in a thin stream. Process for about half the beating time given in chart above or until thickened. Scrape down sides occasionally.

Creamy Fruit-Salad Dressing

YIELD	1 cup	1/2 cup
INGREDIENTS		
Mayonnaise Dressing, page 394	3/4 cup	1/3 cup
frozen orange-juice concentrate, thawed	1/4 cup	2 tablespoons
powdered sugar	2 tablespoons	1 tablespoon
grated orange peel	1/2 teaspoon	1/4 teaspoon
ground allspice	1/4 teaspoon	1/8 teaspoon

Prepare Mayonnaise Dressing. In a medium bowl, combine orange-juice concentrate, powdered sugar, orange peel, allspice and Mayonnaise Dressing; mix well. Cover and refrigerate until serving time. Serve on canned- or fresh-fruit salads.

Tips for Fruit-Salad-Platter Combinations

- **Summer Fruit Platter:** Serve watermelon wedges, cantaloupe or honeydew balls, fresh cherries, fresh peach slices and plum wedges on leaf lettuce. Serve with Creamy Fruit-Salad Dressing, above.
- **Tropical Fruit Platter:** Serve fresh pineapple slices, papaya wedges, mango slices, pomegranate seeds, orange sections and fresh coconut in scooped-out pineapple shells. Serve with Creamy Curry Salad Dressing, page 389.
- **Winter Fruit Platter:** Serve apple slices, pear slices, kiwifruit slices, banana chunks and grape clusters on romaine leaves. Serve with Celery-Seed Fruit Dressing, above.

Mayonnaise Dressing

YIELD	3/4 cup	1/3 cup
INGREDIENTS		
mayonnaise or mayonnaise-style salad dressing	1/2 cup	1/4 cup
dairy sour cream	1/2 cup	1/4 cup

In a medium bowl, combine mayonnaise or salad dressing and sour cream; mix well. Cover and refrigerate until serving time. Serve on lettuce wedges, garnished with shredded cheese. Or, use as base for Creamy Seafood-Salad Dressing, page 386, Creamy Fruit-Salad Dressing, page 392, Green Goddess Salad Dressing, opposite, Thousand Island Dressing, below, and Guacamole Salad Dressing, below.

Guacamole Salad Dressing

YIELD	1-1/2 cups	3/4 cup
INGREDIENTS		
Mayonnaise Dressing, above	3/4 cup	1/3 cup
avocado, peeled, cut up	1 avocado	1/2 avocado
canned chopped green chilies	1/4 cup	2 tablespoons
lemon juice	4 teaspoons	2 teaspoons
onion salt	1/2 teaspoon	1/4 teaspoon

Prepare Mayonnaise Dressing. In a blender or food processor fitted with a steel blade, combine Mayonnaise Dressing, avocado, chilies, lemon juice and onion salt. Cover and process until smooth, scraping down sides once or twice. Cover and refrigerate until serving time. Serve on taco salad or sliced-tomato salad, garnished with additional chopped green chilies.

Thousand Island Dressing

YIELD	2 cups	1 cup
INGREDIENTS		
Mayonnaise Dressing, above	3/4 cup	1/3 cup
chili sauce	1/2 cup	1/4 cup
chopped sweet pickle	1/4 cup	2 tablespoons
chopped green onion	1/4 cup	2 tablespoons
hard-cooked eggs, chopped	2	1

Prepare Mayonnaise Dressing. In a medium bowl, stir chili sauce, sweet pickle, green onion and hard-cooked eggs into Mayonnaise Dressing. Cover and refrigerate until serving time. Serve as spread for sandwiches or dressing for vegetable salads.

Creamy Bacon Salad Dressing

YIELD	1 cup	1/2 cup
INGREDIENTS		
Buttermilk Dressing, page 388	3/4 cup	1/3 cup
crumbled cooked bacon	1/4 cup	2 tablespoons
fines herbes	1/2 teaspoon	1/4 teaspoon
freshly ground pepper	1/2 teaspoon	1/4 teaspoon

Prepare Buttermilk Dressing. In a medium bowl, combine Buttermilk Dressing, bacon, fines herbes and pepper; mix well. Cover and refrigerate until serving time. Serve on sliced-tomato salad or fresh spinach-and-mushroom salad.

How to Make Green Goddess Salad Dressing

1/Spoon Mayonnaise Dressing into a blender or food-processor container. Snip in parsley, watercress and chives. Add tarragon vinegar and anchovy paste. Blend until well-combined.

2/Serve Green Goddess Salad Dressing on a platter of sliced tomatoes and cucumbers on leaf lettuce. To garnish, sieve hard-cooked egg yolk over vegetables.

Green Goddess Salad Dressing

YIELD	1-1/4 cups	2/3 cup
INGREDIENTS		
Mayonnaise Dressing, opposite	3/4 cup	1/3 cup
snipped parsley	1/4 cup	2 tablespoons
snipped watercress	1/4 cup	2 tablespoons
snipped chives	2 teaspoons	1 teaspoon
tarragon vinegar	2 tablespoons	1 tablespoon
anchovy paste	2 teaspoons	1 teaspoon

Prepare Mayonnaise Dressing. In a blender or food processor fitted with a steel blade, combine Mayonnaise Dressing, parsley, watercress, chives, vinegar and anchovy paste. Cover and process until blended, scraping down sides several times. Cover and refrigerate until serving time. Serve on tomato-and-cucumber salad, garnished with leaf lettuce and sieved hard-cooked egg yolk.

Creamy Bleu-Cheese Salad Dressing

YIELD	1 cup	1/2 cup
INGREDIENTS		
Buttermilk Dressing, page 388	3/4 cup	1/3 cup
crumbled bleu cheese	1/2 cup (2 oz.)	1/4 cup (1 oz.)

Prepare Buttermilk Dressing. In a medium bowl, combine Buttermilk Dressing and half of bleu cheese. Whisk until almost smooth. Fold in remaining bleu cheese and leave in chunks in dressing. Cover and refrigerate until serving time. Serve on tossed vegetable salads or avocado slices arranged on leaf lettuce, garnished with ripe olives and tomato wedges.

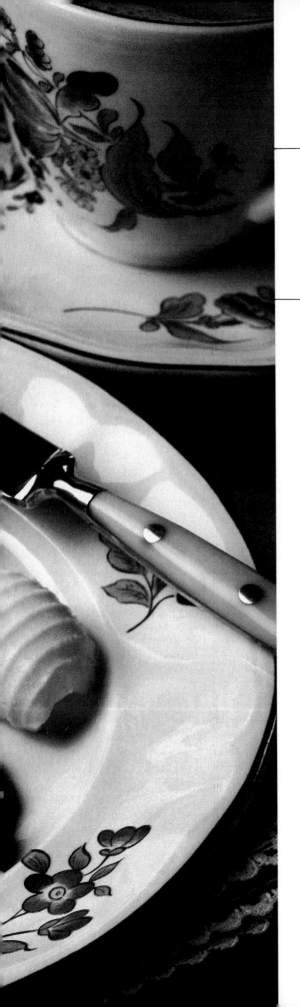

Breads, Pasta & Rice

Nothing has a better aroma than freshly baked bread. Recreate the wonderful smells of yesteryear by trying our bread recipes. With today's fast-rising yeast and easy electric-mixer method, it is no longer an all-day affair. It only takes a fraction of the time it used to. Step-by-step photos show you the basics, so even beginners can experience the indescribable satisfaction of serving beautiful baked breads.

Croissants, page 416.

Breads, Pasta & Rice

Q. How do you use the new fast-rising dry yeasts?

A. The new Quick-Rise™ or RapidRise™ yeast can be substituted in yeast-bread recipes in which the dough is not refrigerated. This yeast acts about twice as fast as regular yeast when dough is rising for the first time. However, we found little time savings when dough shaped into loaves rose for the second time. Check dough halfway through both rising times if you use fast-rising yeast. Omit the standing time before shaping dough with this yeast. During the first few minutes of baking, the extra expansion from the fast yeast may cause a small split or shred in the side of some loaves.

Be sure to check the freshness date on all yeast packages, including fast-rising yeasts, before using.

Q. I like to bake big batches of bread while I am at it. How can I keep all this bread fresh?

A. To keep yeast bread more than 1 day, wrap cooled bread in moisture-vapor proof wrap and freeze. In humid climates, refrigerating yeast breads retards mold, but it also makes bread dry and stale faster.

To keep quick bread, wrap loaves in foil and refrigerate up to 1 week. Freeze for longer storage. Muffins, biscuits and waffles are best stored frozen if not used the same day.

The freezer gives you flexibility, because breads can be frozen up to 3 months. Small families can remove bread slices or rolls as needed, and leave the rest frozen for freshness.

Q. How do I reheat frozen bread and rolls?

A. Allow wrapped bread loaves to thaw at room temperature about 3 hours. To reheat frozen or room-temperature rolls, muffins or biscuits, place in an opened foil package. Bake in a preheated 350F to 375F (175C to 190C) oven 12 to 15 minutes if room temperature, or 15 to 20 minutes if frozen. Reheat waffles in the toaster.

Q. What is bread flour and how is it different from other flours?

A. Bread flour is a specially developed flour with more protein or gluten, the substance that forms the structure in bread. It is not essential for success, but bread flour does make beautiful yeast breads. Bread flour can be substituted for all-purpose flour in recipes. However, expect to use less bread flour than all-purpose flour for the last flour addition in the recipe. Medium rye flour is a fine-textured flour; *medium* refers to the color. Whole-wheat flour is ground from the entire wheat kernel.

Q. Should all flours be stored at room temperature?

A. Store whole-wheat flour, dark rye flour and pumpernickel rye flour in the refrigerator. Store other flours in tightly covered containers at room temperature. Or, freeze flours for longer storage.

Q. Why do you use the electric mixer with these yeast-bread recipes?

A. Using the electric mixer allows warm liquid ingredients (120F, 50C) to be added directly to the dry yeast-flour mixture. This eliminates the first step of softening yeast in warm water. Some of the flour is then beaten into the dough with the mixer, using regular mixer beaters. This provides some kneading action, which shortens kneading time later. If your mixer has dough hooks, follow the manufacturer's directions for using them. Some doughs can also be made successfully in the food processor. Follow manufacturer's directions.

Q. Why does the same bread recipe sometimes require more or less flour from one time to the next?

A. Temperature and humidity affect the flour's moisture level. In humid weather, flour has more moisture, and the bread recipe requires more flour. To compensate, we have provided a range for the amount of flour in each bread recipe. For a rule of thumb, *less is best.* Use as little flour as you can and still make the dough easy to handle. Include flour used in kneading as part of the total. Use the smaller amount of flour listed in the recipe when making the dough, then use some of the remaining flour for kneading.

Q. My family enjoys French bread, but I've never tried to make it myself. Can you give me some tips?

A. If your family likes French bread, they will also enjoy the hard rolls and breadsticks that are made from the same dough, page 406.

French bread, hard rolls and breadsticks should be baked in the upper third of the oven for maximum browning. If you have only one oven, you will be able to bake only one baking sheet of dough at a time. After shaping the dough, refrigerate the extra baking sheets of dough to slow down the rising until the dough can be baked. Keep in mind that French-bread dough has no shortening, butter or margarine, and thus has poor keeping quality. Plan to use French bread, hard rolls or breadsticks the same day they are baked. For longer storage, cool on racks, then wrap in moisture-vapor proof wrap and freeze.

Techniques for Making Yeast Dough

1/For the electric-mixer bread method used in this book, beat flour, sugar, dry yeast, salt and any spices at low speed of an electric mixer about 20 seconds to blend. Heat milk or other liquid ingredients and shortening, butter or margarine until warm (120F, 50C). Fat does not need to melt. The temperature of the milk is very important. Milk must be warm enough to activate yeast. Milk that is too warm will kill yeast. If possible, use a thermometer to check the temperature of the milk mixture.

2/After beating in some of the flour with the electric mixer, stir in as much remaining flour as possible with a wooden spoon. Dough will still be sticky. Sprinkle some remaining flour on a large board. Turn dough over to coat with flour. Knead dough by pushing it away from you with the palm of your hand. Give dough a quarter turn and fold it over toward you. Push dough with the palm of your hand again. Continue pushing, turning and folding dough until smooth.

3/Place kneaded dough in a greased bowl. Turn dough over once to grease the top. For consistent rising results, place bowl of dough on the top rack of a cold oven. Cover bowl with a clean towel. Place a shallow pan of very hot water on the bottom oven rack. Change water to keep it hot. Close the oven door to let dough rise. Do not turn oven on! Dough has risen enough if your fingerprint remains when you touch dough firmly in center. Do not let dough over-rise or the finished product may "fall." This is Whole-Wheat Bread, page 404.

4/Plunge your fist into the center of risen dough to punch down dough. Turn out dough on a floured board. Follow shaping instructions in the recipes. We found bread loaves rose more evenly if they were placed to 1 side of the loaf pan. Dark loaf pans, such as these, will form very dark crusts. Glass loaf dishes or light-colored metal pans will produce a more golden crust. Cover shaped dough with a clean towel and let rise in the oven as before. After rising, remove bread and pan of water before preheating oven to bake bread.

White Bread

YIELD	2 loaves	1 loaf
INGREDIENTS		
water	1-1/2 cups	3/4 cup
milk	1-1/3 cups	2/3 cup
shortening	2 tablespoons	1 tablespoon
all-purpose flour	3 cups	1-1/2 cups
sugar	1/4 cup	2 tablespoons
salt	2 teaspoons	1 teaspoon
active dry yeast	2 (1/4-oz.) pkgs.	1 (1/4-oz.) pkg.
all-purpose flour	1 cup	1/2 cup
all-purpose flour	3-1/2 to 4 cups	2 to 2-1/4 cups
BOWL (for dough rising)	4-qt. bowl	2-qt. bowl
LOAF PANS	2 (9" x 5" x 3") loaf pans	9" x 5" x 3" loaf pan
SAUCEPAN	1-1/2-qt. saucepan	1-qt. saucepan
MIXER BOWL (for dough mixing)	3-qt. bowl	3-qt. bowl
TIME AT MEDIUM HIGH	5 to 6 minutes	2 to 3 minutes
BEATING TIME AT MEDIUM SPEED	2 minutes	2 minutes
BEATING TIME AT HIGH SPEED	2 minutes	2 minutes
KNEADING TIME	8 to 10 minutes	8 to 10 minutes
RISING TIME (in bowl)	1 to 1-1/4 hours	1 to 1-1/4 hours
STANDING TIME	15 minutes	15 minutes
RISING TIME (in pan)	35 to 45 minutes	35 to 45 minutes
TIME IN 375F (190C) OVEN	40 to 45 minutes	40 to 45 minutes
COOLING TIME	2 hours	2 hours

Grease a bowl for dough rising, see size in chart above. Grease 1 or 2 (9" x 5" x 3") loaf pans; set aside. In a saucepan, see size in chart above, combine water, milk and shortening. Heat over Medium-High heat for time in chart above or until warm (120F, 50C). Shortening does not need to melt. In a 3-quart mixer bowl, beat first amount of flour, sugar, salt and yeast at low speed of an electric mixer 10 seconds. Add warm water mixture. Beat at medium speed of mixer 2 minutes. Scrape sides of bowl occasionally. Add second amount of flour. Beat at low speed of mixer 15 to 20 seconds. Turn mixer to high speed. Beat 2 minutes. Scrape sides of bowl occasionally. By hand, gradually stir in enough of third amount of flour to make a moderately stiff dough. Turn out dough on a floured board; coat with flour. Knead dough on floured board 8 to 10 minutes or until smooth and elastic. Place in greased bowl, turning dough once to grease top. Cover and let rise in a warm place 1 to 1-1/4 hours or until doubled in bulk. Punch down dough. Turn out on floured board. Cover and let stand 15 minutes. Divide large recipe of dough in 2 portions. On floured board, roll each portion of dough to a 15" x 9" rectangle. Roll up dough, jelly-roll style, starting with short side. Gently pinch together side seam to seal. Turn seam-side down. Crease and fold ends under. Place, seam-side down, in greased pan. Cover and let rise in warm place 35 to 45 minutes or until almost doubled in bulk. Preheat oven to 375F (190C). Bake in preheated oven 40 to 45 minutes or until loaf sounds hollow when tapped with your finger. Cover loaf with a tent of foil during last 10 to 15 minutes of baking time if loaf browns too quickly. Remove from pan. Cool on a rack 2 hours.

Variations
Herb Swirl Loaf: In a custard cup, for each loaf, combine 4 teaspoons dried leaf oregano, parsley, chives, thyme or basil with 1 tablespoon water; mix well. Let stand while preparing dough. After rolling dough into a rectangle for shaping, brush dough with water. Drain herb mixture. Spread over dough for each loaf. Follow directions above for rolling up dough to shape loaves.
Spicy Swirl Loaf: In a small bowl, for each loaf, combine 1 teaspoon ground cinnamon, nutmeg or cardamom with 1/4 cup packed brown sugar; mix well. After rolling dough into a rectangle for shaping, brush dough with water. Sprinkle dough for each loaf evenly with brown-sugar mixture. Follow directions above for rolling up dough to shape loaves.
Honey-Nut Loaf: After rolling dough into a rectangle for shaping, spread dough for each loaf with 3 tablespoons honey. Sprinkle evenly with 1/3 cup finely chopped pecans or walnuts. Follow directions above for rolling up dough to shape loaves.

Techniques for Shaping Bread Loaves

1/Roll dough on a floured board to a 15" x 9" rectangle. For Spicy Swirl Loaf, brush rectangle with water and sprinkle with brown-sugar mixture. Roll up, jelly-roll style, starting with short side. Seal dough with your fingertips after each roll.

2/Continue rolling and sealing dough until you reach the end. Turn dough so seam of roll is up. Pinch this seam together to seal dough.

3/Turn dough seam-side down. Using both hands, firmly crease dough at ends and fold creased ends under loaf.

4/Turn dough seam-side up. Pinch ends of loaf to bottom of loaf to seal end seams.

Light Rye Bread

YIELD	4 round loaves	2 round loaves
INGREDIENTS		
water	2-1/2 cups	1-1/4 cups
shortening	2 tablespoons	1 tablespoon
all-purpose flour	3 cups	1-1/2 cups
packed brown sugar	1/2 cup	1/4 cup
salt	2 teaspoons	1 teaspoon
active dry yeast	2 (1/4-oz.) pkgs.	1 (1/4-oz.) pkg.
caraway seed, if desired	2 teaspoons	1 teaspoon
medium rye flour	2-1/2 cups	1-1/4 cups
all-purpose flour	1-1/2 to 2 cups	3/4 to 1 cup
BOWL (for dough rising)	4-qt. bowl	2-qt. bowl
BAKING PANS	4 (8-inch) round layer pans	2 (8-inch) round layer pans
SAUCEPAN	1-qt. saucepan	1-qt. saucepan
MIXER BOWL (for dough mixing)	3-qt. bowl	3-qt. bowl
TIME AT MEDIUM HIGH	3 to 4 minutes	1 to 2 minutes
BEATING TIME AT LOW SPEED	15 seconds	15 seconds
BEATING TIME AT MEDIUM SPEED	2 minutes	2 minutes
BEATING TIME AT HIGH SPEED	2 minutes	2 minutes
KNEADING TIME	5 to 8 minutes	5 to 8 minutes
RISING TIME (in bowl)	1 to 1-1/4 hours	1 to 1-1/4 hours
STANDING TIME	15 minutes	15 minutes
RISING TIME (in pans)	45 to 60 minutes	45 to 60 minutes
TIME IN 375F (190C) OVEN	25 to 30 minutes	25 to 30 minutes
COOLING TIME	2 hours	2 hours

Grease a bowl for dough rising, see size in chart above. Grease 2 or 4 (8-inch) round layer pans; set aside. In a 1-quart saucepan, combine water and shortening. Heat over Medium-High heat for time in chart above or until warm (120F, 50C). Shortening does not need to melt. In a 3-quart mixer bowl, beat first amount of all-purpose flour, brown sugar, salt and yeast at low speed of an electric mixer 15 seconds. Add warm water mixture. Beat at medium speed of mixer 2 minutes. Scrape sides of bowl occasionally. Turn mixer to high speed. Beat 2 minutes. Scrape sides of bowl occasionally. By hand, stir in caraway seed, if desired, and rye flour. By hand, gradually stir in enough of second amount of all-purpose flour to make a moderately stiff dough. Turn out dough on a floured board; coat with flour. Knead dough on floured board 5 to 8 minutes or until smooth and elastic. Place in greased bowl, turning dough once to grease top. Cover and let rise in a warm place 1 to 1-1/4 hours or until doubled in bulk. Punch down dough. Turn out on floured board. Cover and let stand 15 minutes. Divide large recipe of dough in 4 portions and small recipe in 2 portions. On floured board, shape each portion of dough into a ball, rolling sides under to form smooth top. Place, smooth-side up, in greased layer pans. Cover and let rise in warm place 45 to 60 minutes or until almost doubled in bulk. Preheat oven to 375F (190C). Bake in preheated oven 25 to 30 minutes or until loaf sounds hollow when tapped with your finger. Remove from pans. Cool on a rack 2 hours.

Whole-Wheat Bread

YIELD	2 loaves	1 loaf
INGREDIENTS		
milk	2 cups	1 cup
water	2/3 cup	1/3 cup
honey	1/2 cup	1/4 cup
shortening	1/4 cup	2 tablespoons
all-purpose flour	3 cups	1-1/2 cups
salt	2 teaspoons	1 teaspoon
active dry yeast	2 (1/4-oz.) pkgs.	1 (1/4-oz.) pkg.
whole-wheat flour	2 cups	1 cup
all-purpose flour	2-1/4 to 2-3/4 cups	1-1/2 to 1-3/4 cups
BOWL (for dough rising)	4-qt. bowl	2-qt. bowl
LOAF PANS	2 (9" x 5" x 3") loaf pans	9" x 5" x 3" loaf pan
SAUCEPAN	1-1/2-qt. saucepan	1-qt. saucepan
MIXER BOWL (for dough mixing)	3-qt. bowl	3-qt. bowl
TIME AT MEDIUM HIGH	5 to 7 minutes	3-1/2 to 4-1/2 minutes
BEATING TIME AT LOW SPEED	10 seconds	10 seconds
BEATING TIME AT MEDIUM SPEED	2 minutes	2 minutes
BEATING TIME AT HIGH SPEED	2 minutes	2 minutes
KNEADING TIME	5 to 8 minutes	5 to 8 minutes
RISING TIME (in bowl)	1 to 1-1/4 hours	1 to 1-1/4 hours
STANDING TIME	15 minutes	15 minutes
RISING TIME (in pan)	40 to 60 minutes	40 to 60 minutes
TIME IN 375F (190C) OVEN	40 to 45 minutes	40 to 45 minutes
COOLING TIME	2 hours	2 hours

Grease a bowl for dough rising, see size in chart above. Grease 1 or 2 (9" x 5" x 3") loaf pans; set aside. In a saucepan, see size in chart above, combine milk, water, honey and shortening. Heat over Medium-High heat for time in chart above or until warm (120F, 50C). Shortening does not need to melt. In a 3-quart mixer bowl, beat first amount of all-purpose flour, salt and yeast at low speed of an electric mixer 10 seconds. Add warm milk mixture. Beat at medium speed of mixer 2 minutes. Scrape sides of bowl occasionally. Turn mixer to high speed. Beat 2 minutes. Scrape sides of bowl occasionally. By hand, stir in whole-wheat flour. By hand, gradually stir in enough of second amount of all-purpose flour to make a moderately stiff dough. Turn out dough on a floured board; coat with flour. Knead dough on floured board 5 to 8 minutes or until smooth and elastic. Place in greased bowl, turning dough once to grease top. Cover and let rise in a warm place 1 to 1-1/4 hours or until doubled in bulk. Punch down dough. Turn out on floured board. Cover and let stand 15 minutes. Divide large recipe of dough in 2 portions. On floured board, roll each portion of dough to a 15" x 9" rectangle. Roll up dough, jelly-roll style, starting with short side. Gently pinch together side seam to seal. Turn seam-side down. Crease and fold ends under. Place, seam-side down, in greased loaf pan. Cover and let rise in a warm place 40 to 60 minutes or until almost doubled in bulk. Preheat oven to 375F (190C). Bake in preheated oven 40 to 45 minutes or until loaf sounds hollow when tapped with your finger. Cover loaf with a tent of foil during last 15 minutes of baking time if loaf browns too quickly. Remove from pan. Cool on a rack 2 hours.

How to Make Basic Jam Breakfast Rolls

1/Roll dough into 10- to 12-inch ropes, working from center of each rope toward ends. Coil each rope into a spiral shape. Tuck end under and seal. Brush with fruit juice and sprinkle with fruit-flavored gelatin.

2/Place on a greased baking sheet after sprinkling with gelatin. Otherwise, any gelatin spilled on baking sheet will burn. After rising, make a small indentation with your fingertip in center of each roll. Spoon preserves into center of each roll. Bake.

Basic Jam Breakfast Rolls

YIELD	16 rolls	8 rolls
INGREDIENTS		
Sweet Dough, page 408	small recipe	1/2 small recipe
fruit juice	1 tablespoon	1/2 tablespoon
fruit-flavored gelatin	4 teaspoons	2 teaspoons
fruit jam or preserves	8 teaspoons	4 teaspoons
BAKING SHEETS	2 baking sheets	1 baking sheet
RISING TIME (on baking sheet)	30 to 45 minutes	30 to 45 minutes
TIME IN 375F (190C) OVEN	12 to 15 minutes	12 to 15 minutes
COOLING TIME	10 minutes	10 minutes

Grease 1 or 2 baking sheets; set aside. Prepare Sweet Dough. If making 16 rolls, divide dough in 4 portions; if making 8 rolls, divide dough in 2 portions. Divide each portion in 4 pieces. Roll each piece into a 10- to 12-inch rope. Coil each rope into a spiral shape, tucking ends under and sealing. Brush with fruit juice. Sprinkle each roll with 1/4 teaspoon gelatin. Place 2 inches apart on greased baking sheet. Cover and let rise in a warm place 30 to 45 minutes or until doubled in bulk. Preheat oven to 375F (190C). Make a small indentation with your finger in center of each roll. Spoon 1/2 teaspoon preserves into center of each roll. Bake in preheated oven 12 to 15 minutes or until browned. Remove from baking sheet. Cool on a rack 10 minutes. Serve warm.

Suggested Combinations
Strawberry Breakfast Rolls: Use orange juice for fruit juice. Use strawberry-flavored gelatin. Use strawberry preserves.
Peach Breakfast Rolls: Use apricot nectar for fruit juice. Use peach-flavored gelatin. Use peach preserves.
Citrus Breakfast Rolls: Use orange juice for fruit juice. Use lemon-flavored gelatin. Use orange marmalade for preserves.

French Bread

YIELD	2 loaves	1 loaf
INGREDIENTS		
cornmeal	to sprinkle	to sprinkle
all-purpose flour	2-1/2 cups	1-1/4 cups
active dry yeast	2 (1/4-oz.) pkgs.	1 (1/4-oz.) pkg.
salt	2 teaspoons	1 teaspoon
warm water (120F, 50C)	2-1/2 cups	1-1/4 cups
all-purpose flour	1 cup	1/2 cup
all-purpose flour	3 to 3-1/2 cups	1-1/2 to 1-3/4 cups
egg white, slightly beaten	1	1
sesame or poppy seed, if desired	to garnish	to garnish
BOWL (for dough rising)	4-qt. bowl	2-qt. bowl
BAKING SHEETS	2 baking sheets	1 baking sheet
MIXER BOWL	3-qt. bowl	3-qt. bowl
BEATING TIME AT LOW SPEED (first amount of flour, dry ingredients)	15 seconds	10 seconds
BEATING TIME AT MEDIUM SPEED	2 minutes	2 minutes
BEATING TIME AT LOW SPEED (second amount of flour added)	20 seconds	20 seconds
BEATING TIME AT HIGH SPEED	2 minutes	2 minutes
KNEADING TIME	10 to 12 minutes	10 to 12 minutes
RISING TIME (in bowl)	1 to 1-1/4 hours	1 to 1-1/4 hours
STANDING TIME	10 minutes	10 minutes
RISING TIME (on baking sheets)	45 to 60 minutes	45 to 60 minutes
TIME IN 425F (220C) OVEN (brushing with water)	10 minutes	10 minutes
TIME IN 425F (220C) OVEN (egg-white glaze added)	20 to 30 minutes	20 to 30 minutes
COOLING TIME	2 hours	2 hours

Grease a bowl for dough rising, see size in chart above; set aside. Grease 1 or 2 baking sheets. Sprinkle with cornmeal; set aside. In a 3-quart mixer bowl, beat first amount of flour, yeast and salt at low speed of an electric mixer for time in chart above. Add warm water. Beat at medium speed of mixer 2 minutes. Scrape sides of bowl occasionally. Add second amount of flour. Beat at low speed of mixer 20 seconds. Turn mixer to high speed. Beat 2 minutes. Scrape sides of bowl occasionally. By hand, gradually stir in enough of third amount of flour to make a moderately stiff dough. Turn out dough on a floured board; coat with flour. Knead dough on floured board 10 to 12 minutes or until smooth and very elastic. Place in greased bowl, turning dough once to grease top. Cover and let rise in a warm place 1 to 1-1/4 hours or until doubled in bulk. Punch down dough. Turn out on floured board. Cover and let stand 10 minutes. Divide large recipe of dough in 2 portions. Roll or pat each portion of dough to a 12'' x 8'' rectangle. Roll up dough, jelly-roll style, starting with long side. Gently pinch together edges and ends to seal. Slightly taper ends by rolling dough between hands. Place diagonally, seam-side down, on prepared baking sheet. Cover and let rise in a warm place 45 to 60 minutes or until almost doubled in bulk. Preheat oven to 425F (220C). With a sharp knife, make 4 diagonal slashes about 1/4 inch deep across top of loaf. Gently brush with water. Bake in upper third of preheated oven 10 minutes, brushing with water 3 times. Brush with egg white and sprinkle with sesame or poppy seed, if desired. Bake 20 to 30 minutes longer or until browned. Remove from baking sheet. Cool on a rack 2 hours.

Variation
Baguettes: For smaller loaves, divide large recipe of dough in 4 portions and small recipe in 2 portions. Follow directions above to shape and bake loaves. Loaves will be long and slender.

How to Make French Bread

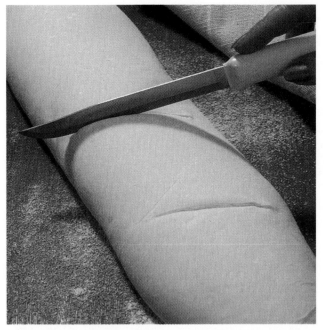

1/Place shaped loaf of dough on a baking sheet that has been greased and sprinkled with cornmeal. Let rise in a warm place until doubled in bulk. While oven is preheating, make 4 diagonal slashes about 1/4 inch deep across top of loaf.

2/Gently brush loaf with water before baking. Place baking sheet in upper third of oven for maximum browning. Brush loaf with water 3 times during first 10 minutes of baking. This gives a more crisp, chewy crust.

Hard Rolls or Breadsticks

YIELD	24 rolls or breadsticks	12 rolls or breadsticks
INGREDIENTS dough for French Bread, opposite:		
hard rolls	large recipe	small recipe
breadsticks	small recipe	1/2 small recipe
RISING TIME (on baking sheets):		
rolls	45 to 60 minutes	45 to 60 minutes
breadsticks	15 to 30 minutes	15 to 30 minutes
TIME IN 425F (220C) OVEN (brushing with water)	10 minutes	10 minutes
TIME IN 425F (220C) OVEN (egg-white glaze added)	20 to 25 minutes	20 to 25 minutes

Follow directions for French Bread until ready to shape dough.

For hard rolls: Grease 1 or 2 baking sheets. Sprinkle with cornmeal; set aside. Divide large recipe of dough in 8 portions and small recipe in 4 portions. Divide each portion in 3 pieces. Shape each piece into a ball, rolling edges under to form smooth top. Pinch dough together at bottom of each ball. Place, 2 inches apart, on a prepared baking sheet. Cover and let rise in a warm place 45 to 60 minutes or until almost doubled in bulk. With a sharp knife, make a slash 1/4 inch deep in top of each roll.

For breadsticks: Grease 1 or 2 baking sheets. Sprinkle with cornmeal; set aside. Divide small recipe of dough in 4 portions and one-half of small recipe in 2 portions. Divide each portion in 6 pieces. On a floured board, roll each piece into an 8-inch rope. Place, 2 inches apart, on prepared baking sheet. Cover and let rise in a warm place 15 to 30 minutes or until doubled in bulk.

To bake hard rolls or breadsticks: Preheat oven to 425F (220C). Gently brush rolls or breadsticks with water. Bake in upper third of preheated oven 10 minutes, brushing with water 3 times. Brush with egg white and sprinkle with sesame or poppy seed, if desired. Bake 20 to 25 minutes longer or until browned. Remove from baking sheet. Serve immediately or cool on a rack.

Sweet Dough

YIELD	large recipe	small recipe
INGREDIENTS		
milk	1 cup	1/2 cup
butter or margarine	1/2 cup	1/4 cup
water	1/4 cup	2 tablespoons
all-purpose flour	2 cups	1 cup
sugar	1/2 cup	1/4 cup
salt	1/2 teaspoon	1/4 teaspoon
active dry yeast	2 (1/4-oz.) pkgs.	1 (1/4-oz.) pkg.
eggs	2	1
all-purpose flour	1 cup	1/2 cup
all-purpose flour	2-1/2 to 3 cups	1-1/4 to 1-1/2 cups
BOWL (for dough rising)	3-qt. bowl	2-qt. bowl
SAUCEPAN	1-qt. saucepan	1-qt. saucepan
MIXER BOWL (for dough mixing)	3-qt. bowl	3-qt. bowl
BAKING DISH OR SHEETS	select size from recipes, pages 405 to 414	
TIME AT MEDIUM HIGH	3-1/2 to 4 minutes	2 to 2-1/2 minutes
BEATING TIME AT LOW SPEED (first amount of flour, dry ingredients)	15 seconds	10 seconds
BEATING TIME AT MEDIUM SPEED	2 minutes	2 minutes
BEATING TIME AT LOW SPEED (egg, second amount of flour added)	20 seconds	20 seconds
BEATING TIME AT HIGH SPEED	2 minutes	2 minutes
KNEADING TIME	4 to 8 minutes	4 to 8 minutes
RISING TIME (in bowl)	1-1/4 to 1-1/2 hours	1-1/4 to 1-1/2 hours
STANDING TIME	10 minutes	10 minutes

Grease a bowl for dough rising, see size in chart above; set aside. In a 1-quart saucepan, combine milk, butter or margarine and water. Heat over Medium-High heat for time in chart above or until warm (120F, 50C). Butter or margarine does not need to melt. In a 3-quart mixer bowl, beat first amount of flour, sugar, salt and yeast at low speed of an electric mixer for time in chart above. Add warm milk mixture. Beat at medium speed of mixer 2 minutes. Scrape sides of bowl occasionally. Add eggs and second amount of flour. Beat at low speed of mixer 20 seconds. Turn mixer to high speed. Beat 2 minutes. Scrape sides of bowl occasionally. By hand, gradually stir in enough of third amount of flour to make a moderately stiff dough. Turn out dough on a floured board; coat with flour. Knead dough on floured board 4 to 8 minutes or until smooth and elastic. Place in greased bowl, turning dough once to grease top. Cover and let rise in a warm place 1-1/4 to 1-1/2 hours or until doubled in bulk. Punch down dough. Turn out on floured board. Cover and let stand 10 minutes. Use dough for Basic Jam Breakfast Rolls, page 405; Basic Spicy Fruit Twists, opposite; Hamburger or Hot-Dog Buns, page 410; Sticky Buns, page 410; Bowknot Rolls, page 412; Crescent Rolls, page 412; Pan Rolls, page 412; Merry Christmas Loaves, page 414; and Hot Cross Buns, page 414.

Powdered-Sugar Glaze

YIELD	1/3 cup	3 tablespoons
INGREDIENTS		
powdered sugar	1 cup	1/2 cup
milk	4 to 6 teaspoons	2 to 3 teaspoons
vanilla extract	1/4 teaspoon	1/8 teaspoon

In a small bowl, combine all ingredients. Beat until smooth. Drizzle on warm rolls.

How to Make Basic Spicy Fruit Twists

1/Roll dough to a 12-inch square. Brush with water. Sprinkle center third of square with brown-sugar mixture and dried fruit. Fold one-third of dough over center third. Brush double layer with water. Sprinkle with sugar mixture and snip on dried fruit. Fold remaining third of dough over and seal edge.

2/Cut dough crosswise in 1-inch strips. Holding ends of each strip, twist tightly in opposite directions. Place dough on a greased baking sheet, pressing ends of twists firmly onto sheet so twists will hold their shape. Let rise until doubled in bulk. Bake in a 375F (190C) oven 15 minutes or until browned.

Basic Spicy Fruit Twists

YIELD	24 twists	12 twists
INGREDIENTS		
Sweet Dough, opposite	large recipe	small recipe
packed brown sugar	2/3 cup	1/3 cup
ground spice	2 teaspoons	1 teaspoon
snipped dried fruit	1 cup	1/2 cup
Powdered-Sugar Glaze, opposite	large recipe	small recipe
BAKING SHEETS	2 baking sheets	1 baking sheet
RISING TIME (on baking sheet)	30 to 40 minutes	30 to 40 minutes
TIME IN 375F (190C) OVEN	15 minutes	15 minutes
COOLING TIME	10 minutes	10 minutes

Grease 1 or 2 baking sheets; set aside. Prepare Sweet Dough. If making 24 twists, divide dough in 2 portions. On a floured board, roll each portion of dough to a 12-inch square. Brush dough with cold water. In a small bowl, combine brown sugar and spice. Sprinkle 1/4 cup brown-sugar mixture in a strip down center third of square. Sprinkle center third with 1/4 cup dried fruit. Fold one-third of dough over center third. Brush double layer with water; sprinkle with 1/4 cup brown-sugar mixture and 1/4 cup dried fruit. Fold remaining third of dough over top. Gently pinch together open edges to seal. Cut crosswise in 12 (1-inch) strips. Hold ends of each strip; twist tightly in opposite directions. Place 2 inches apart on greased baking sheet, pressing ends firmly onto sheet. Cover and let rise in a warm place 30 to 40 minutes or until doubled in bulk. Preheat oven to 375F (190C). Bake in preheated oven 15 minutes or until browned. Remove from baking sheet. Cool on a rack 10 minutes. Drizzle with Powdered-Sugar Glaze. Serve warm.

Suggested Combinations
Cinnamon-Raisin Twists: Use cinnamon for spice. Use raisins for dried fruit.
Golden Apricot Twists: Use mace for spice. Use snipped dried apricots for dried fruit.
Holiday Fruit Twists: Use cardamom for spice. Use chopped, candied, red and green cherries or chopped, candied, mixed fruit for dried fruit.

Sticky Buns

YIELD	15 buns	8 buns
INGREDIENTS		
Sweet Dough, page 408	small recipe	1/2 small recipe
butter or margarine, melted	2 tablespoons	1 tablespoon
chopped pecans	1 cup	1/2 cup
packed brown sugar	1/2 cup	1/4 cup
ground cinnamon	1 teaspoon	1/2 teaspoon
packed brown sugar	2/3 cup	1/3 cup
butter or margarine, melted	1/4 cup	2 tablespoons
light corn syrup	1/4 cup	2 tablespoons
hot water	4 teaspoons	2 teaspoons
BAKING DISH	13" x 9" baking dish	10" x 6" baking dish
RISING TIME (in baking dish)	30 to 45 minutes	30 to 45 minutes
TIME IN 375F (190C) OVEN	20 to 25 minutes	20 to 25 minutes
COOLING TIME (before inverting)	2 minutes	2 minutes
COOLING TIME (after inverting)	5 minutes	5 minutes

Grease a baking dish, see size in chart above; set aside. Prepare Sweet Dough. On a floured board, if making 15 buns, roll dough to a 15" x 12" rectangle. If making 8 buns, roll dough to a 12" x 8" rectangle. Brush dough with first amount of butter or margarine. In a small bowl, combine pecans, first amount of brown sugar and cinnamon. Sprinkle pecan mixture evenly over dough. Roll up dough tightly, jelly-roll style, starting with 15- or 8-inch side. Gently pinch together open edges to seal. Cut roll in 1-inch slices, 15 for large recipe and 8 for small recipe. In a small bowl, mix second amount of brown sugar, second amount of butter or margarine, corn syrup and hot water. Spread mixture over bottom of greased baking dish. Place buns, cut-sides up, on brown-sugar mixture in baking dish. Cover and let rise in a warm place 30 to 45 minutes or until doubled in bulk. Preheat oven to 375F (190C). Bake in preheated oven 20 to 25 minutes or until browned. Cool in baking dish 2 minutes. Invert on a platter without removing baking dish. Cool 5 minutes longer. Remove dish. Serve warm.

Hamburger or Hot-Dog Buns

YIELD	16 buns	8 buns
INGREDIENTS		
Sweet Dough, page 408	large recipe	small recipe
BAKING SHEETS	4 baking sheets	2 baking sheets
RISING TIME (on baking sheet)	45 to 60 minutes	45 to 60 minutes
TIME IN 375F (190C) OVEN	12 to 15 minutes	12 to 15 minutes
COOLING TIME	15 minutes	15 minutes

Grease 2 or 4 baking sheets; set aside. Prepare Sweet Dough. Divide large recipe of dough in 4 portions and small recipe in 2 portions. Divide each portion in 4 pieces.
For hamburger buns: Shape each piece into a ball, rolling edges under to form smooth top. Gently pinch dough together at bottom of each ball. Place buns, smooth-sides up, 4 inches apart, staggered, on greased baking sheets. Flatten each gently to 4-inch diameter.
For hot-dog buns: On a floured board, roll each piece of dough into a 5-inch rope. Place 4 inches apart, staggered, on greased baking sheets. Flatten each gently to 1-1/2-inch width.
To bake hamburger or hot-dog buns: Cover and let rise in a warm place 45 to 60 minutes or until doubled in bulk. Preheat oven to 375F (190C). Bake in preheated oven 12 to 15 minutes or until browned. Remove from baking sheets. Cool on a rack 15 minutes before serving.

Pan Rolls

YIELD	24 rolls	12 rolls
INGREDIENTS Sweet Dough, page 408	small recipe	1/2 small recipe
BAKING DISH	2 (8-inch) round baking dishes	8-inch round baking dish
RISING TIME (in baking dish)	30 to 40 minutes	30 to 40 minutes
TIME IN 375F (190C) OVEN	13 to 17 minutes	13 to 17 minutes

Grease 1 or 2 (8-inch) round baking dishes; set aside. Prepare Sweet Dough. If making 24 rolls, divide dough in 4 portions; if making 12 rolls, divide dough in 2 portions. Divide each portion in 6 pieces. Shape each piece into a ball, rolling edges under to form smooth top. Gently pinch dough together at bottom of each ball. Place 3 balls, smooth-sides up, in center of greased baking dish. Surround with 9 balls of dough. Repeat with remaining dough balls for large recipe. Cover and let rise in a warm place 30 to 40 minutes or until doubled in bulk. Preheat oven to 375F (190C). Bake in preheated oven 13 to 17 minutes or until browned. Remove from baking dish. Serve immediately or cool on a rack.

Variation
Quick Cloverleaf Rolls: Follow directions above for shaping dough balls for Pan Rolls. Place 1 dough ball in each greased 2-1/2-inch muffin cup. Using scissors, snip an **X** 1/2 inch deep in top of each roll. Follow directions above for rising, baking and cooling rolls.

Bowknot Rolls

YIELD	16 rolls	8 rolls
INGREDIENTS Sweet Dough, page 408	small recipe	1/2 small recipe
BAKING SHEETS	2 baking sheets	1 baking sheet
RISING TIME (on baking sheet)	30 to 40 minutes	30 to 40 minutes
TIME IN 375F (190C) OVEN	10 to 12 minutes	10 to 12 minutes

Grease 1 or 2 baking sheets; set aside. Prepare Sweet Dough. If making 16 rolls, divide dough in 4 portions; if making 8 rolls, divide dough in 2 portions. Divide each portion in 4 pieces. On a floured board, roll each piece into a 9- to 10-inch rope. Tie each rope in a loose knot. Place 2 to 3 inches apart on greased baking sheet. Cover and let rise in a warm place 30 to 40 minutes or until doubled in bulk. Preheat oven to 375F (190C). Bake in preheated oven 10 to 12 minutes or until browned. Remove from baking sheet. Serve immediately or cool on a rack.

Crescent Rolls

YIELD	24 rolls	12 rolls
INGREDIENTS Sweet Dough, page 408 butter or margarine, melted	small recipe 2 tablespoons	1/2 small recipe 1 tablespoon
BAKING SHEETS	2 baking sheets	1 baking sheet
RISING TIME (on baking sheet)	30 to 40 minutes	30 to 40 minutes
TIME IN 375F (190C) OVEN	12 to 15 minutes	12 to 15 minutes

Grease 1 or 2 baking sheets; set aside. Prepare Sweet Dough. If making 24 rolls, divide dough in 2 portions. On a floured board, roll each portion to a 12-inch circle. Brush with melted butter or margarine. Cut circle in 12 pie-shaped wedges. Roll up each wedge, beginning at wide end. Place 2 to 3 inches apart, point-sides down, on greased baking sheet. Cover and let rise in a warm place 30 to 40 minutes or until doubled in bulk. Preheat oven to 375F (190C). Bake in preheated oven 12 to 15 minutes or until browned. Remove from baking sheet. Serve immediately or cool on a rack.

How to Shape Rolls

1/**For Pan Rolls:** Shape small pieces of dough into balls by rolling edges under to form smooth tops. Pinch dough together at the bottom of each ball. Arrange balls of dough in a greased baking dish.

2/**For Quick Cloverleaf Rolls:** Shape balls of dough as for Pan Rolls. Place dough in greased muffin cups. Using scissors, snip an **X** 1/2 inch deep in top of each roll.

3/**For Bowknot Rolls:** Roll dough pieces into 9- to 10-inch ropes, working from center of each rope toward ends. Tie each rope in a loose knot. Place rolls 2 to 3 inches apart on greased baking sheets.

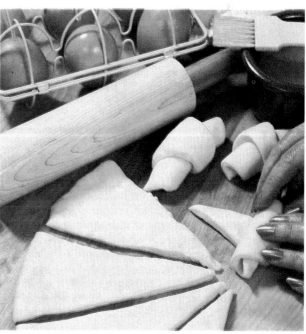

4/**For Crescent Rolls:** Roll dough to a 12-inch circle. Brush with melted butter or margarine. Cut in 12 pie-shaped wedges. Roll up, beginning at wide end of each wedge. Place, point-sides down, on greased baking sheets.

Breads, Pasta & Rice 413

Merry Christmas Loaves

YIELD	4 loaves	2 loaves
INGREDIENTS		
candied mixed fruit and peel	1 cup	1/2 cup
raisins	1 cup	1/2 cup
rum	1/4 cup	2 tablespoons
Sweet Dough, page 408	large recipe	small recipe
ground cardamom	2 teaspoons	1 teaspoon
chopped almonds	1/4 cup	2 tablespoons
grated lemon peel	2 tablespoons	1 tablespoon
almond extract	1/2 teaspoon	1/4 teaspoon
Vanilla Cake Glaze, page 464	large recipe	small recipe
PIE PLATES	4 (9-inch) pie plates or cake pans	2 (9-inch) pie plates or cake pans
RISING TIME (in pie plates)	40 to 60 minutes	40 to 60 minutes
TIME IN 375F (190C) OVEN	25 to 30 minutes	25 to 30 minutes
COOLING TIME	2 hours	2 hours

Grease 2 or 4 (9-inch) pie plates or cake pans; set aside. In a small bowl, combine candied fruit and peel, raisins and rum; set aside to soak. Prepare Sweet Dough, adding cardamom to yeast-flour mixture. Stir candied-fruit mixture, almonds, lemon peel and almond extract into dough before last addition of flour. Continue following directions for Sweet Dough. Divide large recipe of dough in 4 portions and small recipe in 2 portions. Shape each portion into a ball, rolling edges under to form smooth top. Place, smooth-sides up, in greased pie plates or cake pans. Cover and let rise in a warm place 40 to 60 minutes or until doubled in bulk. Preheat oven to 375F (190C). Bake in preheated oven 25 to 30 minutes or until browned. Loaf should sound hollow when tapped with your finger. Remove from pie plates or cake pans. Cool on racks 2 hours. Frost with Vanilla Cake Glaze.

Hot Cross Buns

YIELD	36 buns	18 buns
INGREDIENTS		
Sweet Dough, page 408	large recipe	small recipe
ground cinnamon	2 teaspoons	1 teaspoon
ground nutmeg	1/2 teaspoon	1/4 teaspoon
currants	1 cup	1/2 cup
grated orange peel	4 teaspoons	2 teaspoons
egg white, slightly beaten	1	1/2
Powdered-Sugar Glaze, page 408	large recipe	small recipe
BAKING SHEETS	2 baking sheets	1 baking sheet
RISING TIME (on baking sheet)	30 to 40 minutes	30 to 40 minutes
TIME IN 375F (190C) OVEN	15 to 17 minutes	15 to 17 minutes
COOLING TIME	25 minutes	25 minutes

Grease 1 or 2 baking sheets; set aside. Prepare Sweet Dough, adding cinnamon and nutmeg to yeast-flour mixture. Stir currants and orange peel into dough before last addition of flour. Continue following directions for Sweet Dough. Divide large recipe of dough in 6 portions and small recipe in 3 portions. Divide each portion in 6 pieces. Shape each piece into a ball, rolling edges under to form smooth top. Gently pinch dough together at bottom of each ball. Place buns, smooth-sides up, on greased baking sheet. Arrange on each baking sheet in 6 rows of 3 buns touching. Cover and let rise in a warm place 30 to 40 minutes or until almost doubled in bulk. Preheat oven to 375F (190C). Gently brush rolls with egg white. Bake in preheated oven 15 to 17 minutes or until browned. Remove from baking sheet. Cool on a rack 25 minutes. Drizzle Powdered-Sugar Glaze in a cross shape on each roll. Serve warm.

How to Make Merry Christmas Loaves

1/In a small bowl, soak candied fruit and peel and raisins in rum while preparing Sweet Dough. Add cardamom to yeast-flour mixture. Stir candied-fruit mixture, almonds, lemon peel and almond extract into dough before last addition of flour.

2/After dough has risen, divide large recipe of dough into 4 portions and small recipe into 2 portions. Shape each portion of dough into a large ball by rolling edges under to form a smooth top. Place, smooth-side up, in greased pie plate or cake pan.

3/Cover dough with a clean towel and place over a pan of very hot water in a cold oven to rise. Check to see if dough has risen enough to bake by gently making an indentation in the side of loaf. If your fingerprint remains, loaf is ready to bake. Do not test in center of loaf or you will have an indentation in the finished loaf.

4/Remove loaves and pan of water from oven. Preheat oven to 375F (190C). Stagger loaves on oven racks so they are not directly above or below each other. Bake 25 to 30 minutes or until browned. Loaf will sound hollow when tapped. Cool on a rack. Frost with Vanilla Cake Glaze, page 464. Cut with a serrated knife to serve.

Croissants   Photo on page 396.

YIELD	32 croissants	16 croissants
INGREDIENTS		
active dry yeast	2 (1/4-oz.) pkgs.	1 (1/4-oz.) pkg.
warm water (110F, 45C)	2/3 cup	1/3 cup
milk	2-1/2 cups	1-1/4 cups
all-purpose flour	7 cups	3-1/2 cups
cornstarch	2/3 cup	1/3 cup
sugar	1/4 cup	2 tablespoons
salt	1 teaspoon	1/2 teaspoon
shortening	1/2 cup	1/4 cup
all-purpose flour	1 cup	1/2 cup
butter or margarine, softened	2 cups	1 cup
BOWL (for dough rising)	4-qt. bowl	2-qt. bowl
SAUCEPAN	1-qt. saucepan	1-qt. saucepan
BOWL (for dough mixing)	4-qt. bowl	2-qt. bowl
BAKING SHEETS	4 baking sheets	2 baking sheets
TIME AT MEDIUM HIGH	5 to 7 minutes	3 to 4 minutes
KNEADING TIME	8 to 11 minutes	5 to 8 minutes
RISING TIME (in bowl)	45 to 60 minutes	45 to 60 minutes
REFRIGERATE	30 minutes	30 minutes
RISING TIME (on baking sheets)	30 minutes	30 minutes
TIME IN 375F (190C) OVEN	30 to 35 minutes	30 to 35 minutes

Grease a bowl for dough rising, see size in chart above; set aside. In a measuring cup, combine yeast and warm water; set aside. In a 1-quart saucepan, heat milk over Medium-High heat for time in chart above or until lukewarm (110F, 45C). In a bowl for dough mixing, see size in chart above, combine first amount of flour, cornstarch, sugar and salt; mix well. Add warm milk, dissolved yeast and shortening to flour mixture; mix well. Gradually stir in enough of second amount of flour to make a soft dough. Turn out dough on a floured board; coat with flour. Knead dough on floured board for time in chart above or until smooth and elastic. Place dough in greased bowl, turning dough once to grease top. Cover and let rise in a warm place 45 to 60 minutes or until doubled in bulk. Punch down dough. Divide large recipe of dough in 2 portions. On floured board, roll each portion of dough to a 16″ x 12″ rectangle. Spread with 1/3 cup butter or margarine. Fold one-third of dough, starting at 12-inch side, over center third. Fold remaining third over top. Gently pinch together open edges to seal. Roll dough again to a 16″ x 12″ rectangle. Spread with 1/3 cup butter or margarine. Fold and seal as before. Repeat rolling and spreading once more. Fold and seal as before. Cut crosswise in 2 portions. Seal edges. Wrap each portion in plastic wrap. Refrigerate 30 minutes. On floured board, roll each portion of chilled dough to a 14-inch circle. Cut circle in 8 pie-shaped wedges. Roll up each wedge, beginning at wide end. Place, point-sides down, 2 inches apart on ungreased baking sheets. Curve ends slightly into crescent shapes. Cover and let rise in warm place 30 minutes or until almost doubled in bulk. Preheat oven to 375F (190C). Bake in preheated oven 30 to 35 minutes or until deep golden brown. Remove from baking sheets. Serve immediately or cool on racks.

Basic Quick Bread

YIELD	2 to 4 loaves	1 or 2 loaves
INGREDIENTS		
all-purpose flour	4 cups	2 cups
granulated sugar	1 cup	1/2 cup
packed brown sugar	1 cup	1/2 cup
baking powder	2 tablespoons	1 tablespoon
salt	1 teaspoon	1/2 teaspoon
ground spice	2 teaspoons	1 teaspoon
shortening	1 cup	1/2 cup
eggs	4	2
mashed fruit or fruit sauce	2 cups	1 cup
lemon juice	2 teaspoons	1 teaspoon
additional ingredient	1-1/2 cups	3/4 cup
LOAF PANS	2 (9" x 5" x 3") loaf pans or 4 (7-1/2" x 3-1/2" x 2") loaf pans	9" x 5" x 3" loaf pan or 2 (7-1/2" x 3-1/2" x 2") loaf pans
MIXER BOWL	3-qt. bowl	1-1/2-qt. bowl
BEATING TIME AT LOW SPEED (dry ingredients)	50 to 60 seconds	25 to 35 seconds
BEATING TIME AT LOW SPEED (liquid ingredients added)	30 seconds	30 seconds
BEATING TIME AT MEDIUM SPEED	30 to 60 seconds	20 to 30 seconds
STANDING TIME (before baking)	20 to 30 minutes	20 to 30 minutes
TIME IN 350F (175C) OVEN: 9" x 5" x 3" loaf pan 7-1/2" x 3-1/2" x 2" loaf pan	60 to 65 minutes 50 to 55 minutes	60 to 65 minutes 50 to 55 minutes
COOLING TIME: 9" x 5" x 3" loaf pan 7-1/2" x 3-1/2" x 2" loaf pan	3 hours 1-1/2 to 2 hours	3 hours 1-1/2 to 2 hours

Grease and flour loaf pans, see number and size in chart above. In a mixer bowl, see size in chart above, beat flour, granulated sugar, brown sugar, baking powder, salt and spice at low speed of an electric mixer for time in chart above to blend. Add shortening, eggs, mashed fruit or fruit sauce and lemon juice. Beat at low speed of mixer 30 seconds to blend. Turn mixer to medium speed. Beat for time in chart above, just until blended. Do not overbeat. Scrape sides of bowl often. By hand, stir in additional ingredient; mix well. Spread batter evenly in prepared pans. Let batter stand in pans 20 to 30 minutes. Preheat oven to 350F (175C). Bake in preheated oven for time in chart above or until a skewer inserted in center of loaf comes out clean. Cool 10 minutes on a rack. To loosen, carefully run a sharp knife around edges of pan. Invert and remove bread from pan. Cool on rack for time in chart above. Wrap loaf in foil or clear plastic wrap; refrigerate. Bread will slice better if refrigerated overnight. Drizzle with Powdered-Sugar Glaze, page 408, before serving, if desired.

Suggested Combinations

Pumpkin-Date Quick Bread: Use pumpkin-pie spice for spice. Use canned pumpkin for mashed fruit. Use chopped pitted dates and chopped nuts for additional ingredients.

Apple-Raisin Quick Bread: Use cinnamon and nutmeg for spices. Use applesauce for fruit sauce. Use raisins and shredded orange peel for additional ingredients.

Tropical Banana Quick Bread: Use ginger for spice. Use mashed ripe banana for fruit. Use well-drained crushed pineapple, patted dry on paper towels, and flaked coconut for additional ingredients.

Tips for Quick Breads

- A large crack may develop in the top crust of quick bread that is baked immediately after mixing. Allow the batter to stand in the loaf pan at room temperature 20 to 30 minutes before baking. This produces a loaf with a more rounded top and much smaller crack on top.

- Quick bread seems moister and can be sliced thinner if it is cooled, wrapped in foil or clear plastic wrap and stored overnight. Quick bread will keep up to a week in the refrigerator. It freezes up to 3 months.

- For a pretty hostess gift, wrap small loaves in colored plastic wrap and tie with ribbon.

Basic Muffins

YIELD	12 to 14 muffins	6 or 7 muffins
INGREDIENTS		
all-purpose flour	2 cups	1 cup
sugar	1/2 cup	1/4 cup
baking powder	1 tablespoon	1-1/2 teaspoons
salt	1/2 teaspoon	1/4 teaspoon
grated citrus peel	1 teaspoon	1/2 teaspoon
ground spice	1/2 teaspoon	1/4 teaspoon
milk	3/4 cup	6 tablespoons
egg or egg yolk	1 egg	1 egg yolk
vegetable oil	1/3 cup	3 tablespoons
additional ingredient	1 cup	1/2 cup
toppings, see suggestions below		
BOWL	2-qt. bowl	1-qt. bowl
MUFFIN PAN	12 to 14 (2-1/2-inch) muffin cups	6 or 7 (2-1/2-inch) muffin cups
TIME IN 400F (205C) OVEN	20 to 22 minutes	20 to 22 minutes
COOLING TIME	5 minutes	5 minutes

Preheat oven to 400F (205C). Grease bottoms of muffin-pan cups or line with paper bake cups; set aside. In a medium bowl, combine flour, sugar, baking powder, salt, citrus peel and spice; mix well. In a measuring cup, beat milk, egg or egg yolk and oil with a fork until frothy. Make a well in center of dry ingredients. Pour egg mixture into well. Quickly stir with a fork or spoon just until flour mixture is moistened; batter will be lumpy. Gently fold in additional ingredient. Gently spoon batter into prepared muffin cups, filling each two-thirds full. Bake in preheated oven 20 to 22 minutes or until a wooden pick inserted in center of muffins comes out clean. Immediately remove from pan. Cool on a rack 5 minutes with muffins tilted in pan. Serve warm.

Suggested Combinations
Blueberry or Cranberry Muffins: Use lemon peel. Use pumpkin-pie spice for spice. Use fresh or frozen whole blueberries or chopped fresh or frozen cranberries for additional ingredient. Dip tops of warm muffins in melted butter or margarine, then in sugar.

Apple-Orange Muffins: Use orange peel. Use cinnamon for spice. Substitute orange juice for half of milk. Use grated apple and chopped nuts for additional ingredients. Spread tops of warm muffins with whipped cream cheese, then sprinkle with chopped nuts.

Note: To make miniature muffins, spoon batter into greased 1-3/4-inch muffin cups. Bake in preheated 400F (205C) oven 8 to 10 minutes or until a wooden pick inserted in center of muffins comes out clean. Large recipe makes 30 to 36 small muffins; small recipe makes 15 to 18 muffins. Cool 2 minutes.

Tips for Muffins

- Stir liquid and dry ingredients together vigorously with a fork or spoon, but only until dry ingredients are moistened. This should take 10 to 20 seconds. Batter should be lumpy. Overstirred batter makes muffins with very high peaks.

- Use a large spoon to scoop up enough batter for 1 muffin all in one motion. Rest the spoonful of dough in the muffin cup and gently push batter off with another spoon. Do not add additional batter to the muffin.

- If muffins must stand a few minutes before serving, tilt muffins in muffin cups so they stay warm without becoming soggy on the bottom.

- In our testing, muffins baked in paper bake cups had more evenly rounded tops.

How to Make Basic Muffins

1/With a large spoonful of batter resting on the muffin cup, gently push batter into cup using the back of another spoon. Do not add more batter to muffins or they will form pointed tops during baking.

2/Insert a wooden pick into center of muffins and other quick breads to test for doneness. If muffins are done, pick will come out clean.

Refrigerated Cereal Muffins

YIELD	28 to 32 muffins	14 to 16 muffins
INGREDIENTS		
lemon juice	2 tablespoons	1 tablespoon
milk	2 cups	1 cup
boiling water	1 cup	1/2 cup
granola or whole-bran cereal	3 cups	1-1/2 cups
vegetable oil	1/2 cup	1/4 cup
eggs, beaten	2	1
all-purpose flour	2-1/2 cups	1-1/4 cups
sugar	1 cup	1/2 cup
baking powder	2 teaspoons	1 teaspoon
baking soda	2 teaspoons	1 teaspoon
salt	1 teaspoon	1/2 teaspoon
ground cinnamon	2 teaspoons	1 teaspoon
ground nutmeg	1 teaspoon	1/2 teaspoon
MUFFIN PAN	2-1/2-inch muffin cups	2-1/2-inch muffin cups
TIME IN 400F (205C) OVEN	20 to 22 minutes	20 to 22 minutes
COOLING TIME	5 minutes	5 minutes

In a measuring cup, stir lemon juice into milk; set aside. Pour boiling water into a large bowl. Sprinkle cereal into water. Stir until well-moistened. Stir in milk mixture, oil and eggs; mix well. In a medium bowl, combine flour, sugar, baking powder, baking soda, salt, cinnamon and nutmeg; mix well. Add to cereal mixture. Quickly stir with a fork or spoon just until flour mixture is moistened; batter will be lumpy. Cover and refrigerate up to 3 weeks. Bake muffins, as needed, in greased or paper-lined 2-1/2-inch muffin cups filled two-thirds full. Bake in preheated 400F (205C) oven 20 to 22 minutes or until a wooden pick inserted in center of muffins comes out clean. Immediately remove from pan. Cool on a rack 5 minutes with muffins tilted in pan. Serve warm.

Biscuits

YIELD	9 or 10 biscuits	4 or 5 biscuits
INGREDIENTS		
lemon juice	2 teaspoons	1 teaspoon
milk	3/4 cup	6 tablespoons
all-purpose flour	2 cups	1 cup
baking powder	1 tablespoon	1-1/2 teaspoons
sugar	2 teaspoons	1 teaspoon
salt	1/2 teaspoon	1/4 teaspoon
baking soda	1/4 teaspoon	1/8 teaspoon
shortening	1/3 cup	3 tablespoons
BAKING SHEET	baking sheet	baking sheet
TIME IN 450F (230C) OVEN	12 to 14 minutes	12 to 14 minutes

Preheat oven to 450F (230C). In a measuring cup, stir lemon juice into milk; set aside. In a medium bowl, combine flour, baking powder, sugar, salt and baking soda; mix well. Cut in shortening with a pastry blender or 2 knives until most of mixture resembles peas. Add milk mixture to flour mixture. Quickly stir with a fork just until dough clings together. Turn out dough on a floured board; coat with flour. With your fingertips, gently knead dough on floured board 25 to 30 times. Gently roll out dough 1/2 inch thick. Cut with a floured 2-1/2-inch biscuit cutter. Cut straight down with cutter; do not twist cutter or biscuits will be lopsided. Place on an ungreased baking sheet. Bake in preheated oven 12 to 14 minutes or until golden brown. Serve warm with honey, if desired.

Variation
Drop Biscuits: Follow directions above for mixing biscuits. Do not knead. Drop dough from a tablespoon in mounds, 1 per serving in chart above, on an ungreased baking sheet. Bake as above.

Popovers

SERVINGS	6	3
INGREDIENTS		
eggs	2	1
milk	1 cup	1/2 cup
vegetable oil	2 tablespoons	1 tablespoon
all-purpose flour	1 cup	1/2 cup
salt	1/2 teaspoon	1/4 teaspoon
CUSTARD CUPS	6 (6-oz.) cups	3 (6-oz.) cups
BLENDING TIME AT LOW SPEED	30 to 45 seconds	20 to 30 seconds
TIME IN 450F (230C) OVEN	15 minutes	15 minutes
TIME IN 375F (190C) OVEN	30 minutes	30 minutes
STANDING TIME (in oven)	15 minutes	15 minutes

Preheat oven to 450F (230C). Generously grease 3 or 6 (6-ounce) custard cups. Place custard cups on a baking sheet; set aside. Do not preheat custard cups. In a blender, combine all ingredients. Cover and process at low speed for time in chart above or until smooth. Stop blender and scrape down sides once. Pour batter into greased custard cups. Bake in preheated oven 15 minutes. Reduce oven temperature to 375F (190C). Bake 30 minutes longer or until puffed and golden brown. Turn off oven. Prick each popover twice with tines of a large fork. Let popovers stand in oven with door closed 15 minutes. Remove from custard cups at once; serve warm. Popovers will be hollow in center with a crisp outside shell.

How to Make Biscuits

1/Cut shortening into flour mixture until most of mixture resembles peas. Add milk mixture; stir with a fork just until dough clings together. Turn dough over on a floured board to coat with flour. Dough will be sticky. Knead dough *gently,* using your fingertips, 25 to 30 times. Do not knead vigorously or biscuits will be tough.

2/Using a rolling pin, gently roll out dough on a floured board until 1/2 inch thick. Dip a 2-1/2-inch biscuit cutter in flour. Cut straight down into dough. Do not twist cutter or biscuits will be lopsided. Cut circles of dough as close together as possible. Roll scraps again and cut into more biscuits. These biscuits will be tougher than first batch.

Cornbread

SERVINGS	8 to 10	4 or 5
INGREDIENTS		
all-purpose flour	1 cup	1/2 cup
yellow cornmeal	1 cup	1/2 cup
sugar	2 tablespoons	1 tablespoon
baking powder	4 teaspoons	2 teaspoons
salt	1/2 teaspoon	1/4 teaspoon
eggs	2	1
milk	1 cup	1/2 cup
vegetable oil	1/4 cup	2 tablespoons
BAKING PAN OR MUFFIN PAN	8-inch-square baking pan or 16 (2-1/2-inch) muffin cups	8 (2-1/2-inch) muffin cups
BOWL	2-qt. bowl	1-qt. bowl
TIME IN 425F (220C) OVEN:		
square pan	22 to 25 minutes	
muffin pan	12 to 15 minutes	12 to 15 minutes
COOLING TIME	5 to 10 minutes	5 to 10 minutes

Preheat oven to 425F (220C). Grease a baking pan or muffin cups, see size and number in chart above; set aside. In a bowl, see size in chart above, combine flour, cornmeal, sugar, baking powder and salt; mix well. Make a well in center of dry ingredients. Add eggs, milk and oil to well. Stir with a fork or spoon to moisten, then stir vigorously 30 seconds just until blended. Do not overbeat. Batter may be slightly lumpy. Pour into greased pan. Or, spoon batter into greased muffin cups, filling two-thirds full. Bake in preheated oven for time in chart above or until a wooden pick inserted in center of cornbread comes out clean. Cool on a rack 5 to 10 minutes with muffins tilted in pan. Serve warm.

Waffles

SERVINGS	4 to 6	2 or 3
INGREDIENTS		
lemon juice	2 tablespoons	1 tablespoon
milk	1-1/2 cups	3/4 cup
all-purpose flour	2 cups	1 cup
sugar	2 tablespoons	1 tablespoon
baking powder	2 teaspoons	1 teaspoon
baking soda	1 teaspoon	1/2 teaspoon
salt	1/4 teaspoon	1/8 teaspoon
eggs	2	1
vegetable oil	6 tablespoons	3 tablespoons
vanilla extract	1 teaspoon	1/2 teaspoon
MIXER BOWL	1-1/2-qt. bowl	1-1/2-qt. bowl
WAFFLE IRON	waffle iron	waffle iron
BEATING TIME AT HIGH SPEED	2-1/2 minutes	2-1/2 minutes
BEATING TIME AT LOW SPEED	30 seconds	15 seconds
BEATING TIME AT MEDIUM SPEED	30 to 45 seconds	15 to 20 seconds

In a measuring cup, stir lemon juice into milk; set aside. In a medium bowl, combine flour, sugar, baking powder, baking soda and salt; set aside. In a 1-1/2-quart mixer bowl, beat eggs at high speed of an electric mixer for 2-1/2 minutes or until light. Add oil, vanilla, flour mixture and milk mixture. Beat at low speed of mixer for time in chart above to blend. Turn mixer to medium speed. Beat for time in chart above or just until smooth. Prepare waffle iron according to manufacturer's directions. Using amount of batter recommended by manufacturer, bake waffles according to manufacturer's directions. Serve hot with butter or margarine and maple syrup or Basic Breakfast Fruit Syrup, below.

Basic Breakfast Fruit Syrup

YIELD	4 cups	2 cups
INGREDIENTS		
prepared pureed fruit, see suggestions below	4 cups	2 cups
sugar	2 cups	1 cup
fruit juice	1 cup	1/2 cup
whole spice	4 teaspoons	2 teaspoons
citrus peel	2 (3" x 1/2") pieces	1 (3" x 1/2") piece
HEAVY DUTCH OVEN	5-qt. Dutch oven	3-qt. saucepan
TIME AT MEDIUM	25 to 30 minutes	10 to 15 minutes

In a blender or food processor fitted with a steel blade, process fruit until pureed. Process fruit for large recipe in 2 batches. Measure fruit, see amount in chart above. In a heavy Dutch oven, see size in chart above, combine fruit puree, sugar, fruit juice, spice and citrus peel; mix well. Bring to a boil over High heat, stirring constantly. Reduce heat to Medium. Simmer, uncovered, for time in chart above or until syrup is thick, stirring frequently. Remove peel and spice. Serve warm over waffles or pancakes. Cover and refrigerate leftover syrup up to 2 weeks.

Suggested Combinations

Breakfast Peach Syrup: Use sliced, peeled, fresh or thawed, frozen, dry-pack peaches for fruit. Use orange juice for fruit juice. Use crystallized ginger for spice. Use orange peel.

Breakfast Strawberry Syrup: Use fresh or thawed, frozen, dry-pack strawberries for fruit. Use pineapple juice for fruit juice. Use cinnamon sticks for spice. Use lemon peel.

Breakfast Mixed-Fruit Syrup: Use fresh or thawed, frozen, dry-pack mixed fruit for fruit. Use apricot nectar for fruit juice. Use whole allspice for spice. Use orange peel.

Note: If using frozen fruit, use 2 (16-ounce) packages for large recipe or 1 (16-ounce) package for small recipe. When measuring whole spices, 1 (2-inch) cinnamon stick equals 1 teaspoon.

Waffles with Breakfast Strawberry Syrup

Basic Pancakes

YIELD	20 pancakes (8 to 10 servings)	10 pancakes (4 or 5 servings)
INGREDIENTS		
all-purpose flour	2 cups	1 cup
sugar	1/4 cup	2 tablespoons
baking powder	2 tablespoons	1 tablespoon
ground spice	1 teaspoon	1/2 teaspoon
baking soda	1/2 teaspoon	1/4 teaspoon
salt	1/2 teaspoon	1/4 teaspoon
eggs	2	1
milk	1-1/2 cups	3/4 cup
flavored yogurt	1 (8-oz.) carton	1/2 cup
vegetable oil	2 tablespoons	1 tablespoon
additional ingredient	2 cups	1 cup
GRIDDLE OR HEAVY SKILLET	12-inch griddle or skillet	12-inch griddle or skillet
TIME AT MEDIUM HIGH (first side)	2 to 3 minutes	2 to 3 minutes
TIME AT MEDIUM HIGH (second side)	2 to 3 minutes	2 to 3 minutes

In a medium bowl, combine flour, sugar, baking powder, spice, baking soda and salt; mix well and set aside. In another bowl, whisk eggs until well-beaten. Whisk in milk, yogurt and oil until smooth. Make a well in center of dry ingredients. Pour egg mixture into well. Quickly stir with a spoon just until flour mixture is moistened; batter will be lumpy. Preheat a griddle or heavy skillet over Medium-High heat until a drop of water sizzles on it. Brush griddle with oil. Pour 1/4 cup batter for each pancake onto griddle. Sprinkle 1 to 2 tablespoons additional ingredient on each pancake. Cook on first side 2 to 3 minutes or until underside is golden brown and surface is bubbly. Turn and cook 2 to 3 minutes or until second side is golden brown. Brush griddle with oil and cook remaining batter. Serve according to suggestions below.

Suggested Combinations

Blueberry-Lemon Pancakes: Use cinnamon for spice. Use lemon yogurt. Use fresh or drained, thawed, frozen blueberries for additional ingredient. Serve with additional lemon yogurt and blueberries.

Banana-Berry Pancakes: Use ground dried lemon peel for spice. Use banana yogurt. Use chopped pecans and flaked coconut for additional ingredients. Serve with fresh strawberries, banana slices and whipped cream.

Tips for Non-Stick Waffles

The mess caused by a waffle that sticks to the waffle iron is a cook's nightmare. There are no sure cures, but these tips should help avoid most problems.

- Season the waffle iron according to the manufacturer's directions before using. This takes time, but it is very important.
- Lightly oil the waffle grids before each use.
- To bake big batches of waffles, oil grids occasionally between waffles.
- Use waffle recipes that include at least 3 tablespoons oil, shortening, butter or margarine for each cup of flour.
- Do not lift the waffle-iron lid until steaming stops. Lifting the lid before the waffle is baked may separate the batter, leaving half on the top grid and half on the bottom.
- Use a fork to lift the baked waffle gently off the grid.

How to Make Surprise French Toast

1/Cut French bread in slices 1-1/4 inches thick. Cut a pocket in 1 side of each bread slice, cutting to, but not through, other side. Spoon a mixture of preserves and chopped nuts into pocket.

2/Place stuffed bread slices in a pie plate. Pour a mixture of egg, milk and fruit preserves evenly over bread. Cover and refrigerate 1 hour or overnight. In a skillet, brown stuffed bread slices in hot butter or margarine to serve.

Surprise French Toast

SERVINGS	2 to 4	1 or 2
INGREDIENTS		
French-bread slices, 1-1/4 inches thick	4 slices	2 slices
fruit preserves	1/4 cup	2 tablespoons
chopped nuts	2 tablespoons	1 tablespoon
eggs	2	1
fruit preserves	2 tablespoons	1 tablespoon
milk	1/2 cup	1/4 cup
butter or margarine	2 tablespoons	1 tablespoon
fresh fruit, powdered sugar	to garnish	to garnish
PIE PLATE	10-inch pie plate	7-inch pie plate
HEAVY SKILLET	11-inch skillet	8-inch skillet
REFRIGERATE	1 hour or overnight	1 hour or overnight
TIME AT MEDIUM HIGH	4 to 6 minutes	4 to 6 minutes

Cut a pocket in 1 side of each bread slice, cutting to, but not through, other side. In a small bowl, combine first amount of preserves and nuts. Stuff some preserve mixture into each pocket. Place bread slices in a single layer in a pie plate, see size in chart above; set aside. In a small bowl, whisk together eggs and second amount of preserves. Whisk in milk. Pour egg mixture evenly over bread. Cover and refrigerate 1 hour or overnight until most of liquid is absorbed. At serving time, place butter or margarine in a heavy skillet, see size in chart above. Heat over Medium-High heat until a drop of water sizzles on it. Add bread slices. Cook for time in chart above or until browned, turning once. Serve hot, topped with fresh fruit and powdered sugar.

Suggested Preserves and Fruit: peach, strawberry, raspberry, pineapple, apricot.

Basic Fettuccine Alfredo Plus

SERVINGS	6 to 8	3 or 4
INGREDIENTS		
bacon, cut in 1-inch pieces	8 slices	4 slices
bacon drippings	1/3 cup	3 tablespoons
chopped or sliced vegetables or meat	4 cups	2 cups
snipped fresh herbs OR	1/4 cup	2 tablespoons
dried leaf herbs	4 teaspoons	2 teaspoons
fettuccine, linguine or spaghetti	1 lb. uncooked	8 oz. uncooked
milk	2 cups	1 cup
cream cheese	1 (8-oz.) pkg.	1/2 (8-oz.) pkg.
grated Parmesan cheese	1 cup	1/2 cup
freshly ground pepper	1 teaspoon	1/2 teaspoon
grated Parmesan cheese	1/2 cup	1/4 cup
garnish, see suggestions below		
SKILLET	10-inch skillet	8-inch skillet
HEAVY SAUCEPAN	1-1/2-qt. saucepan	1-qt. saucepan
TIME AT MEDIUM HIGH (bacon)	10 to 12 minutes	5 to 6 minutes
TIME AT MEDIUM HIGH (vegetables, meat)	4 to 6 minutes	3 to 4 minutes
TIME AT MEDIUM LOW	7 to 8 minutes	3 to 4 minutes

In a skillet, see size in chart above, cook bacon over Medium-High heat for time in chart above or until crisp, stirring often. Remove bacon with a slotted spoon and drain on paper towels; set aside. Reserve in skillet amount of drippings listed in chart above. Cook vegetables, meat and herbs in reserved drippings for time in chart above or until vegetables are crisp-tender, stirring often. Do not overcook. Cook pasta according to package directions; drain. In a heavy saucepan, see size in chart above, bring milk almost to a boil over Medium-High heat. Reduce heat to Medium-Low. Add cream cheese. Whisk constantly for time in chart above until melted and smooth. Mixture will appear curdled as cheese melts. Stir in first amount of Parmesan cheese and pepper. Arrange hot cooked pasta in a large serving bowl or on a large platter. Pour vegetable mixture over pasta; toss to mix well. Pour cream sauce over pasta; toss to mix well. Sprinkle with bacon. To serve, sprinkle second amount of Parmesan cheese on very hot appetizer plates. Serve pasta mixture over cheese. Garnish according to suggestions below.

Suggested Combinations
Fettuccine Provençal: Use sliced mushrooms, chopped, seeded, peeled tomatoes and chopped shallots for vegetables. Use basil and minced garlic for herbs. Garnish with snipped chives.
Fettuccine Straw & Hay: Omit bacon. Use butter or margarine instead of bacon drippings. Use sliced mushrooms, thawed frozen peas and cooked-ham strips for vegetables and meat. Use oregano and summer savory for herbs. Use half green and half white pasta. Garnish with paprika.

Tips for Pasta

- To cook pasta, add 2 teaspoons vegetable oil to a large pot filled two-thirds full with hot water. Add salt, if desired. Bring to a boil over High heat. Add pasta, stirring to separate. Reduce heat to Medium High. Boil vigorously just until tender, stirring occasionally. Drain in a large sieve. Rinse under hot water, if desired.

- Most pasta approximately doubles in bulk after cooking.

- For other pasta recipes, see: Basic Macaroni & Cheese, page 268; Basic Quick Macaroni & Cheese, page 269; Cheese-Stuffed Manicotti, page 267; Creamy Pasta Casserole, page 266; Basic Sweet-Sour Pasta Salad, page 366; Basic Macaroni & Cheese Salad, page 366; Spaghetti & Meatballs, page 150; Lasagne, page 154; Basic Meat & Macaroni Bake, page 84; Basic Meat & Noodle Casserole, page 82; Onion-Braised Shanks & Noodles, page 102; Seafood Shells au Gratin, page 208; Basic Tuna-Noodle Casserole, page 210; Chicken & Noodles, page 163; and Creamy Chicken & Macaroni Casserole, page 166.

Fettuccine Provençal

Basic Oven Rice

SERVINGS	4 to 6	2 or 3
INGREDIENTS		
chopped vegetables	1 cup	1/2 cup
butter or margarine	2 tablespoons	1 tablespoon
dried leaf herbs	2 teaspoons	1 teaspoon
broth	1 (14-1/2-oz.) can	1 cup
dry white wine or water	1/4 cup	2 tablespoons
long-grain rice	1 cup uncooked	1/2 cup uncooked
SAUCEPAN	1-1/2-qt. saucepan	1-qt. saucepan
CASSEROLE	2-qt. casserole	1-qt. casserole
TIME AT MEDIUM HIGH	5 to 6 minutes	4 to 5 minutes
TIME IN 350F (175C) OVEN	30 minutes	30 minutes
STANDING TIME	5 minutes	5 minutes

Do not preheat oven. In a saucepan, see size in chart above, cook vegetables in butter or margarine over Medium-High heat for time in chart above or until tender, stirring often. Stir in herbs, broth and wine or water. Bring to a boil over High heat. Place rice in a casserole, see size in chart above. Pour vegetable mixture over rice; mix well. Cover. Bake in a 350F (175C) oven 30 minutes or until rice is tender and liquid is absorbed. Fluff with fork. Cover and let stand 5 minutes.

Suggested Combinations
Golden Oven Rice: Use chopped onion and chopped celery for vegetables. Use rubbed sage and thyme for herbs. Use chicken broth.
Beefy Oven Rice: Use chopped carrot and chopped zucchini for vegetables. Use marjoram and dry mustard for herbs. Use beef broth.

Wild Rice Deluxe

SERVINGS	8	4
INGREDIENTS		
bacon, cut in 1-inch pieces	6 slices	3 slices
bacon drippings	1/4 cup	2 tablespoons
cooked wild rice	4 cups	2 cups
fresh mushroom slices	4 cups	2 cups
chopped vegetables	2 cups	1 cup
condensed cream soup	1 (10- to 11-oz.) can	1/2 (10- to 11-oz.) can (2/3 cup)
milk	1 soup can	1/2 soup can
snipped parsley	to garnish	to garnish
SKILLET	12-inch skillet	10-inch skillet
CASSEROLE	2-qt. casserole	1-qt. casserole
TIME AT MEDIUM HIGH (bacon)	8 to 10 minutes	6 to 8 minutes
TIME AT MEDIUM HIGH (vegetables)	7 to 8 minutes	5 to 6 minutes
TIME IN 350F (175C) OVEN	40 to 45 minutes	35 to 40 minutes

Do not preheat oven. In a skillet, see size in chart above, cook bacon over Medium-High heat for time in chart above or until crisp, stirring often. Remove bacon with a slotted spoon and drain on paper towels; set aside. Reserve in skillet amount of drippings listed in chart above. Place cooked wild rice in a casserole, see size in chart above; set aside. Cook mushrooms and chopped vegetables in reserved drippings over Medium-High heat for time in chart above or until tender, stirring often. Stir in soup and milk; mix well. Bring to a boil over High heat. Pour over wild rice; mix well. Bake in a 350F (175C) oven for time in chart above or until heated through. Garnish with bacon and parsley before serving.

Suggested Vegetables: onion, celery, carrot, green or red pepper, zucchini.
Suggested Soups: cream of mushroom, creamy chicken-mushroom, cream of onion.

Brown Rice & Vegetable Bake

SERVINGS	8 to 10	4 or 5
INGREDIENTS		
chopped onion	1 cup	1/2 cup
chopped green pepper	1 cup	1/2 cup
butter or margarine	1/4 cup	2 tablespoons
hot, cooked, coarsely chopped vegetables, well-drained	3 cups	1-1/2 cups
cooked brown rice	2 cups	1 cup
cottage cheese with chives	2 cups (1 lb.)	1 cup (8 oz.)
eggs, slightly beaten	4	2
sunflower kernels	1/4 cup	2 tablespoons
dried leaf marjoram	2 teaspoons	1 teaspoon
herb pepper	1 teaspoon	1/2 teaspoon
grated Parmesan cheese	1/2 cup	1/4 cup
paprika	to garnish	to garnish
SAUCEPAN	3-qt. saucepan	2-qt. saucepan
BAKING DISH	12" x 7" baking dish	9" x 5" x 3" loaf dish
TIME AT MEDIUM HIGH	7 to 8 minutes	6 to 7 minutes
TIME IN 350F (175C) OVEN	40 to 45 minutes	30 minutes
STANDING TIME	5 minutes	5 minutes

Do not preheat oven. In a saucepan, see size in chart above, cook onion and green pepper in butter or margarine over Medium-High heat for time in chart above or until tender, stirring frequently. Stir in vegetables, brown rice, cottage cheese, eggs, sunflower kernels, marjoram and herb pepper; mix well. Pour into a baking dish, see size in chart above. Sprinkle with Parmesan cheese and paprika. Bake in a 350F (175C) oven for time in chart above or until a knife inserted off center comes out clean. Let stand 5 minutes before cutting in squares to serve.

Suggested Vegetables: chopped Brussels sprouts and corn, chopped broccoli and cauliflower, or peas and carrots. To use chopped spinach, press cooked spinach in a sieve to remove as much water as possible.

Tips for Rice

● Regular long-grain white rice, long-grain brown rice and wild rice increase 3 to 4 times in volume after cooking.

● Quick-cooking white or brown rice doubles in volume after cooking.

● Regular converted white or brown rice triples in volume after cooking.

● For drier, fluffier rice, let stand in a covered saucepan 5 to 10 minutes after cooking.

● Follow package directions for proportions of rice to water and cooking times. They vary for each type of rice.

● For other rice recipes, see: Basic Rice Salad, page 364; Stir-Fried Roast & Rice, page 83; Mediterranean Lamb Soup, page 284; Chicken-Rice Soup, page 286; Florentine Rice Stuffing, page 204; Basic Rice Stuffing, page 190; and Basic Meat Pilaf, page 86.

Desserts

A terrific dessert provides the perfect ending for a successful meal. This chapter is full of delicious desserts. Each basic recipe allows you to choose the size and flavor you want. Practical new techniques show you how to save time, and no-guess directions guide you through every step.

Chilled Apricot Soufflé, page 500.

Desserts

Q. I know it is tricky to adjust cake recipes. How can I make a loaf cake when the recipe calls for a tube cake?
A. The Select-A-Size™ cake recipes in this chapter are versatile. Sponge cake, for instance, can be made as a tube cake, a loaf cake or a jelly roll. You can make standard-size upside-down cakes or little 7-inch rounds that serve four. Chocolate and yellow cakes allow even more choices. Master the basic recipe, and you can make tube cakes, layer cakes, cupcakes, cake bars or everyday serve-in-the-pan cakes. The pudding cakes and mix-in-the-pan cakes are especially good, and you can choose the size you need.

Q. Is it necessary to sift flour?
A. All-purpose flour is presifted, so you do not need to sift before measuring. Stir the flour in the canister, then spoon lightly into the measuring cup. Use a flatware knife or narrow spatula to level the top for accurate measurement. Cake flour must be sifted before measuring. Do not sift biscuit mix before measuring.

Q. Why are dry ingredients mixed with the electric mixer in the one-bowl cake recipes?
A. This is an easy way to mix dry ingredients thoroughly. In seconds, the mixer does the blending.

Q. Why do the charts include only some of the timings mentioned in the recipe for beating a mixture with an electric mixer?
A. Only significant timings, or those in which timings differ from the large-size to the small-size recipe, have been included. The chart calls your attention to important elements in each recipe.

Q. Are there special recipes for the holiday season?
A. Yes. You will find a wonderful pumpkin pie flavored with brandy, as well as an airy eggnog chiffon pie. We have included three flavors of fruitcake. Baking directions are given for large and small loaves, coffee-can cakes and cupcakes. There are two delicious versions of old-fashioned plum pudding, made easy with an up-to-date trick. Set the prepared pudding on a rack in a Dutch oven with hot water, then let your oven do the steaming. You will also find a recipe for cookie-press cookies that melt in your mouth.

Q. Are chiffon pies hard to make?
A. Chiffon pies are not hard to make if you follow the directions exactly. How-to photographs and instructions accompany the recipe for Basic Chiffon Pie, page 486, to show you special techniques. For inspiration, we offer five flavors: strawberry, lemon, orange, eggnog and coffee. To chill a chiffon pie, your refrigerator must be very cold. Don't load it with food, and don't open the door too often. Allow at least 8 hours chilling time.

Q. May I substitute a lattice-top crust in a two-crust pie?
A. No. Lattice-top crusts are best for small, juicy fruits such as cherries and berries. Make two-crust pies for apples, pears, peaches and apricots. Use the type of crust called for in the pie recipe. Do not substitute or you will alter thickening and cooking times.

Q. Why do you cool meringue shells, meringue pies and cheesecakes in the oven?
A. Baking meringue shells is more a drying than a heating process. Cooling the meringue shell in the oven helps dry the shell. A low baking temperature assures a light-colored, soft, crunchy meringue. Warm, just-baked meringue pies and cheesecakes are delicate. Moving them at this point is critical. You must cool them away from air drafts. We had best results in our test kitchens when we cooled meringue pies and cheesecakes in the oven with the door ajar. Cheesecakes may develop large cracks if cooled too quickly, especially in a draft. To prevent meringue pies from shrinking, cool first in the oven as directed, and finish cooling at room temperature away from drafts.

Q. Must I have a food thermometer to make custard sauce?
A. Our testing showed that a food thermometer provided a sure test for doneness. For another doneness test, dip a metal spoon into the custard sauce and pull it straight up; the sauce should thickly coat the spoon. When done, the sauce is creamy and slightly thickened; it thickens more when chilled. Many factors affect cooking time for Stirred Custard Sauce, page 436: how slowly the sauce is stirred; how fast the water is simmering; and how large the surface area is of the double boiler. Because of these factors, a food thermometer is a good investment if you make custard sauce often.

Q. I notice your pudding recipes call for yogurt. Isn't this unusual?
A. We have tried to use the most nutritious approach in each recipe. You will find recipes for yogurt ice cream and yogurt cheesecake. Both contain fewer calories than standard recipes made with whipping cream or sour cream. We have used less salt and sugar in the recipes. We have omitted butter or margarine in puddings and cream fillings. Our fruitcakes have less sugar but more dried fruit than many recipes, which produces a less-sweet—but delicious—fruitcake.

How to Make Vanilla Pudding

1/Mix sugar and cornstarch together in the saucepan to separate starch granules. This helps prevent lumps. Whisking pudding during cooking also promotes smoothness. Be sure milk mixture thickens and bubbles all over, not just around edges, to ensure proper thickening.

2/Whisk some hot pudding into beaten eggs to warm eggs before stirring them into a large amount of boiling pudding. Stirring cold eggs directly into pudding could cause curdling. Vary pudding flavor by adding baking pieces or peanut butter.

Vanilla Pudding

SERVINGS	6 servings (3-1/2 to 4 cups)	3 servings (1-3/4 to 2 cups)
INGREDIENTS		
eggs	2	1
sugar	2/3 cup	1/3 cup
cornstarch	2 tablespoons	1 tablespoon
milk	2 cups	1 cup
plain yogurt	1 cup	1/2 cup
vanilla extract	1 teaspoon	1/2 teaspoon
SAUCEPAN	1-1/2-qt. saucepan	1-qt. saucepan
TIME AT MEDIUM HIGH	14 to 16 minutes	8 to 10 minutes
TIME AT MEDIUM LOW	4 to 5 minutes	2 to 3 minutes

In a medium bowl, beat eggs; set aside. In a saucepan, see size in chart above, combine sugar and cornstarch until well-mixed. Whisk in milk. Cook over Medium-High heat for time in chart above or until thickened and bubbly all over, whisking constantly. Reduce heat to Medium Low. Whisk one-fourth of milk mixture into eggs. Whisk egg mixture into saucepan. Whisk over Medium-Low heat for time in chart above or until pudding thickens slightly more. Place yogurt in medium bowl. Stir one-fourth of pudding into yogurt. Fold yogurt mixture and vanilla into pudding. Pour into sherbet dishes. Refrigerate. Do not cover until pudding is chilled. Garnish with chopped nuts or fresh or canned fruit, if desired.

Variations
Chocolate Pudding: Stir in semisweet or milk chocolate pieces after egg mixture is cooked at Medium Low. Use 1 cup chocolate pieces for large recipe and 1/2 cup for small recipe. Stir until melted.
Butterscotch Pudding: Stir in butterscotch pieces after egg mixture is cooked at Medium Low. Use 1 cup butterscotch pieces for large recipe and 1/2 cup for small recipe. Stir until melted.
Peanut-Butter Pudding: Stir in chunk-style peanut butter after egg mixture is cooked at Medium Low. Use 1/2 cup peanut butter for large recipe and 1/4 cup for small recipe. Stir until melted.

Basic Frozen Yogurt Ice

YIELD	9 cups	4-1/2 cups
INGREDIENTS		
flavoring liquid	4 cups	2 cups
sugar	1-1/2 cups	3/4 cup
fruit jam or ice-cream sauce	1 cup	1/2 cup
half and half	2 cups	1 cup
flavored yogurt	2 cups	1 cup
MIXER BOWL	3-qt. bowl	3-qt. bowl
LOAF PANS	2 (9" x 5" x 3") loaf pans	9" x 5" x 3" loaf pan
FREEZE (almost firm)	4 to 7 hours	4 to 7 hours
BEATING TIME AT MEDIUM SPEED	45 to 60 seconds (each batch)	45 to 60 seconds
FREEZE (firm)	8 hours or overnight	8 hours or overnight
STANDING TIME	20 to 30 minutes	20 to 30 minutes

In a 3-quart mixer bowl, combine flavoring liquid, sugar and jam or ice-cream sauce; mix well. Whisk in half and half and yogurt. Pour into 1 or 2 (9" x 5" x 3") loaf pans. Cover and freeze 4 to 7 hours or until almost firm. Chill same mixer bowl. Spoon partially frozen mixture into chilled bowl. Beat at medium speed of an electric mixer for 45 to 60 seconds or until slushy but not thawed. Beat large recipe in 2 batches. Pour into same loaf pans. Cover and freeze 8 hours or overnight until firm. Let stand at room temperature 20 to 30 minutes before serving.

Suggested Combinations
Frozen Orange-Yogurt Ice: Use orange juice for flavoring liquid. Use orange marmalade for jam. Use orange yogurt.

Frozen Berry-Yogurt Ice: Use lemonade for flavoring liquid. Use strawberry, raspberry or blueberry preserves for jam. Use strawberry, raspberry or blueberry yogurt.

Frozen Pineapple-Yogurt Ice: Use pineapple juice for flavoring liquid. Use pineapple jam. Use pineapple yogurt.

Frozen Apricot-Peach-Yogurt Ice: Use apricot nectar for flavoring liquid. Use peach jam. Use peach yogurt.

Frozen Mocha-Yogurt Ice: Use hot coffee for flavoring liquid. Use thick chocolate-fudge ice-cream sauce. Use coffee yogurt.

Variation
Frozen Yogurt Pops: After beating frozen mixture, pour about 1/2 cup yogurt mixture for each pop into 3-1/2-ounce plastic drink cups. Freeze until firm. Insert wooden sticks in center of yogurt mixture, pushing sticks only about halfway through each pop. To remove pops, run a knife around edge of cups.

Soft-Serve Ice Cream

YIELD	3-1/3 cups	1-2/3 cups
INGREDIENTS		
whipping cream	1/2 cup	1/4 cup
half and half	1/2 cup	1/4 cup
sugar	2/3 cup	1/3 cup
vanilla extract	1 teaspoon	1/2 teaspoon
unsweetened frozen fruit	1 lb.	8 oz.
PROCESSING TIME (cream mixture)	50 to 60 seconds	30 to 45 seconds
PROCESSING TIME (fruit added)	1-1/2 to 2 minutes	1 to 1-1/2 minutes

In a food processor fitted with a steel blade, process whipping cream, half and half, sugar and vanilla for time in chart above or until thickened. Gradually add frozen fruit while processing for time in chart above or until mixture is fluffy and smooth. Do not thaw fruit before using. Serve at once in glasses. Leftover ice cream may be stored in the freezer, but it will become hard and icy.

Suggested Fruit: frozen strawberries, frozen peaches, frozen mixed fruit.

How to Make Frozen Yogurt Pops

1/Freeze yogurt mixture until almost firm, then beat in a chilled bowl until slushy. These pops are flavored with orange juice, orange marmalade and orange yogurt. Spoon about 1/2 cup yogurt mixture into each 3-1/2-ounce plastic drink cup. Freeze until firm.

2/Seal frozen yogurt cups in a plastic bag and keep frozen for snack time. To serve, push a wooden stick into center of frozen yogurt, pushing stick only halfway through each pop. Run a knife around edge of cup to remove pop.

Basic No-Crank Ice Cream

YIELD	3 quarts	1-1/2 quarts
INGREDIENTS		
egg yolks	6	3
flavored syrup	1/4 cup	2 tablespoons
flavored extract	1 teaspoon	1/2 teaspoon
sweetened condensed milk	2 (14-oz.) cans	1 (14-oz.) can
chopped nuts or candies	2 cups	1 cup
whipping cream, whipped	4 cups	2 cups
MIXER BOWL	3-qt. bowl	1-1/2-qt. bowl
LOAF PANS	2 (9" x 5" x 3") loaf pans	9" x 5" x 3" loaf pan
BEATING TIME AT HIGH SPEED	2 minutes	2 minutes
BEATING TIME AT MEDIUM SPEED	1 minute	1 minute
FREEZE (before stirring)	4 hours	4 hours
FREEZE (after stirring)	5 hours or overnight	5 hours or overnight

In a mixer bowl, see size in chart above, combine egg yolks, syrup and extract. Beat at high speed of an electric mixer for 2 minutes or until fluffy. Scrape sides of bowl often. Add condensed milk. Turn mixer to medium speed. Beat 1 minute or until smooth. Scrape sides of bowl often. Stir in nuts or candies. Fold in whipped cream. Pour into 1 or 2 (9" x 5" x 3") loaf pans; cover. Freeze 4 hours. Stir well to distribute nuts or candies. Freeze 5 hours more or overnight until firm.

Suggested Combinations
No-Crank Maple-Nut Ice Cream: Use maple syrup for flavored syrup. Use maple extract for flavored extract. Use chopped nuts.

No-Crank Confetti Gumdrop Ice Cream: Use strawberry syrup for flavored syrup. Use lemon extract for flavored extract. Use snipped gumdrops for candies.

No-Crank Butter-Brickle Ice Cream: Use chocolate syrup for flavored syrup. Use almond extract for flavored extract. Use butter-brickle pieces for candies.

Stirred Custard Sauce

YIELD	2-2/3 cups	1-1/3 cups
INGREDIENTS		
whole eggs	2	1
egg yolks	2	1
sugar	1/4 cup	2 tablespoons
half and half	1 cup	1/2 cup
milk	1 cup	1/2 cup
vanilla extract	1 teaspoon	1/2 teaspoon
GLASS DOUBLE BOILER	1-1/2-qt. double boiler	1-1/2-qt. double boiler
BOWL	2-qt. bowl	1-qt. bowl
TIME AT MEDIUM TO MEDIUM HIGH (over simmering water)	18 to 26 minutes, 175F (80C)	12 to 15 minutes, 175F (80C)
TIME IN ICE WATER	2 minutes	2 minutes
REFRIGERATE	5 to 6 hours	3 to 4 hours

In the top of a 1-1/2-quart glass double boiler, thoroughly whisk together eggs, egg yolks and sugar. Gradually whisk in half and half and milk. Bring water in bottom of double boiler almost to a boil. Water level should be 1/2 inch below bottom of top pan. Do not let simmering water touch bottom of top pan. Cook egg mixture over simmering water on Medium to Medium-High heat for time in chart above or until mixture is slightly thick and creamy. With a wooden spoon, gently stir mixture slowly but constantly in a figure-8 pattern during entire cooking time. Complete 1 figure-8 pattern every 3 seconds. When done, a food thermometer inserted in custard should register 175F (80C) and mixture should thickly coat a metal spoon. Immediately pour mixture into a bowl, see size in chart above, set inside another bowl filled with ice water. Cool 2 minutes, stirring gently. Remove from ice water. Gently stir in vanilla. Place clear plastic wrap directly on custard surface. Refrigerate at least for time in chart above. Mixture will thicken more when chilled. Serve over cake or fruit. Or, use for Basic Fruit Trifle, page 438.

Note: When water in bottom of double boiler is simmering, bubbles should barely break surface of water. To use a metal double boiler, adjust heat so water simmers on Medium to Medium-Low heat. Cooking time may be slightly less.

Tips for Custard Sauce

- Directions for Stirred Custard Sauce are as complete and failproof as possible. However, due to different techniques, two people can use the same recipe, same utensils and same range—but have different cooking times and temperatures! We have tried to give enough guidelines to ensure success. Do not be concerned if your cooking times do not match ours.

- Varying any ingredients in Stirred Custard Sauce will alter cooking times and temperature.

- After pouring custard sauce into an ice-chilled bowl to cool, do not scrape out sauce left in double boiler. Custard left behind may be lumpy and overcooked from being on outside edge of pan.

How to Make Stirred Custard Sauce

1/Water in the bottom of the double boiler should be 1/2 inch below the top pan. Do not let simmering water touch top pan. When water is simmering, bubbles should barely break water surface. If water begins to boil, reduce heat. If custard cooks too quickly, it may curdle or thicken only around edge.

2/Stir custard mixture very slowly with a wooden spoon during entire cooking time. Stir in a figure-8 pattern that reaches all of pan. If custard is stirred too vigorously, it takes longer to cook. When done, custard will be slightly thickened and creamy. Dip a metal spoon into custard and pull spoon straight up. Custard should coat spoon thickly.

3/Best test for doneness is with a food thermometer. This custard is done when food thermometer registers 175F (80C). Do not allow thermometer to touch side or bottom of pan. Custard temperature will stabilize when thickened.

4/Quickly pour cooked custard into a bowl. Set bowl in a larger bowl of ice water. Stir custard gently 2 minutes while it is in ice water. Stir in vanilla. Place plastic wrap directly on custard surface and refrigerate until thoroughly chilled. Custard will thicken more when chilled.

Basic Fruit Trifle

SERVINGS	12 to 16	6 to 8
INGREDIENTS		
Stirred Custard Sauce, page 436	large recipe	small recipe
Sponge Cake, page 460,	small recipe	small recipe
	(loaf cake)	(use half loaf cake)
OR		
ladyfingers, split lengthwise	16	8
fruit liqueur or cream sherry	1/4 cup	2 tablespoons
fruit jam or preserves	1/4 cup	2 tablespoons
fresh fruit	4 cups	2 cups
whipping cream, whipped	1 cup	1/2 cup
additional fruit, if desired	to garnish	to garnish
SERVING BOWL	2-1/2-qt. bowl	1-1/2-qt. bowl
REFRIGERATE	3 hours	2 hours

Prepare Stirred Custard Sauce; refrigerate as directed in recipe, 3 to 6 hours. If using Sponge Cake, prepare and cool. Cut loaf cake in 1-inch slices. Arrange half of cake slices or ladyfingers in a serving bowl, see size in chart above, or in individual sherbet dishes. Cut slices, if necessary, to fit dishes. Pierce cake all over at 1-inch intervals with tines of a fork. Drizzle with half of fruit liqueur. Spread with half of fruit jam. Top with half of fruit. Pour half of custard sauce over fruit, being sure some custard flows through to cake layer. Repeat layers of cake, liqueur, jam, fruit and custard sauce. Spread top with whipped cream, or pipe whipped cream through pastry tube to decorate top. Cover and refrigerate for time in chart above. Garnish with additional fruit, if desired.

Suggested Combinations
Peach-Raspberry Trifle: Use peach brandy for liqueur. Use raspberry jam. Use sliced fresh peaches and raspberries for fruit.
Strawberry-Cherry Trifle: Use kirsch for liqueur. Use strawberry jam. Use sliced fresh strawberries and pitted, dark, sweet cherries for fruit.

Baked Custard

SERVINGS	6	4	2
INGREDIENTS			
eggs	3	2	1
sugar	1/3 cup	3 tablespoons	4 teaspoons
vanilla extract	1-1/2 teaspoons	1 teaspoon	1/2 teaspoon
milk	2 cups	1-1/3 cups	2/3 cup
ground nutmeg	to garnish	to garnish	to garnish
CUSTARD CUPS	6 (6-oz.)	4 (6-oz.)	2 (6-oz.)
	custard cups	custard cups	custard cups
BAKING PAN	13" x 9"	8-inch-square	9" x 5" x 3"
	baking pan	baking pan	loaf pan
TIME IN 325F (165C) OVEN	40 to 45 minutes	40 to 45 minutes	40 to 45 minutes
COOLING TIME	30 minutes	30 minutes	30 minutes

Do not preheat oven. In a medium bowl, thoroughly whisk together eggs, sugar and vanilla. Gradually whisk in milk. Divide egg mixture evenly among 2, 4 or 6 (6-ounce) custard cups. Sprinkle with nutmeg. Place custard cups in a baking pan, see size in chart above, set on an oven rack. Pour very hot tap water to a depth of 1 inch around custard cups. Bake in a 325F (165C) oven 40 to 45 minutes or until a knife inserted off-center comes out clean. Remove custard cups from pan. Cool on a rack 30 minutes, then serve or refrigerate. May be served warm or chilled.

Variation
Brown-Sugar Baked Custard: Sieve a generous coating of brown sugar over custard immediately after removing from oven.

Strawberry-Cherry Trifle

Basic Cheesecake

SERVINGS	12	6
INGREDIENTS		
crumb mixture for Crumb Pie Crust, page 466	large recipe	small recipe
cream cheese, softened	2 (8-oz.) pkgs.	1 (8-oz.) pkg.
sugar	2 tablespoons	1 tablespoon
all-purpose flour	2/3 cup	1/3 cup
vanilla extract	1 teaspoon	1/2 teaspoon
eggs	2	1
flavored yogurt	2 cups	1 cup
fresh or drained canned fruit	to garnish	to garnish
Basic Cheesecake Glaze, below	large recipe	small recipe
BAKING PAN	9-inch springform pan	7-inch springform pan
MIXER BOWL	1-1/2-qt. bowl	1-1/2-qt. bowl
BEATING TIME AT MEDIUM SPEED	30 to 60 seconds	30 seconds
BEATING TIME AT LOW SPEED	30 seconds	30 seconds
TIME IN 325F (165C) OVEN (crust)	10 to 12 minutes	10 to 12 minutes
TIME IN 325F (165C) OVEN (filling added)	55 to 60 minutes	40 to 45 minutes
COOLING TIME (in oven, door ajar)	3-1/2 hours	3-1/2 hours
REFRIGERATE	8 hours or overnight	8 hours or overnight

Preheat oven to 325F (165C). Butter bottom and sides of a springform pan, see size in chart above. Prepare crumb mixture for Crumb Pie Crust. Pat crumb mixture onto bottom and two-thirds of way up sides of buttered pan. Bake in preheated oven 10 to 12 minutes or until golden brown. Cool. In a 1-1/2-quart mixer bowl, beat cream cheese, sugar, flour and vanilla at medium speed of an electric mixer for time in chart above or until smooth. Turn mixer to low speed. Beat in eggs for 30 seconds until blended. Do not overbeat. Stir in yogurt. Spoon mixture into crumb crust. Place springform pan on a pizza pan or baking sheet with a rim. Bake in preheated oven for time in chart above or until center is just set but not firm. Do not test with a knife. Turn off oven. Cool cheesecake in oven with door ajar 3-1/2 hours or until cool. Refrigerate 8 hours or overnight. Top with fresh or canned fruit. Prepare Basic Cheesecake Glaze. Immediately before serving, spoon glaze over fruit.

Suggested Combinations
Melba Cheesecake: Use peach yogurt. Use sliced fresh peaches and raspberries for fruit. Use Peach Cheesecake Glaze.
Strawberry Cheesecake, photo on pages 4 and 5: Use strawberry yogurt. Use fresh strawberries for fruit. Use Strawberry Cheesecake Glaze.
Pineapple Cheesecake: Use pineapple yogurt. Use drained canned pineapple slices for fruit. Use Pineapple Cheesecake Glaze.

Basic Cheesecake Glaze

YIELD	1/2 cup (for 9-inch cheesecake)	1/4 cup (for 7-inch cheesecake)
INGREDIENTS		
fruit preserves	1/3 cup	3 tablespoons
grated lemon peel	1/4 teaspoon	1/8 teaspoon
dry white wine or fruit liqueur	2 to 4 teaspoons	1 to 2 teaspoons

In a small bowl, combine preserves and lemon peel. Stir in enough wine or liqueur to make drizzling consistency. Drizzle over fruit on cheesecake immediately before serving.

Suggested Combinations
Peach Cheesecake Glaze: Use peach preserves. Use peach brandy for liqueur.
Strawberry Cheesecake Glaze: Use strawberry preserves. Use strawberry liqueur.
Pineapple Cheesecake Glaze: Use pineapple preserves. Use dry white wine.

How to Make Basic Cheesecake

1/Butter a springform baking pan. Pat crumb mixture over bottom and two-thirds of way up sides of pan. A small rubber spatula is helpful in forming side crust. Bake 10 to 12 minutes until golden brown.

2/Beat filling until smooth, but do not overbeat. Spoon filling into prebaked crust. Place springform pan on a pizza pan or baking sheet to catch leaks during baking if springform pan is not tight.

3/When done, cheesecake will appear set, but not firm, in center. Do not test with a knife or a crack will form that will widen as cheesecake cools. Cool cheesecake in oven with door ajar to avoid drafts that cause cracks.

4/Refrigerate cheesecake 8 hours or overnight. Immediately before serving, top with fresh or well-drained canned fruit and glaze. This Melba Cheesecake is topped with peaches, raspberries and Peach Cheesecake Glaze.

Basic Fruitcake

YIELD	10 cups batter (see Yield & Baking Guide for Fruitcake, opposite)	5 cups batter
INGREDIENTS		
dried fruit	2 lbs.	1 lb.
candied fruit	12 oz.	6 oz.
brandy or fruit liqueur	1/4 cup	2 tablespoons
all-purpose flour	2 cups	1 cup
packed brown sugar	1-1/3 cups	2/3 cup
ground spice	2 teaspoons	1 teaspoon
salt	1/2 teaspoon	1/4 teaspoon
butter or margarine, softened	1 cup	1/2 cup
eggs	4	2
fruit sauce or mashed fruit	1-1/3 cups	2/3 cup
chopped nuts	1-1/3 cups	2/3 cup
brandy or fruit liqueur	1/4 cup	2 tablespoons
BAKING PANS	see sizes in chart, opposite	
MIXER BOWL	3-qt. bowl	1-1/2-qt. bowl
BEATING TIME AT LOW SPEED (dry ingredients)	25 to 35 seconds	25 to 35 seconds
BEATING TIME AT LOW SPEED (all ingredients)	1 minute	1 minute
BEATING TIME AT HIGH SPEED	3 minutes	3 minutes
TIME IN 300F (150C) OVEN	see timings in chart, opposite	
COOLING TIME (in pan)	10 minutes	10 minutes
COOLING TIME (before wrapping): large cake small cake cupcakes	3 hours 30 minutes	1-1/2 hours 30 minutes

Preheat oven to 300F (150C). Grease baking pans, see sizes in chart opposite. Line bottom of pans with waxed paper. Grease waxed paper; set aside. Or, line a muffin pan with paper bake cups; set aside. In a large bowl, combine dried fruit, candied fruit and first amount of brandy or liqueur; mix well. Cover and let stand while preparing batter. In a mixer bowl, see size in chart above, beat flour, brown sugar, spice and salt at low speed of an electric mixer for 25 to 35 seconds to blend. Add butter or margarine, eggs and fruit sauce or mashed fruit. Beat at low speed of mixer for 1 minute to blend. Scrape sides of bowl often. Turn mixer to high speed. Beat 3 minutes. Scrape sides of bowl often. Stir batter and nuts into fruit mixture; mix well. Spoon batter into prepared pans, filling about two-thirds full. Spread batter evenly in pans. Bake in preheated oven for time in chart opposite or until a wooden pick or skewer inserted in center of cake comes out clean. Cool in pans on a rack 10 minutes. To loosen, run a sharp knife around edges of pans. Invert to remove from pans. Remove waxed paper. Cool on rack for time in chart above. Drizzle second amount of brandy or liqueur over warm cakes. When cool, wrap cake in brandy- or liqueur-soaked cheesecloth, if desired. Wrap in foil; refrigerate.

Suggested Combinations

Applesauce Fruitcake: Use finely chopped dried apples, chopped pitted dates and golden raisins for dried fruit. Use candied cherries and chopped candied pineapple for candied fruit. Use applejack for brandy. Use cinnamon and nutmeg for spices. Use applesauce for fruit sauce. Use chopped walnuts for nuts.

Banana Fruitcake: Use snipped dried apricots, snipped, dried, pitted prunes and currants for dried fruit. Use chopped, candied, mixed fruit and peel for candied fruit. Use banana liqueur for fruit liqueur. Use allspice and cardamom for spices. Use mashed ripe banana for mashed fruit. Use chopped pecans for nuts.

Pumpkin Fruitcake: Use raisins, snipped dried figs and chopped, dried, mixed fruit for dried fruit. Use chopped candied orange and lemon peel and chopped candied citron for candied fruit. Use brandy. Use pumpkin-pie spice for spice. Use canned pumpkin for mashed fruit. Use chopped pecans for nuts.

Note: Rich fruitcakes, like this one, improve with age and can be refrigerated several months. Pour additional brandy or fruit liqueur over cheesecloth during aging, if desired.

How to Make Basic Fruitcake

1/These fruitcakes use mashed banana, canned pumpkin or applesauce as a base, with a variety of dried and candied fruit added. Bake the batter in your choice of 3 loaf-pan sizes, 2 muffin-cup sizes or 1-pound coffee cans. Drizzle warm baked cakes with brandy or liqueur.

2/For extra flavor, wrap cooled cakes in cheesecloth soaked with brandy or liqueur. Then wrap cakes in foil. Refrigerate for best slicing. Decorate tops with candied fruit and nuts. Small individual cakes make delicious gifts to pack in attractive boxes.

Yield & Baking Guide for Fruitcake

PAN	amount of batter	baking time at 300F (150C)
9" x 5" x 3" loaf pan	5 cups	1-3/4 hours
7-1/2" x 3-1/2" x 2" loaf pan	2-1/2 cups	1-1/4 hours
6" x 3" x 2" loaf pan	1-2/3 cups	1 hour
1-pound coffee can	3-1/2 cups	1-3/4 hours
2-1/2-inch muffin cups	3 to 4 tablespoons each	30 to 35 minutes
1-3/4-inch muffin cups	1-1/2 to 2 tablespoons each	20 to 25 minutes

Basic Plum Pudding

SERVINGS	12 to 16	6 to 8
INGREDIENTS		
butter or margarine, softened	1/2 cup	1/4 cup
packed brown sugar	3/4 cup	1/3 cup
white bread, torn in pieces	4 slices	2 slices
fruit juice	1/4 cup	2 tablespoons
eggs	2	1
brandy or liqueur	1/4 cup	2 tablespoons
vanilla extract	1 teaspoon	1/2 teaspoon
fruit relish	1 cup	1/2 cup
all-purpose flour	3/4 cup	1/3 cup
baking soda	3/4 teaspoon	1/2 teaspoon
salt	1/2 teaspoon	1/4 teaspoon
ground spices	2 teaspoons	1 teaspoon
chopped candied fruit	1 cup	1/2 cup
chopped fresh fruit	1 cup	1/2 cup
chopped nuts	1/2 cup	1/4 cup
Hard Sauce, opposite	large recipe	small recipe
RING MOLD	6-cup ring mold	3-1/2-cup ring mold
MIXER BOWL	3-qt. bowl	1-1/2-qt. bowl
DUTCH OVEN	6-qt. Dutch oven	5-qt. Dutch oven
BEATING TIME AT MEDIUM SPEED	2 minutes	1-1/2 minutes
BEATING TIME AT HIGH SPEED	2 minutes	30 seconds
TIME IN 325F (165C) OVEN	2 hours	1-1/2 hours
COOLING TIME (in pan)	10 minutes	10 minutes
COOLING TIME (on rack)	30 minutes	30 minutes

Preheat oven to 325F (165C). Generously grease and flour a ring mold, see size in chart above. In a mixer bowl, see size in chart above, beat butter or margarine and brown sugar at medium speed of an electric mixer for time in chart above or until fluffy. Scrape sides of bowl often. Add bread, fruit juice, eggs, brandy or liqueur and vanilla. Turn mixer to high speed. Beat for time in chart above or until blended. Scrape sides of bowl often. Batter will appear curdled. Stir in fruit relish. In a medium bowl, combine flour, baking soda, salt and spices; mix well. Toss candied fruit, fresh fruit and nuts with flour mixture. Stir into batter. Spoon evenly into prepared ring mold. Cover tightly with foil. Set on a wire rack in a Dutch oven, see size in chart above. Pour hot water to bottom of rack; cover with Dutch oven lid. Bake in preheated oven for time in chart above or until set. Remove from Dutch oven; remove foil from top. Cool in ring mold on rack 10 minutes. To loosen, run a sharp knife around inside edge of mold. Invert to remove pudding from mold. Cool on rack 30 minutes. Serve warm with Hard Sauce.

Suggested Combinations
Mincemeat Plum Pudding: Use pineapple juice for fruit juice. Use brandy. Use prepared mincemeat for fruit relish. Use allspice and cloves for spices. Use candied pineapple and candied lemon peel for candied fruit. Use chopped pear for fresh fruit. Use walnuts for nuts.

Cranberry Plum Pudding: Use cranberry juice for fruit juice. Use cranberry liqueur. Use canned cranberry-orange relish for fruit relish. Use cardamom and cinnamon for spices. Use chopped fresh cranberries instead of candied fruit. Use chopped apple for fresh fruit. Use pecans for nuts.

Lemon Pudding Cake

SERVINGS	8	4
INGREDIENTS		
egg whites	4	2
sugar	1/2 cup	1/4 cup
egg yolks	4	2
grated lemon peel	2 teaspoons	1 teaspoon
lemon juice	1/2 cup	1/4 cup
milk	1-1/3 cups	2/3 cup
sugar	1-1/2 cups	3/4 cup
all-purpose flour	1/2 cup	1/4 cup
MIXER BOWL (egg whites)	3-qt. bowl	1-1/2-qt. bowl
MIXER BOWL (egg yolks)	1-1/2-qt. bowl	1-1/2-qt. bowl
CASSEROLE DISH	deep 2-qt. round casserole dish	deep 1-qt. round casserole dish
BAKING PAN	13" x 9" baking pan	8-inch-square baking pan
BEATING TIME AT HIGH SPEED (soft peaks)	1 minute	1 minute
BEATING TIME AT HIGH SPEED (stiff peaks)	4 minutes	2 minutes
TIME IN 350F (175C) OVEN	55 to 60 minutes	45 to 50 minutes
COOLING TIME	1 hour	30 minutes

Preheat oven to 350F (175C). In a mixer bowl, see size in chart above, beat egg whites at high speed of an electric mixer for 1 minute or until soft peaks form. Gradually add first amount of sugar, beating at high speed of mixer for time in chart above or until stiff peaks form. Set aside. In a 1-1/2-quart mixer bowl, beat egg yolks at high speed of mixer for 45 to 60 seconds or until foamy. Turn mixer to low speed. Beat in lemon peel, lemon juice and milk until blended. Beat in second amount of sugar and flour until blended. Fold lemon-juice mixture into egg whites. Pour into a casserole dish, see size in chart above. Place casserole in a baking pan, see size in chart above. Pour hot water to a depth of 1 inch in baking pan. Bake in preheated oven for time in chart above or until a wooden pick inserted halfway into cake comes out clean. Pudding mixture on bottom of dish will be moist. Remove from water. Cool in dish on a rack for time in chart above before serving. Serve warm in bowls.

Hard Sauce

YIELD	1-1/3 cups	1/2 cup
INGREDIENTS		
butter or margarine, softened	1/2 cup	1/4 cup
powdered sugar	1 cup	1/2 cup
brandy or liqueur	2 tablespoons	1 tablespoon
MIXER BOWL	1-1/2-qt. bowl	1-1/2-qt. bowl
BEATING TIME AT MEDIUM SPEED (butter, sugar)	4 minutes	3 minutes
BEATING TIME AT MEDIUM SPEED (brandy or liqueur added)	30 seconds	30 seconds

Place butter or margarine in a 1-1/2-quart mixer bowl. Gradually add powdered sugar, beating at medium speed of an electric mixer for time in chart above or until fluffy. Beat in brandy or liqueur at medium speed for 30 seconds. Cover and store in the refrigerator. Serve at room temperature with Basic Plum Pudding, opposite.

Note: Use same brandy or liqueur in Hard Sauce as in Basic Plum Pudding.

Basic Ice-Cream-Cake Torte

SERVINGS	12	6
INGREDIENTS		
ice cream, softened	1-1/2 qts. (6 cups)	3/4 qt. (3 cups)
baked cake layers	2 (9-inch) layers	1 (9-inch) layer, cut in half vertically
flavored liqueur	1/4 cup	2 tablespoons
flavored syrup	1/4 cup	2 tablespoons
frozen whipped topping, thawed	1 (8-oz.) carton (3-1/2 cups)	1 (4-oz.) carton (1-3/4 cups)
nuts or chocolate curls	to garnish	to garnish
BAKING PAN	9-inch layer pan	9-inch layer pan
FREEZE (ice-cream layer)	4 hours	4 hours
FREEZE (finished cake)	at least 2 hours	at least 2 hours

If using large recipe, line a 9-inch layer pan with foil. If using small recipe, line half of 9-inch pan with foil, making wall across center of pan to form half-moon-shaped layer. Spread ice cream evenly in layer pan. Freeze 4 hours or until firm. Pierce cake all over at 1-inch intervals with tines of a fork. Drizzle with liqueur. Place 1 cake layer on a metal serving tray. Remove ice-cream layer from the freezer. Invert ice-cream layer on cake layer; peel off foil. Place second cake layer on ice-cream layer. Place in freezer while preparing frosting. In a medium bowl, fold flavored syrup into whipped topping. Spread over cake top and sides. Freeze at least 2 hours before serving. Garnish according to suggestions below. With a serrated knife, slice frozen cake in wedges to serve.

Suggested Combinations
Spumoni Ice-Cream-Cake Torte: Use spumoni ice cream. Use yellow-cake layers. Use crème de cacao for liqueur. Use chocolate syrup. Garnish with chopped pistachio nuts.
Mint-Fudge Ice-Cream-Cake Torte: Use mint-chocolate-chip ice cream. Use chocolate-cake layers. Use white crème de menthe for liqueur. Use crème de menthe syrup. Garnish with chocolate curls.
Maple-Praline Ice-Cream-Cake Torte: Use pecan-praline ice cream. Use spice-cake layers. Use praline liqueur. Use maple syrup. Garnish with chopped pecans.

Chocolate Pudding Cake

SERVINGS	9	4 or 5
INGREDIENTS		
all-purpose flour	1 cup	1/2 cup
granulated sugar	1/2 cup	1/4 cup
unsweetened cocoa powder	1/4 cup	2 tablespoons
baking powder	2 teaspoons	1 teaspoon
salt	1/2 teaspoon	1/4 teaspoon
shortening	1/4 cup	2 tablespoons
chopped walnuts	1/2 cup	1/4 cup
milk	1/2 cup	1/4 cup
vanilla extract	1 teaspoon	1/2 teaspoon
packed brown sugar	1/2 cup	1/4 cup
light corn syrup	1/2 cup	1/4 cup
unsweetened cocoa powder	2 tablespoons	1 tablespoon
boiling water	3/4 cup	1/3 cup
BAKING DISH	8-inch-square baking dish	8" x 4" loaf dish
TIME IN 350F (175C) OVEN	40 to 45 minutes	25 to 30 minutes
COOLING TIME	45 minutes	30 minutes

Preheat oven to 350F (175C). In a medium bowl, combine flour, granulated sugar, first amount of cocoa powder, baking powder and salt; mix well. With a fork or pastry blender, cut in shortening. Stir in walnuts, milk and vanilla; mix well. Spread batter in an ungreased baking dish, see size in chart above. In a small bowl, mix brown sugar, corn syrup and second amount of cocoa powder. Add boiling water; mix well. Pour brown-sugar mixture over batter in baking dish. Bake for time in chart above or until a wooden pick inserted halfway into cake comes out clean. Pudding mixture on bottom of dish will be moist. Cool in dish on a rack for time in chart above before serving. Cut in squares. Invert squares on plates to serve. Serve warm with whipped cream or ice cream, if desired.

Mix-in-the-Pan Yellow Cake

SERVINGS	15	9
INGREDIENTS		
all-purpose flour	3 cups	1-1/2 cups
sugar	1-1/2 cups	3/4 cup
baking powder	5 teaspoons	2-1/2 teaspoons
salt	1 teaspoon	1/2 teaspoon
vegetable oil	2/3 cup	1/3 cup
eggs	2	1
vanilla extract	4 teaspoons	2 teaspoons
milk	2 cups	1 cup
Spiced Nut Topper or Chocolate-Nut Topper, below, if desired OR	large recipe	small recipe
frosting, pages 462 to 464, if desired	see amount in Cake-Frosting Guide, page 463	
BAKING PAN	13" x 9" baking pan	8-inch-square baking pan
STIRRING TIME (oil, eggs added)	3-1/2 minutes	2-1/2 minutes
STIRRING TIME (milk added)	4-1/2 to 5-1/2 minutes	3-1/2 to 4 minutes
TIME IN 350F (175C) OVEN	40 to 45 minutes	30 to 35 minutes
COOLING TIME	2 hours	1-1/4 hours

Preheat oven to 350F (175C). In a baking pan, see size in chart above, combine flour, sugar, baking powder and salt; mix well. Make a well in center of dry ingredients. Add oil, eggs and vanilla to well. Stir with a fork for time in chart above or until dry ingredients are moistened. Add milk. Beat with fork for time in chart above or until batter is smooth and well-mixed. Sprinkle with topper, if desired. Bake in preheated oven for time in chart above or until a wooden pick inserted in center comes out clean. Cool in pan on a rack for time in chart above. If not using topper, prepare frosting, if desired. Swirl frosting on cooled cake.

Spiced Nut Topper

YIELD	to cover 13" x 9" cake	to cover 8-inch-square cake
INGREDIENTS		
Mix-in-the-Pan Cake, above or opposite	large recipe	small recipe
packed brown sugar	1/4 cup	2 tablespoons
granulated sugar	1/4 cup	2 tablespoons
chopped nuts	1/4 cup	2 tablespoons
ground cinnamon	1/2 teaspoon	1/4 teaspoon
ground nutmeg	1/4 teaspoon	1/8 teaspoon

Prepare cake batter for Mix-in-the-Pan Cake. In a small bowl, combine brown sugar, granulated sugar, nuts, cinnamon and nutmeg; mix well. Sprinkle over batter before baking. Bake according to directions for Mix-in-the-Pan Cake.

Chocolate-Nut Topper

YIELD	to cover 13" x 9" cake	to cover 8-inch-square cake
INGREDIENTS		
Mix-in-the-Pan Cake, above or opposite	large recipe	small recipe
semisweet chocolate mini-pieces or grated semisweet chocolate	2/3 cup	1/3 cup
chopped nuts	1 cup	1/2 cup

Prepare cake batter for Mix-in-the-Pan Cake. Sprinkle chocolate and nuts over batter before baking. Bake according to directions for Mix-in-the-Pan Cake.

Mix-in-the-Pan Chocolate Cake

SERVINGS	15	9
INGREDIENTS		
all-purpose flour	3 cups	1-1/2 cups
packed brown sugar	2 cups	1 cup
unsweetened cocoa powder	1/2 cup	1/4 cup
baking soda	2 teaspoons	1 teaspoon
salt	1 teaspoon	1/2 teaspoon
lemon juice	2 tablespoons	1 tablespoon
vegetable oil	2/3 cup	1/3 cup
eggs	2	1
vanilla extract	2 teaspoons	1 teaspoon
milk or cold strong coffee	2 cups	1 cup
Spiced Nut Topper or Chocolate-Nut Topper, opposite, if desired OR	large recipe	small recipe
frosting, pages 462 to 464, if desired	see amount in Cake-Frosting Guide, page 463	
BAKING PAN	13" x 9" baking pan	8-inch-square baking pan
STIRRING TIME (lemon juice, oil, eggs added)	3-1/2 minutes	2-1/2 minutes
STIRRING TIME (milk or coffee added)	4-1/2 to 5 minutes	3-1/2 to 4 minutes
TIME IN 350F (175C) OVEN	40 to 45 minutes	30 to 35 minutes
COOLING TIME	2 hours	1-1/4 hours

Preheat oven to 350F (175C). In a baking pan, see size in chart above, combine flour, brown sugar, cocoa powder, baking soda and salt; mix well. Make a well in center of dry ingredients. Add lemon juice, oil, eggs and vanilla to well. Stir with a fork for time in chart above or until dry ingredients are moistened. Add milk or coffee. Beat with fork for time in chart above or until batter is smooth and well-mixed. Sprinkle with topper, if desired. Bake in preheated oven for time in chart above or until a wooden pick inserted in center comes out clean. Cool in pan on a rack for time in chart above. If not using topper, prepare frosting, if desired. Swirl frosting on cooled cake. Or, serve with Easy Chocolate Sauce, below.

Easy Chocolate Sauce

YIELD	1-1/2 cups	3/4 cup
INGREDIENTS		
sweetened condensed milk	1 (14-oz.) can	1/2 (14-oz.) can (2/3 cup)
unsweetened chocolate squares, broken in pieces	2 (1-oz.) squares	1 (1-oz.) square
liqueur or milk	2 tablespoons	1 tablespoon
vanilla extract	1 teaspoon	1/2 teaspoon
HEAVY SAUCEPAN	1-1/2-qt. saucepan	1-qt. saucepan
TIME AT MEDIUM	13 minutes	11 minutes

In a heavy saucepan, see size in chart above, combine sweetened condensed milk, chocolate and liqueur or milk. Cook over Medium heat for time in chart above or until chocolate is melted and sauce is smooth, blended and slightly thickened, stirring constantly. Stir in vanilla. Serve warm or chilled over ice cream or cake squares. Store leftover sauce, covered, in the refrigerator.

Note: To reheat chilled sauce, spoon 3/4 cup sauce into a heavy 1-quart saucepan. Cook over Medium-Low heat 10 minutes, stirring occasionally.

Carrot Cake

SERVINGS	12 to 16	6 to 9
INGREDIENTS		
all-purpose flour	2 cups	1 cup
packed brown sugar	1 cup	1/2 cup
granulated sugar	1 cup	1/2 cup
baking soda	1 teaspoon	1/2 teaspoon
baking powder	1 teaspoon	1/2 teaspoon
salt	1 teaspoon	1/2 teaspoon
ground cinnamon	2 teaspoons	1 teaspoon
shredded carrot	2 cups	1 cup
eggs	4	2
vegetable oil	1 cup	1/2 cup
vanilla extract	1 teaspoon	1/2 teaspoon
chopped nuts	1 cup	1/2 cup
canned crushed pineapple, well-drained	1/2 cup	1/4 cup
frosting, pages 462 to 464, if desired	see amount in Cake-Frosting Guide, page 463	
BAKING PAN	12-cup fluted tube pan, 13" x 9" pan or 2 (8- or 9-inch) layer pans	8-inch-square baking pan, 1 (8- or 9-inch) layer pan or 15" x 10" x 1" pan
MIXER BOWL	3-qt. bowl	1-1/2-qt. bowl
BEATING TIME AT LOW SPEED (dry ingredients)	25 seconds	25 seconds
BEATING TIME AT LOW SPEED (carrot, eggs, oil, vanilla added)	1 minute	1 minute
BEATING TIME AT HIGH SPEED	3 minutes	3 minutes
TIME IN 350F (175C) OVEN:		
fluted tube pan	50 to 55 minutes	
13" x 9" pan	45 minutes	
8- or 9-inch layer pans	50 to 55 minutes	50 to 55 minutes
8-inch-square pan		45 minutes
15" x 10" x 1" pan		25 minutes
COOLING TIME (in pan):		
fluted tube pan	20 minutes	
all other pans	10 minutes	10 minutes
COOLING TIME (before frosting):		
fluted tube or 13" x 9" pan	2 to 2-1/2 hours	
8- or 9-inch layer pans	1-1/2 hours	1-1/2 hours
8-inch-square pan		1-1/2 hours
15" x 10" x 1" pan		45 minutes

Preheat oven to 350F (175C). Grease and flour a baking pan, see size in chart above; set aside. In a mixer bowl, see size in chart above, beat flour, brown sugar, granulated sugar, baking soda, baking powder, salt and cinnamon at low speed of an electric mixer for 25 seconds to blend. Add carrot, eggs, oil and vanilla. Beat at low speed of mixer for 1 minute to blend. Scrape sides of bowl often. Turn mixer to high speed. Beat 3 minutes. Scrape sides of bowl often. Stir in nuts and pineapple. Pour into prepared pan. Spread batter evenly in pan. Bake in preheated oven for time in chart above or until a wooden pick or skewer inserted in center of cake comes out clean. Cool in pan on a rack for time in chart above. To loosen layer or tube cakes, run a sharp knife around edges of pans. Invert to remove from pans. Leave other cakes in pans. Cool on rack for time in chart above. Prepare frosting, if desired. Swirl frosting on cooled cake.

How to Make Carrot Cake

1/For all basic cakes, select recipe size and baking pan you wish to use. Beat dry ingredients—in this case flour, sugars, baking soda, baking powder, salt and cinnamon—at low speed of an electric mixer for 25 seconds to blend. Add other ingredients, such as carrot, eggs, oil and vanilla for this cake.

2/Beat at low speed of electric mixer 1 minute to blend ingredients. Beat at high speed of electric mixer 3 minutes. Scrape sides of bowl frequently with a rubber spatula. This keeps batter flowing into beaters. Stir in crushed pineapple and nuts.

3/Pour batter into a greased and floured pan, such as this fluted tube pan. Spread batter evenly in pan. Bake in preheated 350F (175C) oven until a wooden skewer inserted in center comes out clean. Cool on a rack only for time given in recipes. Otherwise, cake will be difficult to remove from pan. Loosen sides and center of cake from pan with a knife.

4/Place a rack over top of cake pan. Hold rack and pan tightly together and invert. Lift off cake pan gently. If cake does not come out, loosen sides and center again with knife. Completely cool on rack before frosting.

Chocolate Cake

SERVINGS	12 to 16	6 to 9
INGREDIENTS		
all-purpose flour	3 cups	1-1/2 cups
packed brown sugar	1 cup	1/2 cup
granulated sugar	1 cup	1/2 cup
baking soda	2 teaspoons	1 teaspoon
salt	1 teaspoon	1/2 teaspoon
shortening	2/3 cup	1/3 cup
eggs	2	1
lemon juice	2 tablespoons	1 tablespoon
milk	1-1/2 cups	3/4 cup
vanilla extract	1 teaspoon	1/2 teaspoon
unsweetened chocolate, melted, cooled	4 (1-oz.) squares	2 (1-oz.) squares
frosting, pages 462 to 464	see amount in Cake-Frosting Guide, page 463	
BAKING PAN	12-cup fluted tube pan, 13" x 9" pan or 2 (8- or 9-inch) layer pans	8-inch-square baking pan, 1 (8- or 9-inch) layer pan or 15" x 10" x 1" pan
MIXER BOWL	3-qt. bowl	1-1/2-qt. bowl
BEATING TIME AT LOW SPEED (dry ingredients)	25 seconds	25 seconds
BEATING TIME AT LOW SPEED (shortening, liquids added)	1 minute	1 minute
BEATING TIME AT HIGH SPEED	3 minutes	3 minutes
TIME IN 350F (175C) OVEN:		
fluted tube pan	55 minutes	
13" x 9" pan	45 minutes	
8- or 9-inch layer pans	40 to 45 minutes	40 to 45 minutes
8-inch-square pan		40 minutes
15" x 10" x 1" pan		18 minutes
COOLING TIME (in pan):		
fluted tube pan	20 minutes	
all other pans	10 minutes	10 minutes
COOLING TIME (before frosting):		
fluted tube or 13" x 9" pan	1-1/2 to 2 hours	
8- or 9-inch layer pans	1-1/4 hours	1-1/4 hours
8-inch-square pan		1-1/4 hours
15" x 10" x 1" pan		45 minutes

Preheat oven to 350F (175C). Grease and flour a baking pan, see size in chart above; set aside. In a mixer bowl, see size in chart above, beat flour, brown sugar, granulated sugar, baking soda and salt at low speed of an electric mixer for 25 seconds to blend. Add shortening, eggs, lemon juice, milk and vanilla. Beat at low speed of mixer 1 minute to blend. Scrape sides of bowl often. Add chocolate. Turn mixer to high speed. Beat 3 minutes. Scrape sides of bowl often. Pour into prepared pan. Spread batter evenly in pan. Bake in preheated oven for time in chart above or until a wooden pick or skewer inserted in center of cake comes out clean. Cool in pan on a rack for time in chart above. To loosen layer or tube cakes, run a sharp knife around edges of pans. Invert to remove from pans. Leave other cakes in pans. Cool on rack for time in chart above. Prepare frosting. Swirl frosting on cooled cake.

Tips for Melting Chocolate

- To melt chocolate on top of the range: Place chocolate squares in a small heavy saucepan or skillet. Stir constantly over Low heat until barely melted.

- To melt chocolate in the microwave oven: Place 1 or 2 chocolate squares in a custard cup, or place 3 or 4 chocolate squares in a small glass bowl. Microwave at full power (HIGH) 1 to 2 minutes or until barely melted, stirring once. Stir before using.

- To melt chocolate without watching: Place chocolate squares in a custard cup or small bowl set in simmering water. Heat until barely melted. Stir before using.

Yellow Cake

SERVINGS	12 to 16	6 to 9
INGREDIENTS		
all-purpose flour	3 cups	1-1/2 cups
sugar	1-1/2 cups	3/4 cup
baking powder	5 teaspoons	2-1/2 teaspoons
salt	1/2 teaspoon	1/4 teaspoon
shortening	2/3 cup	1/3 cup
eggs	2	1
milk	1-1/3 cups	2/3 cup
vanilla extract	2 teaspoons	1 teaspoon
frosting, pages 462 to 464	see amount in Cake-Frosting Guide, page 463	
BAKING PAN	12-cup fluted tube pan, 13" x 9" pan or 2 (8- or 9-inch) layer pans	8-inch square baking pan, 1 (8- or 9-inch) layer pan or 15" x 10" x 1" pan
MIXER BOWL	3-qt. bowl	1-1/2-qt. bowl
BEATING TIME AT LOW SPEED (dry ingredients)	10 seconds	10 seconds
BEATING TIME AT LOW SPEED (all ingredients)	1 minute	1 minute
BEATING TIME AT HIGH SPEED	3 minutes	3 minutes
TIME IN 350F (175C) OVEN:		
fluted tube pan	50 minutes	
13" x 9" pan	45 minutes	
8- or 9-inch layer pans	35 to 40 minutes	35 to 40 minutes
8-inch-square pan		30 to 35 minutes
15" x 10" x 1" pan		18 minutes
COOLING TIME (in pan):		
fluted tube pan	20 minutes	
all other pans	10 minutes	10 minutes
COOLING TIME (before frosting):		
fluted tube or 13" x 9" pan	1-1/2 to 2 hours	
8- or 9-inch layer pans	1-1/4 hours	1-1/4 hours
8-inch-square pan		1-1/4 hours
15" x 10" x 1" pan		45 minutes

Preheat oven to 350F (175C). Grease and flour a baking pan, see size in chart above; set aside. In a mixer bowl, see size in chart above, beat flour, sugar, baking powder and salt at low speed of an electric mixer 10 seconds to blend. Add shortening, eggs, milk and vanilla. Beat at low speed of mixer 1 minute to blend. Scrape sides of bowl often. Turn mixer to high speed. Beat 3 minutes. Scrape sides of bowl often. Pour into prepared pan. Spread batter evenly in pan. Bake in preheated oven for time in chart above or until a wooden pick or skewer inserted in center of cake comes out clean. Cool in pan on a rack for time in chart above. To loosen layer or tube cakes, run a sharp knife around edges of pans. Invert to remove from pans. Leave other cakes in pans. Cool on rack for time in chart above. Prepare frosting. Swirl frosting on cooled cake.

Spice Cake

SERVINGS	12 to 16	6 to 9
INGREDIENTS		
Same ingredients as for Yellow Cake, above, except add:	large recipe	small recipe
grated orange peel	2 teaspoons	1 teaspoon
ground cinnamon	1 teaspoon	1/2 teaspoon
ground nutmeg	1/2 teaspoon	1/4 teaspoon
ground cloves	1/4 teaspoon	1/8 teaspoon

Prepare batter for Yellow Cake, except add orange peel, cinnamon, nutmeg and cloves to dry ingredients before beating 10 seconds. Bake, cool and frost according to directions for Yellow Cake.

Basic Upside-Down Cake

SERVINGS	8	4
INGREDIENTS		
butter or margarine, melted	1/4 cup	2 tablespoons
packed brown sugar	1/2 cup	1/4 cup
ground spice	1 teaspoon	1/2 teaspoon
chopped nuts or flaked coconut	1/2 cup	1/4 cup
canned fruit, well-drained	1 (16-oz.) can	1 (8-oz.) can
cake batter, pages 452, 453 and 457	small recipe	small recipe (use 1 cup batter for upside-down cake; use remainder for cupcakes, opposite)
BAKING PAN	9-inch-square baking pan	7-inch pie plate
TIME IN 350F (175C) OVEN	45 to 55 minutes	30 to 40 minutes
COOLING TIME (in pan)	5 minutes	5 minutes
COOLING TIME (before serving)	30 to 40 minutes	30 minutes

Preheat oven to 350F (175C). In a baking pan, see size in chart above, combine butter or margarine, brown sugar, spice and nuts or coconut; mix well. Spread mixture evenly in bottom of pan. Arrange drained fruit in a design over sugar mixture. Prepare cake batter. Spoon batter over fruit; spread evenly in pan. Bake in preheated oven for time in chart above or until a wooden pick inserted halfway into center of cake comes out clean. Cool in pan 5 minutes. Invert on a serving plate. Spoon remaining topping in pan over cake. Cool for time in chart above before serving. Serve warm with whipped cream or ice cream, if desired.

Suggested Combinations
Pineapple Upside-Down Cake: Use ginger for spice. Use coconut. Use sliced pineapple for fruit. Use batter for Yellow Cake, page 453.
Peach Upside-Down Cake: Use cinnamon for spice. Use chopped pecans for nuts. Use sliced peaches for fruit. Use batter for Spice Cake, page 453.
Cherry Upside-Down Cake: Use nutmeg for spice. Use chopped toasted walnuts for nuts. Use pitted, dark, sweet cherries for fruit. Use batter for Chocolate Cake, page 452.
Ginger-Pear Upside-Down Cake: Use ginger for spice. Use coconut. Use pear slices for fruit. Use batter for Old-Fashioned Gingerbread, page 457.

Basic Yogurt Dessert Filling

YIELD	4 cups	2 cups
INGREDIENTS		
frozen whipped topping, thawed	2 cups	1 cup
flavored yogurt	1 cup	1/2 cup
syrup	1/4 cup	2 tablespoons
sliced fresh fruit or berries	2 cups	1 cup
OR		
chopped nuts	1 cup	1/2 cup
grated citrus peel	2 teaspoons	1 teaspoon

In a medium bowl, combine whipped topping, yogurt and syrup. Stir in fruit or nuts and citrus peel. Serve over shortcake, poached fruit or pie. Or, use to fill cream puffs or jelly roll.

Suggested Combinations
Lemon-Blueberry Yogurt Dessert Filling: Use lemon yogurt. Use light corn syrup. Use blueberries. Use lemon peel.
Strawberry-Yogurt Dessert Filling: Use strawberry yogurt. Use strawberry syrup. Use sliced strawberries. Use orange peel.
Maple-Nut Yogurt Dessert Filling: Use vanilla yogurt. Use maple syrup. Use chopped pecans for nuts. Use lemon peel. For this filling, large recipe yields 3 cups and small recipe yields 1-1/2 cups.

How to Make Basic Upside-Down Cake

1/Mix melted butter or margarine, brown sugar, spice and nuts or coconut in bottom of a baking pan. Spread evenly in pan. Drain canned fruit and pat dry on paper towels. Arrange fruit in design over sugar mixture. This is Ginger-Pear Upside-Down Cake.

2/Spoon cake batter over fruit. Spread batter evenly in baking pan. Bake in preheated 350F (175C) oven. When cake is done, a wooden pick inserted halfway into center should come out clean. Cool on a rack 5 minutes, then invert on a serving plate and cool.

Cupcakes

YIELD	6 per 1 cup batter (see yield below)	6 per 1 cup batter (see yield below)
INGREDIENTS cake batter, pages 452, 453 and 457	large recipe	small recipe
frosting, pages 462 to 464	see amount in Cake-Frosting Guide, page 463	
MUFFIN PAN	2-1/2-inch muffin cups	2-1/2-inch muffin cups
TIME IN 375F (190C) OVEN OR	18 to 20 minutes	18 to 20 minutes
TIME IN 350F (175C) OVEN	20 to 23 minutes	20 to 23 minutes
COOLING TIME (before frosting)	30 minutes	30 minutes

Preheat oven to 375F (190C) to bake only cupcakes. Preheat oven to 350F (175C) to bake cupcakes with upside-down cake from same batter. Line muffin pan with paper bake cups. Prepare cake batter. Fill bake cups half full. Bake in preheated oven for time in chart above or until a wooden pick inserted in center of cupcakes comes out clean. Remove from pan immediately. Cool on a rack 30 minutes. Prepare frosting. Swirl frosting on cooled cupcakes.

Cupcake-Batter Guide

YIELD	large recipe	small recipe
BATTER		
Old-Fashioned Gingerbread	28 to 30 cupcakes	14 or 15 cupcakes
Yellow or Spice Cake	32 or 33 cupcakes	16 or 17 cupcakes
Chocolate Cake	38 to 40 cupcakes	19 or 20 cupcakes

Basic Fruit Baba Shortcake

SERVINGS	6	3
INGREDIENTS		
Pound Cake, below	6 small fluted tube cakes	3 small fluted tube cakes
liqueur or brandy	6 tablespoons	3 tablespoons
fresh, frozen or canned sliced fruit	2 cups	1 cup
Double-Cream Dessert Topper, page 484	large recipe	small recipe
brown sugar	to garnish	to garnish

Prepare Pound Cake. Pierce cakes all over at 1-inch intervals with tines of a fork. Drizzle each cake with 1 tablespoon brandy or liqueur. Spoon fruit over pound cakes. Top with some Double-Cream Dessert Topper. Sprinkle with brown sugar. Serve with remaining Double-Cream Dessert Topper.

Suggested Combinations
Wine-Harvest Baba Shortcake: Use brandy. Use seedless green or red grapes for fruit.
Strawberry-Baba Shortcake: Use strawberry liqueur. Use sliced strawberries for fruit.
Peach-Baba Shortcake: Use peach brandy. Use sliced peaches for fruit.

Pound Cake

SERVINGS	14 to 16 (tube cake)	8 (loaf cake)	6 (small tube cakes)
INGREDIENTS			
eggs	6	3	2
sugar	2-1/2 cups	1-1/4 cups	3/4 cup
shortening	1/2 cup	1/4 cup	3 tablespoons
butter or margarine, softened	1/2 cup	1/4 cup	3 tablespoons
vanilla extract	2 teaspoons	1 teaspoon	3/4 teaspoon
all-purpose flour	4 cups	2 cups	1-1/3 cups
baking powder	2 tablespoons	1 tablespoon	2 teaspoons
salt	1 teaspoon	1/2 teaspoon	1/4 teaspoon
milk	2 cups	1 cup	2/3 cup
frosting, pages 462 to 464, if desired	see amount in Cake-Frosting Guide, page 463		
BAKING PAN	10-inch tube pan (angel-food-cake pan)	9" x 5" x 3" loaf pan	6 (1-cup) fluted tube pans
MIXER BOWL	3-qt. bowl	3-qt. bowl	1-1/2-qt. bowl
BEATING TIME AT LOW SPEED	30 seconds	30 seconds	30 seconds
BEATING TIME AT HIGH SPEED	5 minutes	4 minutes	3 minutes
TIME IN 350F (175C) OVEN	70 to 75 minutes	60 to 65 minutes	20 to 25 minutes
COOLING TIME (in pan)	10 minutes	10 minutes	10 minutes
COOLING TIME (before frosting)	3 hours	2 hours	1 hour

Preheat oven to 350F (175C). Generously grease and flour a baking pan, see size in chart above; set aside. If using loaf pan, line bottom with waxed paper; grease waxed paper. In a mixer bowl, see size in chart above, beat eggs, sugar, shortening, butter or margarine and vanilla at low speed of an electric mixer 30 seconds to blend. Turn mixer to high speed. Beat for time in chart above or until very light and fluffy. Scrape sides of bowl constantly. In a medium bowl, combine flour, baking powder and salt. Alternately add flour mixture and milk to creamed mixture. After each addition, beat at low speed of mixer 10 seconds, then turn mixer to medium speed and beat 15 to 20 seconds. Scrape sides of bowl often. Begin and end additions with flour. Pour into prepared pan. Spread batter evenly in pan. Bake in preheated oven for time in chart above or until a wooden pick or skewer inserted in center comes out clean. Cool in pan on a rack 10 minutes. To loosen, run a knife around edge of pan. Invert to remove cake from pan. Cool on rack for time in chart above. Prepare frosting, if desired. Swirl frosting on cooled cake.

How to Make Basic Fruit Baba Shortcake

1/With tines of a fork, pierce small fluted pound cakes at 1-inch intervals. Drizzle with fruit liqueur or brandy. This Wine-Harvest Baba Shortcake is drizzled with brandy.

2/Spoon fruit over shortcakes. Top with some Double-Cream Dessert Topper, page 484. Sprinkle with brown sugar. Serve with more topper. Vary fruit and liqueur to match the seasons.

Old-Fashioned Gingerbread

SERVINGS	9	4 or 5
INGREDIENTS		
all-purpose flour	2-1/2 cups	1-1/4 cups
sugar	1/2 cup	1/4 cup
baking soda	1-1/2 teaspoons	3/4 teaspoon
ground cinnamon	1 teaspoon	1/2 teaspoon
ground ginger	1 teaspoon	1/2 teaspoon
salt	1/2 teaspoon	1/4 teaspoon
ground allspice	1/2 teaspoon	1/4 teaspoon
shortening	1/2 cup	1/4 cup
egg	1	1
molasses	1 cup	1/2 cup
milk	1 cup	1/2 cup
whipping cream, whipped	1 cup	1/2 cup
BAKING PAN	9-inch-square pan	9" x 5" x 3" loaf pan
MIXER BOWL	3-qt. bowl	1-1/2-qt. bowl
BEATING TIME AT LOW SPEED (dry ingredients)	10 seconds	10 seconds
BEATING TIME AT LOW SPEED (all ingredients)	1 minute	1 minute
BEATING TIME AT HIGH SPEED	3 minutes	3 minutes
TIME IN 350F (175C) OVEN	55 to 60 minutes	40 to 45 minutes
COOLING TIME (in pan)	2 hours	1 hour

Preheat oven to 350F (175C). Grease and flour a baking pan, see size in chart above. In a mixer bowl, see size in chart above, beat flour, sugar, baking soda, cinnamon, ginger, salt and allspice at low speed of an electric mixer for 10 seconds to blend. Add shortening, egg, molasses and milk. Beat at low speed of mixer for 1 minute to blend. Scrape sides of bowl often. Turn mixer to high speed. Beat 3 minutes. Scrape sides of bowl often. Pour into prepared pan. Spread batter evenly in pan. Bake in preheated oven for time in chart above or until a wooden pick inserted in center of gingerbread comes out clean. Cool on a rack for time in chart above. Serve warm with whipped cream.

Basic Chiffon Cake

SERVINGS	14 to 16 (tube cake)	8 (loaf cake)	6 (ring cake)
INGREDIENTS			
sifted cake flour	2-1/4 cups	1 cup plus 2 tablespoons	3/4 cup
sugar	1 cup	1/2 cup	1/3 cup
baking powder	1 tablespoon	1-1/2 teaspoons	1 teaspoon
salt	1 teaspoon	1/2 teaspoon	1/4 teaspoon
egg whites	1 cup (about 8)	1/2 cup (about 4)	1/3 cup (about 3)
cream of tartar	1/2 teaspoon	1/4 teaspoon	1/4 teaspoon
sugar	1/2 cup	1/4 cup	3 tablespoons
egg yolks	1/2 cup (about 6)	1/4 cup (about 3)	3 tablespoons (2)
vegetable oil	1/2 cup	1/4 cup	3 tablespoons
flavored yogurt	1 cup	1/2 cup	1/3 cup
grated citrus peel	2 teaspoons	1 teaspoon	3/4 teaspoon
flaked coconut	1 cup	1/2 cup	1/3 cup
frosting, pages 462 to 464, if desired	see amount in Cake-Frosting Guide, page 463		
BAKING PAN (without non-stick coating)	10-inch tube pan (angel-food-cake pan)	9" x 5" x 3" loaf pan	6-1/2-cup ring mold
BEATING TIME AT HIGH SPEED (soft peaks)	1 to 1-1/2 minutes	1 to 1-1/2 minutes	1 to 1-1/2 minutes
BEATING TIME AT HIGH SPEED (stiff peaks)	1-1/2 to 2 minutes	1-1/2 to 2 minutes	1-1/2 to 2 minutes
TIME IN 350F (175C) OVEN	60 to 70 minutes	50 to 55 minutes	30 to 35 minutes
COOLING TIME (inverted, before frosting)	2-1/4 hours	1-3/4 hours	1-1/2 hours

Preheat oven to 350F (175C). Do not use non-stick coated pans. If using a 6-1/2-cup ring mold, grease bottom only; line bottom with a narrow piece of waxed paper. If using tube pan or loaf pan, do not grease. In a small mixer bowl, sift together cake flour, first amount of sugar, baking powder and salt; set aside. In a large mixer bowl, beat egg whites and cream of tartar at high speed of an electric mixer for 1 to 1-1/2 minutes or until soft peaks form. Scrape sides of bowl constantly. Gradually add second amount of sugar, beating at high speed of mixer 1-1/2 to 2 minutes or until very stiff peaks form. Scrape sides of bowl constantly. When stiff enough, egg whites should hold a trench when a spatula is drawn through bowl. Set egg whites aside. Make a well in center of dry ingredients. Add to well in order: egg yolks, oil, yogurt and citrus peel. Beat at low speed of mixer 10 seconds to blend. Turn mixer to medium speed. Beat 1 minute or until satin smooth. Scrape sides of bowl constantly. Stir in coconut. Gently fold yolk mixture into egg-white mixture, one-third at a time. Pour into ungreased tube pan or loaf pan, see size in chart above, or prepared ring mold. Spread batter evenly in pan. Bake in preheated oven for time in chart above or until a long skewer inserted in center of cake comes out clean. Invert cake. Cool in pan, suspended upside-down, for time in chart above. Do not remove from pan until completely cool. To loosen, run a sharp knife around edge of pan. With a wide spatula, wedge loaf cake away from pan. Prepare frosting, if desired. Swirl frosting on cooled cake.

Suggested Combinations
Lemon Chiffon Cake: Use lemon yogurt and lemon peel.
Orange Chiffon Cake, photo on page 465: Use orange yogurt and orange peel.
Mocha Chiffon Cake: Sift instant, presweetened, cocoa drink mix with flour. Use 1/2 cup cocoa drink mix for large recipe, 1/4 cup for medium recipe and 3 tablespoons for small recipe. Use coffee yogurt and orange peel.
Pineapple Chiffon Cake: Use pineapple yogurt and orange peel.

Note: To use leftover egg yolks from this cake, prepare Basic Creamy Butter Frosting, page 462.

How to Make Basic Chiffon Cake

1/Beat egg whites at high speed until soft peaks form; tips of peaks will curl over. Gradually add sugar; beat until stiff peaks form. Stiff egg whites hold a trench when a spatula is drawn across the bottom of the bowl through the egg whites.

2/Sift together cake flour, sugar, baking powder and salt. Make a well in flour mixture. Add egg yolks, oil, flavored yogurt and citrus peel to well in sifted dry ingredients. Beat at low speed of mixer 10 seconds to blend, then at medium speed 1 minute. Add flaked coconut. Fold mixture into egg whites.

3/Pour batter into an ungreased pan. Do not use non-stick-coated pans. Chiffon cake rises by clinging to sides of pan. To test for doneness, insert a long skewer into center of cake. Skewer should come out clean when cake is done. Chiffon-cake flavors include orange, pineapple, mocha and this lemon flavor.

4/Chiffon cakes are cooled upside-down in pan. Some tube pans have supports to hold cake off counter. For loaf cake, use 2 measuring cups or other objects of equal height to support inverted loaf pan. Counter or supports should not touch top of cake. Loosen sides of cooled cake with a knife. Use a wide spatula to wedge loaf cake away from pan.

Sponge Cake

SERVINGS	14 to 16 (tube cake)	10 (jelly roll)	8 (loaf cake)
INGREDIENTS			
all-purpose flour	1-1/2 cups	1 cup	3/4 cup
baking powder	1-1/2 teaspoons	1 teaspoon	3/4 teaspoon
egg whites	6	4	3
sugar	1/2 cup	1/3 cup	1/4 cup
egg yolks	6	4	3
sugar	1 cup	2/3 cup	1/2 cup
water	1/2 cup	1/3 cup	1/4 cup
lemon juice	2 tablespoons	4 teaspoons	1 tablespoon
MIXER BOWL (egg whites)	3-qt. bowl	3-qt. bowl	3-qt. bowl
MIXER BOWL (egg yolks)	1-1/2-qt. bowl	1-1/2-qt. bowl	1-1/2-qt. bowl
BAKING PAN	10-inch tube pan (angel-food-cake pan)	15" x 10" x 1" jelly-roll pan	9" x 5" x 3" loaf pan
BEATING TIME AT HIGH **SPEED (soft peaks)**	1 to 1-1/2 minutes	1 to 1-1/2 minutes	1 to 1-1/2 minutes
BEATING TIME AT HIGH **SPEED (stiff peaks)**	1 to 1-1/2 minutes	1 to 1-1/2 minutes	1 to 1-1/2 minutes
BEATING TIME AT HIGH **SPEED (egg yolks)**	8 minutes	7 minutes	6 minutes
Baking time for tube cake **and loaf cake:** **TIME IN 325F (165C) OVEN**	45 to 50 minutes		40 to 45 minutes
Baking time for jelly-roll cake: **TIME IN 375F (190C) OVEN**		18 to 22 minutes	
COOLING TIME **(inverted, before frosting)**	2-1/2 hours	2 hours	1 hour
REFRIGERATE	omit	1 hour	omit

Preheat oven to 325F (165C) to bake tube or loaf cake. Preheat oven to 375F (190C) to bake jelly-roll cake. In a small bowl, combine flour and baking powder; set aside. In a 3-quart mixer bowl, beat egg whites at high speed of an electric mixer 1 to 1-1/2 minutes or until soft peaks form. Scrape sides of bowl constantly. Gradually add first amount of sugar, beating at high speed of mixer 1 to 1-1/2 minutes or until stiff peaks form. Scrape sides of bowl often. Set egg-white mixture aside. In a 1-1/2-quart mixer bowl, beat egg yolks and second amount of sugar at high speed of mixer for time in chart above or until very thick and lemon-colored. Scrape sides of bowl occasionally. Turn mixer to low speed. Blend in water and lemon juice at low speed. Beat in flour mixture at low speed 20 seconds or until smooth. Gently fold yolk mixture into egg-white mixture, one-third at a time.

For tube cake or loaf cake: Pour batter into an ungreased 10-inch tube pan or 9" x 5" x 3" loaf pan. Do not use non-stick-coated pans. Spread batter evenly in pan. Bake in preheated oven for time in chart above or until a wooden skewer inserted in center comes out clean. Invert cake. Cool in pan, suspended upside-down, for time in chart above. Do not remove from pan until completely cool. To loosen, run a sharp knife around edge of pan. With a wide spatula, wedge cake away from pan. Use for shortcake or Basic Fruit Trifle, page 438.

For jelly-roll cake: Line bottom of jelly-roll pan with waxed paper. Grease waxed paper. Spread batter gently but evenly in pan. Bake in preheated oven 18 to 22 minutes or until cake is light golden brown and springs back when gently touched. Immediately loosen sides by running a sharp knife around edge of pan. Turn out on a towel sprinkled with powdered sugar. Peel off waxed paper. Trim cake edges, if needed. Roll up cake in towel, starting at narrow end. Cool on a rack 2 hours. Unroll and spread with 2 to 2-1/2 cups Basic Special Whipped Cream, page 489, frosting, Basic Yogurt Dessert Filling, page 454, or 1 cup jelly. Leave a 1-inch border between edge of cake and filling. Roll up, starting at narrow end. Refrigerate at least 1 hour before slicing in 1-inch slices.

How to Make a Sponge-Cake Jelly Roll

1/Line a 15" x 10" x 1" pan with waxed paper. Grease waxed paper. Gently spread sponge-cake batter in pan. Bake in a 375F (190C) oven 18 to 22 minutes or until top springs back when lightly touched. Immediately turn out cake on a towel sprinkled with powdered sugar. Peel off waxed paper. Trim cake edges, if needed. Roll up warm cake and towel.

2/Cool cake in towel on a rack 2 hours. Gently unroll cake. Spread with jelly, Basic Special Whipped Cream, page 489, frosting or Basic Yogurt Dessert Filling, page 454. Leave a 1-inch border between edge of cake and filling. Filling will spread to this border as it is rolled.

3/Carefully roll up cake again. Spoon off excess filling that builds up in front of roll as you roll cake.

4/Refrigerate rolled-up cake at least 1 hour. Cut chilled jelly roll in 1-inch slices to serve. Garnish with sprigs of mint, if desired.

Basic Creamy Butter Frosting

YIELD	3-1/3 cups	1-2/3 cups	2/3 cup
INGREDIENTS			
butter or margarine, softened	1 cup	1/2 cup	1/4 cup
powdered sugar	3 cups	1-1/2 cups	3/4 cup
egg yolks	2	1	2 teaspoons
flavoring liquid	2 to 3 tablespoons	1 to 2 tablespoons	1 to 2 teaspoons
MIXER BOWL	1-1/2-qt. bowl	1-1/2-qt. bowl	1-1/2-qt. bowl
BEATING TIME AT HIGH SPEED (butter)	3-1/2 minutes	3 minutes	2 minutes
BEATING TIME AT HIGH SPEED (sugar, yolk added)	3 minutes	2 minutes	2 minutes

In a 1-1/2-quart mixer bowl, beat butter or margarine at high speed of an electric mixer for time in chart above or until fluffy. Scrape sides of bowl occasionally. Turn mixer to low speed. Gradually beat in sugar and egg yolk to blend. Turn mixer to high speed. Beat for time in chart above or until light and fluffy. Turn mixer to low speed. Beat in enough flavoring liquid to make frosting of spreading consistency.

Suggested Combinations
Lemon or Orange Creamy Butter Frosting: Use lemon or orange juice for flavoring liquid. Stir in 1/2 teaspoon grated lemon or orange peel per cup of frosting.
Chocolate Creamy Butter Frosting: Beat in unsweetened cocoa powder when powdered sugar is added. Use 2/3 cup cocoa powder for large recipe, 1/3 cup for medium recipe and 2 tablespoons for small recipe. Use milk for flavoring liquid.
Mocha Creamy Butter Frosting: Prepare Chocolate Creamy Butter Frosting, above, except use cold strong coffee for flavoring liquid.

Fluffy Cloud-Nine Frosting

YIELD	4-1/2 cups	2 cups
INGREDIENTS		
sugar	1 cup	1/2 cup
fruit juice or cold coffee	1/3 cup	3 tablespoons
cream of tartar	1/4 teaspoon	1/8 teaspoon
egg whites	1 teaspoon	1/2 teaspoon
vanilla extract	2	1
food coloring, if desired	few drops	few drops
SAUCEPAN	1-qt. saucepan	1-qt. saucepan
MIXER BOWL	1-1/2-qt. bowl	1-1/2-qt. bowl
BEATING TIME AT HIGH SPEED (while adding hot mixture)	2 minutes	1 minute
BEATING TIME AT HIGH SPEED (stiff peaks)	2 to 3 minutes	1 to 2 minutes

In a 1-quart saucepan, combine sugar, fruit juice or coffee and cream of tartar. Bring just to a boil over Medium-High heat, stirring constantly to dissolve sugar. Place egg whites in a 1-1/2-quart mixer bowl. Beat at high speed of an electric mixer for time in chart above, slowly adding hot mixture and vanilla to egg whites. After adding hot mixture, continue beating at high speed for time in chart above or until stiff peaks form. Beat in food coloring, if desired.

Suggested Fruit Juices: orange juice, apricot nectar, cranberry juice, pineapple juice.

Note: This frosting does not keep longer than 1 day.

How to Frost a Cake

1/Place strips of waxed paper around edges of a serving plate. Place 1 cake layer on serving plate, top-side down. Waxed paper should extend beyond edge of layer. Frost top of this layer with 3/4 to 1 cup frosting. Place second layer, top-side up, on frosted layer. Bottoms of cake layers should be together.

2/Spread a thin base coat of frosting on sides of cake; then swirl more frosting on sides. Use 1-1/2 cups frosting in total for sides. Swirl about 1-1/2 to 2 cups frosting on top of cake. Carefully pull out waxed-paper strips for a clean serving plate. This is Chocolate Cake, page 452, with Chocolate Creamy Butter Frosting.

Cake-Frosting Guide

CAKE	amount creamy-type frosting	amount fluffy-type frosting
tube cake	3-1/3 to 3-3/4 cups	4-1/2 cups
ring cake	1-2/3 to 2 cups	2 cups
2-layer cake	3-1/3 to 3-3/4 cups	4-1/2 cups
9" x 5" x 3" loaf cake	1-2/3 to 2 cups	2 cups
13" x 9" cake	1-2/3 to 2 cups	2 cups
6 small tube cakes	1-2/3 to 2 cups	2 cups
12 to 16 cupcakes	2/3 to 1 cup	2 cups
1-layer cake	2/3 to 1 cup	2 cups
8-inch-square cake	2/3 to 1 cup	1 cup
15" x 10" x 1" cake	1-2/3 to 2 cups	2 cups

Creamy Cheese Frosting

YIELD	3-3/4 cups	2 cups	1 cup
INGREDIENTS			
shortening	1/3 cup	1/4 cup	2 tablespoons
cream cheese, softened	1-1/2 (3-oz.) pkgs.	1 (3-oz.) pkg.	1/2 (3-oz.) pkg.
powdered sugar	3 cups	2 cups	1 cup
fruit juice or milk	3 tablespoons	2 tablespoons	1 tablespoon
grated citrus peel, if desired	1-1/2 teaspoons	1 teaspoon	1/2 teaspoon
powdered sugar	3 cups	2 cups	1 cup
milk	2 to 3 tablespoons	1 to 2 tablespoons	2 to 3 teaspoons
food coloring, if desired	few drops	few drops	few drops
MIXER BOWL	1-1/2-qt. bowl	1-1/2-qt. bowl	1-1/2-qt. bowl
BEATING TIME AT MEDIUM SPEED (shortening, cream cheese)	1 minute	1 minute	30 seconds
BEATING TIME AT MEDIUM SPEED (first sugar, first liquid added)	45 seconds	30 seconds	30 seconds
BEATING TIME AT MEDIUM SPEED (second sugar, milk added)	2 minutes	2 minutes	1 minute

In a 1-1/2-quart mixer bowl, beat shortening and cream cheese at medium speed of an electric mixer for time in chart above or until fluffy. Add first amount of powdered sugar, fruit juice or first amount of milk, and citrus peel, if desired. Beat at medium speed of mixer for time in chart above or until blended. Add second amount of powdered sugar alternately with second amount of milk, beating at medium speed of mixer for time in chart above or until frosting is of spreading consistency. Beat in food coloring, if desired.

Suggested Fruit Juices: lemon juice, orange juice, sweetened coconut juice.

Basic Cake Glaze

YIELD	about 1 cup	about 1/2 cup
INGREDIENTS		
butter or margarine	1/4 cup	2 tablespoons
powdered sugar	2 cups	1 cup
vanilla extract	1 teaspoon	1/2 teaspoon
cooking liquid	2 to 4 tablespoons	1 to 2 tablespoons
SAUCEPAN	1-qt. saucepan	1-qt. saucepan

In a 1-quart saucepan, melt butter or margarine. Stir in powdered sugar and vanilla; mix well. Gradually stir in enough cooking liquid to give mixture smooth, drizzling consistency. Use as topping for cream puffs, éclairs, tube cakes or coffee breads.

Suggested Combinations
Vanilla Cake Glaze: Use milk for cooking liquid.
Chocolate Cake Glaze: Melt unsweetened (1-ounce) chocolate squares with butter or margarine, stirring constantly to melt chocolate. Use 2 squares chocolate for large recipe and 1 square for small recipe. Use milk for cooking liquid.
Orange Cake Glaze: Use orange juice for cooking liquid.

Orange Chiffon Cake, page 458, with Creamy Cheese Frosting.

How to Make Crumb Pie Crust

1/Place cookies for crumb crust in a plastic bag, then crush with a rolling pin. Or, use the steel blade of a food processor to crush cookies. Vanilla wafers, chocolate wafers and graham crackers, layered in the jar, make excellent crumb crusts.

2/Press buttery crumb mixture evenly against bottom and sides of a pie plate. Bake until lightly browned, then press crumbs against bottom and sides of plate again. Cool before adding filling, such as Strawberry Parfait Pie filling, page 488.

Crumb Pie Crust

YIELD	10-inch crust	9-inch crust	7-inch crust
INGREDIENTS			
fine vanilla-wafer, chocolate-wafer or graham-cracker crumbs	2 cups	1-1/2 cups	1 cup
sugar	1/4 cup	3 tablespoons	2 tablespoons
butter or margarine, melted	1/2 cup	6 tablespoons	1/4 cup
PIE PLATE	10-inch pie plate	9-inch pie plate	7-inch pie plate
TIME IN 350F (175C) OVEN	10 to 12 minutes	8 to 10 minutes	8 to 10 minutes

Preheat oven to 350F (175C). Lightly butter a pie plate, see size in chart above; set aside. In a medium bowl, combine cookie crumbs and sugar. Drizzle butter or margarine over crumb mixture. Stir until all crumbs are moistened. Spoon crumb mixture into buttered pie plate. Press crumbs evenly and firmly against bottom and sides. Bake in preheated oven for time in chart above or until lightly browned. Cool pie crust on a rack. When slightly cooled, press crumbs firmly against bottom and sides of pie plate. Fill when cool.

Variations
Crumb Tart Crusts: For small tart shells that hold 3 to 5 tablespoons filling, use 2 to 3 tablespoons crumb mixture for each. Bake in preheated 350F (175C) oven 8 minutes. Large recipe crumb mixture makes 16 to 24 tart shells, medium recipe makes 11 to 16 tart shells and small recipe makes 7 to 10 tart shells.
Filled-Cookie Crumb Pie Crust: Use crushed lemon-, chocolate-, or vanilla-filled sandwich cookies instead of plain wafers or graham-cracker crumbs. Omit sugar. Decrease butter or margarine by half.

How to Make a Pastry Shell

1/After preparing pastry dough, roll it out on a floured board. Invert the pie plate on dough to check size. Dough should be about 2 inches bigger in diameter than inverted pie plate. Trim excess dough with a pastry wheel or knife, if desired.

2/Fit dough into pie plate. Do not stretch dough or it will shrink during baking. Trim dough 1 inch beyond edge of pie plate. Fold edge under and flute. Prick bottom and sides of dough all over before baking.

Pastry Shell

YIELD	10-inch shell	9-inch shell	7-inch shell
INGREDIENTS			
all-purpose flour	1-3/4 cups	1-1/3 cups	1 cup
salt	1/2 teaspoon	1/2 teaspoon	1/4 teaspoon
shortening	2/3 cup	1/2 cup	1/3 cup
cold water	4 to 5 tablespoons	3 to 4 tablespoons	2 to 3 tablespoons
PIE PLATE	10-inch pie plate	9-inch pie plate	7-inch pie plate
TIME IN 450F (230C) OVEN	13 to 15 minutes	12 to 14 minutes	12 to 14 minutes

Preheat oven to 450F (230C). In a medium bowl, mix flour and salt. With a pastry blender or 2 knives, cut in shortening until most pieces are size of peas. Sprinkle cold water evenly over surface, 1 tablespoon at a time, mixing and tossing with a fork until flour is moistened. Shape dough into a ball. On a floured board, flatten ball into a circle. Roll out dough until it is about 2 inches larger than the inverted pie plate, see size in chart above. Fit dough into pie plate. Trim dough about 1 inch beyond edge. Fold edge under and flute.

For baked pastry shell: Prick bottom and sides of pastry all over with a fork. Bake in preheated 450F (230C) oven for time in chart above or until lightly browned. Cool pastry shell on a rack. Fill when cool.

For unbaked pastry shell: Do not prick pastry or bake. Use for pies such as Pumpkin Pie, page 484, or Pecan Pie, page 485, in which pastry is baked with filling.

For prebaked quiche shell: Fit pastry dough into a baking dish, see size in Basic Quiche, page 260. Flute edge, but do not prick pastry. With a piece of foil, line unbaked pastry shell. Add 1-1/2 cups dry beans. Bake in preheated 450F (230C) oven 10 minutes. Remove foil and beans. Cool pastry shell on a rack.

For deep-dish pies, photos on page 479: Prepare pastry dough as above. Roll out dough on a floured board until 1 inch larger than the inverted casserole. Lay pastry dough directly on filling in casserole. Fold edge of dough under and flute edge against side of casserole. Make slits for steam to escape. Bake in preheated 400F (205C) oven for time in desired fruit-pie recipe, pages 470 to 478.

Double-Crust or Lattice Pastry

YIELD	10-inch double crust	9-inch double crust	7-inch double crust
INGREDIENTS			
all-purpose flour	2-2/3 cups	2 cups	1-3/4 cups
salt	1/2 teaspoon	1/2 teaspoon	1/4 teaspoon
shortening	1 cup	3/4 cup	2/3 cup
cold water	7 to 8 tablespoons	6 to 7 tablespoons	4 to 5 tablespoons
PIE PLATE	10-inch pie plate	9-inch pie plate	7-inch pie plate
TIME IN 400F (205C) OVEN	see timings in pie recipes		

In a medium bowl, mix flour and salt. With a pastry blender or 2 knives, cut in shortening until most pieces are size of peas. Sprinkle cold water evenly over surface, 1 tablespoon at a time, mixing and tossing with a fork until flour is moistened. Shape dough into a ball. Divide ball into two-thirds and one-third portions. On a floured board, flatten larger ball into a circle. Roll out dough until it is about 2 inches larger than the inverted pie plate, see size in chart above. Fit dough into pie plate. Trim dough about 1/2 inch beyond edge. On floured board, flatten remaining ball into a circle. Roll out dough until it is about 1 inch larger than top of pie plate.

For double-crust pie: Place filling in unbaked pastry shell. Lay pastry circle over filling. Trim dough about 1/2 inch beyond edge of pie plate. Fold edges of top and bottom crusts together over or under to seal edge. Flute edge. Make slits for steam to escape.

For lattice-top pie: Place filling in unbaked pastry shell. Cut pastry circle in 1/2-inch strips. Twist half of strips; lay about 1 inch apart on pie. Twist remaining strips; lay diagonally across first strips, forming diamond-shaped openings. Trim ends of strips about 1/2 inch beyond edge of pie plate. Fold bottom edge of crust over ends of strips, rolling tightly together to seal. Flute edge.

Note: Each pie recipe specifies double-crust or lattice-top crust. These pastry tops are not interchangeable.

How to Make Pastry

1/Measure your pie plate with water to determine size. In this book, 10-inch pie plates hold 5-1/2 cups, 9-inch pie plates hold 4 cups and 7-inch pie plates hold 2-1/2 cups. Follow recipe size closest to your pie-plate size.

2/Using a pastry blender or 2 table knives, cut shortening into flour and salt until most pieces of mixture are about size of peas. Smaller pieces of shortening make pastry more tender. Larger pieces make pastry more flaky.

3/Sprinkle 1 tablespoon cold water at a time over flour mixture. Toss mixture with water, pushing moistened portions to 1 side. Keep adding water and tossing mixture with a fork until all dough is moistened.

4/Use your hand to form dough into a ball in the bowl. Pick up dough and form into a solid ball. For double-crust or lattice-top pies, divide ball into two-thirds and one-third portions. For pastry shell or deep-dish pie, use all of dough.

5/On a floured surface, press dough ball into a flat circle. With a rolling pin, roll dough from center toward edge. Keep board well-floured under pastry. After several rolls, pick up pastry and give it a quarter or half turn. Roll and turn again until dough is desired diameter.

6/You may bake pie on a pizza pan to catch any juices that overflow. If edge of pie browns too quickly, cover edge with strips of foil. For more even browning, give pie a half turn midway through baking. Most ovens brown food more quickly at the back.

Preparation Method for Fruit Pies

Preheat oven to 400F (205C). In a small bowl, combine granulated sugar, brown sugar, flour or corn-starch and spice. Mix with a fork until well-blended. In a large bowl, toss together fruit and fruit juice or liqueur. Gently fold sugar mixture into fruit mixture. Set aside while preparing dough for Double-Crust or Lattice Pastry, page 468. Fit dough into a pie plate, see size in chart. Trim dough 1/2 inch beyond edge. Spoon in fruit mixture. Lay top crust or lattice top over filling. Trim dough 1/2 inch beyond edge. Fold top and bottom edges together, rolling over or under until even with rim of pie plate. Flute edge. If using top crust instead of lattice top, make slits for steam to escape. Bake in preheated oven for time in chart or until pastry is browned, fruit juices are bubbling through lattice top or steam vents near center, and fruit is tender. Cover edge of pie with strips of foil if crust browns too quickly. Cool for time in chart before serving.

Note: Each fruit-pie recipe specifies double crust or lattice-top crust. These pastry tops are not interchangeable.

Apple Pie

YIELD	10-inch pie (8 wedges)	9-inch pie (6 wedges)	7-inch pie (4 wedges)
INGREDIENTS			
granulated sugar	1/2 cup	1/3 cup	1/4 cup
packed brown sugar	1/2 cup	1/3 cup	1/4 cup
all-purpose flour	3 tablespoons	2 tablespoons	1-1/2 tablespoons
ground spice	1-1/2 teaspoons	1 teaspoon	3/4 teaspoon
sliced, peeled, baking apples	8 cups (2-1/2 lbs., about 8 apples)	6 cups (2 lbs., about 6 apples)	4 cups (1-1/4 lbs., about 4 apples)
lemon juice	2 tablespoons	4 teaspoons	1 tablespoon
Double-Crust Pastry, page 468	large recipe	medium recipe	small recipe
PIE PLATE	10-inch pie plate	9-inch pie plate	7-inch pie plate
TIME IN 400F (205C) OVEN	50 to 60 minutes	50 to 60 minutes	50 to 60 minutes
COOLING TIME	3 hours	3 hours	2 hours

Follow directions for Preparation Method for Fruit Pies, above.

Suggested Spices: cinnamon, nutmeg, allspice.
Suggested Apples: Rome Beauty, Granny Smith, Golden Delicious.

Tips for Pastry Substitution
- To substitute pie-crust sticks for homemade double-crust or lattice-top pastry crust, allow:
    2-1/2 sticks for 10-inch pie
    2 sticks for 9-inch pie
    1-1/2 sticks for 7-inch pie
- To substitute pie-crust sticks for homemade pastry shell, allow:
    1-1/2 sticks for 10-inch shell
    1 stick for 9-inch shell
    1 stick for 7-inch shell
- Commercial frozen pastry shells do not hold as much filling as called for in these recipes. If you use frozen pastry shells, expect to have leftover filling.

How to Make Double-Crust Fruit Pie

1/Thoroughly mix sugars and flour or cornstarch with spice to separate starch granules. Otherwise fruit filling will be thin and have lumps of flour or cornstarch. Toss fruit with fruit juice or liqueur. Fold in sugar mixture. Spoon fruit mixture into unbaked pastry shell.

2/Place top pastry crust over fruit. To transfer crust easily from the board to pie, gently roll crust onto rolling pin; unroll carefully over top of pie. With scissors or a small knife, trim top pastry about 1/2 inch beyond rim of pie plate. If necessary, patch small pieces of pastry around edge to make top even.

3/Fold bottom and top pastry edges together, rolling either over or under until even with rim of pie plate. There are many ways to flute edge of pastry. A classic technique is to push forefinger of 1 hand against thumb and forefinger of other hand.

4/Cut slits in top crust so steam can escape. Make vents in sunburst pattern radiating from center or in random slashes across top of pie. Or, cut out leaf, flower, fruit or other design in top crust to vent steam. Design is usually in center of pie.

Blueberry Pie

YIELD	10-inch pie (8 wedges)	9-inch pie (6 wedges)	7-inch pie (4 wedges)
INGREDIENTS			
granulated sugar	1/2 cup	1/3 cup	1/4 cup
packed brown sugar	1/2 cup	1/3 cup	1/4 cup
all-purpose flour	1/3 cup	1/4 cup	3 tablespoons
ground spice	1 teaspoon	3/4 teaspoon	1/2 teaspoon
fresh or thawed frozen blueberries with juice	6 cups (about 26 oz.)	5 cups (about 22 oz.)	3 cups (about 13 oz.)
fruit juice or liqueur	3 tablespoons	2 tablespoons	1 tablespoon
Lattice Pastry, page 468	large recipe	medium recipe	small recipe
PIE PLATE	10-inch pie plate	9-inch pie plate	7-inch pie plate
TIME IN 400F (205C) OVEN	45 to 55 minutes	45 to 50 minutes	45 to 50 minutes
COOLING TIME	3 hours	3 hours	2 hours

Follow directions for Preparation Method for Fruit Pies, page 470.

Suggested Spices: orange peel, lemon peel, allspice, cinnamon.
Suggested Fruit Juice or Liqueur: lemon juice or orange liqueur.

Note: If using unthawed frozen blueberries, add about 15 minutes to baking time.

Cherry Pie

YIELD	10-inch pie (8 wedges)	9-inch pie (6 wedges)	7-inch pie (4 wedges)
INGREDIENTS			
granulated sugar	2/3 cup	1/2 cup	1/3 cup
packed brown sugar	2/3 cup	1/2 cup	1/3 cup
cornstarch	1/4 cup	3 tablespoons	2 tablespoons
ground spice	1 teaspoon	3/4 teaspoon	1/2 teaspoon
fresh or frozen, pitted, tart, red cherries	6 cups (about 28 oz.)	5 cups (about 23 oz.)	3 cups (about 14 oz.)
fruit juice or liqueur	3 tablespoons	2 tablespoons	1 tablespoon
Lattice Pastry, page 468	large recipe	medium recipe	small recipe
PIE PLATE	10-inch pie plate	9-inch pie plate	7-inch pie plate
TIME IN 400F (205C) OVEN	55 to 65 minutes	55 to 65 minutes	45 to 55 minutes
COOLING TIME	3 hours	3 hours	2 hours

Follow directions for Preparation Method for Fruit Pies, page 470.

Suggested Spices: orange peel, lemon peel, mace.
Suggested Fruit Juice or Liqueur: lemon juice, orange liqueur, crème de cassis.

How to Make a Lattice-Top Pie

1/After making pastry shell with two-thirds of pastry dough, roll out remaining one-third of dough. Cut with a pastry wheel or knife in 1/2-inch strips.

2/Twist half of dough strips; place across pie filling at about 1-inch intervals.

3/Twist remaining dough strips; place 1 inch apart diagonally across first set of strips, forming diamond-shaped openings. Trim ends 1/2 inch beyond rim of pie plate.

4/Fold edge of bottom crust over ends of strips, rolling together to seal. Use a measuring spoon as a prop to flute edge.

Apricot Pie

YIELD	10-inch pie (8 wedges)	9-inch pie (6 wedges)	7-inch pie (4 wedges)
INGREDIENTS			
granulated sugar	1/2 cup	1/3 cup	1/4 cup
packed brown sugar	1/2 cup	1/3 cup	1/4 cup
all-purpose flour	6 tablespoons	1/4 cup	3 tablespoons
ground spice	1 teaspoon	3/4 teaspoon	1/2 teaspoon
fresh apricots, cut in eighths	6 cups (2-3/4 lbs., about 17 apricots)	4 cups (2 lbs., about 12 apricots)	3 cups (1-1/3 lbs., about 8-1/2 apricots)
fruit juice or liqueur	2 tablespoons	4 teaspoons	1 tablespoon
Double-Crust Pastry, page 468	large recipe	medium recipe	small recipe
PIE PLATE	10-inch pie plate	9-inch pie plate	7-inch pie plate
TIME IN 400F (205C) OVEN	50 minutes	50 minutes	45 minutes
COOLING TIME	3 hours	3 hours	2 hours

Follow directions for Preparation Method for Fruit Pies, page 470.

Suggested Spices: nutmeg, allspice, cinnamon.
Suggested Fruit Juice or Liqueur: lemon juice, apricot brandy, orange liqueur.

Peach Pie

YIELD	10-inch pie (8 wedges)	9-inch pie (6 wedges)	7-inch pie (4 wedges)
INGREDIENTS			
granulated sugar	1/2 cup	1/3 cup	1/4 cup
packed brown sugar	1/2 cup	1/3 cup	1/4 cup
all-purpose flour	6 tablespoons	1/4 cup	3 tablespoons
ground spice	1 teaspoon	3/4 teaspoon	1/2 teaspoon
peeled fresh peaches, cut in 1/2-inch slices	6 cups (3 lbs., about 13 peaches)	4 cups (2 lbs., about 8-1/2 peaches)	3 cups (1-1/3 lbs., about 6-1/2 peaches)
fruit juice or liqueur	2 tablespoons	4 teaspoons	1 tablespoon
Double-Crust Pastry, page 468	large recipe	medium recipe	small recipe
PIE PLATE	10-inch pie plate	9-inch pie plate	7-inch pie plate
TIME IN 400F (205C) OVEN	50 to 55 minutes	50 to 55 minutes	40 to 45 minutes
COOLING TIME	3 hours	3 hours	2 hours

Follow directions for Preparation Method for Fruit Pies, page 470.

Suggested Spices: cinnamon, mace, nutmeg, allspice.
Suggested Fruit Juice or Liqueur: lemon juice, peach brandy.

Pear Pie

YIELD	10-inch pie (8 wedges)	9-inch pie (6 wedges)	7-inch pie (4 wedges)
INGREDIENTS			
granulated sugar	1/3 cup	1/4 cup	2 tablespoons
packed brown sugar	1/3 cup	1/4 cup	2 tablespoons
all-purpose flour	3 tablespoons	2 tablespoons	1-1/2 tablespoons
ground spice	1 teaspoon	3/4 teaspoon	1/2 teaspoon
peeled fresh pears, cut in 1/2-inch slices	8 cups (2-3/4 lbs., about 8 pears)	6 cups (2 lbs., about 6 pears)	4 cups (1-1/2 lbs., about 4 pears)
lemon juice	2 tablespoons	4 teaspoons	1 tablespoon
Double-Crust Pastry, page 468	large recipe	medium recipe	small recipe
PIE PLATE	10-inch pie plate	9-inch pie plate	7-inch pie plate
TIME IN 400F (205C) OVEN	40 to 45 minutes	40 to 45 minutes	40 to 45 minutes
COOLING TIME	3 hours	3 hours	2 hours

Follow directions for Preparation Method for Fruit Pies, page 470.

Suggested Spices: mace, cinnamon, nutmeg, allspice.

Grammy's Jam Snacks

SERVINGS	4	2
INGREDIENTS		
leftover pastry dough	4 (2-1/2-inch) squares	2 (2-1/2-inch) squares
fruit jam	2 teaspoons	1 teaspoon
BAKING SHEET	baking sheet	baking sheet
TIME IN 400F (205C) OVEN	15 minutes	15 minutes

Preheat oven to 400F (205C). Press dough scraps into a ball. Roll out again on a floured surface. Cut in 2-1/2-inch squares. Spoon 1/2 teaspoon jam on half of each square. Fold over other half of square. Seal edges with tines of a fork. Place on a baking sheet. Bake along with pie in preheated oven 15 minutes or until pastry is lightly browned. Cool on a rack.

Tips for Making Fruit Pies

- Thaw large frozen fruits, such as sliced peaches, before baking in pies. You may use frozen blueberries in pies if you increase baking time slightly. You may use frozen raspberries and cherries in pies without increasing baking time. Include any juice from frozen fruit in pie.

- For a pretty top, sprinkle baked pie with a mixture of 1 tablespoon sugar and 1 teaspoon of the ground spice used in the pie.

- Lattice-top pies and double-crust pies have different thickening and cooking times. Do not substitute one for the other.

- You can adapt recipes to make two-fruit pies, such as peach and blueberry. Combine ingredients for 1 (7-inch) blueberry pie and ingredients for 1 (7-inch) peach pie into 1 (10-inch) pie. Bake in preheated 400F (205C) oven. Check for doneness at minimum time given for pie with shortest baking time.

- For easier peeling, fruits such as peaches can be blanched. Plunge fruit into a pan of boiling water 1 minute, then cool in cold water before peeling.

Plum Pie

YIELD	10-inch pie (8 wedges)	9-inch pie (6 wedges)	7-inch pie (4 wedges)
INGREDIENTS			
granulated sugar	1/2 cup	1/3 cup	1/4 cup
packed brown sugar	1/2 cup	1/3 cup	1/4 cup
all-purpose flour	6 tablespoons	1/4 cup	3 tablespoons
ground spice	1 teaspoon	3/4 teaspoon	1/2 teaspoon
Italian purple prune plums, pitted, quartered	6 cups (2-1/4 lbs., about 30 plums)	4 cups (1-1/2 lbs., about 20 plums)	3 cups (1 lb., about 15 plums)
fruit juice or liqueur	2 tablespoons	4 teaspoons	1 tablespoon
Double-Crust Pastry, page 468	large recipe	medium recipe	small recipe
PIE PLATE	10-inch pie plate	9-inch pie plate	7-inch pie plate
TIME IN 400F (205C) OVEN	55 to 60 minutes	45 to 50 minutes	40 to 45 minutes
COOLING TIME	3 hours	3 hours	2 hours

Follow directions for Preparation Method for Fruit Pies, page 470.

Suggested Spices: lemon peel, cinnamon, allspice.
Suggested Fruit Juice or Liqueur: orange juice, orange liqueur, crème de cassis.

Raspberry Pie

YIELD	10-inch pie (8 wedges)	9-inch pie (6 wedges)	7-inch pie (4 wedges)
INGREDIENTS			
granulated sugar	1/2 cup	1/3 cup	1/4 cup
packed brown sugar	1/2 cup	1/3 cup	1/4 cup
all-purpose flour	1/3 cup	1/4 cup	3 tablespoons
ground spice	1 teaspoon	3/4 teaspoon	1/2 teaspoon
fresh or frozen raspberries	6 cups (1-1/2 lbs.)	5 cups (1-1/4 lbs.)	3 cups (12 oz.)
fruit juice or liqueur	3 tablespoons	2 tablespoons	1 tablespoon
Lattice Pastry, page 468	large recipe	medium recipe	small recipe
PIE PLATE	10-inch pie plate	9-inch pie plate	7-inch pie plate
TIME IN 400F (205C) OVEN	55 to 60 minutes	50 to 55 minutes	45 to 50 minutes
COOLING TIME	3 hours	3 hours	2 hours

Follow directions for Preparation Method for Fruit Pies, page 470.

Suggested Spices: lemon peel, allspice, cinnamon, nutmeg.
Suggested Fruit Juice or Liqueur: orange juice, crème de cassis, raspberry liqueur.

Rhubarb Pie

YIELD	10-inch pie (8 wedges)	9-inch pie (6 wedges)	7-inch pie (4 wedges)
INGREDIENTS			
granulated sugar	3/4 cup	2/3 cup	1/3 cup
packed brown sugar	3/4 cup	2/3 cup	1/3 cup
all-purpose flour	2/3 cup	1/2 cup	1/3 cup
ground spice	1 teaspoon	3/4 teaspoon	1/2 teaspoon
fresh or frozen rhubarb, cut in 1/2-inch pieces	6 cups (1-3/4 lbs.)	5 cups (1-1/4 lbs.)	3 cups (12 oz.)
fruit juice or liqueur	3 tablespoons	2 tablespoons	1 tablespoon
Double-Crust Pastry, page 468	large recipe	medium recipe	small recipe
PIE PLATE	10-inch pie plate	9-inch pie plate	7-inch pie plate
TIME IN 400F (205C) OVEN	50 to 60 minutes	50 to 60 minutes	45 to 50 minutes
COOLING TIME	3 hours	3 hours	2 hours

Follow directions for Preparation Method for Fruit Pies, page 470.

Suggested Spices: nutmeg, cinnamon, allspice.
Suggested Fruit Juice or Liqueur: apple juice, orange liqueur.

Basic Spicy Dessert Sauce

YIELD	1 cup	1/2 cup
INGREDIENTS		
sugar	1/4 cup	2 tablespoons
cornstarch	2 tablespoons	1 tablespoon
ground spice	1/4 teaspoon	1/8 teaspoon
fruit juice	2/3 cup	1/3 cup
butter or margarine	2 tablespoons	1 tablespoon
fruit liqueur	2 tablespoons	1 tablespoon
SAUCEPAN	1-qt. saucepan	1-qt. saucepan
TIME AT MEDIUM HIGH	5 to 6 minutes	3 to 4 minutes

In a 1-quart saucepan, combine sugar, cornstarch and spice; mix well. Gradually whisk in fruit juice. Cook over Medium-High heat for time in chart above or until thickened and bubbly all over, whisking constantly. Stir in butter or margarine until melted. Stir in liqueur. Serve warm over cake squares, pie à la mode, plum pudding, hot dessert soufflé or ice cream.

Suggested Combinations
Cinnamon-Cider Dessert Sauce: Use cinnamon for spice. Use apple cider for fruit juice. Use applejack for liqueur.
Ginger-Orange Dessert Sauce: Use ginger for spice. Use orange juice for fruit juice. Use orange liqueur.
Double-Lemon Dessert Sauce: Use ground dried lemon peel for spice. Substitute water for fruit juice. Substitute lemon juice for liqueur.

How to Make Deep-Dish Fruit Pie

1/Deep-dish pies are quicker and lower in calories than other pies. Mix fruit-pie filling as usual. Spoon filling into a casserole with no bottom crust. Roll out pastry dough and fold gently in quarters. Place pastry directly on one-fourth of filling. Unfold pastry gently to cover top of fruit.

2/Fold edge of pastry under. With tines of a fork, flute edge of pastry against side of casserole. Or, flute edge with your fingers or a spoon. Cut vents so steam can escape.

Deep-Dish Fruit Pie

SERVINGS	8	6	4
INGREDIENTS fruit-pie filling, pages 470 to 478	large recipe	medium recipe	small recipe
dough for Pastry Shell, page 467	large recipe	medium recipe	small recipe
CASSEROLE	deep 2-qt. casserole	deep 1-1/2-qt. casserole	deep 1-qt. casserole
TIME IN 400F (205C) OVEN	see timing for fruit-pie recipe you select		
COOLING TIME	3 hours	3 hours	2 hours

Select fruit-pie filling and recipe size. Preheat oven to 400F (205C). In a small bowl, combine granulated sugar, brown sugar, flour or cornstarch and spice called for in fruit-pie recipe. Mix with a fork until well-blended. In a large bowl, toss together fruit and fruit juice or liqueur called for in fruit-pie recipe. Gently fold sugar mixture into fruit mixture. Spoon fruit mixture into a casserole, see size in chart above. Set aside while preparing dough for Pastry Shell. Roll out dough on floured board until 1 inch larger than inverted casserole. Lay pastry dough directly on fruit in casserole. Fold edge of pastry under and flute edge against side of casserole. Make slits for steam to escape. Bake in preheated oven for time in fruit-pie recipe or until pastry is browned, fruit juices are bubbling through steam vents near center, and fruit is tender. Cover edge of pie with strips of foil if crust browns too quickly. Cool for time in chart above before serving.

Cream Meringue Pie

YIELD	10-inch pie (8 wedges)	9-inch pie (6 wedges)
INGREDIENTS		
baked Pastry Shell, page 467	10-inch shell	9-inch shell
egg yolks	4	3
sugar	1 cup	2/3 cup
cornstarch	1/2 cup	1/3 cup
milk	4-1/2 cups	3 cups
vanilla extract	1-1/2 teaspoons	1 teaspoon
Meringue for Pies, opposite	large recipe	small recipe
PIE PLATE	10-inch pie plate	9-inch pie plate
HEAVY SAUCEPAN	3-qt. saucepan	2-qt. saucepan
TIME AT MEDIUM HIGH	16 to 19 minutes	16 to 18 minutes
TIME AT MEDIUM LOW	4 to 5 minutes	3 minutes
TIME IN 350F (175C) OVEN	15 minutes	15 minutes
COOLING TIME (in oven, door ajar)	2 hours	2 hours
COOLING TIME (room temperature)	3 hours	2-1/2 hours

Prepare and bake Pastry Shell, see size in chart above; cool and set aside. In a medium bowl, beat egg yolks; set aside. In a heavy saucepan, see size in chart above, combine sugar and cornstarch; mix well. Gradually whisk in milk. Cook over Medium-High heat for time in chart above or until thickened and bubbly all over, whisking constantly. Reduce heat to Medium Low. Whisk one-fourth of milk mixture into yolks. Whisk yolk mixture into saucepan. Cook and whisk for time in chart above or until filling thickens slightly more. Stir in vanilla. Pour hot filling into cooled pastry shell. Place clear plastic wrap directly on filling surface; set aside. Preheat oven to 350F (175C). Prepare Meringue for Pies. Remove plastic wrap from pie filling. Spread meringue evenly over warm pie, sealing to edge of pastry. Bake in preheated oven 15 minutes or until meringue is golden brown. Turn off oven. Cool pie in oven with door ajar 2 hours. Cool on a rack at room temperature away from drafts for time in chart above before serving. Refrigerate leftover pie.

Variation
Cream Pie: Omit meringue. Do not cover hot pie filling with plastic wrap. Refrigerate until chilled, then cover. To serve, top chilled pie with whipped cream or whipped topping.

Chocolate-Cream Meringue Pie

YIELD	10-inch pie (8 wedges)	9-inch pie (6 wedges)
INGREDIENTS		
baked Pastry Shell, page 467	10-inch shell	9-inch shell
filling for Cream Meringue Pie, above	large recipe	small recipe
semisweet chocolate pieces	1 cup	3/4 cup
Meringue for Pies, opposite	large recipe	small recipe

Prepare and bake Pastry Shell, see size in chart above; cool and set aside. Prepare filling for Cream Meringue Pie. Add chocolate pieces to hot cooked filling. Stir until melted. Fill pastry shell, top with Meringue for Pies, and bake according to directions for Cream Meringue Pie.

Note: If pastry edges are not fluted high enough to hold all of filling, serve extra filling as chocolate pudding.

How to Make Chocolate-Cream Meringue Pie

1/Pour hot chocolate filling into cooled pastry shell. Pat clear plastic wrap directly on filling surface. This prevents a film from forming on filling and keeps filling hot. Hot filling will help cook underside of meringue.

2/Prepare Meringue for Pies. Carefully peel plastic wrap off pie filling. Spread meringue mixture evenly over pie, being careful to seal meringue to edge of pastry all the way around pie. This prevents meringue from shrinking. Bake until meringue is golden brown.

Meringue for Pies

YIELD	to cover 10-inch pie	to cover 9-inch pie
INGREDIENTS		
egg whites	4	3
cream of tartar	1/2 teaspoon	1/4 teaspoon
sugar	1/2 cup	6 tablespoons
MIXER BOWL	1-1/2-qt. bowl	1-1/2-qt. bowl
BEATING TIME AT MEDIUM SPEED	1-1/2 to 2 minutes	1-1/2 to 2 minutes
BEATING TIME AT HIGH SPEED	1 to 1-1/2 minutes	1-1/2 to 2 minutes
TIME IN 350F (175C) OVEN	15 minutes	15 minutes
COOLING TIME (in oven, door ajar)	2 hours	2 hours
COOLING TIME (room temperature)	3 hours	2-1/2 hours

Preheat oven to 350F (175C). In a 1-1/2-quart mixer bowl, combine egg whites and cream of tartar. With an electric mixer at medium speed, beat 15 to 30 seconds or until foamy. Gradually add sugar, beating at medium speed of mixer 1-1/2 to 2 minutes. Turn mixer to high speed. Beat for time in chart above or until stiff peaks form. Spread evenly over warm pie, sealing meringue to edge of pastry. Bake in preheated oven 15 minutes or until meringue is golden brown. Turn off oven. Cool pie in oven with door ajar 2 hours. Cool on a rack at room temperature away from drafts for time in chart above before serving.

Lemon Meringue Pie

YIELD	10-inch pie (8 wedges)	9-inch pie (6 wedges)
INGREDIENTS		
baked Pastry Shell, page 467	10-inch shell	9-inch shell
egg yolks	4	3
sugar	2 cups	1-1/2 cups
cornstarch	3/4 cup	2/3 cup
cold water	1/2 cup	1/2 cup
very hot tap water	2 cups	1-1/2 cups
lemon juice	2/3 cup	1/2 cup
grated lemon peel	1-1/2 teaspoons	1 teaspoon
Meringue for Pies, page 481	large recipe	small recipe
PIE PLATE	10-inch pie plate	9-inch pie plate
HEAVY SAUCEPAN	2-1/2-qt. saucepan	2-qt. saucepan
TIME AT MEDIUM HIGH	11 to 13 minutes	12 to 14 minutes
TIME AT MEDIUM LOW	5 minutes	4 minutes
TIME IN 350F (175C) OVEN	15 minutes	15 minutes
COOLING TIME (in oven, door ajar)	2 hours	2 hours
COOLING TIME (room temperature)	3 hours	2-1/2 hours

Prepare and bake Pastry Shell, see size in chart above; cool and set aside. In a medium bowl, beat egg yolks; set aside. In a heavy saucepan, see size in chart above, combine sugar and cornstarch; mix well. Whisk in cold water until thoroughly combined. Blend in hot tap water and lemon juice. Cook over Medium-High heat for time in chart above or until thickened and bubbly all over, whisking constantly. Reduce heat to Medium Low. Whisk one-fourth of lemon mixture into yolks. Whisk yolk mixture into saucepan. Cook and whisk for time in chart above or until filling thickens slightly more. Stir in lemon peel. Pour hot filling into cooled pastry shell. Place clear plastic wrap directly on filling surface; set aside. Preheat oven to 350F (175C). Prepare Meringue for Pies. Remove plastic wrap from pie filling. Spread meringue evenly over warm pie, sealing to edge of pastry. Bake in preheated oven 15 minutes or until meringue is golden brown. Turn off oven. Cool pie in oven with door ajar 2 hours. Cool on a rack at room temperature away from drafts for time in chart above before serving. Refrigerate leftover pie.

Variation
Lemon Cream Pie: Omit meringue. Do not cover hot pie filling with plastic wrap. Refrigerate until chilled, then cover. To serve, top chilled pie with whipped cream or whipped topping.

Tips for Making Meringue Pie
- Whisk cream filling constantly but not vigorously during cooking. Whisking too rapidly may cause filling to break down.
- Pour hot cream filling into cooled baked pastry shell, then place clear plastic wrap directly on filling surface. This keeps filling piping hot and prevents film from forming on top. Both help bond meringue to filling so it does not slide off.
- When making meringue, add sugar very slowly to egg whites during entire beating time at medium speed. This allows sugar time to dissolve before egg whites are overbeaten.
- After beating at medium speed, egg whites will be shiny and syrupy. Turn mixer to high and beat egg whites just until tips stand straight up when beaters are lifted.
- Meringue should be smooth, glossy and pliable. Overbeating makes meringue dry and lumpy-looking.
- Spread meringue over entire surface of pie so filling does not break down in hot oven. Seal meringue to edge of crust so meringue does not shrink and water out.
- Do not store meringue pies tightly covered or moisture beads may develop on top.
- Cut meringue pie with a wet knife to prevent meringue from sticking to knife. Dip knife in water again after each cut.

Pumpkin Pie

YIELD	10-inch pie (8 wedges)	9-inch pie (6 wedges)	7-inch pie (4 wedges)
INGREDIENTS			
unbaked Pastry Shell, page 467	10-inch shell	9-inch shell	7-inch shell
eggs	5	3	2
pumpkin	1 (16-oz.) can (2 cups)	2/3 (16-oz.) can (1-1/3 cups)	1/3 (16-oz.) can (2/3 cup)
half and half	2 cups	1-1/3 cups	2/3 cup
sugar	1 cup	2/3 cup	1/3 cup
molasses	1/3 cup	1/4 cup	2 tablespoons
brandy or orange juice	1/3 cup	1/4 cup	2 tablespoons
ground cinnamon	1 teaspoon	3/4 teaspoon	1/2 teaspoon
ground ginger	1/2 teaspoon	1/4 teaspoon	1/8 teaspoon
ground nutmeg	1/4 teaspoon	1/8 teaspoon	dash
ground cloves	1/4 teaspoon	1/8 teaspoon	dash
PIE PLATE	10-inch pie plate	9-inch pie plate	7-inch pie plate
MIXER BOWL	3-qt. bowl	3-qt. bowl	1-1/2-qt. bowl
BEATING TIME AT MEDIUM SPEED	1 minute	1 minute	1 minute
TIME IN 375F (190C) OVEN	75 to 80 minutes	60 to 65 minutes	55 to 60 minutes
COOLING TIME	3 hours	3 hours	2 hours

Prepare Pastry Shell. Do not prick or bake shell; set aside. Preheat oven to 375F (190C). In a mixer bowl, see size in chart above, beat eggs at high speed of an electric mixer for 45 to 60 seconds or until foamy. Add pumpkin, half and half, sugar, molasses, brandy or orange juice, cinnamon, ginger, nutmeg and cloves. Beat at low speed of mixer 30 seconds. Turn mixer to medium speed. Beat 1 minute or until blended. Scrape sides of bowl often. Place unbaked pastry shell on oven rack. Pour pumpkin filling into pie shell. Bake in preheated oven for time in chart above or until a knife inserted off-center comes out clean and filling is set. See note below for 10-inch pie. Cool on a rack for time in chart above before serving. Refrigerate leftover pie.

For 10-inch pie: Using 4 pieces of foil, loosely cover outside half of pie after 1 hour of baking. Tuck foil pieces about 1 inch under pie plate. Do not let foil touch filling. Continue baking until done as above. Foil keeps outside of pie from overcooking before center is done.

Double-Cream Dessert Topper   Photo on page 457.

YIELD	2 cups	1 cup
INGREDIENTS		
soft cream cheese	1/2 cup	1/4 cup
powdered sugar	1/4 cup	2 tablespoons
whipping cream	1 cup	1/2 cup
MIXER BOWL	1-1/2-qt. bowl	1-1/2-qt. bowl
BEATING TIME AT HIGH SPEED	1 minute	1 minute
BEATING TIME AT MEDIUM SPEED	1 to 1-1/2 minutes	30 to 60 seconds

Immediately before serving, in a 1-1/2-quart mixer bowl, beat cream cheese and powdered sugar at low speed of an electric mixer until blended. Turn mixer to high speed. Beat 1 minute or until fluffy. Scrape sides of bowl often. Turn mixer to low speed. Blend in whipping cream. Turn mixer to medium speed. Beat for time in chart above or until fluffy. Serve over shortcake, poached fruit or pie.

Note: Topper is best used immediately after preparation, but it can be refrigerated up to 1 week. Stir before using leftover topper.

How to Make Pumpkin Pie

1/To avoid messy spills, place unbaked pastry shell on a rack in preheated oven before pouring in pumpkin filling. A large measuring cup or pitcher makes it easy to pour thin filling into pastry shell.

2/To test for doneness, filling should look set—it should not quiver as you pull out oven rack. A knife inserted off-center should come out clean. Center of pie will finish cooking while cooling.

Pecan Pie

YIELD	10-inch pie (8 wedges)	9-inch pie (6 wedges)	7-inch pie (4 wedges)
INGREDIENTS			
unbaked Pastry Shell, page 467	10-inch shell	9-inch shell	7-inch shell
butter or margarine, softened	1/4 cup	3 tablespoons	2 tablespoons
sugar	2/3 cup	1/2 cup	1/3 cup
eggs	4	3	2
dark corn syrup	1-1/3 cups	1 cup	2/3 cup
ground allspice	1 teaspoon	3/4 teaspoon	1/2 teaspoon
pecan halves	2 cups	1-1/2 cups	1 cup
PIE PLATE	10-inch pie plate	9-inch pie plate	7-inch pie plate
MIXER BOWL	1-1/2-qt. bowl	1-1/2-qt. bowl	1-1/2-qt. bowl
BEATING TIME AT MEDIUM SPEED (cream butter)	3 minutes	2 minutes	1-1/2 to 2 minutes
BEATING TIME AT MEDIUM SPEED (syrup added)	1-1/2 minutes	1 minute	30 seconds
TIME IN 350F (175C) OVEN	45 to 50 minutes	40 to 45 minutes	40 to 45 minutes
COOLING TIME	3 hours	3 hours	2-1/2 hours

Prepare Pastry Shell. Do not prick or bake shell; set aside. Preheat oven to 350F (175C). In a 1-1/2-quart mixer bowl, beat butter or margarine and sugar at medium speed of an electric mixer for time in chart above or until blended. Scrape sides of bowl often. Add eggs, 1 at a time, beating 20 seconds at medium speed after each egg. Scrape sides of bowl often. Mixture will appear curdled. Add corn syrup and allspice. Beat at medium speed for time in chart above or until well-combined. Stir in pecans. Pour nut filling into unbaked pie shell. Bake in preheated oven for time in chart above or until a knife inserted off-center comes out clean and filling is almost set in center. Cool on a rack for time in chart above before serving. Refrigerate leftover pie.

Basic Chiffon Pie

YIELD	10-inch pie (8 wedges)	9-inch pie (6 wedges)	7-inch pie (4 wedges)
INGREDIENTS			
baked Crumb Pie Crust, page 466	10-inch crust	9-inch crust	7-inch crust
unflavored gelatin	4 teaspoons	1 (1/4-oz.) envelope	2 teaspoons
sugar	2/3 cup	1/2 cup	1/3 cup
egg yolks	4	3	2
mashed fruit, fruit juice or cooking liquid	3/4 cup	1/2 cup	1/3 cup
grated citrus peel	1-1/2 teaspoons	1 teaspoon	1/2 teaspoon
liqueur, if desired	1/3 cup	1/4 cup	2 tablespoons
food coloring, if desired	few drops	few drops	few drops
egg whites	4	3	2
cream of tartar	1/4 teaspoon	1/4 teaspoon	1/8 teaspoon
sugar	1/3 cup	1/4 cup	2 tablespoons
flavored yogurt or whipped cream	1-1/3 cups	1 cup	2/3 cup
garnishes, see suggestions below			
PIE PLATE	10-inch pie plate	9-inch pie plate	7-inch pie plate
SAUCEPAN	1-1/2-qt. saucepan	1-1/2-qt. saucepan	1-qt. saucepan
MIXER BOWL	3-qt. bowl	1-1/2-qt. bowl	1-1/2-qt. bowl
TIME AT MEDIUM	15 to 17 minutes	11 to 14 minutes	7 to 9 minutes
BEATING TIME AT MEDIUM SPEED	1-1/2 to 2 minutes	1-1/2 to 2 minutes	1-1/2 to 2 minutes
BEATING TIME AT HIGH SPEED	1-1/2 to 2 minutes	45 seconds	45 seconds
REFRIGERATE	8 hours	8 hours	8 hours

Prepare and bake Crumb Pie Crust; cool and set aside. In a saucepan, see size in chart above, combine unflavored gelatin and first amount of sugar; mix well and set aside. In a medium bowl, whisk together egg yolks, mashed fruit, fruit juice or cooking liquid, citrus peel, and liqueur and food coloring, if desired, until blended. Stir into gelatin mixture. Cook over Medium heat for time in chart above or until mixture thickens slightly and gelatin dissolves, whisking constantly. Cool to room temperature, stirring once or twice. In a mixer bowl, see size in chart above, beat egg whites and cream of tartar at medium speed of an electric mixer for 30 seconds or until foamy. Gradually add second amount of sugar, beating 1-1/2 to 2 minutes. Turn mixer to high speed. Beat for time in chart above or until stiff peaks form. Fold egg-yolk mixture into egg-white mixture. Fold in yogurt or whipped cream. Spoon into cooled pie crust. Refrigerate 8 hours or until firm. Garnish according to suggestions below.

Suggested Combinations

Strawberry Chiffon Pie: Use mashed fresh strawberries for fruit. Use lemon peel. Use strawberry liqueur. Use strawberry yogurt. Garnish with whipped cream and fresh whole strawberries.

Lemon Chiffon Pie: Use lemon juice for fruit juice. Use lemon peel. Omit liqueur. Double amount of sugar beaten with egg whites. Use 2/3 cup for large recipe, 1/2 cup for medium recipe and 1/4 cup for small recipe. Beat egg whites at high speed for approximately double the time given in chart above or until stiff peaks form. Use lemon yogurt. Garnish with whipped cream and lemon twists.

Orange Chiffon Pie: Use orange juice for fruit juice. Use orange peel. Use orange liqueur. Use orange yogurt. Garnish with whipped cream and orange twists.

Eggnog Chiffon Pie: Use eggnog for cooking liquid. Use orange peel. Use amaretto liqueur. Use vanilla yogurt. Garnish with whipped cream and toasted almonds.

Coffee Chiffon Pie: Use cold coffee for cooking liquid. Omit citrus peel. Use coffee liqueur. Use coffee yogurt. Garnish with whipped cream and chocolate curls.

Variation

Cold Dessert Soufflés: Omit pie crust. Spoon pie filling into wine goblets or parfait glasses. Chill. Garnish as above.

How to Make Basic Chiffon Pie

1/Beat egg whites and sugar to stiff peaks. Beaten whites should stand up straight and hold a trench when a spatula is pulled through the bowl. Fold gelatin mixture into egg whites. Use a circular down, up and over motion with the spatula to fold mixture in without deflating egg whites. Give bowl a quarter turn after each folding motion.

2/Refrigerate chiffon filling in a crumb crust until firm. A packed refrigerator will probably not be cold enough to chill pie so it can be cut. Decorate Coffee Chiffon Pie in chocolate crumb crust with chocolate curls. Make curls from large milk chocolate or semisweet chocolate bars. Hold bars in your hands to soften slightly. Use a vegetable peeler to make curls.

Frozen Mock Custard Pie

YIELD	10-inch pie (8 wedges)	9-inch pie (6 wedges)	7-inch pie (4 wedges)
INGREDIENTS			
baked Crumb Pie Crust, page 466	10-inch crust	9-inch crust	7-inch crust
sweetened condensed milk	2 (14-oz.) cans	1-1/2 (14-oz.) cans (2 cups)	1 (14-oz.) can
lemon juice	1/2 cup	6 tablespoons	1/4 cup
frozen whipped topping, thawed	2 cups	1-1/2 cups	1 cup
additional whipped topping, lemon twists, if desired	to garnish	to garnish	to garnish
PIE PLATE	10-inch pie plate	9-inch pie plate	7-inch pie plate
FREEZE	8 hours or overnight	8 hours or overnight	8 hours or overnight

Prepare and bake Crumb Pie Crust; cool and set aside. In a large bowl, whisk together sweetened condensed milk and lemon juice until blended. Fold in first amount of whipped topping. Pour into cooled crumb crust. Cover and freeze 8 hours or overnight until firm. Garnish with additional whipped topping and lemon twists, if desired. With a serrated knife, cut frozen pie in wedges to serve.

Basic Fruit Parfait Pie

YIELD	10-inch pie (8 wedges)	9-inch pie (6 wedges)	7-inch pie (4 wedges)
INGREDIENTS			
baked Pastry Shell, page 467 OR	10-inch shell	9-inch shell	7-inch shell
baked Crumb Pie Crust, page 466	10-inch crust	9-inch crust	7-inch crust
water	2-1/2 cups	1-3/4 cups	1-1/4 cups
fruit-flavored gelatin	2 (3-oz.) pkgs.	1-1/2 (3-oz.) pkgs. (1 pkg. plus 3-1/2 tablespoons)	1 (3-oz.) pkg.
ice cream	1 qt.	1-1/2 pints	1 pint
frozen whipped topping, thawed	1 cup	3/4 cup	1/2 cup
additional whipped topping, fruit	to garnish	to garnish	to garnish
PIE PLATE	10-inch pie plate	9-inch pie plate	7-inch pie plate
SAUCEPAN	3-qt. saucepan	2-qt. saucepan	2-qt. saucepan
REFRIGERATE (filling)	50 to 60 minutes	50 to 60 minutes	45 minutes
REFRIGERATE (finished pie)	8 hours or overnight	8 hours or overnight	8 hours or overnight

Prepare and bake Pastry Shell or Crumb Pie Crust; cool and set aside. In a saucepan, see size in chart above, bring water to a boil. Stir in gelatin until dissolved. Add ice cream by spoonfuls, stirring until melted. Stir first amount of whipped topping, then whisk into ice-cream mixture until smooth. Refrigerate for time in chart above or until mixture mounds when dropped from a spoon. Stir gently occasionally. Spoon ice-cream mixture into cooled pie shell. Cover and refrigerate 8 hours or overnight until firm. Garnish with additional whipped topping and fruit.

Suggested Combinations
Peach Parfait Pie: Use peach-flavored gelatin and peach ice cream.
Lime Parfait Pie: Use lime-flavored gelatin and vanilla ice cream.
Strawberry Parfait Pie: Use strawberry-flavored gelatin and strawberry-swirl ice cream.
Cherry Parfait Pie: Use cherry-flavored gelatin and cherry-nut ice cream.

Variation
Parfait Tarts: Allow 3 to 5 tablespoons filling per tart shell, depending on size. Large recipe, above, makes about 5 cups filling, medium recipe makes about 4 cups and small recipe makes about 2-3/4 cups. Refrigerate tarts 2-1/2 hours or overnight until firm.

Frozen German-Chocolate Pie

YIELD	10-inch pie (8 wedges)	9-inch pie (6 wedges)	7-inch pie (4 wedges)
INGREDIENTS			
baked Pastry Shell, page 467	10-inch shell	9-inch shell	7-inch shell
milk	1-1/2 cups	1 cup	3/4 cup
miniature marshmallows	6 cups	4 cups	3 cups
German sweet chocolate, broken up	2 (4-oz.) bars	1-1/2 (4-oz.) bars	1 (4-oz.) bar
vanilla extract	1 teaspoon	3/4 teaspoon	1/2 teaspoon
frozen whipped topping, thawed	4 cups	3 cups	2 cups
additional whipped topping, chocolate curls, if desired	to garnish	to garnish	to garnish
PIE PLATE	10-inch pie plate	9-inch pie plate	7-inch pie plate
SAUCEPAN	3-qt. saucepan	2-qt. saucepan	1-1/2-qt. saucepan
TIME AT MEDIUM	17 minutes	11 minutes	10 minutes
COOLING TIME	45 minutes	30 minutes	30 minutes
REFRIGERATE	1-1/4 hours	1-1/4 hours	1-1/4 hours
FREEZE	8 hours or overnight	8 hours or overnight	8 hours or overnight

Prepare and bake Pastry Shell; cool and set aside. In a saucepan, see size in chart above, combine milk, marshmallows and chocolate. Cook over Medium heat for time in chart above or until chocolate and marshmallows melt, stirring constantly. Stir in vanilla. Cool in pan at room temperature for time in chart above. Whisk in first amount of whipped topping, one-half at a time. Refrigerate 1-1/4 hours, or until mixture no longer separates, stirring 3 times to combine mixture. Stir and pour into cooled pie shell. Freeze 8 hours or overnight until firm. Garnish with additional whipped topping and chocolate curls, if desired. With a serrated knife, slice frozen pie in wedges to serve.

Basic Special Whipped Cream

YIELD	1-1/2 to 2 cups	3/4 to 1 cup
INGREDIENTS		
whipping cream	1 cup	1/2 cup
powdered sugar	1/4 cup	2 tablespoons
flavoring powder	2 teaspoons	1 teaspoon
flavored extract	1/8 teaspoon	dash
MIXER BOWL	1-1/2-qt. bowl	1-1/2-qt. bowl
BEATING TIME AT MEDIUM SPEED	2-1/4 to 3 minutes	1 to 1-3/4 minutes

In a 1-1/2-quart mixer bowl, combine whipping cream, powdered sugar, flavoring powder and flavored extract. Place beaters in bowl and refrigerate until serving time. Immediately before serving, beat cream mixture at medium speed of an electric mixer for time in chart above or until cream holds a swirl in bowl. Scrape sides of bowl often. Cream should mound softly when dropped from a spoon. Do not overbeat or cream will look lumpy or separate.

Suggested Combinations
Orange-Cappuccino Whipped Cream: Use orange-cappuccino instant coffee for flavoring powder. Use orange extract.
Chocolate Whipped Cream: Use sifted unsweetened cocoa powder for flavoring powder. Use almond extract.
Plain Whipped Cream: Omit flavoring powder. Use vanilla extract, using 1 teaspoon for large recipe and 1/2 teaspoon for small recipe.

Basic Fruit Glacé Pie

YIELD	10-inch pie (8 wedges)	9-inch pie (6 wedges)	7-inch pie (4 wedges)
INGREDIENTS			
baked Pastry Shell, page 467	10-inch shell	9-inch shell	7-inch shell
Basic Fruit Glaze for Pie, below, cooled	large recipe	medium recipe	small recipe
soft cream cheese	2/3 cup	1/2 cup	1/3 cup
sugar	1/4 cup	3 tablespoons	2 tablespoons
grated citrus peel	1-1/2 teaspoons	1 teaspoon	3/4 teaspoon
sliced, peeled fresh fruit or berries	7 to 8 cups	5 to 6 cups	3-1/2 to 4 cups
whipping cream, whipped	to garnish	to garnish	to garnish
PIE PLATE	10-inch pie plate	9-inch pie plate	7-inch pie plate
REFRIGERATE	6 to 8 hours	4 hours	3 hours

Prepare and bake Pastry Shell; cool and set aside. Prepare Basic Fruit Glaze for Pie; cool and set aside. In a small bowl, combine cream cheese, sugar and citrus peel; mix well. Spread evenly in bottom of cooled pie shell. Cover and refrigerate while preparing fruit. Spoon fruit into pie shell, drizzling each layer with some cooled glaze. If using fruit that darkens easily, such as peaches and bananas, cover completely with glaze. Refrigerate at least for time in chart above, but no more than 8 hours before serving. Garnish with whipped cream.

Suggested Combinations
Strawberry-Banana Glacé Pie: Use Pineapple Glaze for Pie. Use lemon peel. Use sliced strawberries and sliced bananas for fruit.
Blueberry-Peach Glacé Pie: Use Lemon Glaze for Pie. Use lemon peel. Use sliced peaches and blueberries for fruit.
Plum-Kiwifruit Glacé Pie: Use Orange Glaze for Pie. Use orange peel. Use plum wedges and sliced kiwifruit for fruit.

Basic Fruit Glaze for Pie

YIELD	2 cups	1-1/3 cups	1 cup
INGREDIENTS			
cornstarch	1/4 cup	3 tablespoons	2 tablespoons
frozen juice concentrate, thawed	1/3 cup	1/4 cup	2 tablespoons
water	1 cup	3/4 cup	1/2 cup
light corn syrup	1/2 cup	1/3 cup	1/4 cup
fruit liqueur or wine	1/4 cup	3 tablespoons	2 tablespoons
ground spice	3/4 teaspoon	1/2 teaspoon	1/4 teaspoon
SAUCEPAN	1-qt. saucepan	1-qt. saucepan	1-qt. saucepan
TIME AT MEDIUM HIGH	9 to 10 minutes	7 to 8 minutes	5 to 6 minutes

In a 1-quart saucepan, combine cornstarch and juice concentrate; mix until smooth. Stir in water, corn syrup, liqueur or wine and spice; mix well. Cook over Medium-High heat for time in chart above or until thickened and bubbly all over, stirring constantly. Mixture should be thick and clear. Cool to room temperature, stirring occasionally. Use for Basic Fruit Glacé Pie, above, or cheesecake.

Suggested Combinations
Orange Glaze for Pie: Use orange-juice concentrate. Use orange liqueur. Use allspice for spice.
Pineapple Glaze for Pie: Use pineapple-juice concentrate. Use white wine. Use ginger for spice.
Lemon Glaze for Pie: Use lemonade concentrate. Use white port wine. Use cinnamon for spice.

Strawberry-Banana Glacé Pie with Pineapple Glaze.

Basic Easy Fruit Cobbler

SERVINGS	8	4	2
INGREDIENTS			
sugar	1/2 to 1 cup	1/4 to 1/2 cup	2 to 4 tablespoons
fruit-flavored gelatin	1 (3-oz.) pkg.	1/2 (3-oz.) pkg. (3-1/2 tablespoons)	2 tablespoons
all-purpose flour	2 tablespoons	1 tablespoon	2 teaspoons
sliced fruit or berries, fresh or thawed frozen with juice	5 cups	2-1/2 cups	1-1/4 cups
packaged biscuit mix	2 cups	1 cup	1/2 cup
sugar	2 tablespoons	1 tablespoon	2 teaspoons
butter or margarine, melted	1/4 cup	2 tablespoons	1 tablespoon
grated citrus peel	1 teaspoon	1/2 teaspoon	1/4 teaspoon
milk	1/2 cup	1/4 cup	2 tablespoons
BAKING DISH	12" x 7" baking dish	9" x 5" x 3" loaf dish	7-inch pie plate
TIME IN 425F (220C) OVEN (fruit mixture)	15 minutes	12 minutes	10 minutes
TIME IN 425F (220C) OVEN (topping added)	18 to 20 minutes	15 to 18 minutes	15 to 18 minutes
COOLING TIME	1 hour	40 minutes	40 minutes

Preheat oven to 425F (220C). In a baking dish, see size in chart above, combine first amount of sugar, gelatin and flour; mix well. Toss fruit with gelatin mixture. Spread evenly in baking dish. Bake in preheated oven for time in chart above. Stir well. In a medium bowl, combine biscuit mix, second amount of sugar, butter or margarine and citrus peel. With a fork, stir in milk until dough follows fork around bowl. Drop by small spoonfuls on hot fruit mixture, allowing 2 drop biscuits for each serving, see number in chart above. Bake in preheated oven for time in chart above or until biscuits are lightly browned and no longer doughy in center. Cool on a rack for time in chart above before serving. Top with ice cream to serve.

Suggested Combinations

Easy Peach Cobbler: Use smaller amount of sugar. Use peach-flavored gelatin. Use sliced peeled peaches for fruit. Use lemon peel. Serve with peach ice cream.

Easy Rhubarb Cobbler: Use larger amount of sugar. Use strawberry-flavored gelatin. Use sliced rhubarb for fruit. Use orange peel. Serve with strawberry ice cream.

Easy Blueberry Cobbler: Use smaller amount of sugar. Use lemon-flavored gelatin. Use blueberries. Use lemon peel. Serve with vanilla ice cream.

Easy Cranberry-Apple Cobbler: Use larger amount of sugar. Use strawberry-flavored gelatin. Use cranberries and sliced peeled apples for fruit. Use orange peel. Serve with cinnamon ice cream.

How to Make Basic Easy Fruit Cobbler

1/In a baking dish, combine sugar, fruit-flavored gelatin and flour. Toss gelatin mixture with fruit, such as apple slices and cranberries. This recipe has strawberry-flavored gelatin.

2/Partially bake fruit mixture. Drop small spoonfuls of biscuit mixture on hot fruit. Bake until biscuits are lightly browned and no longer doughy in center. Top with ice cream to serve.

Basic Fresh-Fruit Crisp

SERVINGS	6 to 8	3 or 4
INGREDIENTS		
granulated sugar	1/2 cup	1/4 cup
packed brown sugar	1/2 cup	1/4 cup
all-purpose flour	1/2 cup	1/4 cup
quick-cooking oats	1/2 cup	1/4 cup
ground spice	1-1/2 teaspoons	3/4 teaspoon
butter or margarine	1/4 cup	2 tablespoons
sliced fresh fruit or berries	6 cups	3 cups
fruit liqueur, wine or juice	1/4 cup	2 tablespoons
BAKING DISH	round, 8-inch cake dish	7-inch pie plate
TIME IN 375F (190C) OVEN	30 to 35 minutes	30 to 35 minutes

Do not preheat oven. In a medium bowl, combine granulated sugar, brown sugar, flour, oats and spice. Cut in butter or margarine until mixture resembles coarse crumbs; set aside. Place fruit in a baking dish. Drizzle with liqueur, wine or juice. Sprinkle with sugar mixture. Bake in a 375F (190C) oven 30 to 35 minutes or until fruit is tender. Serve warm with cream or ice cream, if desired.

Suggested Combinations
Raspberry-Blueberry Crisp: Use nutmeg for spice. Use blueberries and raspberries. Use white wine.
Apple-Pear Crisp: Use cinnamon for spice. Use sliced peeled apples and pears for fruit. Use apple juice.
Peach-Cherry Crisp: Use allspice for spice. Use sliced peeled peaches and pitted, dark sweet cherries for fruit. Use peach brandy for fruit liqueur.

Basic Baked Apples or Pears

SERVINGS	4	2
INGREDIENTS		
large baking apples or pears	4 (6- to 8-oz.) apples or pears	2 (6- to 8-oz.) apples or pears
snipped dried fruit or raisins	1/4 cup	2 tablespoons
packed brown sugar	1/2 cup	1/4 cup
ground spice	2 teaspoons	1 teaspoon
fruit juice	1/2 cup	1/4 cup
BAKING DISH	8-inch-square baking dish	9" x 5" x 3" loaf dish
TIME IN 350F (175C) OVEN:		
apples	50 to 60 minutes	50 to 60 minutes
pears	30 to 40 minutes	30 to 40 minutes
COOLING TIME	30 minutes	30 minutes

Preheat oven to 350F (175C). Core apples or pears, but do not cut through bottoms. Peel a small strip around top of each apple or pear. With tines of a large fork, prick sides of fruit at 1-inch intervals. Set apples or pears, cored-side up, in a baking dish, see size in chart above. Spoon dried fruit into center of apples or pears. Mound brown sugar on fruit. Sprinkle with spice. Drizzle with fruit juice. Bake in pre-heated oven for time in chart above or until tender. Cool on a rack 30 minutes before serving. Serve warm with pan juices and ice cream or cream.

Suggested Combinations
Golden Baked Apples: Use Granny Smith apples. Use snipped dried apricots and golden raisins for dried fruit. Use nutmeg for spice. Use apricot nectar for fruit juice.
Fig-Stuffed Baked Apples: Use Rome Beauty apples. Use snipped dried figs for dried fruit. Use cinnamon for spice. Use cranberry juice for fruit juice.
Date-Stuffed Baked Pears: Use snipped dates for dried fruit. Use cardamom for spice. Use orange juice for fruit juice.
Prune-Stuffed Baked Pears: Use snipped prunes for dried fruit. Use allspice for spice. Use pineapple juice for fruit juice.

Rosy Applesauce

YIELD	5-1/3 cups	2-2/3 cups
INGREDIENTS		
tart cooking apples, peeled, cored, quartered	3 lbs. (about 14 medium apples)	1-1/2 lbs. (about 7 medium apples)
apple juice or apple wine	1-1/2 cups	3/4 cup
sugar	1/2 cup	1/4 cup
red, hot, cinnamon candies	1/4 cup	2 tablespoons
ground dried lemon peel	1/2 teaspoon	1/4 teaspoon
HEAVY SAUCEPAN	3-qt. saucepan	2-qt. saucepan
TIME AT MEDIUM (apple quarters)	10 to 15 minutes	10 to 15 minutes
TIME AT MEDIUM (pureed apples)	10 to 12 minutes	10 to 12 minutes

In a heavy saucepan, see size in chart above, combine apples and apple juice or apple wine. Bring to a boil over High heat. Reduce heat to Medium; cover. Simmer 10 to 15 minutes or until apples are tender, stir-ring twice. In a blender or food processor fitted with a steel blade, process apples in several batches until pureed. Return pureed apples to saucepan. Stir in sugar, cinnamon candies and lemon peel. Cook over Medium heat 10 to 12 minutes or until candies dissolve, stirring frequently to prevent sticking. Serve warm or chilled. Refrigerate leftover sauce, covered, up to 1 week. Or, pour into freezer cartons, leaving 1/2-inch space at top. Seal and freeze for longer storage.

Basic Poached Fresh Fruit

SERVINGS	8	4
INGREDIENTS		
granulated sugar	1/2 cup	1/4 cup
packed brown sugar	1/2 cup	1/4 cup
fruit juice	2 cups	1 cup
whole spices, see note below	4 teaspoons	2 teaspoons
port wine or cream sherry	1/2 cup	1/4 cup
lemon juice	2 teaspoons	1 teaspoon
fresh fruit, see suggestions below	6 cups (about 2 lbs.)	3 cups (about 1 lb.)
SAUCEPAN	3-qt. saucepan	1-1/2-qt. saucepan
TIME AT MEDIUM LOW:		
apples, pears	7 to 10 minutes	7 to 10 minutes
peaches, plums	3 to 4 minutes	3 to 4 minutes

In a saucepan, see size in chart above, combine granulated sugar, brown sugar, fruit juice and whole spices. Bring to a boil over High heat, stirring to dissolve sugar. When mixture boils, stir in port or sherry and lemon juice. Gently stir in fruit. Return to a boil. Reduce heat to Medium Low; cover. Simmer for time in chart above or until barely tender, stirring gently once or twice. Remove spices. Serve warm or cover and refrigerate fruit in syrup.

Suggested Combinations
Poached Fresh Peaches: Use apricot nectar for fruit juice. Use cinnamon sticks and whole cloves for spices. Use white port wine. Allow 4 peaches per pound. Peel and quarter peaches.
Poached Fresh Pears: Use orange juice for fruit juice. Use whole nutmeg and cardamom for spices. Use cream sherry. Allow 4 pears per pound. Peel, core and quarter pears.
Poached Fresh Plums: Use white-grape juice for fruit juice. Use whole allspice and cinnamon sticks for spices. Use red port wine. Allow 10 plums per pound. Pit and quarter plums.
Poached Fresh Apples: Use apple juice for fruit juice. Use cinnamon sticks and whole nutmeg for spices. Use cream sherry. Allow 3 apples per pound. Peel, core and quarter apples.

Note: When measuring whole spices, 1 whole nutmeg or 1 (2-inch) cinnamon stick equals 1 teaspoon.

Rhubarb Sauce

YIELD	5-1/3 cups	2-2/3 cups
INGREDIENTS		
packed brown sugar	2/3 cup	1/3 cup
granulated sugar	2/3 cup	1/3 cup
ground spice	1/2 teaspoon	1/4 teaspoon
fruit juice	1/2 cup	1/4 cup
fresh rhubarb, cut in 1/2-inch pieces	8 cups (about 2 lbs.)	4 cups (about 1 lb.)
OR		
frozen rhubarb, cut in 1/2-inch pieces, thawed (with juice)	2 (1-lb.) bags	1 (1-lb.) bag
SAUCEPAN	3-qt. saucepan	2-qt. saucepan
TIME AT MEDIUM	7 to 9 minutes	5 to 7 minutes

In a saucepan, see size in chart above, combine brown sugar, granulated sugar and spice. Stir in fruit juice. Cook over High heat until mixture boils and sugar dissolves, stirring constantly. Stir in rhubarb. Bring to a boil. Reduce heat to Medium; cover. Simmer for time in chart above or until tender, stirring occasionally. Serve for breakfast or dessert.

Suggested Fruit Juice: orange juice, pineapple juice, apple juice.
Suggested Spices: cinnamon, nutmeg, allspice, cloves.

Wine & Fruit Dessert Sauce

YIELD	2-1/2 to 3 cups	1-1/4 to 1-1/2 cups
INGREDIENTS		
fresh fruit, see suggestions below	2 cups	1 cup
sugar	1/2 cup	1/4 cup
dry red or white wine	1 cup	1/2 cup
cornstarch	2 tablespoons	1 tablespoon
cold water	1/4 cup	2 tablespoons
SAUCEPAN	1-1/2-qt. saucepan	1-qt. saucepan
TIME AT MEDIUM:		
peaches, blueberries, plums	3 to 5 minutes	3 to 5 minutes
strawberries	1 to 1-1/2 minutes	1 to 1-1/2 minutes
TIME AT MEDIUM HIGH	1-1/2 minutes	40 to 60 seconds

In a saucepan, see size in chart above, combine fruit, sugar and wine. Bring to a boil over High heat, stirring constantly until sugar dissolves. Reduce heat to Medium. Simmer, uncovered, for time in chart above or until fruit is almost tender. In a small bowl, combine cornstarch and water; mix well. Stir into fruit mixture. Cook over Medium-High heat for time in chart above or until thickened and bubbly all over, stirring constantly. Serve warm or cool over ice cream, or layer in parfaits.

Suggested Fruit: sliced peeled peaches, sliced unpeeled plums, blueberries, strawberries.

Basic Nut Dessert Sauce

YIELD	1-1/3 cups	2/3 cup
INGREDIENTS		
packed brown sugar	2/3 cup	1/3 cup
light corn syrup	1/3 cup	3 tablespoons
butter or margarine	2 tablespoons	1 tablespoon
half and half	1/4 cup	2 tablespoons
toasted nuts	1/2 cup	1/4 cup
liqueur	2 tablespoons	1 tablespoon
vanilla extract	1/2 teaspoon	1/4 teaspoon
SAUCEPAN	1-1/2-qt. saucepan	1-qt. saucepan
TIME AT MEDIUM	7 minutes	6 minutes

In a saucepan, see size in chart above, combine brown sugar, corn syrup and butter or margarine. Cook over Medium heat for time in chart above or until mixture boils and sugar dissolves, stirring constantly. Gradually stir in half and half. Stir in nuts, liqueur and vanilla. Stir before serving. Serve warm or chilled over ice cream or cake squares. Store leftover sauce, covered, in the refrigerator.

Suggested Combinations
Pecan-Praline Dessert Sauce: Use pecans for nuts. Use praline liqueur.
Toasted-Almond Dessert Sauce: Use slivered almonds for nuts. Use amaretto liqueur.

Wine & Fruit Dessert Sauce, made with peaches.

Basic Filled Meringue Shells

SERVINGS	8 to 10	6
INGREDIENTS		
egg whites, room temperature	4	2
cream of tartar	1 teaspoon	1/2 teaspoon
vanilla extract	2 teaspoons	1 teaspoon
sugar	1 cup	1/2 cup
filling, see suggestions below		
MIXER BOWL	3-qt. bowl	1-1/2-qt. bowl
BAKING PAN	15" x 10" x 1" baking pan	15" x 10" x 1" baking pan
BEATING TIME AT MEDIUM SPEED (egg whites)	45 seconds	30 seconds
BEATING TIME AT MEDIUM SPEED (while adding sugar)	5 minutes	3 minutes
BEATING TIME AT HIGH SPEED	3 to 3-1/2 minutes	1-1/4 to 1-1/2 minutes
MERINGUE SIZE	10-inch circle, 1-3/4 inches high at rim	6 (3-inch) circles, 1-inch high at rims
TIME IN 225F (105C) OVEN	2-1/2 hours	1-1/2 hours
STANDING TIME (in oven)	2 hours or overnight	2 hours or overnight

Preheat oven to 225F (105C). In a mixer bowl, see size in chart above, combine egg whites, cream of tartar and vanilla. Beat at medium speed of an electric mixer for time in chart above or until foamy. Scrape sides of bowl. Gradually add sugar, beating at medium speed of mixer for time in chart above. Scrape sides of bowl often. Turn mixer to high speed. Beat for time in chart above or until stiff peaks form. Scrape sides of bowl often. Line a 15" x 10" x 1" baking pan with foil. Spread large recipe of meringue in 1 (10-inch) circle or small recipe in 6 (3-inch) circles on baking pan. Use the back of a spoon to shape meringue into shells, building up meringue at edge. Bake in preheated oven for time in chart above. Turn off oven. Do not open oven door. Let meringue stand in oven at least 2 hours. To serve, peel off foil. Fill meringue shells with scoops of ice cream. Garnish with ice-cream topping and nuts or fruit. Or, fill with whipped cream, frozen yogurt or pudding and fruit.

Suggested Combinations

Praline-Pecan Meringue Shells: Use praline-pecan ice cream, chopped pecans and caramel sauce.

Valentine Raspberry Meringue Shells: Shape individual meringue shell into hearts. To fill, use frozen raspberry yogurt, chopped almonds and thawed frozen raspberries in syrup.

Double-Chocolate Meringue Shells: Use chocolate-chip ice cream, chopped toasted almonds and chocolate ice-cream sauce.

Lemon & Cream Meringue Shells: Use lemon pudding, topped with whipped cream and candied lemon slices.

Strawberries & Cream Meringue Shells: Use fresh sliced strawberries and whipped cream, folded together.

How to Make Basic Filled Meringue Shells

1/Beat egg whites, cream of tartar and vanilla until foamy. Gradually add sugar, beating at medium speed of an electric mixer for time indicated in chart. Add sugar slowly during entire beating time. After beating, egg whites will be syrupy.

2/Beat egg whites at high speed until stiff peaks form. Notice peaks of egg whites in bowl and on beaters stand straight up. Shape egg whites in 1 large shell or individual shells, using the back of a spoon. Shells should look like nests.

3/To make meringue shells in different shapes or more perfect circles, use a cookie gun or pastry tube with a large star tip. Pipe meringue in concentric layers to form desired shapes. Do not let meringue stand before shaping.

4/Bake meringues in a 225F (105C) oven. Do not open oven door during or after baking. Turn off oven and let meringue shells dry out in oven at least 2 hours. Fill meringue shells with sherbet or ice cream, and top with fruit.

Basic Chilled Dessert Soufflé

SERVINGS	6 to 8	3 or 4
INGREDIENTS		
fruit juice	1/2 cup	1/4 cup
fruit-flavored gelatin	1 (3-oz.) pkg.	1/2 (3-oz.) pkg. (3-1/2 tablespoons)
pureed fruit with tapioca (junior baby food)	2 (7-3/4-oz.) jars (1-1/2 cups)	1 (7-3/4-oz.) jar (3/4 cup)
port wine or cream sherry	2 tablespoons	1 tablespoon
grated citrus peel	1 teaspoon	1/2 teaspoon
lemon juice	2 tablespoons	1 tablespoon
egg whites	4	2
cream of tartar	1/4 teaspoon	1/8 teaspoon
sugar	1/3 cup	3 tablespoons
frozen whipped topping, thawed	1 cup	1/2 cup
additional whipped topping, fruit	to garnish	to garnish
SOUFFLÉ DISH	1-qt. soufflé dish	2-cup soufflé dish
SAUCEPAN	1-1/2-qt. saucepan	1-qt. saucepan
MIXER BOWL	3-qt. bowl	1-1/2-qt. bowl
REFRIGERATE (partially set)	45 minutes	35 minutes
BEATING TIME AT MEDIUM SPEED	2-1/2 minutes	1-1/2 minutes
BEATING TIME AT HIGH SPEED	2 minutes	1-1/2 minutes
REFRIGERATE (finished soufflé)	8 hours or overnight	4 to 6 hours

Cut a strip of waxed paper to fit around outside of a soufflé dish, see size in chart above. Coat 1 side of waxed paper with butter or margarine. Sprinkle with sugar. Place waxed paper, coated-side facing center of dish, around outside of soufflé dish to form collar extending 1 inch above rim. Secure with a paper clip or pin; set aside. In a saucepan, see size in chart above, bring fruit juice to a boil. Stir in gelatin until dissolved. Stir in pureed fruit, port or sherry, citrus peel and lemon juice; mix until smooth. Refrigerate for time in chart above or until partially set. In a mixer bowl, see size in chart above, beat egg whites and cream of tartar at medium speed of an electric mixer 20 seconds or until foamy. Gradually add sugar, beating at medium speed of mixer for time in chart above. Scrape sides of bowl often. Turn mixer to high speed. Beat for time in chart above or until stiff peaks form. Scrape sides of bowl often. Fold fruit mixture into egg-white mixture. Stir first amount of whipped topping. Fold into fruit mixture. Spoon into prepared soufflé dish. Refrigerate for time in chart above or until firm. Remove collar before serving. Garnish with additional whipped topping and fruit.

Suggested Combinations

Chilled Plum Soufflé: Use red fruit punch or plum-apple juice for fruit juice. Use lemon-flavored gelatin. Use plum baby food. Use red port wine or sherry. Use lemon peel.

Chilled Apricot Soufflé, photo on page 430: Use apricot nectar for fruit juice. Use apricot-flavored gelatin. Use apricot baby food. Use white port wine or sherry. Use orange peel.

Basic Baked Dessert Soufflés

SERVINGS	8	4
INGREDIENTS		
butter or margarine	1/4 cup	2 tablespoons
all-purpose flour	1/3 cup	3 tablespoons
granulated sugar	1/3 cup	2 tablespoons
milk	3/4 cup	1/3 cup
liqueur	1/4 cup	2 tablespoons
grated citrus peel	1/2 teaspoon	1/4 teaspoon
egg whites	4	2
cream of tartar	1/4 teaspoon	1/8 teaspoon
granulated sugar	2 tablespoons	1 tablespoon
egg yolks	4	2
powdered sugar	to garnish	to garnish
SOUFFLÉ OR CUSTARD CUPS OR SOUFFLÉ DISH	8 (6-oz.) cups or 1 (6-cup) soufflé dish	4 (6-oz.) cups
SAUCEPAN	1-qt. saucepan	1-qt. saucepan
MIXER BOWL	3-qt. bowl	1-1/2-qt. bowl
TIME AT MEDIUM HIGH (butter, flour)	1 minute	30 seconds
TIME AT MEDIUM HIGH (sugar, milk added)	3 to 3-1/2 minutes	1 to 1-1/2 minutes
BEATING TIME AT MEDIUM SPEED	4 minutes	1-1/2 to 2 minutes
BEATING TIME AT HIGH SPEED (stiff peaks)	1 minute	30 seconds
BEATING TIME AT HIGH SPEED (egg yolks)	5 minutes	3 minutes
TIME IN 350F (175C) OVEN: cups soufflé dish	25 to 30 minutes 50 to 60 minutes	25 to 30 minutes

Preheat oven to 350F (175C). If using large recipe, butter 8 (6-ounce) soufflé or custard cups or a 6-cup soufflé dish; if using small recipe, butter 4 (6-ounce) soufflé or custard cups. Sprinkle cups or dish with sugar; set aside. In a 1-quart saucepan, melt butter or margarine over Medium-High heat. Stir in flour. Cook and stir for time in chart above. Whisk in first amount of granulated sugar, milk, liqueur and citrus peel. Cook for time in chart above or until thickened and bubbly all over, stirring constantly. Set aside. In a mixer bowl, see size in chart above, beat egg whites and cream of tartar at medium speed of an electric mixer for 20 seconds or until foamy. Scrape sides of bowl. Gradually add second amount of granulated sugar, beating at medium speed of mixer for time in chart above. Scrape sides of bowl often. Turn mixer to high speed. Beat for time in chart above or until stiff peaks form. Scrape sides of bowl often. In a medium bowl, beat egg yolks at high speed of mixer for time in chart above or until thick and lemon-colored. Scrape sides of bowl often. Stir milk mixture into yolks. Fold one-fourth of egg-white mixture into yolk mixture. Slowly pour yolk mixture over egg-white mixture. Gently fold together. Carefully pour 1/2 cup soufflé mixture into each prepared cup or all of mixture into large soufflé dish. Bake in preheated oven for time in chart above or until a knife inserted in center comes out clean. Sift powdered sugar over soufflés to garnish. Serve immediately.

Suggested Combinations

Baked Grand Marnier Soufflés: Use Grand Marnier or other orange liqueur. Use orange peel. Garnish with orange-peel twists.

Baked Almond Cloud Soufflés: Use crème de almond or amaretto liqueur. Use lemon peel. Garnish with chopped toasted almonds.

Baked Praline Soufflés: Use praline liqueur. Use lime peel. Garnish with chopped toasted pecans.

Cream Puffs or Éclairs

SERVINGS	16 large puffs or 9 large éclairs	7 large puffs or 4 large éclairs
INGREDIENTS		
water	1 cup	1/2 cup
butter or margarine	1/2 cup	1/4 cup
all-purpose flour	1 cup	1/2 cup
eggs	4	2
filling	see amount in chart below	
Basic Cake Glaze, page 464, or powdered sugar	to garnish	to garnish
BAKING SHEETS	2 baking sheets	1 baking sheet
SAUCEPAN	2-qt. saucepan	1-qt. saucepan
TIME AT MEDIUM LOW	1 minute	1 minute
COOLING TIME (flour mixture)	4 to 5 minutes	4 to 5 minutes
TIME IN 400F (205C) OVEN:		
large puffs or éclairs	35 to 40 minutes	35 to 40 minutes
medium puffs	30 minutes	30 minutes
small puffs	25 minutes	25 minutes
COOLING TIME (after baking)	1 hour	1 hour

Preheat oven to 400F (205C). Grease 1 or 2 baking sheets. In a saucepan, see size in chart above, combine water and butter or margarine. Bring to a boil over High heat. Reduce heat to Medium Low. Add flour all at once. Cook 1 minute or until mixture forms a ball that does not separate, stirring vigorously during entire cooking time. Cool at room temperature 4 to 5 minutes. Add eggs, 1 at a time, beating by hand 1 minute after each addition.

For cream puffs: Drop dough in rounded mounds, see number in chart below, on baking sheets.

For éclairs: Form dough into fingers about 4 inches long and 1 inch wide, see number in chart below, on baking sheets.

To bake cream puffs or éclairs: Bake in preheated oven for time in chart above or until puffed and golden brown. Remove from sheet. Cool on a rack for time in chart above. Split crosswise and remove webbing. Immediately before serving, fill with fruit, Basic Yogurt Dessert Filling, page 454, or ice cream, see filling amount in chart below. Drizzle with Basic Cake Glaze or sprinkle with powdered sugar to garnish. Use cream puffs or éclairs the same day they are baked.

Note: To bake 2 sheets at once, stagger sheets on oven shelves for better heat circulation and more even browning. Reverse sheet positions on oven shelves once during baking.

Yield & Filling Guide for Cream Puffs or Éclairs

	large recipe	small recipe	filling per puff
PUFF OR ÉCLAIR SIZE			
large cream puffs (3 tablespoons dough per puff)	16 puffs	7 puffs	1/3 cup
medium cream puffs (1 tablespoon dough per puff)	48 puffs	24 puffs	3 tablespoons
small cream puffs (1 teaspoon dough per puff)	88 puffs	44 puffs	1 tablespoon
éclairs (5 tablespoons dough per puff)	9 éclairs	4 éclairs	1/3 cup

How to Make Cream Puffs & Éclairs

1/In a saucepan, bring water and butter or margarine to a boil over High heat. Reduce heat to Medium Low. Stir in flour. Cook, stirring vigorously, 1 minute or until dough forms a ball that does not separate.

2/Cool dough 4 to 5 minutes. Beat in eggs one at a time. Beat 1 minute by hand after adding each egg. Batter tends to separate after each egg is added, but recombines with vigorous beating.

3/To form cream puffs, drop dough in rounded mounds on greased baking sheets. For éclairs, form dough into fingers 4 inches long and 1 inch wide. You may use a pastry tube with a wide tip for shaping. Bake until puffed and golden brown.

4/To fill baked cream puffs or éclairs, cut off tops. Use a fork to remove webbing inside shells. Fill with Basic Yogurt Dessert Filling, page 454, fruit or ice cream. This is Strawberry-Yogurt Dessert Filling.

Basic Layered Oatmeal Bars

YIELD	60 bars
INGREDIENTS	
cookie mix	1 (14- to 18-oz.) pkg.
quick-cooking oats	2/3 cup
marshmallow creme	1 (7-oz.) jar
flavored baking pieces	1 cup
ice-cream topping	2/3 cup
all-purpose flour	2 tablespoons
chopped nuts	2/3 cup
BAKING PAN	13" x 9" baking pan
MIXER BOWL	3-qt. bowl
TIME IN 350F (175C) OVEN (crust)	9 to 10 minutes
COOLING TIME (crust)	10 minutes
TIME IN 350F (175C) OVEN (filling added)	25 to 35 minutes
COOLING TIME (finished bars)	1-3/4 hours

Preheat oven to 350F (175C). Grease and flour a 13" x 9" baking pan. In a 3-quart mixer bowl, prepare cookie mix according to package directions, omitting water if called for. Stir in oats. Reserve 1 cup mixture; set aside in a small bowl. Press remaining mixture evenly on bottom of prepared baking pan. Bake in preheated oven 9 to 10 minutes or until lightly browned around edges and set. Cool 10 minutes. Spread with marshmallow creme. Sprinkle with baking pieces. In a small bowl, combine ice-cream topping and flour; mix well. Drizzle or spread over baking pieces. Combine reserved crumb mixture and nuts. Crumble mixture evenly over ice-cream topping. Bake in preheated oven 25 to 35 minutes or until top is firm and lightly browned. Cool in pan on a rack 1-3/4 hours before cutting into bars. Store completely cooled bars in baking pan; cover with foil.

Suggested Combinations
Layered Peanut-Oatmeal Bars: Use peanut-butter-cookie mix. Use peanut-butter baking pieces. Use chocolate-fudge ice-cream topping. Use chopped peanuts for nuts.

Layered Butterscotch-Oatmeal Bars: Use sugar-cookie mix. Use butterscotch baking pieces. Use butterscotch ice-cream topping. Use chopped pecans for nuts.

Layered Chocolate-Oatmeal Bars: Use chocolate-chip-cookie mix. Use semisweet chocolate baking pieces. Use chocolate-caramel ice-cream topping. Use chopped walnuts for nuts.

Tips for Making Cookies

- Dark metal or dark-colored non-stick baking sheets produce browner cookies than shiny metal or light-colored non-stick baking sheets.

- For more even baking, baking sheets should be small enough for air to circulate around them on the oven rack.

- To bake 2 sheets of cookies together, reverse top and bottom sheets halfway through baking time so cookies will bake and brown evenly.

- To use baking sheets for another batch, wash and rinse with cold water until cool. Do not bake cookies on warm baking sheets because cookies will spread.

- In warm weather, chill drop- or shaped-cookie dough 1 to 2 hours. Warm cookie dough does not hold its shape and spreads during baking.

- Cool cookies 10 to 15 minutes on racks. Do not stack cookies until they are completely cool, or they will stick together.

- Allow 1/4 cup frosting to frost about 15 cookies. One cup frosting will frost about 5 dozen cookies.

- Store cookies in plastic bags or tightly covered containers. Coffee cans with plastic lids are good makeshift cookie jars.

- Most cookies store well in the freezer up to 2 months. Freeze completely cooled cookies in moisture-vapor proof paper or freezer containers. Unwrapped frozen cookies thaw in about 10 minutes at room temperature. Well-wrapped cookie dough can be frozen 6 to 8 weeks.

Layered Peanut-Oatmeal Bars, Layered Butterscotch-Oatmeal Bars and Layered Chocolate-Oatmeal Bars

German-Chocolate Brownies

YIELD	40 brownies	20 brownies
INGREDIENTS		
butter or margarine	2/3 cup	1/3 cup
German sweet chocolate, broken up	1 (4-oz.) pkg.	1/2 (4-oz.) pkg.
sugar	2 cups	1 cup
vanilla extract	2 teaspoons	1 teaspoon
eggs	4	2
all-purpose flour	1-1/2 cups	3/4 cup
chopped nuts	1 cup	1/2 cup
flaked coconut	1/2 cup	1/4 cup
BAKING PAN	13" x 9" baking pan	8-inch-square baking pan
SAUCEPAN	3-qt. saucepan	1-1/2-qt. saucepan
TIME AT MEDIUM LOW	10 to 12 minutes	10 to 12 minutes
COOLING TIME (butter, chocolate)	10 minutes	10 minutes
TIME IN 350F (175C) OVEN	35 to 40 minutes	30 to 35 minutes
COOLING TIME (finished brownies)	2-1/4 hours	1-1/4 hours

Preheat oven to 350F (175C). Grease and flour a baking pan, see size in chart above. In a saucepan, see size in chart above, combine butter or margarine and chocolate. Stir constantly over Medium-Low heat 10 to 12 minutes or until melted. Cool 10 minutes. Stir in sugar and vanilla. Add eggs, 1 at a time, beating well with a spoon after each addition. Stir in flour, nuts and coconut; beat well. Pour into prepared pan. Bake in preheated oven for time in chart above or until a wooden pick inserted in center of brownies comes out clean. Cool in pan on a rack. Cut in squares while warm, but do not remove from pan until completely cool, see time in chart above. Store completely cooled brownies in baking pan; cover with foil.

Gingersnaps

YIELD	72 cookies	36 cookies
INGREDIENTS		
all-purpose flour	2-1/2 cups	1-1/4 cups
baking soda	2 teaspoons	1 teaspoon
ground ginger	1 teaspoon	1/2 teaspoon
ground cinnamon	1 teaspoon	1/2 teaspoon
ground cloves	1/2 teaspoon	1/4 teaspoon
shortening	1 cup	1/2 cup
sugar	1 cup	1/2 cup
molasses	1/4 cup	2 tablespoons
egg or egg yolk	1 egg	1 egg yolk
sugar	to coat	to coat
MIXER BOWL	3-qt. bowl	1-1/2-qt. bowl
BAKING SHEETS	baking sheets	baking sheets
BEATING TIME AT HIGH SPEED	1-1/2 to 2 minutes	45 to 60 seconds
TIME IN 350F (175C) OVEN	10 to 12 minutes	10 to 12 minutes

Preheat oven to 350F (175C). In a medium bowl, combine flour, baking soda, ginger, cinnamon and cloves; mix well and set aside. In a mixer bowl, see size in chart above, beat shortening, first amount of sugar, molasses and egg or egg yolk at low speed of an electric mixer for 30 seconds to blend. Turn mixer to high speed. Beat for time in chart above or until light and fluffy. By hand, gradually stir in flour mixture until well-mixed. Roll small pieces of dough into 1-inch balls. Roll in additional sugar to coat. Place 2 inches apart on ungreased baking sheets. Do not press balls down. Bake in preheated oven 10 to 12 minutes or until lightly browned and set. Remove from baking sheets. Cool on racks. Store completely cooled cookies in an airtight container.

How to Make Shaped Cookies

1/Peanut-Butter Cookies are made from a stiff cookie dough. Stiff dough needs to be rolled in 1-inch balls before baking. Place balls of dough about 2 inches apart on baking sheets.

2/There are 2 ways to flatten balls of dough. Use a fork to make a crisscross pattern or use bottom of a sugared glass to press balls of dough into round cookie shapes before baking.

Peanut-Butter Cookies

YIELD	96 cookies	48 cookies
INGREDIENTS		
all-purpose flour	2-1/2 cups	1-1/4 cups
baking soda	1-1/2 teaspoons	3/4 teaspoon
salt	1 teaspoon	1/2 teaspoon
granulated sugar	1 cup	1/2 cup
packed brown sugar	1 cup	1/2 cup
shortening	2/3 cup	1/3 cup
peanut butter	1 cup	1/2 cup
eggs	2	1
peanut butter, chopped peanuts, if desired	to frost	to frost
MIXER BOWL	3-qt. bowl	1-1/2-qt. bowl
BAKING SHEETS	baking sheets	baking sheets
BEATING TIME AT HIGH SPEED	1-1/2 to 2 minutes	45 to 60 seconds
TIME IN 375F (190C) OVEN	8 to 10 minutes	8 to 10 minutes

Preheat oven to 375F (190C). In a medium bowl, combine flour, baking soda and salt; mix well and set aside. In a mixer bowl, see size in chart above, beat granulated sugar, brown sugar, shortening, first amount of peanut butter and eggs at low speed of an electric mixer for 30 seconds to blend. Turn mixer to high speed. Beat for time in chart above or until light and fluffy. Scrape sides of bowl often. By hand, gradually stir in flour mixture until well-mixed. Roll small pieces of dough into 1-inch balls. Place 2 inches apart on ungreased baking sheets. Lightly butter bottom of a glass; dip buttered glass in sugar. Press down dough with bottom of sugared glass to 2-inch diameter. Or, with tines of a fork, press down in **X** pattern to 2-inch diameter. Bake in preheated oven 8 to 10 minutes or until lightly browned. Remove from baking sheets. Cool on racks. Frost warm cookies with peanut butter and sprinkle with chopped peanuts, if desired. Store completely cooled cookies in an airtight container.

Basic Cereal Cookies

YIELD	96 cookies	48 cookies
INGREDIENTS		
all-purpose flour	2 cups	1 cup
baking soda	1 teaspoon	1/2 teaspoon
baking powder	1/2 teaspoon	1/4 teaspoon
salt	1/2 teaspoon	1/4 teaspoon
shortening	1 cup	1/2 cup
granulated sugar	1 cup	1/2 cup
packed brown sugar	1 cup	1/2 cup
eggs	2	1
vanilla extract	1 teaspoon	1/2 teaspoon
quick-cooking oats or cereal flakes	2 cups	1 cup
flavored baking pieces or snipped dried fruit	1 cup	1/2 cup
chopped nuts or flaked coconut	1 cup	1/2 cup
MIXER BOWL	3-qt. bowl	1-1/2-qt. bowl
BAKING SHEETS	baking sheets	baking sheets
BEATING TIME AT HIGH SPEED	1-1/2 to 2 minutes	45 to 60 seconds
TIME IN 375F (190C) OVEN	8 to 10 minutes	8 to 10 minutes

Preheat oven to 375F (190C). In a medium bowl, combine flour, baking soda, baking powder and salt; mix well and set aside. In a mixer bowl, see size in chart above, combine shortening, granulated sugar, brown sugar, eggs and vanilla. Beat at low speed of an electric mixer 30 seconds to blend. Turn mixer to high speed. Beat for time in chart above or until light and fluffy. Scrape sides of bowl often. Turn mixer to low speed. Gradually beat in flour mixture until well-mixed. Beat 20 to 30 seconds after each addition. Scrape sides of bowl often. By hand, stir in cereal, baking pieces or dried fruit and nuts or coconut. Drop by teaspoonfuls, 2 inches apart, on ungreased baking sheets. Bake in preheated oven 8 to 10 minutes or until lightly browned. Remove from baking sheets. Cool on racks. Store completely cooled cookies in an airtight container.

Suggested Combinations
Oatmeal Cookies: Use quick-cooking oats for cereal. Use raisins for dried fruit. Use coconut.
Wheaty Cookies: Use wheat flakes for cereal. Use peanut-butter baking pieces. Use chopped peanuts for nuts.
Cornflake Cookies: Use cornflakes for cereal. Use snipped dried apricots for dried fruit. Use chopped pecans for nuts.

Sugar & Spice Cookies

YIELD	96 cookies	48 cookies
INGREDIENTS		
Same ingredients as for Sugar Cookies, page 510, except add:	large recipe	small recipe
ground cinnamon	2 teaspoons	1 teaspoon
ground nutmeg	1/2 teaspoon	1/4 teaspoon

Prepare dough for Sugar Cookies, adding cinnamon and nutmeg to flour mixture. Press down cookies with bottom of glass dipped in cinnamon-sugar. Bake according to directions for Sugar Cookies. Store completely cooled cookies in an airtight container.

How to Make Drop Cookies

1/Basic Cereal Cookies are made from a cookie dough that is soft enough to make cookies without further shaping. Take a spoonful of dough; using the back of another spoon, push dough off spoon onto baking sheet. Leave 2 inches between cookies.

2/After baking, remove cookies to racks to cool. If cookies are cooled flat on the counter, they will be less crisp. Do not stack cookies until they are cool or they will stick together. Store cookies in a covered jar or in plastic bags.

Rob's Favorite Chocolate Cookies

YIELD	120 cookies	60 cookies
INGREDIENTS		
sifted cake flour	3-1/3 cups	1-2/3 cups
salt	1 teaspoon	1/2 teaspoon
baking soda	1 teaspoon	1/2 teaspoon
eggs	2	1
packed brown sugar	2 cups	1 cup
shortening	1 cup	1/2 cup
vanilla extract	2 teaspoons	1 teaspoon
unsweetened chocolate, melted, cooled	4 (1-oz.) squares	2 (1-oz.) squares
milk	1 cup	1/2 cup
Chocolate Creamy Butter Frosting, page 462	medium recipe	small recipe
BAKING SHEETS	baking sheets	baking sheets
MIXER BOWL	3-qt. bowl	1-1/2-qt. bowl
BEATING TIME AT HIGH SPEED	1-1/2 to 2 minutes	45 to 60 seconds
TIME IN 350F (175C) OVEN	8 to 10 minutes	8 to 10 minutes

Preheat oven to 350F (175C). Grease baking sheets; set aside. In a medium bowl, combine cake flour, salt and baking soda; mix well and set aside. In a mixer bowl, see size in chart above, beat eggs, brown sugar, shortening and vanilla at low speed of an electric mixer for 30 seconds to blend. Turn mixer to high speed. Beat for time in chart above or until light and fluffy. Scrape sides of bowl often. Turn mixer to low speed. Beat in cooled chocolate for 25 seconds or until well-mixed. Alternately add flour mixture and milk to chocolate mixture. After each addition, beat at low speed of mixer 10 seconds, then turn mixer to medium speed and beat 15 to 20 seconds. Scrape sides of bowl often. Begin and end additions with flour. Drop by teaspoonfuls, 2 inches apart, on greased baking sheets. Bake in preheated oven 8 to 10 minutes or until tops spring back when lightly touched. Remove from baking sheets. Cool on racks. Frost cooled cookies with Chocolate Creamy Butter Frosting. Store completely cooled cookies in an airtight container.

Sugar Cookies

YIELD	96 cookies	48 cookies
INGREDIENTS		
all-purpose flour	5 cups	2-1/2 cups
cream of tartar	2 teaspoons	1 teaspoon
baking soda	1 teaspoon	1/2 teaspoon
salt	1/2 teaspoon	1/4 teaspoon
butter or margarine, softened	2 cups	1 cup
powdered sugar	3 cups	1-1/2 cups
eggs	2	1
vanilla extract	2 teaspoons	1 teaspoon
MIXER BOWL	3-qt. bowl	1-1/2-qt. bowl
BAKING SHEETS	baking sheets	baking sheets
BEATING TIME AT HIGH SPEED	1-1/2 to 2 minutes	45 to 60 seconds
TIME IN 350F (175C) OVEN	10 to 12 minutes	10 to 12 minutes

Preheat oven to 350F (175C). In a medium bowl, combine flour, cream of tartar, baking soda and salt; mix well and set aside. In a mixer bowl, see size in chart above, beat butter or margarine, powdered sugar, eggs and vanilla at low speed of an electric mixer for 20 to 30 seconds to blend. Turn mixer to high speed. Beat for time in chart above or until light and fluffy. Scrape sides of bowl often. Turn mixer to low speed. Gradually add flour mixture, beating 20 to 30 seconds after each addition until well-mixed. Scrape sides of bowl often. Drop by teaspoonfuls, 2 inches apart, on ungreased baking sheets. Lightly butter bottom of a glass; dip buttered glass in sugar. Press down dough with bottom of sugared glass to 2-inch diameter. Bake in preheated oven 10 to 12 minutes or until lightly browned. Remove from baking sheets. Cool on racks. Store completely cooled cookies in an airtight container.

Chocolate-Chip Cookies

YIELD	120 cookies	60 cookies
INGREDIENTS		
all-purpose flour	2 cups	1 cup
baking soda	1 teaspoon	1/2 teaspoon
salt	1/2 teaspoon	1/4 teaspoon
shortening	1 cup	1/2 cup
granulated sugar	2/3 cup	1/3 cup
packed brown sugar	2/3 cup	1/3 cup
vanilla extract	2 teaspoons	1 teaspoon
eggs	2	1
semisweet chocolate pieces	1 (12-oz.) pkg. (2 cups)	1 (6-oz.) pkg. (1 cup)
chopped nuts	2/3 cup	1/3 cup
MIXER BOWL	3-qt. bowl	1-1/2-qt. bowl
BAKING SHEETS	baking sheets	baking sheets
BEATING TIME AT HIGH SPEED	1-1/2 to 2 minutes	45 to 60 seconds
TIME IN 375F (190C) OVEN	10 to 12 minutes	10 to 12 minutes

Preheat oven to 375F (190C). In a medium bowl, combine flour, baking soda and salt; mix well and set aside. In a mixer bowl, see size in chart above, beat shortening, granulated sugar, brown sugar, vanilla and eggs at low speed of an electric mixer for 30 seconds to blend. Turn mixer to high speed. Beat for time in chart above or until light and fluffy. Scrape sides of bowl often. Turn mixer to low speed. Gradually add flour mixture, beating 20 to 30 seconds after each addition until well-mixed. Scrape sides of bowl often. By hand, stir in chocolate pieces and nuts. Drop by teaspoonfuls, 2 inches apart, on ungreased baking sheets. Bake in preheated oven 10 to 12 minutes or until lightly browned and set. Remove from baking sheets. Cool on racks. Store completely cooled cookies in an airtight container.

Basic Macaroons

YIELD	92 cookies	46 cookies
INGREDIENTS		
egg whites	4	2
cream of tartar	1/4 teaspoon	1/8 teaspoon
vanilla extract	1 teaspoon	1/2 teaspoon
sugar	1-1/3 cups	2/3 cup
shredded coconut	1-1/3 cups	2/3 cup
chopped nuts, snipped dried fruit or flavored baking pieces	1-1/3 cups	2/3 cup
crisp cereal flakes	2-2/3 cups	1-1/3 cups
BAKING SHEETS	baking sheets	baking sheets
MIXER BOWL	3-qt. bowl	1-1/2-qt. bowl
BEATING TIME AT HIGH SPEED (foamy)	30 seconds	15 seconds
BEATING TIME AT HIGH SPEED (stiff peaks)	2 to 2-1/2 minutes	45 to 60 seconds
TIME IN 350F (175C) OVEN	15 to 18 minutes	15 to 18 minutes

Preheat oven to 350F (175C). Generously grease baking sheets; set aside. In a mixer bowl, see size in chart above, beat egg whites, cream of tartar and vanilla at high speed of an electric mixer for time in chart above or until foamy. Gradually add sugar, beating at high speed of mixer for time in chart above or until stiff peaks form. By hand, gently fold in coconut and nuts, dried fruit or baking pieces. Fold in cereal. Drop by teaspoonfuls, 1 inch apart, on greased baking sheets. Bake in preheated oven 15 to 18 minutes or until light golden brown. Remove from baking sheets at once. Cool on racks. Store completely cooled cookies in an airtight container.

Suggested Combinations
Cornflake-Nut Macaroons: Use chopped pecans for nuts. Use cornflakes for cereal.
Apricot-Wheat Macaroons: Use snipped dried apricots for dried fruit. Use wheat flakes for cereal.
Chocolate Macaroons: Use chocolate mini-pieces for baking pieces. Use whole-wheat and barley flakes for cereal.

Lemon-Nut Cookies

YIELD	96 cookies	48 cookies
INGREDIENTS		
Same ingredients as for Sugar Cookies, opposite, except add:	large recipe	small recipe
grated lemon peel	2 teaspoons	1 teaspoon
lemon extract	1/2 teaspoon	1/4 teaspoon
finely chopped pecans	1 cup	1/2 cup
Lemon Creamy Butter Frosting, page 462, or Creamy Cheese Frosting, page 464, made with lemon juice and lemon peel	medium recipe	small recipe

Prepare dough for Sugar Cookies, adding lemon peel and lemon extract to butter or margarine mixture. By hand, stir in nuts after adding flour mixture. Bake according to directions for Sugar Cookies. Frost cooled cookies with frosting. Store completely cooled cookies in an airtight container.

Rolled Gingerbread Cookies

YIELD	60 large cookies	30 large cookies
INGREDIENTS		
all-purpose flour	4 cups	2 cups
baking soda	2 teaspoons	1 teaspoon
salt	1/2 teaspoon	1/4 teaspoon
ground cinnamon	3 teaspoons	1-1/2 teaspoons
ground ginger	2 teaspoons	1 teaspoon
ground cloves	1/2 teaspoon	1/4 teaspoon
shortening	1 cup	1/2 cup
sugar	1 cup	1/2 cup
molasses	1 cup	1/2 cup
egg or egg yolk	1 egg	1 egg yolk
MIXER BOWL	3-qt. bowl	1-1/2-qt. bowl
BAKING SHEETS	baking sheets	baking sheets
BEATING TIME AT HIGH SPEED	1-1/2 to 2 minutes	45 to 60 seconds
REFRIGERATE	at least 2 hours	at least 2 hours
TIME IN 375F (190C) OVEN	6 to 8 minutes	6 to 8 minutes

In a large bowl, combine flour, baking soda, salt, cinnamon, ginger and cloves; mix well and set aside. In a mixer bowl, see size in chart above, combine shortening, sugar, molasses and egg or egg yolk. Beat at low speed of an electric mixer for 30 seconds to blend. Turn mixer to high speed. Beat for time in chart above or until light and fluffy. Scrape sides of bowl often. Turn mixer to low speed. Gradually add flour mixture, beating 20 to 30 seconds after each addition until well-mixed. Scrape sides of bowl often. Wrap dough in plastic wrap and refrigerate at least 2 hours. Preheat oven to 375F (190C). Divide large recipe into 8 portions and small recipe into 4 portions. On a lightly floured surface, roll out each portion of dough 1/8 inch thick. Keep remaining dough chilled until ready to roll. With floured cookie cutters, cut dough in desired shapes. Press dough scraps into a ball. Roll out again and cut into desired shapes. Decorate if desired. With a spatula, transfer cookies to ungreased baking sheets. Bake in preheated oven 6 to 8 minutes or until set and lightly browned around edges. Cool 1 to 2 minutes before removing from baking sheets. Cool on racks. Store completely cooled cookies in an airtight container.

Cookie-Press Cookies

YIELD	72 to 110 cookies	36 to 55 cookies
INGREDIENTS		
all-purpose flour	2-1/2 cups	1-1/4 cups
salt	1/2 teaspoon	1/4 teaspoon
butter or margarine, softened	1 cup	1/2 cup
powdered sugar	1-1/3 cups	2/3 cup
egg yolks	2	1
vanilla extract	1 teaspoon	1/2 teaspoon
almond, orange or peppermint extract	1/2 teaspoon	1/4 teaspoon
MIXER BOWL	3-qt. bowl	1-1/2-qt. bowl
BAKING SHEETS	baking sheets	baking sheets
BEATING TIME AT HIGH SPEED	2 minutes	1 minute
TIME IN 400F (205C) OVEN	6 to 8 minutes	6 to 8 minutes

Preheat oven to 400F (205C). In a medium bowl, combine flour and salt; set aside. In a mixer bowl, see size in chart above, combine butter or margarine, powdered sugar, egg yolks, vanilla and flavored extract. Beat at low speed of an electric mixer for 30 seconds to blend. Turn mixer to high speed. Beat for time in chart above or until light and fluffy. Scrape sides of bowl often. Turn mixer to low speed. Gradually add flour mixture. After each addition, beat at low speed of mixer for 10 seconds, then turn mixer to medium speed and beat 15 to 20 seconds. Scrape sides of bowl often. Do not chill dough. Fill a cookie press with dough. Press small amount of dough through shaped plates in cookie press onto ungreased baking sheets. Bake in preheated oven 6 to 8 minutes or until edges are lightly browned. Remove from baking sheets. Cool on racks. Store completely cooled cookies in an airtight container.

Note: Yield of cookies will vary depending on thickness of dough design. If using a cookie gun, thick setting will yield smaller number of cookies above. Thin setting will yield larger number of cookies above.

How to Make Rolled Cookies

1/Rolled Gingerbread Cookies are made from a stiff dough that has been refrigerated so it will roll out more easily. Cut rolled dough into desired shapes, fitting shapes together like a jigsaw puzzle to make best use of dough. Flour cookie cutters before cutting each cookie, or dough will stick to cutter.

2/Carefully transfer cookies on a spatula to baking sheets. Leave 2 inches around each cookie to allow cookie to spread. Some hard candies can be used for decoration before baking. Bake and cool cookies. Frost with different colors of frosting and decorate with various candies and marshmallows. To store, place cookies on a plate covered with plastic wrap; do not stack.

Rolled Sugar Cookies

YIELD	96 small cookies	48 small cookies
INGREDIENTS		
all-purpose flour	3 cups	1-1/2 cups
baking powder	1 teaspoon	1/2 teaspoon
salt	1/2 teaspoon	1/4 teaspoon
butter or margarine, softened	1 cup	1/2 cup
sugar	2/3 cup	1/3 cup
egg or egg yolk	1 egg	1 egg yolk
milk	2 tablespoons	1 tablespoon
vanilla extract	2 teaspoons	1 teaspoon
MIXER BOWL	3-qt. bowl	1-1/2-qt. bowl
BAKING SHEETS	baking sheets	baking sheets
BEATING TIME AT HIGH SPEED	1-1/2 to 2 minutes	45 to 60 seconds
REFRIGERATE	1 to 2 hours	1 to 2 hours
TIME IN 400F (205C) OVEN	6 to 8 minutes	6 to 8 minutes

In a medium bowl, combine flour, baking powder and salt; mix well and set aside. In a mixer bowl, see size in chart above, beat butter or margarine, sugar, egg or egg yolk, milk and vanilla at low speed of an electric mixer for 30 seconds to blend. Turn mixer to high speed. Beat for time in chart above or until light and fluffy. Scrape sides of bowl often. Turn mixer to low speed. Gradually add flour mixture, beating 20 to 30 seconds after each addition until well-mixed. Scrape sides of bowl often. Wrap dough in plastic wrap and refrigerate at least 1 hour but not more than 2 hours. Preheat oven to 400F (205C). Divide large recipe into 4 portions and small recipe into 2 portions. On a lightly floured surface, roll out each portion of dough 1/8 inch thick. Keep remaining dough chilled until ready to roll. With floured cookie cutters or a pastry wheel, cut dough in desired shapes. Press dough scraps into a ball. Roll out again and cut into desired shapes. Decorate with small candies or colored sugar, if desired. With a spatula, transfer cookies to ungreased baking sheets. Bake in preheated oven 6 to 8 minutes or until lightly browned. Remove from baking sheets. Cool on racks. Store completely cooled cookies in an airtight container.

Chocolate-Cherry Refrigerator Cookies

YIELD	96 cookies	48 cookies
INGREDIENTS		
all-purpose flour	2-1/2 cups	1-1/4 cups
baking soda	1/2 teaspoon	1/4 teaspoon
cream of tartar	1 teaspoon	1/2 teaspoon
salt	1/4 teaspoon	1/8 teaspoon
butter or margarine, softened	1 cup	1/2 cup
powdered sugar	1-1/2 cups	3/4 cup
unsweetened cocoa powder	1/4 cup	2 tablespoons
egg or egg yolk	1 egg	1 egg yolk
milk	omit	1 tablespoon
vanilla extract	1 teaspoon	1/2 teaspoon
red or green candied cherries	32	16
finely chopped pecans	1 cup	1/2 cup
MIXER BOWL	3-qt. bowl	1-1/2-qt. bowl
BAKING SHEETS	baking sheets	baking sheets
BEATING TIME AT HIGH SPEED	45 to 60 seconds	45 to 60 seconds
REFRIGERATE	at least 4 hours	at least 4 hours
TIME IN 325F (165C) OVEN	10 to 12 minutes	10 to 12 minutes

In a medium bowl, combine flour, baking soda, cream of tartar and salt; mix well and set aside. In a mixer bowl, see size in chart above, beat butter or margarine, powdered sugar, cocoa powder, egg or egg yolk, milk, if using, and vanilla at low speed of an electric mixer for 30 seconds to blend. Turn mixer to high speed. Beat 45 to 60 seconds or until light and fluffy. Scrape sides of bowl often. Turn mixer to low speed. Gradually add flour mixture. After each addition, beat at low speed of mixer until well-mixed, then turn mixer to medium speed and beat 20 to 30 seconds. Scrape sides of bowl often. On a piece of waxed paper, pat small recipe into a 12″ x 3″ rectangle. Divide large recipe in 2 portions. On waxed paper, pat out each portion to a 12″ x 3″ rectangle. Make a row of cherries down center of dough lengthwise. Mold dough up around cherries to form 12-inch rolls with cherries in center. Roll in chopped nuts. Wrap rolls in plastic wrap. Refrigerate at least 4 hours or until firm. Preheat oven to 325F (165C). With a serrated knife, slice cookies 1/4 inch thick. Place on ungreased baking sheets. Bake in preheated oven 10 to 12 minutes or until set. Remove from baking sheets. Cool on racks. Store completely cooled cookies in an airtight container.

Note: Rolls of dough may be frozen. Before slicing, let frozen dough stand at room temperature 20 to 30 minutes. Slice and bake as above.

How to Make Chocolate-Cherry Cookies

1/Pat out chocolate cookie dough to a 12" x 3" rectangle on a piece of waxed paper. Place a row of green or red cherries lengthwise down center of dough. Using waxed paper, mold dough up around cherries to form a round roll with cherries in center. Roll dough in chopped nuts.

2/Wrap dough in plastic wrap and refrigerate at least 4 hours or freeze. This makes dough easier to slice. Use a serrated knife to cut cookie dough in 1/4-inch slices. Let frozen dough stand at room temperature 20 to 30 minutes before slicing.

Refrigerator Cookies

YIELD	144 cookies	72 cookies
INGREDIENTS		
butter or margarine	1 cup	1/2 cup
all-purpose flour	4 cups	2 cups
baking soda	1 teaspoon	1/2 teaspoon
ground cinnamon	1 teaspoon	1/2 teaspoon
finely snipped dates, dried apricots or raisins	8 oz. (1-1/3 cups)	4 oz. (2/3 cup)
chopped nuts	1 cup	1/2 cup
granulated sugar	1 cup	1/2 cup
packed brown sugar	1 cup	1/2 cup
eggs	2	1
SAUCEPAN	3-qt. saucepan	2-qt. saucepan
BAKING SHEETS	baking sheets	baking sheets
REFRIGERATE	at least 4 hours	at least 4 hours
TIME IN 325F (165C) OVEN	8 to 10 minutes	8 to 10 minutes

In a saucepan, see size in chart above, melt butter or margarine; cool 20 minutes. In a large bowl, combine flour, baking soda and cinnamon; mix well. Stir in dried fruit and nuts; set aside. Stir granulated sugar and brown sugar into melted butter or margarine; mix well. By hand, beat in eggs until well-mixed. Gradually stir in flour mixture until well-mixed. Divide large recipe into 4 portions and small recipe into 2 portions. Shape each portion into a roll, 9 inches long and 1-1/2 inches in diameter. Wrap each roll in plastic wrap and refrigerate at least 4 hours. Preheat oven to 325F (165C). Slice cookies 1/4 inch thick. Place on ungreased baking sheets. Bake in preheated oven 8 to 10 minutes or until lightly browned. Remove from baking sheets. Cool on racks. Store completely cooled cookies in an airtight container.

Note: Rolls of dough may be frozen. Slice frozen cookie dough 1/4 inch thick. Bake in preheated 325F (165C) oven 12 to 14 minutes.

Basic Never-Fail Fudge

YIELD	64 pieces	32 pieces
INGREDIENTS		
marshmallow creme	1 (13-oz.) jar	1 (7-oz.) jar
packed brown sugar	2 cups	1 cup
evaporated milk	2/3 cup	1/3 cup
butter or margarine	1/4 cup	2 tablespoons
flavored baking pieces	2 cups	1 cup
chopped nuts	1/2 cup	1/4 cup
vanilla extract	1 teaspoon	1/2 teaspoon
BAKING PAN	8-inch-square baking pan	8" x 4" loaf pan
HEAVY SAUCEPAN	3-qt. saucepan	2-qt. saucepan
TIME AT MEDIUM	5 minutes	5 minutes
REFRIGERATE	2 to 3 hours	2 to 3 hours

Butter a baking pan, see size in chart above; set aside. Butter sides of a heavy saucepan, see size in chart above. In saucepan, combine marshmallow creme, brown sugar, evaporated milk and butter or margarine. Bring to a boil over Medium-High heat, stirring constantly. Reduce heat to Medium. Cook 5 minutes, stirring constantly. Remove from heat. Stir in baking pieces until melted. Stir in nuts and vanilla. Pour into buttered baking pan. Refrigerate 2 to 3 hours or until firm. Cut into small squares. Store in the refrigerator.

Suggested Combinations
Never-Fail Chocolate Fudge: Use semisweet chocolate pieces. Use chopped walnuts for nuts.
Never-Fail Butterscotch Fudge: Use butterscotch pieces. Use chopped pecans for nuts.
Never-Fail Peanut-Butter Fudge: Use peanut-butter pieces. Use chopped peanuts for nuts.

Easy Caramel Corn

YIELD	10 cups	5 cups
INGREDIENTS		
popped corn	2 qts.	1 qt.
peanuts	1 cup	1/2 cup
packed brown sugar	1 cup	1/2 cup
butter or margarine	1/2 cup	1/4 cup
light corn syrup	1/4 cup	2 tablespoons
salt	1/2 teaspoon	1/4 teaspoon
baking soda	1/2 teaspoon	1/4 teaspoon
BAKING PAN	2 (15" x 10" x 1") baking pans	15" x 10" x 1" baking pan
SAUCEPAN	2-qt. saucepan	1-qt. saucepan
TIME AT MEDIUM	5 minutes	5 minutes
TIME IN 200F (95C) OVEN	1 hour	1 hour

Do not preheat oven. Grease 1 or 2 (15" x 10" x 1") baking pans. In a large bowl, layer popcorn and then peanuts; set aside. In a saucepan, see size in chart above, bring brown sugar, butter or margarine, corn syrup and salt to a boil over High heat, stirring constantly. Reduce heat to Medium. Cook 5 minutes, stirring constantly. Remove from heat. Stir in baking soda. Pour over popcorn mixture. Toss with 2 forks until well-coated. Spread evenly in greased baking pans. Bake in a 200F (95C) oven 1 hour, stirring and breaking up large pieces every 15 minutes. Cool completely in pan. Store completely cooled caramel corn in an airtight container or plastic bags.

Index

8.63920649671306